MONTEREY PENINSULA COLLEGE LIBRARY
HT_ _ _ 3513 1988_ _ _ _ _ _
Bair_ _ _ _ _ _ul/Cities and economic devel_ _ _
00004 2446

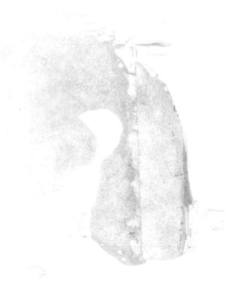

Cities and Economic Development

Cities and
Economic Development

From the Dawn of History

to the Present

Paul Bairoch
Translated by Christopher Braider

HT
111
.B3513
1988

(5-90)

The University of Chicago Press
Chicago

PAUL BAIROCH is professor of economic history at the University of Geneva.

The University of Chicago Press, Chicago 60637

© 1988 by The University of Chicago
All rights reserved. Published 1988
Printed in the United States of America

97 96 95 94 93 92 91 90 89 88 5 4 3 2 1

Originally published in Paris under the title *De Jéricho à Mexico: Villes et économie dans l'histoire*, © Editions Gallimard, 1985.

Library of Congress Cataloging-in-Publication Data

Bairoch, Paul.
  [De Jéricho à Mexico. English]
  Cities and economic development : from the dawn of history to the
present / Paul Bairoch ; translated by Christopher Braider.
      p.   cm.
  Translation of: De Jéricho à Mexico.
  Bibliography: p.
  Includes index.
  ISBN 0-226-03465-8   OcLc 17299591
  1. Urbanization—History.   2. Cities and towns—Growth—History.
3. Urban economics—History.   4. Economic development—History.
I. Title.
HT111.B3513   1988
307.7'6'09—dc19   87-35484
                                                      CIP

Contents

Tables

Introduction

The history of urbanization is without doubt one of the most exciting aspects of the adventure of humanity. When and how were cities born? Does each civilization have a distinctive form of city? How large were urban populations in traditional societies? What was the impact of colonization on urban systems? Did the Industrial Revolution favor urbanization? Has urbanization favored innovation and economic development? Does the urban explosion in the Third World constitute a handicap or an opportunity from the point of view of development? All of these questions, and many more like them, bear on matters touching the very essence of world history and for that reason alone merit our attention.

Nor is this subject of purely historical interest. Two centuries ago, one person in ten lived in a city. Today the ratio is one person in four; in twenty years, it will be one in two—a proportion already surpassed in developed countries. Two centuries ago, neither of the two largest cities in the world, London and Peking, had a population of as much as a million and in the entire world there were fewer than ninety cities with populations in excess of 100,000. By 1985 there were between 32 and 36 cities with populations of more than five million and there are more than 2,300 cities with populations of more than 100,000. Clearly, then, the problem of the city and of its impact on economic life directly shapes the existence of the greater part of humanity.

So there is no shortage of motives for asking such questions. But before going on it would be as well to explain my special interest in the matter—my reasons for having been attracted to such a fascinating, yet also such a difficult, task as a history of the city in its relations with economic development.

The Reasons for the Book

This book is the fruit of the cross-fertilization of two concerns I have pursued side by side for many years.

Twenty-five years ago, after completing a study of the history of economic development, I was led for professional reasons to address my attention to urban problems: I was invited to look into various aspects of the economic decline then afflicting the industrialized regions of southern Belgium. Thus for seven years, I carried on both these regional urban investigations and my own ongoing research into the process of economic development. Although the regional studies remained the subject of strictly confidential reports submitted directly to the regional and national authorities concerned, I did publish the bulk of my work on development. And though this double task at the time weighed heavily upon me, it proved in the end very enriching.

Three years after abandoning these urban studies, I found myself once again called upon to look into the urban question—a question about which, if only in the private capacity of a concerned city dweller, I had in any case continued to keep myself informed. At the behest of the International Labor Office, I undertook a brief study of urban unemployment in the developing countries (Geneva, 1973). This study directly led to my deep interest in another urban problem: that of the effects of the size of cities on the quality of life and on economic development (*Tailles des villes, conditions de vie et développement économique*, Paris, 1977).

Throughout this period, however, I continued to pursue my original preoccupation with the history of economic development, and eventually this dual line of investigation quite naturally induced me to wonder about the connection between urbanization and economic development. Such indeed was the title of a course I gave to students of the Faculty of Economic and Social Sciences and of the Faculty of Letters of the University of Geneva on three separate occasions between the academic years 1974/75 and 1978/79. This course furnished the starting point for the present book—but only a starting point. For the preparation of this book ultimately demanded additional, complementary reading and research far greater in scope than I had initially anticipated. The sheer scale of the phenomenon of urbanization, whether envisaged in its historical or in its geographical extent, obliged me to pass ceaselessly back and forth between the various chapters. The deepened understanding of one period or of one type of society raised unexpected problems elsewhere or shed fresh light on matters imperfectly treated in other parts of the book—all of which led me to draft three successive "semi-definitive" versions before I was finished.

The enormous mass of supplementary material notwithstanding, this book must not be regarded as a mere research report. There are things one can present in carefully documented form for the specialist that have no place in a series of lectures; there are others that can be treated in a series of lectures, but that cannot properly be presented in documented research. It was my aim, however, to resolve and go beyond this apparently irreconcilable contradiction: I wanted to achieve a kind of hybrid combining the best features of a general history on the one hand and of a research document on the other, hoping in this way to provide something that would be a value to the specialist, but would be accessible to a more general public as well. For what I wanted was to write a book of use to anyone intrigued by the dramatic saga of the evolving relationship between urbanization and economic life—the relationship between the city and what today is called "economic development."

The Contents of the Book

This book first sets out to analyze the relationship between the city and the economy as it has evolved in various societies of the world throughout various phases of urban history. But it also attempts to synthesize existing research on the history of urbanization. No sooner had I begun to prepare the material for the course that originally inspired this work than it became clear to me that, while the body of research relating to urban history is very rich, no general survey had yet been undertaken that summed up the vast body of current knowledge on the subject. In addition, then, to my analysis of urbanization in its relations to economic development, one of the chief contributions I hope to make will be to provide a general overview of all urban and preurban societies for the whole of the urban era.

Urbanization. Since there is some risk of ambiguity in the use of the term, I will explain what I mean by it. The term "urbanization" will be employed here in the sense derived from the traditional meaning of the word "urban," which the *Oxford English Dictionary* defines as: "pertaining to or characteristic of, occurring or taking place in, a city." The *OED* defines "urbanization," in the meaning it has here, as: "the process of investing with an urban character"; a definition I will complement with the one given in French, the language in which this book was originally written, by the *Dictionnaire Robert*: "increasing concentration of population in urban agglomerations." Since this book does not concern the political and administrative aspects of urbanism the terms "town," "city," and even "urban agglomeration" or "urban center" will be considered here as roughly synonymous.

A second definition that could be extended to the term urbanization is related to urban studies or urban planning and, more particularly, to what in French (the word does not appear in the most recent edition of the *OED*) goes by the name of *urbanisme,* a word the *Dictionnaire Robert* defines thus: "the systematic study of methods permitting the adaptation of the urban environment to human needs." Envisaging the concept of "urbanization" in this light, I identify it with an aspect (an exceedingly important aspect) of architecture, one that reaches beyond the frontiers of architecture proper to embrace all of the human sciences. Certainly I shall have occasion to refer to urban problems and to speak of urbanization in this sense, and also of urbanization construed as a process of civilization, of making urbane. But the fundamental object of this investigation is urbanization in its original and simplest meaning.

I shall frequently use the terms "development" and "economic development." "Development" is taken here in the widest sense of the word, that is, one that encompasses all of the social and economic phenomena related to the general evolution of societies. Scholars often distinguish, following Perroux (1961), for example, between the concepts of "growth," "development," and even "economic advancement." "Growth" usually means simple increase in production; "development" implies underlying structural change as well; and "economic advancement" adds the idea of broader social and cultural transformation or change. In the context of the present analysis, however, the terms "development" and "economic development" include all of these concepts, as well as the phenomena of underdevelopment. As they are used here these terms may be considered synonyms for "social and economic life," or to use an even more appropriate term, one used by Braudel (1967), "material life." Besides, for the preindustrial world it is inaccurate to speak of economic development in the sense this concept has today.

Plan of the Book

The book has four parts. Part 1 examines the beginnings of urbanism in various regions of the Old and New Worlds. Among the questions to be asked are the following: What were the relations between the emergence of agriculture and the earliest phases in the process of urbanization? Can the invention of the city be traced back to a single origin, or did it spring more or less simultaneously from a number of independent sources? What were the respective roles of Greece and Rome in the urban history of Europe? And what was the city's impact on the economic life of the ancient world?

In Part 2, we shall survey the history of Europe from the fifth century to the eighteenth century—the history, in other words, of the traditional Europe of the Middle Ages and the Renaissance; but a traditional Europe that, despite its resistance to change, underwent a whole series of dramatic, often cataclysmic breaks with the past. For the urban and economic fabric of medieval and Renaissance Europe was continually rent by a succession of violent upheavals. During these centuries Europe witnessed various invasions from the North and from the East, as well as the advent of Christianity; it saw the struggles of the commercial cities of Italy against expanding Muslim influence, the Black Death, and finally that overthrow of the established order of things in the wake of the voyages of exploration at the end of the fifteenth century, when Europe opened to the outside world, a world that Europe broadened by its discovery of the New World.

But the most decisive break with the past was that brought about by the Industrial Revolution, which ushered in the era of "real" economic development and, concomitantly, of real economic underdevelopment. It is to these crucial problems, of which the consequences for urbanization are far-reaching and profound, that the last two parts of the book will be devoted.

Part 3, "The Role of the City in the Development of the Western World," concerns the Industrial Revolution. Was the city of central or merely of marginal importance in the full flowering of the Industrial Revolution in England and in its subsequent diffusion from England to the other countries making up what today is called the developed world? What in general has been the relationship between the city and industrialization, between the city and technological innovation, between the city and new forms of transportation? With the Industrial Revolution, the city itself is no longer the same. Not only does it become for the first time in history the dominant mode of social existence, but it undergoes radical transformations in its own structure and size. In the West, during the first century of the Industrial Revolution, the city devoured its inhabitants, since mortality rates in the city were far heavier than in the countryside. But what precisely caused these changes in the demography of the West, and more to the point, what does this tell us about the nature of Western cities in the post-industrial age? Such are the questions addressed in Part 3.

Colonization and underdevelopment constitute the backdrop against which the urban history of the greater part of the non-Western world unfolds from the sixteenth century to the twentieth. Part 4, the last part of the book, is concerned with this history. But the opening chapters of part 4 will look at the evolution and chief characteristics of urban life in non-Western societies prior to colonization. I shall also consider what evidence we have for the precolonial era regarding the relationship between the city and the economy in these traditional societies, an analysis that will pursue a course somewhat similar to that followed in part 2 with reference to Europe. I shall then examine the multidimensional consequences of colonization (or rather of the various forms of colonization) in the exceedingly diverse urban worlds of Asia, the Middle East, the Maghreb, Black Africa, and Latin America. Finally, I shall close part 4 with a discussion of the crucial and dramatic problem of underdevelopment, with special attention to the urban explosion in the Third World during the twentieth century. Even though certain of its aspects find analogies in the past, this last phenomenon, by virtue of its causes, its ramifications, and its scale, constitutes an event without precedent in the history of humanity.

Acknowledgements

In writing a book, almost any author will contract an enormous number of debts. This is especially true of a book like this one, which would have been inconceivable without the numerous published sources that served as its foundation. Were it not for the hundreds of studies to which generations of anthropologists, archaeologists, historians, economists, sociologists and (last but not least) geographers, urban planners, and architects have devoted many years of research and indeed the best part of their working lives, I should never have been able to bring this rather audacious venture to a successful close. To all the men and women concerned I would like to express my profound gratitude and admiration. Unfortunately, the many references given in the text, and even the bibliography, cannot adequately acknowledge all those who have assisted me.

I would like to express my heartfelt gratitude to all the librarians who helped me to gain ready access to the works I needed to carry out my research, particularly the librarians in those institutions whose resources I most regularly consulted: the Faculty of Economics and Social Sciences of the University of Geneva, the International Labor Office, the United Nations, and the Bibliothèque Publique et Universitaire of Geneva.

The problems treated in this book were discussed for the first time in lecture courses and seminars. I have therefore, like all teachers, profited from the stimulating questions raised by my students. I owe them, too, a debt of thanks, and also this apology for not always having been able to give them the answers they sought and deserved.

Finally, and this is by no means the least of my debts, I have had the good fortune to benefit from the kind interest taken in my work by certain of my colleagues and friends, who read and commented on the first versions of this text. I wish to extend my warmest thanks to Anne-Marie Piuz and Alfred Perrenoud, friends and colleagues at the Department of Economic History of the University of Geneva, to my friend Jean Mayer of the International Labor Office, who read the first version, and to my friend David Landes of Harvard University, who read the last version.*

It goes without saying that, in the time-honored phrase, I accept sole responsibility for whatever errors and omissions remain in this book, and the views expressed in these pages are all entirely my own.

Geneva, January 1979—Saint-Livres, September 1983

*This English edition is based on the French version published in 1985, but it incorporates many revisions as well as additional material and references. As the cutoff date was early 1987, however, a few further revisions were made in page proof (February 1988).

I want to thank Christopher Braider, who performed marvels of translation; Barbara Anderson, my extremely diligent copyeditor; and the staff of the University of Chicago Press.

Part One
From the Birth of Urbanism to the Beginnings of the Great Civilizations

It is hard to imagine anything more fascinating than the birth of urbanism. It is all the more fascinating because there can be little question that the birth of cities and thus the emergence of the historical context that either favored or actively gave rise to cities constitute between them one of the major turning points in the history of humanity. This turning point was as decisive in its way as the Industrial Revolution, from which the world as we know it today emerged, and which clearly could not have taken place without this distant forerunner. Without cities there could have been no real civilization. And even if the reader prefers to reverse the terms of the equation, and argue that it is civilization that makes cities possible rather than the other way around, the fact remains that the city and civilization are intimately bound together, and that this bond is an essential key to the understanding of human history.

But if the city and civilization are indeed intimately connected, it follows that the birth of urbanism leads us to the heart of this book: the links between the city and the economy. What factors made the emergence of cities possible? Or to put it another way, why did it take millions of years after the appearance of man before cities began to appear? We shall see that the answer lies in the absence of agriculture and of certain socioeconomic conditions closely associated with agriculture: the settlement of a large number of people in one place and, since the city contributes little or nothing to its own maintenance, the creation of a storable surplus of food capable of sustaining an urban population. The city emerges, not simply in conjunction with, but as a direct result of advances in agriculture. Where there is no agriculture, we find only a very thin concentration of population, while a high concentration of population is something without which urbanization cannot take place.

The first chapter will examine the factors explaining the birth of urbanism and the Neolithic revolution that was the indispensable precondition. It follows that the history of the relationship between the city and the economy began about twelve thousand years ago. It probably began in the Middle East. For as Fernand Braudel justly puts it, true history is the narrative of events that have had consequences. It is, in the end, the consequences that count. Thus, while episodes of urbanization may undoubtedly have occurred elsewhere prior to its first true flowering in the Middle East, it is only with the advent of urbanism in this region that the process may be said to have had any genuine consequences. For this reason chapter 2 is concerned with the beginnings of cities in the Middle East.

The theme of the second chapter will to a certain extent carry over into the third chapter, the origins of urbanization in Asia. But most of chapter 3 deals with the two great civilizations of the Asian continent, India and China. A break will come in chapter 4, when I deal with Black Africa. But this break will be more apparent than real because Black Africa had close relations not only with the Egypt of the Pharaohs but also with most of the major civilizations of the Middle East and Asia. Since the history and especially the colonial expansion of Europe have drawn Africa and the New World together in many ways, chapter 4 will also treat urbanism in the pre-Columbian New World. Chapter 4 will break somewhat the unity of time more or less closely observed in the others. Whereas treatment of the other continents stops somewhere between 200 B.C. and A.D. 500, the analysis of urbanization in Africa and the New World will be treated up until A.D. 1500, chiefly in recognition of the fact that the real integration of Africa and the New World into world history took place only at this comparatively late date. While it is doubtless the case that such a treatment of the problem betrays a certain ethnocentrism in favor of Europe, it will be noted that this is justified by the nature of my subject, given the enormously influential role that Europe has played in both world and urban history as a whole.

In chapter 5 we come to Europe (to whose history parts 2 and 3 of the book will be devoted). The main emphasis of chapter 5 will be on the history of urbanism in Greece and Rome, a history that has profoundly shaped not only European civilization in general, but its distinctive urban structure as well. The sixth and last chapter in the first part of the book will attempt to draw some conclusions about relations between the city, civilization, and the economy during this crucial phase of the beginnings of urbanization.

1 The Birth of Urbanism and the Economy □

The birth of urbanism! The title of this chapter is certainly too definite, and probably erroneous as well. It is too definite because my speaking of birth may lead the reader to suppose it is possible to establish a date for it. And it is probably erroneous, because in speaking of birth in the singular, I prejudge the question of whether urbanization may be traced back to a single origin or a number of autonomous sources. Over the course of the following chapters it will be seen that many uncertainties remain about dating the first phases of urbanization and identifying the links between different urban centers. But in this first chapter, focused on the relations between urbanization and the economy, it seems preferable to simplify in this way. For the uncertainties will not alter the essential problem dealt with here: to understand the connection between various aspects of economic life and the advent of cities. And in this context, it is necessary to recall that the rise of cities was closely connected to the Neolithic. Such being the case, it will be useful to pause a moment in order to define and date what is often described, and rightly so, as the Neolithic revolution.

The Neolithic Revolution

The term Neolithic signifies "new stone," by which is meant ground stone. But if, in order to facilitate the dating of the phenomenon, the passage from the use of flaked ground stone does constitute a convenient point of reference and a clear token of advance in culture, the chief component of the Neolithic revolution was the progression from an economy based on hunting, gathering, and fishing to one based on farming and the raising of livestock. In sum, it concerns neither more nor less than the invention of agriculture, and for this reason the term "revolution" is by no means too strong. Of the important consequences of the transformation, the most important lay in a pronounced increase in the production of food per unit of land. This increase in production in turn made possible, on the one hand, an ex-

3

changeable food surplus and, on the other hand, a growing density of population. And all of this further implied sedentary life: the adoption of agriculture entailed the abandonment of nomadism.

Thus the Neolithic included three factors that led to the first stages of urbanism. I shall return to this important point later. But I shall first attempt to date more precisely the Neolithic revolution and its dominant constituent, the appearance of agriculture.

As is the case with many other phenomena of prehistory, there is a continual retreat of the date marking the start of the Neolithic. This date has gone from 3000 B.C. to 8000–9000 B.C., and recent research in Egypt would appear to push it back by an additional 7,000 years. In any event, the best estimate, one around which some sort of consensus has formed, would seem to indicate that the Neolithic commenced somewhere between 10,000 and 12,000 years ago, and that agriculture made its first significant appearance between 10,000 and 10,500 years ago.

But if some kind of consensus exists regarding the date for the beginning of the Neolithic and for the agricultural revolution it brought with it, the opposite is the case with respect to determining whether agriculture originally evolved from a single source or from a number of autonomous sources. Most students of the problem have lined up in support of a theory admitting the existence of several autonomous centers. But the existence of several autonomous centers where agriculture was invented simultaneously does not in the slightest rule out the possibility of diffusion of innovations from one region to another, at least on a relatively local level. Furthermore, even if to simplify matters I were to point out that, at present, theses of multiple births of agriculture predominate in the field, this does not imply that it is necessary to abandon the notion of a unique origin. The arguments of G. F. Carter (1977), for example, cannot be dismissed as negligible. For Carter shows (among other things) that, despite the New World's remoteness from Old World centers, it is possible to explain the emergence of agriculture in the New World in terms of a process of transfer and diffusion. And if agriculture could have diffused so early as far as the New World, this must throw a more favorable light on the idea of diffusion in other parts of the world.

It is perhaps wiser to conclude with Carter that "neither a single origin nor several origins can be demonstrated." Although I tend instinctively to lean toward the theory of multiple origins for agriculture, there nevertheless remains the example of that second decisive break with the past in the history of humanity, the Industrial Revolution. And what the Industrial Revolution demonstrates is that the existence of a single source of change does not rule out the possibility of the subsequent diffusion of its influence to the rest of the world. The diffusion may take time; in the case of the Industrial Revolution it took a little more than two centuries (and the agricultural component of that revolution took even a little more than two and a half centuries) to reach the whole of the rest of the world. As for the adoption of agriculture in the Neolithic, that diffusion took several millennia. But however protracted the process, diffusion was clearly possible, and the issue must on this account remain a live one.

Stages in the Rise of Agriculture

I shall, then, leave aside the dispute over the uniqueness or multiplicity of the invention of agriculture in order to provide here, insofar as the current state of knowledge will allow, a summary chronology covering the major stages in the historical rise of agriculture. I must, however, digress briefly to discuss my choice of a notation for dates. Progress in radiochronology has recently led to the generalized use of a dating system for prehistoric phenomena in which the various periods are designated by the initials B.P. (Before Present), the central point of reference being the year 1950. In this new system, then, the year 5000 B.P. would correspond to the year 3050 B.C. in the traditional notation. But despite the obvious advantages the new system affords, I have decided to retain here the traditional notation on the grounds of the persistence of its use in dating historical events.

Turning now to the stages in the development of agriculture, I shall confine myself for the moment to its earliest sites in each region, reserving the right to come back in somewhat greater detail to regions in the chapters specifically devoted to them later, and also to return at several points to the intermediary phase immediately preceding the Neolithic, a phase often called protoagriculture. Although, given the pace of recent discoveries, one ought to concentrate on the numerous journal articles on the subject, I refer the reader in particular to four relatively recent syntheses reviewing the current state of knowledge: the studies of Bender (1975) and Cohen (1977), the collection of essays edited by Reed (1977), and the Cambridge Encyclopedia of Archaeology, edited by Sherratt (1980).

The earliest known site of agriculture is still the Middle East, where tangible evidence both of the domestication of animals (other than dogs, which were already domesticated in hunting cultures) and especially of the methodical cultivation of the soil places the first appearance of farming and the raising of livestock somewhere between 8500 and 8000 B.C. The date for Asia would seems to be about 6000–5000 B.C., for Africa about 5000 B.C., for the New World about 7000–6500 B.C., and for Europe 6500–6000 B.C. As a general rule, there are several more or less early sites in each of these regions.

A number of different hypotheses have been advanced to account for the causes of one or another of these inventions of agriculture, including the effects of chance, changes in climate, or need engendered by demographic pressure. While none of these hypotheses can claim to be anything more than purest conjecture, the last overlaps a problem that touches a matter to which I shall return later in the book: the role of demographic pressure in innovation in agriculture. This problem owes a great deal to a study done by Boserup (1965) concerning certain regions of the contemporary Third World where, according to Boserup, demographic pressure has stimulated the introduction of improved agricultural methods.

Although I do not wish to give undue weight to this explanation of the invention of agriculture, because of the frequency and persistence with which the problem of the impact of demographic pressure comes up, I think I shall linger a moment over this question. Nor can I resist the temptation to quote what is probably the earliest formulation of the thesis that agriculture arose as a result of population growth—a formulation embodied in old Chinese legends. One of the greatest heroes of those legends was Shen Nung, the inventor of agriculture as well as of poetry and the wooden tools used in tilling the soil. The legend dealing with the invention of farming explains its diffusion in these terms: "The people of old ate the meat of animals and birds. But in the time of Shen Nung, there were so many people that there were no longer enough animals and birds to supply their needs. So it was that Shen Nung taught the people how to cultivate the earth."

The discussion of this old problem has lately been infused with new life by the volume edited by Sponner, brought out in 1972 under the title *Population Growth: Anthropological Implications*. The most recent comprehensive analysis, setting forth the best case in favor of this demographic explanation of the rise of agriculture, is that given in Cohen (1977). I will follow Cohen's argument—all the more willingly since, while preparing to tackle afresh the problem of the first phases of urbanization after completing a preliminary draft of this book, I found myself asking precisely the question asked by Cohen: the question of the quasi simultaneity of the independent discoveries of agriculture in various parts of the world.

As the dates given earlier for the emergence of agriculture in various regions of the world would themselves suggest, ranging as they do from 8500 B.C. for the Middle East to 5000 B.C. for the New World, we can only speak of simultaneity in a very long-term perspective—though, to be sure, recent research has increasingly tended to narrow the time scale involved. Simultaneity and also universality. As Cohen writes: "The most striking fact about early agriculture, however, is precisely that it is such a universal event. Slightly more than 10,000 years ago, virtually all men lived on wild foods. By 2,000 years ago the overwhelming majority of people lived by farming."

During the Pleistocene immediately preceding the Neolithic, population growth was incontestably very slow (estimates vary between 0.01 and 0.03% per year). But this would still have enabled world population to reach some 9–15 million sometime around 8000 B.C.

True, this figure seems very small when compared with the population of 4,800 million in 1985, or even with the 750 million at the beginning of the eighteenth century. Nevertheless, in the context of an economy based on hunting and gathering, so the proponents of this thesis argue, 9–15 million represented a population level not permitting continued population growth without some radical transformation of the economy—in short, without the adoption of agriculture. According to the estimates of Hassan (1981), the optimum carrying capacity of the world under hunting and gathering is some 8.6 million (5.6 million in tropical grasslands and only 0.5 million in temperate grasslands). And since population growth did in fact take place wherever the end of glaciation permitted the emergence of vegetation and therefore of game, demographic pressure would indeed seem to explain the simultaneity and multiplicity of the invention of agriculture. For not only does it explain how such an event would have occurred, but it offers reasons for the relatively long time scale involved as well, the advent of farming depending on the retreat of the ice and the rise of population to a level sufficient to generate want, conditions that would by no means inevitably have been met at exactly the same moment in every region.

The thesis is clearly seductive, but it is far from enjoying unanimous support among anthropologists. Reed (1977) concludes his analysis of the literature on the subject in this way: "No consensus emerges, and as far as I can see, no general conclusion is possible at this time." In my view the qualification "at this time" seems too optimistic: Cohen's thesis, like its opposite, will probably never be subject either to conclusive refutation or to definitive proof. In this perspective, Petersen's (1975) conclusion on the matter in an article that, as its title indicates, represents the demographer's point of view on prehistoric demography, strikes me as especially relevant: "Demographic factors, in short, typically are both cause and effect, elements in a material-cultural complex; and to view them as only the consequence of neolithic or urban revolutions is, like any other monistic theory, distortive."

I will now leave the cause behind and return to the consequences. With the rise of agriculture, humanity, for better or for worse, apparently without seeking to (and this is a point about which anthropologists are in agreement) crossed a critical threshold. "For worse" may seem a mere rhetorical flourish, but nothing could be farther from the case. For even without taking into account the problems of the industrial age, a growing number of studies show that, as Reed (1977) puts it, in societies of hunters and gatherers, "people expend less energy per individual per unit of time at successful food getting than do most agriculturists." Translating this into statistical terms on the basis of a review of the data collected by Cohen (1977), whereas in pre-agricultural societies it took 800–1,000 hours of work for an adult to procure a year's supply of food, in primitive agricultural societies it took some 1,000–1,300 hours. So preagricultural man had to put in less work, and what work he did put in was probably less taxing, than was the case in agricultural societies. All appearances tend to indicate, moreover, that his diet was more complete and, surprisingly, less subject to climatic fluctuations. And the better or worse included the city as well; for the new mode of producing food very rapidly carried in its wake the beginnings of urbanization.

Locating the Origins of Urbanization

The first problem concerning the origins of urbanization is the problem of definition: how should urbanism be defined? And naturally enough, the date for the beginning of urbanism will advance or recede depending on how urbanism is defined. There are a great many criteria that could be used to define urbanism. Thus, Thomlinson (1971), for instance, proposes fifteen different criteria, and were one systematically to take up all of the criteria put forward by various writers, one would most likely wind up with between twenty-five and thirty of them.

As for urbanism at its origins, its very first beginnings, most writers have insisted that one or more of the following five conditions must be met:

1. The existence of full-time craftsmen, furnishing evidence of a division of labor
2. The existence of fortifications or walled enclosures, thus distinguishing the city or town from the village, which remains open
3. A population of sufficient size and, above all, density
4. A specifically urban habitat; houses built of durable materials, habitations arranged so as to form streets, and so forth
5. Permanent settlements, as opposed to transient encampments.

It is obvious that none of these criteria in itself constitutes an absolute and sufficient condition. Villages have existed in which a fraction of the population was given over to full-time craftwork. And it will be seen later in this chapter that in many societies the towns were in great part inhabited by peasants. What about fortified enclosures? True, this is an important test, and in China, for example, the same word traditionally designated a city and an encircling wall. Similarly, the Russian word for a city (*gorod* or *grad*) means citadel in Old Church Slavonic. But many Egyptian cities—and even Rome at its inception—had no fortifications, no walled enclosures. On the other hand, there are many instances of fortified villages in various parts of the world. As for the size and density of the population, there exist, notably in Tonking, in Puglia and Campagna (southern Italy) and in Hungary, genuine villages housing more than 10,000 inhabitants, and even in some cases much more. As for the urban structure of the habitat, there are instances of unstructured cities and of villages arranged in streets with adjoining houses. As for permanent settlements, there are ephemeral cities and long-standing encampments.

In the end, as so often happens, it proves necessary to combine all of the criteria, and to qualify them as well. In employing, for example, the test of the existence of full-time craftsmen, one may add to this the requirement that they represent a significant fraction of the total population. Similarly, the size and density of the population should be taken together, never separately. And when it comes to combining all five criteria, the existence of full-time craftsmen is the most important. For the very essence of urbanism is a division of labor, whereby the peasant trades his surplus products for manufactured goods (and services) provided by the city. But here too, as will be seen elsewhere, notably (in chapter 22) in connection with the cities of Asia, this is neither everywhere necessary nor a hard and fast rule.

It is extremely difficult to determine the relative size of the artisan class during the initial phases of the Neolithic: the margin of uncertainty surrounding the first stages of the process of urbanization is pretty wide. Were the towns of the Neolithic already real towns? The question will doubtless remain open for a long time, and it is precisely for this reason that the problem of criteria plays so essential a role. The most realistic way around these difficulties would perhaps be to speak, as Huot (1970) does, of "preurban cities" or, as Anglo-American writers do, of "protourbanization," considering these early settlements as the beginnings of urbanization. The consensus among specialists in the field holds that the emergence of true cities, of true urbanization, dates from the rise of the first great civilization of antiquity, with the cities of Sumer.

It is this emergence that Childe (1950) has called the "urban revolution," and he has located it around 3500–3000 B.C.. Childe draws a clear distinction between what he calls the villages of the Neolithic and the first real cities of the Middle East. In the former case, villages contained an average of 16–30 houses and some 200–400 inhabitants, and the class of craftsmen remained rudimentary. In the latter case, however, there were cities with populations of 7,000–20,000, with a well-developed class of craftsmen and highly developed forms of social organization and government. It was with these later cities, so Childe argues, that the urban revolution truly got under way. I shall return to the urban revolution in the chapters that follow, when the phase will be studied in some detail for each of the major regions. But here it is the immediately preceding phase which is of interest.

Preurban Towns or Protourbanization

The preurban towns that have attracted the most interest lie in the Middle East: these were principally Jericho, Çatalhüyük (Ana-

tolia), and Jarmo (Iraq). Jericho is often regarded—probably errone-
ously, for still older towns will certainly be discovered in the future—
as the first city.

The stages of the history of Jericho may summarized as follows. Archaeological remains point to the presence of a temple and houses
built of stone as early as 7800 B.C. (±210 years). From 6850 B.C. (±
210 years), there is a city surrounded by a fortified enclosure with
walls two meters thick and a shaft or tower nine meters high. The site
covers an area of a little more than three hectares, suggesting a population on the order of 1,000–2,000 (in the next chapter the problems
of estimating urban population will be discussed). The city certainly
possessed an active artisanry, as attested by the remains of pottery and
other manufactured articles found at the site, but of course it is impossible to determine the extent of this activity. Furthermore, and this
is a very important point, there is evidence of an advanced agriculture
complete with irrigation and the domestication of animals from
around 7000 B.C. onwards. But was Jericho a true town or merely a
fortified village? The question has yet to be answered. In any case,
eventual decline reduced the role of Jericho as a factor in the urbanization of the Middle East. The decline of Jericho can be explained by
the specific character of the immediate surroundings of the city: a large
oasis fertilized by local springs in the middle of a semidesert region.

The same basic features can be found in each of the other preurban
towns of the Middle East, but they tend to be of later origin, and their
sites usually, but not always, cover a more restricted area. Thus, Çatalhüyük (6500–5600 B.C.) has an area of 16 hectares. But even here
there are few signs of the activity of skilled craftsmen and no real
ramparts; the houses were crowded tightly together and constructed
without doors or windows (access was through the roof), forming an
enclosure. In the majority of cases, these towns had a subsequent development that unquestionably made true cities of them.

As for the other regions touched by the growth of Neolithic culture,
they have preurban cities closely resembling those in the Middle East;
what differs are the dates at which these towns emerged. Making all
due allowance for the corrections to be made in future research, it is
safe to say that the first preurban cities appeared in India around
2500 B.C. and in China probably 2000–1500 B.C.. The corresponding
date for the pre-Columbian New World is 1500–800 B.C. and for
Black Africa 1000–500 B.C. As for Europe, there was a certain telescoping between the preurban towns and the cities resulting from the
civilizations of antiquity, telescoping also found in other regions, notably in Asia and Africa, but which was more pronounced in the Mediterranean basin than elsewhere. The creation of urban colonies by the
Phoenicians, Greeks and Romans, to cite only these examples, brought
about in most instances the foundation of genuine cities in regions

where the indigenous cultures had yet to engender urban systems of their own. I shall return to this intriguing history of urbanization by colonization in the chapters that follow.

The Relations between the Economy and the Birth of Urbanism: Agriculture and Transport

I shall leave aside here a whole series of theories about the origins of cities in which geographical, ethnological and socioreligious factors predominate. It is certain that the birth of many cities was related to specific factors. But I shall chiefly focus here on the relations between urbanization and the economy, relations that determined the rise as well as the development of urbanism at a still more fundamental level. If, as will be seen, attention is turned not to particular cases but to the emergence of urban civilizations in general, the economic variable will be found to be preponderant.

Some emphasis has already been given to the importance of the rise of agriculture in the advent of urbanism, an importance derived from agriculture's role in increasing population density, in encouraging a settled life, and above all in creating a surplus of food. It is necessary to stress here this especially crucial point: the existence of true urban centers presupposes not only a surplus of agricultural produce, but also the possibility of using this surplus in trade. And the possibilities of trade are directly conditioned by the size of the surplus relative to the amount of ground that has to be covered in transporting it from one place to another, for distance reduces the economic value of the surplus. Here appears what the Australians have described as the tyranny of distance, which is added to the tyranny of agriculture. These twin constraints will now be examined.

The Tyranny of Distance

The tyranny of distance or, if the reader prefers, the cost effects of transportation, are vividly illustrated by the extreme situation of a society whose sole means of transport is the human back. In such a situation it can be estimated that a man can transport 35–40 kilograms of freight over a distance of 30–35 kilometers per day (or 1.1–1.3 ton-kilometers per day). Now in order to sustain himself, man must eat each day 1 kilogram of food, so when the return trip is taken into account, a man needs 1 kilogram for every 17 kilometers of ground he covers in transporting agricultural goods. Taking the simplest possible case, this implies that if food is transported over a distance of 300 kilometers, half of the cargo will be absorbed in the cost of transportation alone, and if the distance reaches 600 kilometers, the cargo will be consumed. The reality is generally far more complex than this, especially where the goods to be transported can be exchanged for food along the way. But on the other hand, this calculation implies a large underestimation, since it should also take into account inactive periods (forced or voluntary), costs and profits of organization, nonfood needs of the carriers, the needs of the carrier's family, and so forth. In the end, there is always the same constraint: the high cost of transportation.

True, the problem may be alleviated by the use of beasts of burden, for not only will this increase the amount of freight that can be carried, but more to the point, animals can graze on vegetation inedible to man, and can at least in part find it along the way. Furthermore, even if the animal is used mainly for transport, it can can also provide food for man, furnishing milk during its lifetime and meat after its slaughter. But with the domestication of animals this supposes, the pre-Neolithic period has been left behind.

It must nevertheless be borne in mind that even with the use of beasts of burden, and thus even after the Neolithic revolution, transportation remained relatively costly, for capacity continued to be limited, and the driver still had to be provided for. A horse can carry a load of 90–150 kilograms per day over a distance of between 20 and 40 kilometers, depending on the terrain and the conditions of the course (and the size of the load), making an average of around 3–5 metric ton-kilometers per day. The performance of oxen is even less impressive. The camel, on the other hand, can carry loads twice as heavy and for far greater distances. Even when animals are harnessed to wheeled vehicles, which requires more drivers, their performance does not increase much. Before the general introduction of collars and horseshoes (in medieval Europe), a horse could transport, on good roads, about 4–7 metric ton-kilometers per day. Besides, as will be seen in chapter 23, the wheel is not always the best solution.

But if the introduction of the wheel did not always constitute real progress, the use of animal transport, despite the preceding reservations, did in fact bring about an important economic gain. According to the substantial body of data assembled by Clark and Haswell (1970), the average cost per metric ton-kilometer—expressed as the equivalent in grain—is on the order of 8.8 kilograms for human portage, 4.8 kilograms for animal portage, and 3.9 kilograms for transportation by cart (in each case the 4 extreme figures were eliminated to make the mean more significant). And in the last case, it is not certain that the indirect costs involved (especially the cost of maintaining roads) have been suitably expressed in the price of transport. But even excluding the indirect costs, it implies in the case of cereals a doubling of price for a journey of 260 kilometers.

The Impossibility of True Cities before Agriculture

The constraints of transportation costs, in conjunction with the very thin population density in pre-Neolithic societies, explain the impossibility of the emergence of true cities during this time. Population density in pre-Neolithic societies varied considerably as a function of climate. The most densely populated tropical regions could support 2–3 and even as many as 9 inhabitants per square kilometer; at the opposite extreme, arctic regions could support only 0.003–0.007 people per square kilometer, or 1 person every 150–350 square kilometers. For Western Europe during the pre-Neolithic, the density must have been less than 0.1 person per square kilometer. Taking this figure as a basis for calculation, and postulating a food surplus of 10% (a hypothetical case in which rural regions produce 10% more food than they need for their own consumption) and a total absence of farming among city dwellers (an extreme assumption, as will be seen), it turns out that in order to maintain a city with a population of 1,000, and without taking the cost of transportation into account, an area of 100,000 square kilometers would have been required. When the cost of transportation is taken into account, the figure rises to 200,000 square kilometers, roughly five times the area of Switzerland, or about that of Great Britain. The significance of this fact will be more clear if it is recalled that in 7500 B.C. the population of the British Isles was only about 10,000.

Given the limited possibilities of transportation available at the time, the task of organizing the flow of trade required to maintain a single city of 1,000 inhabitants over a region that size, or even over a region one-tenth that size, was clearly impossible. For this reason it is not until the Neolithic and the invention of agriculture that the first signs of true urbanization appear. I say true urbanization because, as will be seen when (in chapter 4) the beginnings of the urban history of Black Africa are examined, it is possible to imagine, and there did in fact exist, fairly sizable concentrations of population during the proto-urban phase: 1,000–2,000 people living without agriculture and in the middle of the jungle, in a single, densely populated habitat. One of the conclusions of Reed (1977) in his synthesis is that, where there are adequate local resources, large villages are possible without agriculture. But what defines these settlements as villages, as opposed to true cities, is their dependence on the natural resources of the locality—a dependence entirely distinct from the reshaping of the environment characteristic of true cities.

With the advent of agriculture the givens of the problem change radically. In certain especially fertile regions, population density attained levels of 200–400 people per square kilometer. In the temperate regions of Europe, however, the concentration remained relatively thin. It is estimated that during the Neolithic, France had a population of 5 million inhabitants, or 9 people per square kilometer. But even taking this figure as a basis for calculation (with the same requirement of a food surplus of 10%), an area of only 1,200 square kilometers would have been necessary to support a city of 1,000 inhabitants, still 170 times less than in a society without agriculture.

This explains why cities first emerged in fertile regions and generally downstream in river basins, which permitted a reduction in transportation costs. The reduction was all the more significant in that, in the flow of exchange between town and country, the quantity of goods transported from the country to the town is and always has been greater than that transported by the town to the country. Indeed, even supposing a balance in the value of the goods flowing in the two directions (something that has probably never been the case), the price of manufactured articles per unit of weight has always been higher than that of agricultural commodities. Thus, if we take the situation at the end of the eighteenth century as an indicator of relative price levels, we see that a metric ton of woolen cloth was about 80 times more expensive than a metric ton of wheat and about 2,000 times more expensive than a metric ton of firewood. This means that the cost of transporting a given value of wheat would have been 80 times that of transporting the same value of woolen cloth, while that of transporting a like value of wood would have been 400 times higher.

This leads us to another factor likely to have favored urbanization in warmer regions: the mass of fuel needed to heat cities in colder climates. In traditional, preindustrial northern Europe, for example, the yearly consumption of firewood per person was about 1.6–2.3 metric tons. Let's assume an average annual production of firewood (including kindling and waste) of about 20–25 metric tons per square kilometer of forest (with a higher average for more intensive exploitation, but a lower average the colder the climate becomes). Then, to provide a city of 100,000 people with heating alone, without allowing for transport costs, would have required over 10,000 square kilometers of forest. And paradoxical though it may seem, the consumption of fuel in temperate parts of Europe was not much lower than in northern countries. In fact, the efficiency of the means of heating and cooking were, as a general rule, inversely proportional to average temperature, the open hearth being used in the South, the stove in the North. The most plausible figure for wood consumption in Europe as a whole is 1.0–1.6 metric tons per capita per year (Bairoch, 1988). And while these data properly apply to European urban systems from the sixteenth century to the eighteenth century alone, they do make it possible to establish relative values furnishing an order of magnitude for other urbanized societies. In the contemporary Third World, the consumption of wood in rural regions probably amounts to around 0.6–0.8 metric tons per capita per year.

All of these factors serve to explain why cities first appeared in warmer regions and especially in river basins where two harvests per year were possible. Clearly there was a marked geo-economic determinism at work in the birth of urbanization. The problem that remains, one to which I shall return first when I examine urbanism in antiquity, is that of the interactions between the various elements of the urban equation. What, for example, was the influence of the city on rural development? This is an important question to which answers so far are essentially ambiguous and above all purely specific in their range of application.

In any event, if agriculture removed most of the obstacles in the path toward genuine urbanization, it manifestly failed to resolve all of the difficulties. I have already drawn attention to the difficulties with transportation, difficulties which were only part of the vast problem of the provisioning of cities, which is related to the storage of cereals. It is worth pointing out the hypothesis of Van Leuven (1979), who suggested that to some extent the destruction of certain prehistoric buildings should not be attributed to earthquakes, as is usual, but rather to explosions caused by the accumulation of gases during the storage of grain. As everyone knows, under certain conditions of temperature and humidity, explosions may occur even in modern silos designed and constructed on scientific principles. It is obvious, then, that such occurrences must have been more frequent in the earliest urban civilizations, where storage techniques were far more rudimentary. And in addition to the problems of the supply and storage of food, there were also those relating to the provision of potable water. For if most cities were "born" on the banks of watercourses, this did not always suffice, for a great variety of reasons, to supply all of the needed drinking water.

Peasants Who Live in Cities

The rural world, a world of peasants; the urban world, a world of craftsmen. Certainly this distinction is mainly accurate. The differentiation between the activities normally carried out in cities and those normally carried out in the country, particularly as concerns the nonproduction of food by city dwellers, is the essence of urbanization. But the dichotomy between town and country should not be pushed too far, regarding manufacturing and service-related industries as being exclusively located in the cities and regarding agriculture as a purely rural pursuit. For although rural industry is well known and sometimes considered very important, it is otherwise where the peasant component of cities is concerned, which scholars frequently tend to overlook or ignore. But this is a serious omission. It goes without saying that it is never possible to estimate with any precision the degree to which farmers took part in the first phases of urbanism. But on the basis of the indications available with respect to other stages in the process of urbanization, it can be safely concluded that the contribution of farmers was in fact major.

Indeed, even in the second half of the twentieth century and in developed nations, a significant level of agricultural employment remains, even in very large cities. Around 1960, for example, about 10% of the working population of Italian cities of 100,000–200,000 people were employed in agriculture (Bairoch, 1976a). The proportion is still on the order of 3–5% today in cities with populations of 200,000–600,000. True, Italy is a special case, but the proportion in other developed countries is about 1–3% for cities with populations of more than 100,000, and even reaches 4% in the United States in metropolitan areas with populations of 200,000–300,000.

In the Third World during the 1970s, it is estimated that roughly 25–30 percent of the working population in cities with populations of 5,000–20,000 worked in agriculture. The proportion in cities with populations of 20,000–50,000 is still about 20–25%. Returning to a stage somewhat nearer the origins of urbanism, it will be noted that in many precolonial cities in Black Africa (some of which had populations of more than 10,000, as will be seen in chapter 26), it can be estimated that about 40–50% of these "city dwellers" tilled the fields, and peasants were very numerous in certain Chinese cities as well (chapter 22).

In the traditional societies of Europe from the sixteenth century to the eighteenth century, the proportion appears to have been lower than in the cities of the contemporary Third World. But it is not unreasonable to suppose that in cities with populations of less than 10,000, the proportion of the population working in agriculture was somewhere on the order of 5–10%. Neither of these percentages should be regarded as an outside limit. In certain cities, the proportion may have risen above 15% while in others, for example Geneva (Perrenoud, 1979), the proportion was probably less than 5%.

All of this permits the supposition that, in many preurban towns, as well as a great many small cities during the early phases of urbanization, farmers formed the dominant fraction of the urban population. This would explain the many instances of apparently advanced urban development in economic environments that do not seem wholly to justify it.

What If the City Invented Agriculture?

This chapter will close with a question mark. Is it necessary to totally rule out an extremely unorthodox hypothesis that would invert the direction of the interaction between the invention of agriculture and the emergence of cities? This is the thesis of Jacobs (1969), the first chapter of whose book, *The Economy of Cities*, is titled "Cities First—Rural Development Later."

Jacobs's initial premise is certainly fallacious, for she derives one of her principal arguments from the city's undoubted role as a driving force for agricultural productivity in the contemporary world. For Jacobs, "agriculture is not even tolerably productive unless it incorporates many goods and services produced in cities or transplanted from cities." In order to support this judgment, she compares the current state of affairs in regions that have attained only a modest level of urbanization—which generally have a backward form of agriculture—with that in highly urbanized regions, which have a highly productive agriculture. But while this comparison may shed a good deal of light on the current situation, there is nothing in it that would genuinely support the application of Jacobs's thesis to the preurban world of the pre-Neolithic. The argument is based on a patent anachronism. The author's analysis of the role cities played in the agricultural revolution suffers from a similar lack of evidential foundation and seems to me, therefore, extremely unconvincing. But though Jacobs may have failed to make her case for the pre-Neolithic period that saw the birth of agriculture, this does not exclude the possibility that urbanization may have contributed to progress in agriculture—as in fact it has done, especially from the nineteenth century on (see chapters 16 and 21).

But while the opening premise of Jacobs's analysis proves faulty, and while her arguments do not prove that agriculture was invented in the city, the margin of uncertainty around that period is such that the hypothesis cannot be rejected outright. As was shown earlier, it is possible that towns first formed as the result of concentrations of hunters gathered in encampments of hundreds of people. And nothing rules out the possibility that, in these "towns" or somewhere nearby, demographic pressure may have driven the inhabitants to seek new sources of food while seeking at the same time to develop crafts. But even if this hypothesis were to be confirmed, agriculture—whether invented in the town or in the country—would remain essential for the development of true cities. Without some sort of rural agriculture, it is impossible to envisage the rise of an authentic urban system spanning an entire region. In short, the actual site of the invention of agriculture in no way changes the basic problem of the birth of urbanism.

Besides, in the model Jacobs constructs to explain the urban invention of agriculture, the town as depicted in the role of "theoretical inventor" is essentially a commercial town. But this is to say, as provided for in the model, that the town in question imports food, that is, the surplus food previously produced in some other region. This surplus would be hard to account for without agriculture. In any event, the model requires the prior existence of surplus food and the prior existence of trade in order for the town to have invented agriculture. This second "prior" seems more plausible, however, since, as will be shown in the next chapter, exchange over long distances did in fact precede true urbanization. It should nevertheless be borne in mind that this commercial factor probably favored the diffusion of agriculture more than its actual invention.

2 The Urban Revolution: Its Beginnings in the Middle East □

Why begin the history of urbanism with the Middle East? The answer is simple. In the light of the current state of research on the question, the view accepted for decades—that the first true cities evolved in the Middle East—remains valid. What Gordon Childe wrote in 1928 about the Middle Eastern origin of the urban revolution still holds true today. If we qualify this assessment by adding "in the light of the current state of research on the question," surprises may yet be in store; we cannot rule out the possibility that fresh discoveries may at some future date overturn this chronology. But even if something of the kind did occur, even if one day someone were to unearth traces of a genuine urban system more ancient than any found in the Middle East, this would in no way diminish the preeminence of this region. For even if such a system existed, its influence on the history of humanity as a whole could not have been so decisive as that of the Middle East.

Early Urbanization, Early Agriculture

According to the currently available evidence, the first cities and the first agricultural systems were born in the Middle East. Like its predecessors, the third edition of Grahame Clark's review of existing knowledge on the subject (1977) opens the history of the Neolithic with Southwest Asia. As early as 9000 B.C., sheep had been domesticated in several parts of the Middle Eastern Fertile Crescent. The "first agricultural experiments" date from 8300–7300 B.C. (Aurenche, 1981). As Cohen (1977) points out, agriculture was born almost simultaneously in Iran, Iraq, Kurdistan, Syria, Palestine, and western Turkey. This simultaneity argues against the notion of a diffusion of agriculture from a single source. But whether it sprang from one source or rose simultaneously on all sides, the fact remains that agriculture diffused rapidly in every direction, with the result that we may assume it had already reached the entire region by 5000–4000 B.C., if not before.

But the fact that agriculture reached the whole region by this date does not mean that all of the region's populations were sedentary. The semidesert character of certain parts of the Middle East favored the persistence of nomadic societies—societies that discovered a new source of supplementary income from their role as traders and conveyers for the societies that did change over to agriculture and, subsequently, to an urbanized way of life.

"International Trade" Preceded True Urbanization

The term "international trade" is doubtless anachronistic in this context, since real nations did not yet exist. Nevertheless it is the term that best describes the reality. For trade did take place among various societies and above all between societies very distant from each other. This international or long-distance trade was brought to light by the very first archaeological investigations in the region. The existence of this kind of trade has served as one of the chief explanatory elements in theories emphasizing the role of diffusion, rather than simultaneous growth, in accounts of the origins of urbanization. Obviously, given the concentration of research efforts in this part of the world, it is for the Middle East that we have most information concerning commerce. And the body of evidence assembled in recent syntheses and the papers of Earle and Ericson (1977), Peacock (1977), Kohl (1978), and Yener (1982) is sufficient to affirm beyond any reasonable doubt that trade did indeed occur during this period, despite the fact that true urban systems had yet to be established in those regions.

There is certainly a tendency to overestimate the scale of trade during the Neolithic. The overestimation of the extent of trade constitutes a recurrent feature of historical research. Of all fields of human activity, trade leaves the most traces behind it, and it has for this reason attracted the most attention. But in order to gauge more accurately the limited extent of trade in traditional and, a fortiori, in prehistoric societies, it will suffice to consider the example of Europe, of all continents incontestably the most outward looking. And even as late as the eighteenth century, the time that marks the high point in socioeconomic development prior to the Industrial Revolution, the proportion of exports (or imports) to overall volume of production in Europe was no more than, and probably less than, 2 to 3%.

But despite the tendency to overestimate the amount of trade, during the Neolithic it was nevertheless extensive enough to have enabled diffusion of technological innovation. Even if trade represented only some 0.5–1.0% of total production, this would still imply sufficiently frequent contacts between different regions to assure the dissemination both of the information contained in the goods exchanged and of the information conveyed by merchants and other intermediaries.

However restricted it may have been, there was still enough traffic between the different societies of the Neolithic world to justify the many hypotheses concerning the diffusion of urbanization from one region to another. Trade also played a significant part, in widely diverse geographical settings, as a disseminating agent in subsequent urbanization.

Establishing that trade developed in a context in which urbanization was still unknown is, then, a matter of some importance. And proofs are abundant, especially with regard to trade between regions that were somewhat urbanized and regions still totally unurbanized. Thus in the case of Europe, for example, evidence steadily accumulates which shows that in many parts of the Continent before the emergence of real cities, products of various sorts were imported, most notably pottery from advanced cultures of the Mediterranean. At a later stage, between the fourth and seventh centuries A.D., small trade centers sprang up in Northern Europe, particularly in Sweden, which had trade with the rest of the Continent without having any of the attributes of genuine urbanization (see chapter 5). Many other examples could be cited.

A more delicate question is that of trade over long distances between two nonurbanized regions. But here, too, the evidence increases pointing to the existence of some sort of trade. Recent research has even confirmed that boats capable of transporting cargoes large for the times (boats eight meters in length requiring a crew of at least three men) crossed the English Channel during the Bronze Age (Muckelroy, 1980).

The First Urbanized Cultures: Density and Size

Before going any further, I ought to draw attention to a major source of pitfalls in the analysis of urbanism in the context of the first cultures of antiquity: the extreme difficulty in making generalizations. There is always a great risk of oversimplification. As Mumford points out (1961), the chief distinguishing feature of cities, and especially of cities in traditional societies, is their individuality. On the other hand, to treat the cities of antiquity we must cover a period roughly spanning four millennia (3500 B.C.–A.D. 500). And these were four millennia during which culture and technology evolved greatly. It should be recalled that in 3200 B.C., metallurgy, even bronze, had not yet been invented, that writing was still not in use, that methods of cultivation were still very crude, and that neither the horse nor the camel had yet been truly domesticated. But while a good deal of caution must be observed, it is nevertheless possible to come to a few tentative conclusions about urbanism as it evolved through its earliest phases.

The area covered by the towns of the preurban period was on the order of 3–5 hectares. With the Middle Eastern cultures of antiquity the scale changes radically: beyond any shadow of a doubt, there are true cities. This was the real beginning of urbanization or, to borrow Childe's term once again, the real beginning of the Urban Revolution.

Indeed, from the year 3000 B.C. on, the first Sumerian cities had an area of some 40 hectares, reaching 100 hectares by 2000 B.C. But this difference in area does not indicate a strictly equivalent difference in population. The ratio between area and population is far from being a constant, either from one period or culture to the next, or within the same period, the same culture, and even the same region.

As a general rule, the population density inside the perimeter of a city is determined by three parameters, each of which leaves considerable room for variation:

1. Within a walled enclosure, the space occupied by buildings may be more or less extensive. For example, a city's walls may surround gardens much larger than the ground covered by buildings.

2. The area occupied by the buildings may contain more or less inhabitable space depending on the levels; buildings may have had one, two, three, or even four stories.

3. Finally, the density of occupation may vary considerably. Even today, there are in Europe countries where there are an average of 0.6–0.7 occupants per room (Belgium, West Germany, Switzerland, and the Scandinavian countries) and others where there are 1.4–1.7 occupants per room (Greece and the countries of Eastern Europe). In the nations of the Third World, the average is generally in excess of 2.0 occupants per room.

It can be seen, then, how great the margin of uncertainty is in estimating the population of cities for which the only information is the perimeter of the enclosing wall. It is possible to conceive of deviations ranging between 1 and 3 in estimates of the average number of stories per building, between 1 and 2 in estimates of the density of occupancy, and between 1 and 2 in estimates of the amount of ground covered by the buildings themselves as opposed to gardens, streets, marketplaces, and so forth. Thus, taking the extreme case, the combined deviations in measures of population density relative to the total area of the urban site may range anywhere between 1 and 12.

But perhaps we can be a little more precise in our uncertainty. It may be noted that in dealing with the early cities of antiquity, it is not uncommon for scholars to propose population densities on the order of 400–700 people per hectare. These figures are high, but by no means exceptional. The cities of the European Middle Ages generally had densities of 150–400 inhabitants per hectare, and densities as high as 500–600 people per hectare were not exceptional. Being in Geneva and taking a special personal interest in the history of this city, I observe that, according to information communicated to me by my colleague A. Perrenoud (1979), fourteenth-century Geneva had only 70 inhabitants per hectare; but by the middle of the sixteenth century and up until the middle of the eighteenth, this figure had risen to 350. Geneva in 1789 had as many as 440 inhabitants per hectare, and in 1843 (before the demolition of the city walls) 490. As for the inner-city areas of European cities at the end of the nineteenth century, within a radius of 0.5 kilometers of the city center, the lowest population density (Oslo) was on the order of 205, and the highest (Breslau) on the order of 606 inhabitants per hectare, the average being on the order of 300–400. Back in the fifteenth century, population density in Genoa ran as high as 770 people per hectare. On the other hand, as will be seen later, the population density in what are called the "macro temples" of the pre-Columbian civilizations seems to have been fairly low—40–60 inhabitants per hectare. This figure is only five to seven times higher than the figure for certain of the more densely populated rural regions of the nineteenth and twentieth centuries, and probably long before then as well. Thus for the region of Baghdad during the period that saw the emergence of that city (600 B.C.), Adams (1965) notes concentration of population, supported by a temple and an agrarian settlement, of close to 70 people per hectare, a figure that seems too high. In Asia as a whole, according to the data collected by Colin Clark (1977), urban densities had reached a very high level by the end of the nineteenth century and the beginning of the twentieth century, surpassing in most instances 500 inhabitants per hectare.

I shall now try to reduce this spread somewhat in order to arrive at figures likely to express the dominant, if not the average, situation. The admirable review of the existing literature of Mols (1954–56) (which has not, alas, been brought up to date) permits me to establish for Europe from 1550 to 1800 an average density of urban population on the order of 175–190 inhabitants per hectare, with (not extreme) maxima on the order of 350–400 and minima 70–90 inhabitants per hectare. On the basis of the no-less-admirable synthesis of Russell (1958) (which, unfortunately, has not been brought up to date either), the following indications may be formulated. For Europe from the fourteenth century to the sixteenth century (especially after the great plagues), the average density was some 100–115 inhabitants per hectare, with minima of 60–80 and maxima of 250–300 people per hectare. (The corresponding figure for the period before the outbreak of the plague, a period, however, for which the data are less numerous, was 140–160 per hectare.) The results obtained for the cities of ancient Greece and Rome are not much different. But the density appears to have been perceptibly higher in the cities of the Middle East, and particularly in the Muslim cities where the average would seem to have stood nearer 250 people per hectare.

From these and other fairly plentiful, if rather disparate, data accumulated in the course of my analysis of the various societies of the world, I may draw the following conclusions. The spread is very pronounced, and though the range of deviations may not in fact stretch over the full theoretical scale of 1 to 12 just calculated, it does never-theless reach nearly as far as 1 to 6. Even in unexceptional cases, the population density of individual cities may conceivably range between 70 inhabitants per hectare at one end and 400 inhabitants per hectare at the other. For the urban conglomerations comprising a large num-ber of cities, a density of 100–250 people per hectare may be calcu-lated, and were I to hazard an average, it would fall around 160–180. All of this applies, moreover, only to the cities of traditional societies since antiquity. The concentration of urban population was probably heavier in the cities of the first cultures of antiquity and in the urban systems of the period of protourbanization than they were later; for the preurban era, I would estimate an average density on the order of 200–400 inhabitants per hectare.

I shall now return to the great change in the fabric of socioeco-nomic life that marked the emergence of the cities of the ancient world. Taking an average density of 300 inhabitants per hectare for preurban towns and an average no higher than 150 for the cities of antiquity, this would still suggest that the population of cities rose from 400–1,000 in preurban times to 15,000 or more in the cities of the antique civilizations. Unquestionably, then, their size indicates that these were true cities. And even if certain of the data did not al-ready confirm the existence of cities, this size alone would further imply, ipso facto, yet other features characteristic of genuine urban centers. With dimensions of this kind, a high proportion of the work-ing population must have engaged in nonagricultural pursuits, and the transition to an economy involving such a high proportion of "in-dustrial" activities would have entailed a correspondingly high level of specialization. Such a size equally implies, furthermore, an elaborate socioeconomic organization and a true urban habitat, all of which could not have failed to carry along with them a specifically urban mentality. But these matters will be further discussed later. Now sev-eral more concrete aspects of urbanization in the ancient world will be analyzed.

A Dominant Form of Urbanized Culture: City-States

Whenever one attempts to generalize about the form urban development took in the early cultures of the Middle East, one form in particular assumes predominance: that which historians, and nota-bly Toynbee (1970), call the city-state. By city-states we mean societies that, while exhibiting certain of the essential attributes of states, never-theless retain the character and dimensions of cities; or if the reader prefers, cities that in combination with their respective hinterlands form independent states entirely separate from each other. We have to deal here, however, with a phenomenon that transcends both the geographical context of the Middle East and the historical context of antiquity. City-states first appeared with the emergence of the Mesopotamian cultures (that is, around 3200–3000 B.C.), finally vanishing only in the middle of the eighteenth century, with the reunifications of Germany and Italy and the achievement of a closer federation in Switzerland. A case can be made, moreover, for the idea that the phenomenon survives even into the present in several isolated instances: Hong Kong, Monaco, the Vatican, and Singapore.

As for the Middle East and Europe, Toynbee distinguishes four main types of city-state: the Sumerian and Akkadian cities, whose historical epoch unfolded in 3000–2000 B.C.; the Phoenician and Philistine cities, whose era began sometime around 1000 B.C.; the Greek, Etruscan and Italian cities, which also came into existence sometime around 1000 B.C.; and the city-states of medieval Europe, which first appeared in Italy during the seventh century and in Northern Europe during the thirteenth century.

The city-states of Europe will be discussed in chapter 5 and again, for the medieval period, in part 2. Here, I shall concentrate on the city-states of antiquity, providing a brief historical overview of urbanism in the Middle East up to the time of ancient Greece.

As was seen above, a fifth type can be added, the city-states of the contemporary period. Furthermore, as Griffeth (1981) rightly notes, the African Hausa culture of the fifteenth to nineteenth centuries was composed of city-states. A better knowledge of non-European urban cultures would permit us to find other examples of city-states. I will return to the city-states of Europe in the next section and very briefly to those of Africa in chapter 24. Now, I return to the city-states of antiquity for a brief survey of urbanism before ancient Greece.

From the City-States of Sumer to the Cities of the Egyptian Empire by Way of Babylon

One can never take sufficient precautions when declaring, as scholars usually do, that the first region to have seen the emergence of genuine cities lay in that part of present-day Iraq situated between the Tigris and the Euphrates rivers, that part of Mesopotamia in which the civilization of Sumer took root. For it is always possible that this claim may one day become subject to revision, as has been the case with all earlier attempts to identify the site of the original cities. The fact remains that, in the light of current knowledge on the subject, the first true city still seems to have been Eridu, whose beginnings appear to date from about 3200 B.C., or perhaps even as early as 3500 B.C. In this region, or more precisely a little to the north of Eridu, by 6000

B.C. large villages of four to five hectares emerged which had both craft activities and long-distance trade in luxury goods like copper and turquoise.

The number of Sumerian cities grew steadily thereafter, starting with the famous city of Ur, and there seem to have been some ten to fifteen city-states in the region. As Oates (1980) has observed, most of the cities of Mesopotamia were located in the most fertile parts of the region, notably the alluvial plain between the Tigris and the Euphrates and the moist slopes of the northern plain. All of these were areas in which agriculture was particularly well established.

Each of these cities reigned supreme over the surrounding countryside, creating in this way an integral economic unit within which an exchange of goods and services evolved. To put the matter in more concrete terms, consider Ur as it stood around the year 2800 B.C. The city covered at that time an area of about forty hectares, with a population on the order of 24,000. The territory occupied by the state as a whole, on the other hand, would appear to have had a population of some 500,000, thus making a ratio of rural to urban population on the order of twenty-one to one, the urban population representing a little less than 5 percent of the total—a proportion perfectly in accord with what we know about the economic circumstances of the period.

The following centuries were characterized by steady growth in the size of the various cities, certain of them attaining at their height populations variously estimated at 100,000 and even as much as 300,000. If this last figure seems excessive, it is by no means impossible, given the geographical location and the fertility of the soil in the region. Owning land and exercising control over a sizable artisanry, the temples played an important part in the life of the Sumerian cities, as they did again later in Egypt, and also, after their fashion, as would the churches in the various Christian cultures. But even though the Sumerian kings had close links with the Temple and its clergy, the effective direction of the city lay in the hands of an administration directly answerable to the sovereign. This administration seems to have performed a decisive role in external trade (of which definite signs remain) and probably in the internal commercial life of the city as well. Furthermore, the role of the state, as attested by written records, finds indirect verification in the urban plan of the Sumerian cities, inasmuch as historians have revealed the absence of open markets. This fact does not suffice, however, to prove the absence of a market economy, nor even of a true market established in the streets.

By 1800 B.C., however, Babylon had supplanted this Sumerian culture of city-states; with the rise of Babylon, indeed, we already move on to an entirely new type of culture. For Babylonia was no longer merely one city-state among others, but rather an empire in which one city, imposing itself as the capital, held sway over the life of the region at large. It was, in fact, practically a city-empire. The city itself, moreover, henceforth took on dimensions commensurate with its new imperial status, ruling as it did over an empire that at its height under Hammurabi (1728–1686 B.C.), extended over some 400,000 square kilometers. Babylon was the first giant city of antiquity. Without going as far as Herodotus, who exaggerates considerably, attributing to the city an area of approximately forty-eight thousand hectares (an area ultimately capable of sustaining a population in excess of ten million people), the reality was impressive enough, since Babylon appears to have had a population on the order of 200,000–300,000. To put this statistic in perspective, in the various European societies (except Rome and Muslim Spain), it was not until the seventeenth century that another city, Paris, reached a comparable size.

Before leaving this part of the world, it is worth pausing a moment to consider the case of two ancient city-states, both of which reached their zenith before the fabled city of Babylon, whose history has only recently come to light: Mari and Ebla.

The archaeological adventure of Mari began quite by accident in 1933, when peasants living in the neighborhood of Abdu Kemal, a very small town in Syria near the Iraqi border, happened to dig up a statue. The recently deceased French archaeologist, André Parrot, spent nearly forty years engaged "in what I would dare call my love affair with Mari" (Parrot, 1979), laboring to bring the city back to life. The greatest treasure unearthed at Mari was the city's archives, containing more than twenty-five thousand clay tablets whose decipherment, still in progress, sheds a new light on the history of the city itself and on the economic and administrative life of the region as a whole. It will, in fact, one day enable us to fill in an important chapter in the economic history of the world.

The city dates from at least forty-five hundred years ago, covering an area of about sixty hectares, having a population of at least ten thousand. The city and its civilization flourished during nearly a millennium. The late discovery of this site, like that of Ebla, is due to the fact that the chief building material used in its construction was raw brick.

The archaeological adventure of Ebla is even more recent, beginning only in 1964. Ebla lies in Syria, about fifty kilometers southwest of Aleppo. Here, too, archives have been discovered showing the considerable control city-states exerted over economic life. Both the highly evolved artisanry and the very extensive commercial activity of the city were subjected to state supervision. And in the case of Ebla, the city even had a large livestock holding in the rural areas under its sway. Ebla appears to have been founded even earlier than Mari, and after having been destroyed by fire at least once around 2000 B.C., was abandoned in about 1600 B.C. It was thanks to this fire, which hardened the clay tablets, that the city's archives were preserved for posterity and the greater glory of the Italian archaeologists who found them.

Egypt: A Civilization That First Evolved without Cities?

Egypt represents something of a special case. In the first instance, there is the long duration of this civilization. For the ancient Egyptian Empire began by 2850 B.C., and the age of the pyramids began around 2500 B.C., and yet the empire was still strong enough to conquer the Persian empire sometime around 525 B.C. There is a sense, indeed, in which this civilization may be said to have survived up until the suicide of Cleopatra in the year A.D. 30. But to be more realistic, the line should be drawn prior to the Hellenization of Egypt— sometime around 330 B.C.

It is possible that cities played a different role in Egypt than in the other civilizations of the Middle East. Hammond (1972) even writes that, viewed in a certain light, the interaction between the city and civilization in Egypt was diametrically opposed to that found in the other civilizations in the region. For in the other civilizations, it was the city that brought about civilization, the effects of the city on civilization outweighing the effects of civilization on the city. But in Egypt, civilization gave birth to the city, and this civilization retained, moreover, a predominantly rural character.

Such is, or at any rate such until recently has been, the dominant theory among those Egyptologists who have taken an interest in the first phases of urbanization in Egyptian civilization, notably Wolfgang Helck and especially John Wilson. The latter, moreover, gave to a communication delivered to a symposium held in 1958 the provocative title, "Egypt Through the New Kingdom: Civilization without Cities." The enormity of this suggestion will become more apparent if it is recalled that in the history of Egypt scholars traditionally distinguish between the Old Kingdom or Empire (2700–2100 B.C.), the Middle Kingdom or Empire (2100–1580 B.C.), and the New Kingdom or Empire (1580–1090 B.C.). Thus, according to Wilson, Egypt had no cities until the year 1090 B.C. This notion has been challenged by Kemp (1977), who argues that students of ancient Egypt have placed too much emphasis on the study of inscriptions at the expense of archaeological analysis, and that archaeological analysis shows beyond any doubt that the Egypt of this period was in fact an urbanized society much like any other in the region.

Even admitting the strength of Kemp's argument, one must nevertheless refrain from considering Egypt, and particularly Egypt before 1090 B.C., as being altogether like the other ancient civilizations of the Middle East. What was peculiar to Egyptian civilization, however, was more closely linked to the distinctive character of its urban system than to the degree of urbanization, this system differing in several important respects from the dominant models of the period.

In the first place, Egypt did not have an urban complex composed of a number of separate city-states, or city-empires; instead it was a single state made up of a number of provinces, each one having a city or cities of its own. In the second place, none was a dominant economic metropolis. It was not until the onset of Greek influence and the eventual Hellenization of Egypt that one very great city, Alexandria, emerged, which had a population exceeding 300,000 around 320 B.C., and which exercised economic functions vital to the empire as a whole. Furthermore, when the period of Alexandria's preeminence did in due course arrive, its apogee was very short-lived and its decline very rapid. A third distinguishing feature of the Egyptian urban system was the absence of fortified enclosures. Egyptian cities were open, for peace reigned throughout the interior of the country; wars were rare and their theater of operations generally lay outside Egyptian territory. Finally, taken together the cities of ancient Egypt in all probability comprised an urban population relatively smaller than that of the other civilizations of the region: in other words, Egypt was indeed on the whole a rather rural country.

All of this serves to explain the dominant role played by the temples in Egyptian urban life. The priesthood owned about 15 percent of the land, and their slaves represented just about 2 percent of the total population. Egyptian cities, in short, had religious and administrative functions rather than economic functions in the life of the society at large. In this regard, it is interesting to note the emergence of what are called "pyramid cities." Indeed, a certain number of these monuments gave birth to cities. They were not a result of "worker cities" that were erected during the construction of these enormous monuments and that were destroyed after the work was finished, but rather the use of these pyramids as religious monuments gave rise to these cities (Stadelmann, 1981).

The Phoenicians: The First Commercial Towns

The city-states of the Phoenicians were a type of city that later played a significant part in urban history. These were cities whose economic substratum was not only the neighboring countryside, but also and above all their commercial ties with other, more distant, regions. The Phoenician cities were indeed coastal towns that developed principally as a result of international trade, in which they assumed the role of active intermediaries for the whole of the Mediterranean basin. There exists, in fact, a close parallel between the Phoenician city-states and the cities of Italy in the Middle Ages, and even those of the Netherlands and the Hanseatic League. And as in the case of these later European cities, so in dealing with the Phoenician city-states, one should not neglect the contribution these commercial towns made to the economy of the surrounding region generally, fostering local industrial development aimed at the production of goods destined for the international market the cities themselves did so much to enlarge. The production of glass, for example, was as closely linked with the growth of Phoenician civilization as it would later be linked with the growth of Venice.

Byblos, a city founded on the site of present-day Jebail in Lebanon, was apparently the first important pre-Phoenician commercial town, and thus probably one of the first commercial towns in the world. Dating back as far as the third millennium B.C., it gives evidence of active trade, not only with the sizable economic communities situated in the Middle East (Mesopotamia, Egypt, and Cyprus), but also with regions as distant as the Sudan and the Caucasus. As Hammond (1972) observes, Byblos became the chief port for trade between Syria and Egypt. Traffic with this last country was so intense and so early (2300–2200 B.C.) that a seagoing vessel was called in Egypt a "Byblos boat." And as was also the case in most of the commercial towns of Europe, the Phoenicians city-states were governed not by kings, but by a kind of Council of Elders—a representative council, in other words, whose members were most likely drawn from the merchant class.

The other important maritime commercial cities of the Phoenicians were Acre, Aradus, Beirut, Ugarit, Sidon, and Tyre. The last two played leading roles, as stressed by Bunnens (1979). The various Phoenician city-states reached their heights at different dates, and their commercial relations sometimes involved different partners; but all of the city-states owed their development to external trade. But while the beginnings of the Phoenician civilization came very early, the most dynamic phase of its evolution, the phase including the largest number of cities, began around 1200 B.C. And it was sometime around the year 700 B.C., with the rise of the Greek city-states, that the decline of the commercial power of the Phoenicians began. But though the Phoenician cities went into decline at this time, they did not yet disappear as a major force in the life of the region, for under Persian rule (538–332 B.C.), the Phoenician cities retained a significant commercial function, notably supplying the Persian kings with fleets.

In contrast to the commercial cities of medieval Europe, the Phoenician cities did not figure among the largest cities in the Middle East. It appears that none of them surpassed eighty hectares in area, which suggests that the population of the largest Phoenician cities was probably on the order of fifteen to thirty thousand. Supposing an extremely high population density, which, given the economic context, cannot be ruled out, the population of certain of these cities may have risen to as much as sixty thousand. But most of the Phoenician commercial towns extended over an area of less than sixty hectares.

The Phoenician civilization was not confined to the eight or ten coastal towns founded in the region corresponding to present-day Lebanon and Israel; it also comprised a string of colonies planted around the Mediterranean, and perhaps even farther away. And while it is true that many of these colonies were, and remained, mere ports of convenience, others became true cities in their own right, the most famous being Carthage. The creation of this string of Phoenician colonies or, more accurately, of semiautonomous states ultimately dependent on the city of Tyre, no doubt reflected certain commercial imperatives. But there may also have been additional, more strictly economic motives arising from the difficulties in providing for a growing population with the aid of agricultural imports from regions beyond the immediate vicinity of the mother cities. The colonies may, moreover, have played a part in assuring a regular supply of raw materials for local industries.

As for industry, I have already mentioned the Phoenician manufacture of glass. Pliny's attribution of the invention of glass to the Phoenician merchants is certainly false, since glass was known before the Phoenicians. The fact remains that the Phoenicians improved the techniques used in its manufacture and on this account performed a role of great importance in the history of its production. Greater revenues seem to have accrued, however, from the production and exportation of dyed (especially purple) cloth, to which the Phoenicians joined a trade in luxury textiles and jewelry, that is to say, in articles with a considerable added value commanding a price high enough to justify the cost of transporting them over long distances. Another economic activity that will be seen again later in the commercial city-states and nations that came after Phoenicia was ship construction—an industry, it goes without saying, in which delivery posed no grave problems. The Phoenicians also exported services, since participated in the erection of the Temple of Jerusalem. Commercial relations with the kingdom of Israel were also intense, particularly during the reign of King Solomon (973–935 B.C.). Solomon engaged in a great deal of construction for which "Israel needed building materials, metal, and other commodities, which were supplied and transported to Jaffa by the Tyrians in exchange for agricultural products" (Reviv, 1971).

What Sustained the Commercial Towns of the Ancient World?

These exchanges between Israel and Tyre already afford at least a part of the solution of a problem that will frequently be seen in the treatment of the various commercial cities and nations of the world. The case of the Phoenician cities in general, and of Tyre in particular, demonstrates this unalterable fact of economic life: commercial towns and nations cannot fulfill their economic functions without drawing on the agricultural resources of other regions. The analysis of the external trade of the Phoenicians is rendered difficult by the total absence to date of documentary evidence relating to this question. It is not that the Phoenicians had no form of writing—they are even credited with the invention of the alphabet, the origin of which, it is generally agreed, was located at Ugarit sometime before 1200 B.C. What they apparently did lack, however, were chroniclers. This lacuna was so tantalizing that in the nineteenth century it led to a notorious hoax—frauds of that kind being, it seems, an ill to which archaeology is more often heir than other sciences.

But, fortunately, external trade involves partners, and one of these has left very explicit written records of the nature of commerce between itself and Phoenicia, notably regarding what it imported from the Phoenicians, the composition of its own exports being well known. This is how, in the King James translation, the Bible (Ez. 26–27), describes the commercial relations of the proud and wealthy city of Tyre:

> Renowned city, which was strong in the sea . . . all
> the ships of the sea with their mariners were in thee
> to occupy thy merchandise . . . Tarshish was thy
> merchant by reason of the multitude of all kinds of
> riches; with silver, iron, tin, and lead, they traded in
> thy fairs. Javan, Tubal, and Meshech, they were thy
> merchants: they traded the persons of men and ves-
> sels of brass in thy market. They of the house of To-
> garmah traded in thy fairs with horses and horse-
> men and mules. The men of Dedan were thy mer-
> chants; many isles were the merchandise of thine
> hand; they brought thee for a present horns of ivory
> and ebony. Syria was thy merchant by reason of the
> multitude of the wares of thy making: they occupied
> in thy fairs with emeralds, purple, and broidered
> work, and fine linen, and coral, and agate. Judah,
> and the land of Israel, they were thy merchants:
> they traded in thy market wheat of Minnith, and
> Pannag, and honey, and oil, and balm. Damascus
> was thy merchant in the multitudes of the wares of
> thy making, for the multitude of all riches; in the
> wine of Helbon, and white wool. Dan also and Javan
> going to and fro occupied in thy fairs: bright iron,
> cassia, and calamus, were in thy market. Dedan was
> thy merchant in precious clothes for chariots. Ara-
> bia, and all the princes of Kedar, they occupied with
> thee in lambs, and rams, and goats: in these were
> they thy merchants. The merchants of Sheba, and
> Raamah, they were thy merchants: they occupied in
> thy fairs with chief of all spices, and with all precious
> stones, and gold. Haran, and Canneh, and Eden, the
> merchants of Sheba, Asshur, and Chilmad, were thy

merchants. These were thy merchants in all sorts of
things, in blue clothes, and broidered work, and in
chests of rich apparel, bound with cords, and made
of cedar, among thy merchandise.

As will be gathered from this enumeration, raw materials and food-
stuffs very largely predominated among Phoenician imports. Is. 23:3
declares, moreover, still with reference to Tyre: "the seed of Sihor,
the harvest of the river [the Nile], is her revenue." And to cite an even
more revealing text, Isaiah, after noting the destruction of the power
of the city of Tyre, writes (Is. 23:10): "Pass through [cultivate] thy
land as a river, O daughter of Tarshish: there is no more strength,"
signifying the closure of the city's shipyards and, with it, the loss of its
basic means of support, owing to its massive reliance on food shipped
in from foreign parts.

We are, then, truly in the presence of the first major instance of
commercial cities taking their place in a geographical setting far wider
than that provided by their immediate hinterlands. The existence of
the Phoenician commercial towns can only be explained in the context
of trade within a very large region: a region to whose general economic life they made a significant contribution and from which they
drew the resources necessary for their growth. We find even here,
however, at a time prior to the beginnings of true economic specialization, a phenomenon we shall encounter in the quasi totality of cities
specializing either in industry or trade in later ages: the existence of a
local economic and especially agricultural support base ultimately responsible for the city's original emergence. As Petit (1972) argues, before taking on their role as navigators and traders, thus founding
what Herm (1976) characterizes a little romantically as "cities that take
to the sea," the Phoenicians "were careful farmers and skilled craftsmen. The small plains they occupied were considered very rich, thanks
to irrigation and the regularization of the course of the rivers. Cereals
and the cultivation of shrubs were essential, and the knowledge of the
Phoenicians passed on to the Carthaginians, renowned for it among
the Greeks and Romans, who translated their works of agronomy into
their own languages" (Petit, 1972).

Finally, as was true for other commercial powers during the next
fifteen centuries or so, or so long as the circulation of written information remained limited, Phoenician trade also played an important part
in the diffusion of knowledge and civilization in the widest sense of
the term. The information conveyed by trade was of two kinds: that
which, since it had gone into their production, goods offered in themselves and that which stemmed from human contacts between merchants. So increasing both the flow of goods and the degree of communication among various peoples, the Phoenicians performed a
major civilizing function for the Middle East and the Mediterranean

as a whole. This function was all the more important inasmuch as certain Phoenician colonies, the most famous of them being Carthage, in their turn became magnetic poles in the life of commerce and in the dissemination of civilization.

Israel: Small Towns Inhabited by Peasants and Vine Growers

There is a strange paradox in the resemblance between the way of life of the majority of the Jewish communities of the Diaspora before the twentieth century and that of the Hebrews of the kingdoms of Israel and Judah prior to the dispersal (in the first century) of the Jewish people. Most of the Jewish population of Eastern Europe and of the various Muslim worlds was concentrated in hundreds of small settlements characterized by their urban mode of existence in a rural setting. It appears that this was one of the principal features of the way of life peculiar to the population of the kingdoms of Israel and Judah. Archaeological excavations have confirmed that the whole of the geographical territory inhabited by the Hebrews contained some four hundred cities—if, in fact, we may properly call them cities. For many of them the term seems too strong, since they are mainly urbanized villages. At the height of the demographic curve (around 1000 B.C.), the total population was about 1.8 million. The capital cities were relatively small towns. Jerusalem itself probably never had a population of more than 100,000, even as late as the reign of King Herod, and in 1000 B.C. its population must have been on the order of 25,000–35,000 (Wilkinson, 1974). It seems that the majority of these 400 towns had an average population of 1,000 or less (Baron, 1972), as a great many archaeological excavations have confirmed, with sites of restricted size, generally around 8–12 hectares (Aharoni, 1967). The fact of the matter is that most of the peasants inhabited cities or small towns surrounded by walls from which, in the biblical phrase, "they went out in the morning to their fields and their vineyards, to return again in the evening." So the region housed one of the many societies in which the cleavage between town and country was less pronounced than in the dominant models.

It is interesting to note that four centuries later, when the population had fallen below 1.2 million, the number of these cities had remained pretty much the same. This phenomenon will be seen again later, permitting the formulation of a constant of the history of cities: the stability of urban networks. This stability is very much marked within the same geographical zone and within the same system of culture. But it also often transcends the boundaries between cultures. If new towns come into existence during surges of urban growth, few of them totally vanish during subsequent recessions. Often, moreover, there are renascences. The geographical factors that favored the original foundation of a city at a given place rarely disappear—rarely, though by no means never. The most frequent reason for the disappearance of a localizing factor is the exhaustion of a mineral deposit.

The stability of urban networks may also in its turn be a secondary factor contributing to urbanization. Thus in the case of Jerusalem, recent research in what is known as the "new archaeology" shows that the arable land located around the city did not suffice to support its population at the time of Ezekiel (sixth century B.C.). "The answer was the creation of terraces that transformed hillsides into stepped flat fields supported by retaining walls" (Edelstein and Gibson, 1982). Once such an investment has been made, there is a strong chance that this type of agriculture will survive the city's temporary decline.

The fact that, as a general rule, urban networks remain stable should not induce us, however, to dismiss the exceptions as negligible: for these exceptions are fairly numerous and sometimes important in both size and impact. In the chapters that follow certain of these notorious exceptions will be noted, especially in the urban cultures of Southeast Asia and the pre-Columbian New World. On the other hand, the size factor intervenes directly in this connection, small towns and villages being more liable to disappear completely than big cities. In the case of Israel, for example, an analysis of the spatial distribution of the cities and towns of Palestine under Rome shows, among other things, that "the villages . . . in Roman and Byzantine times were far more numerous than are the Arab villages of today" (I. W. J. Hopkins, 1980).

As will be discussed again later, Roman colonization appears to have erected more cities than it destroyed, and what is more, Roman cities reached substantial proportions. As already noted, Jerusalem probably had a population of 100,000 at the time of Herod; but the great city of the period was the "new" city of Caesaria, credited by some as having at its height a population of 250,000 (Crisler, 1982).

And while on the subject of Roman influence, I should not close my discussion of events in this part of the world without recalling the fate of the "secret" city of Petra, capital of the kingdom of Nabataea, a kingdom whose destiny was indirectly linked with that of Israel. Indeed, even though her troops assisted Titus in the siege of Jerusalem (A.D. 70), the Roman Empire did not long allow Nabataea to retain its independence: in A.D. 106 the Roman legions seized Petra. Until recently it had been supposed that this was the end of Petra. It now appears that the city survived until the middle of the sixth century and that it continued to play a role as a commercial center specializing chiefly in the international trade in incense. Apart from a brief period in which one observes a human presence thanks to a fort established in the twelfth century, Petra was forgotten until its chance discovery by a Swiss explorer in 1812. In a sense, given the part it played in trade as early as about 200 B.C., Petra may be regarded as one of the first nonmaritime commercial cities (Hammond, 1981).

And What of the Other Cultures of the Middle East?

The fact that in this discussion of the cultures of the Middle East I omit mention of the cities of the Assyrians, the Hittites, the Lydians, and so forth, does not in the least suggest that the urbanism associated with these peoples was negligible, nor even that they exhibited no distinctive characteristics of their own worthy of notice. The lack of systematic studies, however, coupled with the necessarily restricted scope I have tried to give this historical overview, obliges me to keep within certain limits. But if we may more or less justifiably leave out the other cultures of the Middle East, the Maghreb is another matter. I feel, moreover, that given the close ties between the Maghreb and the Middle East, it should be within the framework of this chapter that I evoke, if only in passing, the history of the beginnings of urbanization in this part of the world.

The Maghreb: A Delayed Growth of Agriculture and Cities

Was there a delayed growth of agriculture in the Maghreb? In comparison with the Middle East, yes, without any doubt, and also in comparison with the other, eastern part of North Africa itself—when we compare it, notably, with Egypt and the Sudan. This traditional view of the course of events in North Africa remains valid even though, as is the case everywhere else, certain dates have had to be revised. In the Aures region (present-day Algeria), a pastoral, preagrarian economy had grown up by the fifth millennium B.C.—as Roubet (1978) puts it, a "mountain economy of shepherds raising sheep and goats." Moving their flocks seasonally between the mountains and the plains in search of pasturage, these shepherds eventually came to occupy a number of localities in the region; and there developed along with the raising of livestock the "selective and systematic gathering of vegetables and the practice of collecting acorns in the autumn, a practice which led to the production of the first forms of semolina and flour made from sweet acorns." This livestock rearing appeared roughly at the same time or a little later in other parts of the Maghreb as well (Gilman, 1974; Bender, 1975; Harlan, de Wet and Stemler, 1976). As concerns true agriculture, there are apparently too few indications for drawing any definite conclusions, but it seems that it did not emerge before 4000 B.C., and perhaps not even until 2000 B.C. This circumstance authorizes speculation regarding the possibility of transfers not only from the East, but also from the South, since (see chapter 4) the Sahara was not yet a desert and there was an early rise of agriculture there. There is, finally, also the possibility of transfer from the North, since a good deal of evidence has come to light suggesting that there was trade with Spain during the Neolithic, and Spain developed agriculture sooner than the Maghreb.

As for a delay in the advent of cities, there is still little information concerning the stages of the growth of cities in the Maghreb, and the history of this process is in any case difficult to unravel owing to the establishment of Phoenician and later of Greek colonies along the coast. To what extent did the foundation of these colonies involve the birth of urbanism in the region, and to what extent did it involve the implantation of new cities in an already existing, but probably less advanced urban network, as happened later with the rise of Arab influence? In almost every region for which in the past the onset of urbanization has been imputed entirely to a process of importation, subsequent research has pointed to the existence of cities earlier than had been thought. The question of the autonomous development of cities in the Maghreb must therefore remain open. Even if such an autonomous development did in fact take place, however, all appearances suggest that urbanization began later in the Maghreb than in the Middle East; and it seems likely that in many parts of the region, not only the Phoenicians, but the Greek colonizers as well, implanted urban systems in areas previously devoid of cities. The territory corresponding to contemporary Libya serves as an example.

3 The Beginnings of Urbanization in Asia □

When we move on from the Middle East into Asia proper, the problem of the numerous independent "inventions" of the city becomes more conrete. Just how many times has the city been invented? This old question, given fresh currency by Sjoberg in 1960, has yet to receive a definitive answer; uncertainty is the rule. Did urbanization have a single origin, or did it begin in several different places, and if so, how many? For the Middle East, simplifying matters somewhat, there is evidently a single autonomous source. So too in the case of the New World, although surprises are always possible, the answer appears to be fairly clear: the pre-Columbian societies evolved cities of their own independently of the rest of the world. There was, then, a second invention of the city, so there were on the global level at least two autonomous centers of urbanization. By contrast, for Africa, Europe, and Asia, the answer continues to be ambiguous at best. Was the city independently developed in these other regions as well, or did it spread to them from an original source in the Middle East? To confuse matters further, even if today we persist in the belief that the Middle East saw the beginning of cities sooner than any other region, this by no means rules out the possibility of one day discovering urban sites in some other part of the world that are still more ancient than those found in the Middle East. Even in this case, however, the diffusion/invention dilemma would remain intact, the only difference being that the direction of the hypothetical spread of urbanization would be reversed.

Since there is still a great lack of certainty, it might be wisest to proceed from what we know most about to what we know least about. Accordingly, I shall open this summary history of the first phases of urbanization in societies other than those of the Middle East with the early urban cultures of Asia, moving on from there in the next chapter to Africa and the pre-Columbian New World.

The question of the autonomy of the birth of urbanism in Asia is still open. As for the two principal centers of urbanization, India and

China, it has not yet been determined whether their beginnings owed anything to the urban civilizations of the Middle East. This is the first problem I shall discuss regarding both India and China. I will then discuss what is known about the initial stages of their urbanization, stopping at the moment when urbanism has incontestably taken root. The other cultures of Asia will then be treated briefly.

But why place such particular emphasis on India and China? There are at least three reasons. In the first place, there is the dominant position these two civilizations occupied in the continent at large, together accounting (still today) for four-fifths of the total population of Asia. The second reason is the large number of studies on them, and thus the greater availability of data. Finally, and most important, for the urbanization of India and China the question of the originality of the invention of the city poses itself in peculiarly graphic and unmistakable terms. Since India was the first of the two to have experienced true growth of urban civilization, I shall begin with it.

India: The Harappa Civilization as a False Start

The site of Harappa, the city that gave its name to the civilization of which it formed a part, was discovered in the nineteenth century, at just about the same time as the site of the city of Mohenjo-daro. This discovery came too soon, however—archaeological research did not yet have the prestige it enjoys today. A substantial portion of the ruins found on the site was used to construct an embankment for a railway line. No serious excavations were undertaken until the 1930s, but these later excavations pointed to the existence of a fully developed civilization, previously unknown, called the Harappa, or Indus Valley, civilization. Until quite recently, scholars believed that this civilization comprised three major sites: the two at Harappa and Mohenjo-daro and a third at Kalibangan. But recent excavations, begun early in 1979, have brought to light what may well turn out to be a fourth site of considerable size and importance, covering some one hundred hectares in the locality of Dhoraji (Jacobson, 1979), and alongside some 250 sites of which many are smaller than five hectares.

The Harappa (or Indus Valley) civilization, which reached its height sometime around 2100–1750 B.C., lay in the Punjab region, that is, in northern Pakistan, near the border with Afghanistan. But here too it may eventually prove necessary to make some revision. In what Jacobson (adding the qualification "perhaps") calls the most dramatic development in the recent exploration of the Harappa civilization, seven "mature Harappan sites" have been discovered in northern Afghanistan.

The Harappa civilization appears to have been highly urbanized, with several very large cities of which Mohenjo-daro may serve as a typical example. In about 2000 B.C. the city extended over some 180 hectares (some say 80 hectares) and probably had a population of around 30,000–40,000. Mohenjo-daro was a fortified town, and had a functioning network of sewers. It also constitutes (and this applies not only to Mohenjo-daro, but to the other Harappan cities as well) one of the earliest instances of a city built on a regular plan. Although arts and crafts had not yet reached an advanced level of development, this was nevertheless an authentic urban civilization with an economic system based on agriculture and the raising of livestock, and having trade relations with other regions, in particular with Mesopotamia. The Harappan civilization also evolved a form of writing, but this has yet to be deciphered. Archaeologists have even found a large number of weights indicating a decimal system of measures.

While scholars have established, the urban character of the Harappan civilization, two important problems have nevertheless escaped definitive solution. The first of these concerns the extent of Middle Eastern, and especially Sumerian, influence on the emergence of this civilization. It is all but certain that some such influence existed. According to Hammond (1972), the impetus for civilization in the region probably originated in Mesopotamia and involved the abrupt superimposition of an urban system on an already existing network of villages—villages which must have known some form of agriculture before this time. But the absence of many parallels between the Mesopotamian and Harappan civilizations suggests that there were no direct importations of knowledge and example by means of immigrations and invasions, but rather transfers through trades. The cultural links between Sumer and the Arabian coast on the one hand and Harappa on the other have in any event been confirmed by recent investigations (During Caspers, 1979).

The second problem concerns Harappan influence on the urbanization of India. Here, too, near certainty reigns: there was no direct influence. To be sure, the supposed (in historical terms) sudden and brutal "death" of the Harappan civilization has of late been thrown into question, since evidence has accumulated supporting the view that it survived in some sort of "sub-Harappan" civilization. It is nonetheless difficult to consider Harappa as the source for the urbanization of India. As pointed out by Thakur (1981), there may have been links between the two urban systems, but these were only general influences of the Harappan civilization on that of historic India.

Furthermore, any hypothetical transmission of urbanization to the rest of the Indian subcontinent—to the area corresponding to India proper—would quite probably have run up against the obstacle of the absence of a solidly based agriculture. For the Neolithic appeared in India proper much later than in the Indus Valley, where the Neolithic had begun by 4500 B.C., and possibly even earlier. But though the Neolithic arrived in India itself later than in the Indus Valley, it still did so a good deal sooner than was believed even a few years ago.

Compared to research in previous decades, the last ten years have seen a marked increase in both the quantity and the quality of the studies and excavations carried out in this part of the world. On the basis of some brief syntheses of recent archaeological investigations (Vishnu-Mittre, 1977; Jacobson, 1979), and on the basis of other indications, the beginnings of agriculture in India proper may be tentatively placed at about 2000–1500 B.C.

And when were the beginnings of urbanization? This, alas, is a page of the history of India that remains almost entirely to be written. It is worth noting, however, that this particular history was considerably complicated by the successive waves of invasion which totally submerged the country. The most important of these, taking place about 1500–1200 B.C., was the Aryan invasion, which utterly transformed the face of Indian society. The onset of urbanization occurred sometime between this period and 326 B.C., the year Alexander crossed the Indus. The precise date probably fell after 1000 B.C. and before 400 B.C., the year currently favored being around 600 B.C. Here again, however, some recent discoveries, notably those made at Bhukari, could push this date back by a thousand years (Jacobson, 1979). But was the urbanization of India a foreign importation superimposed upon societies not yet urbanized? Or was there rather an original source of urbanization indigenous to India? The problem remains; but the consensus among researchers in the area leans somewhat on the side of a transfer from the Middle East.

The thesis of one or more autonomous urban civilizations was strengthened by Chakrabarti's findings (1976) concerning the emergence in India of an iron industry. Chakrabarti argues that this industry first appeared in India earlier than hitherto estimated (1100–1000 B.C.), and he contends that it was definitely an independent development. Without in the least wishing to discredit Chakrabarti's hypothesis, I feel obliged to mention that the recent tendency in this field has been a phase of nationalism seeking wherever possible to assert national autonomy. Researchers no longer look for links uniting different cultures, but rather for native originality. And this is valid for all cultures. In India an approach of this kind is harder to adopt, for as Naudou (1956) observes, "the history of India is wholly organized according to a single rhythm: that imposed on it by successive invaders and foreign masters." To be sure, this does not mean that India failed to produce a distinctive civilization of its own: "The civilization India evolved and caused to radiate throughout Central Asia and the Far East resembles no other. Still, this did not prevent India from contracting numerous debts: toward Akkado-Sumerian Mesopotamia, of whom the Achaemenids and, after them, the Sassanids were conscious of being the heirs; toward classical Greece and its successors, Rome and the Hellenized East; and later toward Islam, and then modern Europe."

Debts? Imagine what a complex form of accounting we would need to keep track of everything each culture owes to others. Let me give an example, one that will serve at the same time as a transition to China. The accepted view among researchers has until recently been that Indian medicine lay at the root of and provided the fundamental spirit behind Tibetan medicine. Beckwith (1979), however, furnishes fairly conclusive evidence that in Tibet during the first century of the empire (A.D. 634–755), the medicine practised was in fact of Chinese and Greek origin. In this connection, the recent discovery of the city of Taxila, one of the most important of ancient India, which dates from 2500 B.C. (Allchin, 1982), gives new fuel to the debate over the debts the urbanization of India has to the Harappan civilization.

China: Multiple Centers of Agriculture and Urbanization

In dealing with India as a whole, I had to treat as forming a single unit a geographical entity stretching over an area of 4.7 million square kilometers (India prior to the partition of 1947): an area representing 87 percent of the territory covered by Europe (Russia excluded). For China, the space is even more vast: 11.1 million square kilometers, or twice the area of Europe. Up to the period of the Industrial Revolution, the population of China was roughly two to three times that of Europe. For such a huge area it is necessary to at least distinguish between North and South, which will not always be possible without going at times into more detail than is appropriate for this survey. The reader should, then, bear these reservations in mind.

In their studies of the vast territory of China, researchers have lately adopted the view that agriculture arose in three distinct regions rather than in two, as originally supposed. The Neolithic revolution therefore took place separately in three different parts of China. The two "traditional" areas were the coastal region in the South (Taiwan included) and the Hwang Ho valley in the North. The new area, the third center of early agriculture, brought to light by very recent excavations, was situated in the Hwai Ho region and the lower basin of the Yang-tze, that is to say, in east-central China.

In the South, and especially in Taiwan, researchers have discovered signs of changes in the local systems of vegetation as early as 12,000 B.C. The changes, including the development of secondary forests and shrub growth and a marked increase in the number of charcoal fragments deposited in lacustrine sediments, are best explained with reference to some human agency: all of them may easily be interpreted as signs of the clearing of forest to open fields for cultivation. But this is not evidence of true agriculture, which did not appear until about 4000–3000 B.C. In the North, on the other hand, true agriculture emerged as early as 6000–5000 B.C., most notably in the form of the cultivation of millet. According to recent investigations, the third center had agriculture in the form of the cultivation of rice, most likely in irrigated fields, even earlier than the South did—around 4400 B.C.

As Chang Kwang-Chih (1977) remarks, the question of the originality of these various Neolithic revolutions and of the links between them becomes less and less important in the face of the growing preoccupation with the essential mechanisms at work in the adoption of agriculture. It may be said that recent syntheses of research (Chêng Tè-k'un, 1973; Ho Ping-Ti, 1975, 1977) reinforce the likelihood that there was at least one wholly autonomous center of agriculture and perhaps even several such centers in the giant "Celestial Empire."

I shall pass over the preurban towns of China, concerning which, naturally, a great deal of uncertainty exists, to discuss instead the beginnings of urbanization. But the problem remains of determining whether the principal cities of the Shang period (1766–1400 B.C.) were genuinely urban in character. While it is certainly true that these "ceremonial cities," as they are called, seem sometimes to have had fairly sizable populations, the fact remains that, as Wheatley (1971) observes, the division between town and country had not yet appeared at this time. With the cities of the following period, on the other hand, roughly from 1100 B.C. on, these ceremonial cities had in fact turned into dense and, above all, compact urban centers.

It should be emphasized, however, that the cities in question were essentially those found in the North. For there is little doubt that in the North, perhaps as early as 700 B.C. and certainly by 400 B.C., agriculture had attained a level of productivity and yield sufficient to permit setting aside a substantial surplus of food, which may account for the urbanization during this period. Particular stress should be placed, as Ho Ping-Ti (1975) justly insists, on the decisive role played by soybeans in this process. Not only does this plant provide a rich source of protein, but far from depleting the mineral content of the soil, it tends to fertilize and regenerate it. Indeed, its roots have the property of holding nitrogen in the soil, a property that encouraged in this region the continuous rotation of crops. But while soybeans were cultivated in northern China on a fairly general basis by 600 B.C., the rotation of crops did not become a distinct feature of northern Chinese agriculture before 400 or even 250 B.C.

Still, by 400 B.C., these practices and other advances in agricultural methods had brought about a comparatively high yield and productivity. Translating them, as Ho Ping-Ti has done, into contemporary units of value, the data we possess for this period give the following results. The average yield of unhusked millet was roughly 1000 kilograms per hectare. In Europe prior to the agricultural revolution of the eighteenth century, by contrast, the average yield of wheat was 600–800 kilograms per hectare. But of still greater importance was the approximate level of productivity. The average farmer was able to produce enough food to feed more than six people. Even if, for the sake of prudence, I were to reduce the figure to five, this would still imply the existence of a very considerable surplus. It is on these grounds that Ho concludes that "in any case, there can be little doubt about the ability of Yang-Shad agriculture to produce a surplus, thus releasing segments of the population to pursue nonagricultural activities."

Since semifeudal systems foster a considerable margin of local independence, a fairly large number of urban centers grew up. These cities must have been rather large, or in any event extensive, for their enclosures (generally constructed of beaten earth) were several kilometers in length, in certain cases as long as fifteen or even twenty-five kilometers. Prior to the unification of the empire in 221 B.C., a considerable number of very large cities had apparently come into existence. Although there are no population estimates for them, on the strength of the areas surrounded by their walls, I would be inclined, applying the European model, to venture high figures. An enclosing wall fifteen kilometers long contains an area of some fourteen hundred hectares, and assuming what for Europe would have been a thin population density, say on the order of 100 inhabitants per hectare, this would imply a population of about 140,000. In certain pre-Columbian cities, however, the estimates point to populations distinctly smaller than this—about 40–60 inhabitants per hectare, or a population of fewer than 90,000. Assuming a population density lower than that of European cities, the argument may be advanced on the basis of the analysis of most of the cities of China, that agricultural land and ponds used much of the land inside the walls of Chinese cities. However this may be, it seems probable that by the fifth century B.C., though no city had a population of as much as 200,000, China already had four to six cities with populations in excess of 100,000.

According to a review (Chang Kwang-chih, 1977) of the results of recent excavations of cities existing in the North before 221 B.C., there were 20 sites containing large cities. According to my own calculations (using the dimensions of the encircling walls), these cities had the following areas: 1 city of 3,200 hectares, 1 of 1,600 hectares, 4 of 700–950 hectares, 3 of 400–500 hectares, 3 of 200–300 hectares, 6 of 100–150 hectares, and 2 of 50–70 hectares. This obviously was only the apex of the pyramid of the urban network of the region, since some estimates suggest that 78 new cities were founded in northern China between 722 and 480 B.C. alone.

Did this urban development owe anything to other, earlier centers of urbanization? The question remains unanswered. But the possibility of any pronounced foreign influence can be ruled out. As Wheatley (1971) points out, theses holding that the emergence of urbanism in China derived largely from external sources chiefly take as their starting point the observation that cities first appeared in China some 1,500 years after appearing in the Middle East and 1,000 years after appearing in the Indus valley. But this does not necessarily imply the diffusion of cities to China from these other regions, nor even the transfer of particular aspects of urban development. I would be inclined to share Wheatley's conclusion: "among the civilizational nuclei of the old world, the Chinese seems to have been the one most effectively insulated from contact with other foci of high civilization and, despite the lateness of its flowering, to have enjoyed an unusual degree of autonomy in its development." It seems very much more likely, then, that China was an autonomous center of urbanization.

Japan: A Late but Sudden Urbanization

Although permanent villages existed in Japan from 8000 B.C. onwards, these villages belonged to a preagrarian society: a society that derived food wholly from hunting, gathering, and fishing. Agriculture appeared only very late, around 200 B.C., with the arrival of Yayoi, growers of rice (Watson, 1972). More recently this point of view has been challenged, and there seems to be a general tendency to lean toward a "more local" origin of agriculture around 500 B.C.. Thus Japan was probably, but only probably, an autonomous center.

It was not until the fifth century A.D. that a central power emerged, replacing the previous system which was extremely fragmented, the country being divided into about a hundred states. Buddhism was introduced in the second half of the sixth century by way of Korea, and it was likewise from the mainland (especially China) that the Japanese received most of the more highly evolved techniques of agriculture and also of metallurgy. So at this early stage of its history Japan already seemed destined to succeed through imitation.

And yet this imitation might perhaps more accurately be seen as an initiation, so difficult is it to deny the originality of Japan in many areas. The likely absence of an autonomous center of agricultural development (and urbanism) can be accounted for in terms of Japan's isolation and, more particularly, its relatively small size. Indeed, in speculation about the origins of agriculture and cities in Japan, the insular character of the country could very easily be adduced as evidence in favor of spontaneous growth and autonomous development. But by diminishing the mass of human and material resources available, its restricted size militated against such an eventuality. This argument is valid not only for agriculture and urbanization, but also for other great technological innovations of antiquity. Following the expression of Wheatley and See (1978), Japan was "a secondary urban generation."

In any event, the first true cities did not appear in Japan until about A.D. 650–700; and it is worth noting that the plan of the first capital city, Nara (Heijokyo), completed in 710, was of Chinese inspiration, which was also the case for Miyako (present-day Kyoto), which remained the de jure capital of the country from 794 to 1868. Miyako soon became a great city, with a population certainly surpassing 100,000 from the ninth century on, and perhaps reaching as much as 200,000–250,000. Nara at its peak in the second half of the eighth century had a population close to 150,000. So very large cities emerged very early. It should not be forgotten that in Europe in A.D. 800, the largest city, Rome, had only some 50,000 people—and one can argue that this size was a residue of its imperial past. The other large European cities, Paris, Reims, etc., each had only 20,000–25,000 inhabitants. Rozman (1973) explains the sudden emergence in Japan of so great a city as Miyako in terms of the natural transportation network which the country had and in terms of the strength of the central authority. To this may obviously be added the effects of the rapid transmission of techniques imported from China, as well as a factor (see chapter 22) that applied to all of the cultures in this part of the world: the enhanced potential for urbanization introduced by the cultivation of rice. For when one compares this cereal with those cultivated in Europe during this period, one finds that it offered distinct advantages from the point of view of the production of calories per unit of land.

However, aside from the few great cities (in particular Kamakura), it was not until the middle of the Kamakura era (1185–1333) that a genuine network of cities came into place, notably with the emergence of cities (port and market towns) that had a more pronounced economic function and character. Certain of these later cities, moreover, acquired a margin of independence, due above all to the craft guilds that grew up during this period and reached their height in the sixteenth century. The freedom enjoyed by these cities was much greater than that of the cities of China, resembling that found in the European cities of the Middle Ages. This phase lasted until the end of the sixteenth century, when the central political power reinforced its hold over the country as a whole.

Despite the emergence of these commercial cities, most of the urban population of Japan was still concentrated in a few great cities. As a result, the level of urbanization on the island remained comparatively low, in the sixteenth century certainly less than 10%, and probably on the order of 5–8%.

Korea: Essential Borrowings from China

Before returning once more to Southern Asia, we should pause to consider one of the great Asian cultures—Korea, a country whose population ranks fourth in all of Asia.

Especially during the earliest phase of its culture, Korea borrowed from China as much as Japan did, and perhaps even more. Agriculture seems to have come from China around 2000 B.C., with the introduction of the cultivation of millet. Rice appears to have arrived later, around 1500 B.C. according to Choe (1982) and Kim (1982), and possibly as recently as about 1120 B.C. (Nelson, 1982). This diffusion of agricultural techniques was accompanied by the diffusion of certain crafts, pottery in particular.

The emergence of cities in Korea also seems to have been linked to China, most directly during the four centuries of China's occupation of Korea (108 B.C.–A.D. 313). The organized societies that had emerged in various parts of Korea before the occupation by China do not appear to have created true cities. But some of the command centers set up by the Chinese may be considered genuine cities. According to Chinese sources, the largest of them had populations of more than 400,000 (probably a substantial overestimation).

The Cities of Southeast Asia: A Diffusion of Indian and Chinese Urban Systems?

The origins of urban settlement in Southeast Asia are obscure. Most historical evidence indicates that the earlier cities originated as a result of the diffusion into the area of Chinese and Indian forms of political organization and religion from the first century A.D. Prior to this date, political power was scattered throughout the area in a series of tribal cells. These tribal societies existed in a delicate ecological balance with the physical environment because of their limited technology, which forced them to move frequently in search of food and prevented the development of a stable relationship with the environment as well as the emergence of occupational specialization. But the considerable growth of trading contacts with the area from the first century onwards, together with the actual extension of Chinese control into north and middle Vietnam, brought the tribal chiefs into contact with the systems of belief and political organization of these "high civilizations," particularly those systems associated with Indian civilization. The actual manner in which these first cities grew up has not been documented, but it would appear that the growth of trading ports associated with the adoption by the tribal chiefs of Indian forms of political organization, based on Brahmanic and Buddhist beliefs, provided the combination of economic, political, and social forces which brought the first cities into being.

This assessment, taken from McGee (1967), continues in its broad outline to be accepted today. But is it valid?

I do not wish to go as far in my pessimism as Jan Prins, who wrote in the celebrated collection of articles about the city published by the Société Jean Bodin in 1955: "I do not think that someone will some day be able to write a book entitled 'the ancient cities of Indonesia.'" Still, I do have to admit that little is known about the first cities of Southeast Asia. But although there is a great deal of doubt about the modalities and dates of the birth of urbanism in this part of the world, there is no doubt about the existence of ancient urban cultures in Southeast Asia with cities of substantial size.

As Lombard (1970) shows in his brief review of research on the subject, in the Malay archipelago,

> we have found inscriptions dating from the fifth century and an astonishing series of religious monuments dating from the seventh century, some of which, such as Borobudur of Prambanan, could only have been created by societies that had already attained a high degree of complexity. But there is total uncertainty as concerns urban agglomerations, at least so far as their plan and structure go; for there is now general agreement in thinking that they were established near the sea and that it was, precisely, the modification of the coastline that reduced the number of vestiges. Sri Vijaya (the capital of an important thalassocracy, seventh to eleventh centuries) would appear to have been in the vicinity of Palembang and Medan (the city whose inhabitants built Borobudur); it would seem, then, to have been situated on the north coast of Java, near the present-day city of Semarang.

The most recent archaeological excavations in general confirm the urban character of many of these towns.

This region conforms to the general rule in that the date of the birth of agriculture in this part of the world has been put progressively further back. Thus, in the case of New Guinea, the date given has gone from 4000 B.C. to 7000 B.C. (Golson and Hugues, 1980). Moreover, for this region as for many others, the idea that agriculture was diffused into the area (from Southwest Asia) has nearly been abandoned in favor of autonomous development (Yen, 1980). Both of these factors would explain the relatively early urbanization of the archipelago.

Not all of the islands in the Malay archipelago, however, underwent such an early urbanization. This was notably the case in the Philippines, where, before the arrival of the Spanish colonizers at the beginning of the sixteenth century, there were no genuine cities, despite agriculture and commercial ties chiefly with China, but also with Brunei and Japan. These commercial relations had led to the creation of human settlements all along the coast and on the banks of the rivers situated near the coast. But these settlements were not cities. Precolonial Manila, which constituted the principal agglomeration in the region, contained only two thousand inhabitants and had no sizable artisanry. "Manila (and certainly Cebu) was probably a relatively large agricultural and fishing village with an unusually strong secondary trade function" (Doeppers, 1972). The Philippines were thus one of the rare instances in Asia of a region in which the urbanization was entirely due to European colonization.

There is no doubt that urbanization was relatively early on the continent. The reader will recall the famous urban complex founded in Indochina at the start of the ninth century, containing the celebrated temples of Angkor. According to some estimates, at its height around the years 1200–1300 Angkor had a population of as much as 150,000. But there were other cities in Indochina far more ancient than Angkor. By the eighth and ninth centuries, and perhaps even earlier, there were in this region genuine cities, some of which had trade with other great civilizations. Thus, in the city of Oc-éo, situated on the lower Mekong and connected to the sea by a canal, objects of Chinese, Indian, Iranian, and Roman origin have been found—objects whose presence dates back to between the second and seventh centuries. The ramparts of the city surrounded an area of some 450 hectares. Assuming the density of urban habitation to have been low, there could have been a population of 30,000, while if density was high, it might have been as high as 120,000. But many of the cities of Indochina were not so ancient as this. In eleventh-century Cambodia, for example, there was prodigious urban growth. This growth was chiefly due to the personal dynamism of Suryavarman I (about 1007–1050), during whose reign, marked by considerable economic expansion, the number of cities appears to have more than doubled (de Mestier du Bourg, 1970).

Thailand, too, certainly experienced a relatively early urbanization, though the sites there were apparently less numerous than in Indochina. The actual number of ancient Thai cities is unknown, however, because many uncertainties continue to surround the first phase of urban growth in this region. And many urban centers in Thailand, as well as other parts of Southeast Asia, were very unstable (see chapter 22).

The third of the great cultures of the Indochinese peninsula was Burma. Some parts of Burma were among the earliest regions in Asia to give evidence of human settlement. The growth of cities was also fairly early. In any case, by the first century A.D. a large city had emerged, Peikthano, which flourished until the fourth century, when two other cities (Thayekhettaya and Halin) superceded it. All of these cities, located on a river, extended over a very wide area: between six hundred and fourteen hundred hectares. But the density was apparently fairly thin, for only part of the area within the city walls was built up. Judging from their architecture and ground plans, Burmese cities owed nothing to the Chinese model (Kan Hla, 1979). Thus Burma apparently had an autonomous urban development.

However ancient the first cities of Southeast Asia may have been, the cities of India and China were far more ancient. And given the extent of commercial ties between Southeast Asia and these two great civilizations, the evidence seems on the whole to support the idea that urbanization came to Southeast Asia largely as the result of diffusion from India and China. But one very important point has to be made. The comparatively early development of agriculture in Southeast Asia should inspire prudence, and may some day lead to dramatic revisions of current opinion. In any case, the early dates for the first appearance of agriculture find increasing confirmation in recent research, and for much of the region, the hypothesis of a diffusion of urbanization from India and China is yielding ground to that of an autonomous development of cities. Thus in the case of Thailand, for example, the accepted scheme up until about ten years ago went as follows: in about 2000 B.C., the society of hunters and gatherers in the area was revolutionized by the arrival of farmers from China who knew how to cultivate rice; and the Thai culture later borrowed the use of bronze and iron from its two great neighbors, India and China. But no one has as yet ruled out the existence of some form of agriculture, or at least of some form of proto-agriculture, in certain parts of Thailand as early as about 7000 B.C. In any event, the presence of true agriculture around 6000–5000 B.C. induces me to speculate as to the possibility of a Thai contribution to the beginnings of agriculture in India and above all to wonder about the possibility of an autonomous process of urban growth. It is extremely unlikely that an economic system based on agriculture could have existed for two to three thousand years in a relatively fertile region without leading to urbanization.

But for any story which is lost in the mists of time, dramatic revisions are not to be excluded. The natural desire to have as long a history as possible, however, has its dangers. Take, for example, the case of the controversy over the age of the site of Ban Chiang (in northeast Thailand), where excavations began in 1966, and where some very beautiful pottery has been discovered. Since I began this section with a citation, let me terminate it in the same way:

> As a result of the first excavation season, many of
> these pots were deposited at the Bangkok National
> Museum, whence some were sent to the Pennsyl-
> vania University Museum for thermoluminescence
> (TL) dating, with a truly sensational result: they
> were said to be almost seven thousand years old! As
> these pots were not found in isolation, but in associa-
> tion with burials where artifacts in bronze and iron
> and even glass beads were present, the date for the

pottery would be not only that of bronze, but also of iron and glass. (Loofs-Wissowa, 1983)

It should be recalled that the Iron Age is generally considered to have begun around 1700–1500 B.C., while glass seems to have been invented around 2500 B.C.:

> Clearly, something had gone wrong with the dating. This is explicable in that the Pennsylvania TL laboratory was using a slightly different method from that used in Oxford, which could result in a date being mysteriously way out. I happen to know of a very similar Ban Chiang pot acquired by Spink & Co. in London at the same time and dated by Oxford as roughly 1500 to 2500 years old (unpublished). However, the fifth millennium B.C. date was accepted uncritically, and soon there was a ludicrous situation in which Ban Chiang finds, including bronze and iron objects as well as glass beads, were exhibited in the National Museum, labeled as dating to the fifth millennium B.C. The Fine Arts Department even issued an official greeting card with a photo of two painted Ban Chiang pots with spiralic decoration and the legend "Prehistoric Metal Age 5000 B.C.." Countless newspaper and magazine articles appeared throughout the world about these sensational finds, and in Thailand itself a real cult developed around "Ban Chiang, the Place the World Forgot Seven Thousand Years Ago" (the title of an article in *Holiday Time in Thailand*, vol. 13, no. 4, 1972) complete with souvenirs of all sorts, including T-shirts with the inscription "Ban Chiang 7000 Years Old," which could be bought even in Australia.

From the tone of the citation it is clear that Loofs-Wissowa has no doubt that Ban Chiang is less ancient. In addition to the other datings, his historical arguments are convincing. This does not mean that those who hold Thailand to be the birthplace of such important innovations are definitely refuted. The author himself reports that bronze objects have been found which are considered by the archaeologists who discovered them to be even older than those of Ban Chiang.

4　The Beginnings of Urbanization in Black Africa and the New World □

We now turn to the consideration of two parts of the world very different from each other—but which despite their differences, by a process in which Europe played a leading if rather unsavory part, history has nevertheless brought very much closer together.

The links between Black Africa and the New World are of two kinds. In the first place there were the dates at which the Europeans discovered them. Although, of course, the Europeans discovered the two parts of the world at different times, on the giant scale of history the two discoveries took place at pretty much the same time and as expressions of the same historical forces.

In the second place, however, there was the bond forged by the flow of men and goods set in motion by the arrival of the European colonists. On the one hand, there was the prodigious flow of human beings generated over nearly four centuries by the slave trade, which snatched between ten and twelve million Africans from their native soil to make slaves of them on the plantations of America. But on the other hand, moving in the opposite direction there was the flow of food plants (manioc, peanuts, etc.) that soon became principal sources of food for most of Black Africa, to the point, indeed, where today we tend to think of them as typically African.

Black Africa: An Urban History That Remains to Be Written

The urban history of Black Africa is an urban history that remains to be written. But however recent the study of the history and prehistory of Black Africa may be, it has still had time enough to reveal cultures much older than we had previously imagined. Uncertainties abound—uncertainties that, when resolved, raise further questions as exciting as they are instructive. Among these uncertainties (given the rapid pace of developments in the field, the answers have to be sought in journal articles) is that surrounding the Neolithic in Black Africa.

The Neolithic Revolution in Black Africa

In speaking of the Neolithic revolution in Black Africa, one ought properly to use the plural; for amidst all the doubts and obscurities one certainty stands out: agriculture appeared independently at several places in the continent, and it appeared very early. Thus in present-day Ethiopia, for example, an agriculture based on the cultivation of grain and the raising of livestock was present by 5000 B.C. If Ehret (1979) is to be believed, the cultivation of cereals owed its origins, simultaneously yet separately both in Ethiopia and in the Middle East, to the invention of what might be called a proto-agriculture in Northeast Africa. According to Ehret, this proto-agriculture, consisting of the intensive use of wild grain, came into existence around 13,000 B.C., if not earlier.

Among the regions undergoing an early Neolithic, one must not forget the Sahara, which turned into a desert only after 2500 B.C.. The rise in temperature that caused the desertification began around 3000 B.C. and made itself increasingly felt from about 2800 B.C. on. In this predesertic Sahara, as Maitre (1976) notes, "it is possible to imagine that, by about 6000 B.C., after a long period of gestation, some form of agriculture was born, slowly spreading down the valleys." But this was more what Maitre terms a rudimentary proto-agriculture, "essentially consisting of the seasonal exploitation of zones in which wild cereals grew," than agriculture proper. It should be recalled that in northwest Africa, in what would eventually become the Maghreb, it is possible that the Neolithic occurred around 4000 B.C., but it is also possible that it took place much later.

South of the Sahara, it was not until the middle or end of the second millennium B.C. that any societies made use of genuine agriculture. This was notably the case to the south of Lake Chad, a fertile region created by the considerable reduction in the area of the lake following the beginning of the rise in temperature. Nearer to the equatorial forest, moreover, the problem becomes very different. Thus as Oliver and Fage (1975) observe in this context: "The transition to food production depended on vegeculture rather than agriculture, on planting rather than sowing, on roots and fruits rather than on grain, on clearing rather than on hoeing, and on the combination of these activities with fishing rather than with hunting."

On the other hand, as the African geographer, Mabogunje (1980), notes, "the historical geography of Africa especially in its economic aspects yields a picture of a continent in which nature has been unusually kind, at least on the surface. The superficiality of natural bounteousness, so well exemplified in the fragile luxuriance of the tropical forest, has been something of a trap for the human population in Africa. Finding existence so easy to achieve, communities have side-stepped the agonizing demands of social evolution." This does not, however, rule out the emergence of agriculture and in particular the raising of livestock.

Let us look at this in greater detail. In East Africa, in the region corresponding to present-day Kenya and Tanzania, the raising of livestock seems to have emerged earlier than had previously been thought. Radiocarbon dating suggests the presence of domesticated animals sometime around the sixth millennium B.C. Agriculture seems to have arrived on the scene only during the first millennium A.D. Nevertheless there was iron production in nonagricultural societies in Tanzania by 600 B.C. (Mgomezulu, 1981).

It is still difficult to place the beginnings of agriculture in West Africa, with the possible exception of Cameroon. In Cameroon in the equatorial forest societies were practising a rudimentary form of agriculture as early as the end of the second millennium B.C. (de Maret, 1982).

To what extent were there autonomous centers of invention rather than the diffusion of agriculture? There seems to have been diffusion in Northwest Africa, and also in the Sudan. The Sudan had one of the earliest urban cultures of Black Africa. There is a strong probability that there was autonomous development in the other centers of agricultural growth, so there were two, three, or perhaps even four centers for the invention of agriculture. In short, to echo the first of the conclusions reached by the editors of the volume of essays devoted to the origins of the domestication of plants in Africa (Harlan, De Wet, and Stemler, 1976), "African agriculture is basically noncentric."

All of which suggests the autonomous invention of cities as well. But though this seems likely, it is by no means certain. There is still uncertainty about the stages of urbanization following its beginning, uncertainty magnified by the many contacts African societies had with other cultures. There were commercial links, of course, but also the relations imposed by foreign powers, with the classic effects of domination and the positive and negative consequences such relations typically entail. Between the commercial ties with the Egypt of the Pharaohs and the spread of Islam came, especially in the north, contacts with ancient Greece and Rome, and along the east coast, contacts with Persia, Indonesia, India and China. The history of these contacts is, indeed, another of the chapters of the general history of Africa remaining to be written. Some of Africa's early links with centers of civilization have tended to be underestimated: those with China, first of all, but also those with India (Chittick, 1980). Others have been overestimated, especially the extent of Rome's commercial penetration along the African coastline south of the Sahara. Regarding this particular region, recent research reported by Gran Aymerich (1979) makes "the existence of Punic and Roman trade settlements in those latitudes . . . every day less and less probable."

The First Cities of Black Africa

The existence of early Neolithic cultures in Black Africa does not necessarily imply that agriculture had spread through the whole continent even by the sixteenth century. But one of the paradoxical features of the situation in Africa was that, given the high population density made possible by the conditions of life in the jungle (see chapter 1), it is conceivable that fairly large preurban towns came into existence even without agriculture. In this context, it is perfectly legitimate to entertain the hypothesis of concentrated preurban habitats housing some two thousand people in which, while living in a town surrounded by a palisade erected to protect from animals and bands of hostile humans, the entire working population engaged in hunting and gathering. This hypothetical case is based on the following conditions: that there was a population density of three people per square kilometer, and that the maximum distance for the round trip to the hunting ground was fifteen kilometers. But it is true that the persistence of a town of this kind in the long run might have brought about some break in the ecological equilibrium, leading to a thinning out of the available game and consequently to the abandonment of the site.

Thus it may be seen that the task of researchers in this area is not an easy one. Among the additional difficulties urban historians have to face are the late date of the first contacts between Black Africa and Europe, the predominant use of wood in urban construction, the absence of writing, and the impact of slavery (chapter 24). All of these factors have tended to obliterate the traces of the early urban history of Black Africa, making it all but impossible either to date and account for its origins or to chart the stages of its development. Given this state of affairs, and given the broad scope of this analysis, the best course might be to concentrate solely on the certainties.

An initial, important certainty is the following. When over the course of the fifteenth century contacts between Europe and Black Africa finally began and intensified, European explorers found many cultures, some of them already with a very ancient history, exhibiting unmistakably urban features. Even leaving aside for the moment the urban cultures that evolved through contact with Islam (discussed in a later section of this chapter), urbanization was by this time well established in Africa. It is worth recalling that, long before the coming of the Europeans, Arab explorers had left many records concerning Black African cities. Thus as early as the eighth century (Levtzion, 1973), the renown of the kingdom of Ghana, "the land of gold," had reached Baghdad, as attested by references made to it by the geographer Al-Fazari.

Does the kingdom of Ghana furnish the first instance of an autonomous urban culture in Black Africa? The answer is far from certain. This honor may perhaps have to be accorded the kingdom (or empire) of Cush. Hull (1976), in his brief review of the urban life of Black Africa before the European conquest, believes the cities of this kingdom were the first in Africa. Doubt is nevertheless permissible. The proximity of Egypt (the kingdom of Cush lay in the contemporary Sudan), coupled with the trade relations the Egyptians had with this part of the world from 2000 B.C. on, suggest at least the probability of an induced urbanization. This seems all the more likely, indeed, inasmuch as the region for a long time formed part of the Egyptian empire. But in this case, is it still possible to speak of true African cities, even if the cultures that flourished in cities like Napata and Meroe had many original characteristics? On the other hand, there is little doubt that most of the population of these cities and their ruling elites were black. Moreover, the word "cush" appears so frequently in the history of the Middle East, especially in the Bible, that the term "cushi" has been adopted by modern Hebrew as the word for a black person.

In summary, there were sizable cities in Black Africa by 1000 B.C., if not earlier. But despite the fact that agriculture in the Sudan appears more and more ancient as time goes by (Krzyzaniak, 1978), it is not certain that these cities were a purely African urban development. The same questions arise concerning the first phases of the development of cities in Ethiopia, about which even less is known.

The Great Urban Cultures of Black Africa

There were several purely African urban cultures that developed before the sixteenth century, including (chapter 26) the Yoruba, an African urban people who developed their highest culture well before the sixteenth century.

I shall begin with Ghana, traditionally considered the most ancient of the kingdoms south of the Sahara. The capital of Ghana, Koumbi, a city constructed chiefly of stone, was located on the edge of the Sahara, at the extreme southeast of present-day Mauritania. As Oliver and Fagan (1975) note in their history of Africa during the Iron Age, when the Muslims crossed the Sahara for the first time in 753, the kingdom of Ghana had already been established for a great many years. According to the oral tradition of the Middle Ages, the kingdom of Ghana had already counted twenty-two reigns by the time of the arrival of Islam. One cannot, of course, place absolute confidence in this claim, which, if we consider twenty-five years to be the average length of a reign, would make the foundation of the kingdom as early as A.D. 200. What remains certain, however, is that the first cities of the kingdom of Ghana were founded around A.D. 500–600. But there is great uncertainty except about the subsequent stages in the urban evolution of the kingdom. It has been determined, for example, that under the influence of Islam the capital, Koumbi, was transformed into a twin city, Koumbi-Saleh, with an African part and a Muslim part, with a sizable population of merchants living in the latter. The interest the kingdom of Ghana held for merchants derived from its place in the gold trade. It should be remembered that until the discovery of America, Africa was one of the principal sources of this precious metal, the two chief mining centers being the Sudan and Ghana or, more exactly, the regions south of the kingdom of Ghana. This trade facilitated the Muslim penetration of this part of the world and also the establishment of urban centers showing the influence of Islamic civilization.

The probability that there was an autonomous development grows as archaeological research progresses. The urban culture of Ghana seems by 1000 B.C. to have had not only agriculture, but also villages with houses built of stone. And this culture seems in all likelihood to have evolved without major external influences (Munson, 1980).

But was Ghana truly the first of the ancient urban cultures of Black Africa, or was it the Songhai kingdom? For the latter, very recent excavations have confirmed the existence of an urban development that was not only very early (the end of the first millennium B.C.), but was autonomous as well. The excavations were carried out on the site of Jenné-Jeno (in present-day Mali), which was apparently the original location of the city of Jenné (or Djenné). Jenné was considered until recently to have had a marked Islamic influence, Islam having penetrated to this region by the eleventh century. Under Muslim influence, in addition to having substantial commercial functions, Jenné became an important religious and educational center.

The excavations conducted by S. K. and R. J. McIntosh (1981) have revealed that the site was occupied by 300 B.C. by a population using iron and having artisans. By the first century A.D., rice cultivation was firmly established, which was highly favorable for urbanization. A genuine city grew up with a population of 4,000 around A.D. 200. This city reached its height between 750 and 1100. At this time it apparently had an area of 34 hectares. If there were 300 inhabitants per hectare, this would have made a population of 10,000. Other cities seem to have existed in this region, and during the first millenium A.D., the density of rural sites seems to have been ten times as great as today.

The evidence pours in, then, showing that urbanism was both early and autonomous in Black Africa. There are several other instances in which, though proof is still lacking, a comparable situation may be presumed to have existed.

The first we shall look at is Benin, another relatively advanced urban culture of West Africa, but which had no contacts with Islam, or at most insignificant contacts. It should be noted, however, that Benin formed part of the Yoruba states. And since the Yoruba came from the Cush region, the possibility remains of a contribution of the Cushite kingdom by way of the migrations caused by the disappearance of this kingdom. But this possibility seems fairly remote.

The Benin culture was located in the area of present-day Nigeria, more or less in what today is the region of Biafra. A kingdom had been established by the eleventh century, and the second dynasty, coming to power in the thirteenth century, reigned until 1897, when the British forced the monarch to abdicate. The most ancient city of the kingdom of Benin appears to have been Ife. By the ninth century, the population of Ife was apparently large, and very early in its history the city produced a substantial amount of iron and glass, not to mention its celebrated works of art which figure among the masterpieces of world art. The Benin culture reached its apogee during the sixteenth century, by which time it had evolved a culture with many large urban centers. Around the year 1500, the chief city, Benin, had a population of sixty to seventy thousand and was a well-ordered urban center with a system of water conduits and a sizable artisanry working at an advanced technical level. According to one traveller writing at the beginning of the seventeenth century, the principal street was about seven kilometers long. This figure may be an exaggeration, but it is an indication of the large size of the city. Around 1500 the kingdom had about ten other cities. The houses were generally constructed of wood, it is true; but this was also the case at this time in many of the cities of northern Europe and indeed is still the case in most cities in the United States.

Without pretending to attempt an exhaustive treatment of the early urbanized cultures of Black Africa, let us consider a further example of a society with many substantial urban centers, the kingdom of the Congo. For the kingdom of the Congo, archaeological investigations have not yet advanced far enough to enable us to chart with any certainty the course of the beginnings of urbanism in the region. It is known, however, that at its height during the fifteenth century, the Congo was a true empire holding sway over an area of about 500,000 square kilometers, an area roughly the size of modern-day France. At the time of the first contacts with the Portuguese in 1484, the capital city, Mbanza Congo (see chapter 24), probably had a population of some 40,000–60,000. Indeed, certain contemporary estimates place the figure as high as 100,000. As Randles (1972) remarks, however, these estimates are most likely excessive, and he concludes that "we can therefore hazard a fairly safe figure of at least 50,000 for the beginning of the sixteenth century."

These cities were constructed chiefly of wood, but there were some in which stone played a decisive part. To cite but one case, but one which was of major importance, there were the cities of Zimbabwe, a nation situated in the southeastern corner of present-day Zimbabwe. The impressive remains found on its site give some idea of the scale of the city that was once the capital of the empire of the Monomotapa, an empire that at its height had an area of 700,000 square kilometers. Another original feature of this empire, which had numerous cities and towns, was that it developed by exploiting and exporting mineral wealth (principally gold) and ivory destined for India and Persia rather than North Africa or the Middle East. Given the fairly poor quality of the soil in the region, it appears likely that the empire offered all, or a substantial part, of its gold in exchange for food. It is also certain that it imported porcelain from China. The mass of gold extracted from its mines was very considerable: according to Summers's (1963) estimate, the amount was some twenty-five million ounces, or more than seven hundred metric tons, as much gold as was produced by Mexico, Peru, and Potosi combined over the 350 years from the start of the sixteenth century to the second half of the nineteenth century.

The volume of gold produced was, then, very great—great enough, if we accept Summers's estimate, to have provided by itself for a substantial urban population. If we assume that the region could have received during this period half the quantity of grain per gram of gold as Europe did during the same period, the quantities involved are startling. Indeed, in fifteenth-century Europe 100 kilograms of grain cost some 1.5 to 2.0 grams of gold, an average resulting from a fairly wide regional dispersal. If the annual consumption of grain was on the order of 300 kilograms per person, and if all of the gold extracted were exchanged for grain, then Zimbabwe produced sufficient gold to support approximately 400,000 people over a period of 300 years. It is possible that the production figures for gold are an overestimate, since this is only a rough calculation, but it still confirms what has been suggested by excavations in the region. Archaeologists have already run up a list of more than thirty definite sites dating from the Monomotapa Empire, to which must be added more than twenty other probable sites. Many of these sites were most likely true cities, the most important of them being Grand Zimbabwe (given this name by archaeologists to distinguish it from the other cities of the empire). Assuming that the ruins found on the site of Grand Zimbabwe do indeed belong to a single city, the entire urban site covered an area of some 650 hectares. The most impressive of the ruins found on the site are those of the "temple," or "palace," and those of the "acropolis" (so called owing to its location). A wall 10 meters high and 250 meters long surrounded the palace. Even supposing a density of only 40 inhabitants per hectare (the habitat was probably spread out), Grand Zimbabwe would seem to have had at its height a population of some 25,000 people.

It appears that Zimbabwe reached its height between the middle of the fourteenth century and the middle of the fifteenth century, and that the origins of this urban culture go back as far as the eleventh century. Since the capital was abandoned around 1450, that is, some time before the arrival of the Europeans, and since the first European to discover its ruins was a hunter, who stumbled on the site in 1868, it is understandable why so many unknowns remain concerning the history of this culture. But contrary to what happens in most other cases, in this instance recent findings tend rather to dampen the enthusiasm inspired by earlier research. Beach's (1980) summary of what is known about the Monomotapa empire downplays somewhat the scale of what nevertheless remains a substantial urban culture. It is also probably less ancient than had been assumed before, given that it did not really get under way until around A.D. 900.

Islam and Urbanization in Black Africa

The discussion of the urban history of Black Africa would be incomplete without a brief word about the profound impact exerted on the region by the penetration of Islam. This penetration occurred very early, since even before the close of the seventh century the eastern half of the Maghreb had been brought under Muslim domination.

The Islamic influence on urbanization in Black Africa took on four highly distinct forms: (1) the establishment of a number of port bases, notably along the eastern coast; (2) the intensification of commercial relations, especially with the cultures of West and Central Africa, an intensification made possible by the economic development of the Maghreb; (3) the subjection of certain areas, particularly those bordering on the Maghreb, to a colonial type of domination; (4) the exodus of numerous dissident Islamic sects, some of which installed themselves in Africa.

But however different these modes of Islamic influence may have been, they all led to the same two consequences. The first was the conversion to Islam of a part or the whole of the populations concerned. Even if in many cases only the monarch or certain ruling classes were converted to begin with, the consequences were nevertheless substantial. For this initial step eventually either led to the conversion of the entire society, whose cities were thereupon "covered with mosques," or else it led to the creation of large Muslim quarters, or "satellite cities," in or around a large African town, as was notably the case with Koumbi-Saleh, the Muslim quarter of the city of Ghana, whose population must have reached 15,000–20,000.

The second consequence of Islamic penetration into Black Africa was urban expansion. Though it is difficult to measure its exact extent, there is no doubt that expansion did occur, and it was certainly very considerable. Of course, I speak of expansion in this context in order to simplify matters, for it is impossible in most of the regions of Black Africa to distinguish between cases in which Islam brought urbanization to the area and cases in which Islam merely gave added impetus to an autonomous process of urban growth already under way.

The Islamic contribution to urbanism in Black Africa was sufficiently great to justify its inclusion in the present chapter. The scope of the present analysis prevents me, however, from attempting even the most summary historical survey of the various African societies touched by the diffusion of Islam. I shall confine myself, therefore, to identifying the geographical area affected and to furnishing a few explanatory details regarding urban expansion in Africa under Islamic influence.

What was the geographical domain subjected to Islamic influence? Its western boundary more or less followed the course of the Niger river, crossing the continent along the twelfth parallel, north latitude. To the east, this frontier descended along the coast as far as the twelfth parallel, south latitude, even taking in the Comoro Islands. As Bovill (1958) remarks, the African cities trading with Islam during the Middle Ages lay between the latitudes marking the southern limit of transport by camel and the northern limit of tsetse fly infestation. In general terms, this area corresponds to the following modern states: Guinea, Gambia, Senegal, Mauritania, Mali, Burkina Faso, Niger, Chad, the Sudan, Somalia, and the coastal fringes of Kenya and Tanzania.

Among the largest and most important cities of this region, mention should be made of Gao, Gober, Jenné, Kano, Kazargamu, Timbuktu and Zaria. Around the beginning of the sixteenth century, these cities had populations ranging between twenty-five thousand and seventy thousand, with an average somewhere on the order of forty thousand. While certain of them have survived as true urban centers in the twentieth century, others have practically vanished. This is notably the case for Gao (or Gogo) and Jenné (or Djenné); the latter, owing to its extensive commercial functions and its canals, was at its height like the Venice of West Africa.

I shall now sketch in broad outline the factors to account for the urban expansion engendered by Islam in Black Africa. First, there were the indirect consequences of Islamic influence in the continent. By this I mean the effects of the expansion of trade stimulated by the economic development of the Maghreb and the Middle East in the first phase of Islamic influence. The gold deposits in west Africa provided the fundamental impetus for this development. Gold was one of the few products sufficiently valuable to justify the enormous transport costs of the overland journeys involved. It has been pointed out, for instance, that owing to the considerable transport costs, salt was exchanged in certain parts of Africa at a value equal to that of gold. These overland journeys covered distances of 3,000–4,000 kilometers, often through deserts. From Kano to Fez the normal trade route entailed a journey of about 3,300 kilometers, and from Kano to Cairo about 4,200 kilometers. Kano was not itself the center of gold production; the goldfields lay more than 1,000 kilometers from the city. To the list of the principal African exports should also be added ivory (most of it coming from East Africa), slaves, and a few agricultural products, especially gum arabic, and cola nuts. Ivory, like gold, brought a very high price; as for cola nuts, though most of them were intended for internal African trade, Muslim merchants acted as go-betweens. As Levtzion (1973) observes, from the seventeenth century to the nineteenth century, the cola trade played a crucial role in the diffusion of Islam between the Sahel and the borders of the equatorial forest. Among the principal imports to Africa, textiles should be mentioned in addition to the most important, salt.

If trade favored the spread of Islam, Islam in turn favored the spread of trade. And this is the second of the factors furthering the urbanization of Black African societies subject to Islamic influence. The ties of religion and the shared knowledge of Arabic, coupled with the commercial ethic implicit in the Islamic faith and culture, fostered the creation of personal bonds themselves conducive to enhanced commercial bonds. Further, the construction of mosques and of other buildings intended for the use of other religious institutions increased both the size of cities and their urban character.

Urbanism in the Pre-Columbian Civilizations

"When we saw so many cities and towns built over the water, and still other great cities on the dry land, and the paved highway, laid so smooth and level, that ran straight to Mexico, we stood dumbstruck with admiration. We said to ourselves that it resembled the enchanted dwelling places described in the book of Amadis because of the great towers and temples and the edifices built over the water, all of them constructed of lime and stone; some of our soldiers even asked if this vision were not a dream."

The wonder of Bernal Diaz de Castillo, who accompanied Cortez when he first entered the city of Tenochtitlan (Mexico City), grew deeper still when he realized the scale, wealth, and organization of the city. His description, borne out by others every bit as full of praise and astonishment and by archaeological remains found on the site of the city, removes any doubt as to the high level of the pre-Columbian civilizations before the coming of the Europeans. It is the view of many students in the field, indeed, that the cities of the pre-Columbian New World were bigger, richer, and better organized than the European cities of the period.

Until recently it was estimated that around 1519, the date of the arrival of the Europeans, the city of Tenochtitlan, founded in 1345 and capital of the Aztec Empire, had a population of 60,000–80,000. Very recent research, however, following fresh excavations occasioned by subway construction in Mexico City, has led to the revision of estimates of both the area and the population of the city. Tenochtitlan certainly covered more than 12,000, and perhaps even as many as 15,000, hectares of ground. Based on these figures, supplemented by others drawn from manuscript records, Calnek (1978) calculates a population of 150,000–200,000. During this same period, there were only four European cities this size; and on the Iberian peninsula, the two largest cities at that time, Granada and Lisbon, had around 70,000 inhabitants each. And as the eyewitness account quoted above also indicates, since Tenochtitlan lay at the heart of a fairly heavily urbanized region, the numerous smaller cities located in the vicinity could together have had a population of about 400,000.

Nor was the capital, Tenochtitlan, the only large city in the empire. While the Aztec empire as a whole may perhaps have had a less highly urbanized character than sixteenth-century Western Europe, the differences were not pronounced. The Aztec empire took its place in a whole series of urban cultures that had grown up before it, and Mexico was but one of the geographic centers in which urban cultures had evolved. As Millon (1967) very justly remarks in his brief but thorough synthesis, the Spaniards, filled with wonder at their first sight of Tenochtitlan, "could not know that the city they were seeing, with its great pyramid temples, marketplaces, palaces, and gleaming white dwellings, was the product of a long period of growth and development, and that the earliest cities in Mexico antedated it by almost fifteen hundred years."

Let us therefore return to the beginnings of the process of urbanization in the pre-Columbian New World.

The Beginning of Agriculture and Cities in the New World: Were They Invented Here, Too?

Despite the abundance of recent research on the Neolithic in the New World, many mysteries remain. Among these may be cited the question of the origins of certain plants native to the New World. And the reasons have not yet been found for the fact that the domestication of animals in the New World was much more restricted than in the Old World. But there is enough certainty to establish the principal phases in the emergence of agriculture in the New World.

There were at least two seats of agriculture, one in Mexico and one in the Andes, especially Peru. It remains impossible, however, to determine whether any links existed between these two centers or what the nature of such links would have been. In both cases the first signs of agriculture or, more precisely, of proto-agriculture appeared around 7000 B.C., if not earlier. Agriculture proper, together with settlement in villages and the methodical cultivation of specific crops, seems to have emerged sooner in the Andes (7000–6500 B.C.) than in Mexico (around 4000–3500 B.C.).

Moving on to the origins of cities in the New World, it should be noted that researchers in the field agree that urbanism in the pre-Columbian New World was autonomous. Even though, following a line of conjecture pursued practically from the moment the conquistadors first set foot in the New World, scholars continue to wonder about the possibility of links between the New World and Asia, it appears that the development of the pre-Columbian civilizations probably owed nothing to events in the Old World. While there is no longer any doubt that America was originally populated through migrations of peoples crossing the Bering Strait from Asia, these migrations took place more than 20,000 (if not 100,000) years ago. These peoples had no knowledge of agriculture, let alone of urbanism, and remained isolated from the Old World.

The major pre-Columbian civilizations originally evolved in two geographic areas: the Andes, in the region more or less corresponding to contemporary Peru, and in the area more or less corresponding to present-day Mexico. It seems likely that there were relations and mutual influences between these two centers of civilization, but many uncertainties persist.

Located in the northern part of the Isthmus of Tehuantepec (i.e., southern Mexico), the Olmec culture (summit around 800–400 B.C.), considered to have been the first high culture in the New World, is not thought to have had a truly urban character, despite the presence of large temples. The same applies to Chavin, a culture that evolved at about the same time in the Andes, leaving many large temples. Still, the gap between what some scholars have described as "macro-temples," or ceremonial centers, and true cities is not very great. As is the case with other ceremonial centers, there may be great upward revisions of the population estimates. So it is possible to date the onset of urbanism in the New World at about 100 B.C.

Very recent excavations of the site of El Mirador in the extreme north of Guatemala and in Colombia have led researchers to push this date back still further. In Guatemala the excavations have unearthed traces of a very large city with an estimated population of 40,000–80,000. Abandoned by about A.D. 500, this city would appear to have already achieved a considerable size as early as the start of our own era. The discovery of "Ciudad Perdida" dates only from 1975. The enthusiasm of the Columbian archaeologists may be excessive, but it is very likely that this was a very elaborate urban network that was perhaps larger than that of the Incas or the Aztecs. Besides the main center, Ciudad Perdida, this culture, called Tairona, probably had some 200–300 urban centers (Darnhofer-Demar, 1982).

What until now has been considered the first great urban center of the pre-Columbian New World is the city of Teotihuacan. Teotihuacan lay some forty kilometers northeast of Mexico City, where the famous Pyramids of the Sun and Moon are. The civilization that supported Teotihuacan had emerged by 300 B.C.. At its height around the eighth century A.D., the city covered about 1,900 hectares and had a population of 125,000 or even 200,000 (Millon, 1981). These figures have been significantly revised. Previously numbers on the order of 70,000–80,000 were proposed which implied a low density (35–45 people per hectare). However, even if one uses these revised figures, the density remains low (65–100 people per hectare). It is true that in contrast to Tenochtitlan, where the proportion of farmers was low, in Teotihuacan the proportion reached perhaps 75 percent. It is necessary also to consider the vast religious monuments, since many pre-Columbian cities are considered to be either "macro-temples" or "religious cities." The density of Tikal, the largest of the fifteen important Mayan cities at that civilization's apogee (eighth and ninth centuries), appears to have been even lower. Tikal was a religious center whose surface area (about 1,200 hectares), was more than half that of Teotihuacan. In this case there has been even a more dramatic change in the figures. Previously a population of 10,000–15,000 was generally accepted: this figure was then raised to 50,000 (Hartung, 1978) and then to 72,000 (Willey, 1981). Even in this last case there were only 60 persons per hectare.

This brings us to the predominantly religious role played by the majority of the urban centers of the pre-Columbian civilizations. It is likely that future research will tend to attentuate the importance of this feature of pre-Columbian cities. Indeed, if we contemplate the hypothetical case of the destruction of the European civilization of the Middle Ages by conquerors from the New World, the questions that would have been asked four centuries later by the altogether different civilization that would have supplanted it would doubtless closely resemble those asked today concerning the pre-Columbian New World. Think of the huge cathedrals located in cities that were fairly small, and that would appear all the smaller since the urban habitat was constructed largely of wood, and would have left fewer ruins. This does not reduce to nothing, however, the uniquely religious character of urbanism in pre-Columbian societies: though its importance may eventually be much diminished, it can never be cancelled out altogether.

Mention should be made, finally, of one last intriguing facet of pre-Columbian societies: the absence of a genuine form of writing in the civilization of the Andes. In the light of this curious fact, the development of a form of writing does not appear to be an absolute prerequisite of the birth of true urban civilizations. We have already seen that the absence of writing was also a feature of the urban cultures of Africa in the nineteenth century. But the fragility characteristic of urban systems without writing nevertheless lends indirect support to the notion of the essential part played by writing in bringing about lasting urbanization.

Highly Urbanized Societies in the New World: Were There Any? And If So, How Can They Be Explained?

Is it possible to attempt a calculation of the size of the urban population of the pre-Columbian New World? This would be decidedly risky, if only because of the very wide margin of error surrounding the figure for total population. Did the New World south of the Rio Grande have 30–50 million, or 80–110 million people before the coming of the Europeans? Such is the current degree of uncertainty about population estimates for the New World during this period—though for the moment the scales seem weighted in favor of the lower estimate, pointing to a population on the order of some 40 million people.

As for the urban population of pre-Columbian societies, it is estimated that there were something like 4–7 cities with populations of more than 50,000 and some 25–30 (perhaps even 40) cities with populations of 20,000–50,000. Breaking these totals down by major region, the distribution was as follows. In the southern part of North America (Aztecs, Tairona, Tarascans, Zapotecs), there were around 9–11 cities with populations of more than 20,000, 2 or 3 of which probably exceeded 50,000, while in Central and South America (Incas, Mayas, Chibchas, Cakchiquels), there were cities with populations of more than 20,000, one or two of which surpassed 50,000. If we posit a rank-size distribution comparable to that obtaining in medieval Europe, this would yield—applying the criterion of 5,000 inhabitants as the lower limit defining urban populations—an urban population somewhere between 2.1 and 3.5 million. But nothing rules out the possibility of a rank-size distribution very different from that of medieval Europe. In this case the spread could be widened further, say by 10% at either end, giving an urban population of anywhere between 1.7 and 3.5 million, representing a minimum of 2–3% and a maximum of 10–13% of the total population. On the basis of the data that now seem most plausible, the average may have been around 7%: a proportion that appears acceptable given the socioeconomic context, corresponding as it does to the proportion found in the least urbanized countries of Europe prior to the Industrial Revolution or to that of the United States at the start of the nineteenth century.

But none of this excludes either of the two extreme proportions: a level of 10–13% remains a distinct possibility, which is favored by recent estimates by Schaedel (1978) for the Chimu region of the Andes around the city of Chanchan. For this region Schaedel concludes that the level of urbanization was about 14%.

But the likelihood of a high level of urbanization in many pre-Columbian societies and the certainty that such a situation did in fact exist in several regions poses a problem. This problem, which may go far to explain the astonishment of the conquistadors in the face of the scale of urbanism in the New World, concerns what might be called the nonconcordance between the level of urbanization and the level of economic development attained in the pre-Columbian world. Most probably the basis for a solution may be found in the circumstance that the cultivation of maize and potatoes, at that time unknown in Europe, made possible a higher population density than would have been attainable in Europe with a comparable level of economic development. But whatever its origins, this nonconcordance perhaps also explains the fragility of the urban systems of the pre-Columbian civilizations. The most striking example of this fragility was the sudden decline of the Mayan civilization. This civilization, established around A.D. 200–300 and having a highly developed urban system, disappeared sometime around A.D. 900 in the space of a single generation.

As concerns the much-admired Mayan civilization, it should be pointed out that, while the causes for its abrupt and dramatic disappearance remain today as mysterious as ever, the history of the Mayas has lately been enlarged by a further 6,500 years, and also by the addition of an explanatory factor destined to play a significant role in accounts of the development of Mayan cities.

In the past, the history of the Mayas could be traced back no farther than about 2500 B.C., a time at which the Mayas were organized into farming villages. But recent excavations, carried out in early 1980 under the direction of R. S. MacNeish, have pushed the start of the story back to 9000 B.C.

The sequence of events now seems to have been as follows. Between 9000 and 7500 B.C., the economy of the region was based on the hunting of large mammals. The thinning out of the local mammal population, however, led to the use of plants, particularly wild grain. Then gradually a transition was made to fishing. But there was still no farming, although during this period (5000–4200 B.C.) other peoples in the New World already practised agriculture. Agriculture was adopted little by little only from 3300 to 2500 B.C. In the meantime, however, villages of considerable size inhabited by fishers had developed, and it appears that agriculture was eventually adopted when there was an increase of population leading to settlements along the valleys. As MacNeish (*New York Times*, 13 May 1980) said in reply to a question asked him by a scientific journalist intrigued by the delay in the emergence of agriculture in the region, "Why eat beans and squash when you can have lobster?"

A second and more important contribution was made in recent investigations in the area: the discovery of an extremely extensive irrigation network that had remained completely unknown until the beginning of 1980. In tests carried out on a radar device intended for use in the exploration of the planet Venus, the presence of a well-developed system of irrigation canals was discovered over a zone covering a total of 14,000 square kilometers, corresponding to the territory occupied by the Mayas. Archaeologists, rushing to the spot, were able to confirm the existence of irrigation canals supplying water to some 1,250–2,500 square kilometers of fields. In this way a new explanatory element was introduced into discussions of the problem of accounting for the economic base of this major civilization. The evidence steadily accumulates to the effect that it was indeed a truly urban culture. In the light of additional excavations in the region, scholars increasingly tend to abandon the notion that most of the Mayan sites were mere ceremonial centers. As Andrews (1975) writes: "We . . . [have] . . . established the legitimacy of the notion that the larger Maya settlements were essentially urban and should be considered as cities if the general conditions as postulated for the preindustrial or prehistoric city are accepted." Cities with large populations indeed, since it is estimated, for instance, that Tikal had fifty thousand inhabitants and Dzibilchaltun forty thousand or more. The recent discovery of the irrigation canals not only confirms rather high estimates for the urban population of the Mayas, but may even lead to yet higher estimates (Adams, 1980).

North America: Cultures without Cities

The southern part of the territory today occupied by the United States ought properly to be regarded as related to the pre-Columbian civilizations examined in the preceding discussion. Thus in the southwestern United States, for instance (contemporary Arizona, southern Colorado, Kansas, and New Mexico), the Anasazi and the Hohokam cultures were heavily influenced by the culture of the Toltecs. As concerns the Anasazi people in particular, researchers have observed the development of an authentic urban culture, with cities with populations of ten thousand or more, that reached its height between the eleventh and fourteenth centuries. The cultures of the southeastern and eastern United States, on the other hand, appear to have been much less highly urbanized. Here too, however, the influence of the Mayan and Toltec civilizations made itself felt. The adoption of agriculture took place about the beginning of the Christian era, the cultures in these regions reaching their apogee sometime around the twelfth century. But if scholars have confirmed beyond question the existence of numerous towns, it remains risky to speak in this instance of true urban centers.

To the north, in what represents the largest part of the United States and Canada today, we find cultures many of which had not yet adopted or invented agriculture. Thus, in the territory corresponding to contemporary Canada, only the Huron-Iroquois peoples practised agriculture alongside hunting. But even in this case, the kind of agriculture in question was based on the slash-and-burn method of cultivation, a practice that entailed the displacement of the villages every ten to twenty years. True enough, space was hardly wanting. Since the population of North America north of the Rio Grande before the arrival of the Europeans was about 1–4 million, this suggests that, even if one takes the highest estimate, population density was only 0.2 people per square kilometer, a figure that rises to 0.4 people per square kilometer if one excludes all truly uninhabitable regions. In any event, the displacements of villages caused by the practice of slash-and-burn cultivation considerably reduced the likelihood of the creation of urban centers by preventing or impeding any permanent large-scale settlements.

In the United States, with the exception of those areas in the south mentioned earlier, the situation closely resembled that in Canada: the great majority of the indigenous cultures practised no form of agriculture. There were in certain regions, though only in attenuated form, influences originating in Mesoamerica, notably among the cultures of the southern United States. It seems, however, that there were no genuine cities. Even among the most advanced tribes—among those, like the Iroquois, that came closest to urbanization—there was nothing more highly evolved than large fortified villages.

As far as agriculture is concerned, its practice was known to more groups and in larger areas than in Canada. Those groups were mainly between the Great Lakes and the Gulf of Mexico. In this case recent research has not revised the idea of a nonautonomous agriculture (Griffin, 1980).

And What of the Other Continent?

Australia escapes no more than any of the other important regions the hand of dramatic historiographical revision. As R. Jones (1979) remarks, the last fifteen years have witnessed a revolution in Australian prehistory. In 1961 the earliest accepted date for human occupation was 6700 B.C.; in 1962, it was 8000 B.C.; and by 1968 it was nearly 19,000 B.C. Today according to Jones's hypothesis Australia was first colonized by man around 50,000 years ago, if not earlier still.

But despite this early date—a date, however, that compared with the date of man's first appearance in Eurasia and Africa seems rather late—agriculture and urbanization emerged only in the nineteenth century, brought by the European immigrants. Indeed "as a legacy of its geographical position, Australia retained a population of hunter-gatherers living in an environment unaltered by agriculture and organized industry" (Lampert, 1975).

The appearance of man on islands smaller than Australia appears to have occurred later. This does not completely exclude the fact that, unlike in Australia, agriculture was practiced in certain islands, and especially in Western Polynesia, before the arrival of the Europeans. This was certainly a limited form of agriculture, since the sea provided a large, if not overwhelming, part of the food consumed (Davidson, 1981). This agriculture appears to have already existed 2,000–2,500 years ago.

5 Athens and Rome—Two Very Different Civilizations: The Sources of European Urbanization? □

There is surely no need to insist upon the influence of Graeco-Roman (and above all Roman) civilization, not only on Western civilization, but on the urban structure of Europe in its entirety as well. The whole urban texture of Europe was deeply conditioned by the Roman settlements and, to a lesser extent, by the Greek urban colonies. Architecture, and also urban planning, owe an enormous debt to their Graeco-Roman precedents. What is more, in the case of Rome, there were socioeconomic problems of an astonishingly modern character. Finally, there was in the Graeco-Roman world an extremely urbanized way of life. It may not perhaps have been, as Finley (1977) suggests, "more urbanized than any other society before the modern era," but it was certainly in historical terms the first highly urbanized world in human experience.

Were there in fact only two civilizations at the root of the urbanization of Europe? There is no doubt that the urban life of Europe has borrowed a tremendous amount from the civilizations of Greece and Rome. But to see in this fundamental heritage the beginnings of the process of European urban growth is a view that seems increasingly difficult to defend. This explains why I framed the title of the present chapter in the form of a question. It also explains why, after dealing with Greece and Rome, I shall review the first stages in the rise of agriculture and cities in Europe before the miracle of Greece. Over the course of this review, I shall show that agriculture emerged fairly early, making its initial appearance in the Greek peninsula around 6500–6000 B.C. and in Italy around 5600–4600 B.C.

Before addressing the case of Greece, however, and in order the better to establish the link with the world of the Middle East and also to give sharper relief to the mediating and unifying role the Mediterranean has always played in the growth of civilization, it may not be amiss to pause a moment to consider the Aegean civilization. Though the geographic zone of the Aegean civilization largely extended over the same area as that of Greece, and though Greece was in a sense its lineal descendant, the originality of the Greek miracle will in no way appear diminished on that account. It should be recalled that the Aegean civilization reached its zenith during the period known as the Mycenaean age, between 1500 and 1100 b.c. It seems that a part of the population of this civilization came from Asia Minor, settling in the area by 6000 b.c., followed around 4000 b.c. by invaders originating in the Balkans. This was truly the crossroads of the Middle Eastern and European worlds—to the latter of which most of the next two parts of this book will be devoted.

However, the geographic origin of these migrants and the role of the Mediterranean Sea as a link impels me to mention a very interesting thesis proposed in 1964 by the anthropologist John Whiting, a thesis which has been supported by the work of the statistician Stephen Stigler on a model of population dispersion (Whiting, Sodergren, and Stigler, 1982). According to these authors the isothermic line of average temperature ten degrees centigrade during the coldest month constituted a barrier to the migration of preindustrial populations. "Cradles were generally used to carry infants when the winter temperature was colder than 10°C, whereas slings or shawls were more common when it was warmer. Infants were heavily swaddled only in colder regions." Furthermore, it appears "that adult clothing may also be governed by the 10° isotherm. A report of studies carried out for the U.S. Army during World War II specifies that temperature below 10°C requires at least two layers of clothing." The authors present evidence that for those reasons, this temperature of 10°C "has served as a critical isotherm, and that temperature has provided roughly uniform narrow climatic limits to migration throughout the habitable regions of the earth."

This isothermic line cuts the Mediterranean Sea from east to west. Curiously, during the preindustrial era the Mediterranean Sea was more conducive to horizontal interchanges than vertical ones. The urban cultures whose beginnings I have recounted are located to the south of this line. Greece, Rome, and the rest of Europe are on the other side. Now if one recalls that it is these civilizations which put an end to the preindustrial world, one begins to wonder. But that is another story.

The Aegean Civilization: Palaces or Towns?

"The Aegean Civilization: Palaces or Towns?" is the title of a chapter of the excellent synthesis of Hammond (1972), the only available general history dealing with urbanism in Europe and the Middle East before the seventh century. This title asks a question that has been raised with reference to certain of the pre-Columbian and Asian civilizations, a question that in some respects also has a bearing on the towns of the preurban era. To what extent may palaces be regarded as cities? The available data lead me to think that, so far as the initial phases of Aegean civilization are concerned (2000–1450 B.C.), there are not yet true cities. The palaces constructed during this early period were the residences of sovereigns ruling over small regions, in which the court, also small, and the administration, equally small, lived on the tribute exacted from the agrarian communities under their control. These palaces may be said to resemble after a fashion the castles of the nobles of the feudal age in Europe. There are a number of differences, however, including in most cases the absence of fortifications.

Following the troubled period of the years 1700–1450 B.C., a period marked especially by a famous series of volcanic eruptions, there was a new phase of expansion characterized by the construction of larger palaces and also by a larger number of dwellings around them, giving the whole a more urban aspect. But are these really cities? The question remains open as regards most of these palaces, despite the fact that the new communities exhibited many urban features, most notably the rising predominance of an artisan class. But though the question cannot in most instances be answered in the affirmative, Mycenae and Troy (among others) seem to be true cities, as practically all historians agree. Van Effenterre (1980) does not hesitate to use the term "city" in his discussion of those cities, and especially for Mallia, one of the four great palaces. The same is true more generally of Warren (1980).

In short, here as in so many other fields, it is impossible to draw any precise boundaries, whether in general or as regards particular cases. The overall drift toward urbanization nevertheless seems clear. The synthesis of Dickinson (1977) shows that the Aegean towns, especially the largest of them, engaged in long-distance trade. Although this trade was apparently on a relatively small scale, it was nonetheless real. To be sure, as has already been shown, long-distance trade does not necessarily imply the existence of genuine cities. But further evidence derived from recent excavations and other research reinforces the view that the Aegean towns were in fact true cities.

Greek Civilization: City-States with Commercial Functions

In order to situate Greek civilization more precisely in historical time, a few basic points of reference are necessary. Having tended in the past to place too much emphasis on dates, the teaching of history has now swung in the opposite direction, tending too readily to neglect them altogether. But no process of deductive reasoning will in most cases enable us to formulate useful historical frames of reference. While what is called classical Greece may be confined to a period of two centuries marked off at one end by the expulsion of the Tyrant of Athens (510 B.C.) and at the other by the conquest of Greece by Philip of Macedon (338 B.C.), obviously one has to overstep these boundaries in order to situate Greek civilization as a whole. By 700 B.C., Greece had writing and, more to the point, had invented coined money. And Greece did not become a Roman province until 146 B.C. These dates, based more on facts relating to the existence of a specifically Greek civilization than on an interpretation of the political or cultural meaning of that civilization, will serve here to delineate the Greek era.

The priority accorded the invention of money deserves some commentary. Money was of the greatest significance for economic life in general and for urban life in particular. Although the gradual development of a monetary system is still a shadowy area, the Greek contribution lay chiefly in the creation of coins that, by their weight and a determined content of precious metal, had an intrinsic value. This constituted a definite advance not only on the barter system, but also on the system in which exchange was for quantities of raw material. The use of coins made exchange easier and thus favored the growth of cities by giving them the additional function of issuing currency.

Classical Greece had a type of city-state in which the cultural function of the city became important early. The agora, at its inception simply the place where public assemblies gathered, became the focus of urban life because of its cultural functions (theater, place of instruction) which were added to its original administrative and religious functions. To speak of the achievements of Greek civilization is to speak of the achievements of Greek cities: the city plays the cardinal role. But this does not rule out a certain degree of prudence. As Starr (1979) notes in his economic history of Greece: "The one city about which anything can be said in detail is Athens; but in commenting on its evolution one runs the inevitable risk in Greek history of taking a very untypical state as a paradigm."

The First Attempts to Determine the Maximum Size of Cities

It is worth noting that Greece appears to have been the first civilization to raise the question of urban planning from the point of view of size. Both Plato and Aristotle addressed this problem. Aristotle adopted a cautious position, while nevertheless insisting upon the existence of a minimum and especially of a maximum size—a limit that ought never to be surpassed. He proposes no definite figure, however, and even sidesteps the issue by means of a prudent rhetorical pirouette. In *Politics*, VII, 4, 1326b, 10–25, he writes: "But what is this unsurpassable limit? It is easy enough to reckon on the basis of an examination of the facts." In treating size, he gives emphasis to the public function of cities: "It is vital that the citizens know one another." He also stresses problems of security, noting the following as an additional shortcoming of too-large cities: "Foreigners and half-breeds usurp without difficulty the rights of citizens because it is easy for them to escape notice owing to the size of the population."

Plato is far more explicit. He furnishes a definite number, stating in *Laws*, vol. 74, that the ideal republic would have 5,040 citizens. If one interprets citizen as being equivalent to head of household, this implies a population on the order of twenty thousand people, of whom an unspecified number would be city dwellers. He argues, then, for cities of very restricted size. But his concept of the city remains ambiguous in that the ideal republic in his system depends on the integration of the rural and the urban, thus blurring the distinction between them. In any event, for Plato and Aristotle, by far the most important criterion for determining the size of cities is political in character, and it is intimately linked with the problem of communication. The city must remain sufficiently small to permit the holding of public meetings with all of the citizens present.

The Greek cities did in fact remain limited in size. If at its height (around 500–450 B.C.) Athens may have reached or surpassed a population of 100,000, the other cities rarely had as many people as 40,000. Moreover, as a general rule, as soon as a city approached a population of 20,000–30,000, it decided to found a new city rather than to continue the original city's development. This practice not only reflected the political and ideological underpinnings of Greek civilization, but was also apparently motivated by economic constraints. The quality of the Greek soil permitted only a modest agricultural yield and productivity, while transport costs were relatively high. This meant, in turn, that the cost of urban growth was high, in most instances probably prohibitively high.

I shall return to the interesting problem of the Greek colonies, but now I shall concentrate on the metropolis, and especially on this combined problem of supporting urban populations and meeting the high costs of transport. This is another example of economic determinism. Nor could it really be otherwise. While it is true that man does not live by bread alone, he cannot live without it either. Given the peculiar situation of cities, there is inevitably the problem of transport, a fact already clearly perceived by Aristotle. Aristotle (*Politics* VII, 4, 1327a, 5–10) draws up two rules governing the location of the principal city. One concerns the bringing of military aid to all parts of the territory. The other seeks to ensure "that the city provides means of transport with a view to importing the fruits of the soil, and also wood for building, and should the need arise, the materials required for whatever kind of manufacture the city may happen to have."

The problem of acquiring supplies of grain was important to the Greeks because the level of urbanization in Greece was high. Indeed, despite the ecological constraints on urban growth, ancient Greece appears to have been heavily urbanized. Confining myself to the classical Greek period, and basing my estimates on population data available for most of the Greek cities, I find that urban population represented some 15–25% of the total, even when the lower limit defining a city is set at five thousand people. If I reduce the threshold of urbanization it is possible to reach levels as high as 20–30%.

Those "Distant Foreigners" That Cultivated Wheat for Greek Cities

The high level of urbanization in Greece may be accounted for in terms of the commercial function of Greek cities. Greece, with a population of some two million around 500 B.C., was in a sense the trader for the whole of the Mediterranean basin. This circumstance brought with it the profits coming from the role of intermediary, but also an international division of labor. For Greece exchanged its manufactured goods for agricultural products and exchanged certain agricultural products of its own (olive oil, for example) for others more essential for life, such as grain. Thus Herodotus speaks of the eaters of millet in the regions of the north and on the shores of the Black Sea, who cultivated wheat for the cities of Greece.

Attention needs to be drawn here to a general point that ought to be borne in mind in any discussion of traditional societies, whether those of the cultures of antiquity or those of Europe up to the middle of the eighteenth century, or even those in certain parts of the Third World today. To say that urban population represented 25% of overall population does not mean (even supposing a closed economic system) that the proportion of the work force devoted to agriculture represented no more than 75% of the total working population. In fact, as has already been seen, part of the urban population was made up of farm laborers working in the fields near the cities. In cities of small or average size, the proportion of the work force employed in agriculture could have reached or surpassed 25%. Furthermore, and this is important, the agricultural regions in the immediate vicinity of the cities benefited from very substantial supplies of fertilizers derived from the cities themselves. To be sure, this urban agricultural activity was in part offset by the existence of a rural artisanry. But except in the case of what Mendels (1969) so aptly describes as the "proto-industrialization" of the European societies of the eighteenth century, we may by and large regard the amount of full-time agricultural work carried out in the cities as outweighing the full-time industrial work performed in rural areas. The smaller the average size of cities, the greater the proportion of agricultural workers among the urban population. In extreme cases, as in the "cities" of the kingdom of Israel and Judah and as will be seen again later in other parts of the world, it is possible to imagine urban centers inhabited entirely by farming people—although, of course, this involves abandoning as a criterion of urbanization the type of economic activity pursued by city dwellers.

THE BIRTH OF URBANISM

But any city that fulfills all of the essential conditions for the definition of urban centers will without question qualify as a genuine city even if 20, 30, or even 40% of the working population works in agriculture.

While the preceding considerations may somewhat diminish the economic significance of the high level of urbanization attained in ancient Greece, the level was nevertheless high, and is difficult to explain without introducing the kind of foreign trade mentioned earlier, especially the importation of grain. But what was the scale of these imports? It has to be admitted that there is a lack of concrete evidence. Scholars have largely ignored the problem of the functions and economic role of the cities of ancient Greece. Very little research has been done in this area and no recent research of any real breadth. Still, by basing my calculations on the analogous case of seventeenth-century Holland, another urban culture of Europe with a substantial commercial function, and taking into account differences both in the fertility of the soil and in the respective levels of urbanization, I estimate that Greece probably had to import a quantity of grain sufficient to support some 20–40% of its urban population, if not more. In the Netherlands (see chapter 12), net imports of grain during the seventeenth century seem to have been sufficient to cover about 100% of the amount consumed by city dwellers. In the Netherlands, the urban population represented about 50% of the country's total population. But Dutch agriculture was probably more productive than that of ancient Greece.

In any event, the problem of grain imports was so pressing that in Athens the municipal assembly was required to regularly inscribe on the order of the day, alongside the problem of defending the national territory, that of assuring provisions of wheat. These imports seem to have already begun by the end of the seventh century B.C., but it was only later that they became large. "The wheat trade was the only one that Athenian law sought to regulate in this way; the sole concern of the state was to protect the interests of the citizen consumers. It is remarkable that the city should apparently never have addressed its attention to those of its citizens who produced wheat and to the impact that the large-scale importation of wheat would have had on them" (Austin and Vidal-Naquet, 1972). This lack of interest in the situation of the producers of wheat may very readily be explained by the level of urbanization in this agricultural context: it was probably impossible for Athenian farmers to produce any more wheat than they already did.

Local Economic Functions

I have insisted upon the commercial role of Greek cities, especially in foreign trade. It is obvious, however, that Greek trade was not limited solely to long-distance traffic. On the contrary, the commercial activity of Greek cities was above all local in character. As A. H. M. Jones (1940) remarks: "Every city was a market for the surrounding district, whence the peasants came in to sell their products, receiving in exchange the cash with which to pay their taxes, and in some cases rents also, when these were payable in money, and to buy imported goods and such manufactured articles as village industries could not supply. There were thus in every city a number of retailers, who marketed agricultural products, and also groups of artisans, who made such simple articles as the peasants required, and usually also sold them in their own workshops." In short, the cities of ancient Greece presented the same traditional picture as that displayed by the cities of medieval Europe.

Among the urban pursuits of ancient Greece was banking. Bogaert (1968) writes in the conclusion of his study of banking in Greek cities: "The number of Greek cities in which we have found sacred, private or public banks is 53, of which 16 were located on the continent, 12 on the islands and 20 in Asia Minor. Still other cities must have had banks, but their existence is unknown." These were genuine banks and not, as scholars formerly supposed, mere money changers. To be sure, the Greek banks did not give direct credit for investments or for industrial and commercial enterprises. But even in the West it was not until the second half of the nineteenth century that banks fulfilled these functions. In addition to money changing, however, the Greek banks engaged in payment operations for trade and manufacturing, and also (and chiefly) in consumer credit and public-sector lending.

There were other economic pursuits in that heterogeneous mass of professional callings loosely referred to as "specific urban employments" or "specific urban activities." These were those forms of employment that flowed directly from the urban way of life, most of which first appeared after the Industrial Revolution: urban administration, public transport, police, and so forth (see chapter 9). Two of these forms of employment already existed in the cities of ancient Greece: the administration of public thoroughfares (particularly street cleaning and garbage disposal) and the maintenance of public gardens. "The cleaning and upkeep of streets claimed the attention of the ancient Greeks as much as that of our contemporaries. The streets of the cities of antiquity were not perhaps models of hygiene, but neither were they garbage dumps, except in some particular instances which the authorities made every effort to remedy" (Vatin, 1976). As was the case almost until the present, the tasks of garbage disposal and the maintenance of public streets and gardens were often farmed out in ancient Greece in exchange for land.

And unemployment? There was certainly unemployment in Rome (and also underemployment) at a time when this city had become a big metropolis, as we shall see below. In this chapter, dealing with both Greece and Rome, it is legitimate to inquire about unemployment in Greek cities. Unfortunately this problem has been practically neglected. This implies that unemployment was not as important in Greece as in Rome. Another indication that there was less unemployment in Greece is the fact that historians seem to have been mistaken about the sense of the Greek word for "unemployed." According to Nenci (1981), who apparently has written the only article on the subject, one can show that the ancient meaning of the Greek word agoraios (small merchant) is "unemployed, that is, those who wait on the agora—as still occurs today in small villages in southern Italy—for someone to offer them a job for the day." Nenci asks if "when one speaks in general of Greek colonization as a result of overpopulation, it would not be better not to think in abstract numerical terms, but rather in terms of lack of work."

The Greek Colonies

What were the real motives behind the creation of the ring of Greek colonies that were the beginnings of so many cities around the Mediterranean basin? Were they agrarian colonies established to make room for an excess of population? Or were they mercantile colonies established to further trade with the mother country? This old bone of contention has yet to be decided by arguments or discoveries capable of weighting the balance definitively to one side or the other. What makes a conclusive choice all the more difficult, moreover, is the fact that the two camps partially integrate the two functions in their rival explanations of the origins of the Greek colonies. For the proponents of colonization aimed at shifting the burden of population to other regions, the commercial role emerged as a by-product of the establishment of the new settlements. For the proponents of colonization aimed at setting up new trading posts, trade led to the eventual occupation and exploitation of the surrounding countryside. But where does the truth of the matter lie? As so often, neither with the one side nor the other, but probably with both at once, the predominance of one factor or the other depending on the particular region and the particular period.

The first wave of colonization seems to have been of an agrarian type. It began around 750 B.C. and reached Italy, Sicily, and the eastern portion of the Maghreb, giving birth notably to the cities of Syracuse, Tarentum (Taranto), Catania, Locris, and Metapontum. As for Italy, it may be necessary to put further back the date traditionally given for the first colonies. Very recent excavations carried out at Otranto have brought to light evidence indicating that Greeks came from Illyria as early as the ninth or even the tenth century B.C., though this settlement was not necessarily agrarian in character. In the Maghreb, at any rate, the agricultural motive has been established beyond doubt. As Law (1978) observes, "the non-commercial character of the

Greek colonization is also indicated by the location of the two principal cities, Cyrene and Barce, some way inland and not on the coast."

The second wave, more commercial in inspiration, began about 550 B.C., and the Greek colonizers came from Asia Minor. This new wave of colonization principally affected France and Spain, but touched the eastern Mediterranean as well. Among the cities that supposedly owed their foundation to this second movement of colonization was Marseilles. But these cities are only *supposed* to have owed their origin to the Greeks, for nothing rules out the possibility that the Greek settlements engrafted themselves upon small urban nuclei already in existence at the time the Greeks arrived. I shall return to this problem later. But since it is a question that can also be raised with reference to Roman cities outside Italy, I shall postpone the discussion until after a brief account of ancient Rome.

But it must be mentioned that military factors also led to the creation of many cities. Furthermore, and this is an additional hint of motives that were not purely commercial behind many Greek colonial cities, a great number of the cities were located far away from the sea. The recent excavations at Ai Khanoum in northern Afghanistan were "a striking demonstration of the spread of Hellenism to even the most remote areas of the known world" (Mitchell, 1980). And Ai Khanoum was a large city designed on the Greek model and with a Greek-speaking population.

The Etruscan Cities and Rome

"The Etruscan Cities and Rome" is the title given to a study of Rome by Scullard (1967), and it clearly points to an aspect of the development of Roman urban life that cannot be passed over in silence. Supported by an agriculture that had apparently reached a high level of development, the Etruscan cities progressively appeared from 800 to 700 B.C. on. While scholars have established beyond question the Greek influence on Etruscan civilization, this was nevertheless incontrovertibly an urban culture with characteristics uniquely its own, characteristics of considerable interest especially from a demographic point of view. There were nearly twenty full-grown cities among the Etruscans. Estimates made for two of the largest of these cities, Caere and Volaterrae, put the population at about twenty-five thousand. On the basis of our estimates on the area covered by the various urban sites discovered in Etruria, there were at least three to five other cities with populations of more than ten thousand.

It increasingly appears that Rome itself was also, in the beginning, an Etruscan city. In any event, the contribution of Etruscan culture to the early development of Rome was substantial: "In industry and trade Rome owed much to Etruria: the technical skill of the Etruscans in metal and clay had set an example for Roman craftsmen to follow."

The Roman Empire: A Dominant Metropolis

I shall begin by establishing a few historical points of reference. The legend that places Romulus's foundation of Rome in 753 B.C. seems to be fairly accurate. It was indeed sometime around 750 B.C. that the urban history of Rome began; and it was around 500 B.C. that the city began expanding its sphere of influence, extending it by 270 B.C. over practically the whole of Italy. Caesar held power from 59 to 44 B.C., considerably enlarging the frontiers of the empire beyond the Italian peninsula. The empire reached its height roughly 50 B.C.–A.D. 160. Its decline, slow to start with, began by A.D. 200, but picked up speed from A.D. 330 on, particularly from the time Constantine transferred the capital to Constantinople. The Fall of Rome finally took place in 476.

This vast empire had an uncontested center: the city of Rome. Rome gradually evolved from a city-state into a city-empire. Even when the empire had taken on dimensions previously unknown in the history of the world, the role of Rome was in no way diminished; on the contrary. It was not until the establishment of Constantinople that things began to change; but by this time, the Roman Empire had already entered the period of its decline.

The preeminent part played by Rome in the life of the empire led to the rapid growth of its population. By 500 B.C., it had reached an initial summit of some 150,000, probably surpassing 300,000 by 150 B.C. From then on, the growth of the Roman population accelerated still further.

The Population of the First Great Metropolis, Rome

Rome was probably the first very large city in the history of humanity. By about 1700 B.C., Babylon had probably become the first city to have a population of more than 300,000. But at its height, around the second century A.D., Rome had certainly surpassed 800,000, perhaps even reaching—or exceeding—a population of one million. It was not until the period from the seventh century to the ninth century A.D. that there were other (notably Chinese and Muslim) cities with similar populations. And it was not until the Industrial Revolution and the years 1810–1820 that London surpassed a population 1,300,000, a level that Rome itself may have reached.

The uncertainty about the actual population of Rome may serve as a pretext for returning briefly to the discussion of methods of estimating urban populations. For Rome there are two complementary approaches.

I have already analyzed the first of these, which relates to the total area covered by the urban site. As for Rome itself, data are available regarding the amount of land covered by construction. The analysis can be pushed still further, since we know the number of buildings in the city. The sole remaining mystery is, then, the average number of inhabitants per building (resulting from two other unknowns: the number of stories and rooms per building and the number of inhabitants per room). On this basis, the level of uncertainty is high, since it is possible to arrive at figures ranging anywhere between a minimum of 200,000 and a maximum of 1,450,000.

The second approach is based on the existence in Rome of a system for the distribution of grain to large sectors of the population. I shall return later to this important aspect of Roman life, which throws a good deal of light on the parasitic character of this first great metropolis. The number of people enrolled on the list of beneficiaries of this system was around 150,000 by the beginning of the Christian era, rising to 1,750,000 around A.D. 200. But abuses were numerous, and the total number of theoretical beneficiaries may well have surpassed the actual population of the city. These data, together with other, more partial evidence, suggest that by the time Rome reached its height, the city had a population on the order of 800,000–1,300,000.

Given the scale of the Roman population, the provision of the immense amount of food required to support it was a problem. It should be noted, however, that in this case what was said earlier regarding the high proportion of agricultural workers found in the populations of traditional cities does not apply. If only 5 % of the working population of Rome engaged in agriculture, this would already imply some 25,000–30,000 farm laborers. Assuming that each laborer worked no more than 10 hectares of land, a portion of this land remaining uncultivated, this would mean that the farmland in the vicinity of the city would have stretched over an area of 2,500–3,000 square kilometers. Assuming further that these farmlands lay within a uniform radius of the city, this would have entailed a journey of some 50–60 kilometers to and from the farms lying farthest out, a journey it would have taken 10–14 hours to make.

Food for Rome could not, in fact, have been provided within the boundaries of the Italian peninsula as a whole. Postulating the complete absence of any other cities and an average agricultural surplus of 15% once the transport costs have been figured in, I find that the total population of Italy, Rome included, needed to have been about 9–11 million in order to produce the required amount of food. As it happens, Italy during the second century A.D. had barely 6 million inhabitants. And the populations of the other Italian cities taken together certainly surpassed 100,000 or even 200,000. It is true that there are great uncertainties. Thus despite all his efforts to improve the quality of the data on the population of other Italian cities, Duncan-Jones (1974) finds it impossible to make any global estimates.

In fact, Rome was supported not only by Italy as a whole, but above all by its empire, with some 50–55 million inhabitants, which were

THE BIRTH OF URBANISM

exploited chiefly for the provision of food for the capital. This question has raised considerable controversy among historians. Simplifying matters somewhat, there are two schools of thought which confront one another and will probably continue to do so for some time. For the first, it was Rome's military expansion that eventually led to the economic exploitation of its empire. According to this school of thought, therefore, military expansion in some way made possible the growth of the Roman population. For the second school, the growth of the population of Rome explains and necessitated Roman military expansion and the creation of a colonial empire.

Rome: A Parasitic Capital

The second of these two schools enjoys the considerable support of the system of laws governing the distribution of food. At its inception this system amounted simply to a single law intended to regulate the practical problems of the shipping and warehousing of grain. Laws and procedures of this kind are found throughout the urban history of the cities of traditional Europe and probably elsewhere as well. The exigencies of the more-or-less regular cycles of agricultural output demanded foresight of this sort and, returning to an earlier point in time, the reader will recall Joseph's advice to Pharaoh following the dream of the seven fat and seven thin cattle. But in the case of Rome, very early, in 123 B.C., there was a law stating that each citizen had the right to receive a certain quantity of wheat at a fixed official price. This system of grain laws underwent successive amendments and improvements, leading in 58 B.C. to a law stipulating the distribution to each Roman citizen of a certain quantity of wheat or bread free of charge. By about 45 B.C., the list of recipients contained no fewer than 320,000 beneficiaries, and though Caesar reduced this number to 150,000, apparently, it rose again later. The daily ration of bread varied from one period to another (as did the quality of the bread) from one to one and one-half kilograms, representing a number of calories greater than was necessary to meet the average needs of an adult.

Here already the highly parasitic character of the Roman capital is apparent. This kind of free distribution of food entailed in economic terms the breakdown of the trade balance between town and country: agricultural products had ceased to be exchanged for a quantity of manufactured goods or services involving nearly the same amount of work. Rome received much and furnished little. This is the first example of mass unemployment and underemployment. Taken together, they must certainly have exceeded 30 percent, if not 40 percent, of the population of working age. Nor does this figure take into account disguised underemployment in the form of the plethora of servants for the wealthier classes.

It is true, as Paul Veyne (1976) has shown, that there was no overlap between the beneficiaries of the free distribution of bread and the jobless or the poor: "The state distribution of bread never bore, and never would bear, the least resemblance to assistance. Nothing indicates that the poorest citizens were given preference; . . . everything points to the reverse." But the fact remains that with this bread there was a form of redistribution of resources in favor of Rome at the expense of the empire and even Italy itself.

In any case, the principal burden of supplying wheat for the underemployed Roman population fell upon the empire. For owing to socioeconomic changes introduced by the enormous scale of the colonial domain, Italy itself had little by little almost completely abandoned the production of grain in favor of the cultivation of fruits (particularly olives and vineyards) along with a rural exodus toward the cities and a high concentration of landed property in a dwindling number of hands. Furthermore, it should not be forgotten that the Italian peasants also had to support cities other than Rome (see chapter 6). It should be mentioned in passing that in A.D. 332 a similar system of food distribution was set up in Constantinople. In this case, however, the number of recipients was immediately fixed at eighty thousand and grew only slightly in subsequent years.

The parasitic nature of the Roman urban system is to a degree confirmed by the seemingly restricted place occupied by industry and trade in most of the Roman cities (Finley, 1973; Jones, 1974). The limited scope of productive economic activities can only be accounted for by the fact that grain imports intended to fill the likely deficit of food in Italy derived in part not from trade of the classic type, but from the exacting of tribute. I shall return in the next chapter—the general conclusion to part 1 of the book—to this question of the limited role played by manufacturing in the cities of the ancient world. In the present instance, however, this limited role does not imply the total absence either of industrial or of commercial activities. The Roman metropolis was, indeed, probably a net exporter of certain manufactured goods, and particularly of pottery, of which many remains are to be found, not only throughout the Roman Empire, but outside its frontiers as well.

Trade with regions outside the confines of the Empire, and notably with the Far East, did in fact exist. It has been established beyond question that Rome traded with China—providing for the creation of a number of myths (Poinsotte, 1979). There was also trade with India. Schmitthenner (1979) gave his review of current research on the subject the title "Rome and India: Aspects of Universal History during the Principate." In this article, using both Roman and Indian sources, Schmitthenner shows how significant trade of all sorts (commercial exchanges included) were between these two civilizations. Giving definite quantitative figures to these exchanges, however, is another matter. It is certain that trade over long distances could only have involved a limited volume of goods, confined for the most part to luxury items. The pepper, incense, or silk sought in Asia must indeed have represented decidedly modest tonnages. From this point of view, I share the scruples of Finley (1973) regarding the notion of a "world economy" as applied to the ancient world outside the Roman Empire (see chapter 6).

But there is no doubt at all that the heaviest trade was carried on within the Mediterranean basin. As K. Hopkins (1978) very properly stresses: "The unity of the Roman market also depended on the fact that the inhabitants of the Roman Empire could treat the Mediterranean as their own internal sea, free from pirates, from rivalries between competing states, indeed free from the magical dangers which for so long obstructed Odysseus' reunion with Penelope." This shows once again the mediating and unifying role played by the Mediterranean, so vividly described by Braudel (1966) for the time of Philip II of Spain.

While it is true that there was in the Roman world an absence of certain obstacles to trade between nations, there was also an absence of factors capable of fostering economic relations in what was, after all, in the words of A. H. M. Jones (1964) "a vast common market stretching from Britain to Egypt." The term "common market" is indeed an accurate one in this context, since few customs duties were imposed, and the tolls were very moderate, around 2–5% of the value of the merchandise. (For merchandise crossing the imperial frontiers, on the other hand, customs duties were about 12.5%, on both entry and exit.) There was another asset, one today's common market does not yet enjoy: a common currency. Nor should we forget the famous network of Roman roads, though it was conceived more for military and administrative purposes than for trade. Even within the Empire itself, however, long-distance trade occupied a smaller place than these positive factors might lead one to suppose. It would have been difficult for things to have been otherwise, given the constraints imposed by the high costs of transportation in every society prior to the revolutionary technological innovations of the nineteenth century.

Some quantitative indications can be given relating to the extent of this trade, and especially concerning the volume of grain imported by Rome and, at a later date, after the creation of Constantinople, by each of the two great metropolises. As it happens, the data available for Constantinople are better than those for Rome. Annual grain imports originating in Egypt rose in Constantinople during the reign of Justinian (A.D. 527–565) to the level of some 170,000 metric tons. If we postulate an average consumption of 270 kilograms per person, this tonnage represented enough food for nearly 600,000 people, a figure that more or less corresponds to the population of the city at that time. In the case of Rome, the meticulous research of Rickman

(1980) provides, if not precise figures, valuable orders of magnitude. At the beginning of the Christian era, when Rome had a population of approximately 1 million (a figure that Rickman finds plausible), out of a total consumption of wheat of 40 million modii (since a modius is equivalent to some 9 liters, this means some 250,000 tons) some 75 to 95% of this total was imported from outside Italy.

A Parasitic Metropolis, But an Empire with Many Cities

By occupying the whole of the Mediterranean basin, Rome brought under its administration the majority of the regions in the world that were urbanized early: Syria, Palestine, Turkey, Egypt, Greece. While it seems likely that in these regions Roman colonization led to the decline and even the disappearance of a certain number of cities, the better part of the urban networks existing prior to Roman domination remained in place. Some cities enjoyed a measure of growth due at least in part to the *pax Romana*. On the other hand, in the western half of the Mediterranean, and especially in western Europe, a region in which urbanization was more recent and therefore less advanced, Roman colonization brought about the creation of a great number of cities and also the enlargement of most of the cities already in existence.

It will probably require decades of research before the story of the urbanization of the Roman Empire is known. It will require much more than that before anyone will have reliable evidence about the links between urbanization and economic conditions within the empire, and particularly about the impact of Roman colonization. Even the simplest evaluation, a mere assessment of the overall urban population of the empire as a whole proves impossible. On the basis of a measurement by analogy, I would hazard the guess that there were at least 350 cities and towns with populations of more than five thousand in the empire (Italy excluded). I say at least 350, but nothing rules out a figure twice as great. Indeed, the number of *civitates* in the Empire (an administrative unit with all but complete autonomy in local affairs and usually with a town as its administrative center), was very high. According to the estimate of A. H. M. Jones (1964), the number of such units exceeded a thousand, and fewer than a hundred of them contained no city or town of any sort. But many of these towns were in fact nothing more than villages, and there is very little in the way of data about their populations. I shall nevertheless attempt some evaluation of the overall scale of the urban population, but only for the European part of the Empire—the least ill-known part. I shall present the results of this assessment a little later, after a brief review of the history of Europe before the miracle of Greece.

The multitude of cities belonging to such different cultures undoubtedly had varied histories under Roman domination. In *Cities of the Eastern Roman Provinces,* a fundamental resource for researchers in this field, A. H. M. Jones (1971) provides a wealth of information regarding hundreds of cities in the eastern provinces of the empire. The data he has amassed are very disparate, however, and very little evidence exists concerning economic and demographic conditions. But this book shows the great number of cities that, even under the empire, managed to maintain quite a substantial measure, if not exactly of independence, at least of local autonomy. This autonomy was probably less pronounced in the western part of the empire, in Europe notably, owing to its less developed urban tradition. As noted earlier, this autonomy was one of the cornerstones of Roman administration, and it certainly has a significant explanatory bearing on the long duration of the Roman Empire.

The important contribution of Lepelley (1979–81), on the history of the urban areas of Roman North Africa, confirms the existence of a vigorous urban life in this region. Apparently during the last centuries of the empire many cities of Roman Africa were more prosperous than those of the peninsula. Nevertheless it was a costly prosperity, because it was based on heavier and heavier impositions on the countryside. The mark of Roman civilization was so deep that it left for a long time important traces on the urban life of this region.

Europe before the Miracle of Greece

Even a miracle requires a propitious environment; even a graft has need of a solid support. And, as is the case for other parts of the world, the more the study of European prehistory progresses, the more it recalls other societies that were more advanced than had previously been supposed. I will review, therefore, the stages of the emergence of agriculture and cities prior to the miracle of Greece.

There is considerable evidence that the date for the beginnings of agriculture in Greece and the southern Balkans (especially Bulgaria) was around 6500–6000 B.C. More to the west and north, agriculture emerged later. According to the chronological tables of Clark (1977), the sequence of events was as follows. In certain parts of Italy, the first farming appeared by 5600 B.C., and in a more general fashion around 4600–4000 B.C. In southern France there was agriculture by 4500–4000 B.C., if not sooner, while in the north, it did not appear for a further thousand years. Agriculture appeared in certain parts of the Netherlands and Czechoslovakia around 4500–4000 B.C., gradually diffusing over the rest of Europe between 3600 and 2600 B.C.

This chronology projected onto the spatial plane accords well with explanations of the rise of agriculture suggesting a two-stage process of diffusion, spreading in an initial phase from the Middle East toward Greece and the southern Balkans by way of Crete, and in a second phase from there toward western and northern Europe. This view largely prevailed until about ten years ago, the question remaining at issue having to do with whether agriculture diffused across different populations or whether it spread by means of migrations. Since the start of the seventies, however, notably owing to the work of Renfrew (1979), it is no longer possible to speak of a general consensus in the field. Backed up by recent findings, Renfrew comes down on the side of autonomous centers of agriculture, insisting on the part played by an autonomous evolution of techniques, local economies, and socio-cultural factors specific to each region.

I shall refrain from attempting to settle the matter one way or the other. I am all the less willing to do so since I vividly recognize how difficult it would be to provide irrefutable proof for either hypothesis. But in any case, what is chiefly of concern here is not the origins of agriculture, but the fact that its presence had been established throughout Europe long before the Greek miracle burst upon the scene and the urban settlements of Greece and Rome began to swarm over the face of the continent. The question that remains unresolved, however, is that of the urbanization of Europe, especially the regions of Europe outside the Greek and Italian peninsulas, before the advent of Greece and Rome.

Nor is the problem at all simple, for the proliferating spread of the Greek polis and of Roman cities or towns was both prodigious and very extensive. On this point the maps in Pounds (1969) are most eloquent. The geographic zone of the diffusion of the Greek polis, which reached southern Italy and the east coast of the Baltic around 700 B.C., covered by 600 B.C. practically all of Italy and the Mediterranean shores of France and Spain. Around 400 B.C. the line had penetrated far into the interior of Europe, in the center as much as in the south, reaching northwestern Europe and southern England around A.D. 100. To be sure, Pounds's map of the geographical extent of the diffusion of the polis should not leave the impression that all of these cities were Greek settlements; many of them were simply towns based on the Greek model. As for Roman cities, at least 130 of them have been found in Roman Gaul (France), and there were more than 140 in the Iberian peninsula and some 45 in England. These figures probably underestimate the reality by a considerable margin: more recent data will perhaps double these numbers. Rare indeed are the European cities in the regions of the Roman Empire in which excavations have not revealed Roman, or less frequently, Greek remains.

Confining myself to the sites listed in that wonderful research tool, *The Princeton Encyclopedia of Classical Sites* (Stillwell, 1976), I find 270 sites in Gaul, 100 in the Iberian peninsula, and 250 in Britain. Furthermore, recent research has shown that both the commercial and the colonial expansion of Greece assumed larger dimensions than used to be thought (Morel, 1975). Once it is realized (see Part 4) to what extent any colonization entails the partial destruction of indigenous cities, the reader will readily conceive how difficult it is to write a history of European urbanization before Greece, and why such a history is to all intents and purposes nonexistent. As Alexander (1972) remarks, "in studies of urban development in Europe, it has been common to begin with the towns of the medieval period. Either directly or by tacit assumption the towns of the Roman Empire, modelled on the Mediterranean polis, have been accepted as the origin of the medieval ones, even in those regions never occupied by Rome."

The Late Urbanization of Non-Romanized Europe

In support of the view that Rome played a role of decisive importance in the urbanization of Europe is the disturbing fact that independent and noncolonized Europe had an unmistakably retarded growth of cities. This was notably the case in Russia where, as Tikhomirov (1959) has shown in a review verified in this respect by subsequent studies, the onset of urbanization only took place after the eighth century A.D. One should note that for Kiev, which can be considered as the first Russian town, recent research indicates an earlier date of birth. Kiev emerged as a city somewhere between the fifth and sixth centuries (Rybakov, 1983).

The example of central and northern Europe confirms the relationship between the absence of Roman colonization and a delay in urbanization. For a few cases recent investigations have made it possible to write at least the introductory chapters of an urban history of Europe before Greece. Though this history remains almost entirely to be written, the destruction wrought by the Second World War paradoxically led to a promising renewal of archaeological research, the results of which are reviewed in Barley (1977).

In Sweden, archaeological excavations have lately brought to light sites previously unknown. These sites prove the existence, from A.D. 300–700 on, of small farming settlements or very small trade centers. These communities cannot be considered urbanized (Ambrosiani, 1977). The first site that may truly be called urban, Birka seems to date from A.D. 800 to 975 and to have had a population of around 1,000. Even as late as the beginning of the fourteenth century, Sweden had only four or five cities. The largest of them, Visby, had perhaps as many as fifteen thousand inhabitants, but all the others unquestionably had fewer than three thousand. Nor was it until the sixteenth century that a new surge of urban growth got under way.

To sum up the situation at this time in the various Nordic countries considered together, the Swedish experience may be taken to represent the average case. It is worth pointing out that the beginnings of urbanism in Scandinavia received a good deal of impetus from trade with the rest of Europe. Practically all of the cities emerging before the thirteenth century were located along the Scandinavian coastline.

With respect to the territory corresponding to present-day East Germany, an area which has been the subject of a recent vast program of research, Herrmann (1977) insists that in both German and Slavic regions the development of cities was intimately associated with the increase in agricultural productivity during the seventh and eighth centuries. Herrmann gives a chronology of urbanization in this part of the world: "Rise of the first nonagrarian centers, of embryonic cities during the eighth and ninth centuries both in the German and Slavic regions; development of the first urban centers by the middle of the tenth century and during the eleventh century; beginning of free cities during the eleventh and twelfth centuries, and advent of the free city as a specific living place of a bourgeois community." A closely similar chronology is valid for northern Germany as a whole and for all of the Slavic countries not colonized by Rome.

This unquestionable delay in the urbanization of non-Romanized Europe does not by any means constitute proof that Rome played a decisive role in the genesis of urbanism in those regions that did fall under its dominion. The tardy Neolithic in eastern and northern Europe may furnish an adequate explanation for the delay of urbanization in this large sector of the Continent. It is also possible completely to reverse the direction of the causal relation, reinforcing in this way the presumption that some form of urbanization antedated the Greek settlements and especially colonization by Rome even in the Romanized regions of Europe. For the Greek settlements and Roman colonization would not have been possible if the regions concerned had not had easily exploitable agricultural and mineral resources. All colonial expansion has centered on rich regions, that is, on regions where the likelihood of an autonomous growth of cities was relatively strong. I think it altogether legitimate, therefore, to advance the hypothesis that the limits of the Roman Empire approximately covered those regions of Europe marked by early urbanization.

Some evidence, still fragmentary, but nevertheless fairly abundant, has come to light enabling me to affirm that preurban towns existed in these regions as early as 2000–1500 B.C. and that rather small, but authentic cities were there by 1000–500 B.C. This was particularly true in the Iberian peninsula, but also elsewhere. But it would be better not to fall into the opposite extreme. Speaking of the cities of northern France, Leman (1979) writes that they had "Roman origins in lands that, though devoid of any urban system, were not entirely uninhabited."

Recent archaeological research points toward the occupation of the sites of the cities of western Europe at a very early date. Excavations in Paris, for example, have disclosed traces of human habitation dating back to 2000 B.C. In Bulgaria a chance discovery made in the city of Varna during demolition work with a bulldozer brought to light an archaeological site in which tombs were found containing golden jewels of a richness without precedent in the Europe of its time. On the other hand, even though most of the cities created by the Romans in England were established in or near tribal centers, London was created ex nihilo in a sparsely populated region (Morris, 1982). Certainly, much research remains to be done in this field. It is unlikely, however, that there will be a revision sufficiently dramatic to alter the following conclusion: the establishment of Greek and Roman cities took place in regions that already knew agriculture and the initial stages of urbanization. Nor is there any doubt that the introduction of Graeco-Roman technology and the intensification of commercial relations resulting from these settlements carried in their wake additional agricultural development and a sharp acceleration of already-existing processes of urbanization.

However advanced the growth of cities may have been in the regions colonized by Greece and Rome, cities would assuredly not have attained the same level of development as in the urban civilizations of the Middle East or China at this time. But there was nothing even remotely comparable to it in any of the non-Romanized regions of the Continent.

In fact, one can generalize to the whole of the future Romanized Europe the conclusions drawn by Goudineau and Kruta (1980) for France, a country which represented a good quarter of Romanized Europe outside Italy. "Actually, one can only conclude by putting forward the following affirmation: some centers were probably near (and ready) to become cities, and they were more numerous in the South than elsewhere. The Roman conquest put this readiness in evidence, and where the structures were not adapted at the end of protohistory, the Roman action failed or relatively failed."

In order to place this in the clearest possible light, I shall now attempt a rough computation of the extent of urbanization in Romanized Europe in the third century A.D., the century during which it may be said to have reached its height. This will enable me to draw in some way my survey of the history of Europe to a halt at a time close to the period at which I shall take it up again in chapter 7.

A Rough Computation of the Urbanization of Romanized Europe

Outside of the Roman Empire, in independent Europe, there was during the third century no city worthy of the name. In Roman Europe, on the other hand, even without counting those found in Italy itself, there were hundreds of Roman cities—certainly 300 and probably many more than that. Most of them were very small, many only barely qualifying as cities at all. But many were very large cities, some of which had populations surpassing 50,000—though cities of this size were relatively rare. Using the data collected by Russell (1958) regarding the area of Roman cities, and adopting a coefficient of 170 inhabitants per hectare (see chapter 2), I find that there were 8–10 cities with populations of more than 30,000, the two largest of which may even have had populations of 60,000. To this one should add 10–12 towns with populations of 20,000–30,000 and certainly more than 25 cities with populations of 10,000–20,000. This would suffice by itself to give Romanized Europe (excluding Italy) an urban population on the order of 800,000–1,100,000. Taking into account only those of the other cities and towns with populations in excess of 5,000, the figure rises to 1–1.4 million people out of a total population estimated by Russell to have been around 9–12 million. The level of urbanization, then, appears to have been fairly high: around 8–15%.

There is no doubt that without Rome the natural evolution would not have led in the space of two centuries to such an urban network. Rome was not only a catalyzing element, but also a factor in development, because it introduced a whole array of agricultural and transport techniques that fostered urban growth.

6 The Beginnings of Urbanization: The Relations between Agriculture, Civilization, the Economy, and Cities □

Recent research has revolutionized the history of the beginnings of urbanization. To be sure, many uncertainties persist, and there are some things about the earliest phases of the evolution of cities that will remain unknown forever. But the information gained by new generations of archaeologists, anthropologists, and historians has thrown light upon a number of important stages in the process, unearthing facts rich in implications that future explorations will never put in doubt. Among these facts, the most important is perhaps the early rise of agriculture simultaneously in many different parts of the world.

The Earliness, Multiplicity, and Simultaneity of the Rise of Agriculture

The rise of agriculture was early, multiple, and simultaneous. All of these attributes must naturally be placed in the historical context of a greatly protracted time scale and in the geographical contexts of both the Old and New Worlds. As for being early, true agriculture—the methodical cultivation of plants supplying most of the food to support the population—was already in existence 10,000 and perhaps even 10,500 years ago, say around 8500–8000 B.C. As for its multiplicity, agriculture appeared independently in nine, ten, or perhaps even twelve different places in the Old World and in two or three different places in the New World. As for its simultaneity, if attention is confined to those regions that would eventually become centers of civilization in antiquity in the Old and New Worlds, that is to say, to those regions in which, during the fifteenth century, five-sixths of the population of the world lived, then only some 2,000–3,000 years separated the earliest known beginning of agriculture from the latest.

But what were the causes of these beginnings of agriculture? Demographic pressure? Changes of climate? Or still other factors acting in combination with these? Was the multiplicity of centers of agriculture the result of its invention by different peoples independently or of diffusion from one or several "original" sources? These two problems, repeatedly met with over the course of the preceding discussions, constitute what I am tempted to call "everlasting riddles," to which no incontrovertible answers will ever be found. But it seems likely that cases of the autonomous invention of agriculture predominated over cases of diffusion.

The Earliness, Multiplicity, and Simultaneity of the Rise of Cities

The rise of cities was also early, multiple, and simultaneous. And this is sufficient to foreshadow the interesting problem that is one of the main preoccupations of this book: the links between the city and the economy.

But the history of the first stages of urbanization in the various regions of the world, which recent research makes every day more comprehensible, indicates the existence of a reverse relationship.

No Cities without Agriculture, But No Agriculture without Cities

It becomes more and more clear that the rise of agriculture all but inevitably carried in its wake a process of urbanization. For while it is true that urbanization could not get under way without the concentration of population and the surplus of food resulting from agriculture, it is equally true that the emergence of agriculture set in motion forces that sooner or later led to the growth of cities. In practically every case in which there was agriculture a few thousand years later cities appeared. Rare are the regions in which two thousand years after the emergence of farming, cities did not develop.

The length of this delay was doubtless conditioned by a number of factors, among which the fertility of the soil and the efficiency of the form of agriculture adopted would have played an important role: the more substantial the food surplus and the more densely populated the region, the earlier the urbanization. The existence of a natural transportation system, especially rivers, was another element whose presence seems to have been capable of precipitating urbanization. This is because of the constraints of transport costs, the tyranny of distance that reigned until the nineteenth century, when steam was introduced into the economics of transportation.

This delay in the rise of cities was from time to time shortened "artificially" by diffusion—whether through migration or through trade is of little consequence, since the parties responsible are usually difficult to detect. But such diffusion was probably much less important than scholars have tended to suppose. As has been shown, one of the most significant conclusions resulting from the recent renewal of interest in prehistory is that the rise of agriculture in different parts of the world was nearly simultaneous. This simultaneity would have considerably reduced the need for artificial transfers of urbanization. The city, like agriculture, was probably invented on many separate occasions, perhaps even on many separate occasions within each of the great regions of the world.

Is the City the Characteristic Trait of Humanity?

Is the city the characteristic trait of humanity? Is man the only creature to have invented cities? Yes, if we define the city in the truest sense, supposing a specialization of activities leading to this specific feature of all human concentrations: that such concentrations are incapable of sustaining themselves, and require the support of the inhabitants of neighboring regions. This is precisely the distinctive mark of urbanism, the trait that sets it apart from the anthill or the beehive. Without forcing the issue too much, useful analogies may be drawn between the preagrarian village and the anthill. But these analogies lose all meaning when we pass on to cities proper, in which craftsmen exchange the fruits of their toil for those of the farmers of the fairly vast rural area surrounding the city. Braudel clarifies this important distinction in the two sentences opening the chapter on cities in his book, *Civilisation matérielle et capitalisme* (1967): "Cities are like so many electrical transformers: they turn up the tension, precipitate exchange, increasingly set the lives of men on the boil. They were born of that most ancient, most revolutionary of divisions of labor: the tilling of fields on one side, the so-called urban callings on the other."

Nor should there be any need to underscore the fact that this specialization of tasks carried in its wake profound, not to say decisive, consequences for the history of humanity. Cities and civilizations are so closely connected that it is practically impossible to dissociate the two phenomena. And Braudel, after writing the passage just cited, continues with a quotation from Marx: "The opposition between town and country begins with the transition from barbarism to civilization, from the rule of tribes to the State, from the locality to the nation, and is found throughout universal history right down to our own times."

But before going any further, it may be as well to recall the limits of the present study and therefore of the conclusions I may legitimately reach here. The relations between the city and the economy—that is my subject. To be sure, the multiple bonds between the urban revolution and the realm of the economy do indeed constitute a group of related questions, not only very vast and extremely interesting in their own right, but also of crucial importance for human history at large. The fact remains, however, that in focusing my attention exclusively on these questions, I am obliged to pass over a great many problems that do not strictly fall within the compass of my particular concern here. In this context, Buccellati (1977), for example, is perfectly justified in noting, in an attempt to place the urban revolution in a sociopolitical perspective, that "the qualification 'urban' added to 'revolution' captures only a part of the phenomenon at stake" and on this account leaves out the political implications of the process of urbanization, such as the creation of bureaucratic states.

Cities and Civilizations

There is no doubt that the existence of genuine cities, presupposing a substantial agricultural surplus and the real and enduring possibility of using this surplus for exchange, equally presupposes the existence of certain social and technological structures—structures that in some sense form the backbone of civilization. This means that once genuine cities have developed, the societies affected must already have achieved some degree of civilization.

This brings up the question of the role of the city as a factor in the evolution of civilization, a role played, as one would expect, in the context of a series of interactions. It is extremely unlikely that the invention of writing or such decisive technological innovations as metallurgy or the manufacture of glass could have occurred and, more significantly, could have been maintained in a purely rural setting. In this perspective the city appears to gather together all of the factors conducive to significant sociotechnical advance. It was the city, after all, that created the real demand for and consequently defined the genuine usefulness and value of social and technological innovation. Similarly, it was the city that engendered the social contacts necessary to assure the kind of circulation of information and experience that both conditioned innovation and encouraged its generalized adoption and use. And finally, it was the city that brought into existence a work force wholly devoted to nonagricultural forms of labor.

The technological progress originating in cities, or that cities made possible, had a pronounced impact upon the rural milieu. Metallurgy, for example, permitted improvements in farm equipment, thus increasing the volume of agricultural production both by increasing agricultural productivity and by making it possible to cultivate neighboring areas that without improved equipment would not naturally have lent themselves to farming. And without the increase in the density of human habitation cities brought with them, there would have been little likelihood of perfecting modes of transportation more highly developed than the human back. The invention of writing made it possible to record the advances made in methods of cultivation, and both assured the safeguarding of these innovations and improved the chances of their diffusion throughout the countryside. On the other hand, progress in agriculture and in modes of transportation led to the continued growth of cities, which induced a further division of labor and increased the likelihood that a fraction of the urban population would engage in activities in which the prospects of innovation were even greater than before. This important problem of the innovative function of cities will be further discussed in chapter 20.

Thus, admittedly simplifying matters in the extreme, I arrive at the following schema. By making it possible to produce a storable surplus of food, and by creating a population density far greater than would otherwise have been possible, the adoption of agriculture engendered an embryonic form of urban life. But both the constraints and the advantages of urban life favored the development and diffusion of technological innovations that exerted a positive influence on agriculture. All of these interactions taken together led to the emergence of cultures in which cities played a central and determining part. Once a certain stage had been reached, regional diffusion of information, brought about through mass migrations, military conflicts, or the wanderings of individual bearers of oral or written knowledge, accelerated the development of civilization. From this point on, the interactions stopped being merely local, because by this time long-distance trade had become increasingly important. For trade not only fostered a division of labor, but also encouraged the diffusion of technological innovations—writing and methods of political and economic management as well as techniques of farming and industrial production.

In speaking of the role of trade, however, I must take care to avoid anachronism. It is necessary to place this international trade in the economic and technological context of the times—a context that was more or less unchanged in traditional societies until the Industrial Revolution. Until the Industrial Revolution brought about, with the introduction of the steam engine, a fundamental reduction in the costs of transportation, the volume of goods handled in long-distance trade remained very modest. This was true even for the wide open, resolutely extroverted world of Europe between the sixteenth century and the eighteenth century; and it applied even more directly to the economies of antiquity. For in the field of maritime navigation, at the start of the eighteenth century Europe had reached a level distinctly superior to that attained in any other society—a circumstance that resulted in real transportation costs lower by half than those obtaining even as late as the close of the fourteenth century.

In concrete terms this means that in the ancient world grain alone was the object of a quantitatively significant trade. Sometimes, as with Greece and probably Phoenicia, the trade was intended to fill a chronic deficit induced by commercial specialization. Sometimes, as with Rome and Constantinople, the flow of grain consisted of colonial tribute levied to ensure the political stability of the capital. But in either case the grain came from regions of fairly vast extent compared with the regions for which it was destined. As for other goods, the quantities involved were very limited, even though important in terms of value. As noted in chapter 5, I entirely share the doubts voiced by Finley (1973) about the idea of a world economy, and also his aversion to vague expressions capable of misleading the unwary about the true state of affairs in the ancient world. But why not let him speak for himself? The examples he cites are especially telling and instructive:

> Wheeler tells the cautionary tale of the discovery on the Swedish island of Gotland of 39 sherds of terra sigillata pottery scattered over an area of some 400 square metres, which turned out in the end all to be broken bits of a single bowl. Around the year 400 the wealthy Bishop Synesius of Cyrene (in modern Libya) wrote to his brother from Alexandria (*Epistles* 52) asking him to purchase three light summer mantles from an Athenian, who, Synesius had heard, had arrived in Cyrene. That is the man, he added, from whom you brought me some shoes last year, and please hurry before all the best ware has been sold. Here are two examples of "ready sale" in a "world market." I cite them neither to caricature nor to imply that ancient trade was all on that level, but to concretize my demand for more specification, more qualification, where possible quantification, of such otherwise misleading vague phrases as "intensive exchange," "exceedingly active," "examples have been dug up." The imperial city of Rome lived on grain imported from Sicily, Spain, North Africa, and Egypt, but in Antioch, during the famine of A.D. 362–363, it required the forcible intervention of the emperor Julian to have grain brought in from two inland districts of northern Syria, one fifty, the other a hundred miles away. To be meaningful, "world market," "a single economic unit" must embrace something considerably more than the exchange of some goods over long distances.

Having granted him these reservations, however, we should avoid going to the opposite extreme, denying the existence in the ancient world of genuine international trade of any sort. International trade, however limited its scope, did in fact exist, and if we are to understand the civilizations of antiquity it must be accorded its proper place and standing.

In any event, once this stage of development had been reached, the ancient world had already advanced to the next phase in the general evolution of civilization: that in which urbanism, though not yet established everywhere, was nevertheless present in many parts of the world, and especially in many parts of the Old World. In historical terms this is 500 B.C.–A.D. 200, a period during which, if it were possible to gauge the true extent of urban growth, it would be seen that a level of urbanization had been achieved in the Old World that was not too distant from the level reached at the start of the fourteenth century or around the start of the eighteenth. And to anticipate matters discussed in the concluding chapter, it might be pointed out that one of the incidental (though by no means marginal) conclusions here is that traditional societies were much more heavily urbanized than specialists in urban history generally tend to believe.

This and other facts about the history of various cultures of the ancient world lead me to ask one of the essential questions underlying this book: what influence has urbanism had on the economic life of societies past and present? But while it may be possible to *ask* this question, a great many obstacles still stand in the way of *answering* it. The number of studies (journal articles included) in which a genuine attempt has been made to determine the impact of cities on economic development can be counted on the fingers of one hand. It is not that the problem lacks interest—far from it! But the lack of reliable data coupled with a general concentration of research on the problems associated with the political, philosophical, literary, and artistic aspects of the life of cities has tended to keep the study of purely economic matters to a minimum.

And yet however difficult it may be to find an answer to this question, it is nevertheless possible to shed some light on the probable influence of cities on economic life. It already seems clear that this influence is usually somewhere between two opposing extremes: one at which the city functions as a ferment actively promoting economic development, and the other at which the city is a parasite, drawing off the supplies of energy required to stimulate economic activity and growth.

Urbanism and the Economy: The Economically Generative City and the Parasitic City

Given the total lack of data for many of the societies concerned, placing the many cultures of antiquity, both in the Old World and the New World, along a scale running from the city as a primordial factor in economic development to the city as a parasite that hinders or even causes a decline of economic life proves not only difficult, but largely arbitrary. This is why I shall focus my attention on the two cases about which we are least ignorant, Greece and Rome: cases that analysis enables me to place, if not at either of the two extremes of the scale, at least on either side of the mean, at which the city would have exerted no appreciable influence on the economy one way or the other.

The Case of Greece

I shall first look at Greece. Despite the advances made by Greek civilization, it still closely resembled the societies of antiquity before Greece. True enough, the rise of cities in Greece did give birth to a civilization; and to the extent that one is prepared to apply this modern concept in the context of the ancient world, urbanization did indeed on the whole promote economic development. Owing to the creation of new cities around the Mediterranean basin, one can say that, in a sense, Greece exported industrial and agricultural technologies. And the impact the invention and use of money had on international trade should not be forgotten. Finally, in Greece there was even a distinct, dynamic asymmetry—characteristic of the urban societies of a later age—in the normally balanced interaction between the city and agriculture. For in Greece, the city unquestionably played a greater role in the development of agriculture than agriculture played in the growth of cities.

In the main, then, Greek cities favored economic development. But as will be seen later (see chapters 12 and 31), we cannot properly speak of development in the modern sense of the word even with reference to Europe on the eve of the modern industrial age from the fifteenth century to the eighteenth century. So long as the Industrial Revolution had not yet taken place, bringing with it a substantial rise in the ceiling set on the level of development societies might conceivably attain, the difference between minimum and maximum levels of development remained very small. There is no doubt, however, that by around 350 B.C., Greece found itself on the average in a better economic position than in 750 B.C.: the amount of goods and, above all, the number of services available to the Greek citizen were greater in 350 B.C. than they had been four centuries earlier. Still, this progress was by no means spectacular. The standard of living enjoyed by the average Greek citizen probably did not rise as far in the space of four hundred years as did the standard of living of the average European during the twenty years between 1950 and 1970 or the standard of living of the average Japanese during the ten years between 1961 and 1971, that is, a multiplication by two and a half.

Nor had any especially revolutionary advances been made in agricultural and industrial techniques. As Deshayes writes in the chapter devoted to Greece in *Histoire générale des techniques* (Daumas, 1962–79), "the methods of manufacturing practised in the Greek world rarely progressed beyond the stage of simple artisanry, and very little advance was achieved in this area relative to earlier civilizations. Even the Hellenic age failed to make up the delay in development." It was only in the field of construction that perceptible progress was made, both in terms of the construction of buildings per se and in terms of the urban infrastructure. In order to solve the problem of supplying

MONTEREY PENINSULA COLLEGE LIBRARY

cities with water, for instance, the Greeks performed many magnificent feats of engineering and brought a great number of technological innovations to a high level of perfection. The Samos tunnel serves as a particularly well-known example. Without being the first tunnel ever dug to provide a city with drinking water (the procedure was employed before this in Israel, most notably in Jerusalem), the Samos tunnel nevertheless stood as a technological novelty both by reason of its length (1,100 meters) and because it was dug out from both ends simultaneously. Perceptible progress was also achieved in the techniques used in the design and construction of ports. As Deshayes puts it, "while Hellenic ships display hardly any changes relative to Phoenician vessels, decisive strides were made during the Greek period in the realm of port installations."

On the whole, then, there was no spectacular rise in the standard of living, this being impossible in the framework of traditional societies; nor, for reasons it is difficult at this distance to elucidate, was spectacular progress made in technology. But does this mean that the advances brought about by urbanization were, after all, only marginal? The answer is no. For as I have already pointed out, the historical context must be taken into account; nor above all should we overlook the noneconomic contributions made by the city to the general life of ancient Greece. And from this latter point of view, the word "spectacular" proves perfectly appropriate, whether applied to intellectual or to artistic endeavor. These two fields of human enterprise in any case incontestably fall within the compass of development as defined in my general introduction. The stunning achievements of Greek civilization in this sense—the true miracle of Greece—had a great deal to do with the high level of urbanization exhibited by the population of the Hellenic world. Since it is hard, moreover, to detect any negative consequences stemming from the growth of cities in ancient Greece, the impact of Greek urbanization would on balance appear to have been positive.

The Case of Rome

The case of the Roman Empire appears more ambiguous, for it is possible—and even probable—that the city of Rome had a detrimental impact both on agriculture and on the economy at large. This does not alter the fact, of course, that the city also produced some manifestly beneficial effects. I will first look at the beneficial effects.

It is almost certain that the pressure of demand generated by the enormous size of the city of Rome acted as a powerful stimulus for the great technical advances realized by Roman agriculture. Roman agriculture was, in fact, probably the most highly developed in the world; it was not until eighteenth-century Europe (or thirteenth-century China) that agriculture attained an equivalent or a more advanced stage of development. In this context, the case of Rome tends to substantiate the thesis of Boserup (1965) according to which demographic pressure played a role of primary importance in the evolution of agriculture. I shall weigh the strengths and weaknesses of this thesis later in the book, but it may be as well to mention here and now that I do not give it my unqualified assent. As so often in other areas, there is in economic matters no hard-and-fast rule. Thus, while there is obviously much truth in Boserup's view, it must nevertheless be remembered that it only applies to a limited number of specific cases— and it so happens that, at least up to a certain period in its history, the case of Rome is one of these. Indeed, extending the use of Boserup's thesis beyond the Italian peninsula itself, during a subsequent phase of Roman development the pressure exerted by the vast size of the Roman population even had a favorable impact at the international level. For it seems likely that, owing to the increasing burden placed on her colonies by the exaction of tributes of grain, the growing need for food in Rome contributed to the spread of more advanced agricultural methods throughout the Empire.

The urbanization of Rome also had positive effects on industry. Though we do not have at our disposal all of the data we could wish for, it seems by no means unreasonable to assert that the average Roman of A.D. 150 had access to a somewhat greater quantity of manufactured articles than his counterpart of 500 B.C. And not only did he own a greater number of manufactured goods, but they were probably of superior quality as well. Technological advance in the industrial sector, however, was more limited than in agriculture. Taking the simplest view, one could even argue that under Roman influence industrial techniques made no forward strides whatever. "On the whole, the metallurgic industry achieved no remarkable technical progress . . . In the textile field, no new invention emerged bringing about improvements in spinning, weaving or fulling." (Duval, 1962)

Is this absence of progress related to the absence of industrial specialization in Roman cities? One can and should, moreover, ask this same question with respect to the cities of Greece as well. As always, the scarcity of reliable information has led to a divergence of interpretations. Many writers believe that specialization occurred as soon as cities exhibit written or material records of the manufacture of products for foreign consumption. But just as a single robin doesn't make a spring, so too the regular export of a few manufactured goods does not by itself make an industrially specialized city. And once again I am inclined to share the point of view championed by Finley—the most eminent proponent and the chief investigator of the thesis of the absence of specialized cities in Greece and Rome. Finley (1973) rightly contrasts the specialized cities of the Middle Ages with the cities of the Graeco-Roman world:

It has been claimed, rather exuberantly, that such excavated districts as the potters' quarter of Corinth evoke, in their physical appearance, "the artisan quarters of medieval cities." But it seems commonly to be overlooked that the excavators of Tarsus have found no Cloth Hall, that all ancient cities lacked the Guildhalls and Bourses which, next to the cathedrals, are to this day the architectural glories of the great medieval cities of Italy, France, Flanders, the Hansa towns, or England. Contrast the Athenian Agora with the Grande Place in Brussels.

But coupled with the slight progress achieved in industrial techniques, does not this absence of specialized industrial cities call into question what I just claimed regarding the positive effects of Greek and Roman urban growth on the industrial sector? The answer is no. For if the degree of technological progress was indeed slight, it was by no means nonexistent. Moreover, leaving aside the question of technological advance altogether, the fact remains that the process of urbanization automatically led to the diffusion of industrial activities in spatial terms, if nothing else. And in the context of traditional economies, even a slight progression in the level of technological development, when accompanied by the diffusion of techniques, already constitutes an unquestionable step forward.

Without in the least pretending to present a detailed explanation of the modest technological advances achieved by the Romans, which is beyond the scope both of this analysis and of my own particular expertise, I cannot bring myself to move on from this aspect of the problem without mentioning the very large number of slaves in the Italian peninsula. It is generally estimated that slaves represented about 20 percent of the total labor force. Roman military conquests, moreover, entailed a regular and substantial influx of slaves ensuring the renewal of the available stock. And the existence of this large and inexhaustible pool of cheap labor was, naturally enough, far from constituting an incentive for the inevitably costly business of research and experimentation in new modes of production.

Before I go on to assess the negative effects of urbanization, a word should be said about the beneficial influence of the city on construction and navigation. In the field of construction, let me cite the vaulted cupola, glass, and the aqueduct bridge as examples of important Roman innovations. As for navigation, owing to the increased demand for wheat in Rome, the capacity of ships, which in Greece was on the order of 130 burden, rose under Rome to 340 burden, and certain especially large vessels were even able to carry in excess of 1,300 burden.

Now for the negative aspects of Roman urbanization. I already showed some of the detrimental impact of the city on Roman life when I spoke (chapter 5) of the imbalance between town and country induced by urban growth and of the parasitic character of Rome. While during an initial phase urbanization in general and the growth of the city of Rome in particular most probably had a beneficial effect on agriculture, giving added impetus to progress in farming, once the size of Rome exceeded a certain threshold there was a fundamental change for the worse. It should be remembered that Rome was the first very great city in the history of the world—perhaps the first to have a population of more than of 300,000–400,000, and certainly the first to have a population of more than 600,000–700,000. At exactly what point did the size of Rome cross the threshold beyond which the city's impact became destructive? It is impossible to say. But it does seem clear that by around 90–70 B.C., and maybe even as early as 210–150 B.C., there was a decline in Italian agriculture, the essential cause of which lay in the free distribution of grain imported from the imperial provinces.

Of course, one should not overplay the importance of this factor, for as Rickman (1980) notes, the high cost of overland transport "makes the hypothesis that imports of corn to Rome from overseas ruined local production in Italy implausible. Only the growers in the immediate environs of Rome could conceivably have been affected and it was more profitable for them to supply fruits and vegetables to the city anyway." But it was just this fact that could also have affected more distant regions. While the high transport costs prevented these distant regions from supplying Rome with wheat, they could not have had too great an impact on the supply of expensive agricultural products such as fruits, vegetables, and in particular wine and oil. And the growth of Rome led to a strong increase in the demand for these products.

Another important factor in hypotheses accounting for the decline of Roman agriculture was the extension of slavery as a source of agricultural labor. After the Punic Wars (around 200 B.C.), many small independent peasant holdings were expropriated. But as Rathbone (1981) observes, this question too remains open. I believe the exceptional character of Roman urbanism owing to the combined effects of size and the free distribution of bread constitutes the most important explanatory factor.

At the same time that this free distribution of grain reduced the demand for Italian agricultural products, it also acted as a powerful force inducing an exodus of the rural population toward Rome. In theory this flight from the countryside could also have had beneficial consequences for Italian agriculture. A reduction in the population density on arable land may lead to gains in productivity. But this factor plays a greater role where there is a high population density. This was not the case in Italy during this period. And the rural exodus encouraged a partial substitution of slaves for the departing peasants, and this did not necessarily have a positive influence on agricultural productivity, for the reasons just given.

It is certain, moreover, that the free distribution of grain seriously diminished the incentives for an eventual industrialization of the city in which the largest part of the urban population of Italy lived—the capital, Rome. The citizen from the Italian countryside could become a city dweller without having to seek a job in some existing industrial enterprise and without having to seek to create an industrial enterprise. And the positive influence the flight to the city might otherwise have had in bringing about a general rise in wages was effectively forestalled by the presence of vast numbers of slaves. As a result, an initial phase in which the city probably fostered the development of industry was succeeded by another phase in which the city acted rather as a brake on industrial growth. But these surmises require in-depth studies of a kind that are unfortunately lacking. A second Gibbon is needed who will analyze in greater detail than his predecessor the purely economic factors involved in the decline and fall of the Roman Empire. One thing, however, is already clear: the parasitic character of the Roman metropolis was not only responsible for a weakening of the Italian economy; it also played a central part in bringing about the disequilibrium that may later have precipitated the collapse of the empire.

On the whole, then, for the Roman Empire I am tempted to take the view that urbanization exerted an influence more negative than positive on the process of economic development in Italy. Nor should mention be omitted of the detrimental economic consequences of the defence of the empire. The regular army appears to have numbered some 600,000 men by the end of the imperial era, and the costs of maintaining so large a body of men under arms must, for the period, have been gigantic. The conclusion reached on this score by K. Hopkins (1978) certainly merits close consideration: "Huge pre-industrial empires accumulate huge resources; they spend a large part of that accumulated surplus on self-preservation, not on economic growth."

Still, one cannot fairly assess the value of the Roman Empire without taking into account its contribution to the entire Mediterranean basin. Allowance should also be made for a number of achievements Rome handed down to later generations—achievements for which the European Renaissance, in particular, is deeply indebted. There is no doubt that, along with certain negative effects endemic to any colonization, Roman domination facilitated the transmission of new knowledge and new techniques to regions that would otherwise have been denied them. Although this may perhaps have been even more true of Greece, the role Rome played in the diffusion of civilization should also be remembered. And in this diffusion of civilization, the urban factor occupied a preeminent place.

Is Generalization Possible?

In the light of all of these reservations, and in the light of the contrast between the contributions of Greece and Rome, is it possible to reach some sort of general conclusion concerning the influence of the first phases of urbanization on economic development? I am strongly tempted to avoid the issue altogether. What, after all, can really be said with any reliability or precision about China, or India, or the Egypt of the Pharaohs, or the civilizations of the pre-Columbian New World? An attempt to put in place the very few pieces of this vast puzzle that are available, however, produces a general picture that filling in the remaining gaps is unlikely to change in any radical way. Once exception has been made for a couple of extreme cases limited in time and space, like Italy after 100 B.C., it seems difficult to question the positive contribution made by urbanism. Thus agriculture makes the rise of cities possible and after a certain length of time makes it inevitable. Agriculture and urbanization are fundamentally and inextricably linked, since agriculture constitutes the indispensable precondition for the emergence of cities. And once cities are in place, they in turn are the source of still further progress in the vast domain of socioeconomic development—a domain embracing not only the multiple interactions between the city and the countryside, but the development of civilization itself.

Part Two

Europe from the Fifth Century to the Eighteenth Century

In moving on from part 1 of of this book, in which the scope of my investigation covered some six or seven thousand years and encompassed the world in its entirety, to part 2, in which the horizon will be confined to Europe alone and to the space of a single millennium, the reader may quite understandably expect to find an analysis in greater depth and detail than has hitherto been possible. This expectation will, however, prove illusory. The diversity of sixteenth-century Europe, for example, is as great as that of the world as a whole around 2000 B.C. Sixteenth-century Europe probably counted, moreover, some one hundred million inhabitants, while the whole world in 2000 B.C. probably had fewer than eighty million. The reader should not, therefore, hope to find here an exhaustive study of the urban history of the remarkably multifarious Europe of the fifth century to the eighteenth century; I shall instead try to illuminate only its outstanding features. To do more than this is out of the question. For each city has its own history, often rich in incident and always unique in character. By the close of the seventeenth century, Europe had 130–160 cities with populations of more than twenty thousand, and had nearly a thousand more with populations of five thousand to twenty thousand.

One aspect of the urban history of Europe during these centuries that will have a relatively exhaustive treatment is the relation between urbanization and economic development. This thoroughness will reflect more the poverty of the data available than the wealth of analysis devoted to the question. But entering into some detail in my examination of the relationship between the city and the economy in medieval and Renaissance Europe seems justified by the absence of comprehensive studies of this period, and above all by recent, albeit still fragmentary, research on this problem.

In the first chapter of part 2 (chapter 7), I shall focus on the specific case of Europe from the fifth century to the tenth century. This is in essence a Europe in process of formation and about which a great many mysteries remain about fundamental aspects of urban, social, and economic life. In chapter 8, I shall give a general overview of the period from the tenth century to the eighteenth century. But before going on to discuss in the following chapters topics for which the available data enable me to attempt a deeper and more elaborate analysis, I will digress to discuss several methodological matters of some importance. These matters form the subject of chapter 9, in which I examine the main lines of research on the location, the spheres of influence, the distribution by size, and the economic functions of cities.

The surge of urban growth that took place during the Middle Ages, especially in the years 1000–1340, played a decisive role in the formation of the urban structure of Europe and will be the theme of chapter 10. I shall confine myself to a rapid survey of the period of the catastrophes associated with the Black Death, concentrating in chapter 11 on the sixteenth and seventeenth centuries—when largely owing to the discovery of the New World and the impact that the opening up of the Atlantic had on European trade, there was a radical shift in the center of gravity of the cities of Europe. I shall then conclude part 2 with an analysis in chapter 12 of the relations between urbanization and development in Europe prior to the Industrial Revolution.

7 Europe from the Fifth Century to the Tenth Century: A Period of Transition Marked by Declines and Renaissances □

To speak of Europe from the fifth century to the tenth century is to begin with the Fall of Rome, drawing to a halt once more at the close of the period of invasions: I shall start this chapter, in other words, with the twilight of one urban civilization and end with the dawning of another. This was an era in which the center of gravity of the urban world around the Mediterranean shifted from Europe toward the Middle East. This shift was the result of the partition of the Roman Empire into two halves, the eastern capital of which survived the Fall of Rome by nearly a thousand years, from 476 to 1453. During three or four centuries, roughly from 400 to 700, Constantinople was probably the largest city in the world, before it was overtaken by Changan (present-day Sian) in China and then by Baghdad. With this last named city, we come to the other center of urban gravity in the Mediterranean, the Muslim civilization, whose spread held significant implications for the continent of Europe. The direct consequences of Muslim expansion lay in the fact that with the start of the eighth century the Arabs began a series of conquests that would ultimately place a part of Europe in their hands. But there were indirect consequences as well, arising from a distortion of traditional trade patterns brought about by the rise of this Arab Empire, which broke up some of the trade routes linking Europe and Asia while calling other, rival networks into existence.

The Question of Economic Decline in Europe after the Fall of Rome

The traditional image is that the Fall of Rome brought with it the economic decline of Europe as a whole. The reality, however, was more subtle and complex. To be sure, a decline settled upon Italy. Deprived of its empire, the city of Rome collapsed. An indication of the extent of this collapse may be gathered from what happened to the city's population. At its height during the second century A.D., Rome probably had a population of about a million. About the year 700, however, only some 50,000 people remained, and despite the presence of the Papacy the population had slipped to around 35,000 by the start of the eleventh century. Rock bottom was reached about 1377, the year of the return of the Popes from Avignon, where they had resided since 1304; in 1377 the city seems to have had a population of no more than 15,000–20,000. But this does not mean that the rest of Italy suffered as heavily as its sometime capital. On the contrary, it has been estimated that the population of the other Italian cities underwent a reduction much less severe than that of Rome, some maintaining their former levels.

By the same token, the economic decline experienced elsewhere in Romanized Europe, assuming there was such a decline, was considerably less pronounced than in Italy, if only by virtue of the relatively modest level of development attained outside the Italian peninsula. If the provinces of the empire that represented roughly two thirds of the population of Europe experienced some sort of decline in the aftermath of the economic and administrative disorganization following the Fall of Rome, this decline may have been offset by the diminution or complete removal of the tribute levied by Rome. Additional compensation derived from the investments made by Rome during the period of its domination, notably the system of roads constructed under the empire, a portion of which retained its economic value and helped maintain communication networks within and between the various former provinces. In a similar vein, the monetary system introduced by Rome remained intact, as did many of the technological advances achieved under imperial rule. One should not forget, on the other hand, the disruptive impact of the German invasions (though these did make a positive contribution by helping to spread the triennial rotation of crops), still less the destruction wrought by Viking, Magyar and Saracen raids. Even so, on balance Romanized Europe suffered less of a decline than is habitually supposed, and the likelihood of decline in non-Romanized Europe is even more remote, given the meager progress of any kind previous to the Fall of Rome.

Outside Italy itself, then, rather than speaking of decline, it seems more appropriate to speak of a return to the previous state of autarky. On this score, the evidence is clear. There was unquestionably a decline in European trade with the rest of the world, and especially with the East. While Ibn Khaldoun, an Arab thinker and historian of the fourteenth century, may have been exaggerating when he claimed that the Christians were no longer capable of launching so much as a plank on the Mediterranean, it is certain that Europe's trade with the outside world underwent a considerable reduction. This is evidenced in particular by the increasing rarity in European cooking and pharmacy of products from the Middle East and Asia, spices being especially notable for their absence. Further indication of this reduction in the flow of trade lies in the growing scarcity of silks and the consequent rise in their price. It is also found in the disappearance of paper, which had to be replaced by parchment.

What remains at issue is the cause of this diminution in the flow of trade. Two conflicting views have grown up around this point. The first holds that, because of the German invasions, the European trade with the outside world came to a sudden halt in the fifth century. The second view holds that the trade ended later (the beginning of the eighth century) and only gradually. It is argued, moreover, that the cause lay in increasing Muslim control over the Mediterranean due to the spread of Islam. A certain consensus has lately formed in support of this second interpretation.

From 500 to 700–800: A Decline in the Population of Europe or Only a Decline in the Population of European Cities?

Another indicator of the likelihood of economic decline in Europe at large comes from estimates of the European population. I shall leave out of this analysis the territory of nineteenth-century Russia, owing both to the greater unreliability of the data and to its geographical distance, which caused it to be less affected than the rest of the continent by the processes that concern me here (the population of Russia fluctuated around 11 million during these three centuries). The population of Europe except Russia, then, having apparently reached a high point of some 40–55 million people by the start of the third century, seems to have fallen by the year 500 to about 30–40 million, bottoming out at about 20–35 million around 600 (see table 8.1). In the year 700 it seems to have remained at roughly the same level. But by the start of the ninth century the population of Europe seems to have increased by some 2–5 million people, rising around the year 1000 to 35–45 million and returning to the level of the year 200 around 1100–1150.

This fall in population clearly resulted in part from the general disorganization of the economic, social, and political structures of the Continent in the wake of the Fall of Rome. But it was also brought about by the series of widespread epidemics that descended upon Europe from the middle of the sixth century on, the most disastrous of them going by the name of the Justinian plague, given it for dating purposes. The Justinian plague first occurred in 541 at Pelusium, a port in Egypt, reaching Spain by 542 and Italy, France, and Germany by 543. It returned sporadically thereafter, striking Europe and the Mediterranean basin during the next two centuries with varying degrees of severity, but without penetrating far into the interior. How many deaths may be imputed to it? Biraben (1975) estimates that "it is unlikely, given the limited extent of the plague and the modest number of outbreaks, especially in the West, that it could by itself, like the great plague of the fourteenth century, have carried off a third or a quarter of the total population." So the decline in the population of Europe from the third century on has to be accounted for by a combination of factors.

To the extent that one is prepared to accept these figures and make use of them as indicators of the overall economic situation, one observes a general decline from around 200 to around 600–700, followed by a recovery that seems to have begun sometime in the eighth century. A large question mark hovers over this point, however. Population estimates for the various countries and regions of Europe—serving as the basis for calculating the population of the Continent as a whole—are largely founded on estimates of urban populations. This holds two important implications for my analysis.

The first is that even if the decline reflected in these figures were confined to cities, the course of events in the urban milieu would nevertheless still provide a valid index of the likelihood of a general economic decline affecting the countryside as well as the towns. It is difficult (though not impossible) to imagine that this urban decline was accompanied by rural prosperity. The second implication is that this way of assessing total population has probably induced scholars to overestimate the extent of the recession. It seems likely that in many regions the Fall of the Roman Empire led to an increase in the population of rural areas around the declining cities. For with the disappearance of an extralocal economic base resulting from the Fall of Rome, the chances are that a fraction of the urban population would have turned once more to farming for their livelihood. And even more often the decline of a city might have been accompanied by a stable population of the surrounding countryside.

The fact nevertheless remains that, whatever the situation in the countryside may have been, a decline in the urban population of Europe did indeed occur. This decline is attested not only by the admittedly incomplete population estimates available, but also by other significant indicators. A great many documents indicate that a certain percentage of the houses formerly used as habitations in the smaller cities were converted into stables. Archaeological research has revealed that in many cities the encircling walls were rectified during this period in order to adapt them to the steadily shrinking amount of ground covered by buildings. Some cities, finally, vanished altogether.

No systematic study of the scale of these disappearances has yet been done. Scattered examples prove, however, that sometimes large towns were affected as well as small ones. History has kept a record of the most vivid episodes, those marked by especially dramatic reversals of fortune. Such is notably the case of Saint-Bertrand-de-Comminges (in the Haute Garonne region of southwestern France). Saint-Bertrand-de-Comminges was originally founded by the Romans under the name of Lugdunum Convenarum, probably sometime before the year 20

B.C. During the first two centuries of the empire, the city "grew prodigiously rich thanks to the intensive exploitation of the mineral, thermal, woodland, and pastoral resources of the central Pyrenees, and by means of trade with Spain and the neighboring regions. . . . [It] was a center of Roman influence from which Roman civilization radiated to the furthest reaches of the surrounding valleys" (Lot, 1945–53). At its height the population of Lugdunum Convenarum probably rose above thirty thousand, and some estimates place it as high as sixty thousand.

Largely destroyed around 405 during the Vandal invasions, the city regressed considerably, eventually ceasing to exist as a true urban center altogether. However, the accidents of church history gave it a new lease on life. Converted to Christianity as early as the third century, it owed its second birth to Bertrand of l'Isle-Jourdain, bishop of Comminges, who decided in the eleventh century to raise up again the ruins of what had by then become the Vallis Capraria (the valley of goats). The bishop was canonized in 1220, and the city thereupon took his name. Being, moreover, the episcopal seat of future pope Clement V, the city became, through the efforts of this Pope, an important pilgrimage site. But Saint-Bernard-de-Comminges never recovered its former economic functions, which were taken over by other cities in the region, and this ultimately led to another, though slower, demise. At the end of the eighteenth century, the city (or what was left of it) still had a thousand inhabitants, but by 1911 the number had dropped to 555, of whom only 337 lived in the town itself. Today the population is under 400.

This case prompts me to evoke the general problem of cities located in regions where a political boundary appears (or disappears). Such an event can obviously modify the economic function of a city by leading to a stoppage or a regression (or an increase) of commercial exchange. Spain was part of the "free trade" area of the Roman Empire, but was later very often an enemy of France.

The task of computing with any accuracy the decline in the urban population of Europe as a whole during this period is at present all but impossible, and will doubtless remain so for a long time to come. All that can be safely said is that by around 700–750 urban population must have been lower by at least 20% than it had been in the year 500. It should likewise be borne in mind that by this date urban population must already have been some 40% lower than in the year 200, when the empire was at its height. In order to hazard a few figures with a view to determining at least the relative orders of magnitude involved, I have made an estimate for the year 800 (see below) yielding for Europe (except Russia) an urban population somewhere on the order of 3.3 million. Around the year 200 the number may have been 4.7–5.8 million, while in the year 500, it could have been as high as 3.4–3.9 million. It should be noted, however, that in reaching these figures, as well as those cited later in this chapter, I treated as urban any settlement with a population of at least 2 thousand; in the rest of the book, I have drawn the line at 5 thousand.

The fall in population between the start of the third century and the start of the sixth century may seem rather steep. But it should not be forgotten that during this period Rome alone lost a million inhabitants, which is roughly two-thirds of the total loss suggested by the figures just given. Calculated on the basis of highly fragile and fragmentary evidence, however, even this estimate of the decline in urban population is less than the decline in the average area covered by the fortified towns of western Europe would lead one to expect. Thus following the calculations done as much as fifty years ago by Grenier (1931–34) (calculations that have yet to be attempted by anyone else), the average area of these fortified towns ranged from 50–200 hectares at the height of the imperial era (A.D. 29–192) to 5–50 during the period leading up to the Fall (A.D. 193–235). This reduction in area does not necessarily imply a parallel diminution in population— all the less so inasmuch as, given the troubled character of the times, in the later years of the empire the city wall played a role of great importance in urban life: "Wherever it diminished the area of the city in order the better to assure its defence, it enabled the old 'civitas' to come down through the ages" (Dollinger-Léonard, 1958). Still, the weight of evidence indicates that, although its exact extent may never be known, a decline of major proportions did in fact take place at this time in the population of the cities of Europe.

An Urban Decline That Nonetheless Set the Scene for Later Urban Development

The decline in the urban population of Europe is of considerable interest on a number of grounds. It shows, first of all, how individual cities have undergone periods of recession, sometimes to the point of complete extinction. But it equally demonstrates that recessions of this kind have in the past afflicted great economic systems taken in their entirety—a lesson confirmed by the experience of other civilizations. It likewise illustrates the fundamental fragility of urban systems during the initial stages of development and above all the dramatic fluctuations to which the populations even of large cities are subject in traditional societies.

The part played by the economy in all of this stands out in bold relief. During this period of general decline in the urbanization of Europe, moreover, a new network of cities was in the process of taking shape. These new cities found their essential support, their fundamental economic base, in trade with Byzantium, a city that, during these centuries of recession, enjoyed periods of prosperity and growth. Venice serves as the most typical and, owing to its subsequent evolution, the most important example of this process. Thanks to its commercial ties with Byzantium, Venice—until then only a large conglomeration of twelve very small village communities—was federated in 466, electing its first Doge in 687. In the meantime, trade had brought about a substantial increase in its population, which reached forty thousand during the tenth century. Therein lay the seeds of the growth of the Italian trade cities, those independent commercial city-states that were thereafter to contain the largest part of the urban population of Italy.

I have already discussed Venice. But mention should also be made of Amalfi, even though, as the Michelin Guide puts it, it is at present no more than "a small town (population seven thousand), rather Spanish in appearance, whose high, white houses scale the rocks opposite a bay of deepest blue, composing a wonderful panorama framed by an old Saracen tower and the Capuchin monastery today converted into a hotel." This small town, beginning its development in the seventh century, was by the tenth century, with its population of sixty thousand to eighty thousand, the largest city in Italy. It owed its expansion and its wealth to trade with Byzantium and also with the Muslim world beyond. "The citizens of Amalfi were the first Westerners to establish a permanent presence in Constantinople, probably as early as the first decades of the tenth century" (Balard, 1976). The luxury goods they brought back from Byzantium and the Middle East were not only to be found throughout Italy, but even "made their way to the transmontane countries" by way of the "pilgrims who came to meditate on the tomb of St. Peter."

Balard writes: "Owing as much to the nature of the goods involved as to the lines of communication it followed, Amalfi's traffic with Byzantium closely resembled that of the Venetians. A distinction has to be drawn, however, to the extent that Amalfi engaged in commercial distribution without developing any productive base of its own and to the extent that Amalfi's trade evolved in the context of that vast commercial network, that enormous 'free trade community' (Goitein) constituted in the 10th and 11th centuries by the Mediterranean world. Amalfi owed everything to the energy and business acumen of a group of merchants who founded a new economy based on exchange and money at a time when the whole of the rest of the Western world had as yet to develop beyond the various forms of agrarian economy. Precocious and brilliant, Amalfi's trade was also very frail. It sufficed for change to occur in the general conditions of economic activity to land the merchants of Amalfi in serious difficulties announcing the coming crisis and decline of the city."

How frail Amalfi's trade really was we may gather from the fact that at the beginning of the sixteenth century, when Venice had a population of 150,000, Amalfi had no more than 2,000–3,000. Historians often explain this decline in political terms, as the result of Amalfi's subjection to Norman domination. But the economic explanation should not be cast aside. Having failed to generate an economic base in industry, Amalfi was inevitably rendered highly vulnerable to the caprices of history—all the more so in that its hinterland, separated from it by a mountain, was relatively devoid of resources.

Concerning trade in the European interior, while one cannot detect a dynamism even remotely comparable to that of the Italian cities, one must nevertheless take note of positive trends. According to Fixot (1980), "one of the most important developments was the appearance in Gaul, in the second half of the seventh century (in all likelihood around the year 670), of the minting of silver coins in the form of denarii. Whatever the origin of the switch from gold to silver coins, it is clear that the change must have been sharply felt. Owing to the emergence of monetary divisions corresponding to low monetary values, money penetrated to practically every level of society. This induced a potential liquidity of exchange marked by a renewal of trade reflected shortly afterwards by references to local markets. What people were at that time able to buy with a denarius corresponded to a volume of food (wine, bread, meat) consumable between two markets occurring at weekly intervals."
The whole of Europe participated in this monetary revolution and the map charting the spread of the minting of coins in a sense traces the dynamics of urban growth. Thus the use of money is obviously both a factor in and an index of urbanization.

Besides the traffic with the Middle East, another factor conducive to the creation and development of urban centers increasingly made its presence known. This new factor was the Church, whose role steadily grew in importance with the approach of the eighth and ninth centuries. But this brings us to a second phase in the urbanization of medieval Europe, namely the urban expansion that began around 700–800, and earlier still in some regions such as Ireland, where by the fifth century the Church already exerted a perceptible influence on local urban growth.

From 800 to 1000: An Urban Renaissance

Thanks to the data assembled by Chandler and Fox (1974), it has become easier to draw the curve of urban population from the start of the ninth century. Chandler and Fox have collected all existing estimates of population for each of the larger cities of the world from 1360 B.C. to A.D. 1850. But it is only after the year 800 that this survey may be regarded as truly systematic. This monumental and extremely useful work nevertheless leaves a number of important gaps unfilled. These gaps result from the omission of a fairly sizable frac-

TABLE 7.1   Approximate Growth of European Cities (except Russia)
according to Population (in Thousands)
(800–1000)

Size of Cities	800	1000
	Number of Cities	
10–20	(50)	(72)
20–50	25	35
50–100	1	3
100 or more	1	1
Total	77	111
	Urban Population	
2–5	(1,030)	(1,600)
5–10	(750)	(1,200)
10–20	(600)	(930)
20–50	660	970
50–100	50	215
100 or more	160	460
Criterion for urban population		
2,000	3,250	5,365
5,000	2,220	3,765
Total population	(32,000)	(39,000)

Sources: Calculations and estimates by the author; see the methodological appendix.
Note: The fact that these figures have been only slightly rounded off does not imply a correspondingly small margin of error. The figures in parentheses have a much wider margin of error than the other data.

tion of the cities of the world (probably 20% of the larger cities and 60% of the smaller ones) and especially from the failure to undertake a systematic review of recent studies on the history of various individual cities. Bringing the data of Chandler and Fox up to date and carrying out complementary estimates designed to take likely omissions into account (see the methodological appendix), I arrived at the figures given in table 7.1.

As for the population of cities with fewer than 10,000 inhabitants, I based my estimate on what might be called Davis's Law. I shall explain this law in detail in chapter 9. For the moment I shall simply say that Davis's Law makes possible a good approximation of the population of any set of cities of a given size if there are reliable population data for another set of cities of a greater size. Needless to say, the figures presented in my table involve a substantial margin of error, amounting to some 15% for the number of cities and some 20% for population. Moreover, these margins of error are a little higher for the cities of the year 800. (As I shall continue to do for every year prior to 1800, I left out of this analysis data for Russia, owing to the high degree of uncertainty affecting the information available with respect to both its total population and its urban population). For additional details on methodology and sources, see the methodological appendix.

According to my estimate as given in table 7.1, between 800 and 1000, the number of cities with populations of more than 10,000 rose from 70–80 to 100–120, making an increase of 40–50%. During this same period, urban population (defined as that of all "cities" with populations of 2,000 or more) grew by 60–70%. This makes for an impressive increase indeed. But the reader should remember that the period in question spanned more than two centuries. In terms of urban population, therefore, this meant an annual growth rate of only 0.2–0.3%. It will be noted that total population rose at an even slower rate—around 0.07–0.11%. The level of urbanization also significantly increased. Around the year 800 the relative proportion of the overall population in cities as defined in this chapter was on the order of 9–11%, reaching 12–15% about the year 1000. If I calculate urban population on the basis of a definition of cities requiring a population of 5,000 or more (the criterion applied in my treatment of later periods), the level of urbanization went from 6–8% at the start of the ninth to 9–11% at the start of the eleventh century. In addition to the unreliability of the available data on urban population, however, the reader should bear in mind the high degree of uncertainty about total population.

Muslim Spain: An Urban Culture

During the fifth century to the tenth century Europe was divided into two distinct parts. The reader will recall that by the start of the eighth century the expansion of the Arab Empire led to the establishment of a colonial type of domination over Spain and the imposition of a new form of culture in which the city played a more important role than in the rest of traditional Europe at this time. In 800 Spain had been subject to Islamic influence for eighty years, and the structure of the society already bore the stamp of this new culture imported from outside. By the year 800 roughly a third of the population of all cities in Europe (except Russia) with populations of more than 10,000 were located in Spain. Though Spain accounted for only about one-quarter of the total population of Europe, the proportion of the urban population of the Continent found on the Iberian peninsula had grown by the year 1000 to nearly 40%, rising even as high as 50% in the case of cities with populations of more than 20,000.

About this date, the two largest cities in Europe were both Spanish: Cordoba, with a population of some 400,000–500,000, and Seville, with a population of nearly 100,000. After the reconquest of Spain, the population of Cordoba fell to around 40,000, and it was not until 1700 that another European city reached a population of 500,000—a feat accomplished by Paris and London at practically the same time. But at the start of the eleventh century, Paris and London had populations of only 20,000–25,000, and none of the larger cities in Europe outside Spain had as many as 40,000 people. Along with Cordoba and Seville, among the other large cities of Spain, mention should also be made of Toledo, Merida and Elvira, all of which were probably more heavily populated than either Paris or London.

The difference was perhaps less pronounced, however, as concerns the overall percentage of urbanization, for it appears likely that Muslim Spain had a more modest proportion of smaller cities than the rest of Europe. But this feature would not by itself have reduced the degree of urbanization reached in Spain to the level obtaining in Europe as a whole. According to my estimates based on the criterion of 2,000 (highly approximate estimates because of the dubious quality of the available data), the level of urbanization in Spain around the year 1000 must have been on the order of 15–17%, and perhaps even higher. By contrast, the level in the rest of Europe (except Russia) was about 11–13%. All of this throws vivid light on the unique character of urbanization in Spain. This uniqueness derived from Spain's connection with the Muslim world (see chapter 23).

It will also be seen (in chapter 23) that, in Spain as in many other Islamized regions, Arab conquest did not lead to the creation of many new cities. I have estimated that the number of large cities created after the Arab conquest represented only 10% of the total. One must, moreover, distinguish cities that endured from those whose existence was short-lived. The new cities were of the sort that Glick (1979) has described as "palatine-administrative complexes": cities like Madina al-Zahra and Madina al-Zahira, which failed, moreover, to survive the depredations caused by Berbers in the eleventh century. Some other new cities, notably Calatrava and Calatayud, were to start as fortresses. What this amounted to, in short, was a classic process of urban implantation in an already urbanized region.

The expansion of the cities of Muslim Spain can be explained mainly by the progress in agriculture brought with a more advanced technology. But one should not overlook the contribution of international trade, especially with the Maghreb. Spain exported not only agricultural products (oil and wood), but also manufactured goods: textiles and iron objects. Among the latter were the celebrated swords of Toledo; the use of iron was encouraged by the rich deposits of iron ore lying in neighboring regions. In fact, Muslim Spain belonged to the vast Islamic free-trade zone covering a large part of the Mediterranean basin. By contrast, trade with Christian Europe was very limited, though not nonexistent.

Christian Europe: An Urban World Reborn Thanks to the Church and Trade

The special situation in Muslim Spain, however, should not induce us to believe that no change took place in the rest of Europe in the years 800–1000. On the contrary, the urban population of Christian Europe increased very strongly during these two centuries. On the basis of the data least open to dispute, it is clear that, in Europe excluding Spain (and Russia), the number of cities with populations of more than ten thousand grew from 60–70 at the beginning of the ninth century to 85–100 at the start of the eleventh century. The population of these cities in all likelihood increased by about 50–55%. Growth in urban population as a whole appears to have been on the order of 30–40%.

It is possible that a part of this growth did not result from true urbanization. The climate of insecurity created by Norman, Magyar and Saracen raids drove the rural population around the towns to seek refuge within the shelter of their walls. Thus while the influx of peasants seemed to increase the population of the cities, a large proportion of these city dwellers continued to work in the fields. One of the principal functions of cities at this time became defence. It is impossible to compute the number of refuges of this type or the size of this component of the urban growth experienced during the period. It was unlikely, however, that it represented more than 20–30% of the total increase—especially since similar movements often occurred in the opposite direction, with city dwellers seeking refuge in the countryside.

Despite all the precautions we have taken, there may remain in my estimates for the year 800 a bias resulting in an underestimation of the urban population of Europe at this time. Experience shows that biases of this sort generally arise because of the omission of a substantial proportion of the total number of cities, a kind of error that, given our uncertain knowledge, is very hard to avoid. The amount of bias that may remain in my estimates is unlikely to prove sufficient to distort the overall picture. I do not hesitate to claim, therefore, that there was a genuine renewal of urban growth, only tentative as yet, but nevertheless real.

This resumption of urban growth may apparently be accounted for in terms of three series of factors which have already been suggested. The first has to do with the expansion of the commercial cities of Italy. The urban population of Italy most probably increased by 70–80% during the ninth and tenth centuries. Venice was certainly the largest and most important of these commercial city-states. But in the context of the age, the other cities were by no means small towns. Around the year 1000, Amalfi, Genoa, Milan, Naples, Pavia, and Verona each had a population of 20,000–35,000. The population of Palermo was on the order of 70,000–80,000. From 835 to 1062 Palermo was a Muslim city and consequently represents something of a special case.

Elsewhere, long-distance trade, without being totally absent, did not play anything like the same driving role as in Italy. Thus Duby (1959) notes with reference to southeastern France that "the market and the port never had at that time as much importance for the city as the wall and the towers." While long-distance trade never came to a complete halt during the troubled centuries following the fall of the Roman Empire, it in no way constituted a major factor, even during the ninth and tenth centuries. "Long-distance trade," Duby writes, "seems for a long time to have been too limited, too intermittent, to become a significant source of urban vitality." Later in his study, still with particular reference to southeastern France, Duby remarks that the point at which trade got genuinely under way—the moment at which, at last set free, traffic by land and sea began to have a serious impact on the conditions of urban life in the region—did not come before 1150.

The Church, too, had a leading role to play—a role probably of greater importance than that of trade. Throughout Christian Europe, episcopal and archiepiscopal seats conditioned the progress of urbanization. The region corresponding to contemporary France alone contained as many as eighty dioceses and archdioceses. As early as the trying period of the invasions, as Doehaerd (1971) points out, "if it can indeed be said that the medieval city survived, it was thanks to its bishop . . . who . . . assumed responsibility for maintaining contacts with the Barbarians and took charge of providing food for the besieged population." The Church retained this dominant position in urban life throughout the next three or four centuries, and the bishops "upheld in the city the notion of the 'public good' at the same time as they created centers of worship for the faithful. So true is this that those cities which, over the course of the Middle Ages, lost their bishops sickened where they did not die out altogether." The monasteries also had a major hand in agricultural output and especially in the dissemination of improved methods of agricultural production, such as clearing new land for cultivation. The third factor was both the most decisive and the most cloaked in mystery. This third factor was progress in agriculture, both in overall production and, even more crucially, in yield and productivity. Given the current state of research on this question, uncertainty is great. The evidence accumulates, however, pointing to the beginnings of a positive evolution in farming techniques and production from the ninth century on. A development of this kind must have been of critical importance in stimulating urban growth.

The Slavic World: The Birth of the City

For the Slavic world, the problem of urbanism is entirely different. It is not a matter of seeing how the cities of the Roman period survived and developed after the fall of Rome, for there were none. The question centers, rather, on charting the course of the emergence of urbanism in this part of the world. Agriculture first appeared in the region, and especially in the north, considerably later than elsewhere in Europe (see chapter 5). This was most likely the factor accounting for the delay in the urbanization of the Slavic countries. But whatever the reason, cities grew up in the Slavic world only between the seventh and eleventh centuries—toward the beginning of this period in present-day Czechoslovakia and later in Poland and Russia. Many, though not all, of these cities originated as fortresses, some of which can be traced back as far as the close of the sixth century. Moreover, the Russian word for city, *gorod* or, in Old Church Slavonic, *grad*, meant "citadel." But it was not until the eighth century that there were true cities.

Among the earliest Slavic cities, mention should be made of Mikulcice (Czechoslovakia), where a small town—erected on the site of a still earlier settlement—seems to have existed by the seventh century and to have had an area of some seven hectares. By the ninth century the town had unquestionably become a true city, stretching over one hundred hectares. Prague appears to have grown to the size of a genuine city by the tenth century, a period during which it already performed the office of commercial center linking east and west. Prague had by this time unmistakably become the largest city in this part of the world, with a population of more than ten thousand in the eleventh century (Hensel, 1977).

The birth of urbanism began later in Poland; cities did not emerge there until at least the eighth century and probably as late as the ninth century. Among the cities emerging then were Krakow, Poznan, Gdansk, Gniezno, Wroclaw, and Opole: cities not only late on the scene, but of limited size as well, none of them attaining a population of fifteen thousand before the nineteenth century, even at their height around the middle of the twelfth century. Three quarters of these cities had populations of perhaps three thousand to five thousand, the others only a few hundred. Warsaw did not appear in Polish history until the thirteenth century, and only became a city in the true sense of the word during the fifteenth century.

At about the same time (or a century later), cities began to emerge in Russia. But this stage is beyond the historical limits of this chapter (see chapter 10).

Bulgaria: A Rival of Byzantium

But one cannot leave the Slavic world and the centuries examined here without speaking of the urban flowering of the Balkans, and in particular of Bulgaria, whose early urban upsurge was mentioned earlier. Two fundamental differences, each of which had a crucial impact on urbanism, distinguish this part of the Slavic world from the one just discussed: the early rise of agriculture and colonization by Rome.

The creation of the Bulgar kingdom, or empire as some call it, induced a fresh surge of urban growth. At the end of the seventh century a new capital, Pliska, was built from scratch following a classical and Byzantine model. Around the year 800 this capital city seems to have had a population of thirty to forty thousand. Later, in 893, at the start of the reign of Simeon, the "Bulgar Charlemagne," the capital of the kingdom was transferred to Preslav, which rapidly became a very large city. Around the middle of the tenth century, Preslav's population is estimated to have been some sixty thousand. If, as seems likely, this figure is close to correct, Preslav around 950 would have been the largest city in non-Muslim Europe, Constantinople alone excepted, since the largest French cities of the period had populations of less than thirty thousand and the largest Italian cities less than fifty thousand.

Alongside Preslav existed other fairly large urban centers, so Bulgaria must have been, along with Italy, the most urbanized region of Christian Europe. One of the factors contributing to the development of Bulgarian cities was trade with Italy (Dejevsky, 1980). But the economic history of this urban culture has yet to be written, because too many gaps remain. In 972 the Byzantine empire subjugated the Bulgar kingdom, and this date marked the beginning of the end for what had gradually become a rival of Byzantium.

8 Europe from the Eleventh Century to the Eighteenth Century: A Survey of the Economy and Urbanization □

From the eleventh century on, the historical points of reference are both more numerous and more reliable. That data are now more reliable does not mean, however, that uncertainty disappears altogether, but only that the degree of uncertainty diminishes somewhat.

In this chapter, I shall sketch the background for the economic and urban history of the seven centuries between 1000 and 1700—centuries rich in rival tendencies and trends. This era witnessed the deep and decisive break with the past brought about at the end of the fifteenth century by the opening of Europe to the world and by the introduction of printing. Since the economic history of this period, particularly the centuries before 1500, is little known, I shall mainly fill out a broad outline of the most salient facts.

The seven centuries discussed in this chapter fall into three distinct phases. The first of these, which probably began sometime around the ninth century, coming to a close only at the start of the fourteenth, was an age of expansion. Then came the sudden hiatus resulting from the outbreak of the great plagues, which were preceded by a series of poor harvests. The second phase began about 1320–1350 and continued until 1470–1490. The third phase, in which Europe opened up geographically to the rest of the world, closed with the first faltering steps of the English Industrial Revolution, which made the eighteenth century a century of transition to the modern industrialized world.

I shall first look at the chief changes in the economy and then review the urban history of Europe.

1000 to 1320–40: A Period of Economic Expansion

There is no doubt whatever that the years from 1000 to 1320–40 had a positive character, witnessing as they did considerable progress in every area of production, and also a sharp rise in population.

There was a great improvement in agricultural techniques, leading to significant gains in production, in yield, and probably in productivity as well. It is in recognition of these advances that Duby (1954) gives the title "the Medieval Agricultural Revolution" to an article on farming in the Middle Ages. The changes introduced during the period were indeed substantial: improvements in equipment, especially ploughs; the diffusion of the triennial rotation of crops throughout practically the whole of Europe north of the Loire; improvements in the harnessing of horses by means of shoulder collars; and the generalized adoption of iron horseshoes.

If I base my calculations on data on population (see below) and postulate an increase in production of only 10% per capita, the agricultural output of Europe (except Russia) went up by 90–130% between 1000 and 1300, making an annual rate of increase of 0.2–0.3%. Rates of yield (whose course it is now possible to chart on the basis of the work of Slicher van Bath (1963) and his followers) improved by some 50%. As for gains in productivity, there is no way of estimating them scientifically, but the modest rise in the level of urbanization suggests that they were not especially great. Indeed it is unlikely that the proportion of the working population engaged in farming diminished by more than two or three points, passing from 79–85% at the start of the period to 77–82% at the end, the level of urbanization having risen at this time by only one point. Assuming a theoretical increase of 10% in per capita output, this implies a gain in productivity of no more than 13–15% over the course of three hundred years.

At the boundary between agriculture and industry, there was a generalized introduction of windmills and water mills. Water mills were already in use in some parts of the Roman Empire before this time, but their adoption became truly widespread from 900 on. The use of windmills, on the other hand, extended throughout the Continent only two centuries later. (Known in southern France by 1050, windmills did not appear in the Netherlands until sometime around the year 1200.) It is worth noting in this connection, moreover, that distinct improvements in the construction, design, and application of mills during this period were the work of Europeans themselves, rather than innovations imported from other parts of the world, as would normally have been the case previously.

Indeed, the conventional image of a stagnant industrial technology is another idea about the European Middle Ages that has to be abandoned. The widespread introduction of mills has already been mentioned. Mills not only provided power for grinding grain, but also served (especially water mills) various industrial purposes: in paper mills, in hemp mills, driving hammers in iron mills, and so on. But there were technological innovations of all sorts in many economic activities. To be sure, many (though by no means all) of these innovations originated outside Europe, and to a certain extent the Crusades (1096–1204) helped accelerate the diffusion of technology to Europe from the Middle East and China. But while the new technology may have come from abroad, it was in Europe that they bore their greatest fruit.

I should emphasize in this context an important factor enabling Europe to attain a higher level of industrial production (and consumption) than would have been readily possible in other regions, and particularly in the Middle East. I refer to the availability of energy. This may seem paradoxical in view of the fact that today Europe depends more than any other continent on foreign sources of energy—a circumstance that has made it vulnerable to political pressures so massive and unrelenting that their only justification is the total absence of scruple Europe displayed during the colonial era. But in this period the abundance and regularity of watercourses (and also, though to a lesser degree, of winds), coupled with the great availability of wood, gave Europe a high energy capacity. This favored a more intensive use of non-European inventions, on the one hand, while stimulating the creation of new products and procedures on the other. As a further consequence, there was during this period a gradual shift in the industrial center of gravity toward northern Europe, where sources of energy were more numerous.

It is even more hazardous to try to measure the amount of growth in industrial production than that in agriculture. For in agriculture there is no possibility of inordinate variation in per capita consumption. This is not the case in industry, however, where it is conceivable that between the beginning of the eleventh century and the end of the thirteenth century the per capita consumption of manufactured goods rose by a minimum of 10% and a maximum of 100%. I believe that the margin of error is of this order, which means that between 1000 and 1300 total industrial output may have increased anywhere from 110 to 280%, making an annual increase of 0.2–0.5%. For obvious reasons, I shall not speak of the uncertainty regarding gains in productivity. Though the technological advances during this period suggest a rise in productivity, the amount is impossible to compute.

One final aspect of the economy for which at least a few general points of reference should be provided is trade. The expansion of trade over the course of these three centuries rested upon two major foundations. The first was the continuation of the ancient trade between Europe and Asia, where merchants went in search of spices impossible to cultivate in Europe and certain luxury goods infrequently manufactured by Europeans. Despite many political obstacles, the upsurge in demand backed by growing reserves of cash led to an increase in trade, making a substantial base for the expansion of the cities of Italy, which held a virtual monopoly over trade with the East. Of the five European cities with populations of more than 100,000 around 1300 (see below), three were Italian, Venice, Florence, and Milan. And it should be noted that the combined population of these three cities was only about 90,000 at the start of the eleventh century.

The other foundation of European trade, one that underwent an even greater degree of development during this period, was trade among the different regions of Europe, especially between the North and the South. If I may enormously oversimplify a highly complex state of affairs, the merchants of the South offered wine and salt in exchange for the raw materials and manufactured goods produced in the North. In the tide of exchange, the textiles manufactured in the new industrial pole that grew up in Flanders played a significant part. This international trade, a large proportion of which was transported overland, led to the creation of fairs in the central part of Europe, where the two flows met. The cities of Champagne on one side and cities like Geneva and Lyons on the other became sites of trade fairs several times each year. The golden age of these fairs was in the thirteenth century.

This commercial expansion was helped by technological improvements in transportation. But though technological improvements in transportation undoubtedly had a hand in furthering the growth of trade, it is possible that progress in transportation was brought about by the increase in trade. Here again is the tangled problem of interactions—a problem difficult to solve in this particular instance, since it arises in an era with many question marks. As for transport by sea, mention should be made of improvements in ship design and, from the last decade of the eleventh century, the generalized use of the compass. As for transport by land, there was the widespread introduction of shoulder harnesses and iron horseshoes, which probably played an even more significant part in transportation than they did in agriculture. This period also witnessed the earliest large-scale construction of canals (in Italy from 1458 and in the Netherlands from 1560). Finally there was the wheelbarrow. While it obviously had no direct influence on trade, even at the regional level, its use, apparently dating in Europe to sometime around the thirteenth century, nevertheless made a very important contribution in construction and industry.

A Rapid Growth in Population

And what about population, the starting point and ending point of all economic activity? It is certain that pronounced population growth took place between 1000 and 1300–1340. Future research may reduce the margin of error somewhat, but it will not alter our perception of the fundamental demographic trends (see table 8.1).

If only Europe excluding Russia is considered, in order to reduce the margin of error, the exceptional character of the period from 1000 to 1340 stands out in bold relief. Not only had Europe climbed back by the first half of the twelfth century to the summit reached two centuries earlier, but by the close of the period it had substantially

TABLE 8.1 Growth of the Population of Europe (except Russia), with a Rough Estimation of the Margins of Error surrounding the Data (200–1980)

Date	Population (millions)	Margin of Error (%)
200	48	35
500	36	30
800	32	30
1000	39	20
1300	75	20
1340	79	20
1400	56	20
1500	76	10
1600	95	8
1700	102	8
1750	120	7
1800	154	4
1850	203	3
1913	320	2
1980[a]	456	1

Sources: Calculations and estimates by the author; see the methodological appendix.
Note: The population of Russia (its Asian part included) grew approximately as follows (in millions):

Year	Population	Year	Population	Year	Population
1000	10–20	1500	13–12	1800	48–58
1300	12–22	1600	18–27	1850	70–75
1340	12–22	1700	25–35	1913	158–164
1400	10–18	1750	30–40	1980*	297–305

*USSR and Poland
[a]Applies to Europe except the USSR and Poland.

surpassed it. Around 1340 population was 65–95 million, as against 30–70 million around the year 200 and 32–46 million around the year 1000. To the extent that one can be at all precise in the use of figures as uncertain as these, this rise in population between 1000 and 1340 indicates an annual growth rate of 0.22%. This rate of growth may seem rather modest, but it has to be viewed in the perspective of long-term increase prior to the radical socioeconomic transformations brought about by the Industrial Revolution. World population as a whole grew by only 0.04% between the start of the Christian era and 1340; and even allowing for a high degree of bias in the data and correcting for trends in the opposite direction, the world growth rate still clearly fails to exceed 0.10%. It is estimated that world population at the beginning of the Christian era was on the order of 270–330 million, rising to some 400–500 million by 1340. If I assume that the beginning figure is a marked overestimation and therefore use a figure of 150 million, and if I likewise assume that the final is a marked underestimation and therefore use a figure of 600 million, I calculate an annual growth rate of 0.10%. So there is no doubt that the European expansion in population between 1000 and 1340 can be considered rapid. This rapid expansion in population went hand in hand with an acceleration of the process of urbanization—a point to which I shall return later.

1300–1340 to 1470–90: The Upheavals of the Period of the Black Death

Europe seems to have suffered a series of poor harvests starting at the beginning of the fourteenth century. During the three-year period from 1315 to 1317, the harvests were catastrophic and led to severe famine. Thus as Pirenne (1914) has shown, the city of Ypres, a Flemish textile center, lost 12% of its population between May and October 1316. Rossiaud (1980), in his introduction to France's urban history during the two centuries following 1330, insists that "the thirties of the fourteenth century were a period of peasant pauperisation . . . leading to urban stagnation." And 1337 began what was destined to become the Hundred Years War (1337–1453). By September 1347 began a disaster unparalleled in human history: the Black Death, which would ravage Europe during the next 15 years or so. Virulent outbreaks of the plague reappeared in 1361, 1373, and 1380. After that the plague continued to strike Europe, though with less ferocity and at wider intervals, until 1770, the date conventionally set for the last outbreak. Between 1330–40 and 1380–1400, the population of Europe as a whole fell by a third, and in some regions the loss was greater still. The regions chiefly affected by the plague were precisely those that had achieved most development—those the most deeply engaged in trade. In these regions the towns were as a rule more gravely afflicted than the countryside.

The economic and social impact of this calamity was far-reaching and profound. There was a decline in the amount of land under cultivation, accompanied by a five-to-one drop in the price of land. A monetary problem arose as well: de facto devaluations were common and substantial. Both industrial output and the volume of trade fell. Yet despite these major setbacks, the dominant trends before the onset of the Black Death continued. Agricultural methods, industrial techniques, modes of transport, economic organization and management, all underwent further development. This may be explained by an important fact deserving mention here: the catastrophe of the Black Death was very likely accompanied by a rise in the average standard of living of the survivors, especially and most unmistakably among the disadvantaged classes. The evidence supplied by all of the studies dealing with the secular evolution of wages converges on this point: the decades spanning the end of the thirteenth century and the first half of the fourteenth century saw real earnings reach a peak to which they would not again return until the latter half of the nineteenth century after the Industrial Revolution. This rise in wages and the likely concomitant improvement in the standard of living resulted from the more favorable balance between population and resources caused by the sharp fall in population, caused in turn by successive epidemics and the other disturbances that preceded and followed them.

During this period many different social, technological, and economic developments took place that eventually led to the radical break in world history that took place at the close of the fifteenth century. These included advances in the design and construction of ships, in navigation, and in artillery. They all made fundamental contributions to the great discoveries of the fifteenth and sixteenth centuries, which in their turn stimulated European expansion overseas and therefore fostered the rise of European colonization, which supplanted previous forms of colonization. As early as the start of the fifteenth century, Henry the Navigator, a son of the king of Portugal, founded at Sagres his famous school of navigation and geography, a veritable NASA of maritime exploration. With a view to the systematic exploration of the Atlantic Ocean and above all of the African coast, Henry drew to this small town, situated on the extreme southwestern edge of the Continent, the foremost European cartographers, geographers, and navigators of the time. In addition to these developments in shipbuilding, navigation, and geography, in 1440 Europe reinvented printing, and the second half of the fifteenth century saw the introduction of the blast furnace. Nor, finally, should we forget that the Renaissance had begun in Italy by the latter half of the fourteenth century. The chemical mix had formed; it only remained to await the reaction.

1470–90 to 1700: An Expansion of Trade in an Otherwise Stagnant Economy

The most decisive turning point in this period was reached during the last decade of the fifteenth century, with the more or less simultaneous discovery (or rediscovery) of direct maritime routes to Asia and to America (the latter being incidental to the search for a western route to the East). These discoveries, coupled with the continuation of the technological progress that had made them possible, unleashed an unprecedented expansion of European trade with the outside world. I have yet to come across any assessment of the scale of the growth in international trade that flowed from this dual discovery. But whatever its precise extent, it was unquestionably very great. Did international trade grow twice, three times, or five times over? Each of these three orders of magnitude is possible.

But in addition to increasing the volume of trade, the discovery of America and the discovery of a sea route to Asia also (and perhaps above all) created new patterns of exchange whose novelty lay both in the geographical location of the other partner and in the nature of the commodities involved. The new partner, of course, was the New World, and the new commodities were chiefly precious metals and sugar. In the space of a single century, American gold and silver flowed into Europe from the New World in such quantities that, while the exact figure has yet to be established, the stock of precious metals rose by a factor of two at the very least. This influx of precious metals also induced a phase of price rises whose impact on the European economy continues to be the object of often contradictory analyses.

Sugar and of course other products of the tropics should be cited: coffee, cocoa, and so on. But sugar was most important, for in terms of the quantities involved, the traffic in sugar was by far the largest. Thus taking the data for 1700 or thereabouts, according to my provisional calculations, Europe annually imported from the rest of the world some 100,000–120,000 metric tons of agricultural and mineral commodities, of which sugar alone accounted for nearly two-thirds, that is, for about 70,000–90,000 metric tons. In 1500, on the other hand, these imports only amounted to a few hundred metric tons.

But sugar was important for another reason, which scholars have tended to overlook in their analyses of the socioeconomic impact of the discovery of the New World. For sugar was the first product of the tropics that became a staple that was capable of making a significant contribution to the nourishment of urban populations. Indeed, during the sixteenth and seventeenth centuries, from a rare and high-priced luxury item sugar became an ordinary consumer product. In Europe before the sixteenth century, for example, a kilogram of sugar cost the equivalent of thirty to forty days' wages paid to an urban manual laborer. During the first half of the eighteenth century in England, on the other hand, the same amount of sugar cost less than one day's wages—wages that had not greatly increased in the interval. This fact largely explains the rapid rise in the consumption of sugar. In commercial countries, and especially in the cities of commercial countries, consumption had reached substantial levels by the beginning of the eighteenth century. Thus in 1730 the average European consumed less than half a kilogram of sugar per year, while the average Englishman went through nearly five kilograms per year. But the average citizen of one of the commercial cities would probably have consumed some ten to fifteen kilograms per year, that is, enough to cover 7–9% of his annual caloric needs.

I will attempt a more meaningful—or in any case a less imprecise—calculation. Europe imported in 1700 some 80,000–85,000 more metric tons of sugar than in 1500. This difference represents enough sugar to supply throughout an entire year 1,900 calories per day to about 480,000 people—a figure corresponding to 11% of the increase in the total urban population of Europe (except Russia) and roughly a quarter of the increase in the population of cities of more than 50,000 inhabitants between the start of the sixteenth century and the start of the eighteenth century. The growing volume of sugar imports seems all the more significant when it is remembered that growth in European agricultural output during this same period was, to say the least, very modest.

But of much greater significance from the point of view of European urban history was the shift in the center of gravity of international trade from its former location in the Mediterranean to a new location on the Atlantic. From Venice and Genoa the heart of commercial Europe, and consequently the center of financial services and transport, moved first to Lisbon and Seville, and finally to Amsterdam and London (not forgetting the important interlude of Antwerp). And this shift carried in its wake the formation of new networks of commercial cities.

The unquestionable role of commerce in European urban life perhaps explains the exaggerated importance assigned to international trade in the economic life of the traditional preindustrial societies of Europe. To be sure, industry participated in international trade, but not in all industrial sectors. And even within those sectors of industry that were affected by international trade, most production continued to be for the local market. As for farming (which absorbed nearly 80% of the work force), since agricultural produce was exchanged over short distances, only a very small fraction of total output, perhaps 1–2%, may be said to have appeared on the international market. But what nevertheless justifies the importance accorded international trade in the economic life of Europe, apart from the role it played in hastening the diffusion of innovation, especially technological innovation, is the incontestable fact that during this period international trade progressed more rapidly than any other sector of the economy.

But what were the trends in the principal sectors of the economy during the two centuries from 1500 to 1700? The European economy of the sixteenth and seventeenth centuries was an economy in expansion, but the rate of expansion was moderate. This is especially true when one considers the period as a whole and neglects differences in the pace and direction of events at specific times and places. Unfortunately I must pass over the many differences in detail, though I shall return to them later. To do them even superficial justice would require several chapters, particularly when it is observed that in economic terms the history of the sixteenth century begins before the close of the fifteenth, while the seventeenth century does not truly come to an end until 1710–1730. In any case, the European economy of the sixteenth and seventeenth centuries experienced modest growth, with not only a rise in the volume of production, but also diversification, technological change, and probably small gains in productivity as well. All of this must be seen in the context of traditional societies, that is, of a world in which conservatism hindered change of any sort.

Stagnation in Agriculture?

As against the 77–82% of the total working population engaged in farming at the turn of the fifteenth century, agriculture (which naturally remained the dominant sector of the economy) perhaps employed "only" 76–80% in 1700. Agriculture seems to have made little progress during this period. "Blockage in Production and Productivity" is the title of the first of the chapters Jacquart (1978) devotes to agriculture in his review of the economy of seventeenth-century Europe. "On the whole, the [agricultural] techniques of 1700 or 1750 were still those of the 1300s," Fourquin (1977) affirms. This judgement may be a bit excessive, but it appears that the consensus among specialists runs in this general direction.

It is true that the yield of grain per unit of land improved not at all, or at most very little, though this was not the case for all regions at all times. On the other hand, and this is a very important point, the amount of seed required to grow grain crops diminished considerably, falling from around 150 kilograms per hectare at the beginning of the sixteenth century to about 100 kilograms at the start of the eighteenth. At the risk of offending the sensibilities of specialists in the field, having as they do to resolve, among other difficulties, the thorny problem of converting data from volume into weight, I would hazard the following estimate of the spread in the average yield in Europe during this period: between 700–800 kilograms per hectare. This means a gain in requirement of seed implying an increase of 7–10% in the quantities of wheat available per acre of cultivated land. The figure may be a little higher when all the other forms of grain are taken into account.

The data relating to yields expressed in terms of the quantity of grain harvested per unit of grain sown are more numerous. Here too developments seem not to have been very positive. If we ignore gains made in individual regions and occasional fluctuations, stagnation was the rule from the end of the fifteenth century to the beginning of the eighteenth century.

But if European agriculture improved very little with regard to cereals, substantial benefits resulted from the diversification of agricultural production. Legumes in particular had a growing importance, and there was a great increase in their yield. Nor should we forget the various plants introduced from the New World. The cultivation of potatoes became truly widespread only at a later date, but they were already being adopted during this period, as were maize, tomatoes, and beans.

As with the Middle Ages, it is impossible to reach any definite conclusions concerning agricultural productivity during these centuries. There was probably stagnation or at best very modest growth. Using my estimates regarding the proportion of the working population employed in agriculture (derived in part from my data on urban population) and if one further postulates that Europe produced locally 10% more food per capita during 1700–1720 than for 1470–1490, then the productivity of labor increased only 11–13% or 15–20% as the outside limit—and this over a period of two centuries. This gain seems meager if it is recalled that over the course of the first century following the agricultural revolution in England, the increase in productivity exceeded 100%.

In this context it is understandable that to "feed the town dwellers" remained even (or rather especially) at the end of the ancien régime one of the priorities of the city authorities. As my colleague A.-M. Piuz (1983) notes, it is certainly, in addition to being a social and economic problem, a political one. "Political problem no one would doubt? The technological constraints are certainly there, transportation, communication, but the political constraints were still more important in the last century of the ancien régime." She finishes her article by citing this declaration of a procurator of Geneva in front of the Conseil des Deux-Cents during a period of severe shortages: "Everyone must take it upon himself to prevent people's grumbling about the famine and to make the people understand the obligations they have towards the magistrate for his unending efforts to provide for the common good."

Industry: Progress, But No Fundamental Change

Paradoxically (as was also the case for the preceding period), it is even more difficult to gauge progress in the industrial sphere than it was in agriculture, whether with reference to production or productivity. For the uncertainties about variation in per capita consumption and patterns of employment are much greater in the industrial than in the agricultural sector. And within the industrial sector, moreover, each branch of manufacturing has its own story to tell. Developments in textiles and in metallurgy, to cite only the two most important examples, unfolded at different rates. And even within a single area of industry, events followed a different course for silk than for wool, for iron than for tin. In the main, both production and productivity increased, the former probably more substantially than the latter. But progress was strictly limited: no revolutionary changes occurred. As Sella (1974) puts it: "Around 1700 industrial technology, in spite of some significant innovations, was still very much what it had been in the late medieval period."

Nor did anything especially dramatic take place in technology generally, whether industrial or otherwise. There was instead a multitude of minor innovations in a multitude of areas, accompanied by a wider dissemination of advanced techniques that, while failing to bring about absolute equality in every corner of Europe, nevertheless diffused throughout the Continent. All of this meant that by 1700, on the eve of the Industrial Revolution, Europe had attained a higher level of technological development than it had ever known. At the end of this period, Europe was among the most advanced regions in the world, if not the most advanced of all. While in 1500 the sum of technical knowledge was no doubt greater in China than in Europe, by the start of the eighteenth century this was no longer clearly the case.

With respect to population, I will once again confine myself to Europe excluding Russia, in order to reduce the margin of uncertainty, if not eliminate it altogether. The margin of error for the population figures available for this period, even at the level of Europe as a whole, is still on the order of 8–10% (table 8.1). Over the course of the two centuries between 1500 and 1700, the population of Europe in all likelihood rose from around 70–84 million to around 95–110 million. Population growth during these two centuries was, then, quite moderate, 32–40%, making an average annual increase of 0.13–0.17%—a rate of growth lower than that registered for the period 1000–1340. Real growth did take place, however, since the population of Europe had by 1700 substantially surpassed the peak of 66–95 million previously reached in 1340.

Nor could any of this have failed to have some impact on urban life, just as urban life had an active role on the economic scene. It is therefore time to proceed to a survey of the urban history of the seven centuries between 1000 and 1700.

900–1000 to 1300–40: A Period of Strong Growth in Urban Population

There is a similarity between the evolution of the economy as described above and developments in urbanization. Emphasis should be given to the surge of urban growth that marked the period up to 1340 and that began a little before the year 1000 (see chapter 7).

As early as the eleventh century, and even more during the twelfth, rapid urban growth unquestionably took place. All available studies and contemporary records testify to the expansion of those cities already in existence and to the creation of a great many new urban centers. In some instances obscure villages turned into (or on occasion turned back into) bustling cities. In France, this was notably the case for Montpellier, Dijon, and Lille; in Germany for Berlin, Leipzig,

Nuremberg, and Munich; and for practically all of the cities in the Netherlands. To this far from exhaustive list could be added the names of yet other cities of great size and importance today: Antwerp, Copenhagen, Edinburgh, Moscow, Oslo, Stockholm, Vienna, Warsaw, and so on. There were also cases of small cities becoming great metropolises. Between 1000 and 1200 the population of Venice went from 45,000 to 70,000, while that of Paris went from 20,000 to 110,000, and that of Cologne from 20,000 to 50,000.

Naturally these figures cannot be regarded as precise: they only serve to indicate general orders of magnitude. But they are still more reliable than those for earlier periods. This proves especially true when we add together all of the data for Europe as a whole, the margins of error arrived at in this way dropping to acceptable levels. Since almost all of the population data derive from estimates done independently of each other by different observers, often using different methods, and since, moreover, the number of cities in existence by this date is already relatively high, individual errors would, statistically speaking, tend to offset one another at the aggregate level. For instance, if the margin of error for each European city with a population of more than 20,000 in the year 1300 averages about 30 %, then so long as each of the observations is independent of the others, the margin of error for all of the cities taken collectively falls to 2%. The possibility remains of systematic bias due to the omission of certain cities. I have tried to eliminate this bias by starting with present-day data and postulating what levels of correction seem necessary to allow for likely omissions. (For further details consult the methodological appendix.)

Whereas in the year 1000 Europe had some 35–45 cities with populations of more than 20,000, the number had probably risen to around 100–110 by 1340 (see table 8.2). Further, there was only one city with a population in excess of 100,000 in the year 1000, and the city in question was the Muslim city, Cordoba, which may be considered foreign to European society. About the start of the fourteenth century there were five European cities with populations exceeding 100,000: Paris, with around 160,000; rechristianized Granada, replacing Cordoba as the Spanish metropolis, with around 150,000; Venice, with around 110,000; and Milan and Genoa, each with a population of around 100,000.

Despite this sharp increase in the number and size of European cities, the level of urbanization remained stationary. This is not surprising, however, since these three centuries were all characterized by rapid growth in total population. From a population of about 34–42 million in the year 1000, Europe probably had a population of 70–80 million in 1300.

From this point on I shall define as urban any town with a population of five thousand or more. I shall return to the problem of

TABLE 8.2 Growth of the European Cities (except Russia) according to Population (in Thousands) (1000–1700)

Size of Cities	1000	1300	1500	1600	1700
		Number of Cities			
10–20	(72)	(150)	(146)	(177)	(200)
20–50	35	80	74	85	98
50–100	3	7	17	21	21
100–200	—	4	3	9	7
200–500	1	1	1	2	2
500 or more	—	—	—	—	2
Total	111	242	241	294	330
		Urban Population			
5–10	(1,200)	(2,540)	(2,500)	(3,150)	(3,350)
10–20	(930)	(1,960)	(1,900)	(2,300)	(2,600)
20–50	970	2,250	2,100	2,430	2,830
50–100	215	415	1,090	1,350	1,540
100–200	—	460	345	1,120	750
200–500	460	230	225	545	410
500 or more	—	—	—	—	1,080
Total	3,765	7,855	8,160	10,895	12,560
Total population	(39,000)	75,000	76,000	95,000	102,000
Level of urbanization (%)[a]	(9.7)	10.4	10.7	11.5	12.3

Sources: Calculations and estimates by the author; see the methodological appendix.
Note: The fact that these figures have been only slightly rounded off does not imply a correspondingly small margin of error. The figures in parentheses have a much wider margin of error than the other data.
[a] A criterion of 5,000 is used for urban population.

defining urban population in chapter 13. It ought to be stressed now, however, that the choice I have made suffers from a grave defect: the purely relative character of any single criterion. But this weakness is practically unavoidable, being endemic to any analysis seeking to describe and compare, over space and time, the modifications undergone by a social or economic structure with specific regional components and subject to change as a result of the process of economic development. Such is the case for urban population, but it is also the case for working population, foreign trade, industry, and savings.

In my view, the ideal solution to this kind of problem is to define a mobile criterion or several mobile criteria based objectively on a large number of parameters. If, for example, I choose to define urban population in terms of the size of the agglomeration, this size should be a function of the level of economic development in the country at large, the composition and quality of the soil, the configuration of the local terrain, the dominant type of spatial arrangement characterizing the urban habitat, and the political structure both of the city itself and of the country as a whole. The reader will readily realize the practical impossibility of such an approach. Even if in determining a mobile criterion, one were to confine oneself to a single parameter, such as the level of economic development, the absence of reliable data concerning levels of economic development would make it difficult, if not impossible, to apply the relevant test.

The least unsatisfactory solution, one that is far from being the easiest, consists of adopting a single criterion and applying it over both time and space. In this way the differences brought to light would stand a good chance of conveying some sense, however uncertain, of how things were developing. In fact, given the current state of research, there is only one practical alternative to this plan, which, as it happens, is also the easiest solution. This would simply consist of noting not only that what we mean by urban population varies from one region to another, but also that in sizing up situations that are similar in either spatial or historical terms, statisticians have adopted different criteria. One would thereupon conclude that no proper comparison can be made, and that would be that.

Granted, the limit of 5,000 is too high for the societies of interest here. A limit of 2,000 or even on occasion 1,000 would be more appropriate. Having lived for five years in a village with a population of 1,700 (Riscle, in the Gers region of France), I would be the last to deny how urban such a village may be even in the France of the years preceding World War II. A village may take on a distinctly urban character by virtue of the dominant activity of its population, the patently urban configuration of the site, or the cast of mind of its inhabitants. To cite an even more extreme example, consider the present-day village of Menerbes in the Vaucluse region of southern France: despite its population of 400 (800 in summer), Alexander (1972) rightly describes it as a "fully urban settlement." But quite apart from the difficulties the limit of 5,000 creates from the point of view of comparability, there is also a problem of sources. The margin of error is perceptibly greater for cities of 10,000–20,000 people than for cities with more than 20,000 people. And for towns with 2,000–5,000 people, calculations must be based entirely on Davis's Law (see chapter 9), which has been chiefly verified as applied to cities of greater size.

Defining urban population, then, by means of the criterion of 5,000, with all the uncertainties this entails, I find that the urban population of Europe (except Russia) about the year 1000 was on the order of 3.8 million, representing roughly 9–11% of the total population. By 1300 it had reached 7.9 million. The relative level of urbanization, however, had increased only marginally. On the eve of the first outbreak of the Black Death, the proportion of the overall population of Europe living in cities had probably risen only to 9.5–11.5%.

1340 to 1400–20: A Period of Nongeneralized Urban Recession

The period of the great plagues precipitated an urban recession in just about every part of Europe. At the individual level, however, different cities were very differently affected. To the general consequences of the Black Death felt throughout Europe must be added the special economic circumstances peculiar to each city. Thus the steep decline experienced by the textile towns of Flanders, for instance, was not entirely due to the havoc wrought by famines. From 1258 on, England began to take measures to prohibit the exportation of raw wool. But English raw wool figured prominently among the materials required by the Flemish textile industry. Between 1307 and 1327 further measures were taken to promote English textile manufacturing, leading to the migration of Flemish weavers to England. As a result of all of these factors, Ypres, which had a population of 30,000 in 1300, had only 9,000 by 1500 and only 5,000 in 1600.

But to each city its own events. Thus for Geneva, as Binz (1974) points out, "the fourteenth century was an era of confirmations: confirmation of the success of the fairs, confirmation of the commune recognized by the bishop in 1309 and given franchises in 1387." As for the fairs, "still merely a regional market at the beginning of the century, by century's end they had become a center of international exchange and had spread the city's name over ever-widening distances." Thanks largely to this economic base, the city of Geneva, with barely 2,000 inhabitants in 1340, had by 1550 increased this number to 12,000–13,000. Yet in the interval Geneva too had suffered from the plague, experiencing (though only temporarily) a decline in population.

In Europe as a whole, it seems likely that between 1340 and 1400–1420 the number of cities with populations in excess of 20,000 fell from 100–110 to 80–90. But the recovery appears to have begun by 1420–1450, and by the end of the fifteenth century, the urban population of the Continent had returned to a level very close to that of 1340. But the urban structure of Europe had changed. The relative importance of very large cities had grown. For around 1500 there were 20–22 cities with populations of more than 50,000, as against only 10–14 around 1300. This rise in the number of very large cities was probably offset by a fall in the number of small towns.

The Sixteenth and Seventeenth Centuries: A Shift in the Center of Gravity of Urban Europe

The sixteenth century (and a part of the seventeenth) saw a new surge of urban growth, this one linked with the opening of Europe to the rest of the world. By 1600 Europe (except Russia) had 110–130 cities with populations in excess of 20,000, that is, some 25–30% more than in 1300. There were, moreover, 10–12 cities with populations of more than 100,000, twice as many as at the start of the fourteenth century.

The changes were more profound with regard to the spatial distribution of the major European cities. The Atlantic usurped the role of window on the world formerly played by the Mediterranean. Lisbon, with a population of some 15,000 in 1200, became with its new population of 130,000 one of the dozen or so great cities of the first years of the seventeenth century. Amsterdam, a simple fishing village with a population of perhaps 1,000 in 1300, had nearly 50,000 around 1600 and 200,000 by the start of the eighteenth century. But each city has its individual history. Bruges, though a port on the North Sea in direct communication with the Atlantic, saw its population fall from 125,000 in 1400 to some 26,000 in 1600. This evolution against the trend is explained in part by political events (the revolt of 1484), in part by ecological events (the silting up of the canal), and in part by economic events (competition with Antwerp at a time when the latter was not yet hindered by rivalry with Amsterdam).

The occasional exception notwithstanding, the gradual shift toward the north pursued an irresistible course (see table 8.3). Braudel (1979) argues that the break came around 1600, when Europe

> rocked on its axis to the benefit of the north. The rise of Amsterdam was certainly no casual accident, a simple transfer of the center of gravity from Antwerp to Holland. It testifies rather to a crisis of far wider, far more decisive importance. With the passing of the powers of the Inner Sea, the fading out of the last glimmer of the light of Italy that had for so long dazzled the rest of the world, Europe would have only one center of gravity, to the north. And it was henceforth relative to this new magnetic pole that, for centuries, right down to the present, the circles and lines of the deep-seated asymmetries of Europe would be drawn.

At the beginning of the fourteenth century, only some 40% of the cities with populations of more than 20,000 were in the western European countries with access to the Atlantic (Germany, Belgium, France, the Netherlands, the United Kingdom). More than half of them were in these countries by the start of the eighteenth century. Italy was by

TABLE 8.3   Number of Cities with Populations of More than 20,000
(1000–1700)

	1000	1300	1500	1700
Italy	10	24	21 .	22
Spain	10	17	17	15
Western Europe[a]	14	37	41	70
(Europe except Russia)	39	92	95	130
Russia	(4)	(11)	(12)	(17)

Sources: Calculations and estimates by the author; see the methodological appendix.
Note: The figures in parentheses have a much wider margin of error than the other data.
[a]Germany, Belgium, France, the Netherlands, and the United Kingdom.

far the biggest loser: it had more than a quarter of all of the larger European cities in 1300, but its share had dwindled to one-seventh by 1700. What is more, the largest cities were now located in the North. For the first time since the Fall of Rome the population of some of the cities of Europe exceeded 500,000. Around 1700 London and Paris each had populations of some 500,000–570,000. The third largest European city at this time was Naples, with 300,000 people, followed by Amsterdam with 200,000.

As in the preceding phase of urban growth, the one taking place during the sixteenth and seventeenth centuries saw a concomitant rise in total population. As a result, while the urban structure of the Continent changed profoundly, the level of urbanization changed very little. Representing 10–12% of the total population in 1500, urban population still represented only 10–13% in 1600 and 11–14% in 1700. But this average for Europe (except Russia) conceals considerable national differences. Thus in 1700, between the countries of Scandinavia, where no more than 5–8% of the population lived in cities, and the Netherlands, where 38–49% did, the other European countries ranged over the whole gamut of intermediate situations. And to the East lay the vastness of Russia, where the level of urbanization rose no higher than 4–7%. I shall return in greater detail (in chapters 10–12) to these and other aspects of the urban adventure of Europe. Before that I must digress (chapter 9) to discuss matters of method.

9 Cities—Their Locations, Spheres of Influence, Size, and Economic Functions: A Few General Remarks on Matters of Method □

Before undertaking in somewhat greater detail the analysis of the European urban structure and the various modifications it underwent during the centuries between the Fall of the Roman Empire and the dawn of the Industrial Revolution, it seems an appropriate time to consider a few general matters of method. I shall examine in this chapter the theoretical implications of the following problems: What factors determine the location of cities? What do we know about urban spheres of influence (including the urban hierarchy)? What conditions the size of cities? And finally, what are the characteristic economic functions of cities? It will be found that urban spheres of influence and the size of cities are in part connected.

I must insist from the outset, however, that this will not constitute an exhaustive treatment of these problems. I intend here merely to set out the principal elements, hoping in this way to ensure the reader's comprehension of my references to these theoretical matters in subsequent discussions.

The Location of Cities

What factors may explain the precise spatial location of a given city within a particular region? I ask this question without now taking into account the effects of other cities, a problem of spheres of influence. I have largely based my observations here on the article of Ullman (1941) and the important paper of Ridgley (1925)—which was unfortunately neglected in Ullman's synthesis sixteen years later.

It appears that the first modern approach to the problem was that of J. G. Kohl (1841). In his analysis of the relations between forms of transport and human settlements, Kohl insists on the part played by transport as a factor in the location of cities. More systematic than Kohl's work, however, are the analyses of the German geographer F. Ratzel (1891) and the American geographer C. Cooley (1894). Ratzel, like Kohl, assigns a leading role to transport, but defines in more precise terms under what conditions it assumes this importance.

According to Ratzel, a city is established (or develops) wherever we find one of the three following situations:
1. The end of a transport route
2. The junction of two transport routes of the same kind
3. The junction of two transport routes of different kinds
In a monograph published in 1894, Cooley advances a theory that, despite certain superficial differences, is related to Ratzel's. For Cooley, population and material resources tend to accumulate wherever there is a break in transport lines.

These fundamentally convergent viewpoints, each of which is perfectly explicable in terms of the economic considerations set forth earlier in this book, have been extensively developed in later research. But throughout all subsequent changes, the basic principles have remained the same: transport lines constitute the essential factor governing the location of cities. And this is as true for the cities of traditional societies as for those following the Industrial Revolution. This brings us back to the tyranny of distance, whose effects I discussed in part 1.

In traditional societies, waterways are the determining element. Cities are born and grow in size and importance at the mouths of rivers, at the confluence of rivers, at places, such as waterfalls, where rivers become unnavigable, on the shores of lakes (as a rule at exit points), near sites suitable for the establishment of seaports, and so on. Many towns are created near fords for crossing rivers. Naturally the importance of waterways derives not only from their own intrinsic properties, but also from the economic value of the hinterlands they serve: an excellent natural harbor in a desert region without resources will remain rural. After the Industrial Revolution, canals and, especially beginning with the second half of the nineteenth century, railroads have fulfilled a function similar to that of rivers.

The critical role played by transport in the location of cities does not rule out exceptions, but statistically speaking these are in the minority. The exceptions are for the most part religious centers, military centers, and mining towns (precious metals), and capitals built by princely decree. Another sort of exception, but one that has rarely resulted in a large city, is a relatively inaccessible site as a shelter from attack. And without pretending to draw up an exhaustive list, I might mention one last factor that has been far from negligible: thermal springs, or spas. Well-known examples abound in Europe—Vichy and Evian in France, Spa in Belgium, Baden-Baden in Germany, Baden in Switzerland, among others—some of them tracing their origins back to Roman times. This factor is not unique to Europe, but is also found in other parts of the world. In Japan, for instance, thermal springs have fostered the emergence of many cities, some of which have populations of more than 50,00 and even 100,000.

With regard to the religious factor, one must not confuse religious cities proper with cities having some sort of economic base in which religious institutions are established in tandem with the city's secular growth. In the latter case, economic factors, generally transport lines, determine the town's location; religious establishments develop along with the city itself, which is stimulated by its own wealth and that of the neighboring region. Religious cities proper, on the other hand, are those whose location devolves from some specifically religious factor that may vary from one culture to another, ranging from an ideal site for astronomical observations to the tomb of a saint.

What I have just said with reference to religious centers equally applies to certain administrative centers. From time to time, cities have been artificially created, as it were, in order to fulfill purely administrative functions. It is usually the case, however, that some already-existing town has been chosen to carry out these functions. Thus while its subsequent development may result from its status as a seat of administration, it originally owes its existence and location to economic factors. This distinction leads me to a general principle whose formulation brings this section to a natural close: one must never confuse the factor determining the location of a city with those factors favoring its subsequent growth, even though the factor responsible for its location may well be among those fostering its later development.

From Spheres of Influence to the Urban Hierarchy

Given the abundance of research dealing with the urban hierarchy, I shall confine myself here to following a single conducting thread enabling me to cover the essential points without entering into too much detail. This thread will be found in two works that have profoundly shaped the research in this field: Reilly's article, "The Law of Gravitation," published in 1929, and Christaller, *Die Zentralen Orte in Süddeutschland* (1933).

The vast field of research on urban spheres of influence, which have far-reaching implications from the point of view of economic and, more specifically, commercial history, was chiefly opened up by Reilly's article. The analogy with the Newtonian model of gravitation is obviously deliberate and requires no commentary. But it should be noted that the term "law" is used more by geographers than by economists or historians.

Reilly's law was elaborated on the basis of the analysis of zones of attraction of trade and services. It holds that competing cities attract buyers from a given rural region in a direct relation to size and in inverse relation to the square of the distance to be travelled in getting to them. In other words, a city of 100,000 people will have a sphere of influence twice as great as a city of 50,000 people. But the intensity of the attraction exerted by a city diminishes rapidly with distance. At 20 kilometers from the city the attractive force will be 4 times weaker than at 10 kilometers, 4 being the square of 2, and 2 being the ratio of 20 to 10. Similarly, at 40 kilometers the attractive force will be 16 times weaker than at 10 kilometers, 16 being the square of 4, and 4 being the ratio of 40 to 10. All of this, of course, supposes uniform conditions: no imbalance in means of transport, the absence of natural or political barriers, and so on.

Since it relates to Reilly's law in many particulars, I shall cite in this connection the interesting study of von Thunen, which, although published as long ago as 1826, nevertheless retains a place in the first rank of spatial analyses of urbanism. Starting from the admittedly (but deliberately) simplistic postulate of an "isolated state," von Thunen estimates that the exploitation of the soil around a city is characterized by concentric rings with specific functions depending on their distance from the city. The first ring, occupying 1% of the total area within the city's zone of attraction, is given over to intensive farming: market gardening and intensive livestock rearing for the production of milk. Because of the ready availability of large supplies of manure, this symbiosis enables farmers to avoid letting land lie fallow. (Von Thunen bases his assumptions on the situation in Prussia during the first years of the nineteenth century.) The second ring, representing 3% of the area of the urban zone of attraction, is covered by forests providing a high yield of wood both for heating and construction. Next comes the vast ring devoted to extensive farming, covering 58% of the zone of attraction, itself divided into three subrings in which cultivation of various types is carried out with gradually diminishing intensity the farther one goes from the city. The last of these three subrings is given over in part to livestock rearing, which constitutes the predominant activity in the fourth and final ring, representing 38% of the total area of the urban zone of attraction.

I will now move on to Christaller's law, which serves as the starting point for research on the urban hierarchy and brings us closer to determining what governs the size of cities.

According to Christaller, in the hypothetical case of a territory free from disruptions due to accidents of terrain (mountains, rivers, and so forth), the spatial distribution of cities is established as a function of their zones of attraction in conjunction with the types of services they render. In Christaller's analysis, the point of departure is the burg serving as market town for the surrounding countryside. The spheres of influence of each burg extends over an area with a radius of four kilometers—four kilometers being the equivalent of an hour's walk, a reasonable distance to cover in going to market. But there is always more than one burg, and the spheres of influence radiating from the various rival agglomerations take the form of an equilateral triangle with sides 6.9 kilometers long (the geometric formula being $4 \times \sqrt{3}$). Starting from this basic unit, a network of larger and larger towns grows up, spreading their spheres of influence over a progressively wider domain. Six of these burgs, each complete with its own zone of attraction, together make up a hexagon whose center is occupied by what Christaller calls a "greater burg." And so it continues through the 7 urban size levels allowed in the model, leading at last to the regional capital, with a population on the order of 300,000 and a sphere of influence encompassing a total of 2,025,000 people, each burg containing 800 people and each zone of attraction 2,700 people. All of this results in a geometric distribution of cities—assuming the absence of physical and political obstacles. Since its original conception, Christaller's law has received a number of improvements, notably through the efforts of A. Lösch (1940), M. Beckmann (1958), B. Berry (1958), and A. K. Philbrick (1957). The basic premise, however, has remained intact.

Is There a Law Governing the Size of Cities?

There were many antecedents for Zipf's law (1949), which is the reference par excellence on the law of city size distribution. As early as 1913, F. Auerbach arrived at its first formulation, followed by A. J. Lotka in 1925, R. Gilbrat in 1931, and H. W. Singer in 1936. It is unlikely that this is a complete list. I shall nonetheless call it Zipf's law, since that is the name by which it generally goes in the field.

The law is in fact a very simple one. On the basis of empirical observation, it will be realized that in a given discrete geopolitical whole (a country, say, or a large region), the size of the various towns is a direct function of the size of the largest among them. The relation or formula may in its turn also be stated very simply: the size of the second city is that of the largest divided by two, the size of the third that of the largest divided by three, and so on. This relation derives fairly directly from the spatial distribution of the various cities and their respective spheres of influence.

But like so many other laws, this one suffers from exceptions, one of which has engendered a law of its own: Jefferson's law (1939), or as I would rather call it, giving it the title of Jefferson's first article, "The Law of Primate City." Beginning like Zipf, with empirical observations, Jefferson notes that in many cases the existence of one very large city (very large for the country in question at least) leads to the absence of cities of intermediate size alongside the large city, and to the presence of much smaller cities. Large cities of this kind, called primate cities, may of course result from many different causes. As Berry (1958) points out,

> countries which have until recently been politically
> and/or economically dependent on some outside
> country tend to have primate cities, which are the
> national capitals, cultural and economic centers,
> often the chief port, and the focus of national con-

sciousness and feeling. Small countries which once had extensive empires also have primate cities, which are on the one hand "empire capitals" (Vienna, Madrid, Lisbon, etc.), and on the other hand centers in which such economies of scale may be achieved that cities of intermediate size are not called for.

Scholars have attempted to reconcile Zipf's and Jefferson's laws. This has proved possible because, once one overlooks the absence of cities of a size close to that of the metropolis, one discovers that, by the time we get as far as the fifth to the tenth largest city, a relation of rank to size emerges compatible with that prescribed by Zipf's law. Researchers can and no doubt will go further in this direction; for it is possible to imagine a generalized Zipf-Jefferson law integrating the relative size of the first city both with the size of the country as a whole and with the level of urbanization reached in the country as a whole.

Given that these laws were elaborated with specific reference to existing urban models, one may obviously question their validity in different historical contexts. What we have already seen with respect to Rome, for example, squares very well with Jefferson's account of primate cities, and the same holds true for Babylon, Constantinople, and some of the cities of Asia. Russell (1972a) has carried out a systematic investigation of Zipf's law in the context of medieval cities. The results of this test seem conclusive: the law does in fact work, requiring at most a fairly slight modification of the formula expressing the relationship between rank and size. Russell proposes the following equation:

$$N_R = C - \left(\frac{1 + \dfrac{\sqrt{R-1}}{10}}{R} \right)$$

where N_R is a city of rank (R), and C the size of the capital.

The application of this equation leads to a slightly less pronounced reduction in size for the first few cities. Thus according to Russell, instead of having a population equal to the population of the largest city divided by 5, the fifth largest city has a population equal to that of the largest divided by 4.2. But by the time we get to the tenth largest city, instead of dividing by 10, we only find it necessary to divide by 7.7. In other words, Russell's equation involves little change for the first few cities, but as soon as we reach the eighth, ninth or tenth, the difference becomes substantial, growing rapidly thereafter. For the thirtieth city, we divide the population of the capital by 19.5, and for the one hundredth by 50.1.

The question obviously arises of what would have constituted a normal distribution of cities by size in periods even more remote than the

Middle Ages. Carothers and McDonald (1979), for example, have asked precisely this question with reference to one of the regions of Greece at the end of the Bronze Age, coming to more or less the same kind of conclusion as Russell.

Zipf's law has a significant contribution to make, for from a statistical point of view it enables us, given the population of only a few cities, to arrive at relatively valid estimates of the population of all of the cities of a particular region or country despite the absence of reliable data. Russell has used it in this way for Western Europe during the Middle Ages, just as experts at the United Nations use it today in studies of the contemporary Third World. But in cases of this kind, we find it even more useful to resort to what we call Davis's Law (1972).

Though Davis's law follows directly from Zipf's law, Davis does not invoke it, basing his relations entirely on statistical observations. Davis's law may be expressed in the following two propositions:

1. Within a given country or large geographical unit, the number of towns is inversely proportional to their size by a factor of 2. If, for example, there are 80 towns with populations of 10,000 to 20,000, there will be 160 more with populations of 5,000–10,000. Further up the scale, there are 40 cities with populations of 20,000–40,000, and so on.

2. The second proposition derives from the first. The total population of a given class of cities remains stable with each variation in size by a factor of 2. For instance, if in a given country the cities with populations of 5,000–10,000 together have a total population of 300,000, then the cities with populations of 10,000–20,000 will have a total population of 300,000. And the same principle applies whether we move down the scale to the set of cities with populations of 2,500–5,000 or up to cities with populations of 40,000–80,000, or of 80,000–160,000, and so on.

Since Davis based this law on the situation obtaining during the 1950s and 1960s, however, the question inevitably arises to what extent it may be considered valid for other historical periods. To my knowledge, no one has yet put this to the test. On the basis of the data I have myself prepared for cities with populations of more than 100,000 in the developed world since 1800, and for cities with populations of more than 20,000 in Europe since 1500, it seems that, while I discover a relationship close to that predicted by Davis's law, the parameters determining it have to be modified in such a way as to produce a pyramid with a wider base. In other words, for the number of cities, the factor involved appears to be 2.4–2.6 rather than 2, and for population, 1.2–1.3 rather than 1. Insofar as it is possible to discern a historical trend, moreover, it seems to run in the direction of an increase in the size of the ratios the further we travel back in time, with a distinct acceleration in the rate of increase during the most nearly contemporary period.

Given that the data bank I have assembled is practically exhaustive with respect to Europe in 1800, it seemed useful to divide the cities of this period into size categories more appropriate for a test of Davis's law than those I shall use later for the analysis of the European urban structure. In addition to allowing for regular growth, the determination of these categories responded to two imperatives: (1) that I use a lower limit that, while remaining as low as possible, would nevertheless be high enough to reduce as near to zero as possible the number of likely omissions; (2) that I choose upper and lower limits defining the various categories that would not be too close to the round figures (10,000; 20,000; 50,000; 100,000) usually serving this purpose, avoiding in this way the possibility of reinforcing the effects of certain biased estimates contained in my data base.

This eventually led me to include only cities with populations of 12,000 or more: those cities for which I believed I had a virtually complete set of data. The possible omissions involve certainly no more than 1–2% of the number of cities making up the first two size categories. On the other hand, given the greater margin of error affecting the data for Russia, I left this country out of my sample. The reader will also find in table 9.1 that I carried out a second series of calculations in which the United Kingdom was left out, the problem being that by 1800 the urban system of Britain had already begun to register the impact of the Industrial Revolution.

These calculations confirm that Davis's law must indeed be extensively adapted. In traditional Europe at the close of the eighteenth century, the factor relating the number of cities in each category seems to lie closer to 2.5–2.6, and the factor for urban population seems to fall between 1.2 and 1.4. It appears likely, moreover, that these factors should be a little higher still for cities smaller than those included in my sample.

Since there is a direct relation between Zipf's law and Davis's law, it follows that Russell's observations concerning the need to modify Zipf's equation when dealing with the urban networks of the Middle Ages imply, ipso facto, a similar need to modify Davis's law. I have therefore transformed the Zipf-Russell equation into a revised Davis equation. The result closely approximates my empirical observations, yielding a coefficient of 2.6 for the number of cities (giving in turn a coefficient of 1.3 for their population). In other words, if there are 50 cities with populations of 10,000–20,000, then there will be 130 of 5,000–10,000 rather than 100 as stipulated in Davis's law.

I also attempted to determine the probable value of these coefficients for the cities of the nineteenth and twentieth centuries both in developed countries and in the Third World. As described in the

TABLE 9.1 Distribution by Population of Cities with Populations of
TABLE 9.1 Distribution by Population of Cities with Populations of
12,000 or More in 1800
(Population in Thousands)

Size of Cities	Europe except Russia		Europe except Russia and United Kingdom	
	No.	Pop.	No.	Pop
12–24	255	3,983	221	3,470
24–48	88	2,728	75	2,314
48–96	39	2,548	31	1,977
96–192	14	1,832	13	1,667
192–384	4	1,061	4	1,061
384–768	1	550	1	550

Sources: Calculations and estimates by the author; see the methodological appendix and the text.

methodological appendix, I used coefficients of this sort in estimating the population of the size categories of those cities for which the available data are too doubtful, and also to correct the number (and population) of cities wherever there appears to be an underestimation of size groups. Obviously the sole purpose of this procedure was to reduce the margin of error surrounding existing data: it is nothing more than an expedient, so I can justify it only so long as there are no more reliable data available. For the chief merit of this solution lies in the fact that it is at any rate better than simply assuming that those cities for which I have no solid information do not exist; and it would require long and arduous research into the urban structure of traditional societies to arrive at more exact results.

Basic and Nonbasic Functions of Cities

While for Alexander (1954), as for most Anglo-American social scientists and historians, the notion of basic functions traces back to the work of Aurousseau (1921), it appears that the celebrated German economist and sociologist Werner Sombart used the notion as early as 1902 in a key work entitled *Der moderne Kapitalismus*. This European precedent notwithstanding, the development and use of this highly illuminating concept are essentially the work of American geographers. To give the reader some idea of how rich this concept is, it might not be amiss to point out that I find at least six different translations for it in French—*fondamentale, spécifique, exportatrice, non banale, non résidentielle, basique*—none of which by itself exhausts its meaning.

If the terms by which we might render its meaning are legion, the concept itself is as simple as it is useful. The various economic activities pursued in cities may be divided into two types of functions: basic and nonbasic functions. Basic functions may be defined as those producing goods or services destined to be exported from the city, while nonbasic functions are those producing goods or services consumed inside the city. The basic functions therefore play a role of primordial importance in the city's development.

While some functions, notably most services, may be considered to belong exclusively to the category of nonbasic functions, the demarcation between basic and nonbasic functions does not solely reflect the nature of the activities themselves, but mainly the destination of their outlets. Thus in a city where almost all of the industrial production is given over to textiles, for example, some 85–95% of its overall activity (depending on the size of the city and also on other parameters) may be regarded as basic. On the other hand, in a city with highly diversified activities one can imagine an extreme situation in which none of its textile production could be defined as basic, being instead wholly intended for consumption by the local urban population.

Since the very beginnings of urban history, the proportion of basic employments has varied considerably depending on the urban system to which a city belongs and even on the level of development a city has reached. It is certain, however, that basic employments represent on the average a relatively higher fraction of overall economic activity in industrial societies than in traditional societies, and especially in traditional societies before the Industrial Revolution. Similarly, both today and in the past, the size of a city influences the relative scale of each type of employment. As a general rule (Bairoch, 1977a), the proportion of basic forms of employment tends to decrease as the size of the city increases. By way of very rough averages, in the cities of the contemporary industrialized world, basic employments account for 60–75% of overall employment in cities with populations of 50,000, 50–55% in cities with populations of 500,000, and 40–45% in cities with populations of more than a million.

Specific Urban Functions

Earlier analyses of the problems of urban employment led me to elaborate an additional concept, namely specific urban functions or activities, that is, functions stemming directly from the urban way of life. The way of life implied by cities engenders the need for activities that would be useless in rural settings. An example is urban transport, but this is far from being the sole instance of a function peculiar to the urban environment.

In fact, the problem raised here is in many respects akin to the distinction just drawn between basic and nonbasic functions or activities. Thus while nearly 100% of the occupations in urban administration may be considered specific urban occupations, a certain proportion (say 25–30%) of all occupations in the retail trade may also be defined in this way. For even today the consumption of local production is much greater in rural areas than in the city, which reduces the need for and consequently the scale of retail distribution in the country-side. The same holds true for police forces, since both traffic regulation and the protection of persons and property require a much higher ratio of police officers to civilians in urban than in rural districts. Many more examples could be cited to the same purpose. But a clear distinction has to be drawn between activities or forms of employment that happen to be found in cities and activities or forms of employment in themselves specifically urban. Whereas banks, for instance, are almost invariably located in cities, only a fraction of banking activities may be regarded as specific urban functions—that fraction directly called into existence by the conditions of urban life.

It may be deduced from the notion itself that specific urban functions are more numerous and of greater consequence in contemporary urban systems than they were in the past. But this does not mean that no such activities existed in the past. It has already been shown, for example, how in the cities of ancient Greece (and probably elsewhere in the ancient world) special organizations existed that were responsible for street cleaning, refuse disposal, and the maintenance of public gardens. For obvious reasons, no estimates are available concerning the number and scope of specific urban activities in the traditional urban systems of antiquity. The only data available for traditional societies are those I have succeeded in collecting and preparing for the cities of the contemporary Third World where, according to my estimates, specific urban activities make up about 16% of total employment (Bairoch, 1977a). And as one would expect, and contrary to the case with respect to basic economic functions, the relative proportion of specific urban forms of employment tends to increase with the size of cities.

10 The Surge of Urban Growth in Medieval Europe □

There can be few historical epochs as interesting as the European Middle Ages—as interesting and as diverse. Since they spanned some ten and a half centuries the Middle Ages could hardly have escaped being diverse. Traditionally the Middle Ages began in 395, the date of the fall of the Western Empire, and came to a close in 1453 with the capture of Constantinople. The cities of medieval Europe in one sense were subject to the accidents of the many dramatic upheavals and changes marking medieval life, yet they also played a leading role in the story. I have already discussed (in chapter 7) the course of events during the first six hundred years of this period. But the last four remain. And though perhaps the last four centuries had no more momentous happenings, more is known about them and they were ultimately of greater significance for subsequent ages. Of these four centuries, moreover, the first three, those roughly from 1000 to 1340, were especially critical for the general urban history of Europe. It is to these centuries, therefore, that I shall devote the best part of the present chapter.

Medieval Cities and the Future Urban Structure of Europe

The period between 1000 and 1340 witnessed those events that had the most crucial contribution to make in setting in place what until the start of the nineteenth century was the fundamental urban structure of Europe. I have attempted, for example, to determine what in 1300 was the state of those European cities that in 1800 had populations of 20,000 or more (table 10.1). Out of a total of 182 cities with populations of 20,000 or more in 1800, 77% already had populations of more than 5,000 and 13% of 2,000–5,000 around 1300. The majority of the remaining 10% were probably villages, but only the majority, for about a third of them were already small towns. Thus about 93% of the cities with populations of 20,000 or more in 1800 already existed by the start of the fourteenth century.

The permanence of the medieval urban structure from the point of

TABLE 10.1 Populations around 1300 of European Cities with Populations of 20,000 or more in 1800 (Europe except Russia)

Population in 1800	Number of Cities in 1880	Distribution of cities by population around 1300					
		Unknown or Villages	Under 2,000	2,000 to 5,000	5,000 to 10,000	10,000 to 20,000	Over 20,000
Europe							
20,000–50,000	127	8	5	13	29	31	41
50,000–100,000	37	2	4	7	4	6	14
100,000 or more	18	—	—	3	2	—	13
Total	182	10	9	23	35	37	68
Europe except UK and Netherlands							
20,000–50,000	105	5	2	9	22	26	41
50,000–100,000	28	—	2	4	3	5	14
100,000 or more	15	—	—	2	2	—	11
Total	148	5	4	15	27	31	66

Sources: Calculations and estimates by the author; see the methodological appendix.
Note: In 1800 Europe (except Russia) probably had some 190–200 cities with populations of over 20,000 instead of the 182 reported above, but there is insufficient information on those missing cities to incorporate them in this table.

view of location clearly does not imply, however, that what Barel (1977) calls the "medieval urban system" remained intact. On the contrary, it is certain that this system, with its specific socioeconomic structure, disappeared, more or less rapidly and more or less completely depending on the region, under the impact of the changes that took place during the sixteenth and seventeenth centuries. Nor should the catastrophes associated with the Black Death be forgotten in the changing urban system.

Moreover, the industrialization of the United Kingdom dating from the second half of the eighteenth century and the late urban development of the Netherlands somewhat distort the overall picture. If these two countries are excluded, the role played by the urban structure of the Middle Ages stands out in even bolder relief. Only 3% of the cities with populations of 20,000 or more in 1800 had populations of less than 2,000 around 1300. In other words, probably 97%

of all cities outside Britain and the Netherlands with populations in excess of 20,000 at the start of the nineteenth century were already in existence about the start of the fourteenth.

Of the eighteen cities with populations of more than 100,000 in 1800, only three had less than 5,000 in 1300: Amsterdam, Copenhagen, and Madrid. Amsterdam remained a fishing village right up to the close of the twelfth century. But in 1204 Giesebrecht II of Amstel erected a castle there, and in 1240 his son constructed a dike (in Dutch, "dam"); and though the population had not yet reached 2,000, the city received its first charter in 1300. Copenhagen, meaning "merchants' harbor" (the original name was Havn, or "harbor"), was a fishing village until the middle of the thirteenth century. In 1167, however, the future Archbishop of Lund constructed a castle on the present site of the Christiansborg palace in the heart of the contemporary city, and merchants gradually began to take up residence in the town thereafter. But the city did not receive its first charter until 1250, and its growth was slow to start with. One interesting feature of Copenhagen was the fact that the charter of 1294 forbade the setting up of corporations, thereby entitling every citizen to obtain authorization to pursue the economic or commercial activity of his choice. And even when the authorities permitted the establishment of a few guilds, freedom of choice in employment by and large remained the rule. In contrast to Amsterdam and Copenhagen, Madrid may have already been a small town in antiquity. But between the retaking of the city by the Christians in 1083 and the decision of Philip II to make it his capital in 1560, even though it served as a hunting station for Henry IV and a temporary residence for Charles V, it had not yet become a city.

But Madrid and Copenhagen are not the only examples of capital cities whose populations were still extremely small around the start of the fourteenth century. Of the nineteen countries of some size and importance in Europe in the second half of the nineteenth century, there were nine in which the future capitals had only 5,000 inhabitants or less around 1300: besides Madrid and Copenhagen there were also Berlin, Berne, the Hague, Helsinki, Moscow, Oslo, and Stockholm. Rulers often chose not to establish the seat of government in the metropolis for fear of the potential for unrest any large city breeds. Moreover, the difference between a revolt in the countryside or a small town and insurrection in the capital is practically the difference between a jacquerie and a revolution.

Of the nineteen cities with populations of more than 20,000 at the start of the nineteenth century that at the start of the fourteenth either had not yet come into existence or had populations of less than 2,000, seven were in Britain, among them Belfast, Birmingham, Edinburgh, Liverpool, and Sheffield. Others that should be mentioned are Besançon and Brest in France and Altona and Mannheim in Germany.

Should one wish to take a look in the opposite direction to see how many of the cities already in existence around 1300 were still there in 1800, the results prove even more revealing. Indeed, while many cities were less highly populated in 1800 than in 1300, rare were those that had totally vanished. Of the 600-odd cities with populations of more than 5,000 Europe seems to have counted at the start of the fourteenth century, only about ten at most had disappeared or descended to the rank of villages by 1800. Some fifty to sixty of these cities, on the other hand, had smaller populations in 1800 than in 1300. To be sure, most of them remained genuine cities, almost all of them regaining or surpassing in the nineteenth century the highest population levels recorded at earlier points in time. But while this applies to most, it does not apply to all. About 40–50% of the cities whose populations went into decline between the fourteenth century and the beginning of the nineteenth century were in Italy or Spain, which reflects the general shift in the center of economic gravity in Europe.

And yet how many fascinating and often tragic destinies are hidden behind the bland statistics about those cities that went into decline between 1300 and 1800. Many of them, once great centers of influence and power, have become mere tourist sites, providing a delightful journey six, seven, or eight centuries back into the past, but deprived of their former might and glory. There is the story of Roskilde, for instance, until 1445 the capital of Denmark. At its height Roskilde was a wealthy city with a population of some 30,000–35,000. By 1800 it had dwindled to a village inhabited by 2,000 to 3,000 people, only to rise again later thanks to the railways. Or take the story of Tvorno or Preslav in Bulgaria, two cities brought low under Ottoman domination, that were at one period during the Middle Ages the successive capitals of a prestigious country.

The causes for decline were various, sometimes political or religious, sometimes military, and sometimes (see chapter 8 with reference to the Flemish cities) economic. And sometimes natural disasters had a hand in directing a city's fate. But whatever the particular causes, the list of cities whose populations fell sharply between 1300 and 1800 is highly evocative. To demonstrate this, I need only cite the cities that lost more than a third of their population during this period: Winchester in England; Erfurt, Goslar, Spires, Trier, and Worms in Germany; Gran, or Esztergom, in Hungary; Almeria, Burgos, Granada, Malaga, Medina del Campo, Salamanca, and Toledo in Spain; Bruges and Ypres in Belgium; Laon, Narbonne, Provins, and Valenciennes in France; Athens and Corinth in Greece; Arezzo, Cremona, Perugia, and Pisa in Italy; Curtea-de-Arges in Rumania; Visby in Sweden; and Skoplje in Yugoslavia.

But now I shall return to the cities of the Middle Ages and in particular to the surge of urban growth that began in the tenth century and became powerful during the eleventh century.

A Surge of Urban Growth without Increase in the
Level of Urbanization—And Yet . . .

Between the years 1000 and 1300, the number of cities with populations of more than 20,000 certainly doubled at least. And the same probably holds true for urban population as a whole, no matter what criteria we apply in determining it (see table 8.2). But while the overall urban population of Europe doubled, the level of urbanization remained much the same, passing from 9–11% in the year 1000 to 10.5–11.5% in 1300.

But does this really mean that Europe at the start of the fourteenth century was no more highly urbanized than at the start of the eleventh? Just as we must take pains to avoid certain traps laid for the unwary in absolute numbers, so must we also avoid those hidden in relative numbers. Although by around 1300 the proportion of Europeans living in cities had gone up hardly at all, in spatial terms urban density had doubled. Over an identical territory, the number of cities had doubled. Thus the peasantry, for instance, while still representing about 80–85% of the total population of Europe, was now in an entirely new situation. Around the year 1000 the city was for most rural people something far removed from their normal experience and was therefore often completely unknown to them. But things were different for the fourteenth-century peasant. The halving of the distance from the city often implied fundamental change. For in practical terms the obstacle posed by the length of the journey from one place to another is not linear. For example, if the journey to and from the city takes more than half a day and, a fortiori, if it takes more than a whole day, the trip is something highly exceptional. By halving the distance between town and country, then, one more than doubles the city's accessibility to the rural populace.

Nor was the change confined to the life of the peasantry; it also reached into the urban world. Since cities were now more densely distributed over the Continent, they lay nearer one another, which facilitated and consequently increased the intensity of contacts between them. Among other things this enhanced the chances of transmitting innovations of every kind from one part of Europe to another.

Another significant change was the general increase in the size of cities. Certainly chiefly owing to its political fragmentation, fourteenth-century Europe did not yet possess any very great cities. Around 1300 the largest city was Paris, capital of the most heavily populated European country. At this time, France had a little more than a fifth of the population of the entire continent, and Paris itself contained 180,000–220,000 people. The second largest city, with a population of 150,000, was Granada. But since the Spanish armies did not enter the city until 1492, Granada remained at mid-century the last bastion of Muslim Spain and does not therefore offer a true indication of how things stood in Europe. The three other large cities of this period were Italian: Venice, Milan, and Genoa, each with a population of around 100,000. It will be noted, moreover, that China had at least four cities with populations in excess of 300,000 at this time; and nearer Europe, Cairo had a population of 400,000 and Fez of 200,000.

The absence of very large cities nevertheless did not entail the absence of change in the urban structure of Europe with regard to size. Around the year 1000 Europe counted only three cities with populations of more than 50,000: Cordoba, Seville, and Palermo, none of which was really a part of European culture. By around 1300, on the other hand, there were thirteen such cities. Whereas in the year 1000 there was only one city with a population of more than 100,000—Cordoba—there were five in 1300. Three were in Italy, one in France, and only the last, Granada, still belonged to the Muslim world. And if Russia were included, I would have to add another city to this list—Sarai. Like Granada, however, Sarai was a Muslim rather than a truly European city.

But the change brought about in the urban structure of Europe with regard to size quite naturally leads me to consider the geographical component of this surge of urban growth. For as the preceding remarks already suggest, pronounced differences arose at the regional level.

The Geographical Component in the Surge of Urban Growth (1000–1300)

While the number of cities with populations of more than 20,000 in Europe as a whole roughly doubled between 1000 and 1300, in the western part of continental Europe (Germany, Belgium, the Scandinavian countries, and France) it tripled. The increase was also very rapid in Italy (see table 10.2). Another country in which events moved very rapidly (but for which the data are highly unreliable) is Russia, to which I shall return later. The absence around 1300 of large cities (in this case cities with populations of more than 20,000) in countries like the Netherlands and Switzerland, however, does not imply the absence of a process of urbanization. In the Netherlands, for example, around the year 1300 there were at least four cities of more than 10,000 people, as against none around the year 1000. Similarly, in Switzerland around the year 1000, the population of all cities appears to have been less than 10,000, while around 1300 it most likely exceeded 35,000.

One region in which the urban evolution was unusual was the Balkans. As was the case for Spain between the eighth and thirteenth centuries, the Balkans between the end of the fourteenth and the beginning of the nineteenth centuries did not really participate in the main currents of European culture, belonging rather to the Ottoman

TABLE 10.2   Growth of the Number of Cities with Populations of
20,000 or More
(1000–1500)

	1000	1300	1500
Austria-Hungary	0	2	3
Balkans	(7)	(9)	(10)
Belgium	0	5	6
France	7	21	21
Germany	4	10	13
Italy	10	24	21
Netherlands	0	0	0
Portugal	0	1	1
Scandinavia	0	1	1
Spain	10	17	17
Switzerland	0	0	0
United Kingdom	1	2	2
Europe	39	92	95
Russia	(4)	(11)	(12)
Europe as a whole	43	103	107

Sources: Calculations and estimates by the author; see the methodological appendix.
Note: The territorial limits of these countries are those in effect at the end of the 19th century.
The figures in parentheses have a much wider margin of error than the other data. The figures are approximate, especially for the year 1000.

Empire. Even before this time, however, the urban life of the Balkan countries had already taken a turn different from that observed elsewhere in the Continent. Though the data are fairly incomplete, it seems that between the eleventh and fourteenth centuries the growth of cities was much more limited in this region than in the rest of Europe.

At the other end of the Continent, Ireland also had an urban history different from that of the rest of Europe, despite the many points of contact through which it participated in the general current of European life. The spread of Christianity played a driving role in the initial phase of the urbanization of Ireland. Most local historians trace the foundation of their cities back to Saint Patrick. And in many cases they have ample justification for this. In the twelfth century, at a time when Europe as a whole was recovering from the period of the Viking raids, Ireland suffered an Anglo-Norman invasion that led to the decline of numerous cities, most notably Armagh, a city supposed to have been founded by Saint Patrick, in which a synod was held as early as 448. Armagh had for centuries been a center of religion and education. Its college enjoyed such renown that among its 7,000 students a high proportion of foreigners was to be found, and this at a time when travel was extremely difficult. After the Anglo-Norman conquest, however, the city, deserted by its bishop, progressively fell into decay and was for hundreds of years nothing more than an "insignificant collection of cabins with a dilapidated cathedral." Under pressure from various archbishops, Armagh was reconstructed during the second half of the eighteenth century and became the "best built and the most respected town in the country" (*Encyclopedia Britannica*, 1926).

The rapid increase in the number of cities in Italy obviously obscures the true dimensions of urban expansion in this country. Since in Italy the urban network had been largely in place since the eleventh century, most of the growth was in the population of existing cities. Between 1000 and 1300, the population of Venice rose from 45,000 to 110,000, that of Genoa from 15,000 to 100,000, that of Milan from 30,000 to 100,000, that of Florence from 13,000 to 95,000, that of Pisa from 9,000 to 38,000, and that of Ferrara from 12,000 to 36,000. Bologna and Messina, large market towns or villages around the year 1000, by about 1300 had populations of 40,000 and 30,000, respectively.

The rapid growth of the Italian trade centers led to a very high level of urbanization. Defining as urban any agglomeration with a population of at least 5,000, Italy, with 23–25 cities of more than 20,000 people, around the start of the fourteenth century probably had an urban population on the order of 1.6–1.8 million. This represented 15–16% of the total population, as compared with 8% in the rest of Europe. It is unlikely that this marked difference may entirely be explained by a difference in levels of agricultural productivity. Certainly, this factor had a hand in it, but commercial expansion produced most of the economic resources needed for the dramatic rise in the population of Italian cities.

As for the role of commerce in the cities of Italy, I have given particular emphasis in previous chapters to international trade. This does not mean, however, that Italian cities did not have a more regional commercial function. On the contrary, it has been estimated, for example, that the trade of Venice with Lombardy alone generated sufficient revenue to support several thousand people. It is possible, moreover, as is the case today, that Italian cities had a greater proportion of farmers and farm laborers than cities in other countries. If true, this would have reduced the size of the likely deficit of cereals that the most heavily urbanized regions of Italy must have known.

But even in the case of Italy, its prodigious urban expansion during this period notwithstanding, it should not be forgotten how individual is each city's destiny. During this period of general urban growth, some cities stagnated or went into decline. In 1160, for example, Palermo, with its population of some 150,000, was still the largest city in Italy; indeed, with Seville, it was one of the two largest cities in Europe. By the start of the fourteenth century, however, it no longer had a population of more than some 50,000. But like Seville, Palermo in 1160 was not a truly European city. Occupied by the Saracens in 835, it became a Muslim capital, and its eventual decline stemmed from the stormy political and military events following its return to Christian Europe in 1062. Nor should it be forgotten that Christian Europe was at this time less developed economically than the Muslim world.

Palermo and Salerno: two cities whose names are so close, and whose destinies, too, were nearly parallel (a godsend for cabalists). But though their histories were similar with respect to the hazards each had to undergo, the actors responsible for their initial successes and ultimate falls were very different. Salerno, while managing to resist Saracen attack, was taken by the Normans in 1075; they made this ancient city the capital of Norman southern Italy. The city prospered, probably reaching a population of 50,000 after the second half of the eleventh century. Palermo's return (in 1071) to the fold of Christianity, however, eventually cost Salerno its role as capital. Moreover, Salerno came under attack once more in 1194, and the sacking (by Henry VI of Germany) of the city proved almost fatal to it. Salerno succeeded in repopulating itself only with great difficulty, and had barely 3,000–4,000 inhabitants by the middle of the fifteenth century.

The population of Rome continued to stagnate, remaining at about 35,000 throughout the period. And it is worth recalling in this context the case of Amalfi. Amalfi's population probably reached 70,000 during the tenth century, but it fell to 10,000–15,000 by about the start of the fourteenth. All of this induces me to wonder about the connection between such individual urban histories and the economy—a connection at the very heart of this book. What exactly were the economic components of the various evolutions of the various cities? But in order to come to effective terms with this question (see chapter 12), it is first necessary to ask what types of cities there were during this period.

From the Fortified Castle to the Burg, from the Burg to the New Burg, from the New Burg to the Merchant's Agglomeration, from the Merchant's Agglomeration . . .

At the start of the fourteenth century, Europe (except Russia) had some 220–260 cities with populations of more than 10,000, 340–370 with populations of 5,000–10,000, and 900–1,100 with populations of 2,000–5,000. In the context of the times, a great number of towns with populations of 2,000–5,000 would have counted as genuine cities.

There were, then, some 1,400–1,500 cities in fourteenth-century Europe. These cities were far from uniform, however, not only with regard to size, but with regard to their functions as well. Both their size and their functions generally resulted from a very slow process of evolution—a process that appears rapid to us today only because of the distance from which we look back upon it. Pirenne (1914) gives this summary of the evolution of cities in medieval Europe:

> Western Europe at this time [the beginning of the tenth century] was covered with fortified castles erected by the feudal princes to provide shelter for their men. These castles or, to use the term by which they are habitually known, these "burgs" usually consisted of a rampart of earth or stone encircled by a moat, with gates let in at various points. The laborers in the surrounding territory were requisitioned for its construction and maintenance. Inside, a garrison of knights was stationed at a fixed post. A keep served as a dwelling place for the local lord; a church housed the canons who saw to the religious needs of the community; finally, barns and granaries received the grain, smoked meats and rents and taxes of all sorts levied upon the domainal peasantry in order to assure supplies of food for the garrison and for the people who in times of danger would crowd inside the castle walls with their livestock. Thus, the lay burg, like the ecclesiastical city, was supported by the land. They had no economic activity of their own. Both were wholly consonant with an agrarian civilization: far from opposing it, one could claim that they provided for its defence.

On the basis of the data assembled by Le Goff (1980), in the region of what is today France and Belgium more than twenty of those burgs emerged between 750 and 1000 and almost seventy in the eleventh century. And as is always the case, the spatial diffusion was unequal: the northern part was more affected.

Let us return to Pirenne, for his description holds good:

> As trade began to recover, however, it did not take long for these burgs to undergo a profound change in character; indeed, the first symptoms of this change can be detected during the second half of the tenth century. The itinerant way of life led by the merchants, the risks of every kind to which they were exposed at a time when pillage constituted one of the basic means of existence for the minor nobility, drove them from the first to seek out the shelter of the walled enclosures placed at intervals along the rivers and natural roadways they traveled. During the summer these enclosures served as trading posts and during the harsh season as wintering places. In this way, the best situated of these enclosures—those at the head of an estuary or creek,

at the confluence of two rivers, or at the point where
a watercourse became unnavigable and the cargoes
of the boats had to be unloaded before proceeding
further—evolved as sites of passage and sojourn for
the merchants and their merchandise. . . . The newcomers grew more and more numerous and cum-
bersome as traffic grew heavier, however, and the
towns and burgs soon ceased to afford enough room
to accommodate their swelling ranks. The merchants
were obliged to overflow the boundaries of the old
burg and to establish alongside it a new one or, to
use an expression that denotes exactly what is involved, a *faubourg*, deriving from the Latin *foris-
burgus*, meaning the "outer burg." In this way were
born, beside the ecclesiastical cities and feudal fortresses, a species of mercantile agglomeration in
which the inhabitants engaged in a way of life in
complete contrast with that led by the inhabitants of
the inner city.

And these new burgs were in a sense the prototype of the dynamic
mercantile cities of the Western world and the shantytowns of the
Third World: "More than the others, they were the offspring of the
new age: born of the economic upsurge, of the broadening of horizons, they welcomed immigrants from further afield, and money
played a greater role here than elsewhere. Fortunes were made and
unmade here more rapidly, and disorderly hovels surrounded the
houses—some of them already built of stone—belonging to those
who had succeded. Here assuredly lived both the most wretched and
the most audacious of people" (Chedeville, 1980). From this it is but a
short step to the city.

To close the description of this progressive change, let me quote Le
Goff (1980), who knows the Middle Ages so well:

The city was first of all a society teeming with life,
concentrated in a little space amid vast tracts of
thinly-inhabited land. Next it was a place of production and exchange, where crafts and commerce
mingled, fueled by a monetary economy. It was also
the center of a unique system of values from which
emerged the laborious and creative work ethic, the
taste for trade and money, an appetite for luxury, a
sense of beauty. Further, it was a systematic way of
organizing a space enclosed by walls and bristling
with towers, a space into which one entered through
gates and about which one travelled through streets
and squares.

As will be gathered from this account, the process of differentiation unfolded very gradually. I shall try to distribute the 1,400–1,500 cities of fourteenth-century Europe (except Russia) according to an approximate classification of their functions. The classification, involving descriptions of the dominant economic functions of cities, is to some extent more valid for the fifteenth century than for the beginning of the fourteenth, on which for statistical reasons this classification is based. As has been seen, the Black Death, while it caused dramatic short-term changes in population, did not constitute a break in the overall evolution of the economic system. In short, this description is valid for the last century and a half of the Middle Ages and the first years of the Renaissance.

Small Towns with Highly Local Functions

The great number of cities and towns leads me to define a first urban category, or type: the many very small towns of between 2,000–4,000 and 6,000 people—towns whose functions were in almost every instance highly localized. At once seat of one or more churches and site of the local market, such a small town housed a part of the artisanry whose products were destined for consumption by the neighboring rural people. Nor should one forget the inns, the apothecary shops, or the barbers, the latter performing a number of medical functions in addition to their obvious function. Out of a total of about 1,450 cities, some 900–950, representing more than 60% of the total, belonged to this category. There were, however, certain exceptional cases in which towns of 3,000–4,000 inhabitants had attributes corresponding to one of the other categories outlined below. This is particularly true of certain small cities that were sites of international fairs— for example, Geneva, which around 1300 had only 4,000 inhabitants, but was already the location of an international fair.

Regional Centers

Immediately above this first level, there were what might best be termed "regional centers." These were generally towns of somewhat more substantial size that, in addition to the functions of the very small towns just described, performed other more various and sophisticated functions. The cities and towns in this category had populations of 4,000–6,000 at one end of the scale and 8,000–12,000 at the other. The number of towns that performed a regional function can be estimated as around 300–330.

Owing to their larger size, these regional centers required a certain number of specifically urban forms of employment—in other words, as the definition of this concept at the end of chapter 9 indicates, forms of employment created by the urban way of life as such. In the context of the Middle Ages this essentially meant public administration, the police, street cleaning, and in most cases the construction and maintenance of the surrounding walls, pales, and moats. Besides these specifically urban employments, however, the city had crafts more elaborate than those of the smaller towns, and also a number of commercial functions involving goods not produced locally, but redistributed by the traders and peddlers living in these regional centers. In this class of cities were the traders whose business it was to buy up the local agricultural surplus and export it to larger cities and abroad. And here lived the administrators responsible for collecting taxes.

As for religious affairs, regional centers were often episcopal sees. I have already noted how in many instances bishops played a vital role in assuring the survival and development of certain cities, especially those belonging to this category. But the presence of a bishop also tended to be associated, both directly and indirectly, with specific kinds of employment. Education was one of the functions performed by regional centers. As a rule these towns did not have universities, but rather what corresponded to present-day primary schools, and occasionally what today would be considered secondary schools. The universities, on the other hand, gravitated mainly toward cities of more substantial size, with larger, more highly developed infrastructures. I shall return to this aspect of the urban scene toward the end of this chapter.

Finally, the relatively high income level of a segment of the population of these regional centers led to a large class of domestic servants. This class, it may be recalled, accounted for a very large fraction of overall urban employment in traditional societies. Thus in Geneva the domestic class represented roughly 20% of the total population, and nearly 50% of the female working population. The proportion was even higher in Coventry, where at the start of the sixteenth century a quarter of all working people were engaged as servants, a percentage also found in fifteenth-century Reims.

A very geat majority of these urban domestic servants came from the neighboring countryside and thus participated in the migratory influx by which the city made up its deficit in people and in food (see chapter 12). In the French cities of the seventeenth and eighteenth centuries, domestic servants represented 7–14% of the total population, and thus 15–30% of the labor force. As Gutton (1981) observes, "drawing on villages for domestic servants was for city dwellers one of the many forms by which the cities dominated the countryside." Moreover, the important place domestic servants occupied in traditional cities—a place they continued to occupy up to the first stages of the Industrial Revolution—applied to non-European Western societies as well. In Canada at the start of the nineteenth century, domestic servants represented some 5–8 % of the total urban population (Lacelle, 1982), and thus some 10–17% of the labor force. To be sure, as the analysis of census records of the nineteenth century demonstrates, the dividing line between domestic service and unskilled labor is very often blurred. And what Garden (1975) observes concerning the marginal difference between a female servant and a female worker in the silk industry of eighteenth-century Lyons applies equally well to many other sectors and to many other periods.

And as in smaller towns, there existed among these intermediate-sized cities a certain number whose functions were those generally belonging to larger cities. It is to these larger cities that I shall now turn.

Large Cities

The remaining 210-odd cities generally had populations in excess of 8,000–12,000, which in the context of the times made them large cities. These cities may be divided into three main groups. Needless to say, this does not rule out the possibility that some cities belonged to several groups at once, every system of classification being to some degree arbitrary. These last three types of city were:
1. Commercial cities proper, that is, those cities in which international trade played a decisive part
2. Industrial cities, that is, those cities exporting manufactured goods over a very wide area
3. Administrative cities, that is, those cities that were either national or regional capitals

Commercial Cities

Many of the commercial cities of the Middle Ages were city-states which have already been discussed. I shall begin with the city-states of Italy.

Practically all of the large cities of the Italian peninsula fell into the category of commercial cities, since international trade played a decisive role in almost every one of them. But the kind of international trade in question was one that today retains only a marginal significance. Like the Phoenician cities before them and the Dutch cities after them, the Italian cities before anything else were intermediaries between the West and the East. Venice, Pisa, and Genoa imported spices, dyes, silks, and other goods of Middle Eastern and Eastern origin generally aimed not only at the regional market, nor even simply at the Italian market, but at a large part of Europe. And the products the Italian cities exported to the Middle East came not only from Italy, but also from the rest of Europe. The principal goods exported by Europe during this period were precious metals, woolen goods, and raw materials, especially wood. Slaves, which had once represented a very sizable fraction of the flow of goods to the Middle East, by this stage occupied only a marginal place in the pattern of exchange.

But elsewhere in Europe at this time, another important trade center had come into existence, one also directly related to the class of maritime commercial cities: the Hanseatic League. The foundation of the Hanseatic League can be traced back to the accord signed in 1241 between the cities of Lübeck and Hamburg with the object of protecting the passage between the Baltic Sea and the North Sea. These two cities retained their predominance in the League, which numbered a further twenty cities, most of which figured among the largest German towns of the period. Among them were Bremen, Cologne, and Rostock. In addition to their commercial activities the Hanseatic cities, taking advantage of the abundance of wood found in this part of Europe, engaged in shipbuilding. In the cities of the Hanseatic League were found the same characteristically urban secondary effects that played so large a role in the life of the Italian cities. Just as Venetian industry, resulting from local needs generated by the profits from international trade, in turn contributed increasingly to augmenting the city's exports, so too, shipbuilding served to amplify the impact of foreign trade on the cities of the league.

Beside these two maritime poles, mention should also be made of several isolated maritime commercial cities that played an analogous role in France, Spain, and England: Marseilles, Montpellier, Barcelona, Bristol, among others. And to this class of maritime commercial cities may be added a number of towns that served in some of the larger regions as ports of exit for regional surpluses: Bordeaux for wine, the English ports for wool, Bruges for Flanders cloth, and so on.

And then, last but not least, one should recall the commercial cities of the continental interior: cities that did much to further overland trade between northern and southern Europe. In this category must notably be placed Chalon-sur-Saône, Lyons, Provins, Troyes, Geneva, Milan, Frankfurt, and Leipzig. Not only did these cities derive their wealth from internal European trade, they also served as relay stations in the flow of trade with the rest of the world. And in this system of relays the Italian merchants had a decisive hand.

Industrial Cities

Industrialization did not begin to play a key role in the life of European cities until the nineteenth century, when it made a decisive contribution to the surge of urban growth in the countries of the developed world. One must not on this account neglect its impact on urban life in the Middle Ages. But it may perhaps be as well first to define industrial city. A definition is all the more important inasmuch as industrial activity ultimately lies at the very heart of urbanism. By industrial city, we mean one in which industrial activity outweighs all other factors and is essentially aimed at the production of goods intended for exportation to regions lying beyond the city's traditional sphere of attraction. To use a more technical language, an industrial city is one in which the basic functions, as defined in chapter 9, predominate over others and relate chiefly to manufacturing.

The prototype for this kind of city is provided by Ypres, Ghent, and the Flemish textile towns generally. Within a radius of less than thirty kilometers there were three cities, the two just mentioned and Bruges, with a combined population of 220,000 around the middle of the fourteenth century, in which most economic activity centered on textile production, the raw materials coming from abroad and the finished products being sent back abroad. This region supplied some part of the woolen goods not only for the upper classes of Europe, but also for the rest of the world. The subsequent decline of these cities was the result of changes in the economic policies of England aimed specifically at wresting control of the textile market from them (see chapter 8).

Industrial concentration of this kind was unique in medieval Europe. The concentration of mining towns in southern Germany, for example, was much lighter. Still, albeit on a more limited scale, a number of European cities performed analogous functions. To name only a few: Saint Gall in Switzerland exported linen; Liège in Belgium exported arms; Florence in Italy exported textiles; Leyden in the Netherlands exported black broadcloth; and Delft, also in the Netherlands, exported earthenware.

Administrative Cities

The most important administrative cities were capital cities. At the end of the Middle Ages capital cities predominated among the largest cities in Europe (I refer here to the capitals of that period). Paris, for example, was the largest city in Europe, while London was the largest city in England, and Lisbon the largest in Portugal. But perhaps one ought rather to speak in this context of royal cities; for it was the court as much as the administration that fostered the growth of these cities. Later, for political reasons, the courts of Europe increasingly established themselves at some distance from the capitals.

In analyzing the development of these capital cities of the various centers of regional administration, one should not overlook the part played by garrisons. Indeed, there were many instances in which cities owed their birth to this military presence, not only under the Roman Empire, but during the Middle Ages as well. This brings me back to the remark with which I opened this discussion. While it may happen that in many cities one particular function sets the tone for all the others, in the majority of cases there are several such functions. Among these, where the great cities of the Middle Ages are concerned, one should bear in mind the universities. For the thirteenth and fourteenth centuries saw the first great flowering of the European universities, and the university is above all an urban phenomenon.

Cities and Universities

The university was, in fact, urban, and much more so than one might imagine. For while it is fairly clear that, by and large, universities originally flourished in cities (adding to the list of basic urban functions), one tends to forget that by the close of the fifteenth century there were universities in almost all of the larger cities of Europe. As Barel (1977) notes, "the medieval university stood at the crossroads between the Church, the great political power centers, and the urban system, and used its strategic position to secure at least partial self-determination, perhaps becoming in this way a subsystem on its own." And a very widespread urban subsystem at that, since according to my calculations Europe counted before the end of the fifteenth century some 70 to 73 cities with one or more universities. And even before the end of the fourteenth century there were already some 35–37 such cities.

But universities also qualify as urban by reason of their correlation with the size of cities. I looked into the sizes of various cities at the time of the foundation of their first university. I did this analysis for the period leading up to the year 1500, covering all universities founded before this date. Of the seventy cities I was able to include in this census, around 85–90% had populations of more than 5,000 when their university was first established. More important still, about 75% of these university towns had populations of more than 10,000 when their first university was founded. The distribution was as follows: 13% had populations of less than 5,000; 13% had 5,000–10,000; 37% 10,000–20,000; 14% 20,000–30,000; and 23% populations of more than 30,000. To put the matter in another light, by around 1500 roughly one half of all the cities in Europe (except Russia) with populations of more than 20,000 had one or more universities.

The prestige of the university should not, however, lead one to forget the rest of education. And in this area the tenth and eleventh centuries constitute a decisive turning point. In his study of schools and learning in the High Middle Ages, P. Riché (1979) opens his chapter on urban schools with this statement: "The monastic community represents the past, the city, the future." He shows very clearly how a system of education gradually came into place in the West largely in response to the demand developing at this time in the cities.

The Medieval City: A School of Democracy?

A discussion of medieval education may easily induce one to pass on to another social function of the cities of the European Middle Ages: that of "school of democracy." Indeed, during this period, a very great number of cities had received or had or seized on their own account a real autonomy. These cities became free worlds in which relatively democratic forms of government were established. And these worlds were, in fact, both very free and highly democratic compared with rural society, which was dominated by serfdom and feudalism. Still, however fascinating this aspect of medieval urban life may be, its treatment would oblige me to overrun the scope not only of this book, but also of my personal competence: the great interest and intrinsic significance of this subject are no excuse for amateurism. The one matter I cannot pass over in silence is the considerable role played by the guilds both in the movement toward independence among medieval cities and also in economic affairs. With regard to economic affairs, however, it is not at all certain that the contribution of guilds was on the whole positive or beneficial.

Nevertheless, though the system of guilds may have had a detrimental impact on the development of some cities by introducing a measure of inflexibility into the economy, the fact remains that the independence of medieval cities unquestionably exerted an influence more positive than negative on economic life. An independent city can more readily redirect its economic policies, take initiatives designed to stimulate flagging economic activity, attract skilled craftsmen and businessmen, and so on. But here as in all other facets of economic life, a place must be set aside for chance. And indeed, how many choices, whether wise or unfortunate, are fundamentally owed to mere luck.

And What of Distant Russia?

Russia was distant from Europe not only because of its distance from the rest of Europe, but also because of the scarcity of studies (at least available studies) concerning events there. In Russia there was a definite delay in the emergence of a genuine urban way of life, a delay resulting mainly from the absence of Roman colonization, which left a profound mark on the rest of the Continent (see chapters 5 and 7). All of this and especially the highly unreliable character of the numerical data induce me to separate medieval Russia from the rest of Europe.

But during the medieval period, distant Russia still appears to have had a history in some ways similar to that of Europe as a whole. Tikhomirov (1959) concludes his review (somewhat out of date) of research on the Russian cities of the Middle Ages by observing that, while they dated from high antiquity, they did not truly come into their own as centers of industry and trade until between the tenth and twelfth centuries. The term "trade" should not lead one astray, however: with the exception chiefly of Novgorod, Tver, and Smolensk, the spheres of influence of the cities of Russia remained chiefly local, and very few cities participated in international trade. This does not mean that before that period there was a total absence of commercial relations. The discoveries in the Dnieper basin of numerous hiding places of Roman coins of the second century to the fourth century permits Russian historians to conclude that there was trade (Rybakov, 1983). But this trade was probably even smaller in scale than that in the tenth century to the twelfth century.

Another difference lay in the more limited role played by guilds. Though guilds did exist in some Russian cities, they had no power comparable to that of those of Western Europe. This had beneficial effects in some areas, making it possible for foreign merchants and craftsmen to establish themselves in Russian cities. Nevertheless, as Langer (1976) remarks, "since the bulk of the Russian peasantry was at that time not enserfed, the Russian town was not the island of freedom in the sea of serfdom that the town was in the West." But many cities enjoyed a measure of freedom, if not a relatively wide margin of independence.

The revolt of Kiev in 1068 marked a turning point in the evolution toward this kind of independence. Among the larger cities in Russia at the start of the fourteenth century (with the borders those of 1913) were (in addition to Kiev) Smolensk, Ryazan, Novgorod, Polotsk, Gorodno, Vilna, the two cities of Vladimir, Galich, Pskov, Chernigov, Pereslavl, and Tver. But large, here, is a relative term, since Novgorod, for example, apparently the largest of the Russian cities, had by the year 1300 a population of only some 30,000–40,000. Vladimir, the capital between 1157 and 1328, had perhaps 30,000, a population Kiev may also have reached before its destruction by the Mongols in 1240. During the fourteenth century there were in all perhaps eight to ten, but certainly not as many as twelve, cities with populations of more than 20,000, and none of these reached the 50,000 mark. At the same period Europe, whose population was only four to five times larger, had some ninety to ninety-five cities with populations of over 20,000, of which twelve exceeded 50,000. Finally, even as late as the close of the fifteenth century there were still no universities, the first being founded in 1578 at Vilna in Lithuania, followed in 1775 by the University of Moscow. Europe at the end of the fifteenth century had some seventy to seventy-three university towns.

This delay in the start of Russian urban history is explained not only by the late emergence of urbanism in Russia, but also by the troubled character of the general history of the country. The Mongol invasions, which began in 1237, brought Russia under direct or indirect domination by the Golden Horde for nearly two centuries. And while the Tartar raids never had the devastating impact tradition has given them, they nonetheless profoundly disturbed the economic life of the country, urban as well as rural. Yet it was during this same period that Moscow emerged as the dominant urban center. Practically nonexistent up to the middle of the twelfth century, the city probably surpassed a population of 20,000–30,000 around the middle of the fourteenth century, exceeding 35,000 at the end of the fifteenth century. In any case, to the various invasions must further be added the Black Death (see below) and the civil wars that marked the years 1425–1462, so that the return to a normal life did not take place until the end of the fifteenth century. Even then the respite was but short-lived, the nefarious reign of Ivan the Terrible (1533–1584) bringing with it a dramatic fall in the population of certain cities. Thus it was that Novgorod, Kolomna, and Mozhaisk, for example, lost 80–90% of their populations at this time.

The Black Death: A Staggering Demographic Catastrophe from Which the Cities Recovered Quickly

Asia, from which Europe had already begun to borrow a great many technological innovations by the tenth century, also brought it the worst demographic catastrophe of all time—the Black Death. Did the Black Death come from India, from China, or, as seems most likely, from Central Asia? This will remain for some time a question without an answer. What "seems to be in no doubt, however, is that this new epidemic cycle was of Asiatic origin" (Biraben, 1975). And what is also in no doubt is that by the month of September 1347 the plague had reached southern Italy. In November it was in Marseilles, and by the end of the year 1348, Italy, France, Germany, Austria, and England were heavily afflicted, not to mention eastern Russia, first affected by 1346. The rest of Europe followed in 1349, with the exception of western Russia, which escaped contagion until 1352. Though certainly rapid from a historical point of view, in contemporary terms the spread of the plague was slow, conforming to the pace of the travellers who carried it. According to Biraben's calculations, based on fifteen cases of the spread of infection, there was an average speed of 2.4 kilometers per day (with a maximum of 3–4 kilometers and a minimum of 1 kilometer per day). The Black Death continued to ravage Europe during the next fifteen years, and severe epidemics broke out in 1361, 1373, and 1380 (see chapter 8).

According to recent estimates, between 1340 and 1400 the plague and the political and ecological disturbances associated with it reduced the population of Europe (except Russia) by 25–33%; and if one takes the average of the two extreme estimates, European population fell from 79 million in 1340 to 56 million in 1400. It is traditionally held that the town was more gravely affected than the country. This is possible. But what is certain is that the cities recovered very quickly.

Indeed, on the basis of my data bank, I compared estimates of the population of European cities between 1300 and 1400. This proved possible for 101 cities, and the surprising result was that they had even larger populations around 1400 than they did around 1300—3.11 and 2.97 million respectively. In the main, the larger cities recovered more completely than the smaller ones. It is conceivable that the urban universe comprising my sample contains a bias favoring a slightly higher number of omissions of the cities that suffered most heavily from the plague. For by the end of the period covered in my analysis, such cities may have become so small that, in the absence of reliable information, it was not possible to include them in the sample. Furthermore, around 1340, on the eve of the first epidemic outbreak of the plague, the population of the cities studied was perhaps a little greater than in 1300, though this remains to be proven one way or the other. Still, if population did in fact rise between 1300 and 1340, the increase could only have been very modest since the total population of Europe grew by no more than 4–6%, the period offering an unfavorable climate for economic progress. Thus once I have eliminated these sources of bias, I find between 1340 and 1400 either demographic stability or at most (by systematically adjusting my figures in order to prevent a disguised fall in population from remaining hidden in my data), a decline of 5–10%. But even in the latter event, so long as the estimates of total population remain within the same limits, this decline must be compared with the fall of 27–35% in the rural population. And while this begs the question of whether I ought to revise the figures for rural population, I have been unable to uncover any fresh evidence justifying such a revision.

It seems that, as usual, recent information regarding the fate of cities during this period is very sound. The existing demographic studies show that the rate of natural recuperation was very rapid, and that the towns also managed to draw heavily on the population of the countryside. This recovery was all the easier since in the wake of the fall in population food surpluses grew substantially, a fact confirmed by the peak reached at this time in real income.

As the history of a certain number of cities attests (Higounet-Nadal, 1980), moreover, one cannot rule out the possibility that the decline in urban population began before the full force of the plague made itself felt in the cities. This does not cast doubt on the heavy and painful cost of the plague in all of the cities of Europe (and probably Asia and the Middle East as well). But it does oblige one to wonder whether there may not have been a substratum to the plague. In particular, as I noted earlier, there was a series of poor harvests in the years leading up to the first outbreak of the plague. And given that the urban growth of the three centuries preceding the plague had brought the level of urbanization in Europe as a whole to a point never recorded before, it may well be that the cities had come to draw too heavily on rural resources. Indeed it is possible, and even probable, that the rate of growth in urban population had exceeded that of growth in agricultural productivity, leading to a decrease in the amount of food available per capita. But though this may be probable, given the lack of data it remains very difficult, if not impossible, to prove that it it was in fact the case.

11 European Cities from the Sixteenth Century to the Eighteenth Century □

The Break with the Past at the Beginning of the Sixteenth Century

In the space of a few decades between 1490 and 1530, Europe underwent a profound change in its relations with the rest of the world. The consequences of this change were to prove considerable, not only with regard to the structure of trade and the stock of precious metals in Europe, but also with regard to the rest of the world, certain parts of which began at this time the slide toward an economic system that would later result in underdevelopment. Sixteenth-century Europe was about to join that long line of colonial powers in which her predecessors (in reverse historical order) were the Ottoman, Arab, and Roman empires. The only difference, but one heavy with implications, lay in the Industrial Revolution that touched certain of the European metropolises during the eighteenth and nineteenth centuries. For the Industrial Revolution made possible an intensification of economic relations to levels unknown until then and contributed to the diffusion throughout the world of medical practices that in time led to an unprecedented fall in mortality rates, leading in turn to an equally unprecedented demographic explosion.

As early as the 1420s, efforts intensified to explore the Atlantic and consequently Africa as well. Prince Henry of Portugal, called the Navigator, created at Sagres a veritable NASA of maritime exploration in which he assembled the most skillful seamen, navigators, and geographers of the day (see chapter 8). Italy had preceded Portugal in attempts at exploration, and Spain too was soon to take part in the enterprise. Alongside religious motives, whose role in the voyage of exploration should not be overlooked, one major objective underlay all of these efforts: the discovery of a maritime route to Asia permitting direct access to the coveted spice and calico markets of the East. For both the profits from trade with these markets and the scale of European access to them had been reduced both by the fees and duties charged by the middlemen of the Middle East and by the high cost of overland transportation.

At the close of the fifteenth century these efforts bore fruit: on 28 May 1498, having rounded Africa, Vasco da Gama arrived in an Indian port. But six years earlier, in 1492, this quest of a sea route to Asia had led to another, wholly unexpected discovery that would ultimately prove of even greater consequence: America. It matters little that Columbus's discovery of America was not really the first contact made by Europeans with the New World; the fact remains that it was the first to lead to the establishment of lasting relations between the Old World and the New World. As Braudel so justly stresses, the truly historic event is the one that has consequences. Thus the discoveries made by the Vikings (not to mention the Phoenicians) and even their likely settlement in a few isolated regions of North America do not constitute an important historical event, because they produced no significant consequences and remained unknown to the rest of Europe.

I shall return later (in part 4) to the impact these discoveries had on non-European societies. Here it is their impact on Europe itself that demands our attention: their very substantial impact on the economy and above all on urbanization. There is no doubt that together with the Industrial Revolution, the Black Death, Roman colonization, and the Neolithic revolution, the break with the past that took place in the sixteenth century represents one of the four or five most decisive socioeconomic events in the entire history of Europe—all the more so, indeed, inasmuch as these geographical discoveries took place in the context of that vast upheaval of European civilization that was the Renaissance.

A New Surge of Urbanization

By the beginning of the sixteenth century Europe had returned to the level of urbanization and population reached around 1340, before the series of catastrophes ushered in by the first outbreak of the great plague (see chapter 10). Now, despite a new increase in the size of the overall population of the Continent, which increased by roughly 33–40% between the start of the sixteenth century and the close of the seventeenth century, there was a perceptible rise in the proportion of urban population to total population, indicating a fresh, substantial surge of urban growth. In Europe (except Russia), urban population, defined as the population of all towns with populations of five thousand or more, went up from 10–11.5% in 1500 to 12–13% in 1700 (see table 11.1). The number of people living in cities grew by about 55% and the number of cities by some 37%. Thus even if the level of urbanization overall increased only slightly (0.5–1 point, or by roughly 15%), urban density rose strongly in spatial terms.

If one compares the pace of this new surge of urban growth with that of the Middle Ages, a certain similarity may be seen in the lev-

TABLE 11.1 Growth of the Urban Population and Levels of
Urbanization in Europe (except Russia)
(1300–1750)

	Total Population (millions)	Urban Population		Level of Urbanization	
		Millions	Annual Variation (%)	% of Total Population	Annual Variation (%)
1300	75	7.9		10.4	
1500	76	8.2	0.02	10.7	0.01
1600	95	10.9	0.29	11.5	0.07
1650	(98)	(11.6)	0.12	(11.8)	0.06
1700	102	12.6	0.16	12.3	0.08
1750	120	14.7	0.31	12.2	−0.01

Sources: Calculations and estimates by the author; see the methodological appendix.
Note: The fact that these figures have been only slightly rounded off does not imply a correspondingly small margin of error. The figures in parentheses have a much wider margin of error than the other data.
A criterion of 5,000 is used for urban population.

els of increase in urban population: 0.22–0.26% per year between 1000 and 1300 and 0.20–0.24% per year between 1500 and 1700. But there was also a noticeable difference in the rise in the level of urbanization which grew very little between the start of the eleventh and the start of the fourteenth centuries. This difference reflects the fact that the urban growth of the sixteenth and seventeenth centuries was in countries previously only slightly urbanized, especially Britain and the Netherlands.

Urban Growth and the Divisions of Time

But the period from the sixteenth century to the eighteenth century was by no means uniform. For some time now, historians have spoken of a long sixteenth century with a favorable economy followed by a less-favored seventeenth century. And this is supported by Fernand Braudel (1982), who with his usual genius for finding a phrase that clarifies history, speaks of a "division of time" affecting Europe and perhaps the rest of the world as well. What is relevant here is the pluri-secular cycle in which there is a "secular trend": a cycle that (for traditional societies) lasted between 230 and 260 years, of which the first half is characterized by an economic expansion and the second half by an economic contraction. The secular cycle of interest here lasted from 1507–10 to 1733–43, the positive phase of the cycle coming to an end around 1650.

What were the trends in urbanization? They conformed for the most part to the general pattern. Still (see table 11.1), the cities seem to have entered a negative phase in the first half of the seventeenth century. A wide margin of error must be allowed for these data, especially those for the year 1650, since in this case I had to resort to less complete sources of information. But the likelihood is strong that the urban cycle of Europe as a whole began its return movement sometime before 1650.

In speaking here of Europe as a whole, of course, I introduce a major qualification, especially where the first half of the seventeenth century is concerned, given the wide range of differences in urban growth observed at the regional level during these years. For the modest rise in the urban population of the Continent as a whole resulted from the combination of fairly rapid increase in England, the Netherlands, and France and the likely decline in Germany, Italy, and Spain. With regard to the declines registered in these last three countries, more perhaps than to economic factors they are to be imputed to the hazards of history: military history in the case of Germany, where the Thirty Years' War had a catastrophic impact on the population of vast areas of that country; and epidemiological history in the cases of Italy and Spain, for the plague broke out in Europe once again sometime around the 1630s, afflicting the countries in the South more severely than those in the North.

A second qualification is called for. The trends I have just described apply solely to cities with populations of more than ten thousand. As for smaller cities (and it should be remembered that during this period smaller cities accounted for nearly a third of the overall urban population of Europe), it is impossible to determine with any degree of certainty whether they conformed to the same pattern as the larger cities.

It may be seen that any attempt to chop history up into small pieces is bound to increase the number of accidents and inaccuracies. The safest course might be to think in terms of centuries, especially since there is a greater body of evidence available for the years 1500, 1600, and 1700 than for the years in between. Viewed at this level, then, the seventeenth century appears in the main to have been more languid than the sixteenth; and for the purposes of analyzing the general geographic and economic changes taking place during this period, there is sufficient conformity to type within each century to permit me usually to treat these two centuries as single, undivided units.

Urban Growth Resulting from the Rise of the New Commercial Powers

The new patterns of trade centering on the Atlantic exerted a highly visible influence on the changes during this period in the urban geography of Europe. The four commercial powers with easy ac-

TABLE 11.2   Growth of the Approximate Levels of Urbanization of
European Countries
(1300–1700)

	1300	1500	1700
Austria-Hungary	4–7	5–8	5–8
Balkans	8–11	7–12	7–12
Belgium	25–35	30–45	26–35
England	6–9	7–9	13–16
France	9–11	9–12	11–15
Germany	5–8	7–9	8–11
Italy	15–21	15–20	14–19
Netherlands	8–12	20–26	38–49
Portugal	8–11	11–13	18–23
Scandinavia	5–7	5–8	5–8
Spain	13–18	10–16	12–17
Switzerland	5–7	6–8	6–8
Europe	9–12	10–12	11–14
Russia	3–6	3–6	4–7
Europe as a whole	7–9	7–9	9–12

Sources: Calculations and estimates by the author; see the methodological appendix.
A criterion of 5,000 is used for urban population.
Countries are understood within their boundaries of 1913.

cess to the Atlantic, Portugal, Spain, the United Kingdom, and the
Netherlands, figured among the five countries recording the strongest increase in the level of urbanization (see table 11.2).

The most rapid urban growth took place in the Netherlands.
Around 1500, the level of urbanization in the Netherlands (8–12%)
was close to the European average; but by 1700 the Netherlands was
the most heavily urbanized country in Europe, some 38–49% of its
total population living in towns with populations of five thousand
or more. In 1500 probably no Dutch city had a population of as much
as 25,000. Amsterdam, Rotterdam, and Leiden, which together had
populations of as much as 290,000 around 1700, had a combined
population of only 15,000 in 1500. This rapid growth and high level
of urbanization were essentially accounted for by the role this country
of fewer than two million people played as intermediary for Europe at
large, carrying out a substantial proportion of the Continent's foreign
trade, though it had only one-sixtieth of its population. That this high
rate of urban growth had a considerable impact on the domestic economy of the Netherlands seems likely (see chapter 12).

The Netherlands stood at the midpoint in the succession of the European commercial powers of the period—between Portugal, which
had opened the way for extra-European trade by the Atlantic route,

and England, which in the second half of the seventeenth century would seek to supplant all rivals. And the urban structures of both Portugal and England were dramatically transformed as a result of this expanded commercial activity.

The decline or at best stagnation that had marked urban life in Europe between 1340 and 1450–1500 apparently failed to affect Portugal. Thus Lisbon, with a population of some 35,000 around 1300, had 50,000–60,000 in 1400 and 60,000–70,000 at the start of the sixteenth century. Without registering so positive an evolution as this, most of the other Portuguese cities certainly suffered no decline. But the real period of urban expansion took place during the sixteenth and seventeenth centuries, with accelerated growth in Lisbon. Lisbon had some 120,000–140,000 inhabitants around 1600 but something like 190,000 by around 1700. The urban structure of Portugal was of the primate type, however, since around the start of the eighteenth century, probably 50–60% of the urban population and some 11% of the total population of the country was concentrated in the capital. To the list of Portuguese cities should also be added the many founded or occupied by the Portuguese in Africa and Asia (see part 4).

In chapter 8 I discussed the displacement of the center of gravity of the urban world of Europe, which shifted to the North away from the Mediterranean. Along with the Netherlands, England was clearly responsible for this change. England at the start of the sixteenth century figured among the least urbanized countries of Europe (see table 11.2). Phythian-Adams (1979) calls this a period of urban crisis for England. The extreme case, which he studied in depth, was Coventry, at one point during this period one of the country's larger cities. The population of this "city of desolation" dropped from 10,000 around 1440 (after the plague) to 4,000–5,000 in 1550. "In the opening years of the sixteenth century not only did a major geographical alteration to the urban network take place, but many of the leading cities in the hierarchy were at least in trouble. . . . Thereafter, and perhaps until about the first decade of Elizabeth's reign, there is little to suggest an improvement in the condition of English towns." And as in the case of sixteenth and seventeenth century Portugal, the major part of the urban growth taking place in subsequent centuries was concentrated in London, a city that, like Lisbon, combined the functions of capital with those of principal port of trade and seat of the royal crown. When sometime around 1700 the population of London surpassed 500,000, the city had roughly 65% of the urban population and 9% of the total population of England. In part 3 I shall dwell at some length on the later growth of London, when I discuss the Industrial Revolution.

Urban expansion proved much more modest in Spain. Though urban life felt the influence of relations with the extra-European world, for Spain these relations were more of the colonial type and involved the importation of precious metals rather than commerce. I would have liked at this point to explore in some detail the profound consequences of the colonial contribution to urbanism in Spain, especially those relating to its economic development. This would have taken me too far, however; and there are so many unknowns, especially with regard to developments in the agricultural sector, that I thought it impossible to make a contribution to this question. I shall merely fill in the gaps in the data in table 11.2. Because it omits figures for 1600, the table masks a part of the urban growth of Spain, namely the more positive character of the sixteenth century as opposed to the seventeenth century. For the seventeenth century saw the decline of a number of large and important cities, in particular Seville, Toledo, Valencia, and Valladolid, whose combined population was on the order of 320,000 in 1600, but fell to around 160,000 by 1700.

Not only was this surge of urban growth unequal in different parts of Europe, but in some regions there was a pronounced fall in the relative size of the urban population. Such was the case for what is present-day Belgium, where the level of urbanization diminished by roughly a fifth. The population of Bruges dwindled from about 125,000 in 1400 to about 30,000 in 1700, while Ghent went from 80,000 to 50,000 between 1500 and 1700 (see chapter 8). And while during this same period Antwerp and Brussels enjoyed growth in population, they too suffered a reversal between 1700 and 1750. Moreover, around 1750 the urban population of Belgium as a whole stood at roughly 25% (or less) of the total population, as against some 30% fifty years earlier. Another region that suffered urban decline at this time was the Balkans. But in this case the data are less reliable, and it is necessary to speak only of the likelihood of a decrease in urban population.

A Western Europe Far More Urbanized Than the Rest of the Continent

The lack of uniformity in the way things evolved in the different parts of Europe naturally led to highly dissimilar situations. But whereas following the Industrial Revolution the dividing line between developed and less developed regions came to run from East to West, at the beginning of the eighteenth century it crossed Europe from North to South, roughly along the western border of present-day Germany. To the West lay Belgium, France, the Netherlands, the United Kingdom, Spain, Portugal, and Italy, where Europe teemed with large cities: a Europe in which the levels of urbanization in the various countries ranged from 10–12% to 35–45% with the average for the region as a whole falling around 14–17%. Within the boundaries of Western Europe were at this time both the newly urbanized commercial powers of the Renaissance and those countries that had already achieved a high level of urbanization in former centuries: countries that, despite the shift of the urban center of gravity toward the North, had retained a substantial urban network.

To the East was a scattering of small towns spread out thinly over the face of the countryside, where levels of urbanization ranged between 4–5% and 7–8%. The average, not counting Russia, was 6–7%, falling when Russia is included to 5–6%. Many of the cities of vast Russia were not only small, but also at the fringe of the rural world, because of the dominance of agricultural activities of their inhabitants. Contemporary Soviet historians reject the qualification of "agrarian towns" given by the "bourgeois" historians of the end of the nineteenth century to a certain number of those cities (Milov, 1982). This is probably justified, and as seen elsewhere, cities with a large proportion of peasants can be found in other societies and for other periods.

Of the 35-odd cities with populations of more than 50,000 in Europe as a whole at the start of the eighteenth century, only 6 or 7 were in the East, despite the fact that the East accounted for about 58% of the European population. Furthermore, practically all of the largest cities were concentrated in Western Europe. Out of a total of 11 cities with populations in excess of 100,000, 9 lay in the West and only 2 in the East: Vienna, with a population a little over 100,000, and Moscow, which had a population of perhaps 130,000. The average size of the 9 largest cities of Western Europe, by contrast, was 250,000. The emergence of these very great cities constitutes one of the principal features of this phase of urbanization.

In Central and Eastern Europe, where despite the relative absence of very large cities the overall trend ran toward a rise in the general level of urbanization, mention should also be made of a number of cases in which large cities suffered declines in population. The population of Prague, for instance, which between 1400 and 1600 had fluctuated around 80,000–90,000, fell by 1700 to no more than 50,000. And the population of Budapest, at one time between 20,000 and 25,000, dropped below 20,000 in 1700, tracing in this way a pattern repeated in many Polish cities as well. These declines reflected the unhappy fate of the cities of any region or country absorbed into large empires (in this case the Russian and Austro-Hungarian empires) whose capitals take over a significant portion of all economic and administrative functions. Thus during the seventeenth century the population of Vienna went up from some 30,000 to more than 100,000, and that of Moscow from 80,000 to 130,000.

Italy gives more examples of the uniqueness of each city's individual destiny. When Italy was short-circuited by the opening up of the Atlantic, the Italian economy fell into a negative course. Recent research showing that Italy kept during this period a commercial role of some importance indicates that the Italian economy was by no means as enfeebled as scholars have thought. But even if no pronounced regression took place, the economy nevertheless remained relatively stagnant; and this stagnation was unquestionably accompanied by suspended growth in the level of urbanization and by only marginal increase in total population. But while the populations of Florence, Milan, Genoa, Bologna, and Venice stagnated, and while the populations of Brescia, Cremona, Catania, and Lucca declined, the population of Naples actually doubled and that of Rome even tripled.

The First Very Great Cities in Europe

The reinforcement of the power and executive activity of the state and the growth of international trade are the two chief factors accounting for the formation of very great cities. For the first time since the Fall of Rome, European cities had populations of more than half a million. Paris reached this size sometime around 1660–1680, and London did so soon afterwards, sometime between 1670 and 1690. Around 1500 there were only four cities with populations of more than 100,000. In 1700 there were ten, and by 1750, fourteen. Practically all of these cities were capitals, and five of them were also ports. The number of people living in these great cities represented 18% of the total urban population in 1700, as compared with only 7% in 1500. In absolute terms, their population rose from 600 thousand to 2.2 million (see table 8.2).

The general rise in the overall urban population of Europe between 1500 and 1700 may chiefly be imputed to these great cities, and more particularly to one small group of them. Thus the rapid growth of only nine cities, all of them capitals, accounted for a third of the increase in total urban population. Amsterdam, Copenhagen, Dublin, Lisbon, London, Madrid, Paris, Rome, and Vienna, which together had a population of half a million around the start of the sixteenth century had two million by the end of the seventeenth century.

The rest of the urban growth registered during this period was very unevenly distributed among the multitude of lesser cities. Thus, even the 15 cities that after the 9 just mentioned recorded the sharpest rise in absolute terms, accounted for only one-fifth of the overall increase in urban population. And of the 186 other cities about which there is relatively reliable data for the period 1500–1700, 104 increased in population, 46 declined, and 36 remained stagnant. This means that, taking the situation as a whole and including the 24 cities that experienced especially rapid growth during this period, roughly 4 out of every 10 cities in Europe between 1500 and 1700 either declined or stagnated in population.

In both the sixteenth and seventeenth centuries the larger cities (those with populations in excess of 100,000) expanded at a faster rate than cities in the other size categories (see table 11.3). The method of

TABLE 11.3 Annual Percentage Growth of European Cities
(except Russia) by Size at the Start of Each Time Period
(1500–1700)

Size of Cities (in thousands)	1500–1600	1600–1700
10–20	0.35	0.19
20–30	0.27	0.14
30–50	0.27	0.00
50–100	0.13	0.00
100–200	0.46	0.26
200 or more	0.11[a]	0.23
Total, cities over 30	0.23	0.11
Total, cities over 20	0.24	0.12
Total, cities over 10	0.26	0.13
Overall urban population[b]	0.29	0.14

Sources: Calculations and estimates by the author; see the methodological appendix.
Note: The fact that these figures have been only slightly rounded off does not imply a correspondingly small margin of error.
See in the text the reservations regarding the degree of significance to be attached to these data, especially those for the period 1500 to 1600.
[a] Only one city, Paris.
[b] Includes newly emerging cities.

analysis used consisted simply of taking, for example, all cities that in 1600 had populations of 20,000–30,000, then adding up their combined total both in 1600 and in 1700 without including any cities entering this category in the meantime, without excluding any cities leaving it. I then compared the two totals and worked out the annual rate of increase for the category as a whole.

The average rates of increase for the sixteenth century show marked variations. The differences among the rates of increase for the various size categories should not therefore be considered very significant. For the seventeenth century the results merit close attention, but only with respect to cities with populations of less than 100,000. Both for the cities with populations of 100,000–200,000 and for those with more than 200,000, the best part of the increase can be traced to only a few isolated cases. Indeed, the concentration of urban growth in a limited number of cities in the fifteenth and sixteenth centuries was even more pronounced during the seventeenth century. During the seventeenth century three cities, Amsterdam, London, and Paris, were responsible for 40% of all growth in urban population in Europe as a whole.

All of this confirms what I noted at the beginning of this section: the seventeenth century witnessed the emergence of the first very great cities in Europe. By the start of the eighteenth century the twenty largest cities had a combined population of three million, representing one quarter of the total urban population of the Continent at large.

This new type of city brought with it a mode of existence very different from that in smaller towns, where ties with rural life remained closer. The opposition between town and country became much more marked, and town and country both registered the change. In the urban milieu this much larger size most likely fostered technological innovations of various kinds, owing to the greater division of labor and also the increased intensity in the flow of information. (I shall return to this question of the relations between the size of cities and the pace of innovation in chapter 20). In the countryside the existence of a great city implied increasing demand for food and consequently growing pressure on both the supply and the means of transporting it to town. Great cities also implied an accelerated rate of migration from rural districts to the towns. (See the end of chapter 12 for a discussion of specific features of urban demography at this time.) Before going on to look into the purely demographic aspects of the problem, I shall say a few words about those factors most capable of explaining the many contrasts in the evolution of cities during this period.

What Factors Explain the Diversity in the Growth of Cities between 1500 and 1700?

The data concerning the population of European cities (see the methodological appendix) indicate the importance of geography; this is reflected in the correlation between the growth of cities and the countries in which they happened to be. Although on the average 4 out of 10 European cities stagnated or declined in population between 1500 and 1700, the ratio was a little more than 4 out of 10 in Belgium and Germany, was 5 out of 10 in Italy, and was 7 out of 10 in Spain. In France, however, the proportion was only 3 out of 10, and in the United Kingdom and the Netherlands was less than 2 out of 10. (The number of cities whose individual histories it is possible to follow in other countries is too small for me to calculate meaningful ratios.) In other words, 45 percent of the cities suffering stagnation or decline were concentrated in Italy and Spain, whereas most of the cities that grew at this time were in Western Europe.

Needless to say, the importance assumed by geography reflects the force of the economic trends at work in the various countries of Europe. In view of this fact, I shall attempt, through the analysis of the general characteristics of the various cities involved, to disengage the factors that explain these geographical differences in urban evolution.

To be sure, it will prove impossible to identify all the factors responsible for the diversity in urban growth. From the theoretical point of view, the number of such factors may be very great indeed. The Canadian scholar Trigger (1972), for example, has drawn up a list of eleven factors related to urban growth in preindustrial societies. Since they are all instructive, I shall cite the entire list: (1) an increase in the food supply, (2) increasing population and/or rural unemployment, (3) a division of labor, (4) marketing and trade, (5) landlords who live in the city, (6) administration, (7) defense, (8) religion, (9) secular tourism, (10) education, and (11) domestic service.

I would add to this list three further factors: the discovery (or exhaustion) of mineral deposits; the redrawing of political boundaries; and ecological change (the silting up of a harbor, earthquakes, changes in local climate, etc.). Nor should we forget the role of chance: a city's leader more or less well equipped to turn the city's course in a positive or negative direction.

An adequate analysis of the factors determining the development of a city cannot be undertaken except by means of an in-depth study of its particular economic and social history. But studies of this kind exist only for a minute fraction of the cities of the period. Under these circumstances the correlation of the dominant features of a city with the growth of its population may afford precious evidence, so long as a sufficient number of such correlations have been carried out. And I was able to carry out analyses of this sort for about 90% of all European cities with populations of more than ten thousand, and for a number of smaller ones as well. Russia and the Balkan countries had to be left out. The exclusion of Russia was justified by the unreliable nature of the population data and the exclusion of the Balkans by the fact that during this period they were in the Ottoman Empire.

I determined the classes into which the cities in the sample were to be divided by consulting the headings under which they were treated in various historical dictionaries and encyclopedias. I decided the dominant function of each city by determining which of the following categories it falls into, giving the greatest weight to the first and progressively less weight to each subsequent category: (1) capitals; (2) port towns; (3) other commercial cities; (4) industrial cities; (5) administrative cities; and (6) religious, university, and military cities (see table 11.4).

These comparisons enable me to confirm what analyses of a more classical sort have already suggested: the part played by the reinforcement of the power and executive activity of the state on the one hand and by the expansion of international trade on the other. While representing only 7% of the cities studied, capitals made up 19% of the cities recording a rise in population exceeding 100%. And all of the capital cities registered population increases greater than 50%. As a general rule, those capital cities that were also ports grew even more than the others.

Port cities, many of which also had other, purely commercial functions, constitute after capitals the class of cities with the greatest growth: roughly 55% of them doubled or even tripled in population. Another, even more significant indicator is the fact that, while representing only 27% of cities other than capitals, port cities nevertheless

TABLE 11.4 Growth of the Population of European Cities (except Russia and the Balkans) according to Dominant Function (1500–1700)

	Cities in Sample	Capitals		Other Cities[a]				
		Ports	Other	Ports	Comm	Ind	Adm	Other
Growth								
Over 200%	33	5	3	16	1	3	4	1
100 to 200%	30	2	2	13	1	6	5	1
50 to 100%	37	2	1	12	5	10	4	3
10 to 50%	30	—	—	2	6	8	8	6
Stagnation								
10 to −10%	35	—	—	5	4	8	11	7
Decline								
−10 to −20%	11	—	—	—	4	—	5	2
−20 to −40%	10	—	—	4	—	1	3	2
−40 to −60%	13	—	—	—	1	6	6	—
Over −60%	8	—	—	—	1	4	2	1
Total sample	207	9	6	52	23	46	48	23

Sources: Calculations and estimates by the author; see the text.

[a] Comm = commercial; Ind = industrial; Adm = administrative; Other = religious, university, or military.

made up about 57% of the cities (other than capitals) whose population rose more than 100%. Even in those regions, such as Italy, in which downward trends were in force, ports grew more than other cities.

To the extent that agriculture achieved very little real progress during this period (see chapter 8), the especially rapid growth observed in port cities, clearly explained by the general rise in international trade, was in particular made possible by growing imports of foreign products. The consumption of sugar, all of it coming from abroad, grew to the point where it could by itself supply enough calories to support 11% of the increase in total urban population that took place during the sixteenth and seventeenth centuries. Furthermore, during this period the most heavily urbanized regions and countries of Europe imported appreciable quantities of grain from northeastern Europe and especially from the territory corresponding to present-day Poland—that is to say, from regions that had only a very low level of urbanization: on the order of 5–6%. This is half the level of the rest of Europe. Over the course of the eighteenth century, an average of some 125,000 metric tons of grain per year passed through the Sund, the strait joining the Baltic with the North Sea. Since the volume of grain following this same route had been much smaller during the fifteenth century, this tonnage represented a significant contribution to the provisioning of the cities of those parts of Europe experiencing rapid urban growth at this time. Those 125,000 tons could provide each dweller in all cities with a population of over fifty thousand in Western Europe with some seventy kilograms of bread per year. But one should not overlook the fact that the population of those cities represented more than one-third of the total urban population but only 4–5% of the total population. I shall return in chapter 12 to the problems of the more heavily urbanized regions in supplying food for their populations.

As for the other types of cities, commercial towns (those that were not ports as well) and industrial cities during these two centuries grew more than the rest, that is, more than administrative centers, ecclesiastical cities, university towns, and garrison towns. It would require more information than I currently have to refine this analysis further. Still it seems fairly clear that apart from the role played by ports (and thus by commerce generally) and by capitals, the growth of cities during this period depended more on a city's region than on its specific functions. Finally, the diversity displayed in table 11.4 and the differences resulting from geographical location together illustrate yet again the unalterably idiosyncratic character of each city's individual destiny.

12 Urbanization and Development in Europe before the Industrial Revolution: 1000–1700 □

The break with the past that took place at the beginning of the sixteenth century suggests a division of the seven centuries between 1000 and 1700 into two distinct periods. This break with the past was decisive for the future course of urbanization and also largely determined the direction of European civilization as a whole. During the period from 1000 to 1700 European civilization as we know it today received its essential distinguishing stamp and character. The question arises, then, as to the contribution urban history made to this process: to paraphrase the title of the very beautiful essay devoted to this matter by Le Goff (1972), what role did the city play as an agent of civilization in the traditional, preindustrial Europe of the medieval and Renaissance eras? This question is clearly of the first importance, and the opening section of this chapter will attempt to provide some sort of answer. Our considerable debt to Le Goff will be evident throughout this section.

The City: Agent of Civilization

There is no doubt that during the period between 1000 and 1500 cities had a major hand in the diffusion of knowledge—technical information, literary conventions and innovations, musical modes and styles, religious doctrines, and philosophical speculations—that frames a civilization. Nevertheless, especially at the outset, cities were not alone in disseminating knowledge. The castles of the nobility and above all the monasteries occupied a very important position in this process. Le Goff places the time at which the cities gradually began to wrest the leading role from the monasteries somewhere in the twelfth century.

The cities succeeded in supplanting the monasteries chiefly owing to growth in urban education at both the primary and university levels. Large numbers of city children learned how to read and write. It is estimated that in 1340 in Florence, for example, 8,000–10,000 boys and girls learned how to read. It happens that at this time Florence had a population of roughly 60,000 people, and it can be estimated that children between the ages of five and ten represented 8–12% of the total population. This implies that practically all of the children were given some sort of education. As for higher learning (see chapter 10), around seventy universities were created in Europe between 1200 and 1500. By the start of the sixteenth century, roughly half of the cities of more than 20,000 people in Europe (except Russia) had at least one and in many instances several universities. And almost no universities were established in towns of fewer than 5,000 inhabitants.

The rise of education in the cities had great consequences for the spread of knowledge, since it appears likely that education was much more restricted in the countryside. This is only likely, however, for a great deal less is known about the rural world than about cities. Still, what remains in doubt is not the reality of the gap between urban and rural education, but its extent. Even where religious life was concerned (a factor capable of introducing a measure of uniformity), it is certain that the priesthood was more limited in rural districts in both numbers and ability. And whatever the human qualities of the country curate, the cities had the most highly educated members of the clergy.

At the beginning of the sixteenth century the city's role as agent of civilization was probably strengthened. Feudalism had by this time almost completely vanished and the role of the monasteries had, in relative terms, diminished. Moreover, to the seventy to seventy-three universities founded before 1500 (practically all of which remained active) were added another fifteen to seventeen new ones during the sixteenth century and fourteen to sixteen during the seventeenth century. Around the start of the eighteenth century there were about one hundred university towns in Europe (except Russia). Thus, roughly 45% of all cities with populations of over 20,000 had one or more universities. But the largest cities were not necessarily the only ones with seats of higher learning. Around 1700, among the large cities that still had no universities were London, Amsterdam, Rotterdam, Antwerp, Brussels, Stockholm, and Madrid. In many cases, however, a university town was to be found near one of these cities. This fact, coupled with the residential character of most of the universities of the period, meant that certain universities of very great renown continued for many years to be located in small towns. Among the most noteworthy were the universities of Oxford, Cambridge, Louvain, Lundt, Uppsala, and Heidelberg. While it is true that universities contributed a great deal to urbanization, they nevertheless rarely constituted poles of urban growth in themselves.

By virtue of the intensification of trade with the rest of the world, the contribution of the civilizations of Asia and the pre-Columbian New World spread throughout Europe, and in the dissemination of this new influence on European civilization commercial cities played a key role. Out of eleven European cities with populations of more than 100,000 in 1700, seven were ports in direct communication with Asia and America, and most of the other cities were in direct communication with these first. Thus, from the sixteenth century on, the part played by the city as agent of civilization was considerably reinforced. The whole of the Renaissance was closely linked with urban life.

Certain technological innovations, on the other hand, exerted a more ambiguous impact. The widespread adoption of printing, for example, strengthened the position of cities relative to the monasteries with respect to the production of books. But the consequent lowering of the price of books fostered the spread of knowledge and information in the country just as much as in the town. Similarly, the cities were not alone in profiting from the apparent increase in the volume of textile manufacturing at this time. Owing to the need for ready access to sources of water power, the rural textile industry grew considerably during this period. Indeed, the protoindustrialization so skillfully described by Mendels (1969) was in a sense just this expansion in rural industrial activity.

The shift of certain industrial activities toward rural districts began very early: "As early as the thirteenth century in some places, but certainly from the fourteenth and fifteenth centuries on, we witness throughout Western Europe the relocation of a series of skilled activities, and in particular textile manufacturing, out into the countryside" (Barel, 1977). Braudel (1966) estimates, albeit with some reservations, that in sixteenth-century Europe the number of rural craftsmen was roughly equal to that of urban craftsmen: three million in town and three million in the country—though according to Braudel this numerical equality did not entail equality "in qualifications or earnings." And it is interesting to note that this proportion is similar to that observed in China under Mao, where numerous industrial employments were transplanted to rural districts in order to achieve a better balance between town and country.

Putting the question in a more general perspective, the paradox of an equivalence between the number of industrial jobs in town and in the country is more apparent than real. Indeed, given that industry occupies in the city only some 50–60% of the work force, if 90% of a country's total work force is made up of rural people, it is only necessary for 6–7% of these rural workers to engage in industrial forms of labor for the number of industrial jobs in town and country to be equal. And in the Third World today it can be estimated that some 5–8% of all jobs in rural districts are provided by the industrial sector (Anderson and Leiserson, 1980). As a result it can be estimated that, as in sixteenth-century Europe, the number of industrial jobs in rural areas is the same as in urban areas, though technological differences between these two types of industrial jobs are more pronounced today than they were in the sixteenth century.

But this aspect of the city's impact on life in the societies of traditional Europe has more to do with economic than with purely cultural factors. To be sure, the economy unquestionably forms an integral part of civilization as a whole. To treat it in these terms, however, I would have to broaden my definition of civilization beyond the relatively narrow scope of this section, and discuss civilization in its material more than in its strictly cultural dimension. But one should not neglect the more general influence of rural industrial labor on the tenor of rural life. For the growth of rural industry increased both the intensity and the frequency of contacts between town and country; and while these contacts usually took place only through the mediation of merchants and other employers, their effect must have been wider and deeper than their immediate, narrowly economic motive would by itself suggest.

Were artisans present in the rural world? Yes, but peasants were also present in cities. And in the same way as the artisan of the country was not the same as the artisan of the city, the peasant of the city was not the same as the peasant of the country. In societies where serfdom prevailed the peasant of the city was generally a free man. Other differences were of a more economic nature. The peasant of the city had a distinct advantage in transport costs when selling his products. He could use the organic refuse of the city. Finally, his products were different: more perishable goods, especially milk. It is worth noting that the presence of milk cows inside European cities (and probably also in non-European cities) has survived the agricultural revolution for centuries. The author of this book was born in Antwerp in a house whose owner lived from such an activity.

The City and Development in Europe from 1000 to 1500

There is no doubt that just as the economic disorganization following on the Fall of the Roman Empire lay at the root of the urban recession of the fifth to ninth centuries, so too the surge of urban growth taking place during the next three hundred years received its fundamental impetus from economic progress, especially from progress in agriculture. For even though productivity may not have increased very much, if at all, yields increased substantially, and increasing yields permitted a greater urban density.

But it may be as well at this point to pause a little for the distinction that has to be drawn between yield, or return, and productivity in agriculture. Confusion is frequent in this connection, probably owing to the famous law of "diminishing agricultural returns" (first formulated by Turgot, but chiefly popularized by Ricardo). This law in fact concerns diminishing productivity. The term "return," or "yield," on the other hand, ought to be reserved for yields properly, that is, production in relation to the amount of land under cultivation or to the amount of seed used. Thus one may say, for example, that the yield of wheat in Western Europe went up from 700–900 kilograms per hectare for the period 1810–20 to 1,200–1,300 kilograms per hectare for the period 1900–1910. Or one may say (and this method is used especially with reference to preindustrial eras) that in Europe during the Middle Ages the yield of wheat was four grains for every one grain sown.

By contrast, productivity measures the product obtained for a given quantity of work or of some other factor of production (capital, techniques, etc.). As a rule, productivity chiefly refers to the relationship between the volume of output and the amount of work done. It is in this sense that one will speak of the number of hours of work required to produce one ton of wheat; and it is clearly productivity that serves as the measure of economic progress. Furthermore, and this is an important point, where agriculture is concerned there is often conflict between the state, or sometimes the growth, of yield on the one hand and productivity on the other. There may be certain modes of cultivation (or regions or countries) that achieve both high yield and low productivity, and vice versa. Intensive farming, for instance, is generally characterized by high yield and low productivity, while extensive farming is generally characterized by low yield and high productivity. In the United States, for example, the yield of wheat for the period 1979–1982 was only about 2,300 kilograms per hectare, that is, about half the yield achieved in many countries of Western Europe (such as France, Belgium, and Germany). Yet it is well known that productivity is much higher in the United States than in those European countries, being at least three to five times greater.

In the present context, increased yield in medieval Europe even without an increase in productivity would have had a significant impact on urbanization. Chief among its effects was the possibility of creating a denser urban network than before; and since any rise in the density of the urban population would have led to reduced transport costs for food and also for manufactured goods sold to the urban population, this in turn made it possible to attain a higher level of urbanization. It follows that this growth in yield encouraged specialization in the kinds of activities pursued in the city. Even the textile towns of Flanders conformed to this pattern. Despite their mercantile origins (generally accepted since the analyses of Pirenne), Nicolas (1978) has concluded that these cities "developed in regions with a prosperous agriculture and with ancient and dense settlements of people." In this case too, however, the impetus provided by international trade and industry was necessary for the dozen small towns found in the region in the twelfth century to turn into the three great cities that grew up in Flanders during the late Middle Ages and early Renaissance.

Instances of industrial cities being supported by international trade were extremely rare, however. The case of the Flemish cities notwithstanding, the whole problem of the impact of urbanization on economic development remains open. Two lines of investigation should receive particular emphasis: the effect on agriculture because of the demand for food, and the consequences of the demand for luxury goods the urban way of life supposes.

The principal problem with regard to the effects of the city on agriculture is to learn to what degree urban demand stimulated changes in agricultural techniques: to see if it is not possible to reverse the direction of the relationship between town and country. The emergence of cities depends on and presupposes the existence and growth of agriculture; and to this extent conditions in the country determine conditions in town (see chapter 1). Even though agriculture is needed before the origins of cities, cities in turn have brought about a number of advances in agriculture. For the period of interest here, it is necessary to invoke once more the hypothesis of Boserup (1965) with respect to certain countries of the contemporary Third World. Put in its simplest terms, it is Boserup's contention that the demographic pressure stemming from the recent population explosion in the Third World has induced farmers to adopt new, more productive methods of cultivation. This was in part because more food was needed for greater numbers of people than before. But it was also partly due to the demand for space generated by the increase in population, which made it very difficult, if not impossible, to expand the amount of land under cultivation. Grigg (1980), who analyzed in detail the relations between demographic growth and agricultural changes, notably in preindustrial Europe, concludes that the growth of population between 1000 and 1300 occasioned only minor changes in agricultural techniques. "Most of the increase in food output must have come from expanding the area under cultivation, but by 1250 there was little good land left, and in some regions intensification took the form of reducing the fallow by shifting from the two-field system to the three-field; this was not always accompanied by adequate means of maintaining soil fertility. By 1300 the technological possibilities of medieval agriculture were largely exhausted."

With regard to the limited effect of demographic pressure, it is important to recall that in Europe from the tenth to the fifteenth century, the demographic growth was nothing like that which exists today in the Third World. In Europe the population grew at a yearly rate of 0.2% (doubling every 350 years), while now in the Third World it grows at 2.5 percent (doubling every 28 years). Europe (except Russia) in the year 1000 had only 8 people per square kilometer, the India of 1960 already had 131, and the India of 1980, 201; for the Bangladesh of 1980, the figure is 600. It is likely that the India and Bangladesh of the year 2000 will have, respectively, 280 and 1,000 people per square kilometer.

Nevertheless, considering only urban regions with a high rate of expansion, analogies may still be drawn between the two situations. And in this context it is possible to conceive of an urban impact on agriculture, especially where the city was supported in part by long-distance trade. For in such cases increasing yields, even when unaccompanied by increases in productivity, would have been useful. A city's growth entails a rise in the price of agricultural commodities at its periphery: first of all because the city has to enlarge the zone from which it draws supplies, which leads to increased transport costs; and second because land of only marginal value often has to be put to use, increasing production costs. But once prices rise, the peasants living near the city will have both an interest in and the financial possibility of adopting more productive methods, even when this involves, on the average, higher initial outlays.

This is probably what happened during this period in certain parts of northern Italy and in Flanders. It is also what most likely happened during the sixteenth and seventeenth centuries in the Netherlands. I shall return later to this last case, however, in order to illustrate the limits of this effect. For there were indeed limits, since despite the advances in agriculture in the more heavily urbanized regions, the supply of food to the cities depended on massive imports of grain from abroad. Fifteenth-century Flanders is another example. To be sure, Marie-Jeanne Tits-Dieuaide (1975) notes that the English libel of 1436 to the effect that "in a year, Flanders did not produce enough wheat to feed itself for a single month" was in all likelihood an exaggeration. But the evidence of Tits-Dieuaide shows that Flanders had to import substantial amounts of grain in order to support its population, especially its city dwellers.

As soon as cities reached a certain level of development, social differentiation became more pronounced, leading to different patterns of consumption among the different social classes. Social classes or groups with higher incomes purchased luxury goods, whether textiles or food. The production of industrial goods for the luxury market led to, or at any rate encouraged, greater regional specialization and consequently more substantial trade covering greater distances. Some textiles in particular were imported from outside Europe. All of this was obviously a factor in the diffusion of progress in the widest sense of the word. What defined luxury foods as luxuries (what defined their price) was essentially the impossibility of growing them in temperate climates, which led to long-distance trade with different countries and different cultures.

This trade was at the root of the fairs, which in their turn supported the development of a good number of European cities. In many instances industrial activities were added to this commercial function; and it was to these industrial activities that certain of the cities with their fairs owed their survival and development when they were deprived of their initial commercial role as a result of subsequent displacements in the patterns of trade. Such was notably the case for Geneva, Rouen, Lyons, among other cities. That other cities with fairs failed to survive, or at any rate failed to develop further, may be attributed to various factors—among which probably ought to be included critical mass. Some "international" fairs were held in towns too small to readapt to changing circumstances. Although this problem has never received thorough treatment, the existing evidence seems to indicate that decline predominated: fair cities having a fall in population following the loss of their commercial function outnumbered those maintaining or increasing their population under similar conditions. And it is worth noting that only one medieval fair, that of Leipzig, has really survived as such down to the present.

These contrasting destinies induce me to emphasize once more the unique character of each city's individual history. Every city is subject, especially in economic matters, to a combination of events peculiarly its own. In an urban system in a process of expansion, some cities may stagnate or decline; in another system in a general recession, some cities may grow.

It is necessary to return to the problem of the ruralization of textile manufacturing. Some of its causes seem self-evident, among them the lower wages paid rural workers and the absence of guild regulations in the countryside. Still, I am on the whole inclined to share Barel's view (1977) based on certain remarks of Braudel concerning the possibility that the cultivation of grapes and olives in southern Europe was a substitute for the rural textile manufacturing so much more prevalent in northern Europe. Barel wonders

> whether the development of the rural textile industry may not have been linked with the excessive demands made by the city on the economic surplus generated by agriculture, and also with possible underdevelopment among the rural work force, the Malthusianism of the urban guilds preventing unemployed rural workers from emigrating to the city in search of jobs in skilled labor. These are only conjectures. But strengthened by what is known about the wage differential between town and country and about the regulation of specifically urban occupations, they pave the way for an analysis of the ruralization of textile manufacturing based on the hypothesis that the urban model of industrialization was losing its grip on the situation: that it was growing incapable of compensating through its own internal dynamics for all that it extracted from the country.

Before leaving behind the period brought to a close at the end of the fifteenth century, I ought to say a few words about the role of international trade as an economic factor in urban development. Even though international trade at this time was less important than in subsequent centuries, it was nevertheless substantial enough to have had a visible effect. It is only necessary to compare the figures for urban growth in Italy, where international trade had taken deepest root, with those for the rest of Europe. And while these figures are certainly unreliable, they do provide a valid measure of relative orders of magnitude sufficient to show the urbanizing impact of international trade in the Middle Ages. Thus around 1300 some 15–21% of the population of Italy (with its current boundaries) lived in cities and towns with populations of 5,000 or more, whereas the proportion in the rest of Europe (except Russia) was only 6–8%. As seen in earlier chapters, however, Amalfi, Venice, Genoa, etc., were not merely Italian cities: they were European cities, cities whose merchants handled most of the trade between Europe and the rest of the world, although at this time only within the Old World. But it was to the European stature of its cities as centers of international trade that Italy owed her comparatively high level of urbanization. As this example from thirteenth-century Italy shows, moreover, at the close of the Middle Ages, what Braudel (1982) calls an "economy world" already existed.

This economy world should not be confused, however, with the "world economy" that developed during the nineteenth century, and even as late as the second half of the nineteenth century. A system of economic relations directly or indirectly connecting every corner of the globe, the world economy was the product of the Industrial Revolution. It was, indeed, wholly inconceivable without the Industrial Revolution, presupposing as it did precisely those increases in the volume of production, in productivity, and in the technology of transport that the Industrial Revolution alone made possible. And I might point out that this fruit of the Industrial Revolution bears a terrible stain: underdevelopment. Underdevelopment was something else wholly inconceivable prior to the Industrial Revolution, if only because before the Industrial Revolution development as we understand it today did not exist and in fact could not have existed.

The economy world, on the other hand, in Braudel's words "concerns only a fragment of the universe, one economically autonomous piece of the planet by and large capable of supporting itself on its own, upon which its internal links and networks of exchange confer a certain organic unity." And according to Braudel, "an economy world always possesses an urban pole, some city at its heart, directing the logic of its business affairs: information, merchandise, capital, credits, men, orders, merchants' letters flow into and flow back out of it." This center does not remain immutable: various cities have succeeded one another in occupying a position of primacy. To begin with, starting from the eleventh century there was in Europe a bipolar economy world dominated by Bruges and the Flemish cities on the one hand

and the cities of Italy on the other. Then, starting from the middle of the thirteenth century, primacy in Europe settled exclusively on Italy, remaining there for more than two hundred years, with Genoa and later Venice—the unrivalled commercial capital of Europe—as center. The true successor to Venice was Amsterdam, which took this position from 1570–1580 on, yielding to London only some two centuries later. But between Venice and Amsterdam, two brilliant comets flashed across the European heavens: Lisbon and especially the author's native city, Antwerp. Antwerp was during three separate periods (1505–1521, 1535–1576, and 1870–1955) the principal port of Europe and one of the busiest in the world.

Those great metropolises of international trade should not put in the shadow the vast number of cities of all sizes where nonlocal trade contributed in varying degrees to their economic bases. These ranged from the small cities with international fairs (which made fundamental contributions to the cities' economic life) to large industrial cities for which commercial activity was marginal.

The City and Development in Europe from 1500 to 1700

As during the period 1000–1500, there is no doubt that between 1500 and 1700 economic development strongly conditioned urban development. One of the most powerful factors was unquestionably the growth of trade with the rest of the world. But the rest of the world was enlarged by the maritime discoveries made at the end of the fifteenth century.

Those discoveries brought a shift of urban Europe's center of gravity toward the Atlantic coast. But the important role of trade does not exclude the persistence of the agricultural factor, which remained the determining element. Furthermore, in those regions that were losers in this new orientation of international trade, the role of agriculture became more important. Thus to take only one example: in the Tuscany of the sixteenth century and the first half of the seventeenth century, agriculture strongly influenced the new distribution of urban population (Della-Pina, 1982).

But what was the impact of urbanization on economic development? In the industrial sphere, it is clear that the surge of urban growth during the Renaissance had significant consequences. As had been the case during the Middle Ages, the increase in urban population manifestly stimulated the demand for manufactured goods, and in particular for a wider variety of manufactured goods. The large size of the Renaissance cities, moreover, encouraged the division of labor within the cities, since the cities themselves now provided sufficient markets for a wide range of products, especially luxury items. As a result it became possible to reduce prices of goods generally, and of luxury goods more particularly, because it was no longer necessary to incorporate either the high costs involved in shipping goods over long distances or profits for the numerous middlemen long-distance trading inevitably involved. A large city could produce at the same time luxury woolen goods, fancy laces, and glassware, and thus not need to import them from Flanders, Switzerland, or Italy. This did not, of course, mean the elimination or even the reduction of long-distance trade in these goods, but rather that the overall consumption of such goods increased, thereby reducing the proportion of imported ones. And as the number of economic activities increased, so too did the amount of information in circulation. Thus by stimulating the economy the larger cities of the Renaissance also promoted the diffusion of technological innovation both within each sector of industry and from one sector to another. Finally, the larger the city, the better were the chances that a balance would be struck between the demand for skilled labor and the supply of more skilled jobs. And this too would have furthered economic development by increasing the opportunities open to skilled workers.

The effect of this surge of urban growth on agriculture, however, was less straightforward, the problem being that the impact of urban growth was not uniform in the various regions affected. In the main, a distinction has to be drawn between southern Europe and the North —between Spain and Portugal on the one hand and the Netherlands on the other. I shall for the moment leave England aside, because commercial expansion did not begin there until the second half of the seventeenth century. I shall consider it in part 3.

In southern Europe urban growth during this period did not lead to positive changes in agriculture. In the Netherlands, however, agriculture made rapid progress. Such being the case, it is tempting to seek the sources of this difference in the pace of urban growth and thus in the levels of urbanization achieved in these two parts of the Continent. And sure enough, whereas between 1500 and 1700 the urban population of Spain grew by only 10–20% and that of Portugal by only 30–50%, the corresponding increase in the Netherlands was between 200 and 400%. And while the level of urbanization in Portugal certainly never reached 25%, in the Netherlands it was 40% or more. The level of urbanization was undoubtedly more important than the pace of growth, since even a 500% increase, spread out over two centuries, is after all an annual growth rate of less than 1%. And although some cities experienced growth rates higher than this, given the sound state of communications throughout the Netherlands, coupled with the small size of the country, in this instance it is more to the average that we should look.

This high level of urbanization unquestionably exerted pressure on the means of agricultural production, tending to encourage the adoption of new, more productive techniques. This is all the more likely, indeed, inasmuch as the profits from international trade would have led to a fairly high standard of living in Dutch cities. But there was not necessarily growth in agricultural productivity or even a higher average price level in this country than in the rest of Europe. The profits from trade made it possible to pay not only for a large part of the food for the cities, but also for manufactured goods for the rural populations. But all of this remains in the domain of the merely possible effects of urbanization: a great deal of research will have to be done before it will be a certainty. Nor can the hypothesis be ruled out that these advances in agriculture, far from stemming from urban growth, were themselves at the root of the first phases of urban expansion.

I must emphasize that despite the significant progress it probably realized during this period, Dutch agriculture, like that of Flanders before it, was by no means capable of supporting by itself the massive population of Dutch cities. According to the figures assembled by Jan de Vries (1974), during the second half of the seventeenth century, net imports of grain in the port of Amsterdam alone amounted to some 120,000 metric tons per year; the figure for the Netherlands as a whole was perhaps 150,000 to 200,000 metric tons. If one assumes as reasonable an average annual consumption of 250 kilograms per urban inhabitant, this tonnage would have represented enough grain to support 600,000–800,000 people, that is, roughly 40% of the total population of the Netherlands, or nearly 100% of the population of all cities and towns with populations of 5,000 or more. These net imports of grain (and also of meat, probably amounting to 30,000–50,000 head a year) were only slightly offset by exports of other agricultural commodities. It is true that the Netherlands exported some 8,000–12,000 metric tons of cheese and probably half as much butter each year, but compared with the amount of grain imported annually these quantities pale into insignificance. Besides, as de Vries remarks, "the dense population and specialized economy could not have arisen had the region not been able to draw upon all of Europe, and Poland in particular, for its grain."

Two other factors might help explain the difference between developments on the Iberian peninsula and in the Netherlands: the importation of precious metals and the drain on population resulting from the conquest and settlement of colonial empires. Supposing them to be valid, these explanations would apply to Spain more than they would to Portugal. Scholars have often insisted on the negative role played by the enormous quantities of precious metals imported from overseas by Portugal and Spain, this unwonted influx of wealth providing easy short-term solutions for deep-seated economic difficulties. But the same line of reasoning could be followed with respect to the commercial profits of the Dutch during their golden age. The possibility of easing, through emigration to the colonies, the pressure of population on the land may perhaps have played a larger role. But here too more specific studies are necessary. If I were to formulate a conclusion about the effects of urban growth on all of Europe—which certainly formed an economic entity—I would share the opinion of Grigg (1980), who for this period as well as for the preceding one finds a limited impact of demographic growth on agriculture.

What Conclusions Can Be Drawn?

Since with the close of the present chapter I shall leave behind what might be called the traditional European economy, the time has come to draw some conclusions regarding all of the relations between the city and the economy at this stage of European development.

There is no doubt that urbanization remained closely related to agriculture and to the existence of agricultural surpluses. And to the extent that before the transformations introduced by the Industrial Revolution such surpluses continued to be limited, so, too, the size of the urban population of Europe continued to be limited. Taking Europe (except Russia) as a whole and applying the criterion of five thousand, the level of urbanization in Europe grew by only a few points in seven centuries, rising from 9–11% of the total population in the year 1000 to 11–14% in 1700. But if the limit is put at two thousand inhabitants, the rise in the level of urbanization appears even weaker, rising from 12–15% in 1000 to 15–17% in 1700. Most of the change consisted of a heavy increase in the urban population, total urban population having multiplied by 2.6. But rises and falls in urbanization were determined first and last by general economic conditions, and especially by the state of agriculture. Thus on the strength of the economic conditions peculiar to them, some regions—most notably the city-states specializing in international trade—succeeded in surpassing the average levels of urbanization of 15–17%. But these city-states have to be placed in the context of Europe as a whole, for which they performed certain functions and from which they drew the food necessary to support their populations.

But what of the other side of the coin—the impact of urbanization on economic development? In this case both the facts themselves and the mechanisms underlying the facts have been less clearly established. It proves necessary, therefore, to distinguish between those effects that are almost certain and those that are merely probable.

To begin, then, with the certainties (or near certainties, rather), the city provided a fruitful soil for the dissemination of innovation generally, both technological and cultural, and was a significant factor in the diffusion of civilization. The city stimulated (as it continues to today) the generation of technological advances in the industrial field, constituting, indeed, an indispensable contributor to improvements in industrial technology. Owing to the increasing demand among upper-income groups within society, the city also stimulated long-distance trade in luxury goods, both manufactured and agricultural, which in turn accelerated the pace of European exposure to other cultures and made possible the diffusion of innovations of all kinds throughout the Continent.

Among the merely probable economic outcomes of urbanization, the most important appears to have been the promotion of improved methods of agriculture. It is possible that this effect had a hand in developments both in parts of northern Italy and in the Netherlands especially. The improvements in agriculture in these regions certainly owed something, maybe a great deal, to urban expansion. For urban expansion in northern Italy and the Netherlands brought with it enormous demand backed by money, inasmuch as it originated in rich commercial towns. But if improved methods of agriculture led to higher yields, they did not lead to real progress in productivity. And it is this lack of progress in agricultural productivity that explains the near stagnation in the level of urbanization during those seven centuries. Furthermore, as in the case of ancient Rome, the possibility cannot by any means be ruled out that by increasing food imports this demand created the opposite effect: that of causing a decline in agriculture. Detrimental effects of this kind would have been most likely and most severe when these imports were directly or indirectly tied in with colonial levies, as may have been the case in Spain and Portugal, which also had very rich commercial cities.

Care should be taken, however, to avoid treating the cities of this period as centers of dynamism. They would have merited this distinction only as compared with the countryside and in the particular context of traditional societies, that is, of a universe in which immobility was the rule. And as Perrot (1975) very rightly emphasizes with regard to urban structures of production, "in a highly unprogressive world, every victory is paid for by a crushing defeat somewhere else."

But May We Really Speak of Development in Traditional Societies?

One of the observations to which I have not yet drawn sufficient attention is the astonishing stability of the levels of urbanization reached in Europe as a whole revealed by the statistics I have elaborated. The restriction "as a whole" is important, for the center of gravity in urban Europe did not stay in one place. And if the term "stability" seems a little excessive, there is nevertheless no doubt that the scale, the amplitude of secular variations in the level of urbanization in Europe remained very modest. From the tenth century to the eighteenth century the level of urbanization rose by only 2 to 3 points. There is a strong likelihood, moreover, that the level of urbanization reached in the tenth century was lower than that reached in the third century under Rome. In the general conclusions (chapter 31) I shall return at greater length to this stability of the relative size of the urban world of medieval and Renaissance Europe, relating it to the situation in traditional societies outside Europe.

I shall also return (in chapter 31) to the theme of this section. For it appears more and more clear (Bairoch, 1979a) that the levels of development attained in traditional societies, both in Europe and elsewhere, fell within a fairly narrow range. Between a rich traditional society and a poor traditional society the difference in terms of average per capita income probably never exceeded 50%, and was perhaps not even as much as 20%. Such being the case, even supposing that the widest gaps between the richest and the poorest nations were larger than they have so far proven to be, can one really speak of development at all?

Splendid but Impoverished Cities

The modest gap between rich and poor nations, duplicated in slightly more exaggerated form at the regional level, raises an important question. How under these circumstances do we explain the testimony provided by the urban remains left to us from former times, a testimony pointing to great differences in wealth? The answer lies in the low cost of investments in tokens of urban power and prestige. Between a rich city with sumptuous monuments and a poor city without monuments of any kind, the difference in terms of investments would have amounted to no more than a few percentage points of national income. Quite independently of the choices individual societies might have made in this regard, even a slight rise in the standard of living would have permitted the erection of cities of great magnificence. Indeed it was enough to mobilize only a relatively small fraction of national urban revenues to set massive construction schemes on foot, an additional allocation of some 3–7% to construction probably sufficing to build urban edifices that in later years signified prodigious wealth.

Thus in Bruges, for example, the proportion of the working population employed in construction was something like 10% in the fourteenth century and between 5% and 10% in the fifteenth (Sosson, 1977). According to my colleague A. Perrenoud (1979), in Geneva during the years 1700–1725, a period of urban expansion and large-scale public works, 10.7% of the male labor force was engaged in public works and building, a figure that must have represented something less than 8% of the overall working population of the city. And during the 1770s, another period of urban growth, the figure was 8.3%, that is, probably less than 7% of the total work force. By contrast, during less prosperous phases of Geneva's history the proportion ranged between 3.7% and 6.4% of the male labor force, probably representing less than 3% and certainly less than 5% of the total active population.

And in Caen around the middle and end of the eighteenth century the corresponding proportions most likely stood at around 4–5% (Perrot, 1975). Now in the case of "poor" cities, the smallest possible fraction of the labor force employed in the building sector—a minimum permitting nothing more than the repair and replacement of existing edifices—was on the order of 3–4%. If one assumes that the mean income of construction workers was close to the overall urban average, and if one considers the enormous amount of time required to construct most of the largest monuments, this would have meant that the mobilization of 3–7% of total urban revenues would have made it possible to erect a rich, and even a very rich city.

And How Was the Pie Divided?

"The way in which the cities of the West imposed their will on rural areas prefigured the renewed activity of the urban markets: markets serving as instruments that by themselves made it possible to subjugate the countryside on a regular basis. 'Industrial' prices rose; agricultural prices fell. By this means, the cities won hands down." This aspect of Braudel's (1979) conclusions regarding the history of the various "tools of exchange" in use from the fifteenth century to the eighteenth century has a significant and illuminating bearing on the problems of the distribution of resources between town and country. This is indeed an important problem, one that has at least to be mentioned in passing even if, for obvious reasons, I harbor no illusions about being able to deal with it properly here. A valid analysis of what economists would call the cost benefits of relations between town and country in preindustrial societies is at present wholly out of the question; and given the lack of relevant data, it will remain so for a long time to come, if not forever. And yet it is precisely this lack of relevant data that makes Braudel's reflections on the matter interesting.

Even though there was a deterioration in the terms of trade between town and country, especially with regard to the value of goods manufactured in the cities relative to the value of agricultural products grown in the countryside, this does not tell the whole story. As in the case of the contemporary Third World and its commercial dealings with developed nations, however, at the heart of the problem lies the question of the extent to which this deterioration in the terms of trade necessarily entailed a loss of resources in the countryside to the benefit of the town. Indeed, if this deterioration were accompanied by an increase in the productivity of rural labor more rapid than like progress in the productivity of urban industrial labor, the countryside would have suffered no loss of resources whatever. But the presumption among students of this period is that the two sectors had similar (and very slow) rates of growth in this area. It follows, then, that the deterioration in the terms of trade between town and country led to a division of the pie in which the city received an ever-increasing slice.

But while city dwellers may thus be said to have profited from the country by taking away a disproportionate share of the natural resources, they failed nevertheless to get what was the most coveted thing of all: a longer life span. On the contrary, people died younger in the cities than in the countryside; in particular, fewer urban children reached adulthood. And as a direct result, the city was forced to draw on the countryside not only for food, but also for population. This brings me to a feature of relations between town and country that deserves to be treated in some detail—for what aspect of development matters more than people? I shall devote the remainder of this chapter to a discussion of the characteristics of urban demography in preindustrial societies.

Was There a Specific Urban Demography?

Even though much is unknown about urban demography, and even though no general review of research in this area has recently been done, it is nevertheless possible to sketch in the broad outline of an urban demography of the societies of traditional Europe. In particular, it is now possible to answer with a reasonable degree of certainty parts of two questions relating to urban demography after the fifteenth century. Did the growth of cities result mainly from natural developments or from immigration? And did natural developments (births and deaths) display any specifically urban characteristics?

What, then, was the nature of urban growth during this period? On this point, research findings tend to converge. Most studies show very clearly that migration played a role of primary importance in urban growth at this time. An increase in the population of any city was very largely the result of an influx of migrants, not only from neighboring areas, but often from other, very distant regions as well. And while, to be sure, most of the migrants came from rural districts, a good many of them also came from other cities. This migratory movement between cities—a movement lasting into the industrial phase of development—must be viewed in the context of the uneven growth of cities during this period. As I have already noted, some cities stagnated and even declined in population; and especially rapid decline sometimes created the need for immigration, particularly of specialized craftsmen.

Given the small number of cases for which reliable data exist, it is still risky to quantify the relative contribution made by each of the two components of urban growth, natural developments and migrations. But the role of migration finds confirmation in one important aspect of urban demography: the disproportionately high mortality rate among urban populations at this time. While it is difficult to come to any definite conclusions about the existence of a specifically urban birth rate, the exceptionally high urban death rate stands out more and more distinctly as a solidly established fact—one which at the level of the national average unquestionably constitutes a historical reality of some significance. And as a reality of history it continued to shape the general conditions of urban life until the very recent past. For, as will be seen later (chapter 14), this disproportionately high urban death rate did not finally level off until the twentieth century, at which point it vanished almost completely.

A Trend Established Long Ago: People Died Younger in Cities

As a general historical condition of urban life, disproportionately high mortality rates most likely date back to ancient times, since the study of average life spans has revealed very perceptible differences between urban and rural death rates in ancient Rome. Szilagyi (1962), for instance, examining funeral stellae, concludes that in Italy from the first century to the fifth century the average life span in the city of Rome was some 20–25% shorter than in Italy as a whole. The average life span of slaves, for example, was 17.5 years in Rome, as against 22.5 years in Italy at large, while the figures for freemen were 25.2 and 32.6 years, and for artisans and traders 31.2 and 39.2 years. Certainly the means by which Szilagyi arrived at these figures may be questioned on methodological grounds; but they point to a state of affairs comparable to that obtaining in other periods and may on this account be used as a token of the persistence of this specific feature of urban mortality.

And it is worthy of note that in 1662 John Graunt could write in his "Observations upon the Bills of Mortality" (considered a "seminal work, at the root both of statistics and of demography") with respect to urban mortality:

> It follows therefore . . . that the country is more
> *healthful* than the city, that is to say, although men
> die more regularly and less *per saltun* than in the
> country, yet, upon the whole matter, there die fewer
> *per rata*; so as the fomes steams and stenches above-
> mentioned, although they make the air of *London*
> more equal yet not more *healthful*.

This disproportionately high urban death rate apparently affected all age groups, but seems to have been especially pronounced among young children, the high infant mortality rate accounting, moreover, for a great part of the difference between urban and rural death rates. In traditional European societies, infant mortality (defined as the number of deaths per thousand births among children less than one year old) was probably on the order of 200–270 for the population as a whole. It appears that infant mortality in urban settings, on the other hand, lay somewhere between 230 and 450. Thus in German-speaking countries during the eighteenth century, urban infant death rates varied between 250 and 450 per thousand (close to 250–300 in small towns and 350–400 in larger ones) (François, 1978). For Leipzig between 1751 and 1800, the number was 348 per thousand; for eighteenth-century Breslau, 295 per thousand; for Vienna between 1752 and 1754, 409 per thousand; and for the small town of Menninge between 1747 and 1800, a staggering 459 per thousand. In the Tuscan city of Fiesole infant mortality rose from 237 per thousand for the period 1621–1649 to 333 per thousand for the period 1650–1699. In Geneva between 1580 and 1599, the rate was 290 per thousand, with averages of 285 per thousand during the seventeenth century and 225 per thousand during the eighteenth century.

But the hecatomb did not stop there. Only one child in two reached the age of ten years during the eighteenth century (Perrenoud, 1979). In the case of France, the practice of baby farming, sending babies out to nurse in the countryside (a matter to which I shall return), makes the data somewhat deceptive. But there is no doubt that infant mortality surpassed, on the average, 300 per thousand. In any event, the number of infants sent out to nurse who died before the end of their first year would appear to have been around 650–700 per thousand according to certain authors, and around 400–500 according to others. In view of these remarkably high mortality rates, one may well wonder, following the lead given by Philippe Ariès at a recent colloquium, whether we are not dealing with some kind of disguised infanticide; for when I add to the number of deaths occurring during the first year those occurring during the second, I find that only one nursing child in ten survived. By contrast with the situation in France, however, infant mortality in England seems to have been fairly moderate.

Nevertheless—and this concerns not only infant mortality, the easiest to measure, but death rates among other age groups as well—there were as many different demographic situations as there were cities; and the size of the city in particular had a differential impact in this regard. Comparative analyses of urban as against rural death rates during the sixteenth and seventeenth centuries are as yet too few and far between to enable me to provide any reliable indication of the probable difference between mortality rates in town and country during the period leading up to the eighteenth century. In the spirit of purest conjecture, however, I may hazard a guess based on the data (chapter 14) about nonindustrialized societies during the eighteenth and early nineteenth centuries. I surmise that urban mortality was greater than that in the surrounding countryside by anywhere from

20 to 60%. It may be noted that the figure marking the upper limit of this range of differences related to infant mortality, while the figure marking the lower limit related rather to young people and adults.

And What of Urban Fertility?

As was just indicated, it is not yet possible to reach any definite conclusions regarding urban fertility. But it seems likely that differences in the area of fertility were smaller than those for death rates. Several decades of research will doubtless prove necessary, however, before any verdict can be given—the principal problem being that patterns of behavior may have differed very widely from one city to another, and there is little chance that the national averages will present any similarities. Thus, as was seen in the preceding section, for example, recent investigations have shown the frequent and widespread practice of baby farming in many French cities during the seventeenth century and particularly during the eighteenth century. And it is interesting to observe that this practice was common among all social classes, the cost of sending a baby to a wet nurse being well below the wages paid working women in the cities. But while baby farming was also fairly common in Geneva, for instance, it appears to have been, if not totally absent, at least of no significance in England. And preliminary indications suggest that it was equally infrequent in Germany and Spain. The importance of these differences emerges when one considers that baby farming resulted in an increase in fertility among women; an increase capable of offsetting the more widespread use of contraceptive practices in the city.

The disappointment Bardet met with in 1974 when he analyzed the data available at that time for France, the country to which the greatest number of studies have been devoted, seems still valid today: the higher urban fertility rates that the first investigations led one to expect have failed to materialize. As Bardet himself puts it, "regional regroupings would appear to have prevailed over a generalized urban model."

A Negative Natural Balance Sheet: The Country Nourished the City with People as Well as with Food

Given the higher death rates in the cities, the lack of any fundamental difference between urban and rural birth rates reinforced the role of immigration in urban growth. For even in those cases where urban population did not increase more rapidly than that of the rest of the country, the higher mortality rate in the cities still created the need for a migration from the countryside. And in those cases where rapid urban growth took place, the influx of migrants must have been very substantial. Thus according to recent estimates based on the in-depth analysis of the situation in seventeenth-century London done by Wrigley and Schofield (1981), London needed to have received a net total of nearly 900,000 immigrants in order to have grown as it did from a population of around 190,000 in 1600 to one of some 550,000 in 1700. During this period London absorbed 80% of the natural increase in the population recorded for England as a whole.

Each day brings fresh evidence of the negative balance for natural population growth in cities since the Middle Ages at least, and probably since the very beginnings of urban history. In the case of medieval France, for example, "research conducted more systematically and in greater depth has revealed that immigration was thus a vital necessity in the strictest sense of the term. This has just been brought to light strikingly in the case of Arles. Periodically depopulated by famines and epidemics, perhaps having low birth rates, high mortality, and highly variable, often short individual life spans, the cities were in need of a constant supply of people to fill the voids created in their population" (Higounet-Nadal, 1980).

And in their synthesis of research on the period 1500 to 1700, Roger Chartier and Hugues Neveux (1981) reach the same conclusion concerning the indispensability of immigration. To be sure, one should not consider these migrations to have been only in one direction: people moved out of cities as well, though most often to move to other cities. But those arriving outnumbered those departing.

This convergence of findings should not lead one to suppose that there is perfect unanimity in the field. Thus Sharlin (1978) has advanced the paradoxical hypothesis that the negative natural population growth in traditional Western cities was indirectly due to migrations. In his view, the analysis of natural developments (births and deaths) among indigenous urban populations, or to borrow the terminology of demographers studying this period, among "natives" or "resident populations," shows a positive balance. Among indigenous populations births outnumbered deaths, the contrary being true for newcomers.

This thesis has, however, been subjected to pertinent criticism by Finlay (1981) and my colleague Perrenoud (1985). The first objection that can be leveled at it concerns the bias in the data relating to the natural events in indigenous populations. Owing to migration (natives, too, emigrate), there is a much greater likelihood of underestimating deaths than births. Certainly, given the uniqueness of each city's history, one cannot rule out the possibility that some cities during some periods had natural growth in their indigenous population and even in their population as a whole. But finer analyses, like that of Perrenoud for Geneva, confirm the dominant trend toward an excess of deaths among natives as well as migrants.

And I consider it entirely arbitrary to separate the inhabitants of cities artificially into these two classes. For while, because of their socioeconomic status, new arrivals may indeed have been characterized by a specific demography, in particular by a deficit of births, in the absence of these migrants a part of the indigenous population would have had to fill the socioeconomic niches left vacant. And since like causes lead to like effects, these natives would have suffered the same demographic shortfall.

In any event, the traditional city, like the city of the first phases of the Industrial Revolution (say between 1750 and 1850) (see chapter 14), was characterized by negative natural population growth.

The dwindling of the population of cities in the absence of an influx of immigrants constitutes part of the explanation of the rapid decline experienced by those cities whose economic base disappeared or diminished. There is in such cases no need to resort to the hypothesis of a heavy exodus from the cities to account for large-scale decreases in population. In the case of London once more, notably between 1650 and 1675, a period during which the natural movement of population was unfavorable, the city lost on the average some nine thousand inhabitants per year (or 3% per year) as a result of an excess of deaths relative to births. Without a steady flow of immigrants London would at this rate have lost more than half of its population over the course of this twenty-five-year period. Given the size of London this represents an extreme case, but one which nevertheless well illustrates the prevailing situation. For those cities were in the minority in which the natural growth of population was positive, and this despite the influx of migrants and the fact that the newcomers were generally of child-bearing age.

From the European Middle Ages to the Third World of today, the city has drawn on the countryside for people. "The country's penetration of the town occurred first of all at the human level. The urban France of the Middle Ages was in large part a rural France transplanted to the city" (Le Goff, 1980). And *Cities of Peasants* is the title of a work by B. Roberts (1978) on urbanization in the Third World.

Part Three

The Role of the City in the Development of the Western World

As early as the end of the seventeenth century, the English economy had begun to undergo the first of those profound changes that would eventually lead to the Industrial Revolution. By the 1770s and 1780s, a type of economy had already taken root which was without precedent in the history of humanity: an economy which, placed in the perspective of the period, had a pace of growth in yield and productivity that was exceedingly high.

Agriculture was the first sector of the economy to experience radical changes. In the space of a century—between 1700 and 1800—agricultural productivity doubled, freeing workers in rapidly increasing numbers for employment in nonagricultural forms of labor. England was thus to be the first major country in the world in which more than 30% of the working population worked elsewhere than in farming. And this happened in a sizable nation (total population of seven million), and despite the absence (and this is of great importance) of food imports. There had certainly never been such a ratio before, but by the 1770s and 1780s, such was the case in England. And by 1800, although imports still accounted for only about 3–5% of food consumed, already more than 60% of the English work force had ceased to be employed in agriculture. All of this was naturally reflected in a surge of urban growth. By 1800 around 23% of the population of England lived in towns with populations of five thousand or more (in 1850, 45%).

While the Industrial Revolution was for some fifty to eighty years confined exclusively to England, it had begun to spread outwards by 1760–80. The first countries outside England to feel its influence were France, Belgium, Switzerland, and the United States. Another fifty years or so would pass before a second, much smaller group, including Germany and certain parts of Austria-Hungary, joined in the movement. But this is already well into the nineteenth century. The third group of nations to experience the effects of the Industrial Revolution was distinctly heterogeneous, comprising Russia, Sweden,

Spain, Italy, and Japan. This third group entered the industrial age in the second half of the nineteenth century, between 1850 and 1880.

But what place did urbanism occupy in this highly uneven spread of economic development? This is the question I shall attempt to answer in part 3.

The spread of the Industrial Revolution was indeed uneven not only in temporal terms, but also with regard to the extent to which different countries succeeded in industrializing. Some nations (including those of the Third World) remained almost entirely nonindustrialized. I shall discuss this matter more particularly in chapter 16, after a discussion of the Industrial Revolution in England (chapter 15). These two chapters will be preceded by a general overview of the evolution of urbanization in the developed world between 1700 and 1980 (chapter 13) and by a global appraisal of the specific features of modern urban demography (chapter 14). Chapters 17 and 18 will focus on the relations between industrialization and urbanization in the nineteenth century. In chapter 19 I shall examine trends in urbanization during the twentieth century. Over the course of the discussion it will be shown that sometime around 1968 a profound change took place in attitudes toward the city. General problems concerning the relation between urbanization and economic development will occupy the two closing chapters of part 3 (chapters 20 and 21). And given the importance of this question, chapter 20 will concentrate entirely on the relations between the city and technological innovation.

13 Urbanism in Developed Countries: 1700–1980 □

    The economic explosion made possible by the Industrial Revolution eventually brought about a fundamental transformation in the nature of cities. Nor indeed were the cities alone in undergoing radical change. For where the urban way of life had for thousands of years been the exception, it now became the rule. Today in most developed countries more than two of every three persons live in cities. What is more, half of these city dwellers live in large urban agglomerations with populations in excess of 500,000. In transforming the urban landscape, the Industrial Revolution transformed the nature of society as a whole.

    At the beginning of chapter 15 I shall sketch in broad outline the important characteristics of the Industrial Revolution. But this seems a good time to indicate something of the unprecedented scope of the change wrought by the Industrial Revolution, not only in what gradually became the developed world, but also in the life of the whole world. For the Industrial Revolution led to a population explosion and a quantum leap in industrial and agricultural production that have completely remade the social structures of almost every country on earth.

    I shall start with the population explosion. At the beginning of the Christian era, world population had reached a summit of 200–350 million people. Over the next millennium the world's population increased hardly at all. But around 1340 it had reached a new summit of 400–500 million. Then after the hecatomb of the Black Death a further surge of growth took place resulting around 1700 in a world population on the order of 700 million. By 1985 the world had a population of some 4.8 billion, and so long as no catastrophe intervenes, we may be sure that by the year 2000, the population of the world will have surpassed 5.7 billion, the most likely figure being 6.1 billion. At present world population increases every ten years by a figure greater than the number of people inhabiting the entire world in 1700.

    But however prodigious the population explosion has been, the explosion in production was even greater. Between the years 1000 and 1700 the output of iron per capita (to take but one example) may perhaps have doubled, and this is probably an overestimation. Between 1700 and 1980, on the other hand, the output of iron per capita increased 180 times over. In the developed nations of the West today, one man in fourteen works in agriculture, as against eleven in fourteen two centuries ago. Yet despite the small proportion of the work force engaged in farming, farmers in the privileged societies of the developed world supply to each person a greater quantity and variety of food than their forebears, and even manage to export an amount of grain close to one-third of that produced by the entire world around 1700.

As another measure of the enormous changes resulting from the Industrial Revolution, consider life expectancy. Life expectancy at birth was practically identical under the Roman Emperor Augustus or under Wang Mang (in China during the same period) as under Louis XIV in France or K'ang Hsi in China (two nearly parallel reigns of similar length: 1643–1715 and 1662–1722). In the developed world, however, it has jumped from 28–35 years in 1700 to about 75 years today. But this holds true only for the developed world, the privileged world of the West. In the Third World life expectancy is only 45–50 years. And this is only one aspect (and not the most important) of the differences in the levels of development. But these crucial problems of the Third World will be discussed in detail in part 4.

The Eighteenth Century in Europe: Contrasts in Regional Development

Even as late as the nineteenth century, Europe still accounted for 80% of the developed world. During the eighteenth century the Industrial Revolution had not as yet transfigured the demographic landscape of Europe by altering the distribution of population between town and country, for it affected at that point only a few limited regions. In fact taking Europe as a whole no perceptible change in the relative size of the urban population occurred during the eighteenth century; the level of urbanization in 1800 was just about the same as in 1700 if not perhaps a little lower (see tables 13.1 and 13.2). This stagnation resulted from two contradictory trends tending to cancel each other out. England, still the only part of Europe to have truly felt the impact of the Industrial Revolution, experienced rapid growth in urban population. The number of people living in English cities went up from roughly 750,000–850,000 in 1700 to around 2,100,000 in 1800, a rise in the level of urbanization from 12–15% at the beginning of the century to 23% at the end. But England in 1800 represented only one-twentieth of the population of Europe at large. And on the Continent the eighteenth century was a period of stagnation

TABLE 13.1   Growth of the Levels of Urbanization
of European Countries
(1700–1800)

	1700	1750	1800
Austria-Hungary	5–8	6–7	6–7
Balkans	7–12	7–12	8–11
Belgium	26–35	18–23	18–22
England	13–16	17–19	22–24
France	11–15	12–16	11–13
Germany	8–11	8–10	8–10
Italy	14–19	15–20	16–20
Netherlands	38–49	33–41	34–39
Portugal	18–23	13–15	14–17
Scandinavia	5–8	6–9	8–10
Spain	12–17	12–18	12–19
Switzerland	6–8	6–9	6–8
Europe	11–14	11–13	11–13
Europe except England	11–14	10–13	10–13
Russia	4–7	5–7	5–7
Europe as a whole	9–12	9–12	9–11

Sources: Calculations and estimates by the author; see the methodological appendix.
A criterion of 5,000 is used for urban population.

and even of decline in urbanization. In France, in Germany, and in
Switzerland, urban population increased at more or less the same pace
as the total population, if not a little more slowly. And while the
situation appears to have been more positive in the Scandinavian countries and in Austria-Hungary, the rest of Europe recorded a fairly pronounced fall in the level of urbanization. This was particularly noticeable in Belgium, Portugal, and the Netherlands, but applied to a lesser
extent in Italy and Spain as well (see table 13.1).

The several instances of decline and the general stagnation in the
level of urbanization in continental Europe suggest that the region
had reached a threshold difficult, if not impossible, to surpass within
the framework of traditional economies. European agricultural production had come to a bottleneck. And one may well wonder whether,
without the revolution in agricultural techniques and productivity associated with the Industrial Revolution, the Europe of the first half of
the nineteenth century might not have succumbed to the same unfavorable changes as had gripped China three centuries earlier (see
chapter 22). Thus the disturbing parallels observed by Braudel (1967)
between the dominant currents in the socioeconomic histories of Europe and China would have lasted longer in Europe if it had not been
for the Industrial Revolution.

As for Russia, which has been left out of Europe to facilitate analy-

TABLE 13.2   Growth of the Urban Population and Levels of
Urbanization in Europe (except Russia)
(1700–1980)

	Total Population (millions)	Urban Population		Level of Urbanization	
		Millions	Annual Variation (%)	% of Total Population	Annual Variation (%)
1700	102	12.6	—	12.3	—
1750	120	14.7	0.3	12.2	0.0
1800	154	18.6	0.5	12.1	0.0
1850	203	38.3	1.5	18.9	0.9
1880	243	71.4	2.1	29.3	1.5
1900	285	108.3	2.1	37.9	1.3
1910	312	127.1	1.6	40.8	0.7
1930	333	159.7	1.1	47.9	0.8
1950	367	186.0	0.8	50.7	0.3
1970	427	271.8	1.9	63.7	1.2
1980	453	301.0	1.0	66.5	0.4

Sources: Calculations and estimates by the author; see the methodological appendix.
Note: The fact that these figures have been only slightly rounded off does not imply a correspondingly small margin of error.
A criterion of 5,000 is used for urban population.
Russia is considered within the frontiers of 1913.

sis, it is difficult to make any definite judgement one way or the other. The data I was able to assemble are too incomplete and the margin of error surrounding the figures on population is too great to permit any but the rashest conclusions. The only thing I can safely say in this connection is that nothing momentous happened in Russia during this period.

The Urban Explosion in Nineteenth-Century Europe

But if, England apart, one observes few changes in Europe during the eighteenth century, the situation changed dramatically during the nineteenth, and to begin with of course in England. Somewhere between 1837 and 1842 the level of urbanization in England surpassed 40%, and by 1880 fully 68% of the population lived in cities. But changes were also taking place in other countries, as they too increasingly began the process of industrialization. Thus by 1850 the level of urbanization in Europe had grown by 60%, (19% as against 12% in 1800). And on the eve of the First World War, roughly 42% of the population of Europe would be living in cities.

The nineteenth century constitutes the pivotal period between a rural Europe, very close to the Europe of former centuries, and a highly urbanized Europe prefiguring the urban Europe of the late twentieth century. Since overall population growth was also very rapid, the number of people living in cities increased sevenfold between 1800 and 1910, rising from 19 million to 127 million. Between 1300 and 1700 the population of European cities rose from 8 million to 13 million. Over the course of the nineteenth century, urbanization was especially rapid between 1830–1840 and 1900. Urban population during this period increased at the rate of 2% per year, and the level of urbanization increased by 1.4% per year.

A Digression: The Criteria Used to Define Urban Population

The nineteenth century was a pivotal century in the history of Europe. But it was also a pivotal period in the history of the world as a whole, marking the moment of transition between traditional societies (to which part 2 and much of part 4 are devoted) and the developed world (on which part 3 focuses). Now upheaval on this scale entails, ipso facto, consequences touching the very nature of urbanization and thus the criteria used to define it as well.

Also, it is interesting to note that in his study "The Evolution of the Notion of Cities in the Geographical Descriptions of France (1650–1850)" (1979) Bernard Lepetit describes very well how the notion evolved over time, and also how early there was awareness of the problem. He cites a writing of 1678: "It would be necessary to propose and decide which are the places we have to qualify as cities and which do not merit such a name."

In chapter 8 I discussed the general problems of the criteria used to define urban population. At that point, I justified the compromise I had to make in a case like this where the analysis not only covers a very long time span and very different societies but must also often rely on fairly dubious data. Under these circumstances the only workable criterion proved to be the size of urban agglomerations. And given the wide margin of error surrounding the figures available for smaller cities and towns, I adopted a population of 5,000 as the limit starting from which an agglomeration would qualify as urban. As I stressed at that time, this limit is certainly a little high for traditional European societies; a limit of 2,000 would unquestionably have been more suitable, and I have in fact occasionally made use of it. The time has come, however, to justify this limit of 5,000 more thoroughly, after which I shall examine the effects alternative criteria would have on measures of urban evolution.

The first and most important justification is the fact that in those instances where use is made of the criterion of size (that is, in most censuses), the limit of 5,000 most nearly approximates the average of the various limits employed. Thus in the censuses taken at the beginning and during the latter half of the nineteenth century, for example, for the fourteen countries for which information of this kind is available, five chose the limit of 2,000, two the limit of 5,000, one 6,000, one 8,000, four 10,000, and one 20,000, making an average of 6,700 if I include this last case and 5,700 if I do not. In censuses taken in the twentieth century, the limit of 5,000 predominates even more clearly. On the other hand, we preferred the limit of 5,000 over that of 2,000 on purely practical grounds, since the countries using limits above 2,000 often do not furnish statistics on the distribution of population among centers falling below the limit adopted for the census.

The evidence presented above, and also the comparisons that can be made for nations in which for recent censuses urban population has been determined using many different and complex criteria, prove that the limit of 5,000 provides a very good approximation, though there is probably a slight bias tending to underestimate urban population. And while a limit of 3,000 or 4,000 would provide an even closer approximation, neither has shown itself to be practicable. Also, even if one adopted a limit of 2,000, this would make only a fairly small difference in my measures of the levels of urbanization in developed countries. For once the levels of urbanization in the developed countries of the nineteenth century have been reached, most of the urban population has already been concentrated in larger cities. Thus even at the level of Europe except Russia, the adoption of the criterion of 2,000 would entail for 1900 an increase of only 2 points, or 7% in the level of urbanization as measured here (see table 13.3). For 1950 the increase would only be 4%, and for 1980 only 2%.

On the other hand, the use of the criterion of 2,000 to gauge levels of urbanization in 1700 and 1800 would lead to a deviation on the order of 30% and for 1300 even around 40%. Certainly these differences are highly approximate. One of the essential reasons for adopting the criterion of 5,000 is that the margin of error for the number of people living in cities of 2,000–5,000 people is much greater than that for the number living in cities of more than 5,000 people. Indeed, before the nineteenth century there are no data at all available for cities of 2,000–5,000 people: I had to supply them myself by postulating what the population of cities of 2,000–5,000 people would have been in the nineteenth century, based on the data for various countries at different levels of urbanization and on my own calculation to correct Davis's law (see chapter 9 and the methodological appendix).

Although it does involve a certain underestimation of urban population, so long as we are dealing with the evolution of urban population in the context of traditional societies, the criterion of 5,000 does not significantly distort either the patterns of urban development or comparisons between countries. This is because the size of the overall population of cities of 2,000–5,000 people relative to that of cities of more than 5,000 people remained, on the whole, almost constant. With the urban explosion of the nineteenth century, on the other

TABLE 13.3   Growth of the Urban Population of Europe (except Russia) according to Each of the Two Criteria for Urban Population (1000–1980)

	Criterion of 2,000		Criterion of 5,000	
	Millions	% of Pop	Millions	% of Pop
1000	5.4	13.7	3.8	9.7
1300	10.9	14.5	7.9	10.4
1500	11.3	14.8	8.2	10.7
1700	16.2	16.2	12.6	12.3
1800	24.2	15.5	18.6	12.1
1850	45.3	22.1	38.3	18.9
1900	115.9	40.6	108.3	37.9
1950	193.0	52.6	186.0	50.7
1980	307.0	67.3	301.0	66.5

Sources: Calculations and estimates by the author; see the text concerning restrictions.
Note: The fact that these figures have been only slightly rounded off does not imply a correspondingly small margin of error.

hand, this situation changed entirely. For in the nineteenth century two new phenomena enter on the scene. In the first place, the relative size of the population living in cities of 2,000–5,000 people diminished, owing to the larger size of cities generally. And in the second place, as a result of the growing size of cities in general, the real lower limit of urbanization moved upwards. All of this meant that the urban expansion of the nineteenth century was in fact a little slower than the figures based on the criterion of 5,000 would suggest. Thus during the period 1800–1900, instead of the annual rise in urban population of 1.8 percent calculated using the limit of 5,000, the growth rate would have been nearer 1.6%. The difference for the period 1800–1850 is even more pronounced; the growth rate obtained using the criterion of 5,000 is 1.5%, whereas the actual growth rate was 1.2%.

The Twentieth Century: A Variety of Cyclical Patterns

Over the course of the twentieth century, the pattern of urbanization has reflected the different phases of economic growth very closely. The depression of the thirties and the two World Wars brought about a perceptible slowdown in the growth of urban population and in the level of urbanization. The period of very rapid growth in developed countries since the end of the Second World War brought about a fresh acceleration in the rate of urbanization.

And yet with regard to developments since the Second World War, considering the economic growth in developed nations urbanization did not proceed at the same rate as during the latter half of the nineteenth century. A slowdown of this sort, however, especially one affecting growth in the level of urbanization, can be explained in terms of the fact that urbanization is ultimately subject to an absolute limit. While expansion in industrial production, for example, can at least in theory continue forever, it is obvious that urbanization can never surpass 100%. And it seems very likely that the real limit on urbanization lies well below this theoretical ceiling.

The slowdown observed during the decade of the seventies should be viewed in this perspective. But allowance should also be made for the impact of changes in the attitudes and behavior of urban populations themselves. To be sure, the analysis of developments during the seventies is risky, owing to the aura of crisis surrounding the events of this decade. There was the recession of 1974–75, of course, and the energy crisis. But also, and more fundamentally, there has been a growth of interest in ecology and concomitantly in the rural way of life. This renewed interest in rural life probably resulted from urban expansion itself: hyperurbanized societies very likely contain within their own growth the seed of this sort of reaction against the conditions of urban existence. I shall have more to say on this matter in chapter 19, where I discuss the possible future course of urbanization in the developed world.

Another thing that can be noted about the general evolution of cities in the twentieth century is that the absolute limit on urban growth has promoted a certain harmonization of levels of urbanization. Thus whereas in the Europe of 1910 (see table 13.4) the maximum deviation in the levels of urbanization reached in the various nations of the developed world was about 480 percent of the minimum, in 1980 it was only 240%. This does not mean, however, that levels of urbanization had become totally independent of levels of development, only that the closer urbanization comes to its absolute limit, the greater the role played in any country by national factors peculiar to it. These factors have tended to be either purely geographical in character (qualities of the soil, for example) or of a political cast (the size of the country, its form of government, its economic policies, etc.). In any event, for the years around 1900, a period for which my criteria for defining urban population have practically no distorting effects, the analysis of the linear correlation between the levels of development (expressed by the indicator of per capita gross national product) and the levels of urbanization of the countries of Europe yields a coefficient of 0.62. The corresponding coefficient for 1970, on the other hand, is only 0.27. In other words, for 1900 differences in levels of development account for more than one-third of the differences in levels of urbanization, while for 1970 they explain less than one-tenth. I shall examine the links between development and urbanization in greater detail in chapter 21.

But before moving on to the analysis of developments in the size of cities, a few words about the urban evolution of developed nations

TABLE 13.4 Levels of Urbanization in the Principal Developed Countries (1800–1980)

	1800[a]	1850	1910	1950	1970	1980
Belgium	20	34	57	64	71	70
England	23	45	75	83	81	79
France	12	19	38	48	68	69
Germany	9	15	49	53	68	75
Italy	18	(23)	(40)	(56)	65	65
Netherlands	37	39	53	75	83	82
Portugal	16	(16)	16	25	29	34
Rumania	7	(11)	16	28	47	56
Spain	18	(18)	(38)	(55)	70	73
Sweden	7	7	23	45	62	64
Switzerland	7	12	33	48	59	58
Yugoslavia	10	(10)	10	16	37	44
Europe	12	19	41	51	63	66
USSR	(6)	(7)	(14)	(34)	54	61
United States	5	14	42	57	66	65
Canada	6	8	32	46	56	58
Australia	—	(8)	(42)	59	79	80
Japan	(14)	(15)	18	38	72	78
Developed countries as a whole	11	16	32	46	62	65

Sources: Calculations and estimates by the author; see the methodological appendix.
Note: The fact that these figures have been only slightly rounded off does not imply a correspondingly small margin of error. The figures in parentheses have a much wider margin of error than the other data.
A criterion of 5,000 is used for urban population.
[a] Very approximate levels.

outside Europe seem in order. And something should be said in particular about North America, which today still represents the largest part of the non-European developed world.

The Urbanization of the Rest of the Developed World

Around 1700 North America north of the Rio Grande was still very thinly populated, there being some 250,000 Europeans, some 30,000 blacks, and perhaps one to three million native Americans. But in contrast to what was the case south of the Rio Grande, the white newcomers did not confront indigenous urban cultures. As was seen in chapter 4, while certain of the cultures of northern North America had attained a high degree of development in art and in a number of techniques, they remained on the whole essentially rural and even, in most cases, preagrarian. Furthermore, the very nature of the first waves of European immigrants to the present-day United States and Canada led to a fundamentally rural society. As a result of all of these factors, in 1700 the two largest cities in northern North America—Boston and Quebec—had about 6,000–7,000 people each. The two other "big" cities, New York and Philadelphia, had some 4,000–5,000 each, followed by Newport and Charleston with 2,000 each.

But the eighteenth century witnessed rapid growth in North American cities. By 1800 Philadelphia had around 68,000 people, New York 64,000, Boston 35,000, Montreal 15,000, and Quebec 12,000. Despite this growth, however, northern North American society continued to be rural in character. For in the interval, the population (European and that assimilated into the European system) had risen from 250 thousand to 5.5 million, with the result that even as late as 1800 the level of urbanization remained very low: on the order of 5–6% as compared with 12% in Europe.

This low level of urbanization is explained not only by social factors (immigration of religious minorities with rural backgrounds) or by historical factors (nonurbanized indigenous cultures, leading to the late emergence of urbanism), but also by economic factors. The very large amount of available land led to a low population density, which is not favorable to the emergence of cities. The colonial policy of England, confining the development of the industrial sector to a minimum, put a brake on industrial activity in the United States until Independence. To take one example, in 1750 England, facing at that time a substantial deficit in iron which obliged her to import from abroad more than half of her iron, passed an act of Parliament allowing the American colonies to produce iron. But this same act prohibited any manufacturing use of this iron in the colonies themselves.

The Spanish and Portuguese pursued a similar policy in Latin America, where the level of urbanization was nevertheless on the order of 12–14% (see chapter 24). To explain this difference, two further elements must be called into play. The first is the absence of any large-scale mining of precious metals in northern North America, for the American gold rush did not take place until 1849. The second relates to climate. The predominantly temperate climate of the United States kept its agricultural exports within very narrow limits until around 1790, when King Cotton began, tentatively at first, his reign in the South. Thus during the first half of the eighteenth century, the United States furnished only 6–7% of England's overall imports, that is, less than half of what England received from her small colonies in the Antilles.

But things greatly changed over the course of the nineteenth century. The United States experienced rapid economic growth during the nineteenth century—more rapid, indeed, than that of Europe. Above all, it absorbed a massive influx of immigrants, 31.5 million of them arriving between 1840 and 1914, roughly 60% of whom stayed. Further, thanks to tariff policy changes made possible by independence, the economic situation swiftly changed, especially in the latter half of the nineteenth century, when the country underwent rapid industrialization. There was, moreover, a paradox at work here, inasmuch as after independence, owing to the growing need for cotton on the part of British industry, the United States furnished a much larger share of the United Kingdom's total imports: some 19–21% by the end of the 1850s. And those total imports had themselves seen a twentyfold increase in value (as compared to the first half of the eighteenth century).

As a result of all of this, by the start of the twentieth century the United States was more heavily urbanized than Europe. To the factors discussed above should further be added the high level of agricultural productivity achieved in the United States. This high level of productivity very soon enabled the United States, in common with most of the other countries of temperate climate colonized and populated by Europeans, to have a large urban population. Consequently at a comparable level of development, the United States and the other countries with European settlement generally had a larger urban population. One effect of this was the formation of very great cities, which was favored even more by the fact that these cities were located at the mouths of rivers with vast inland basins. Thus by 1900, of the eleven largest cities in the world, all of which had at that time populations of more than a million, four were in countries settled by Europeans: New York, Chicago, Philadelphia, and Buenos Aires.

But now I shall take a closer look at the question of great cities, for this has been one of the dominant features of the process of urbanization since the Industrial Revolution.

The Emergence of the Megalopolis

It little matters what term we use to describe the new giant cities (metropolis, megalopolis, megacity, connurbation, urban nebula). The fact is that, with the Industrial Revolution, there appeared an entirely new phenomenon characterized both by a considerable rise in the upper limit on the size of cities and by a marked increase in the number of very great cities.

When one speaks of the size of a city, agreement must first be reached as to the definition of its perimeter. At present, a distinction is drawn between three main concepts used to define cities: the "city proper," the "urban agglomeration," and the "metropolitan area." Very schematically these three concepts may be defined as follows.

As a general rule, the city proper is delineated by administrative boundaries and involves the districts forming an urban center. This is the narrowest definition of the city, corresponding to what in the modern world could be described as a city without suburbs. In historical terms this concept of the city covers practically all cities before the nineteenth century.

The urban agglomeration may be defined as the city together with its suburbs. In general it covers zones of a distinctly urban character that, while falling outside the limits of the city proper, nevertheless lie adjacent to it. Obviously the suburb is essentially the result of the urban evolution of the nineteenth century, even if it can be traced to the Middle Ages.

The metropolitan area, a concept first used in the United States, applies in principle only to cities of fairly large size—in the United States to cities whose administrative center has some 50,000 inhabitants. The perimeter of a metropolitan area reaches out to include those regions in which "there exists a manifest relation of interdependence between local functions and those of some central city." For practical purposes this means that the metropolitan area embraces not only the adjacent suburbs, but also those smaller agglomerations that, owing to their proximity, have come to depend on the central city. In historical terms this notion does not apply before the twentieth century. To put it another way, during the nineteenth century, the urban agglomeration and the metropolitan area were virtually indistinguishable, just as in preceding centuries there was virtually no difference between the urban agglomeration and the city proper. Today, however, very pronounced differences exist between these three urban categories. Thus it was that, according to estimates done by the United Nations (1970) for cities with populations of 100,000–500,000 in developed regions in 1955, the population of urban agglomerations surpassed that of cities proper by 3% while the population of metropolitan areas surpassed that of urban agglomerations by 21%.

The term "city" as I shall use it here will as a rule have a meaning close to that of the term "metropolitan area," in the same way that throughout the book I have for each period given the word "city" the widest meaning appropriate to that period. Naturally this does not mean that the limits for each city are stable or are based here on the very large sizes of the contemporary era. Rather the figures used in each case were adjusted to include a certain percentage, variable over time, of populations that, while not part of the city proper, nevertheless had close relations with it and were located only a short distance away.

The emergence of a great number of very large cities (cities, let us say, with a population of more than 500,000 people) was in fact fundamentally related to the phase of development following the Industrial Revolution. To be sure, as has been seen in previous chapters, one will find among the civilizations of the West or (as will be seen in part 4) among the civilizations of Asia a few very limited examples of cities reaching and even surpassing this size prior to the Industrial Revolution. But each of these examples is a capital city or the metropolis of a far-flung empire: cities like Rome, Paris, London, Constantinople, Peking, Baghdad, and perhaps two or three others, each of

TABLE 13.5   Growth of Cities in Developed Countries according to
Population
(1800–1980)

Size of Cities (in 1000s)	1800	1850	1900	1950	1980
			Number of Cities		
100–200	17	35	101	288	491
200–500	9	18	61	186	376
500–1,000	1	3	24	68	121
1,000–5,000	1	2	8	47	101
5,000 or more	—	—	1	5	9
Total	28	58	195	594	1,098
			Urban Population (in millions)		
100–200	2.3	4.8	14.2	39.2	69.7
200–500	3.0	6.2	19.1	55.8	114.5
500–1,000	0.6	2.0	14.3	45.2	84.4
1,000–5,000	1.1	4.0	18.1	84.9	182.0
5,000 or more	—	—	6.6	40.5	84.7
Total	6.9	17.0	72.4	265.7	535.3
Urban population[a]	26.2	51.5	163.3	388.4	762.0
Total population	241.8	331.9	549.2	843.1	1,165.0

Sources: Bairoch (1977a) and additional data; see the methodological appendix.
Note: The fact that these figures have been only slightly rounded off does not imply a correspondingly small margin of error.
[a] A criterion of 5,000 is used for urban population.

which at its height (of longer or shorter duration) had a population of some 500,000 to 1,000,000, and sometimes even a little more. These cities had their climaxes at different periods, so one can estimate that before the Industrial Revolution there were never more than five to seven cities in the world which at the same time had populations of more than 500,000. Now as early as 1910 Europe alone (except Russia), although it had only one-sixth of the world's population, had some twenty-nine cities with populations of more than 500,000, of which four had populations in excess of 1 million. It seems that before the Industrial Revolution no city had a population surpassing 2 million, (probably not even 1.5 million). By 1860, on the other hand, London already had a population of more than 3 million, surpassing 7 million before 1910. And on the eve of the First World War, Europe had five cities with populations of more than 2 million (Berlin, Leningrad, London, Paris, and Vienna), to which should be added three others outside Europe (New York, Chicago, and Tokyo).

The growth in the size of cities continued after the First World War (see table 13.5). New York was the first city in the world with a population of more than 10 million—that is to say, as many people as lived in all of the 500-odd cities of Europe and North America in 1600. New York had already reached this size by about 1930, having overtaken London—the largest city in the world between 1830 and 1920—ten years earlier. London itself had in 1830 snatched the honor of being the largest city in the world from Peking; the latter, like London, had retained this title for about a century. New York continued to grow until between 1964 and 1966 it became the first city in history to surpass 15 million. Since then, however, its growth has slowed down considerably. This slowdown, which has been seen in other cases as well, raises the question of whether there is an "upper limit" to city size, and also the question of the optimal size of cities. But these are large questions beyond the scope of this book. I have done a fairly extensive and detailed study of these matters (Bairoch, 1977a). A short summary of this research will be presented in chapter 19.

The combination of rapid growth in the level of urbanization and increase in the size of cities led to radical changes in the way of life of the population. Around 1800 less than 3% of the total population of developed countries lived in cities with populations of more than 100,000. By 1900 the proportion had risen to 14%, approaching 50% in 1980. In the most highly developed countries, the proportion is even on the order of 60%, and in 1980 there were in the developed world as a whole some 110 cities with populations of more than 1 million.

Thus industrialization not only profoundly changed the scale and form of consumption, but also brought about a totally new type of society. It will be necessary to look into the links uniting these two cardinal facts of postindustrial life: the links between the city and the full flowering of the Industrial Revolution, between the city and the spread of industrialization, between the city and technological innovation, and so on. Such will be the subject of the following chapters. But before moving on to these matters, in the next chapter I shall consider the specific characteristics of urban demography in the developed world since the Industrial Revolution. But I cannot close the present chapter without mentioning a minor paradox: the surprisingly limited change in the average size of cities in the postindustrial world.

Large Cities, But No Dramatic Change in the Average Size of Cities

The average size of cities is not necessarily meaningful. And this seems an appropriate time to recall the old chestnut about the statistician who drowned in a lake whose average depth was only one foot. It was perhaps due more to idle curiosity than anything else that I calculated the growth of the average size of cities since the Industrial Revolution. And since my findings surprised both me and the col-

TABLE 13.6   Growth of the Average Population of European Cities
(except Russia)
(1300–1970)

	Average Population of Cities with Populations of More Than		
	2,000	5,000	20,000
1300	6,600	12,900	36,500
1500	6,700	13,500	39,600
1700	7,600	15,400	51,000
1800	7,800	16,700	54,900
1900	15,400	21,200	78,900
1970[a]	30,800	42,800	113,200

Sources: Calculations and estimates by the author; see the methodological appendix.
Note: The fact that these figures have been only slightly rounded off does not imply a correspondingly small margin of error.
[a] Not strictly comparable; data for large cities were adapted from data for metropolitan areas, which were converted into data for cities.

leagues to whom I communicated them, I decided to present them here (table 13.6). In order to simplify my task a little, but also in order to keep the region as homogeneous as possible, I confined my calculations to Europe alone, excluding Russia. In any case, before 1900 the inclusion of the rest of the developed world would not have altered the results.

The surprise is the small amount of growth in the average size of cities. Between 1300 and 1800 the average size of cities increased by only some 20%. Naturally enough, things moved faster after that. Even between 1800 and 1900, however, the average only doubled, doubling once more between 1900 and 1970. The explanation for this unexpectedly slow rate of growth lies in the emergence during the nineteenth century and part of the twentieth of a great number of small cities and towns. But if it is true that in 1970 the average population of European cities was only 43,000, it should not be forgotten that at this same time roughly 75% of the urban population lived in cities with populations of more than 43,000 (and 80% of these lived in cities with populations of more than 100,000). This means that only 25% lived in cities with populations of fewer than 43,000.

14 Urban Demography in Developed Countries from the Eighteenth Century to the Twentieth Century □

Is there a specifically urban demography? As was shown at the end of chapter 12, the notion that there is anything uniquely urban about the demography of populations living in cities in traditional societies can still be called into question on many counts. No doubt is possible, however, regarding the period from the onset of the Industrial Revolution to 1920–1950. During these two centuries, there was practically no aspect of the demography of cities that did not exhibit specifically urban traits: fertility, infant mortality, marriage, and so on. Each was different in town from its counterpart in the country.

And among the components of this uniquely urban demographic landscape there was in particular the heavy and terrible urban death rate. The young country couple deciding in the middle of the nineteenth century to move to an industrial city did not suspect that in making this move they shortened their life expectancy by some six to nine years, and that their children yet unborn (probably fewer than if they had remained in the country) stood a one-and-one-half-times greater risk of dying in their first year. Not all cities were as deadly as this, but all cities were much more deadly than the surrounding countryside. And if today mortality rates are a little lower in the city than in rural districts, this reversal is of relatively recent date. It is symptomatic in this regard that in 1924, in a country as affluent as Canada (at that time among the two or three wealthiest countries in the world), the authors of the Official Annual Report could write: "It is one of the greatest triumphs of our age that, while the urban scene may not be as healthy as the rest of the country, yet it is no longer necessarily more dangerous to human life and especially to the lives of children."

It is with this terrible aspect of city life that I shall begin my analysis of urban demography. For this aspect of city life the data are both more abundant and more reliable, even though no proper historical synthesis of urban demography in general exists. This state of affairs led me to attempt such a synthesis here. For what in life is more important than birth? And what is more tragic than death, and in particular the death of children?

The City: Graveyard of Babies

Infant mortality, that is, the number of children dying before their first birthday per thousand live births (or, if one prefers, the proportion of children dying before the age of one) is a type of demographic statistic widely available and subject to fairly minor distortions. We need only know the number of live births (thus excluding stillbirths) and the number of deaths occurring before the age of one. Statistical biases may derive especially (though not exclusively) from an incomplete registration of deaths (something more frequent in rural than in urban districts) and from migrations. Since the city tends to be a place that people immigrate to, there may be an overestimation of the urban infant mortality rate owing to the inclusion of babies born in rural areas but dying in the city after their parents had moved there. It is true that in the past this form of distortion was partly offset by the number of babies born in the city but dying in the countryside after being farmed out for wet-nursing, a very widespread practice (see chapter 12). But in the nineteenth century in most developed countries, these distortions and others like them accounted for deviations on the order of 5–10% at most.

Before dealing with infant mortality, it may be well to mention here that the Industrial Revolution did not lead to any increase in infant death rates—quite the opposite. Even if the causes of the lowering of infant mortality remain open to debate, and even if more negative phases sometimes occurred, the fundamental trend was toward a rapid reduction in infant deaths, especially after 1860–1870. In France, for instance, the rate fell from 270 deaths per thousand in 1770 to 200 in 1800, and to 134 in the 1910s. In Sweden the rate was 208 per thousand between 1751 and 1780, falling to 200 by 1800, and to 75 in the 1910s. Taking western Europe as a whole, according to my calculations, infant mortality evolved as follows:

mid-eighteenth		around 1929	95
century	240	around 1939	80
around 1800	210	around 1950	55
around 1850	190	around 1970	23
around 1870	190	around 1980	12
around 1913	130	around 1985	9

In the traditional Europe of the sixteenth and seventeenth centuries, cities—and particularly the larger cities—constituted a highly unfavorable environment for the health of children (see chapter 12). Infant mortality in urban districts must in all likelihood have exceeded that in the neighboring countryside by roughly 60%—though there were as always differences from one region and one phase of socioeconomic life to another. I shall leave the eighteenth century aside

TABLE 14.1   Infant Mortality Rates in Urban and Rural Regions
(1811-1960)

	Norway[a]		Netherlands[b]		Sweden	
	Urban	Rural	Amster-dam	Whole Country	Urban	Rural
1811–1820	—	—	251	—	243	177
1831–1840	—	—	228	—	229	161
1851–1860	135	95	228	197	219	137
1871–1880	135	91	214	203	193	119
1891–1900	126	83	155	158	130	95
1901–1910	—	—	107	125	101	80
1911–1920	73	58	64	92	76	67
1921–1930	—	—	41	60	58	59
1931–1940	39	40	31	41	40	49
1941–1950	30	32	—	—	25	29
1951–1960	19	20	18	21	17	19

Sources: For Norway: United Nations (1973), p. 134.
For the Netherlands: Bureau Municipal de statistique d'Amsterdam (1923), p. 208; Annuaire statistique de la ville d'Amsterdam, various numbers; Quarterly Bulletin, vol. 66, part 4. Amsterdam, October–December 1960, Supplement (p. S182); and vol. 86, part 4. Amsterdam, October–December 1962, Supplement (p. S218).
For Sweden: Historisk Statistik för Sverige, vol. 1, 2d edition, Stockholm, 1969 (p. 115).
Note: Infant mortality rate: deaths of children less than one year old per thousand live births.
[a] For 1851–60 onwards, the data cover 1856–60, 1876–80, etc.
[b] For before 1891, the data cover 1850–59, 1870–79, etc.

here, concentrating on changes in this domain from the beginning of the nineteenth century on.

Throughout most of the nineteenth century, infant mortality in the cities exceeded rural infant mortality by some 30–60%. In Sweden between 1850 and 1880 the urban infant death rate exceeded the rural infant death rate by 60%. In Norway in the same period the gap was around 45% (see table 14.1). According to the data prepared by Knodel (1977), the gap in Germany was only 10% for the whole country between 1875 and 1877. It is true in this case that the rural infant mortality rate was very high (222 per thousand), and that in industrial regions like Prussia and Schleswig-Holstein, the difference between urban and rural death rates was twice the national average. And while Knodel's analyses show very clearly that, as one would expect, urbanization was not alone in accounting for differences in infant mortality, nevertheless infant mortality (especially neonatal mortality) represented, along with levels of fertility, one of the two demographic phenomena most subject to urban influences. The veritable gold mine of information provided by Weber (1899) indicates well the general situation throughout Europe and North America.

It was not until the end of the nineteenth century that the gap began to close noticeably, disappearing around 1920–1930. In certain

TABLE 14.2   Infant Mortality Rates in European Countries and
Larger Cities
(1880–1938)

	1880–84	1890–94	1900–1904	1911–13	1924–26	1937–38
Austria	251	294	216	193	123	88
Vienna	189	216	179	157	103	62
Belgium	163	163	153	139	93	76
Brussels	—	194	174	177	129	106
Antwerp	—	—	210	165	94	—
Denmark	140	138	121	98	83	63
Copenhagen	220	184	160	101	75	51
England	142	149	143	111	73	55
London	152	155	144	109	67	—
Birmingham	163	180	178	138	78	61
France	170	170	144	124	90	66
Paris	172	138	111	107	91	—
Lyons	123	144	127	106[a]	113[b]	—
Germany[c]	206	204	192	104	102	62
Berlin	291	243	208	151	90	57
Frankfurt	178	166	170	110	75	45
Leipzig	228	235	230	205	108	—
Hungary	—	250	212	198	182	133
Budapest	259	216	149	151	131	—
Italy	181	180	169	141	124	108
Rome	179	150	131	133[a]	83	81
Naples	246	206	154	99	124	107
Turin	151	139	152	136[a]	90[b]	70
Russia	266	275	(255)	(240)	215	—
Moscow	351	350	356	298	146	—
Leningrad	303	232	208	230	149	—
Switzerland	173	155	138	104	59	45
Zurich	208	160	142	94	42	33
Basel	184	163	130	87	48	35

Sources: Data for cities drawn from Bureau Municipal de Statistique d'Amsterdam (1911), pp. 140–61; Office permanent de l'Institut international de Statistique (1927), pp. 242–75, 310–26; Institut international de Statistique (1954), pp. 78–91, and (1957), pp. 56–66; National data: League of Nations (various issues); Statistiques générales de la France (1907–14), pp. 463–65.
[a] Figures cover 1907–9.
[b] Figures cover 1925–27.
[c] I.e., Prussia until 1924–26.

countries, however, infant mortality was lower in the cities than in the country by the end of the nineteenth century. This was notably the case in relatively developed countries which nevertheless did not yet have manufacturing towns: Austria, the Netherlands, and Switzerland. By contrast, during this same period (around 1890), the urban infant death rate surpassed the rural rate by 19% in Germany, 13% in

Belgium, 17% in England, and 3% in France (Weber, 1899). In England, according to Williamson's calculations (1980), even as late as 1906 urban districts still had higher infant mortality rates than rural districts. This was particularly the case for London (owing to its size) and other heavily industrialized regions. In industrialized regions infant mortality in the principal cities still exceeded that outside of the cities by 25%. In 1890 in the northeastern states of the United States infant mortality (adjusted for underregistration) in urban regions exceeded that in rural regions by 63%; and mortality for children (aged 1–4) was excessive by 107% (Condran and Crimmins, 1980). And in Japan, industrialized later, infant mortality in the larger towns surpassed that in the countryside by 24% in the early 1920s (Tauber, 1958).

In order to determine more exactly the time at which the disproportionately high urban infant mortality rate in cities finally disappeared, I prepared table 14.2, for the period 1880–1938. At the beginning of the 1880s disproportionately high infant mortality rates were apparently the rule throughout Europe. The four instances in which the situation was different were either marginal or, as in the case of Paris, due to an underregistration of the actual number of deaths. With respect to Paris, it is written in the statistical record compiled at the time that "there is reason to take into account the fact that many infants born in Paris are given out to nurse and may die outside Paris." On the eve of the First World War, on the other hand, in the majority of cases urban and rural infant death rates had equalized—though, as will be seen below, mortality was higher in large cities than in smaller ones. By far the most important transition occurred between 1900 and 1913. Even during the period between the two world wars, however, large cities frequently had infant mortality rates higher than the national average. As always, allowance must be made for regional differences; and here too, each city has a character all its own. Thus during 1880–1914, Edinburgh, for instance, had an infant mortality rate roughly 10–20% lower than that of other British cities of comparable size.

The disproportionately high infant mortality rates of the nineteenth century for the most part affected babies more than one month old. The mortality rates relate, in other words, to what specialists call "postneonatal" mortality, the neonatal stage spanning the first month after birth (or the first 28 days, depending on usage). The fact that death struck more frequently at this later stage offers proof, if proof were needed, that the disproportionate urban mortality rate was linked to living conditions, since deaths during the first month essentially result from endogenous factors—those associated with congenital malformations, accidents during delivery, or premature birth. I shall return later to the general causes of the high number of deaths in cities.

As a general rule, during the nineteenth century infant mortality was higher in large cities than in small cities, and much higher in manufacturing cities than in those with little industry. Thus according to the data assembled by Weber (1899), in the United States infant mortality, which in 1890 was 121 per thousand in rural areas, reached 237 per thousand in cities with populations of more than 100,000 and 264 per thousand in New York. In Prussia in 1880–1881, infant mortality was as follows: in rural areas, 195 per thousand; in cities with populations less than 20,000, 216 per thousand; in cities with populations of 20,000–100,000, 224 per thousand; and in cities with populations of more than 100,000, 267 per thousand. For the whole of Germany during 1900–1909, according to my own calculations, infant mortality in cities with populations of more than 100,000 was 184 per thousand in cities with populations of 100,000–150,000 and 211 per thousand in cities with populations of 200,000–300,000 (Bairoch, 1977a). But after this period the effect of the size of the city no longer applies. Probably the negative consequences of urban congestion were offset by the greater availability of medical facilities.

After a phase of roughly thirty years (from 1910–20 to 1930–50) in which urban infant mortality rates fall perceptibly below those recorded in rural areas, there was fairly general equalization, with differences being mainly regional. To the extent that one can discern a difference, it is in favor of the city. But it is both small in scale (mortality rates being 10–15% higher in the country) and does not affect every country. And even differences correlated with the size of cities have almost (though not entirely) disappeared. In short, actually no clear pattern exists (United Nations, 1982a).

Lower Life Expectancy in the Cities Even for Adults

In immigrating to the city, the average person suffered a decline in life expectancy; the decline was very substantial and remained so for a long time. And except for children, a disproportionately high urban death rate still exists today (albeit in attenuated form) in almost every developed country and even appears over the last few years to be increasing.

But to return to the past, I shall first look at crude mortality rates. Given differences in age structure, these crude rates do not provide a valid means of measuring real differences. But they provide useful data about the natural growth of urban population.

I have assembled the chief available data on this question, and they enable me to identify the following trends. By the beginning of the nineteenth century, the urban death rate was distinctly higher than that recorded in rural districts—as was also the case with infant mortality, which of course contributed to the overall pattern. The difference between urban and rural mortality, large at the start of the nineteenth century, gradually decreased until it vanished during the first years of the twentieth century. The average difference, which around 1810–1830 seems to have been on the order of 40– 60%, fell to around 10–30% by about 1890. From the start of the twentieth century on, the difference disappeared altogether or had even reversed its direction. Here as elsewhere there were substantial national differences, resulting in part from differences in urban structure relating to the nature of the dominant form of employment, to the size of the cities, or to their rates of growth.

Owing to urban populations being on the average younger than rural populations, the data on crude mortality rates distinctly underestimate the extent to which the urban mortality rate was higher than the rural mortality rate. There is little data with regard to either mortality according to age or life expectancy distinguishing between urban and rural districts. What data is available, however, converge on the same point. Extracts from the principal data sets are given in table 14.3, in which I have focused on mortality after infancy. Given the greater difference between urban and rural infant mortality, the comparison of life expectancy at birth would have revealed still greater differences than those in table 14.3. In Sweden, for example, for the period 1881–1890 life expectancy in the city at age 15 was 4.2 years shorter than in the country. At birth, on the other hand, it was 5.7 years shorter.

The more fragmentary data available for other countries, and in particular for the United Kingdom, confirm that disproportionately high urban mortality rates were a constant.

What finally emerges from these data? There is first of all the fact that urban mortality for adults did not come down to the level of rural mortality until after the 1930s, that is, nearly 20–30 years after urban infant mortality went down. Around 1800–1830, life expectancy at age 15 was probably lower by some 20–30% in the city than in the country; or more strikingly life expectancy in the country surpassed that in the cities by some 25–40%. In terms of numbers of years, this meant that rural youths could expect to live some 8–12 years longer than urban youths. Around 1880 this gap had already been perceptibly reduced, and around 1900 it had probably fallen to no more than 10%. These are only approximate orders of magnitude for the average in developed countries, however; differences between nations can be large.

Thus the difference between urban and rural mortality became negligible after the 1930s. And demographers as well as medical researchers lost interest in this problem. It is significant in this respect that a recent study done jointly by the United Nations and the World Health Organization (United Nations, 1982a), while tackling the various aspects of mortality differentials (income, education, occupation, etc.), totally ignores the urban-rural component of this problem. This lack of interest is surprising, because the data for the last decade for

TABLE 14.3 Life Expectancy and Mortality Rates according to Age in Urban and Rural Regions (1850–1960)

Life Expectancy (years)	Urban	Rural	Life Expectancy (years)	Urban	Rural
Sweden			United States		
at 15 years:			(white)		
1881–1890	45.9	50.1	at 10 years:		
1891–1900	47.3	50.3	1901	40.5	46.0
1900–1910	49.0	51.2	1910	42.0	46.4
1911–1920	49.3	50.4	1930	45.8	49.3
1921–1930	52.7	53.6	at 50 years:		
1931–1940	54.2	54.9	1901	19.4	23.2
1941–1950	56.8	57.5	1910	19.6	22.9
1951–1960	59.2	59.5	1930	21.1	24.1
at 50 years:			Japan[a] (men)		
1881–1890	21.4	23.1	at 10 years:		
1900–1910	22.8	24.8	1925–1926	45.8	48.4
1951–1960	26.3	26.7	1935–1936	46.9	48.4
			at 50 years:		
			1925–1926	16.3	18.9
			1935–1936	17.0	19.3
Mortality by Age (per 1,000)	Urban	Rural	Mortality by Age (per 1,000)	Urban	Rural
Sweden[b]			France[c]		
20–30 years			20–30 years		
1851–1860	12.1	6.6	1874–1875	10.1	8.8
1871–1880	9.9	6.1	1886	10.8	8.2
1891–1900	6.5	6.1	United States		
Germany			5–15 years		
20–30 years			1890	6.2	4.0
1863	8.6	6.7			

Sources: For Sweden: *Historisk Statistik för Sverige* (1969), p. 118; Sundbarg (1908), p. 146.
For Germany: Mulhall (1898), p. 186.
For the United States: Dublin and Lotka (1936), p. 91; Weber (1899), p. 346.
For France: Levasseur (1891), p. 402.
For Japan: Tauber (1958), p. 299.
[a]Cities with populations of 100,000 or more are considered urban.
[b](Unweighted) average for Stockholm and other cities.
[c]Paris for urban regions; all of France for rural regions.

the developed countries show a reversal of the tendency: the mortality rates for urban adults are again higher than for rural adults. Certain calculations made by the American Department of Health and Human Services, reported by Weinstein (1980), indicate that having lived in a city for 65 years leads to a 1800-day (five-years) reduction in life expectancy in comparison with the same amount of time spent in the country. This may be a bit excessive, but an analysis of the most recent data on mortality for Western Europe by age and residence suggests a probable 2–3 year lower life expectancy at the age of 20 for city people compared to rural people. Obviously this is a problem that would require and merit careful study.

The Causes of Disproportionately High Mortality Rates in the Urban Environment

Industrialization most certainly contributed directly to the disproportionately high mortality rates of the urban environment. In the factories of the nineteenth century accidents were frequent and working conditions very exhausting and unwholesome. There is no doubt that, other things being equal, the nineteenth-century worker suffered a greater loss in life expectancy than the craftsman of earlier eras. But these were not the decisive factors, as the disproportionately high urban death rates of the centuries immediately preceding the Industrial Revolution demonstrate. The real causes were, in fact, those so skillfully analyzed by Wrigley (1969), who after examining the impact of industrialization on urban mortality concludes:

> It is perhaps more accurate to say that high mortality was caused by urbanisation rather than by industrialisation. It was in the bigger cities that mortality was so very high. Many of these big cities were not heavily engaged in the new industries, but were administrative and commercial centres. Paris, Berlin, Marseilles, and Liverpool all had high death rates and low expectation of life, though none was a typical product of the industrial revolution in the narrow sense. In a broader sense, of course, all were able to develop only because of the improvements in transport and growth in productive capacity which characterise the industrial revolution. To a notable extent, but now in a different context, mortality was still density-dependent. Wherever there were large cities there were slum areas with very high densities of population and severe overcrowding which allowed diseases like tuberculosis to spread very widely and exposed children and young people to a great range of infectious illness.

The role of the size of cities had been thrown into relief as early as 1772 by Richard Price, philosopher and forerunner of demography, who came to the conclusion that as a general rule, "the proportion of people who die annually . . . [is] . . . as follows . . . great towns, from 1/19 or 1/20 to 1/23 to 1/24. Moderate towns, from 1/23 to 1/28. The country from 1/30 or 1/35 to 1/50 or 1/60." And Price was also aware of the individual character of cities, since he adds: "This must however be understood with exceptions. There may be moderate towns so ill situated, or whose inhabitants may be so crowded together, as to render the proportions of death in them greater than in the largest towns."

At a time when the artificial feeding of infants has come under heavy attack in the Third World, it is worth pointing out that one of the causes given to explain the exceptionally high infant mortality in the cities of the nineteenth century is just this type of feeding, a practice made necessary by working conditions in the city more often than in the country. Thus in Würtemberg, for instance, the mortality rate among breast-fed children was 135 per thousand, as opposed to 427 for artificially-fed children (Bailey, 1906).

If there is no doubt that during the nineteenth century and even in the beginning of the twentieth century the hygienic environment made artificial feeding an important cause of higher infant mortality, the impact of the mother's working in industry is less clear. There is no doubt, as Margaret Hewitt (1958) has shown in her beautiful book *Wives and Mothers in Victorian Industry*, that the working conditions of women in the mills influenced very negatively the living conditions of children and especially of infants. She begins her chapter, "The Sacrifice of Infants," with the terrible testimony of a clergyman of the second half of the nineteenth century. "What do they do?," asked Charles Dickens of the rector of a parish in a large English town, "what do they do with the infants of the mothers who work in the mills?" "Oh," replied the clergyman, "they bring them to me, and I take care of them in the churchyard!" Although the scope of the negative impact of women working in industry has been challenged by Carol Dyhouse (1978–79), it is true for the end of the nineteenth century. It may be best to leave the last word to a third woman, Elisabeth Roberts (1982), who rightly insists that in addition to women's working in industry and working-class standards of living, "the strategies adopted by working-class families to ensure their survival were also of critical importance."

Before moving on from deaths to births, a brief digression on suicides seems in order. For in a recent analysis Anderson (1980) has called into doubt "one of the oldest, best-known and most widely accepted sociological theories, which is the belief that the transition from a traditional society to a modern society is associated with rising suicide rates." In order to discover whether suicide increased with industrialization in Victorian England, Anderson assembled data showing that, with the exception of the very largest cities, industrialized regions, and notably urban regions with a high level of industrialization, had suicide rates even lower than those recorded in rural areas.

The Urban Origins of the Second Demographic Revolution

The second demographic revolution is the name given (or rather that was given) to the radical change in popular behavior constituted by the fall in fertility beginning at the end of the nineteenth century. Roughly one hundred years after the fall in mortality rates, there was for the first time in history, in very large sectors of the population, the generalized practice of birth control, leading to a sharp decline in fertility. The "demographic transition" is the name given today to those two profound changes in the demographic revolution. The decline in fertility, confined in the main to developed countries, began between 1870 and 1890. For reasons that have yet to be clearly understood, France is an exception to the rule, its divergence from the general pattern occurring as early as the late eighteenth century. Naturally enough, and for reasons that are obvious in this case, birth rates began to fall later in economically less advanced nations, notably in southern and eastern Europe.

But the cities everywhere anticipated this general pattern by forty to fifty years, creating a substantial difference between urban and rural birth rates, a difference that still exists today. This means that as early as 1840–1860, not only did people die in greater numbers in the city (as had already been the case in earlier centuries), but fewer of them were born. The scale of this difference is still the subject of debate among experts in the field. The problem is not a simple one. A part of the difference, for example, derives from the higher proportion of single people in cities.

From my point of view, however, it matters little what the components of this decline in fertility were; it is the fact of such a decline that counts. And there can be no question that there was a decline by the second half of the nineteenth century (see table 14.4). But when exactly did urban birth rates begin to decline in different countries? On this score unknowns remain. It seems likely (but not certain) that the difference between urban and rural levels of fertility was less before the middle of the nineteenth century. But it is possible that in some countries the change had already begun by the beginning of the nineteenth century.

As was the case for mortality, the fall in fertility affected large cities more than smaller ones. And also as in the case of mortality, the urban factor proper was not the only one involved, as was confirmed by Mosk (1980) in a study comparing urban and rural birth rates in Sweden, Germany, Japan, and Korea. In a country like Belgium, where the role of the church was very influential in the nineteenth century, secularization is an important explanation of the lower urban birth rates in that country (Lesthaeghe, 1977).

Furthermore—and this general remark applies to all aspects of urban behavior—by engendering different kinds of socioeconomic ac-

Table 14.4 Evolution of Indicators of Urban and Rural Fertility
(1800–1970)

Year (approx.)	Sweden[a]		Bavaria[a]			United States Urban as a % of Rural[b]
	Stockholm	Rest of Country	Munich	Other Cities	Rural	
1800	—	—	—	—	—	59
1840	—	—	—	—	—	55
1860	358	443	—	—	—	—
1870	313	440	341	344	433	—
1880	325	447	338	342	451	—
1890	298	423	290	318	421	—
1900	252	407	285	—	—	—
1910	221	363	199	262	387	65[c]
1930[d]	97	201	115	165	245	61
1950	194	241	—	—	—	59[e]
1970	143	221	—	—	—	—

Sources: For Sweden: Hofsten and Lundström (1976), pp. 23 and 99–106; data for the rest of the country calculated by the author, eliminating Stockholm; data for total population: Historisk Statistik för Sverige (1969), pp. 50–51; for Bavaria: Knodel (1974), p. 283; for U.S.: Jaffe (1942), p. 56.
[a]Children per 1,000 women aged 15–49.
[b]Net reproduction rate of white urban population as a percentage of the rural figure.
[c]1920.
[d]1925 for Bavaria.
[e]1940.

tivities, new modes of human relations, and forms and levels of education unique to urban populations, the city brought about a change in both attitudes and patterns of personal conduct. Certainly this change was not in the strictest sense the result of conditions in the city. But to deduce from this that the decrease in fertility was not as specifically urban as the rise in population density, for example, seems a little forced. Did the urban factor make a direct or indirect contribution? This is an artificial distinction. One attractive hypothesis, advanced by Livi-Bacci (1977), deserves mention, even if it has not yet been possible to put it to any valid test. In this view, the flow of migrants to the cities would have worked in favor of couples with few children, it being much more difficult for large families to move to the city than small ones.

> An old theory which now has little currency attributed the relatively low fertility of city dwellers in general and of the upper economic and social strata in particular to a supposed weakening of sexual desire or procreative power due to effete modes of life. In the modern view, the explanation is sought rather

in different attitudes and patterns of behavior pertaining to marriage and birth of children, and differences in knowledge of means of limiting births.

Thus opens the explanatory section of the United Nations study, published in 1963, on levels and trends of fertility worldwide. This assessment still holds today.

In contrast to the disproportionately high levels of urban mortality,
the inordinately low level of urban fertility has not yet disappeared in
the societies of the developed world. But while it has not yet disappeared, the gap has perceptibly narrowed, particularly since the end
of the Second World War. As always, the city anticipated this trend,
leading the way in the baby boom that affected many countries in the
immediate postwar period without closing the gap altogether (Johnson, 1960). Thus in his in-depth analysis of the developed countries at
the start of the sixties, Kuznets (1974) shows, for instance, that the
number of children under the age of 5 per 1,000 women aged 15–49
was 31% higher in rural areas than in urban areas. A study carried
out for the United Nations (1977a) concludes that the gap has shrunk
even further since the sixties. Around 1970 the number of live births
per married woman under 45 (data standardized for length of marriage) was greater in rural districts by 10% in France, 11% in Belgium,
13% in the United States, 14% in Denmark, 20% in Czechoslovakia,
21% in Hungary, and by as much as 33% in Yugoslavia and 40% in
Poland. Levels of development, in conjunction with other factors,
largely account for these differences. Place of birth also seems to have
retained an influence: women born in rural areas but living in cities
tend to have more babies than women born in cities and living in them.

Until the present, then, city dwellers have continued to have fewer
children. And since the difference between urban mortality rates and
rural mortality rates did not become marginal until shortly after urban fertility rates had largely dropped to a point lower than rural fertility rates, the result has been that, from the start of the nineteenth
century until the very recent past, the city has experienced a slower
rate of natural growth than the country. The city, particularly during
the nineteenth century, has acted as a brake on its own growth.

The City: A Brake on Its Own Growth

The city of London had a large natural deficit (see chapter
12). This situation prevailed throughout the developed world for a
great many years. Rare indeed were the cities, especially those of a
certain size (say, with populations of more than 20,000), that did not
chronically suffer from an excess of deaths relative to births—and this
despite the influx of migrants, most of whom, being young, had a
higher level of fertility and a lower level of mortality than normal.

TABLE 14.5   Annual Percentage of Natural Growth of the Swedish
Population in Urban and Rural Regions
(1751–1960)

	Stockholm	Urban	Rural
1751–1760	−1.11	—	0.90[a]
1801–1810	−1.67	—	0.08[a]
1821–1830	−1.14	—	1.16[a]
1831–1840	−1.29	—	0.91[a]
1816–1840	−1.17	−0.35	1.11
1851–1860	−0.61	0.13	1.22
1871–1880	−0.15	0.81	1.29
1891–1900	0.72	0.97	1.11
1901–1910	0.85	1.10	1.09
1921–1930	—	0.36	0.63
1931–1940	—	0.21	0.31
1951–1960	—	0.64	0.37

Sources: Calculations based on: Historisk Statistik för Sverige (1969), pp. 62, 89, and 100; Sundbarg (1908), p. 142; Hofsten and Lundström (1976), p. 96; Thirring (1913), p. 73.
[a] Country as a whole, except Stockholm.

Once again, owing to the wealth of statistics available for that country, the case of Sweden provides a clear illustration of this trend as it evolved over a very long period of time. In the city of Stockholm until the 1870s and in the other cities until the 1850s, urban population maintained itself (or grew) by virtue of the continuing influx of migrants from the countryside. The fragmentary data available for the rest of the developed world confirm this chronology. As a general rule, deaths ceased to outnumber births roughly 1850–1880.

But it should be emphasized that these are migratory balances, for as we have already seen with respect to the demography of the cities of traditional Europe, the migrations were not in one direction. It is likely that the scale of migration in both directions was even greater in the emerging industrialized world than in the traditional world, if only owing to the rapid urban growth. Thus if one takes the decade 1901–1910, for example, it can be calculated, thanks to the first edition of Annuaire Statistique des Grandes Villes (Office Permanent, 1927), that over the course of this ten-year period, Berlin gained 2.6 million new inhabitants, but lost 2.1 million others. Even a city (Gorlitz) whose population practically stagnated and was in 1910 only 86,000, had over this ten-year period gained 160,000 new inhabitants, while losing 152,000. Brussels gained 398,000 while losing 303,000; Amsterdam lost a few more than it gained (277,000 as opposed to 267,000). Zurich gained 408,000 people, while losing 390,000.

In less dynamic regions, notably Italy, where other social factors may perhaps have intervened, the migration was of smaller proportions. Though it had a population of nearly 600,000 around 1900 and was a major center of industrial growth, Milan gained only 162,000 new inhabitants and lost only 62,000 others. Certainly problems relating to the definition of cities may distort the data a little, but they do not alter the scale of these migratory flows.

The eventual disappearance (around 1850–1880) of the deficit of births notwithstanding, the natural growth rate in urban populations did not reach a level comparable to that in rural populations. As I just noted, the gradual disappearance of the gap between urban and rural mortality rates was accompanied by a decline in urban fertility relative to rural fertility. Thus migrations continued to furnish the greater part of the population required for the cities to expand. Since the end of the Second World War, rural districts have in part come to mirror the demographic patterns of the cities, with the result that the gap between urban and rural growth rates has become of minor significance. There are even a few countries whose cities experience a rate of natural population growth greater than that recorded in rural areas. Still, these rare and short-lived exceptions apart, from the start of the phase of urban expansion linked with industrialization to the present day, the city has on the whole been a brake on its own growth.

15 The City and the First Phases of the Industrial Revolution in England □

The Industrial Revolution has correctly been called one of the most decisive events in the history of humanity. From the socio-economic point of view, of the three major turning points in the evolution of human societies (the other two being the Neolithic revolution and the break with the past at the start of the sixteenth century), the Industrial Revolution unquestionably left the deepest mark. And yet for five to eight decades England alone underwent this momentous change. England being the cradle of the Industrial Revolution, an inquiry into the relations between the birth of the Industrial Revolution and urbanism in that country seems in order. I shall begin with a brief recapitulation of the facts of that revolution. It is not at all easy, however, to deal with so complex a phenomenon in a few pages. I hope I will be excused if I omit certain secondary aspects and emphasize the basic facts rather than the underlying mechanisms, about which there is still great uncertainty.

The Industrial Revolution in England: A Rapid Survey of a Complex Phenomenon

The name given to any complex phenomenon will never fit perfectly. Thus scholars have very often criticized the use of the term "revolution" to describe those changes—profound and laden with consequences, but very gradual—that, from the middle of the eighteenth century in England and a little later in other Western countries, progressively turned the traditional, essentially agrarian societies of the Middle Ages and the Renaissance into the predominantly industrial societies of the modern world. Indeed, the slow and gradual character of the first phase of this great transformation contrasts with the notion of revolution, which the *Dictionnaire Robert* defines as an abrupt or sudden change.* For my own part, taking into account the

* Neither the definition given in the *OED* ("alteration, change, mutation," or "an instance of great change or alteration in affairs or in some particular thing," nor that

243

pace of historical events before the Industrial Revolution, I view the word "revolution" as perfectly adequate. But another, better-founded objection could be made to the term Industrial Revolution. For the Industrial Revolution was above all an agricultural revolution that, where it took place, permitted and even generated unprecedented development in the industrial and mining sectors.

Indeed, as early as the end of the seventeenth century, and certainly by the first years of the eighteenth, a profound change had begun to transform English agriculture. To start with this change consisted of adopting methods of cultivation already used in the Netherlands. But the transference of Dutch methods to the English scene had crucial consequences. In the Netherlands the land was very densely populated, which restricted agricultural productivity. In England the countryside was less densely populated than in the Netherlands, and more land was open for cultivation. Therefore the application of the Dutch methods in England resulted in a rise both in agricultural yield and, more important still, in agricultural productivity. And very early on—by the first decade of the eighteenth century—local innovations replaced imitation of the Dutch example, leading to even greater progress.

This profound change in a sector of the economy engaging some 70–80% of the working population could not fail to cause change in the other sectors. The decisive change in manufacturing and transport associated with the Industrial Revolution took place largely as the result of increased demand in the agricultural sector and in the rural world generally. The two most important of these changes, with regard to both their direct and indirect consequences, were the mechanization of spinning and the use of coal in the production of iron.

The history of the practical success of mechanical spinning began in 1769 with Arkwright's patent on the waterframe and the establishment of his cotton mill. This led in a few decades to a complete and radical transformation of the cotton industry, which in the context of traditional economies employed some 65–75% of all industrial labor. But twenty years before Arkwright's invention of the water frame, the iron industry had begun to undergo a far-reaching transformation of its own. Darby had probably succeeded in producing cast iron using coal as early as 1709, but practical progress was slow and did not accelerate until about 1750. Around 1760 there were still only some 17 blast furnaces out of a total of 70–80 producing pig iron using coke

---

found in *The American Heritage Dictionary* ("an assertedly momentous change in any situation") quite answers to the author's meaning. But the idea of great suddenness and speed is not altogether foreign to the connotations of the word in English. The *AHD*'s "momentous" in particular, indicating dramatic happenings, suggests a certain spectacular swiftness—TRANS.

instead of charcoal. By 1806, however, 97% of iron was produced in coke blast furnaces, and the production had increased tenfold.

All of this engendered a complex interplay of actions and reactions that transformed the whole English economy. In agriculture by 1730–1740, England had become (in the terms of the age) a granary for Europe, for she was by then in a position to export regularly 10–12% of her grain output. And while in later years England stopped being a net exporter, England did not become a net importer until after 1846—that is, until after the repeal of the corn laws that had placed strict limits on grain imports in order to protect the interests of landlords. Until the 1840s, then, English agriculture continued to be able to support the English people despite a marked rise in population, and this even though it required by this stage only a small fraction of the work force needed a century earlier. Thus between 1740 and 1840 the population of England (that is, of England and Wales) went up from around 6 million to 15.7 million. But while the agricultural labor force represented 60–70% of the total work force in 1740, by 1840 it represented only 22%, a proportion the other developed countries did not reach until well into the twentieth century (around 1930 in the United States, 1955 in France, 1968 in Italy, 1976 in Spain, and not yet in the the USSR). This meant that, even assuming only a very modest increase in the per capita consumption of agricultural products, English agricultural productivity rose more than threefold during this period. And this in turn made possible the urban growth accompanying the process of industrialization.

And the process of industrialization was very rapid. By 1790–1810, England had become what would later be called the "workshop of the world." Indeed, by around 1825, while England had only 2% of the world's population, the volume of production in English ironworks was equal to that of all the rest of the world. The productivity of the average worker in a modern English spinning mill around 1825 equalled that of 200–300 workers employing the traditional equipment used at the end of the eighteenth century. In order to facilitate transport in England, which was well provided with natural waterways, nearly 4,000 kilometers of canals had been constructed before 1835, and the first railroad line had been opened by 1825.

An inevitable consequence of these radical changes in the economy was a geographic change. Working in industry or trade almost always meant working in town. The growing scale of modern enterprises quickly transformed rural zones with industrial activities into true cities. This was the first case of urbanization linked to modern industrialization—the first case of what was eventually the fate of all those countries that followed England's lead and modernized their economies.

Traditional England: An Essentially Rural Country Despite Its Commercial Role

Urban growth in the Middle Ages had been fairly moderate in England and at the start of the sixteenth century, England was more rural than the European average. While in Europe at large some 10–12% of the population lived in cities with populations of over 5,000, in England the proportion was only 7–9%. London, the largest city in the country at least since 1000, had only a population of 40,000–60,000 in 1500, when the population of Paris was 200,000–240,000 and Europe contained four cities with populations of more than 100,000. And while Europe as a whole counted at this time more than seventy cities with populations of 20,000–50,000, the largest English city next to London was Norwich, with a population of roughly 10,000–12,000.

The situation changed noticeably in the sixteenth century and especially in the seventeenth century, a period during which expanding trade and a definite increase in traditional manufacturing induced a phase of urban growth.

This commercial expansion suggests a digression on the role of foreign trade in launching the Industrial Revolution. I first wrote on this problem more than a decade ago (Bairoch, 1973b), focusing on the period 1700–1710 to 1780–90, covering the best part of the beginning of industrialization in England. These are the conclusions I reached based on an empirical analysis of the data.

Whatever approach one uses, empirical analysis indicates that the contribution of foreign trade to the genesis of the Industrial Revolution was minimal. If one is not willing to accept the mere succession of two exceptional events as proof of a causal link, the traditional thesis according to which the commercial expansion of the sixteenth and seventeenth centuries was an important cause, if not the sole cause, of the Industrial Revolution does not stand up to objective scrutiny. Commercial expansion was certainly not a sufficient cause. If it had been, Holland, to mention only one example, should have been industrialized before England. But commercial expansion was probably not even a necessary cause, for if it were, the list of industrialized European countries would have been shorter than it is.

But the reader may well ask, what about the profit from foreign trade and the demands on industry resulting from the growth of the English fleet? With regard to the first part of the question, even if all of the profits from commercial expansion had been invested in the English economy, they would only have represented 10–20% of total investments. And that portion actually invested was probably only 6–8% of the total. Moreover, the literature dealing with this important functional link has generally been distorted by its methodology: it was necessary to analyze the origins of the capital and entrepreneurs in those sectors of the economy providing the driving force behind the Industrial Revolution at large, instead of investigating those cases in which commercial capital was actually invested in the emerging industries. If one uses the correct approach, one finds that capital originating in international trade was not preponderant in the initial phases of industrialization.

What is more, there is a very distinct disparity between the geographic zones in which commercial capital was accumulated and those in which industrialization took place, and this holds for countries as well as for smaller regions. A disparity of this sort, at a time when the spatial transfer of investment capital was extremely rare, is an important piece of evidence. The causes of this lack of contribution were largely sociological. Changes in activities are extremely rare when the old sphere of employment or profits suffers no abrupt deterioration.

As for the demand resulting from the creation and renewal of the English fleets, both mercantile and military, although the development of the fleet was rapid, the resulting demand had only marginal industrial consequences. On the basis of admittedly fragmentary data, I estimate that this demand amounted to less than 0.5% of the national product. The impact was also very modest on the sectors driving industrialization, amounting to about 1% for textiles and about 2% for iron and steel.

Approaching the question in a perspective both narrower in geographical terms and broader in historical terms, O'Brien (1981) concludes that had England been excluded from trade with the future Third World between 1489 and 1789, English investments would have declined by at most 7%.

Although the commercial expansion of the sixteenth and seventeenth centuries made no major contribution to the genesis of the Industrial Revolution, it did bring about a surge of urban growth. But on the eve of the Industrial Revolution and those transformations that would utterly reshape the English socioeconomic landscape, England in the context of the times was still only modestly urbanized. Even around 1700 the level of urbanization in England probably rose to about 13–16%, only a little higher than the European average of 11–14%, but lower than the level in Belgium, Italy, the Netherlands, and Portugal, and roughly the same as that in Spain and France.

As for the general level of urbanization, of the 820,000–900,000 people living in English cities with populations of 5,000 or more, 550,000 lived in London. London at this time had been perhaps for one or two decades the largest city in Europe. Paris had a population of some 530,000. But England in 1700 had a little fewer than 6 million people, while France probably had a little more than 21 million. Thus London had 9% of the total population of England. This was a rare situation, which had arisen in Europe only twice before the Industrial Revolution, if one excludes Rome in antiquity. In the Netherlands in 1750 Amsterdam had roughly 11% of the population (9% around 1700) and in Portugal in 1700 Lisbon had 12%. These three countries at this point in history were perfect examples of the type of urban structure described by Jefferson (see chapter 9) in which one primate city dominates all the others. The second largest English city, Norwich, had a population of only about 30,000 during this period. The same situation obtained in Portugal and also, though to a lesser extent, in the Netherlands, where the population of Rotterdam stood a little below 50,000.

London's rapid expansion had begun by the sixteenth century, its population going up from around 50,000 to nearly 190,000, making an annual growth rate of 1.3%. London's growth was even stronger between 1600 and 1650, a period during which the city's population probably doubled (an annual growth rate of 1.4%). The rate slowed down during 1650–1800, but accelerated once more in the nineteenth century, reaching 2% per year. London was thus very likely the first city in the world to have a population of two million, crossing this threshold sometime around 1840, and was unquestionably the first city to exceed the three million mark (around 1865).

By the second half of the eighteenth century urbanization had reached other parts of the country, creating new urban nuclei directly linked with industrialization. And by 1800 there were besides London —which at this time had a population of roughly 900,000—fifteen-odd cities with populations of more than 20,000, five with more than 50,000. This made for an overall population of 2.1 million living in cities with populations of 5,000 or more, representing around 23% of the total population. And if we add towns of 2,000–5,000, the level of urbanization rises to about 26–28%.

So high a percentage without benefit of massive imports of food was strictly impossible before the Industrial Revolution and indicates therefore that by 1800 England had already crossed over into the industrial age. Moreover, England had probably sometime around 1750–1770 transcended the limit of urban growth attainable by traditional societies in the absence of food imports. This brings me to my first question about relations between the city and the English Industrial Revolution: the role of London in the English agricultural revolution.

London and the English Agricultural Revolution

London is of interest in connection with a general question raised earlier: the question of the role of demographic pressure in promoting changes in agricultural techniques. The rapid growth of the population of London, bringing this city by 1690–1710 to the first rank of European urban centers, definitely bears scrutiny in this connection. As long ago as the thirties, Fisher (1935) insisted on the role of London in the development of a market for agricultural products. But it remained for the historian and demographer Wrigley (1967) to formulate hypotheses concerning a more direct link between the growth and relative size of London and the agricultural revolution.

As Wrigley himself points out, London was obviously not the only factor explaining the agricultural revolution. To define the precise contribution its rapid growth made, it is necessary to observe a certain number of restrictions.

In the first place, London cannot be regarded as truly unique. Leaving aside northern Italy and Portugal (and completely overlooking non-European cultures with analogous situations), one should remember the Netherlands, where the pace of growth was still more rapid and where the level of urbanization was considerably higher. The onset of the English agricultural revolution dated from 1690–1710. Between 1603 and 1695 London's annual rate of growth was on the order of 0.5% (the percentage being higher during the first two or three decades). Between 1695 and 1740–50 the rate was still 0.5%, and it was only 0.4% over the second half of the eighteenth century. Amsterdam, on the other hand, grew at the rate of 1.9% per year between 1514 and 1622. And whereas about 13–16% of the English population lived in cities in 1700, the corresponding figure in the Netherlands at this time was some 40%, (in Holland proper more than 50%). And while London had a population of around 500,000 in or about 1690, more than double the population of Amsterdam, it should be remembered that Amsterdam was itself only the nucleus of a metropolitan area in the modern sense, containing within a radius of thirty-five kilometers cities whose collective population amounted to some 440,000. Nor should it be forgotten that England as a whole had three times the population of the Netherlands. For all of these reasons, then, de Vries (1974) seems entirely justified in regarding the two cases as closely similar.

The second restriction, less fundamental than the first, follows from the fact that the most decisive innovations associated with the agricultural revolution were initially introduced in regions rather distant from London—some 150–200 kilometers away. But although, given the size of London at this time, the distance was relatively great, this does not necessarily mean that London exerted no influence on events in the regions concerned.

But there is reason to believe (moving on to my third restriction) that what influence London did exert on the agricultural revolution was of a negative sort. While it is certain that the presence of a large city, and particularly of a large city with external resources resulting from trade, led to improvements in agricultural techniques, these improvements usually related to gains in yield rather than to gains in productivity. It is not even excluded that the gains in yield were made at the expense of productivity, because the proximity of a London market enabled local farmers to maintain a competitive edge over their more distant rivals who, owing to their greater distance, had to include transport costs in their prices. But the essential part of the agricultural revolution was gains in productivity. So London must be denied any especially conspicuous role in the agricultural revolution.

My last restriction stems from the observation I shall make later concerning the modest degree of development in traditional cities during the early phases of the Industrial Revolution. London did not depart from this general rule, as can be seen from the slow growth of its population in the eighteenth century. But this is related more to the global impact of urbanization on the Industrial Revolution than to the specific part played by London.

The Place of Urbanization in the Explanations of the Industrial Revolution in England

The best way objectively to approach research into the place of a given factor in any complex process is perhaps to make use of syntheses whose aim lies precisely in analyzing the impact of the whole array of contributing factors. This is what I shall do below, presenting the conclusions reached in eight of the most general inquiries into the causes or origins of the Industrial Revolution in England. I shall then sum up the results of the most important analyses of specific aspects of the problem.

In one of the earliest of the eight general studies, that of Flinn (1966), the city occupies the greatest number of pages. Despite the large amount of space given to the city, however, it should be noted right away that Flinn concludes that, while urbanization favored the Industrial Revolution, its contribution was not particularly decisive. According to Flinn, the role of urbanization lay chiefly in the increasing demand resulting from a more highly developed urban infrastructure and in the demand for supplies required to maintain urban populations. Thus, Flinn recalls that the first true canal built in England (1761) was built to convey coal to Manchester. (This was also the reason for the construction of the first canal in Ireland, in 1742, for shipping coal to Dublin.) The same period saw the creation of the first provincial newspapers—an urban fact: the newspapers were soon used for publicity for local markets.

And this brings me to an essential point: the market that cities offered for industrial goods. It is obvious—and all writers have explicitly or implicitly drawn attention to this fact—that the concentration of a large population in one place facilitated the rapid turnover of industrial products, and this in turn was conducive to the development of new techniques for manufacturing increasingly standardized products. On balance, then, Flinn argues that the existing evidence points to the positive role played by urbanization. But urban growth was not a significant factor contributing greatly to explaining the Industrial Revolution.

In his general survey, Hartwell (1967) gives no role whatever to urbanization as a cause of the Industrial Revolution. This is also the position of Deane (1967). By contrast, Landes (1965) believes urbanization can explain why the Industrial Revolution was so early in England. But even here it is only one factor among many, coming eighth in Landes's list of nine factors. According to Landes, who estimates 15% as the level of urbanization in Great Britain in around 1750, "it was not only that England had more people living in cities than any other European country except perhaps Holland; it was the character of British urban life that made the pattern of settlement particularly significant." But to Holland should be added Italy, Spain, and Portugal; and the gap between Great Britain and France was narrower than Landes (with a lack of data) could know when he wrote. But he is perfectly right in insisting that the English cities were more open to economic activity because there were fewer government functionaries, clergymen, and military personnel among their citizens. But Landes limits the role of urbanization once more when he writes:

> Nothing is more striking about the map of Britain in the eighteenth century than the modernity of the urban pattern. The medieval county seats—Lancaster, York, Chester, Stafford—were overshadowed by younger places like Liverpool, Manchester, Leeds, and Birmingham, and there was already a substantial shift of population in favor of the North and the Midlands. Much of the increase, moreover, did not take place within the cities proper, but took the form of a thickening of the countryside. Numerous overgrown industrial villages sprang up . . . The pattern throughout was one of close contact and frequent exchange between city and land.

If, in short, urbanization was not altogether removed from this process, it certainly played no leading role, nor even too important a supporting role. Landes still takes this position (personal communication).

In his excellent review of the economic history of Britain, Peter Mathias (1969) makes practically no mention of the city. The same limited emphasis on urbanism, or more precisely its total absence, can be found in the new collective economic history of Great Britain edited by Floud and McCloskey (1981). Quite the opposite is the case in the study of Pawson (1979), and with good reason: the author is a geographer chiefly addressing himself to other geographers. For Pawson "the large towns of the early industrial revolution were far more than a symbol of change, they were to a substantial degree the cause of it." And the impact of urbanization as a cause of growth, so

Pawson argues, made itself felt in four ways: through the demand for agricultural products; through the status of cities as major centers of both the production of and demand for greater numbers of manufactured goods; through the impetus given to the building up of the infrastructure for transport; and finally through the modernizing influence of cities on society at large. But, still according to Pawson, urbanization was only one of the factors promoting the Industrial Revolution in England, nor did it figure among the most important of these.

The position of Corfield (1982), who gives a good synthesis of the impact of English towns from 1700 to 1800, is very near that of Pawson. "The growth of towns, even on a small scale, is therefore likely to have some economic impact, however minor; and when both the scale and the continued pace of urbanization become substantial, there is a good case for pointing to this as one of the key 'disequilibria,' promoting, as well as responding to, fundamental economic mutation. Urbanization was emphatically not, however, the long-sought but ever-elusive 'first cause' of England's Industrial Revolution."

Thus on the whole none of the general studies on the origins of the Industrial Revolution in England give prominence to urbanization. The same conclusion emerges (and the one thing explains the other) in the various analytical studies on specific aspects of the problem. Considerations of space prevent me from summarizing one by one the principal analyses in this area. But it may be simply said that in none of them does the city appear as a significant contributor. To the extent that any qualification of this assessment may be made, it concerns the hand the city had in creating the infrastructure for transport. The city gave decisive impetus to the construction of the network of canals constructed beginning in the 1760s. The same was true later, in the 1830s, for the railroads. For in both instances only very heavy traffic would have justified the expense involved in constructing man-made transport lines, as opposed to natural land routes and waterways. Generally speaking, the latest analyses, by insisting less than earlier efforts on the part played by the expansion of trade, minimize the urban factor further still. Many analyses leave out the city altogether. This is notably the case for my own research (1963) into the causes of the English Industrial Revolution. In my discussion, I completely neglected urban problems, deeming the city not a significant driving force. Naturally this does not mean that urbanization failed to emerge as an important element of the first stages of industrialization; but it did so more as a consequence than as a cause.

Traditional Cities and the Industrial Revolution

Whatever the exact role played by cities in the Industrial Revolution in England, one thing is certain: the traditional cities did not constitute the poles around which this new type of development gravitated. It may be noted, indeed, that during the eighteenth century most of the urban growth took place outside of the major urban centers already in existence at the start of the century. I noted earlier that London, accounting for 65–75% of total urban population in 1700, recorded only very modest growth in the eighteenth century, expanding at the rate of 0.4% per year. It may be possible to explain this modest growth in terms of the city's size, since sometime before the middle of the eighteenth century London had already reached a size equalled by no other European city except ancient Rome. But as may be observed in table 15.1, the other seven largest cities in England also had slow rates of growth during this period.

During the eighteenth century, the seven largest English cities (aside from London) recorded an annual growth rate of something like 0.5%. This rate drops to 0.3% if Bristol is excluded. Bristol was the exception that proves the rule. But the seven towns that, with London, figured among the largest cities after 1800 registered an average growth rate of 2.1% per year during the eighteenth century, which rose to 3.0% from 1800 to 1850. To these seven cities should be added others that, while less important from the point of view of size, nevertheless made a substantial contribution to the Industrial Revolution. And in almost every case these cities were originally very small towns, and often simply villages.

Similarly, when we analyze the geographical locations at which the most important technological innovations first took hold, we find that the traditional urban centers are absent from the list. Darby—the inventor of the method of fabricating cast iron using coal—was the son of a farmer settled in Coalbrookdale, at that time a little village. But it was normal in traditional societies for smelting works to be established in rural areas, wood being in quantitative terms the most important raw material used in the production of iron. Even during later phases, however, improvements in industrial techniques continued to come from semirural districts, which remained the site of the iron industry until the start of the nineteenth century.

While Arkwright may not have been the inventor of the first spinning machine, he was unquestionably the first to have understood how to use this machine for the commercial production of thread. He therefore provided the starting point for the mechanization of this sector of industry, a sector destined to play a role of primordial importance in the industrialization of England. As Mantoux (1928) puts it, "with Arkwright, mechanization ceases to belong solely to the history of techniques, becoming a fact of economic life in the broadest sense of the term." Now Arkwright, a barber by trade before he became the proprietor of a spinning mill, was born in Preston, a small town which had a population of less than 2,000–3,000 in 1732, the year of his birth. It was here that in 1768 he established the first spin-

TABLE 15.1 Growth of the Population (in Thousands) of
English Cities according to Function
(1700–1850)

	1700	1800	1850
London	550	860	2,320
Major urban centers before the Industrial Revolution			
Norwich	29	36	67
Bristol	25	61	150
Newcastle	25	33	110
Exeter	14	16	16
York	11	16	35
Colchester	8	10	12
Coventry	7	16	36
Total for these seven cities	119	188	426
Major urban centers in the first phase of the Industrial Revolution			
Birmingham	10	71	230
Liverpool	6	76	422
Manchester	9	81	404
Leeds	7	52	185
Sheffield	8	45	141
Bradford	4	13	100
Stoke	3	22	65
Total for these seven cities	47	360	1,547
Total urban population	880	2,100	8,000

Sources: See the methodological appendix.
Note: The fact that these figures have been only slightly rounded off does not imply a correspondingly small margin of error.

ning mill. Preston by this time had a population of some 5,000–6,000. He founded the second spinning mill, larger and more modern than the first, in 1771 in Cromford, a little village near Derby, itself only a very small town of 6,000–7,000 people at this time. What drew Arkwright to Cromford was the presence of a watercourse capable of powering a mill to drive his machinery, for in his first factory the machines were driven by horses. Here was one of the major reasons why rural areas were so important in the early phases of industrialization: the ready availability of sources of energy. It will be remembered that steam engines came into use only as of 1785–1790. And for decades after this, watermills still outnumbered steam-driven machines by a wide margin. This dependence on water mills explains how in English the term "mill" came to mean "factory."

But even the birth of the steam engine was tied to the rural environment. The true first steps in its development were taken by Newcomen, who after 1710 built steam-powered machines that were not really supplanted by Watt's machines until around 1790. Now Newcomen was a blacksmith and locksmith in Dartmouth, a very small port and local market with a population of around 1,000–2,000. The next decisive step, linked with Watt, took place (so far as its economic exploitation went) in an urban setting, but outside the great centers of the traditional urban world.

This is a good time to take note of the interactions between science on the one hand and the city and technology on the other—interactions destined (see chapter 20) to play a central role in subsequent phases of the process of industrialization. Watt was born in a very small town, but he emigrated to London at the age of nineteen. He was not only a city dweller, but his career was closely tied to university life. By 1757 he had been appointed instrument maker for the department of mathematics at the University of Glasgow (Glasgow at that time had a population of 23,000–25,000). While performing these duties he repaired a model of Newcomen's steam engine; he recognized its imperfections, which he largely succeeded in eliminating. Though Watt's invention took place in a traditional urban center, its production began elsewhere. And even afterwards, when large-scale production actually got under way, it was in the budding manufacturing town of Birmingham, which had a population only 2,000 in 1600. Birmingham only developed during the very first stages of the Industrial Revolution, reaching a population of 10,000 sometime around 1750.

But while Watt may be considered a city dweller, the third great name in the epic saga of the steam engine, Trevithick (inventor of the high-pressure engine), though in direct contact with coal mining, was country born and bred. He was chiefly concerned with the use of the steam engine in agriculture. For he was convinced that if the steam engine were used to its full potential in this sector, "one could double the population of the Kingdom and make our markets the cheapest in the world."

The great name in the history of pottery, Wedgwood, was born in Staffordshire, and it was here that he established and developed his manufacturing works, whose renown reached round the world.

> At the time of his birth in 1730, this region was
> backward and poverty-stricken. The soil, full of clay
> and resistant to cultivation, only barely nourished a
> scattered population. Roads were rare and so bad
> that merchandise had to be carried on the backs of
> men. There were no towns, only a few villages of
> thatch-roofed cottages. About fifty potters lived in
> Burslem, seven in Hanley. Stoke had fewer than ten
> houses. (Mantoux, 1928)

Many more examples could be added to this list, and in almost every case the schema would still be the same. There were few cities in the urban network at the start of the eighteenth century that played an important part in the Industrial Revolution in England. And nowhere was this more true than in the city that by itself made up the greatest part of this network—London. It is worth pointing out in this regard that in Mantoux's book (*The Industrial Revolution in the Eighteenth Century*), of the 140 citations of cities in the index, only eight are connected with London. The proportion is higher in Deane (1967), but remains under 30%. The significance of this fact emerges when we consider that, having 56% of the total population of Great Britain in 1700, London still accounted for 50% as late as 1750. And it may be noted that in both of these books a number of the references to London solely concern political matters, while practically none of the references to other cities do.

It may be further noted that the two men associated with the enterprise that ushered in the age of canals in Great Britain—an age unquestionably linked with the growth of British cities—both came from rural backgrounds. Francis Egerton, Duke of Bridgewater (predestined name), who, following an unsuccessful courtship, had retired very young to his estate, decided in the late 1750s to construct a canal linking his coal mines in Worsley to the city of Manchester. Joseph Brindley, who not only designed, but also supervised, the construction of this first canal of the industrial age (and many others after it), was born in 1716 in the village of Thornsett. Largely uneducated, Brindley became first a mill builder and then a wheelwright in Leek, probably a small town at that time with fewer than 3,000 people, where his reputation for repairing machines grew.

The Reasons behind the Lack of a Role for Traditional Cities

As has been vividly illustrated, the dominant urban centers in English society at the start of the eighteenth century made no significant contribution to the initial phases of the Industrial Revolution. They may even have proved resistant to the changes introduced by industrialization, a problem to which I shall return when I discuss the role of cities in the international spread of the Industrial Revolution. The lack of a role for the dominant urban centers of traditional England did not mean, however, that the innovations associated with the Industrial Revolution and the development of the first poles of industrialization took place exclusively in rural districts. On the contrary (see chapter 20), cities generally provided the setting for most technological innovations and were often the setting for their applications. But this setting was in general semiurban or was in small towns that did not figure prominently in the predominant urban network. Writing in 1914, Pirenne observed of capitalists that "to each of the successive periods in an economic history corresponds a clearly distinct

　　　　　DEVELOPMENT OF THE WESTERN WORLD

capitalist class. In other words, the group of capitalists existing in any given historical epoch will not have issued from the group of capitalists of the preceding epoch." Similarly, each economic stage has favored a certain number of urban nuclei, without bringing about the disappearance of the preceding urban nuclei.

The fact that the new industries ushered in by the first stages of the Industrial Revolution evolved outside the network of traditional urban centers and often in essentially rural settings can easily be explained in terms of a fairly large, but well-defined, group of factors. I have already drawn attention to the need for waterpower, a factor that played a determining role in the location of textile mills (and some other mills) practically to the middle of the nineteenth century. Another energy-related factor was the transformation in the technology of the iron and steel industry, a transformation that placed a premium on coal. As a result, the new iron works increasingly gravitated toward the coalfields, which did not necessarily lie near any of the existing cities. Mention should also be made of other, purely economic motives, such as the lower wages paid in rural districts or in small towns, the lower cost of industrial sites and buildings there, and the absence of the regulations that in many cities would have hindered the establishment of industrial concerns. Nor should one overlook the fact that during these early phases the new industrial enterprises were small and the labor force largely unskilled. The growth of industry in areas outside major urban centers was, then, readily understandable and is not in the least paradoxical.

But this does not mean that there was no change in English cities between the Middle Ages and the start of the Industrial Revolution. I have mentioned commercial expansion and the rapid growth of London. Further, it appears that during the same period important changes took place in the cultural life of provincial cities (Borsay, 1977). An evolution of this sort was almost inevitable if one calculates, as I have done, that between 1500 and 1700 the average population of the twenty-five largest provincial towns grew from 5,200 to 10,800. But such changes often occurred elsewhere, not only in other European societies, but outside Europe as well.

I close this chapter with the conclusion reached by Daunton (1978), which is perfectly in accord with my own. After analyzing the relations between the city and economic growth in eighteenth-century England, Daunton writes: "Certainly, the towns of the eighteenth century merit study—but perhaps not as useful analytical tools in explaining economic growth." Nor, I would add, are they likely to prove useful in explaining to any significant degree the English Industrial Revolution.

16 Urbanization and the Diffusion of the Industrial Revolution □

The problem I shall deal with in this chapter is ultimately more important than the role of cities in the inception of the Industrial Revolution in England. It is more important not only because it concerns more countries, but more significantly, because the mechanisms conditioning the transfer of industrialization to traditional societies remain today a crucial aspect of the problem of underdevelopment.

The question I shall try to answer here is this: to what extent did the levels of urbanization and the urban structures in existence before the international diffusion of industrialization influence this diffusion? Did urbanization help or hinder the diffusion of the Industrial Revolution from England to other countries during the eighteenth and nineteenth centuries? I shall for the time being leave aside the problem of the Third World (discussed at length in part 4). I shall also deal with the relations between levels of urbanization on the one hand and the pace of growth and levels of industrialization in developed countries on the other.

Urbanization and Diffusion in Europe

I shall open this discussion by making a very important observation: all of those countries today considered developed had begun the process of development before the 1880s. This in itself is reason enough to treat these cases separately from those of the countries of the Third World. These beginnings of modern development spanned a fairly long period of time, taking a little more than a hundred years. On the other hand, during a first phase in the diffusion of the Industrial Revolution there were in fact two processes at work which, to simplify matters somewhat, can be regarded as different. For the transmission of the agricultural revolution from England to other countries preceded the transmission of industrialization.

Leaving aside non-European nations, to which I shall return later, one can divide the countries of Europe into four groups as a function of the time at which modern development began. There are first the three countries earliest affected by the Industrial Revolution: Belgium, France, and Switzerland. For this first group of countries, the diffusion of the agricultural revolution (or at least certain aspects of it) got under way during the period 1740–1780, and the diffusion of industrialization sometime around 1770–1800. The second group was basically Germany and certain parts of the Austro-Hungarian Empire, especially Czechoslovakia. In this group agriculture began to be affected by 1800–1820 and industry by 1840–1860. It will be noticed that in both these groups the time lag between the two revolutions (somewhat artificially separated here) was shorter than it had been in England. This was even more the case in the third group of countries, where the two revolutions overlap, agriculture beginning to register change between 1860 and 1870 and industry between 1860 and 1880. This third group was composed of Spain, Italy, Russia, and Sweden. The fourth group was decidedly heterogeneous, the sole common denominator being the fact that in each of the countries in this group industrialization had progressed very little before 1914. This does not mean, however, that modern development failed to reach these countries, nor did it prevent some of them from joining the ranks of the richest countries in Europe on the eve of the First World War. The wealthy countries in this fourth group were Denmark, the Netherlands, and Norway. These countries were affected relatively early by the change taking place in England, which led to the rapid expansion of their exports of food and raw materials. The poor countries in this last group were basically Portugal and those countries formerly in the Ottoman Empire, which partly explains their delay in joining the rest of industrialized Europe.

As can be seen, there is a definite correlation between the time when the process of change got under way and the distance from England: the countries nearest to England were as a rule the soonest affected by the Industrial Revolution. This circumstance argues against the importance of any hypothetical contribution of the urban structure to the time of the diffusion of industrialization. It may simply be noted that among the first six countries to follow the English lead (i.e., the first two groups mentioned above plus the United States), the great majority—five out of six—had attained only a modest level of urbanization. This by itself suggests that a high level of urbanization was neither a necessary nor even a positive factor with respect to early development. Indeed, the opposite relation stands out just as clearly: highly urbanized countries figured very prominently among those in which development was slow in getting started (see table 16.1). It may be recalled that the last two groups included Italy, Spain, Portugal, the Netherlands, Russia, and Sweden. Now as early as the eighteenth century, and even before, the first four of these six countries already had high levels of urbanization persisting into the nineteenth century.

But however interesting the likely influence of urbanization on the time when modern economic development began in the various countries of Europe may be, its impact on growth rates and on the process of industrialization is more important still. For the time when modern economic development began can largely be explained, as was just noted, in terms of geographical location: the closer to England, the sooner the start of development. Once development had finally begun, on the other hand, developments reflected indigenous conditions alone. It was therefore at this point that urbanism came into its own.

Urbanization and Economic Growth

Comparing growth rates is not an easy thing to do, even when, as begins to be the case in this period, the available data are more abundant. What makes this task so difficult is that one cannot use the same set of dates for all the countries concerned. For during any given period each country will be found to have reached a different phase of development. The obvious alternative would be to use the same phase regardless of date, which is, in fact, what I shall do. The trouble is that approaching the problem this way I run up against interference in the form of general growth cycles, which certainly existed in the nineteenth century. All things considered, however, this second source of statistical bias is much less severe than the first, and in fact analysis of the data shows that the distortions imputable to it are relatively insignificant.

I have used the first five decades following the start of the process of development. For those countries in which a long time elapsed between the increase in agricultural productivity and the beginnings of industrialization, I placed the start of the process of development at the midpoint between these two times. In the other cases the date was set some ten years prior to the time at which economic development began. I then divided the countries of Europe into two groups, according to the pace of growth, with the change in the volume (that is, in constant value) of the per capita gross national product serving as the index of the growth rate.

Arbitrarily fixing the dividing line between the two groups at 1.0% per year one finds that each group contains roughly the same number of countries. The group of countries experiencing rapid growth (i.e., growth at the rate of 1.0% or more per year of GNP per capita) includes first of all Sweden and Denmark, with growth at the rate of some 2.0% per year. Then come Switzerland, Germany, and Belgium, with growth at the rate of 1.5 % per year, France and Norway at 1.2% per year, and finally Austria-Hungary and Russia at 1.0% per year. In the second group, that of countries with slow rates of growth, one finds the Netherlands, Rumania, and Greece at the top of the list, with growth at the rate of 0.8% per year, followed by Italy, Serbia, and Bul-

TABLE 16.1 Economic Development and Urbanization

	Start of Modern De-velopment	Level of Urbaniza-tion Then	Growth of per Capita GNP	Level of Industrialization[a]
Austria-Hungary	1830	7	0.6	average
Belgium	1790	18	1.0	high
Bulgaria	1880	8	0.8	low
Denmark	1850	15	1.7	low
France	1780	12	1.1	high
Germany	1830	10	1.2	high
Greece	1880	20	0.8	low
Italy	1850	20	0.6	low
Netherlands	1850	39	0.9	low
Norway	1850	9	1.0	average
Portugal	1880	16	0.6	low
Rumania	1880	12	0.7	low
Russia	1860	8	0.8	average
Spain	1850	18	0.4	low
Sweden	1850	7	1.2	high
Switzerland	1790	6	1.2	high
Yugoslavia	1880	8	0.6	low
United States	1790	5	1.2	high

Sources: For levels of urbanization, table 13.4; For GNP, Bairoch (to appear); For levels of industrialization, Bairoch (1982).

[a] Around 1914 or around 1950, as a function of when development began.

garia at 0.5% per year. Spain and Portugal bring up the rear, with growth at the rate of only 0.1% per year.

Since the United States is the only non-European country with a population of European origin to have achieved any real importance during the first half of the nineteenth century, I decided to include it in the present analysis.

Now that I have defined my sample (see table 16.1), when I compare growth rates with levels of urbanization, a series of interesting observations emerge. To begin with, there is a definite correlation between the level of urbanization before development began and the rate of growth once development got under way. By and large, the less urbanized the country, the more rapid the pace of economic growth during the first half-century of development. Thus in the nine countries in which the level of urbanization before development was under 11%, the average growth rate was 0.96% per year. In the nine countries in which the level of urbanization was over 11%, the growth rate was 0.86% per year. When the dividing line (for urbanization) is put at 15%, the differences become even more striking and significant, the annual growth rate for countries above and below this line being 0.61% and 1.01% per year, respectively. While this inverse relation also emerges from the calculation of coefficients of correlation, it is not quite significant statistically. I shall examine the link between levels of development and levels of urbanization at greater length in chapter 21.

Urbanization and Industrialization

In statistical terms, the correlation between levels of industrialization after the start of economic development and levels of urbanization before the start of economic development is more significant than the inverse relation between the level of urbanization before it and the rate of growth after it. The less urbanized any given country was before economic growth began, the more industrialized it was by the end of the first phases of development (see table 16.1).

Five of the six countries that had a high level of industrialization quite soon after beginning development had only a low level of urbanization at the start of the process. These five countries were France, Germany, Sweden, Switzerland, and the United States. As for the sixth, Belgium, though it had a high level of urbanization, Belgian industry was little diversified, with a predominance of semimanufactured goods.

Among the nine countries in which industrialization progressed very little, six were highly urbanized: Denmark, Greece, Italy, the Netherlands, Portugal, and Spain. It should be noted in this context that in many cases industrialization evolved independently of the rate of economic growth: certain countries developed economically without industrializing a great deal. Thus among the twelve to fourteen richest (if not most highly developed) countries in the world around 1913, six had a dominant agricultural sector: Australia, Canada, Denmark, the Netherlands, New Zealand, and Norway. Canada, however, was the most highly industrialized of the six and is something of a special case. But although not all of the highly developed countries in my sample were necessarily industrialized, two facts remain: all of the industrialized countries were highly developed, while not all of the agricultural countries were.

To the extent that in traditional societies, urbanization was itself a factor in development of the demand for and supply of manufactured goods, the prominent place of heavily urbanized countries among the late developers in my sample raises a number of serious problems. Unfortunately, to my knowledge at least, no analyses have yet been done to solve these problems. (So far as I can tell, no one has even recognized their existence.) Nevertheless, two complementary explanations can be suggested.

The first involves the observation (see chapter 15) that in the first phases of the Industrial Revolution in England, industrialization generally took place outside traditional urban centers. It is worth recalling in this connection that this did not apply merely to London, but to all large cities. Now as it happens, much the same thing was true in most of the countries industrialized in the nineteenth century.

In Germany, of the thirty-eight cities with populations of more than 100,000 in 1905, seventeen were very small towns around 1800, half of them with populations of less than 6,000. Essen and Bochum, where a great part of the German iron and steel industry came to be concentrated, had populations of 300,000 and 140,000, respectively, by about 1910, while in 1800 their combined population was only some 5,000. The cities in which the iron and steel were processed—Solingen, Heilbronn, Esslingen, and so forth, did not by and large figure among the German cities of importance at the start of the nineteenth century. The cotton industry more often tended to be located in traditional cities, but not exclusively. The chemical industry, on the other hand, chiefly developed outside traditional urban centers. Thus, Ludwigshafen and Höchst, for instance, were decidedly small towns before chemical manufacturing concerns were established in them and they began to expand.

In France the poles of industrial development in the nineteenth century lay in regions little affected by traditional urban growth. The principal centers of the iron industry, Le Creusot, Pont-à-Mousson, Longwy, and so on, were only villages or very small towns at the start of the nineteenth century. An analogous situation obtained in the case of the textile industry. Although this industry did in fact take root in regions already with some degree of urban development, the great cities of traditional France were not involved. The only exceptions to this rule, large traditional cities which became manufacturing towns of considerable importance, were Lyons and Lille.

Industrial development in Belgium closely followed the French pattern in that, there as in France, there were two notable exceptions to the general rule: Liège and, to a lesser extent, Ghent. If one sets these exceptions aside, however, the best part of Belgian industry at the beginning the twentieth century lay in what had at the start of the nineteenth been rural, or at most semiurbanized areas.

In Sweden, Malmö, with its population of 85,000, had by around 1910 become the country's second largest city and after Stockholm the most important center of industry, both in textiles and in iron and steel. Around 1800, however, with a population of 4,000, it was only the ninth or tenth largest city in Sweden. The iron industry and the majority of the concerns involved in the industrial use of iron and steel were established in semiurbanized areas. In the case of the textile industry, the two chief centers, Norrköping and Borås, were, respectively, at their origin a fairly large traditional city and a small town, barely more than a village, with a population of some 2,000. Of the three cities in which the manufacture of matches developed, only two existed in 1800, and their combined population at that time was under 6,000 as against 46,000 by 1910.

For obvious reasons this cleavage was much less pronounced in those nations, like Italy and Spain, that achieved only a modest degree of industrial development. But even here a good number of manufacturing towns had been of only marginal importance in the preindustrial age. In 1910 Bilbao had a population of nearly 100,000, making it the seventh largest city in Spain. In 1800, on the other hand, with a population of roughly 10,000, it was somewhere between thirty-third and thirty-six place.

One obvious explanation for this turn of events lay in the new geographic determinism introduced by one of the chief constituents of the process of industrialization—coal. Since in the nineteenth century the production of one ton of cast iron required six tons of coal, the iron industry was mainly located near coalfields. Even after the lowering of transport costs associated with the use of the steam engine, it was not until the second half of the twentieth century that the shipping of heavy materials such as coal or iron ore over long distances became an economically viable proposition. (I shall return to this problem in the next chapter.) The production of iron and steel in coal-producing regions, moreover, clearly favored the establishment of other industrial plants in the same areas. Further still, during the initial phases of its development and indeed right up to the early 1950s, the chemical industry used coal as a raw material. Thus although raw materials represent only a very small fraction of the return on the finished product in chemical manufacturing, this sector was also drawn to coal-producing regions.

Thus coal constituted a major factor underlying the location of the new industrial cities, one particularly capable of explaining the movement away from traditional urban systems. As in the case of England, furthermore, other elements have to be introduced. The first of these was waterpower, which, though less decisive in the nineteenth century than in the eighteenth, still played an important part in determining the location of urban industries. It can be estimated that as late as 1870 water provided half of the mechanical power used in the industries of the developed countries (Bairoch, 1983). But it is obvious that for countries whose industrial takeoff took place much later than England's, the steam engine gave considerably more geographical freedom for the location of the textile industries. The next factor was the lower wages paid rural workers and the lower costs of buildings and industrial sites in rural districts and small towns. Nevertheless, while all of these factors serve to explain why industrial growth took place in areas formerly untouched by traditional urban systems, none of them contributes very much to explaining why a high level of traditional, preindustrial urbanization should have acted as a brake on economic development. It is at this point that a second group of explanatory elements should be introduced.

Instances of Parasitic Urbanization

This second explanation for the effects of preindustrial urbanization on economic development remains in the province of deductive analysis and on this account proves hard, if not impossible, to verify by empirical means. The highly urbanized countries that encountered great difficulties in pursuing development were essentially those countries that had inherited their original urban systems from some economic function that in the meantime had either largely vanished or at any rate had been greatly reduced in importance.

It may be recalled that the countries in question were chiefly Italy, Spain, and Portugal. Nineteenth-century Italy had long ago stopped being the foremost commercial power in Europe, while Spain and Portugal had a century before become of marginal significance from the point of view of international trade. As a result, these three countries found themselves saddled with an urban sector that had in a sense become parasitic. Around 1850, for example, they had an urban population some 40–50% greater than it normally should have been given their level of development. Indeed, an excellent correlation exists between levels of urbanization and per capita GNP (see chapter 21). Basing my calculations on this relation, I find that, around 1850, 11–13% of Italy's population should have been living in cities, whereas in fact the proportion certainly exceeded 20%. For Spain the figures were 12–14% as against 18%, and for Portugal, 10–12% as against 16%.

There is a sense in which the Netherlands could also be included in this group. Over the course of the nineteenth century industrialization made very little headway in the Netherlands. And while the Netherlands was definitely richer around 1900 than Italy, Spain, or Portugal, the difference was not all that great since the Netherlands in terms of wealth was in only eighth or ninth place among the nineteen countries of Europe, having fallen from between second and fourth place in 1800. Now in 1850 about 40% of the total population was still concentrated in Dutch cities, a proportion at least twice that justified by the level of development. The gap was, then, very much wider for the Netherlands than for Italy, Spain, or Portugal.

The Netherlands was also distinguished from Italy, Spain, and Portugal by two factors that explain in part, though not completely, this high level of urbanization. At the beginning of the nineteenth century only fifty years or so had passed since the Netherlands lost its supremacy in commercial affairs. This to a certain extent enabled the Dutch to recover during the nineteenth century a portion of their role as commercial intermediaries. This recovery was facilitated by the geographic location of the Netherlands, which induced countries like Switzerland, Austria, and even Germany to ship a substantial fraction of their exports and imports through Dutch ports, along Dutch rivers, and later on Dutch railroads. Thus it has been estimated that by the

close of the nineteenth century the volume of exports the Netherlands handled for other countries represented roughly 50% of overall
national exports, if not more. By contrast, the corresponding volume
in the United Kingdom was about 24%, and it generally fluctuated between 10 and 30% in the other countries of Europe.

The second distinguishing feature of the Dutch situation was the
economic importance of the Dutch colonial domain. The brutal, but
effective policy pursued by the Dutch with a view to the development of
export crops in present-day Indonesia had by the 1840s made possible
a heavy flow of exports. In 1850 the value of these exports amounted to
about eight dollars for every inhabitant of the Netherlands as against
four dollars in the United Kingdom and Spain, less than one dollar in
Portugal and nothing at all in Italy. By 1913, the gap had widened
further still in favor of the Netherlands: forty-four dollars per capita
in the Netherlands, six dollars in Portugal, forty cents in Spain, and
ten cents in Italy.

These facts help to reduce somewhat the artificial character of the
level of urbanization in the Netherlands, but they do not remove it
altogether. The most that can be said is that they bring the gap between the level of urbanization actually achieved in the Netherlands
and the level theoretically justified by the level of development back
into line with similar gaps observed in the case of Italy, Spain, and
Portugal.

In those countries there was an urban hypertrophy somewhat similar to that existing for several decades now in the Third World (see
part 4). And while the causes of this hypertrophy were different, the
consequences were mainly the same. It is certain that the pressing
need for supplies and sometimes for equipment held back the flow of
investments in the productive sector of the economy. The excessive
size of the urban sector led to underemployment in the urban work
force, leading to a reduction in the productiveness of the economy as
a whole. This underemployment must also have led to more workers
being engaged in the tertiary, service-related sector of the economy,
producing a subsequent rigidity and lack of mobility in the supply of
labor. My colleague Busino (1971) has told of many observations made
at the end of the nineteenth century by the great economist Pareto,
at that time head of an industrial concern, regarding the preference
shown by Italian workers who were occasionally employed in industry
for jobs in the tertiary sector. In general the most talented members
of the working population sought work in services, which added a further handicap to the industrialization of a country already deficient in
natural resources.

Furthermore it should be noted—and this constituted an important
aspect of the parasitic character of the urban systems of the more
slowly developing countries of Europe—that these heavily urbanized
nations were also distinguished by the predominance of very large

cities. This was especially true of Italy and Portugal. Around 1800 Naples had a population of some 430,000 and Lisbon nearly 200,000. At the start of the nineteenth century in Italy the population living in cities with populations of more than 100,000 represented roughly 30% of the total urban population. In Portugal at this time the proportion was 45–50%, and in Spain 15–17%. In Germany, on the other hand, the proportion was only 11–14%, and while it ran as high as 20–23% in France, it was nil in Switzerland, Sweden, and the United States. And these differences become even larger when the population of cities with populations of more than 100,000 is related to total population.

The Persistence of Urban Networks in Countries in Decline: How May It Be Explained?

The persistence of such a high level of urbanization in these countries poses a problem in its own right, one it is not easy to solve given the present state of research. For quite apart from its adverse effects on industrialization, this abnormal and excessive urban growth must have been a heavy burden on the societies concerned. But what is the explanation of the fact that the larger Italian cities usually resisted urban decline more successfully than medium-sized cities or small towns? Though Brescia, Cremona, Ferrara, and Lucca had considerably smaller populations in 1800 than at the start of the sixteenth century, Venice and Florence had about the same populations, while Milan, Naples, and even Genoa (not to mention Rome, of course) had larger populations. Events in Portugal evolved along the same lines: Lisbon in 1800 had twice the population of that in 1550, and had even a greater population than in 1700. But capital cities represent something of a special case, and elsewhere on the Iberian peninsula some of the larger cities registered declines. Thus in Spain, for example, while Barcelona, Madrid, and Valencia grew, Granada, Cordoba, Salamanca, Segovia, and Toledo, among others, suffered a fall in population. In the Netherlands, Amsterdam held its ground and even had a slight increase in population, rising from 210,000 in 1750 to 224,000 around 1850. The population of Rotterdam doubled during this same period, as a result of the development of its port activities and more particularly the part it played in the transit business mentioned earlier, Rotterdam lying at the mouth of the Rhine. The other Dutch cities were by and large stagnant, however, though there may have been more-or-less pronounced progressions and regressions at the local level.

There was probably a whole series of factors, economic as well as social and political, responsible for these differences. But overall, there was a certain persistence of structural elements. The cause for the differences must most likely be sought in the reaction time required for cities or other structural elements to adapt to gradual changes in the environment. This reaction time is probably longer than that needed for the other socioeconomic changes associated with industrialization, a time going beyond the period of immediate interest here. But in seeking the source of this persistence it is necessary to descend to a more detailed level of analysis, looking for clues among the conditions peculiar to each region and even to each city.

Another hypothesis provides a partial explanation for this paradox of societies in decline in which the relative size of the urban population does not fall as sharply as their economic recession would lead one to expect. A declining or stagnant urban population may bring about substantial savings in outlays for construction in housing and in the urban infrastructure. This would make it possible for the urban population to adjust to a fall of 3–5% in the level of available revenues without reducing its standard of living. In short, this is, albeit to a considerably lesser degree, a case analogous to that in which a fall in rural population leads to a rise in the ratio of land to inhabitants. Needless to say this hypothesis can account for only a portion of the paradox, and it does not exclude the intervention of other factors, notably a fall in the standard of living of urban populations, a more intense drain on the population of rural districts, or a combination of the two. It should be noted, moreover, that the preservation of the level of urbanization was in some cases more apparent than real, inasmuch as it was accompanied by an increase in the relative place of agricultural activities in urban areas.

17 Industrialization and the Cities in the Western World in the Nineteenth Century □

In this chapter I shall discuss relations that are the inverse of those dealt with in chapter 16. The fact that industrialization was one of the fundamental causes of urbanization in the nineteenth century may seem so self-evident that it merits only the most cursory consideration, a mere reminder of the essential part it played. But even though industrialization was not the sole factor responsible for urbanization in various developing societies in the nineteenth century, its contribution deserves to be discussed in some detail. For the very self-evidence of the link between industrialization and the urbanization of the Western world during the nineteenth century may lead to taking it too much for granted, at the risk of obscuring a number of significant aspects of the process.

Industrial Cities Different from Traditional Cities

Among the important elements in urbanization should be mentioned the dominant functions of cities. While in traditional societies these functions were above all administrative, commercial, religious, and craft-related, with the onset of industrialization manufacturing became preeminent. Indeed the nineteenth century witnessed a sharp increase in the number of people working in industry. In Europe (except Russia), whereas industrial manufacturing employed only a little more than six million people around 1800, this figure had risen to roughly thirty-eight million by 1913. And around 1800 a fairly large proportion of the six million industrial workers lived and worked in rural districts. But one of the characteristics of the nineteenth century was precisely the nearly total disappearance of this type of rural labor. It is probably no exaggeration to say that the number of workers employed in industries located in urban centers increased nine, if not ten times over. Urban population grew during this period by a factor of 7.4. And overall employment in the service sector went up from around seven million in 1800 to around thirty-five million in and around 1913. In this case, however, it seems likely that a larger fraction of all tertiary economic activity was located in rural areas in 1914, for example, than in 1800. This leads me to postulate that the number of city dwellers employed in services actually rose only fourfold during the nineteenth century.

In the cities of Renaissance Europe it can be estimated that the traditional productive activities corresponding to industrial manufacturing must on the average have employed 35–45% of the working population. By contrast, at the end of the nineteenth century (around 1913), industry probably accounted on the average for roughly 50–55% of all employment in the cities. But these percentages only indicate the average situation. It may be remembered that in traditional societies there were cities specializing in specific economic pursuits. Thus while manufacturing would have represented only a small fraction of employment in some market towns, for instance, it would have accounted for a very high percentage of overall employment in towns given over to textile production. As for the cities of the industrialized world of the nineteenth century, though specialization had somewhat diminished, it had not vanished. And there were pronounced differences at both the national and the regional level. In Russia, for instance, according to the census of 1897 industrial manufacturing accounted for only 25% of all urban employment. And even if analysis is confined to cities with populations of more than 10,000, in only one-fifth of these cities does industrial manufacturing account for more than 30% of overall employment (In rural areas industrial manufacturing engaged 10% of the working population.) By contrast, in Germany according to the 1882 census at least 53% of the working population in cities of 5,000–100,000 people worked in industry and mining. And if allowance is made for various inaccuracies in the definitions of the different categories of employment, the proportion was probably more than 60%.

But the change industrialization introduced was not quantitative alone; it brought about a profound change in the social condition of the people employed in the industrial sector. For dating from the nineteenth century at least, industry meant wage labor, and the proportion of wage earners employed in trade increased at this time as well. The rural world of the nineteenth century, on the other hand, was dominated by small independent farmers. Thus one of the distinctive features of life in the traditional economies of the West was reversed: in the nineteenth century the urban world was in many respects less free than the rural world. Another change in social conditions, more positive this time, was a reduction in the number of domestic servants: a trend offset, it is true, by a rise in the number of workers in services, and especially in the commercial sector.

Profound change also took place in housing. Particularly after the middle of the nineteenth century, in cities housing was constructed specifically for industrial workers, especially miners. As a general rule, right up to 1920–30 the initiative in this area came from employers. In a sense worker housing formed part of the enterprise, and it provided an additional way to apply pressure on the working class, even though humanitarian motives often lay at the root of such projects. To leave one's job meant giving up one's home, and thus in many cases it necessitated moving from one place to another, with all of the painful consequences such a move could entail. And the nature of the dominant industrial sector also exerted a definite, sometimes significant social impact. There was the predominance of female workers in textile manufacturing, for example, or the higher wages paid in industries requiring highly skilled labor, and so on.

During the nineteenth century industrialization also implied the industrial plant, which came to form an integral part of the urban space. In the first stages of industrial development industries were set up in existing buildings: stables, barns, old religious edifices, and, particularly owing to energy needs, in old mills as well. As was noted earlier, the term "mill" in English has come since the Industrial Revolution to mean both mill in the traditional sense and factory. But in England from the end of the eighteenth century and in Europe generally from 1830–1850 on, things changed. The steam engine freed the factory from watercourses, and both technical and commercial developments led to the establishment of larger enterprises than before, whence the construction of buildings specifically designed to be factories. In the smaller towns this often led to the concentration of housing and service buildings around the factories, while in the larger cities the factories had to be set up near housing in order to reduce the length of the journey to and from work. In both cases, then, the factory occupied a central place in the spatial arrangement of the urban milieu. And sometimes efforts were made to make the factory beautiful. *The Castles of Industry* is the title of a survey of the architecture of the region of Lille, an industrial city of the north of France, for the period 1830–1930 (Grenier and Wieser-Benedetti, 1979). The pictures illustrating the book are proofs indeed that some factories were disguised into castles of all styles.

The Human Costs of Urbanization
Stemming from Industrialization

The constraints resulting when the worker's residence was provided by his employer have just been discussed. But however painful conditions may have been in this housing, they nevertheless marked a considerable improvement over the housing conditions for a large fraction of the urban working class during the first decades of the nineteenth century. On this score there is the eyewitness testimony of Villermé, a member of that scattered group of upper-class liberals who denounced the scandalous living conditions endured by the working class at the start of industrialization. In France and England, as in most other countries touched by the Industrial Revolution, doctors predominated in this group; they were brought by their profession into direct contact with the wretchedness of life among the working people.

In his description of the living conditions of workers in the cotton, wool, and silk industries, Villermé (1840) describes the housing conditions of workers in the mid-1830s in these terms:

> I saw at Mulhouse, in Dornach and in neighboring houses, some of those wretched dwellings in which two families slept each in one corner of the room, on straw thrown down on the tile floor and held in place by a pair of planks. A ragged blanket and often a sort of feather mattress of disgusting filthiness, such is all that covers this straw. Moreover, a single dirty and uncomfortable pallet for the whole family, a little stove serving both for cooking and for heat, a crate or large box for a wardrobe, a table, two or three chairs, a bench, a little crockery commonly comprise all of the possessions furnishing the rooms of workers employed in the spinning and weaving mills of this same town.

We now move on to Villermé's often-quoted description of the conditions in Lille, and particularly in the rue des Etaques and the surrounding courtyards:

> This is how the workers are housed there. The poorest of them live in the cellars and attics. In these cellars there are no doors or stairs communicating with the interior of the houses: they open directly on the streets or courtyards, and one enters them down a stairway, which very often serves as door and window both. They are made of stone or brick, are vaulted, paved or tiled, and all of them have fireplaces, which proves that they were built to serve as dwellings. They are commonly from six to six and a half feet high from the middle of the vault, and they are from ten to fourteen feet along the side. The usual furniture consists, along with the objects of the inhabitant's occupation, of a sort of wardrobe or a plank where food is kept, a stove, a small ceramic portable stove, a little crockery, a small table, two or three chairs in bad condition, and a dirty pallet made up of nothing more than a straw mattress and the tatters of a blanket. I should like to add nothing to this detailed account of hideous things revealing, to the most cursory glance, the profound wretchedness of the unfortunate inmates; but I must mention

that in several of the beds of which I have just
spoken I have seen sleeping together individuals of
both sexes and of very different ages, most of them
without nightshirts.

Villermé continues:

Well, the cellars are not the worst dwellings: they are
not the worst, far from it. . . . The worst dwellings
are the attics, where there is no protection against
the extremes of temperature; for the inmates, every
bit as wretched as those in the cellars, even lack the
means of keeping a fire to heat themselves during
the winter. Finally, I would not convey a complete
idea of the dwellings in question were I not to add
that, for all the people inhabiting several of the
courtyards I have mentioned, that is to say, for hundreds of persons sometimes, there are only one or
two of those closets indispensable for the cleanliness
of cities.

To be sure, what Villermé describes were not the average housing
conditions for all workers or, a fortiori, for all city dwellers. And one
should not retrospectively endow rural dwellings with a charm they
never had: thatch-roofed cottages are romantic only for those who do
not have to live in them. This said, there remains no doubt that the
housing of the urban worker suffered from the terrible constraints of
the price of space and its consequences, consequences of which, as has
been seen, inordinately high mortality rates were one of the more
terrible expressions.

But these deplorable housing conditions were only one facet of the
wretched life led by workers in the cities of the times. For while industrialization created many jobs for the peasant's sons driven from the
countryside by the combined effects of increases in the productivity of
agricultural labor and the more rapid increase in rural population,
these jobs were very ill-paid. Throughout most of the nineteenth century, despite the fact that city dwellers had to meet higher expenses,
the wages paid unskilled laborers in industry exceeded those paid farm
laborers by very little (10−15%). Working hours, moreover, were unquestionably much longer for workers during the first stages of industrialization than for the farm laborers of traditional societies. Putting
in 13−15 hours a day, six days a week, the urban laborer spent an
average of 3,700−4,500 hours a year in the factory, during which
time he worked some 3,400−3,900 hours. Farm laborers, on the other
hand, owing to seasonal slow periods, probably worked no more than
2,100−2,600 hours a year.

But it is very likely that the Industrial Revolution caused an intensification of labor in agriculture. It is indeed very likely that the annual number of working hours of the European peasant of the nine-

teenth century was higher than that of his ancestors at the beginning of the eighteenth century.

These sons of peasants who (see chapter 14) by migrating to the towns, reduced their life expectancy by a number of years, were compelled on top of this to send their children out to work at a very young age. By reason of its conditions, child labor constituted one of the scandals of the first century of industrialization and thus of the process of urbanization that formed its framework. Those children who had the good fortune (or perhaps one ought rather say the misfortune) to escape the death awaiting such a terrible number of babies in the cities were driven by the wretched plight of their parents to work in the factories. The technology of the period, especially in the textile industry, itself encouraged child labor. The use of children made it possible to compensate at low cost for the lack of automation in most of the machines in use at the time.

It is worth pointing out that while, in traditional societies, children also participated in economic activities, the beginning years of the Industrial Revolution were characterized by a lowering of the age at which children went to work. Children under eight or even six years of age commonly worked in the cotton industry. In traditional societies, on the other hand, apprenticeship in textile manufacturing began at twelve to fourteen years of age.

Children going to work for the first time while very young were also in most cases forced to do so outside the framework of the family. Since children helped adults, they worked to an identical timetable. Furthermore, they were paid ridiculous wages, as a rule one-fifth or one-seventh of what unskilled adult laborers earned. A daily wage of this kind sufficed to buy less than one kilo of bread, and wages were in many instances unable to meet even the minimum cost of keeping a child. In this perspective, a father's decision to send his child out to work may appear irrational and immoral. This was not the case, however. For without the wages children brought in, family earnings would have been insufficient to enable the household to survive.

The exploitation, not to say the martyrdom, of children was not confined to a limited period. In fact it was not until the close of the nineteenth century, at the time when technological advances on the one hand reduced the usefulness of child labor and on the other made their general education necessary, that an end was brought to this scandal, and mandatory primary schooling became the general rule.

In order to complete this all-too-brief account of the human costs of the first phases of industrialization in the urban environment, I would have to discuss still other great hardships for which I do not have room enough here: the way in which, as its size increased, the industrial plant came to resemble a forced-labor camp; the bullying to which workers were subjected on the job; the scale of unemployment which, though essentially cyclical, nevertheless created great misery among working people. In short, the term martyrdom just used seems in no way too strong. The social costs of the Industrial Revolution were enormous: the reverse side of the coin was very dark indeed. From the condition of slavery to which children and, lest we forget, women as well (whose wages were one-third those paid men) were subjected to the martyrdom of the working class as a whole, from the grim periods of unemployment to the vexations and costly fines imposed on workers by vindictive bosses, from the strikes motivated by despair to the pitiless lockouts, from the cellars of Lille to the slums of London, there was an endless course of wretchedness. The thousands of tons of cast iron and the millions of meters of cotton fabrics were paid for with the infinite mass of suffering accompanying the growth of cities under the impetus of industrialization.

Human Costs, but Human Benefits as Well

That the human costs were high, then, is undeniable. But there were human benefits as well, such as the enhanced possibilities for education and above all the greater chances of upward social mobility. The move to the city also brought more numerous recreations with it and wider and more diverse human contacts.

It is not an easy matter to draw up the balance of the costs and benefits of migrating to the city, and the result certainly varies from period to period. Take, for example, the case of England. The costs definitely outweighed the benefits at the start of the nineteenth century, and probably as late as about 1840–1850. But by the start of the twentieth century, urban and rural mortality rates had equalized and urban housing had become more spacious and wholesome (see below). And both of these changes for the better reflected the fact that in real terms urban wages had increased fairly sharply, substantially surpassing rural wages at this time, even though rural wages had also increased.

But at what point had the balance finally become positive? This is very difficult to determine, and varies a great deal not only from country to country, but from region to region. If I take the two most meaningful indicators, namely the average differences between wages paid to urban and rural workers, and the average differences between urban and rural infant mortality (see chapter 14), I can draw up the following approximate table for Western Europe as a whole:

	Differences in Wages in Favor of the City	Differences in Infant Mortality in Favor of the Countryside
circa 1815–40	15–20%	50–70%
circa 1900–14	25–30%	10–20%

To these considerations should be added the fact that, owing to the enhanced possibilities for upward social mobility, the wages paid to agricultural workers around the years 1900–1914 ought properly to be compared with those paid workers in a higher socioprofessional bracket than urban manual laborers. This widened the gap between urban and rural worker still further, with the result that by the start of the twentieth century, rational choice already favored the city. But is man solely *homo economicus*, and can one really think here in terms of choices? Industrialization drew men toward the cities, but it also tended, often imperiously, to drive them from the countryside.

And since this discussion opened with a passage from Villermé, it will close with another:

> It must not be thought, however, that the cotton industry created all of these poor people. No. But it did call them together, gathering them up from other regions. Those who could no longer find the means of earning a living at home, who were driven from home, who no longer had a right to parish assistance (among others, many Swiss, natives of Badois, inhabitants of the German part of Lorraine), all of them moved, whole families at a time, to Mulhouse, to Thann, and to the neighboring manufacturing towns, drawn there as they were by the hope of finding work.

Cities near Coalfields

Industrialization also brought with it new factors determining the location of cities. The cities whose economic activity was based on heavy industry were situated, even as early as the second half of the nineteenth century, near coal mines. Why this particular localizing factor at a time when transport costs were falling so steeply? The reason was that, despite this drop, transport costs for products with little intrinsic value were still very substantial.

A concrete example will better illustrate how matters stood. In France around 1880, the rate for slow freight on the railroads was on the order of six centimes per metric ton-kilometer. The price of coal at the mine, on the other hand, was on the average around twelve francs per metric ton. Thus a journey of only one hundred kilometers represented a price increase of 50%, even before taking into account loading and unloading. It is true that the cost was perceptibly lower for goods shipped on full railroad cars and was even lower by canal, but the cost for goods shipped by road was much higher. Since more coal was required to produce cast iron than iron ore, the decisive consideration in the iron and steel industry was the coal mine. At the start of the nineteenth century, as was noted before, six tons of coal were needed to produce one ton of cast iron; and it still took two tons at the end of the century.

The difference between the iron and steel industry and the textile industry (the two most important sectors of industrial activity in the nineteenth century) will be easily grasped if one considers that during this same period raw cotton cost roughly 1,500 francs, linen 2,200 francs, and silk 4,500 francs per metric ton. In other words, while transporting coal over a distance of one hundred kilometers raised its price by 50%, transporting cotton increased its price by only 0.4%, linen by only 0.3%, and silk by only 0.1%. The ratios were in real terms a little different, for I have not allowed in these theoretical calculations for the specific price schedules applied to each of these commodities. But the orders of magnitude involved would not be appreciably altered. Such being the case, one will readily understand the wide dispersal of the textile industry during the nineteenth century, its chief raw material (raw cotton) being for the most part imported from abroad.

But even those industries in which the cost of transporting raw materials or sources of energy played a more restricted part conformed to the general type. For as we have seen in previous chapters, in order to profit from certain economic advantages and free themselves from certain constraints, most of the new industries were established outside the traditional urban network. As a result, the urban network of the developed world was substantially modified during the nineteenth century, and (see chapter 18) a series of new cities came into existence. And in the emergence of these new cities the railroads played a leading role.

The Railroads: New Cities and Giant Cities

In England the railroads did not affect the economic life of the country until long after the fundamental transformations due to industrialization had occurred. But in the rest of the developed world the two phenomena went hand in hand. The first railway line in England (and in the world) was opened in 1825. By 1870 there were 105,000 kilometers of track in Europe and 88,000 kilometers in North America, growing to 363,000 and 467,000 kilometers, respectively, by 1913. The rail network spread only modestly thereafter, beginning to shrink at the start of the thirties in the United States and around 1960 in Europe. (The retreat began as early as 1921 in the United Kingdom, however.)

Mainly intended to link existing cities together, the railroads also became a new localizing factor in their own right. The railroads joined with natural transport routes in stimulating the creation of cities. The point at which two railway lines crossed constituted a propitious site for urban development, and many new cities owed their foundation or their rapid growth to this factor.

In regions where a surplus labor force existed (a surplus generated by the new demographic pattern, which led to a faster increase in the supply of labor), the railroads made possible the establishment of industries in those sectors (textiles, notably) making use of raw materials with a high intrinsic value or (as in the case of elaborate forms of manufacturing in metal) involving a substantial added value through labor costs. This promoted the urbanization of certain regions that had previously had only marginal economic functions, and especially those in which agriculture was less productive than elsewhere. One of the effects of the creation of the railroads was to make of marginal value any agricultural region with poor terrain, climate, or soil composition, leveling out the price of agricultural products. The railroads placed at a disadvantage any region in which the cost of exploiting the land was high.

The railroads had an even more direct impact on the chances of growth in very large cities. By 1840 the population of London had reached two million, rising to more than seven million on the eve of the First World War. And there were already at that time five other cities in Europe with populations of more than two million. Now it is certain that, without the railroads, the task of supplying so many large cities with food especially, but also with fuel and raw materials for industry, would have posed all but insuperable difficulties. And although this was obviously not the only factor responsible, it is nevertheless interesting to note that the population of London began to grow more rapidly from the time when (around 1840) the city was largely linked up with the British rail system.

Obviously the impact of railroads was not the same in every country and region. It was in the developed countries outside Europe, where the starting level was low and the urban growth in the nineteenth century was very rapid, that the impact was the strongest. On the other hand, in the countries already highly urbanized, where the growth of cities was during the nineteenth century the slowest, railroads played a more minor role. Thus, for instance, in France, as Denise Pumain (1982) has shown for the nineteenth century, "if one considers French cities as a whole (which does not exclude specific cases for which there is an obvious relationship) the presence or absence of a railroad line has not been a determining element in demographic evolution."

In this same general connection, emphasis should also be given to the role played by the railroads (and by steamships) in enabling Europe to broaden considerably the scope of its food imports. From the 1870s onwards, Europe imported enormous amounts of grain, chiefly from the United States. And these imports unquestionably had a hand in accelerating the process of urbanization in Europe (see chapter 18).

On the other hand, emigration from Europe to the New World and elsewhere reduced the level of European urbanization.

The Need for Urban Transportation: A Late Development

The growth of cities made possible in part by the modifications in transport gradually created the need for urban transportation networks. The problem of transporting people within a city obviously does not arise until cities reach a certain, relatively large size. Even in traditional cities with populations on the order of 100,000, a rarity before the Industrial Revolution, city dwellers could move about on foot without any difficulty. If we assume a density of around 350 people per hectare, such a city could be contained within a square 1.7 kilometers on each side. This would mean that the center would be less than one kilometer from the farthest point out on the boundary, making roughly a twelve- to fifteen-minute walk. Once the population reaches one million, however, and retaining the same parameters as before, the distance from the center to the farthest point out on the perimeter would be nearly four kilometers, requiring nearly an hour's walk.

It has been postulated, moreover, that the limit on the size of a city (in spatial terms, and thus in terms of population as well) is ultimately a direct function of the time it takes to cross from end to end. And it has been argued that, as a rule, an hour's walk one way has always corresponded to the radius of the largest cities, corresponding to some four to five kilometers for travel by foot in traditional cities and fifty to sixty kilometers for travel by automobile in cities like Los Angeles today.

But between these two private modes of transportation—walking, open to all from the start, and the automobile, open to all only since the 1920s in the United States and the 1960s in Western Europe—came the imperative of public urban transportation. This need became pressing once cities had populations of more than 500,000, and especially once the nature of industrial enterprises changed as a result of the Industrial Revolution. The artisan lived in the heart of the medieval or Renaissance town and worked where he lived. So the artisan of traditional cities had almost no journey to make between his place of work and his place of residence (to use modern terminology). Indeed, not only was there no journey between his place of work and his place of residence, but (to use another modern term, not very adequate when applied to traditional societies) he did not have far to go in search of entertainment, either. For living at the heart of the city, he already found himself close to whatever amusement the city had to offer. The factory, on the other hand, owing to both its size and its unpleasant by-products (pollution, noise, etc.), has often been situated at the periphery, pulling workers away from the city center and necessitating longer journeys both to and from work and between places where people live and places where entertainment is offered.

A Glimpse into the History of Urban Transportation

Owing to the narrow streets in traditional cities, to the fragility of the pavements, and also to the noise, wheeled vehicles were generally either banned from the cities or were very little used. Whether in ancient Rome or in the cities of China, there were everywhere regulations imposing extremely strict limits on the use of wheeled vehicles in town. The upper classes, enjoying both the requisite resources and a greater mobility than their social inferiors, used horses or sedan chairs. Thus in France until the seventeenth century, the king and certain nobles alone were permitted to travel in carriages. It was also apparently in France that the first attempts to provide public transportation were made. In about 1620 a certain Nicolas Sauvage set up stables in a house called the hôtel Saint Fiacre with a view to hiring out horses and carriages (and the word *fiacre* in time became the French equivalent of the English "hackney cab"). The first form of urban public transportation appears to have been the product of the fertile genius of Pascal, who had the idea of letting carriages circulate through the streets along fixed routes with fixed stops taking passengers at a fixed price: three principles essential for urban public transportation. This system was inaugurated in May 1662, and at its height had five different lines. But the success of the enterprise in a sense brought about its ultimate undoing. For "people of low estate" were eventually forbidden to use it, and the service was withdrawn in 1677 owing to the resulting financial losses.

The true beginnings of urban public transportation came 150 years later, in 1828, once again in Paris, whose population had grown in the meantime from around 500,000 to nearly 800,000. A single "omnibus" line was created, providing fourteen seats. The history of this first line, destined to be the real starting point for public transportation, has an interesting origin underlining the high price of energy at the start of the nineteenth century. Two kilometers from the center of Nantes, a certain Stanislas Baudry owned a flour mill equipped with a steam engine. In order to make use of the excess hot water, he opened a bathing establishment. Subsequently, seeking to attract clients, he set up between the city and his concern a transportation service with cars containing sixteen seats, drawn by two horses. This line, which Baudry eventually came to call the "omnibus" (from Latin for "all"), proved considerably more successful than his baths, which gave him the idea of setting up a similar transportation service in Paris. (Nantes at this time had only eighty thousand inhabitants.)

Despite the fact that some French cities (notably Bordeaux and Lyons) and also several American cities appear to have preceded the

French capital by a few years, the true beginning of public urban transportation still occurred in Paris, inasmuch as it was from Paris that the system spread throughout the Western world. As early as 1829, impressed by the success of the Parisian omnibus network, an English carriage manufacturer, who probably had a concern in Paris, introduced the system in London. In 1831 New York imitated London's example, and within the next twenty years or so all of the principal cities of Europe and North America followed suit. These new public transportation networks expanded rapidly: there were already some forty million passenger rides per year, for instance, in Paris and in London by the end of the 1850s. The clientele, however, continued to be drawn essentially from the middle and upper classes: in the middle of the nineteenth century one omnibus ride cost the equivalent of an hour's pay for an urban laborer. This high price may be explained by the low seating capacity of the first omnibuses and especially by the high cost of upkeep for horses, whose life span did not exceed three to four years.

Naturally enough, rails attracted the attention of enterpreneurs in urban transportation, and by 1832 New York saw the opening of the first streetcar line, the original streetcar being nothing more than a horse-drawn omnibus traveling on rails. It was not until 1852, however, that the streetcar system began to assume major proportions, thanks to the innovation of a French engineer living in New York. This innovation consisted of placing the rails in two sunken grooves in order to prevent the streetcar from impeding traffic. And it was in 1855 that, complete with this improvement, the streetcar crossed the Atlantic, the first European line being established in that year in Paris. From this point on the streetcar spread to the other large European cities. By 1870 some lines had adopted steam, but the nuisances associated with the use of steam blocked its diffusion. The solution to the problem had to await electrification, just as the electric automobile will probably solve in the future a part of today's urban pollution problem. The German firm Siemens gave a demonstration of the electrified streetcar in 1879, and in 1881 the first line opened in Frankfort. Six years later nine European cities had electrified streetcar lines, which from then on gradually became the most important means of urban public transportation.

The numerous technological innovations introduced, coupled with the amount of traffic in those cities experiencing rapid population growth, led to a lowering of costs and thus to the democratization of urban transportation. This in turn made further expansion possible. During the years 1880 to 1890 the cost of a ride fell to the equivalent of the wages paid an urban laborer for twenty minutes' work.

The increasing size of cities, combined with the introduction of large department stores and the proliferation of sporting, musical, and theatrical entertainments offered in city centers, further spurred the demand for urban transportation (Barker and Robbins, 1963). But once cities reached a certain scale, the solution of public transportation problems entered a new phase in which certain parts of the urban thoroughfares were reserved exclusively for public transportation vehicles. And given the congestion in the streets, this quite naturally led to the metropolitan railway, preferably below ground in the form of a subway in order to diminish the unpleasant side effects. The London underground is considered to have been the first. In London, as in the other great metropolises, the railroad companies established urban railway lines that gradually linked up to form genuine urban transportation systems. Some of these lines were constructed in trenches, and sections of them passed under the Thames through a tunnel. One of the familiar names designating the London metropolitan railway, the "tube," comes from the construction technique developed at this time: submerging into rivers a cylinder made up of giant tubes soldered together. The first section of the first truly underground line was opened in 1863. However, owing to pollution problems (solved in some cases by the use of traction cables), it was not until electrification that the underground network really took shape, the first line in London opening in 1890. On the eve of the First World War, twelve cities in the world had installed underground communal transportation networks or subways of greater or lesser size: in addition to London, there were New York (1868), Istanbul (1875), Budapest (1897), Glasgow (1897), Vienna (1898), Paris (1900), Boston (1901), Berlin (1902), Philadelphia (1907), Hamburg (1912), and Buenos Aires (1913). Between the two wars six other cities were added to the list: Madrid (1919), Barcelona (1924), Athens (1925), Tokyo (1927), Osaka (1933), and Moscow (1935). Almost sixty cities have joined these first two groups between the Second World War and 1987.

While private automobiles did not begin to figure among the various modes of urban transportation until the end of the twenties (and even then for the most part only in the United States), the use of vehicles powered by internal-combustion engines for urban public transportation dated from the very beginning of the saga of the automobile. As early as September 1904, the London police authorized the circulation of the famous double-decker buses. Their number had reached five hundred by the middle of 1906, leveling off at around one thousand between 1908 and the outbreak of the First World War. Even before the First World War buses were used in other cities as well.

It was at about the end of the nineteenth century that the railroad companies became aware of the possibility of using their train networks not only to link cities together, but also as a means of urban transportation. The railroads began to exploit the new market offered by expanding large cities by creating the so-called "suburban lines." Even before the creation of the suburban lines, the growth of urban transportation systems had encouraged the breakup of the urban habitat. But the opening of the suburban lines resulted in a further acceleration of this process. The private automobile would subsequently push this process to its extreme limit about fifty years later, practically erasing in many regions the distinction between the urban and the rural so far as the character of residential areas goes. It is also worth noting in passing that with the development of urban transportation there was a new specifically urban function and a new specifically urban source of jobs.

The rise in the standard of living of the working class was another factor whose contribution to the growth of urban transportation systems should not be overlooked. For the great mass of unskilled workers who during the nineteenth century constituted the largest part of the industrial labor force, any commute between home and work place involving payment of a fare was too costly. The existing evidence shows that until the years 1880–1890, only well-paid skilled workers could afford to commute over a distance of more than a few kilometers. As Hobsbawm (1964) puts it, for the unskilled workers of London in the 1860s, "all that lay beyond a tiny circle of personal acquaintances or walking distances was darkness." It was not until 1870–1890, then, that the rise in the standard of living made sufficient resources available to enable large sectors of the population to use urban transportation.

But even then, moving away to some distance from the working place was not easy for working-class families. And it even appears that

> wives were far less inclined to remove a distance
> than men, since by doing so they forfeited extra
> earnings from charring and washing which usually
> amounted to three or four shillings a week. A family
> which moved only two miles lost these tangible ad-
> vantages: correspondence was cumbersome and vis-
> iting an extravagance on a twenty-shillings-a-week
> budget, out of which one-third was earmarked for
> rent. Thus, even the stronger ties soon weakened
> and old associations were forgotten. . . . Of those
> who had migrated to the suburbs, large numbers
> in the 1880s wished to return to their old areas.
> (Dyos, 1953)

The Ability to Build Higher, Thanks to Industry, But the Creation of New Problems as Well

Paradoxically, at the same time as industrialization, the rise in the standard of living, and technological innovation and change generally promoted the breakup of cities, technology also made possible a sharp increase in the density of habitation in city centers, where the price of land tends to grow at least in proportion to the size of cities. There were to begin with changes in construction techniques. First used in industrial construction (in England as early as the start of the 1780s) and in the erection of monuments, iron definitively came to be used in the construction of large urban buildings with the Crystal Palace at the Universal Exposition held in London in 1851. At the start of the 1880s the United States inaugurated the age of skyscrapers with the use of metal frameworks (a twenty-one-story building was erected in Chicago as early as 1892). In the meantime cement, originally invented in 1820, had come into increasing use. In fact one should specify Portland cement, since the Romans had developed a type of cement whose properties were halfway between plaster and cement. Cement was subsequently combined with iron, eventually leading to (from 1880) reinforced concrete: a new building material that, combining the properties of stone and metal, would prove indispensable for the new modes of construction. But concrete had already been combined with iron in construction by the start of the 1850s. Building higher inevitably brought the problem of assuring access to the upper stories, and in the United States Otis installed the first elevators in 1857, giving a demonstration as early as 1854. But providing access for people was only one of the difficulties associated with the new modes of construction. The distribution of water to all stories, for instance, very quickly emerged as a major problem for the engineer. And here too, progress in industrial technology made a decisive contribution in the form of more powerful pumps and of conduits both more watertight and more resistant to pressure.

But in the end the solutions to the problems of providing access and water to the upper stories of the new tall buildings of the industrial age paled in importance when compared with other, much more serious difficulties caused by the increasing density of urban population that tall buildings made possible. The rapid growth of cities narrowly missed bringing about an ecological catastrophe that, with all due allowances made for scale, might well have reached the proportions of the Black Death of the fourteenth century. Cholera was the Black Death of the nineteenth century, leaving such a deep imprint on the collective memory of some parts of Europe that its name became in many Slavic countries, for instance, a familiar term of abuse.

Cholera, endemic to a vast region in Asia between Bombay and southern China, struck Europe for the first time in 1830, reaching London in January 1832. From 1847 on, the epidemics grew both more numerous and more deadly. In 1847, 53,000 people died of cholera in England, including 14,000 in London. It is estimated that the epidemic of the years 1883–1895 took 300,000 lives in the developed world as a whole. The epidemic of 1892–1895 claimed 270,000 lives in Russia and nearly 20,000 more in the rest of Europe.

Since water was the principal carrier of the contagion, it proved necessary to redesign the entire system of supply and sewage in those cities where rapid growth made the traditional system inadequate. It may be recalled that around 1847 London had a population of more than 2 million. Around 1880, the authorities having improved its water supply and sewage systems, the population of London reached nearly 5 million; the population of Paris surpassed 2.5 million, those of New York, Berlin, and Vienna, 1 million, and that of Saint Petersburg (Leningrad) was near 1 million. All of the larger cities (and also some of the smaller ones) were gradually forced to make improvements in their sewage and water supply. At the same time, the chemical industry contributed the solution to the problem of purifying water. And inside dwellings, the U-bend, a system invented by the end of the eighteenth century, which created a siphon and effectively blocked effluvia both in toilets and in sinks, came into general use during the first half of the nineteenth century.

During this phase occurred "the relatively abrupt shift from an age in which people openly bargained over the value of excrement to an age in which it was boycotted in silence" (Gleichmann, 1982). As this writer also notes, in the nineteenth century towns became "clean and odorless." This does not mean that the problem of getting rid of human excrement had received no adequate solution before the nineteenth century. Let me cite Gleichmann once more:

> One finds at Mohenjo-daro, in India, toward the end of the period 3250 to 2750 B.C., houses equipped with water closets linked to drainage installations; one discovers similar facilities in the palace of the Sumerian king, Sargon, around 2350–2130 B.C. The first account of the palace at Knossos in Crete mentions the traces of a water closet dating to before 1650 B.C. At Tellel-Amarna, in the house of a high Egyptian official constructed around 1370 B.C., a seat has been found carved in stone with a shape matching the human anatomy and fitted out with a drain. The Bible says (Deut. 23:12–13): "Thou shalt have a place also without the camp, whither thou shalt go forth abroad: and thou shalt have a paddle upon thy weapon; and it shall be, when thou wilt ease thyself abroad, thou shalt dig therewith, and shalt turn back and cover that which cometh from thee."

But in practically all traditional societies, the place for ridding oneself of garbage and excrement in the city was the street, the gutter. Nor did things really change until the nineteenth century. It is, however, true that the "production" of garbage was very low before the

Industrial Revolution and even before the second half of the twentieth century.

It was also at this time that gas lighting became widespread thanks to the creation of distribution networks and, of course, gas plants, since coal gas was used. By 1801 Lebon in France had demonstrated this type of lighting. Great Britain followed a year later. Despite the overoptimistic claims of the manufacturers, according to whom natural gas would reduce the cost of lighting by a ratio of twenty-one to one, some systems set up in Great Britain between 1805 and 1812 did not survive. The true start-up date was 1814 (Falkus, 1982).

At that date certain quarters of London already received this service, and by 1823 fifty-two cities in Great Britain had a distribution system, more than three hundred by 1850. Gas lighting spread rapidly throughout the rest of the developed world, reaching Baltimore in 1816, soon afterwards Boston and New York, Paris in 1817, Berlin in 1826, and Moscow in 1866. Then came electric lighting. In New York in 1882 Edison began operating the first central electrical power station designed to distribute electricity.

Together with the telephone and central heating, all of these technological advances vividly illustrate the development over the course of the nineteenth century of industries whose essential mission it was to satisfy purely urban needs. I find in all of this a species of feedback loop. Industrialization fosters urbanization, and cities promote further industrialization, engendering in the process a growing number of specifically urban forms of employment: jobs for streetcar drivers, meter readers for water, gas, and electrical systems, men to install water, gas, and electrical appliances and equipment, and so on.

Thanks to all these technological innovations, urban housing became more comfortable than rural housing. The urban dwelling, well heated, lighted by electricity, equipped with running water and gas, thus became an additional attraction of the city. Censuses have only begun very recently to investigate these aspects of housing. For this reason it is only since the eve of World War II that it is possible to have a valid description. At that time, on the average, in the developed countries 75% of the dwellings in cities had running water, but only 25% of the rural dwellings did. The gap was even larger for bathrooms: 25% of dwellings in cities, but 5% in the country. The situation was more egalitarian for electricity: some 85% and 65%, respectively. It is true that some 45% of the electricity was hydroelectricity and therefore rural. On the other hand, for gas (produced mainly in cities), on the average some 65% of dwellings in cities had it, as against some 3% in the country.

Urbanization through Industrialization, Made Possible Only Thanks to Agricultural Progress

I have already underlined the decisive place of progress in agriculture, that is, of the agricultural revolution, in urbanization in England during the early phases of the Industrial Revolution. Indeed it is axiomatic that in a closed economic system there can be no substantial rise in the relative size of the urban population without a substantial reduction in the relative number of farmers and farm laborers required to produce the food to support the population as a whole. Yields and productivity must increase in order to avoid the fall in production that would otherwise result from a shrinking agricultural work force. It should be noted, however, that the qualification "in a closed economic system" is an important one. For (see part 4) the fact that the contemporary Third World has access to large quantities of food from developed nations has utterly transformed this problem.

Now in the nineteenth century, the Western world was indeed a closed economic system, especially when compared with what it would become in the second half of the twentieth century. Contrary to current opinion, it was a closed economic system even where raw materials were concerned. (But however interesting it may be, this is another question that has to be left aside here.) Even when sugar (which, beginning with the second half of the nineteenth century, was chiefly produced in Europe) and other tropical staples (oils, fruits, etc.) are taken into account, the Western world formed a practically closed economic system with regard to food as well. I have estimated that as late as a few years before the First World War the developed world produced 94–97% of all the food it consumed. (But this percentage only applies to the developed world as a whole; see chapter 18. Europe acquired an appreciable portion of its food in the form of grain imported from non-European countries—the United States, Canada, and so forth—settled by Europeans. But this was the case only after the 1870s.)

While around 1800 agricultural workers still represented in the developed world 75–80% of the working population, by about 1910 the proportion had fallen to no more than 53–55%. But despite this fall, the agricultural workers of the developed world remained capable of supplying to each person an amount of agricultural produce probably higher by some 40–60% than the amount supplied in 1800—and this even though the population of the West had risen from 212 to 575 million in the interval. Until the years 1850–1870, these advances in agricultural productivity and yields were achieved by means of the diffusion of what had originally been the gains of the English agricultural revolution. But after this period occurred what has come to be known as the "second agricultural revolution," that is, the introduction of mechanization and the use of artificial fertilizers. Without these revolutionary changes in agriculture, the urban explosion experienced in the developed world would have been impossible.

Indeed, the second agricultural revolution brought about a new jump in both productivity and yields, but particularly in productivity, owing to the introduction of reapers, and then combines, which by mechanizing the most labor-intensive part of agricultural work, made it possible to reduce considerably the time required for this task. Thus in the United States, while around 1840 it took nearly sixty hours of work to harvest one hectare of wheat, on the eve of the First World War it took only seventeen hours. In Europe, artificial fertilizers and other factors made it possible to increase wheat yields by a third between the mid-nineteenth century and the eve of the First World War.

18 Urbanization in the Developed World in the Nineteenth Century □

Just as the urban expansion of the Middle Ages had marked the whole urban structure of Europe right up to the start of the nineteenth century, so too the urban expansion of the nineteenth century fashioned the urban landscape of the developed world as we know it today. The nineteenth century was unquestionably a period of pivotal importance in the urbanization of the developed world. The developed world (not counting Japan, which did not really join it until after 1918) around the year 1800 had some twenty-one million people living in cities with populations of more than five thousand. By around 1914, there were ten times as many, roughly 212 million. Certainly overall population had also recorded powerful growth in the interval. But where urban population had increased tenfold, total population rose by a factor of a little less than three, going from 212 million to 606 million. Thus the level of urbanization went up from 10% in 1800 to 35% in 1914: an urban explosion resulting both from the growth of existing cities and from the rise and development of new cities.

Rapid but Uneven Urbanization

The developed world, which during the nineteenth century was rapidly urbanized, was far from a homogeneous unit, and this was even more true at the end of the nineteenth century than at its beginning, due to the increased inequality in the standard of living resulting from economic development. This inequality in standards of living stemmed as much from differences in the time at which development began in the various developed nations as from unequal rates of economic growth. Since (see chapter 21) a close link existed between levels of development and levels of urbanization, the unevenness in the degree of economic expansion in different parts of the developed world led to differences in urban growth.

I have already presented in chapter 13 (table 13.4) data on the levels of urbanization in the principal countries of the developed world. See table 18.1 for data on the principal regions of the developed world.

	1800	1850	1880	1900	1910
	Urban population				
United Kingdom	3.1	10.2	21.0	27.8	31.2
Continental Europe	15.5	28.1	50.5	80.5	95.9
Europe	18.6	38.3	71.4	108.3	127.1
Russia	(3.0)	(5.2)	(11.0)	(17.0)	(21.8)
North America	0.3	3.4	13.2	28.6	40.9
Other developed countries[a]	—	0.1	0.7	1.9	3.3
Total for developed countries other than Japan	21.9	47.0	96.3	155.8	193.0
Japan	(4.4)	(4.5)	5.9	7.4	8.6
Total for developed countries	26.2	51.5	102.2	163.3	201.6
	Levels of urbanization (in percentages)				
United Kingdom	19.4	37.1	60.6	67.6	69.4
Continental Europe	11.2	16.0	24.2	32.9	36.0
Europe	12.1	18.9	29.3	37.9	40.8
Russia	(5.7)	(7.2)	(10.6)	(13.2)	(14.3)
North America	5.3	13.3	24.2	35.1	40.9
Other developed countries[a]	—	8.0	14.3	20.3	29.4
Total for developed countries other than Japan	10.3	15.6	23.7	30.8	33.6
~~n~~	(14.5)	(15.0)	16.0	17.0	17.5
Total for developed countries	10.8	15.5	23.0	29.7	32.3

Sources: Calculations and estimates by the author; see the methodological appendix.
Note: The fact that these figures have been only slightly rounded off does not imply a correspondingly small margin of error. The figures in parentheses have a much wider margin of error than the other data.
   A criterion of 5,000 is used for urban population.
[a] Australia, New Zealand, and South Africa.

Since the Industrial Revolution continued for many years to be confined to England, the United Kingdom accounted until 1860–1880 for a large proportion of the increase in urban population in the developed world at large, and particularly in Europe. Between 1800 and 1850, 35% of all growth in urban population in the developed world was concentrated in the United Kingdom alone, despite the fact that in 1800 the United Kingdom represented only 7% of the total population of the developed world. Even as late as 1910, the early economic development in England was evident in levels of urbanization; the United Kingdom had at this time twice as great a ratio of urban to rural population as continental Europe.

Urbanization was also unequal between continental Europe and vast Russia, on the eve of the First World War one of the least urbanized regions of the future developed world. Czarist Russia was even less urbanized than the Japan of the Mikados. But in this instance the difference mainly reflected historical factors, and urbanization was already present at the beginning of the nineteenth century. Finally, before moving on to consider the course of events in each of the parts of the developed world, I should point out that the dynamism of the United States was already manifest in the nineteenth century: only half as urbanized as continental Europe in 1800, the United States had overtaken it by 1910.

The Emergence of New Cities

Of the approximately 268 cities with populations in excess of 100,000 in the developed world (Japan included) around 1910, about 98 did not exist or were still villages at the start of the nineteenth century (or in the middle of the eighteenth century in the case of England). The proportion must have been higher among smaller cities, so it can be estimated that roughly 40% of all cities with populations of more than 50,000 were new cities that came into existence during the nineteenth century. Except in Russia, moreover, very few new cities emerged after the First World War. It is true that since the thirties in developed countries there has been planned construction of new cities (see chapter 19). But such construction has essentially been directed toward decongesting existing large urban centers rather than toward the creation of new cities.

Among the approximately 98 large cities that emerged during the nineteenth century, more than half were in North America (48 in the United States and 3 in Canada). In Europe the share of new large cities was only 24%, or 36 out of 157. This and other important differences quite naturally lead me to make a distinction in my review of the urban history of developed nations between Europe and the rest of the developed world, and in particular between Europe and the United States.

The Urbanization of Europe in the Nineteenth Century

The nineteenth century played the pivotal role in the urbanization of Europe. Around 1800 only 12% of the population of Europe (except Russia) lived in cities. By 1910 the figure had risen to 41%. Most of this urban growth took place between 1830–40 and 1900. During this period the population of European cities rose from some 28 million to some 108 million, making an annual growth rate on the order of 2.1%.

The emergence of the large new cities responsible in part for this rapid growth occurred essentially in two countries: England and Germany. In England, of the 41 cities with populations of more than 100,000 in 1910, 16 were new or had only been very small towns at the start of the century. In Germany, 18 of the 40 cities with populations of more than 100,000 were new in this sense, and in France 3 out of 16. Practically all of these cities were located in or near coalfields. To these three countries should be added Belgium, whose new industrial towns around 1910 had yet to reach a population of 100,000.

In addition to the emergence of these new manufacturing towns, few of which became great metropolises, the process of industrialization led in many countries, directly and indirectly, to an upheaval in the urban hierarchy. Thus in England, for example, with the exception of London and Birmingham none of the six largest cities of the year 1700 figured among the six largest cities of 1910. Liverpool and Manchester—which, with populations of more than 700,000 in 1910, figured among the four largest English cities—had populations of only 5,000–8,000 in 1700. The same applies to Leeds and Sheffield, each with populations of more than 400,000 in 1910. The upheaval was less profound in other countries, but the new surge of urban growth associated with industrialization everywhere had the effect of rearranging the old urban hierarchy. These rearrangements stemmed from a number of different factors, among which should be mentioned the nature of the industries established in a given city and the city's location relative to the new transportation lines. There was, then, considerable variety in the destinies of the various cities of the nineteenth century. But even though, as has been noted, the destiny of each city is unique, the cities of the developed world nevertheless formed a largely interdependent system, and all of the available evidence suggests that this interdependence grew stronger with time as development continued.

Until the middle of the eighteenth century, the dividing line separating the most heavily urbanized regions of Europe from the least urbanized ran from north to south. By the second half of the nineteenth century, however, it had made something like a 45 degree rotation, crossing Europe from southwest to northeast, starting about at the border between France and Spain and reaching on the other side the northern border of Germany and Poland. North of this line lay the most heavily urbanized countries: France, Belgium, the Netherlands, the United Kingdom, Switzerland, Germany, and the Scandinavian countries. In 1910 the level of urbanization in this region was 47%, as against 30% in the rest of Europe minus Russia, 22 percent in the rest of Europe when Russia is included.

The Role of New Nations

One cannot speak of the urbanization of Europe in the second half of the nineteenth century without mentioning the dual flow of people and goods that so decisively marked the Western world at this time. On one hand, beginning with the great famine of 1846–1850 in Ireland, there was a massive flood of emigrants leaving Europe to settle abroad, especially in North America. From 1848 to 1914 some 45–50 million Europeans emigrated overseas, making a flow of unprecedented proportions in the universal history of migration. On the other hand, from the 1870s Europe imported increasing amounts of grain, chiefly from those countries to which the European emigrants went. Around 1860 net imports of grain (and flour) in Europe (except Russia) amounted to less than two million metric tons, representing 3% of production, and almost all of this grain came from Russia. On the eve of the First World War, however, some twenty-three million metric tons were involved, representing 22% of production, and Russia furnished a little less than half of all European grain imports. Alongside these massive grain imports should also be mentioned the growing imports of other foods, such as meat from Argentina and Australia and dairy products from New Zealand. I shall leave aside the imports of the various tropical products since, except for sugar, they cannot properly be considered staple foods. And as for sugar, Europe itself became the chief world producer during the nineteenth century.

There were therefore two phenomena which had a significant impact on urbanization, but their consequences were diametrically opposed. Emigration unquestionably helped to reduce the flow of rural people to European cities, but the possibility of importing substantial quantities of food permitted a higher level of urbanization than before. The result of these two contrary forces appears to have been a slowing down of the pace of urban growth. Indeed, the slowdown in the growth of European agricultural output following on massive grain imports and the resumption of growth in agricultural output whenever imports were curbed imply that production was sufficiently elastic. On the other hand, increased grain imports did not lead to similar increases in the exportation of manufactured goods. According to my own calculations (Bairoch, 1976b), in the United States, for example, for each dollar's worth of exports to Europe, there was only twelve cents' worth of imports from Europe. Thus in Europe very few new industrial jobs resulted from purchases of grain.

I shall try to quantify very approximately the impact of this wave of emigration on urbanization in Europe—excluding Russia, which in any case supplied only around 5% of the European emigrants.

There were some 45 to 50 million emigrants, but not all of them stayed on the American side of the Atlantic; a great many of them came back to Europe. Among those who returned were certainly a few "rich American uncles," but most of them were people disenchanted by the reality of life overseas. Very often the reality did not measure up to the idea of the Eldorado the travel companies used in order to cash in on this very considerable source of profits. It can be estimated that about 40% of the emigrants returned. Taking this into account, together with such factors as the age structure of the emigrant population, the natural increase of population, and so forth, it can be concluded that by 1913 Europe (excluding Russia) had lost some 42–46 million people owing to these migrations. It seems likely (based solely on deductive reasoning) that had they stayed in Europe, some 80–90 percent of these 42–46 million people would have gone to live in cities. Furthermore, a certain fraction of the emigrants were city dwellers. For Europe (except Russia), this would have meant some 35 million more city dwellers, yielding by around 1913 a level of urbanization of 46–48% instead of the 42% actually recorded.

Russia: A First Surge of Urbanization

Nineteenth-century Russia was in economic terms a very backward country: a country still predominantly agrarian by a wide margin, and a country in which serfdom persisted until 1861. All of this is true in broad outline, but it does not mean that urban life remained unchanged in the vast reaches of Russia, which in 1913 had as many people as all of the rest of Europe around 1810. In the first place, there was a sharp rise in population, the most rapid of any experienced in Europe. With a population of about 53 million around 1800 and 81 million in 1860, Russia had a population of 161 million in 1913. This alone sufficed to increase the population of existing cities and to bring about the emergence of a certain number of new ones. But of much greater importance was the break with the past dating from 1861, when the central authorities attempted to modernize Russian society.

The edict of 3 March 1861 emancipated the serfs and implied in addition to their freedom the possibility of their moving to the cities. At the same time, the appeal for foreign capital for modernizing Russian industry and setting up a network of railroads had the same consequences in Russia as the beginnings of the process of industrialization had everywhere else. In 1860 Russia had 1,590 kilometers of railway lines—in other words, less than Italy, Spain, or Belgium, and only 3% of the European total. By contrast, in 1913 the Russian network was one of the largest in Europe, extending over 58,400 kilometers of track, or 17% of the European total. The production of cast iron, in 1860 less than 300,000 metric tons, or 4% of the European total, rose in 1913 to 4.2 million metric tons, or 9% of the European total.

The number of cotton spindles, on the order of 1 million in 1860, had grown to 9.2 million in 1913 (from 2% to 9% of the European total).

This resulted in a very rapid increase in urban population, which rose from under 6 million around 1860 to more than 23 million in 1913, making an annual growth rate of 2.3%, as compared with 1.9% in the rest of Europe. The older dominant urban centers grew rapidly. Saint Petersburg (Leningrad), with hardly more than half a million inhabitants in 1860, was to have 2 million by the outbreak of the First World War. By this time the population of Moscow had surpassed 1.5 million, as against less than 500,000 in 1860. Even at the periphery of the empire, Warsaw and Riga saw their populations increase four times over. And alongside the growth of the older cities came the creation of new cities—cities in which the new industries were established, where the railroads were born and prospered, and through which grain was shipped to the rest of Europe.

Thus the period 1860–1913 in Russia saw a first surge of urbanization linked to industrialization. But this surge of urban growth did not turn Russia into a heavily urbanized country. To be sure, by around 1914 Russia could not be considered underurbanized. Its cities accounted for 15% of the total population, a proportion exceeding by only a quarter the maximum generally reached in the rest of Europe in the framework of traditional societies. Nevertheless, by this same date the level of urbanization in the rest of Europe had reached 42%, a difference reflecting history, since at the start of the nineteenth century the ratio of urban to rural population in Russia was half that in the rest of Europe. But a large amount of urban growth had occurred during preceding decades. While development certainly accelerated after 1861, events were already moving rapidly before then. Between 1800 and 1860 the number of city dwellers doubled, and the level of urbanization increased by a third.

The Rapid Urbanization of Developed Countries outside Europe

Among the newly emerging nations in this section the countries in the temperate regions of Latin America (Argentina, Uruguay, Chile) will be excluded, and also Japan. The reasons for excluding Japan are obvious, the most important being Japan's late development and especially the very different type of traditional society found in that part of the world. The omission of the temperate Latin American countries, however, requires some explanation, since during the period in question these countries differed in no fundamental way from Canada and Australia, for instance. But their omission seems justified by their subsequent evolution, that is, by the fact that from 1920–1930 they slid toward underdevelopment. The fascinating problem of the widely diverging destinies of countries like Argentina and Chile on the one hand and Canada and Australia on the other has yet to be properly elucidated. But despite its interest, it would lead us beyond the scope of the present analysis. In any event, in this section the developed world outside Europe is treated as containing only five countries: the United States, Canada, Australia, New Zealand, and South Africa.

Over the course of the nineteenth century, the developed world outside Europe experienced a very rapid urbanization, leading to an urban structure perceptibly different from that of Europe. Less urbanized than Europe at the start of the century, these regions had caught up with their European counterparts by the 1880s. The level of urbanization between 1800 and 1910 rose at the rate of 1.8% per year, as against 1.1% per year in Europe (except Russia). And given the rapid increase in overall population, urban population grew at the exceedingly fast rate of 4.6% per year. There were some 300,000 people living in all of the cities of these regions combined around 1800; in 1910 there were 44 million. At the start of the nineteenth century the heaviest concentration of urban population of European origin outside Europe was still found in Latin America (see chapters 24 and 25). By 1860–1865, however, developed America had surpassed Latin America in urbanization.

The preponderant place of the United States among developed countries outside Europe (accounting for 38.5 million of the 44 million city dwellers in the year 1910) quite naturally leads me to take the experience of this country as an illustration of urbanism as it evolved during the nineteenth century in the countries outside Europe.

The Urbanization of American Society: From Covered Wagons to Station Wagons

The United States remained very little urbanized until the 1820s and 1830s. Even before the arrival of the Europeans in the sixteenth century, the cultures to the north of the Rio Grande were nonurban; and most of them were preagricultural (see chapter 4). The first waves of immigrants did not greatly modify the rural character of the United States, and (see chapter 13) around 1700 the largest American city, Boston, had a population of only some 6,000–7,000. The British government reinforced this state of affairs by forbidding the American colonials to engage in most industrial activities.

The political independence of the United States, of which an economic motivation was paramount, brought about a sharp change in direction favoring industrialization. The modern doctrine of industrial protectionism originated in the United States, the work of the highly influential Secretary of the Treasury, Alexander Hamilton, notably, having made a strong impression on Friedrich List during his long stay in the United States. (List was the major figure in the theory advocating tariff protection to stimulate national industrial development.) But for a good many years—nearly half a century—the United States continued to be predominantly rural. The structure of American exports contributed to this tendency, since at the start of the nineteenth century about 80% of the goods exported by the United States were agricultural. And despite the rapid industrial growth, which in any case concentrated almost entirely on the domestic market and was located in the northeastern part of the country, change was fairly slow.

Around 1820 a mere 6% of the population of the United States lived in towns with populations of 5 thousand or more, while in Europe the figure was 13–14%. But from this point on the process of urbanization accelerated. By 1850, the level of urban population had risen to 14%, and the United States caught up with Europe by around 1905. And the rapid spread of urbanization was combined with a dramatic expansion in overall population. While in 1820 the United States had a population of a little under 10 million, it was 97 million in 1913. Growth of urban population was especially rapid between 1820 and 1870, a period during which the population of American cities increased fourteenfold, making an annual growth rate of 5.5%, as against 3.8% between 1870 and 1900.

This period of rapid growth coincided with the phase of urbanization (1830–1870) that American historians link with the development of the railroads and steamships. The preceding phase (1790–1830) was marked by the use of sailing ships and wagons, and succeeding phases by the introduction of steel and electricity (1870–1920) and the automobile (1920–1960). Given the enormous size of the territory of the United States, it is only natural that means of transportation should have had a decisive effect on urbanization. For example, the United States became in 1830 the first country after England to have a railroad, and by 1860 the rail network extended over 15,000 kilometers and then to as much as 420,000 kilometers by 1913. And among the 48 new cities with populations of more than 100,000, (a total of 59 in 1913), many owed their existence and vitality to the railroads.

The most typical is Chicago, which was influenced by both water and rail transportation. In 1804 a fort was established on the banks of the Chicago River, especially for trade by French Canadians. The fort was first abandoned in 1814 and then totally in 1837. The settlers who had built homesteads near the fort on the shore of Lake Michigan numbered only a few hundred right up to the start of the 1830s. The town did not really emerge until improvements had been made in the infrastructure for transportation. The construction of the Illinois-Michigan canal and the improvement of the port of Chicago (on the Great Lakes) caused the population of this small settlement to explode: with a population of less than 5,000 in 1840, Chicago had a population of some 30,000 in 1850. Then in 1852 the railroad reached the city, and by 1860 its population had grown to 109,000, surpassing one million less than thirty years later (around 1887) and two million by around 1907. Chicago had become the second-largest city in the United States around 1890, overtaking Philadelphia, which had been the largest city in the country until around 1810.

Chicago is only an extreme example of the growth of very great cities in the United States. While around 1800 no city had a population of 100,000, by 1850, six were larger than this. And in 1910 there were fifty, of which three had populations of more than a million. In 1850 Los Angeles had no more than about 2,000, and Minneapolis was only a little village. But by 1910 each of them had a population of more than 300,000.

The important place of transportation in the wide open spaces of the United States should not obscure the more traditional process of urbanization in which local markets made a decisive contribution. Thus the recent statistical analysis of Riefler (1979) confirms what Williamson (1965) had already made clear: in the antebellum era preceding the Civil War, "interregional exchange was an important determinant of the urbanization process." During the postwar era, on the other hand, the decisive factor was industry.

To the expansion of American cities, linked with the rapid growth of the population and of the domestic market, immigration contributed in many different ways. The first was through the general increase in overall population, for which it was substantially responsible. First it should be noted that a large fraction (but not the majority) of the European emigrants were city dwellers whose objective was to settle in an American city. And it should be remembered that a considerable fraction of the immigrants of rural background who went to the United States convinced that America was a country where they could easily become owners of their own farms changed their plans once they arrived. Their stay first in the port of embarkation and later in the port of arrival put them in contact with an urban milieu many of them had not known before. The chances of finding work in American port cities, and particularly in New York, encouraged many newcomers to settle in the cities, even if the decision sometimes was originally made in order to save money before moving farther West, to the Promised Land of wide open spaces—distant and, on occasion, dangerous. Even if the statistical analyses of Gallaway and Vedder (1971) have demolished the thesis, largely backed by public authorities, that the latest immigrants—those coming after 1890, mostly from eastern and southern Europe—were more inclined to settle in the cities than those who preceded them, it nevertheless remains true that foreign born Americans generally tended to become city dwellers more often than native born Americans. And this was a completely natural outcome. In a new country, a foreign newcomer will be made to feel doubly foreign in rural areas.

Agriculture Is Once Again Important

Another important contributor to the rapid expansion of American cities was the high level of agricultural productivity in the United States, as well as in other developed countries populated by European settlers. This high level of productivity resulted from the combination of two factors: the vast amount of available land and, because of the European agricultural revolution, farming techniques readily adaptable to the climates of those countries. According to my calculations (Bairoch, 1965), by 1840 the agricultural productivity of the United States exceeded that of the United Kingdom by 20%, while that of the United Kingdom exceeded that of the rest of Europe by more than 100%. Around 1910 the United States exceeded the productivity of the United Kingdom by about 80%. In more concrete terms, this means that in 1910 each American farmer produced about three times more than his European counterpart, despite the fact that the latter had already doubled or tripled his own productivity over what it had been at the start of the nineteenth century.

High levels of agricultural productivity also explain how, despite being much less industrialized than the United States, other countries settled by Europeans were nevertheless considerably urbanized. The most extreme case is that of New Zealand. By around 1910 (and even today) the level of industrialization in New Zealand was extremely low, if not nonexistent. And yet about 40% of its population lived in cities with populations of 5,000 or more (according to the definition used in the census of the period, 54% of the population was urbanized). What accounts for this extensive urbanization is that, because of the high level of agricultural productivity and the fact that a substantial proportion of the country's output was exported, a sizable nonparasitic service sector developed in New Zealand. Around 1910, 40% of New Zealand's work force was employed in services, as opposed to only 22% in Europe (except Russia).

Despite its earlier settlement by Europeans and its more substantial industrialization, Canada was urbanized less rapidly than New Zealand, Australia, or the United States. In 1910 less than a third of all Canadians lived in cities. This difference is essentially explained by geographic factors, and in particular by the climate, which made the economic cost of urbanization higher than it was elsewhere. But history may also be in part responsible for a certain delay in urban growth. At the start of the eighteenth century, the mother countries concerned (simplifying somewhat, England for the United States and France for Canada) exhibited differing degrees of interest and dynamism in their dealings with their respective colonies. Then, after 1763, the English victory over the French brought about a certain withdrawal of the French-speaking population toward rural districts. In addition, since the two dominant urban centers, Quebec and Montreal, were peopled by the French, Canada's incorporation into the English colonial domain led to a certain marginalization of these two cities. From having the second and fourth largest populations in North America around 1700, they had slipped by around 1800 to the sixth and seventh places and around 1850 to tenth and fifteenth places.

Returning before closing this chapter to the United States, I should mention another consequence of space. For the enormous size of the United States was a major factor in the rapid spread of the automobile. Of nearly 2.5 million automobiles in use worldwide around 1914, 1.8 million were in the United States. During this first phase, however, the automobile was not yet an important means of urban transportation. Even by the start of the twenties many purely agricultural states like Iowa and Nebraska had more cars per capita than heavily industrialized and urbanized states. In 1924 the State of New York, while it had 10 % of the American population, had only 8% of the 17.7 million cars in use in the country. But from this point on, things changed rapidly. The devastating reign of the automobile over the city began, and it was not until the sixties that its sway began to be challenged, although even today its grip on urban life has yet to be really loosened, much less broken. It is an irony to note that during the twenties many urbanists, particularly in the United States, saw in the automobile a providential means of reducing urban pollution. Indeed, the growing number of horses used in urban transportation (especially in moving merchandise and making home deliveries) posed serious problems. Once it had dried out and been pulverized by passing wheels, horse manure formed, under the effects of wind, an ocherous and malodorous cloud. In the long run the cure was worse than the disease. But this already takes us deep into the twentieth century. The automobile may serve as a transition to the next chapter, devoted to urbanization during the twentieth century.

19 Urbanization in the Developed World in the Twentieth Century □

Chapter 18 stressed the importance of the nineteenth century in the urbanization of the developed world of today. But this does not mean that the urban history of the developed world between 1913 and 1980 is unimportant. There was a slowdown in the growth of urban population and also of levels of urbanization. Certainly once a certain threshold has been reached, the pace of urbanization must inevitably slow down. On the average a halt (or a decline) must occur because, as has been noted, the level of urbanization is one of the many characteristics of social and economic structures that has an absolute limit. The level of urbanization cannot exceed 100%.

This absolute limit had another important consequence in the twentieth century, namely, the equalization of levels of urbanization on the international plane. I shall discuss this equalization in this chapter when I discuss the general evolution of urbanization during the twentieth century. I shall look into what appears to be a fundamental change in popular attitudes and behavior toward the city, a change that can be said to date from 1968–1970.

The twentieth century has witnessed both the emergence of very great cities and their eventual stabilization, if not decline. Similarly, there was during the twentieth century a breakup of cities in spatial terms—cities seem also to have reached their limits. Unlike the nineteenth century, the twentieth has not seen the birth of many new cities. But the problems posed by the enormous size of certain cities has brought about a policy of decentralization in which new towns are created near older cities. And the rapid industrialization of the Soviet Union, a country very little urbanized at the turn of the century, has also led to the creation of a certain number of new cities. Finally, starting from the twenties, the number of jobs in the service sector has increased rapidly in the cities, which has changed the nature of cities.

Trends in Urbanization from 1910 to 1980

The period from 1910 to 1980 had four fairly distinct phases. The first, lasting until the Depression of the thirties, was in some ways a continuation of the phase of rapid urbanization at the close of the nineteenth century. The second period includes the Depression and the Second World War—years marked by a pronounced slowdown in urban growth. The third phase, including the brisk economic growth following the Second World War, was a phase of renewed acceleration in the process of urbanization. It is rather difficult to determine when this third phase ended. For it seems that even before the crisis of 1974–1975, a slowdown in the process of urbanization had set in, connected to the change in behavior just mentioned. This slowdown marked the fourth phase, which very likely extended beyond 1980. But this cannot be established until the results of the next census become available around 1992–93.

It may be noted that developments within each of these phases have not necessarily been uniform from one country to another (see table 19.1). I shall now look at each phase in greater detail.

TABLE 19.1 Urban Population and Levels of Urbanization in Developed Countries (1910–1980)

	1910	1920	1930	1950	1960	1970	1980
	Urban Population (in millions)						
Europe	133	144	166	193	234	288	321
USSR[a]	16	24	33	61	96	131	161
North America	41	53	69	92	122	147	162
Japan	9	10	15	31	59	75	91
Other developed countries[b]	3	4	6	11	15	21	27
Total for developed countries	202	236	290	388	526	662	762
	Level of Urbanization (in percentages)						
Europe	39	43	46	49	55	63	66
USSR[a]	13	17	20	34	45	54	61
North America	41	46	51	54	62	65	64
Japan	17	18	24	38	64	72	78
Other developed countries[b]	29	33	38	46	51	56	59
Total for developed countries	32	36	39	46	55	62	65

Sources: Calculations and estimates by the author; see the methodological appendix.
Note: A criterion of 5,000 is used for urban population.
[a] Not including Poland in 1910.
[b] Australia, New Zealand, and South Africa.

If the effects of the First World War are disregarded, the years 1910–1930 appear to have been a period of rapid urbanization. Indeed, taking the developed world as a whole (except Japan and the Soviet Union) and regarding the First World War as a loss of four years, one finds a growth rate of 1.2% per year in the level of urbanization—a rate of growth similar to that found for the nineteenth century. Growth was particularly strong in those developed countries that escaped the direct impact of the war. Thus despite a reduction in the number of immigrants after the First World War (400,000 per year 1920–1929 as against one million per year 1905–1914), the level of urbanization in the United States still increased by 1.1% per year during the twenties.

Urbanization in the Thirties: Stabilization in Europe and North America, Expansion in the Soviet Union and Japan

For Western Europe and North America the thirties were a period of stabilization in the process of urban growth. The scale of the crash of 1929 (the worst crisis the capitalist system has ever known) and the length of the ensuing Depression of the thirties (the longest depression many developed countries have ever had to face) obviously account for this stabilization. Events followed a very different course, however, in two other parts of the developed world, the Soviet Union and Japan.

In the Soviet Union the program of industrialization begun in 1928–29 resulted in very rapid urban expansion. The populations of most of the larger cities (with populations of more than 100,000) already in existence grew by about 50% between 1930 and 1939, making an annual growth rate of 4.8%. The population of Moscow rose from 2.8 million to 4.1 million, and the population of Leningrad from 2.2 million to 3.2 million. Many new cities were created. At the time of the first five-year plan (1928–1932), sixty new cities had been founded. Some of these grew very rapidly. Thus of some thirty-three cities with populations of 200,000–500,000 in the Soviet Union in 1939, five either did not exist or were only small towns before the Revolution. It has been estimated that between 1926 and 1966 nine hundred towns were created, a certain number of which incorporated small old townships.

In 1941, on the eve of the German invasion, around 30–34% of the population of the Soviet Union was concentrated in cities, as against 15–16% on the eve of the October Revolution. And many of these city dwellers lived in large cities. When one considers the ideas the revolutionaries held on urban matters, this is a paradoxical state of affairs. For the revolutionaries, following Marx, considered the conflict between town and country one of the fruits of capitalism. Accordingly the new framers of urban policy ingeniously sought to reconcile the need for industrialization with new forms of urbanization in which large cities were notably absent. But it is true that in this area, as in so many others, Stalinism involved the abandonment of certain ideals.

With idealism and ingenuity, there was a great deal of research attempting to find ways to give a new form to the Soviet urban world. For many architects the object was to "change the city in order to change life." After the phase of "paper architecture" of the first years of the new regime, the more practical research of the late twenties and early thirties can be divided into two main streams: the urbanizers and the deurbanizers (Kopp, 1975).

For the urbanizers the major aim was to do away with the large cities and the villages by creating socialist agglomerations "resulting from the fusion of industrial and agricultural activities": agglomerations whose average population would be around 40,000–60,000. The aim of the deurbanizers was to suppress the city as a living area and to disperse the city dwellers into a habitat somewhat on the lines of the large American suburbs of the fifties, but with elaborated social and collective infrastructures. Thus they criticized the communes that were in favor in the 1926–29 period. Those communes can be related to previous socialist utopias and foresaw projects of large collectives (for 750–3,000 people) where space for individual activities would be restricted in favor of collective space: dining room, day nursery, laundry, club, library, and so forth.

Japan, like the Soviet Union, was urbanized late in its history. But however late the emergence of cities may have been, once they did emerge their growth was extremely rapid. Thus whereas the Soviet Union was industrialized before it was fully urbanized, traditional Japanese society was already heavily urbanized. At the start of the eighteenth century, when only 4–7% of the Russian population lived in towns, in Japan around 11–14% did. The Meiji Revolution (1868), a reaction on the part of the ruling elites to the progressive abandonment (dating from 1854) of a part of the national sovereignty, deliberately put Japan on the path to modernization (what today would be called Westernization) and industrialization, which were regarded as the sine qua non of genuine independence in the face of the developed world. During the first half century or so this industrialization did not precipitate any profound upheaval in Japan's urban structure. In 1920 only 18% of the Japanese population lived in cities. But after this time events moved swiftly. During the twenties urban population grew by 4.4% per year. This is an extremely rapid rate. But between 1930 and 1940 the rate accelerated further still, reaching nearly 6% per year, the highest rate of urban growth ever recorded up to that time by any society on the road to industrialization. This urban expansion took place without the emergence of any new large cities. But the growth in traditional Japanese cities was prodigious. In 1940 five cities had populations of more than a million. Tokyo, with a population of around 600,000 at the time of the Meiji Revolution, had a population of nearly seven million by 1940. And the population of Osaka had grown from 30,000 to more than 3 million.

1946–1975: A Genuine Economic Explosion

One often tends to overlook the exceptional force of the economic growth of the three decades following the Second World War. Between 1946 and 1975 the volume of the per capita gross national product in developed countries grew by 3.7% per year, making an overall increase of 190%. This means that during this 29-year period alone, the standard of living rose by as much as it had during the 120 years before 1946. Growth on this scale could not fail to have an impact on urbanization. Its consequences were all the more pronounced in that this general economic expansion was accompanied by another new phenomenon too often overlooked by social scientists and historians: beginning in the forties in the United States and in the fifties in Europe, agricultural productivity increased roughly twice as fast as industrial productivity, reversing the previous trend. Given the modest degree of elasticity in food consumption, this resulted in a sharp decline in the size of the agricultural work force.

All of these factors explain why despite an already high level of urbanization the proportion of overall population living in cities rose very steeply, especially from 1950 to 1970. During these two decades the level of urbanization rose by 1.5% per year, a rate faster even than that registered in the nineteenth century. Certainly this pace reflects in good part increases recorded in Japan and the Soviet Union, which were still relatively little urbanized by 1950 (see table 19.1) and had experienced extremely high rates of economic growth (8.7% per year in Japan and about 5.2% per year in the Soviet Union). When these two countries are excluded, the rise in the level of urbanization in the developed world comes down to an annual rate of 1.3%.

To these two important cases of rapid urbanization—Japan and the Soviet Union—should also be added almost all of the countries of Eastern Europe, together with Spain, Italy, and Greece. All of these countries shared not only a high rate of urbanization, but also rapid economic growth and, above all, a relatively low level of urbanization around the fifties. Thus during this new phase of economic development following the Second World War there was once more a relation between low levels of urbanization and rapid rates of economic growth (see chapter 21, which concludes part 4). What is of interest here is the fact that the link between low levels of urbanization and high rates of growth led to an equalizing of levels of urbanization among developed nations. Whereas in 1950 the ratio of the level of urbanization between the three least urbanized and the three most urbanized countries in the developed world was 1 to 3.3, in 1970 it was only 1 to 2.0, falling by 1980 to 1 to 1.9.

But beyond the equalization caused by differences in rates of growth, and also by an upper limit on the possible levels of urbanization, one may wonder whether another factor might not also have been involved. During this period there was an obvious change in the relation between economic growth rates and urban growth rates. In the nineteenth century and during the first half of the twentieth century (except the decade of the great Depression) each increase of 1% in per capita gross national product (GNP) led on the average to a rise of 0.8–1.1% in the level of urbanization. By contrast, during 1950–1970 an increase of 1% in per capita GNP only resulted in a rise of 0.4% in the level of urbanization. And from 1970 to 1980 in particular, an increase of 1% in per capita GNP has brought about a rise of less than 0.3% in the level of urbanization. As I remarked earlier, this can be accounted for in part by the stage of urban growth already reached. One may also be permitted to ask, however, how much this slowdown owes to a change in popular attitudes and behavior.

A New Attitude toward the City?

There is no doubt that in most developed countries since 1968–70, there has been a new attitude toward the city that has brought about a profound change in the direction of urbanization. The numbers speak for themselves. According to the forecasts made in 1975 by the United Nations, the urban population of North America ought to have grown by 18% between 1970 and 1980 (United Nations, 1975a). The increase has in fact amounted to only 8%. In Western Europe there was an 8% rise, as against a predicted 13% rise, and Germany alone accounted for nearly all of the recorded growth. Among developed nations only Germany and Japan now escape the new trend. Many countries have even begun a process of deurbanization, notably the United States, the United Kingdom, Belgium, Switzerland, and the Netherlands.

In the United States—where as always the greatest number of studies have been done—this trend seems to reflect changing attitudes toward the city among all age classes of the population (Zuiches and Rieger, 1978). The analysis of migrations in France during the period 1968–1975 leads one to expect to find a similar change there (Desplanques, 1979). The results of the 1980s census have confirmed this trend. For the first time in the history of American censuses (the first was taken in 1792) there has been a decrease in the level of urbanization. The most cursory study of the press and the other mass media, moreover, suffices to show that the city has lost much of its popular appeal. It is significant, for instance, that people no longer write—or at any rate sing—songs in praise of one or another city. Paris and New York are only rarely in the titles of hit records these days.

Reasons for such a change are not lacking. Where should we start? With the causes of the declining quality of life in the city? With those developments that have helped remove many of the traditional handicaps associated with life in the countryside? Or with the general affluence of the developed world, an affluence that has made it possible to fulfill a wish that always existed, but that economic constraints prevented from being fulfilled? I shall look at a few of the factors in each of these groups before going on to mention certain reservations regarding the nature of deurbanization and the exceptional character of the decade of the seventies, which remains unique in the annals of history, owing not only to the change in popular attitudes toward the city, but for other reasons as well.

What are the causes of the declining quality of life in the cities? The chief one is size. A growing proportion of city dwellers live in cities that exceed the optimal size, that is, the size beyond which the disadvantages begin to outweigh the avantages. Certainly the old problem of determining what is the optimal size of cities remains unsolved, which, after spending many years looking for a solution, I would be the last to deny (Bairoch, 1977a). There is no doubt, however, that at present in the developed world the optimal population lies below 500,000, probably around 200,000–300,000. I have looked into the impact of size on more than twenty of the multiple facets of the quality of life (ranging from pollution to crime rates, from education to the standard of living) and found that all of them deteriorate as soon as population gets over half a million. But today nearly half of all city dwellers live in cities of more than half a million people. I shall return later to this question of the optimal size of cities, one of the most important aspects of the urban problem.

The congestion in the center of the larger cities drove toward the periphery a whole population composed of middle-class people hungry for more space, and these newcomers joined other populations that had in the past been obliged to live far from the inner city because of a lack of resources. The periphery became the suburbs, and the mirage of green spaces turned into towers of concrete or into endless rows of houses without character that, once the children had grown up, lost much of their value. In the words of the sociologist Chombart de Lauwe (1982), the periphery of the cities became a space "between an incomplete urban life and a degraded rural life." Here too size was a repulsive factor.

But size is not the only factor. For if a city with a population of 800,000, for instance, is as a general rule more polluted than a city of 200,000, this does not mean that the latter is not more polluted today than two or three decades ago. And while traffic may be more congested in a city of three million than in a city of 100,000, traffic has become dense in the smaller city just as much as in the larger one.

What of those socioeconomic developments that have helped remove many of the handicaps traditionally associated with life in the countryside? I shall begin with leisure and entertainment. For decades recreation was a factor drawing people into the cities. But what today do average city dwellers do with their leisure time? They spend it in front of their television sets watching more or less the same programs as the average dweller in the country. And the automobile, largely responsible for the nuisance of life in the cities, has paradoxically had a liberating effect in the country. Further, agricultural mechanization has considerably reduced the constraining character of labor in the fields and partly equalized working hours which since the thirties and forties had probably become shorter in town than in the country.

One could add still other factors, but I shall move on to the consequences of the increase in economic resources. More than anything else, the growing affluence of developed nations has made it easier to maintain in rural districts a fraction of the population that under other circumstances would have been compelled to emigrate. Because of the sharp rise in the standard of living, even very marginal agricultural enterprises no longer imply the imperious necessity of quitting the land. The rise in the standard of living has also acted as a brake on the exodus toward the cities of the nonagricultural inhabitants of villages and small towns. Finally, on the side of the city, the rise in the standard of living has made it possible for some city dwellers to live in rural areas even though the city remains their source of income.

But this last case brings up those reservations just mentioned. For can one properly regard this last category of country dwellers as true country dwellers? A part of the slowdown in the process of urbanization has been due to this kind of dispersal of urban populations. With Bauer and Roux (1976) one can speak of rurbanization or the scattered city, rather than of a halt in the process of urbanization proper. Moreover, the decade of the seventies experienced the oil crisis and one of the gravest recessions of the postwar period. And while, like the ecological movement to which it is related, an unmistakable movement away from cities in the traditional sense has unquestionably begun, one cannot rule out the possibility that this new turn of events (if, indeed, there has been a new turn of events) may lead back to the urbanizing trends in force before 1970. Nor can one rule out the possibility that the preference for rural living may grow more marked still.

Growth and Stagnation of Great Cities

In 1900 the largest city in the developed world (and in the whole world) was London, with a population of 6.6 million. And only 2 other cities, New York and Paris, had populations of more than 3 million (see table 19.2). Only 10 cities in all (the three just mentioned included) had populations of more than 1 million. By 1950, on the other hand, 52 cities had populations of more than a million, and by 1980 there were 110, 9 of them with more than 5 million and twenty with more than 3 million. New York had a population of more than 10 million as early as 1930, and more than 15 million by around

TABLE 19.2   Growth of the Population of the Largest Cities in the Developed World (in Millions) (1850–1980)

	1850	1900	1930	1950	1970	1980
Athens	—	0.1	0.9	1.3	2.1	2.5
Barcelona	0.2	0.6	1.0	1.6	2.7	3.0
Berlin	0.4	2.4	4.5	3.4	3.2	3.2
Birmingham	0.3	1.2	1.9	2.5	2.8	2.9
Boston	0.2	0.6	0.8	2.4	2.9	2.8
Chicago	—	1.7	4.3	5.0	6.8	6.8
Cleveland	—	0.4	0.9	1.4	2.2	2.1
Detroit	—	0.3	2.0	2.8	4.0	3.8
Hamburg	0.2	0.9	1.7	1.8	2.2	2.2
Leningrad	0.5	1.3	2.2	2.6	4.0	4.7
London	2.3	6.6	8.2	10.3	10.6	10.3
Los Angeles	—	0.1	2.0	4.1	8.4	9.5
Madrid	0.3	0.6	0.9	1.5	3.4	4.3
Manchester	0.4	1.3	2.6	2.5	2.5	2.5
Melbourne	—	0.5	1.0	1.5	2.3	2.9
Milan	0.2	0.5	0.9	3.6	5.5	6.7
Montreal	—	0.8	1.0	1.3	2.7	2.8
Moscow	0.4	1.1	2.8	4.8	7.1	8.2
Naples	0.4	0.6	0.8	2.8	3.6	4.0
New York	0.7	4.2	10.3	12.3	16.3	15.6
Osaka	0.3	1.1	2.5	3.8	7.6	8.7
Paris	1.3	3.3	5.6	6.0	8.4	8.7
Philadelphia	0.4	1.6	2.7	2.9	4.0	4.1
Pittsburgh	—	0.6	1.3	1.5	2.1	2.0
Rome	0.2	0.5	0.9	1.6	3.1	3.6
Saint Louis	—	0.6	1.0	1.5	2.1	2.0
San Francisco	—	0.4	1.2	2.0	3.0	3.2
Sydney	—	—	1.2	1.7	2.7	3.4
Tokyo	0.6	1.8	4.0	6.3	14.9	17.7
Toronto	—	0.2	0.9	1.1	2.6	3.0

Sources: Before 1950: See the methodological appendix. 1950 to 1980: United Nations (1986b) (with some rectifications by the author), and some national sources.

Note: Cities with populations of more than 2 million in 1970; population within the perimeter of the agglomeration.

1964–66. London went over 10 million shortly before 1950, and Tokyo sometime around 1962–63. It should be noted in this connection that the first city in the Third World to surpass 10 million was probably Shanghai, which did so around 1950. Shanghai was joined between 1950 and 1985 by 5 or 6 other Third World cities: Mexico City, Buenos Aires, Sao Paulo, Rio de Janeiro, Calcutta, and Seoul.

But a set of factors, the most important of them being the deterioration of the structure of urban life, has led to a very pronounced slowdown in the growth of these great cities as soon as they reached a population of 8–10 million. Such was notably the case of London by the sixties and of other very great cities by the start of the seventies. Thus taking all cities that in 1970 had populations of more than 8 million, one finds that their populations increased by only 5% between 1970 and 1980, while for all cities in developed countries there was an increase of 15 %. Even cities with populations of 3–8 million in 1970 had growth slower than that of smaller cities, amounting to only 9%.

This directly raises the problem of the optimal size of cities mentioned earlier, a problem I regard as crucial since it will determine living conditions for what will in the future be the greater part of humanity. This is a problem I have tried to analyze in depth elsewhere (Bairoch, 1977a). I refer the reader interested in these matters to what I have written there, for these questions go beyond the scope of this book. But they are by no means unrelated to it—far from it. I shall therefore summarize here the chief findings of the study.

The Optimal Size of Cities and the Upper Limits of City Size

My object in Bairoch (1977a) was not only to establish the optimal size of cities, but also to determine the upper limits of city size. By upper limits I mean the maximum size beyond which it is likely, if not certain, that any supplementary advantage of an increase in size will for some variables become negligible or nonexistent. On the other hand (and this applies to other variables as well as those for which size may up to a point prove advantageous), the upper limit lies at that size level at which the disadvantages flowing from size become unquestionably significant. Certainly this notion of an upper limit or maximum size of cities is not very far removed from the upper extreme of the division defining the optimal size of cities. It must nevertheless be distinguished from it on at least three counts:

1. Where it is possible to imagine two or more optimal levels for each variable, there can be only one upper limit.
2. The upper limit will in general lie beyond the optimal limit.
3. Situations may exist in which there is no optimal size, only a maximum size.

Needless to say, in order to determine such thresholds it is necessary to take into account a multitude of factors related to the economy as well as to general living conditions. My analysis involved more than twenty factors related to living conditions, among which may be cited, in no particular order, climate, pollution, commercial services, crime rates, education, housing, traffic, income, political representation, recreation, health, urban services, and so on. With regard to economic matters I looked into seven factors, some of which were studied in this context for the first time. From among these economic factors, I shall mention in particular jobs and unemployment, productivity, savings, patterns of consumption, and imports.

In the end, as one would have expected, it proves necessary to negotiate a very delicate balance between two largely contradictory sets of conclusions. Indeed the chief general finding I made was that there is a distinct conflict between, on the one hand, the size levels favorable to various aspects of employment and above all to the process of development, and on the other hand the size levels favorable to better general living conditions. Thus again with respect to the size of cities, there is a conflict between economic growth and the well-being of citizens.

One may argue that where certain forms of employment and economic development are concerned there is no optimal size. On the whole, a large city is a positive factor in these areas. The advantages derived from size only become modest or negligible once the population exceeds 500,000 to one million. And even then size probably has no negative effects, at least not until the population reaches five million.

By contrast, with regard to general living conditions there is indeed quite a low optimal population level, somewhere around 200,000–300,000. Further, it can be argued in this case that the upper limit on the size of cities—especially that point beyond which the disadvantages flowing from size become genuinely significant—lies around half a million people. In most cities larger than this, urban life becomes a veritable hell for the majority of citizens. One finds growing levels of pollution, noise, crime, and traffic congestion; the climate becomes more unhealthy, the habitat less spacious, the sense of social isolation and physical crowding more intense, and so on. Nor is any of this offset by the added benefits enjoyed in large cities in contrast to smaller ones.

In order to surmount this conflict between economic imperatives and the physical and psychological well-being of the citizenry, one is forced into a dilemma whose insoluble character is somewhat mitigated by the fact that the optimal and maximum size levels converge to a certain extent. For the upper limit beyond which general well-being and living conditions suffer is not too far removed from the lower limit favorable to employment and economic development.

For developed countries the answers are not all that much in doubt. One may regard the imperative of economic development as distinctly less important in developed countries than the well-being of the population. It may even be considered marginal to the extent that employment can be optimized at fairly low urban size levels. In this light the optimal population of cities in developed countries can be placed at around 300,000. And more important still, it would seem highly recommendable that cities not exceed an upper population limit of 400,000 to 500,000.

I have insisted that these findings concern only developed countries. This is a major qualification inasmuch as, having also studied the situation in Third World countries, I have found that the problem seems to be different there. In the Third World the trade-off between the economy and the quality of life is more difficult to make (see chapter 30).

With regard to developed nations and the observed slowdown in the growth of great cities, it should be recalled that what was said about the negative effects of growth beyond a population of five million applies also to economic problems. This probably does much to explain why the very largest cities have had slower rates of growth.

The New Towns

In some cases the slowdown in the growth of great cities has been deliberate. Thus regarding London, a commission of inquiry recommended as early as 1940 that limits be put on the expansion of industry in that city. And by 1945 it had been decided to create a network of new autonomous cities forty to fifty kilometers from London. These new towns to a large extent are part of the garden cities movement founded in 1899 under the instigation of Ebenezer Howard, father of the modern trend toward establishing new towns. In 1898 was published Howard's famous book, *Garden Cities of Tomorrow*, in which he drew up plans for new cities, seeking to realize the old dream of creating an urban habitat combining the advantages of the city with those of the country. As Galantay (1975) has very clearly shown, Howard takes his place in a long line of visionaries setting out in search of the ideal city, and his influence has been decisive.

It is interesting to follow the fortunes of the first of the two cities conceived according to Howard's plan, Letchworth. Founded in 1903, Letchworth was for many years considered a semifailure owing to the difficulties encountered in attracting jobs. In the long run, however, it has proven a success. Indeed, the straitlaced *Financial Times*, in an article of 1 August 1980 entitled "A Thriving Garden City after 77 Years," noted that unemployment was much lower in Letchworth than in the rest of the country. The article ends with these lines: "Letchworth is not London commuter territory in the way some of the towns to the south of the Thames are. It has its own life, its own industrial base, and its own sense of purpose. Ebenezer Howard would have been well pleased with the progress it has made in 77 years."

The example given by the English in their attempts to decongest London was followed very soon afterwards in other countries. By 1950 plans had been drawn up for decongesting Stockholm. At that time, however, Stockholm had a population of only 740,000 and one of the lowest population densities of any city of comparable size in the world. Several satellite towns of 50,000 people were planned, some of which today exceed that size. The model used is different from that for London in that these satellite towns were to lie at most thirty minutes' distance from the center of Stockholm. Finland quickly followed the Swedish lead, conceiving a similar scheme for Helsinki. Only one new town was constructed, however, though the question of building others has recently arisen.

In trying to decongest Osaka, the Japanese modelled their scheme on both British and Swedish lines. The construction of new towns had begun by 1963. France came to this solution only fairly late, despite the fact that Paris is one of the most densely populated cities in Europe. It was not until 1965 that a plan was devised and not until 1970 that work began. Other new towns are also projected near the larger provincial cities.

As has already been seen, the creation of new cities began very early in the Soviet Union. The problem of slowing down the growth of Moscow was first tackled by other means, however, notably those possible in regimes in which freedom of residence can be restricted. But this did not prove effective enough, and the authorities decided in 1956 on a plan providing for the construction of twenty new towns.

In the United States, where private initiative is king, there are no real projects to relieve the congestion of large cities by the creation of new planned cities. This does not, of course, mean that new planned cities have not been created in the last few decades or even at the end of the nineteenth century. The most interesting case of a planned city is that of Pullman City, described by Claude Massu (1983) as a "model city of untamed American capitalism." Paternalistic city par excellence, it was designed for employees of the constructor of the famous railroad cars. This town was intended to resolve the conflicts between labor and capital. Founded in 1880, it was designated at the International Fair at Prague as the most beautiful model city of the world, because a real effort had indeed been made in this sense. However, the management of the city was based on profit-making principles, since the rents were to cover the costs of operation. In addition, a certain puritanism presided over the design of public areas (notably the absence of bars). Social conflicts, and especially the strike of Pullman workers in 1894, who also demanded a reduction in rent, brought to the surface the crisis which had been undermining the city. The city survived the death in 1897 of Pullman by only a few years. The lake was filled in, public buildings were sold and by around 1910 Pullman City was no more than another suburb of Chicago, one among many others.

The Automobile and the Breakup of Cities

The two least populated cities in 1900 among those in table 19.2 were Detroit and Los Angeles. Both of these cities illustrate in different ways the power of the automobile and its impact on urban life resulting in the breakup of cities. Detroit lies at the heart of the principal automobile-producing region in the world. Los Angeles is probably the most sprawling city in the world, some of its streets being eighty kilometers long.

As was noted in chapter 18, by 1914 there were some 2.5 million automobiles in use worldwide. Despite the First World War this figure had risen to 10.9 million by 1920, and to 35.1 million by 1930; 33.9 million of them were in developed countries and 27.8 million in the developed areas of North America alone. This meant that there were 210 cars for every thousand people in developed North America as against only 13 in the rest of the developed world (except the Soviet Union, where there was only 0.1 car per thousand). This explains why the spatial breakup of cities began first in North America, as early as the twenties. The process did not get perceptibly under way in Western Europe until the sixties. Western Europe as a whole did not have as many cars per person as developed North America had in 1930 until around 1969. One of the chief reasons for this is differences in population density; the wide open spaces of North America encouraged the extensive motorization of its rural population.

The mechanism underlying the breakup of cities has everywhere followed a similar pattern. The discomfort of life in large cities has led a growing number of city dwellers to move out to the periphery, to which the automobile has provided easier access. This displacement of city dwellers (mostly young couples with children) in turn brings on the establishment of a part of the commercial facilities that were formerly in the cities, their establishment at the periphery being further encouraged by parking problems in the city center. The inner city thereby loses an important part of the amenities it once offered, and as a result it becomes less appealing, thus accelerating the flow of people out toward the periphery.

The low population density in these enlarged suburbs makes the setting up of public transportation lines unprofitable. And the increasingly frequent use of private cars in the city leads to a reduction in the use of public transportation. Thus in the urban regions of the United States the number of passenger rides per person on public transportation lines, which practically doubled between 1900 and

1920, then went into a decline, which considerably increased in tempo after 1950. As the title of Foster's (1981) history of American city planners and urban transportation expresses it, between 1900 and 1940, we passed "from streetcar to superhighway."

So far as I know, no overall statistics exist for Europe, but a decline in urban public transportation became manifest around 1960 to 1965. Thus in the provincial cities of France, despite an increase of 10% in vehicle-kilometers traveled, ridership dropped by 12% between 1967 and 1973. Since I am writing this book in Geneva, I shall also give the relevant statistics for that city. In 1950 there were 221 passenger-rides per person. This figure rose to 281 passenger-rides per person in 1964. By 1970, it had fallen back to 230. And compared with what has been happening in most other European cities, the situation in Geneva appears favorable.

The decline in ridership has forced public transportation authorities to cut back on the frequency of service, to close some lines and/or to raise fares. This has naturally led to still further use of private cars. Since private cars take up ten to thirty times more space than public transportation, this has forced municipal authorities to increase the amount of room intended for traffic. This has reduced the width of sidewalks and the size of green spaces ("cars eat trees"). And the flood of automobiles, creating more noise and pollution, has made the city even less livable than before. Whence a fresh wave of migrants heading for the periphery and, as a direct result, increasing automobile traffic. In short, cities find themselves caught in a vicious circle well on the way to destroying them.

Since the early seventies, however, in the United States one observes the first signs of a reversal of this trend: the return of former urbanites to the inner city. But the scale of this new trend is as yet quite small, and in any case there is good reason to wonder to what extent future changes in the employment sector will slow down this flow back to the city. Indeed, given the new possibilities computers are creating, the likelihood of the decentralization of many jobs appears very strong. This decentralization would be more accurately described as domiciliation, since computers make it possible for an appreciable fraction of the work force to work at home. Certainly this process of domiciliation is not incompatible with a return to the inner city. And the efforts made in both American and European cities to rekindle life in central city areas, reinforced by the growing cost of fuel, may eventually prove a powerful enticement.

It should be pointed out that this turnabout is also reflected in the number of people using public transportation. I shall take another look at the three cases cited earlier. In the cities of the United States, having bottomed out sometime around 1972, use of public transportation has tended since 1974 to move upwards once again. In the provincial cities of France the number of passenger-rides grew by 7% between

1973 and 1975. Finally, in Geneva, after use of public transportation first stopped declining between 1973 and 1976, it has since increased by 2.5% per year (between 1976 and 1985).

Cities and the Growing Predominance of Services

Before closing this chapter I shall mention one last important change taking place in the cities of the developed world: the declining relative number of jobs in industry in favor of those in services. By 1960, jobs in the service sector accounted for about 50% of all jobs in the cities in developed countries. This proportion has today in all likelihood reached 65%. Thus the situation obtaining a century ago has practically been inverted, 60–65% of all jobs in the cities of the developed countries of the West now being in the service sector, as against 30–35% in the industrial sector.

But one must again insist on the uniqueness of each city's individual experience. These figures are only averages resulting from a fairly wide numerical spread. Many cities still specialize either in industrial activities or in transportation. And some cities heavily concentrate on administrative services. But service-related jobs are everywhere on the rise, and this trend, begun during the twenties and thirties, cannot be expected to slow down for a few more decades.

Just as the industrialization of the cities of the nineteenth century brought about profound changes in social structure and in the urban way of life generally, so too the predominance of services has in its turn changed the city of the second half of the twentieth century. The transformation is already reflected at the level of urban architecture; the office block is very different from the factory, not least because it more readily blends into its surroundings. The general integration of services in the urban life is enhanced, moreover, by the fact that much of the growth in this sector is linked to education, which in turn depends by and large on the government. The higher salaries paid to service workers imply new patterns of consumption further encouraged by the greater stability of jobs in this sector of the economy. Indeed, cyclical variations affect services less strongly than industry, leading to less cyclical unemployment.

Looked at in a certain way, growth in the service sector creates more new service-related jobs, for the higher standard of living implies greater consumption of services in the broadest sense of the word. This is notably the case for the restaurant and hotel trades, for instance. People eat in restaurants not only because of the higher incomes associated with service-related jobs, but also because service employees work in urban districts and follow schedules flexible enough to allow for longer breaks for meals. But differences may result from a great many factors. Between the diversity of the bistros of Paris and Geneva or of the food stalls in the streets of Athens or Tel Aviv, and the scarcity of restaurants in Bergen or Moscow, a great many intermediate situations exist.

The growth of jobs in the service sector has not had only positive effects. In many places it has accelerated the decline of the inner city. The need for space per worker in this sector is less than in the industrial sector; and the demand for raw materials is almost nil. This has encouraged the establishment in the heart of the city of offices that have progressively driven out residents and shops. Thus once the offices close for the day, the inner city, already deprived of a part of its animation by television, takes on still more the aura of a ghost town, its facades devoid of life.

As one long-standing and pertinacious student of the problem of the megapolis, Gottmann (1979), observes, "the study of offices, work, and related activities greatly helps to understand the modern evolution of cities." The service sector, moreover, is currently assuming new forms more closely related to information processing and decision making, which have earned it the name of "quaternary sector." And while until now these activities have been located in the inner city, the new orientation introduced by the information revolution by no means rules out the possibility of a dispersal of jobs in this sector, a dispersal that would leave the offices empty.

"In the Shadow of the Factories, as Though Nothing Had Happened"

This suggestive title is that of an article by Geneviève Delbos (1979) describing the survival down to the present of a peasant way of life in a village near the industrial complex at Longwy (France). But it is a peasant life without agriculture, for three-quarters of the residents of the village no longer farm. Certainly the persistence of rural life is more a feature of less urbanized societies or of societies only recently urbanized. Thus with reference to Moscow at the end of the nineteenth century, Johnson (1979) notes that the factory workers remained rural both in their behavior and in their solidarity with each other. For according to Johnson the solidarity of the Russian working class of the period reflected village life more than social class. And these workers moved back and forth between the city and their native villages.

These facts were unquestionable realities, but they concerned only a fraction of the 260 million-odd city dwellers that the developed world gained between 1800 and 1930. As more people were drawn into the cities essentially by the prospect of factory jobs, factory workers fairly quickly became urban people attached to their neighborhood, which at the start was nothing more than a worker ghetto. As Yves Lequin (1982) remarks:

The essence of the manufacturing town was the ghetto, the generalized segregation of its populations, and particularly the radical separation from the city itself and from the rest of society of a working class that drew to one side the rootless and atomistic individuals on whom the city's growth fed. This sharp division was the sign of a dual exclusion: taken to its extreme, the suburb (or the degraded quarter of the historical city center) was no longer part of the city, just as the proletariat was no longer anything more than a pathological excrescence of a normal social hierarchy. One turns to Saint-Marc-Girardin, who spoke in the 1830s of the Barbarians camping in the industrial suburbs of the larger cities of Western Europe, or to those English philanthropists of the late nineteenth century who proposed to solve at the same time the problem of slums and that of unemployment by deporting what they called the social "residuum" to the colonies.

But then how are we to explain the fact that in the nineteenth century the workers of Paris and elsewhere had so much trouble leaving the squalid neighborhoods in which they were born? That they were so strongly attached to their neighborhoods that, when these were transformed by gentrification, they would whenever possible reestablish themselves only one or two streets away? That the retirees of some mining towns of today refuse to leave on retirement the company dwellings where they lived, when they do not simply resist the sanitary improvement of their housing?

How difficult it is to leave, for "around the workers' quarter proliferates the discourse of reassuring intimacy, of the warmth of neighborhoods, of the familiarity of streets and courtyards through comradeships developed on vacant lots, staircase friendships, passing companionships, in short, all the opportunities for the meetings and exchanges of everyday life." And in this context should be recalled what I said (in chapter 17) about the high costs of urban transportation and the supplementary incomes of working-class wives.

20 Technological Innovation and the City □

The city has greatly benefited from the enormous technological advances of the nineteenth and twentieth centuries. There is no doubt that without this rich harvest of technological innovations the process of urbanization would have come to a standstill, owing in particular to a halt in the growth of the larger cities. Traditional technology (preceding the Industrial Revolution) could not have solved the many problems caused by the urban explosion of the postindustrial world. If such an explosion had occurred without the technological developments of the past two hundred years, how would one have organized the transport required to ship the food and fuel needed in cities of two to five million people or more? And how would urban transportation have been provided in these cities? And how would the serious public sanitation problems in cities of this size have been solved without progress in engineering and chemistry? Even communication would have been very difficult without the telephone, which came into practical use as early as the late 1870s, at a time when the largest city in the world, London, had a population of three million, and the second largest, Paris, had a population of two million. By 1885 there were already some 260,000 telephones in service, almost all of them in the cities of developed countries. The number had risen to about two and a half million by 1900 and fourteen and a half million on the eve of the First World War.

One may object that, necessity being the mother of invention, the bottlenecks created by urban growth would have produced their own solutions. Here indeed lies the crux of the problem of the link between technological innovation and the economy in general, and between technological innovation and the city in particular. While it is unquestionably the case that the city has profited from technological advances, has it not also had a considerable hand both in stimulating innovation and in assuring its diffusion?

This leads me to open this chapter with a brief review of the relations between technology and economic development. The problem is very important. For if technology were to turn out to be an independent variable in economic life, that would make more important the role of the city in technological innovation. Indeed, if technology is an independent variable, this implies that progress in technology results from the general progress of science. But it has already been seen how intimately the growth of science is connected to urban life. It should be noted, however, that, even if technology depends on economic factors, this does not reduce the city's role to nothing. But the contribution would be made, not by the urban factor itself, but by the economic component of urban life. This is an important aspect of the question I shall return to later.

Technology, Science, and the Industrial Revolution

The old, classic view is that the Industrial Revolution was the fruit of the progress of science during the century of the Enlightenment, a century itself the fruit of continuous progress since the end of the Middle Ages. Although this view contains important errors, it should not be abandoned altogether. There is no doubt that Western Europe had by the start of the eighteenth century reached a level of culture it had never known before. Because of Western Europe's openness to the rest of the world (an attitude unique to Western Europe) it was able to seek out and assimilate the offerings of other cultures. European culture was thus at that time one of the most advanced cultures in scientific and technical terms. Although the gap between Europe and Asia was not at this time very wide, Arabic algebra, Chinese printing, the American potato, the renewed interest in antiquity—all of these things, together with many other borrowings, fertilized by the original research of the Europeans of the sixteenth and seventeenth centuries, had by the start of the eighteenth century probably brought European society to a height probably no other civilization had reached.

Doubtless so high a level of scientific and technological development, and above all such open-mindedness, at the same time the cause and the consequence of scientific and technological growth, made the West fertile ground first for the agricultural revolution and then for the Industrial Revolution that came after it. But economic history and the history of technology compel me to modify this picture. Certainly it is very tempting to think of a continuous evolution, a direct thread running from the Gutenberg printing press to Stevenson's locomotive, by way of the achievements of Leonardo da Vinci, Copernicus, Galileo, Bacon, Descartes, Newton, Papin, Lavoisier, and Watt, to cite only a few names picked at random from the cast of characters in the saga of European progress in science and technology. The fact remains, however, that practically all of the technological advances in the agricultural revolution, and especially the Industrial Revolution during its first seventy to a hundred years, were not the work of scientists; they were rather the work of sometimes illiterate craftsmen who, proceeding along purely empirical lines, perfected or improved the machines on which these revolutions relied. And I speak of perfecting and improving rather than inventing them, because in most cases the machines used during the opening phases of the Industrial Revolution had been invented long before the date of their first real practical application; and they did not necessarily originate in the West.

So science played almost no part in the technological developments associated with the beginnings of industrialization, or any other sector of development. The first operational steam engines, constructed around 1710 by Savary, and especially those of Newcomen (as was noted, a blacksmith), owed nothing to science. And this was the case for other improvements over the next six decades and more.

In the textile industry, which acted as a driving force in industrialization until the middle of the nineteenth century, craftsmen guided by experience were also responsible for perfecting and improving the first mechanization. Like Arkwright, whose career we described in chapter 15, they were still far removed from scientific life. During the first decades of the mechanization of the textile industry, the machines were as a rule manufactured by textile concerns themselves. It was only later, probably largely as a result of the substitution of iron for wood in the construction of industrial equipment, that independent workshops took over the fabrication of these machines. The independent workshops could specialize and introduce improvements requiring a higher degree of technical qualification. But the fact remains that the original impetus came from inside the industry itself, as the product of purely practical training and experiment.

The same process occurred in the iron and steel industry and in other areas as well. Nor was this lack of relations to science characteristic of industrial technology alone; in their early stages agricultural techniques were also very little influenced by science.

But gradually, the more complex the new technologies became, the more they drew on science, which had also progressed very rapidly. The successive transitions from the use of wood (until around 1820), to iron or cast iron, and then to steel (beginning in 1860) in the construction of machines represented stages in a process of growing complexity involving, both in manufacturing and in maintenance, more highly developed techniques and more highly evolved equipment.

Thus the nearer one comes to the end of the nineteenth century, and the further one goes into the twentieth century, the more one finds an evolving technology characterized by growing complexity. This complexity gradually led to a break with traditional techniques, a break accentuated during the early years of the twentieth century by the generalized introduction of electricity and the internal combustion engine; and the break became total with the numerous applications of electronics and nuclear energy. The chief result of this evolution lies in the growing independence of technology from the economy.

Technological Innovation and Economic Growth

One may nevertheless wonder whether the independence of technology was not already very great in the second half of the nineteenth century and even during the first half of the twentieth century. Over the last three decades this independence has apparently been extremely great, owing notably to the scale of the by-products of arms research and space exploration, and also to the large amount of basic research done during this period. It suffices in this context to think of the growing numbers of researchers in science and technology (the barriers between them being very porous and often nonexistent) to realize the great increase in research since before the Second World War. What matters here is the period of urbanization spanning the nineteenth century and the beginning of the twentieth century, that is, the period during which the contemporary urban world was formed.

Despite the enormous value and interest of the empirical analysis of the links between technological innovations and the economy, studies in this area are paradoxically rare. The most important, which was a starting point for the main inquiries into specific aspects of relations between technology and the city, was the study of Schmookler (1966). This study is a review of inventions and economic change between 1800 and 1955 in four sectors of the United States economy: agriculture, the petroleum industry, the paper industry, and railroad equipment. Schmookler comes to two chief conclusions:

1. Despite the widespread belief that the impetus for technical inventions designed for specific applications has come from scientific breakthroughs and major technological innovations, the study of developments in these four sectors of the American economy reveals no case in which a relation of this sort unequivocally came into play. On the other hand, cases abound in which the stimulus for new inventions was provided by specific technical problems demanding solutions. More precisely, there were new inventions when there was the promise of large savings (procedures were costly before the invention) or where there was a promise of profits to those who found new techniques to solve definite technical problems.

2. There was a very close relation between the state of the economy and the rate at which patents were filed. (This relation has been often observed.) The important point emerging from Schmookler's analysis, however, is that the economy turns out to have been the driving force, upswings in the economy preceding surges in the pace of invention.

Schmookler explains these findings by the fact that invention is largely an economic activity carried out, like all economic activities, for profit. And the profits expected are a function of sales. Schmookler's explanations even more than his findings (flowing as they do directly from his empirical analysis) have the unmistakable ring of the "American way of life." But it should be noted that for the first half of the nineteenth century, a consensus has been formed—even in the case of Europe—regarding the primacy of economics over invention. Further, from 1850–1860 the United States has had an important role in technological innovation in the West, its role becoming decisive between 1890 and 1910.

I shall now move on to analyze more specifically the relation between technological innovation and the city. One has unfortunately had to rely almost entirely on American research. While this is not necessarily a bad thing in itself, the fact that American students of the problem quite naturally direct most of their attention to the United States has proved something of a drawback.

Technological Innovation and the City

The first modern analysis of the relation between technological innovation and the city was done by Pred (1966). His analysis formed part of his seminal work on the dynamics of urban and industrial growth in the United States. Pred computed the relation between the number of patents pending and the population of the thirty-five largest American cities from 1860 to 1910. While the course of invention is only imperfectly seen through patents, Pred's calculations point unmistakably to the concentration of invention in the cities. In about 1860 the number of patents per capita in the thirty-five principal cities of the United States was 4.1 times the national average, even though the national average included the figures for cities. This ratio nevertheless exhibited a downward trend, falling by 1910 to only 1.6, thus reflecting a diminution of the inventive function of cities. But around 1910 the thirty-five largest cities accounted for a higher proportion of the overall urban population than in 1860. And since the urban part of the population of the United States had also increased sharply during this time, the thirty-five largest cities made up a correspondingly greater share of the national average, thereby mitigating somewhat the force of this downward movement. In any event, though its role declined to some extent toward the end of the period, the city played a predominant role in invention in the United States, a predominance linked, according to Pred, to the amount of industrial employment located there.

Still with regard to the United States, Higgs (1971) has shown that throughout the period 1870–1920 the relation between the level of urbanization in the United States as a whole and the number of patents pending was very close and highly significant. The relation was even tighter than that between the number of patents pending and the proportion of the working population employed in manufacturing.

Two more specific analyses were done by Feller (1971, 1973). The first confirms the findings of Pred and Higgs. But Feller tries to isolate more exactly the urban contribution to invention. And he argues that while—as Schmookler shows—invention is unquestionably determined by contact with technical need, the urban way of life increases the frequency of such contact. Similarly, while invention occurs only when bottlenecks develop in industry, the city makes it possible for a greater number of people to become aware of these bottlenecks.

Since there were few studies of these problems in the framework of European societies for the period before 1850, I had some research done in this area in the Department of Economic History at the University of Geneva. This work was the topic of the master's thesis of Martin (1977), aided by a visiting assistant to the department, Gilbert Eggimann. The aim of this study was to explore the relation between the size of cities and technological innovation. It can serve my purpose here because the lower limit defining urban centers was fixed at a population of five thousand, and because account was taken of developments in rural districts.

A systematic census was taken of all inventors in the field of technology, using the histories of technology available for the three countries included in the study—the United Kingdom, France, and Germany. Martin tried to discover the biography of each inventor, which proved possible for 535 of the 1,358 inventors on the list. For each country and for intervals of twenty-five or fifty years, Martin compared the size of the city where an inventor was born and the city where he made his most important invention with the size of the cities of the country as a whole.

Technological innovation was of distinctly urban origin in the three European countries studied (see table 20.1). In all three, for both the inventor's place of birth and the place of his invention the city largely predominates. The predominance of cities in the places of birth must be explained in large part by the close link between place of birth and place of residence. Almost all of the future inventors born in an urban environment still lived there when they made their discoveries or inventions. On the other hand, given the fact that the migratory flow of the population ran predominantly from the country to the towns, one would normally expect to find a greater role for cities in the places of invention than in the places of birth. But this is not the case (see table 20.1). This may in part be accounted for by statistical bias. But it also reflects the gradual decline over time of the specifically urban contribution to innovation, since at least twenty and as a rule thirty to forty years separate the inventor's birth and the date of his invention.

This brings me to another conclusion: the decline over time of the

TABLE 20.1 Indices of Urban Concentration of Technological
Innovation according to Inventor's Place of Birth and the Place
of Residence at the Time of Their Most Important Innovation
(1700–1900)

	Place of Birth		Place of Innovation	
	Period	Concentration index[a]	Period	Concentration index[a]
United Kingdom	1700–1780	2.6	1760–1820	3.9
	1780–1820	3.3	1820–1880	2.3
	1820–1860	1.8	1880–1900	1.4
France	1800–1830	5.3	1800–1850	6.1
	1830–1880	3.6	1850–1900	3.6
Germany	1800–1840	5.5	1800–1850	7.1
	1840–1860	4.9	1850–1900	3.2

Sources: Martin (1977).
[a] Relation between relative population of urban places where the inventors were
born or resided and the relative urban population.

specifically urban contribution to innovation. The case of these three
major European countries thus confirms the results of the analyses
done for the United States. Another finding Martin's study enables
me to verify (but which leads a little beyond the framework here) concerns the positive impact of the size of cities on innovation. In this
area too, the only available studies (less thorough than the others
cited) bear only on the United States. Like their successors, using statistics on patents, Rose (1948) and Ogburn and Duncan (1964) had
already reached the conclusion that the larger the city, the greater the
number of patents pending per capita. Viewed in a certain light, this
relation between the size of cities and innovation is very important,
for it ipso facto gives further evidence of the urban component of innovation. Indeed, assuming the city made no particular contribution
to innovation, there would be little reason for the size of cities to have
such an effect.

Empirical analysis, then, fully confirms the predictions suggested
by deductive reasoning, which has in just about every case assigned
the city a leading role in innovation in the broadest sense of the word,
including technological invention. And this has proven true for preindustrial societies as much as for those affected by the Industrial
Revolution.

The reader may sense a certain contradiction between these conclusions about the preponderant place of the city in technological innovation and the conclusions reached earlier (chapters 15 and 16)
regarding the absence of a relationship between the existing urban network and the establishment of new industries during the first phases of
the Industrial Revolution. The contradiction is only apparent, how-

ever, for the two phenomena are not necessarily related. The inventor and the person who puts the invention to practical use are not always the same. And this is an especially important point: I have shown that economic considerations and also the availability of energy have very often induced entrepreneurs to establish new industries in rural areas or in very small towns.

And now before closing this chapter I must deal with one other important aspect of the problem: the diffusion of technological innovations.

The City and the Diffusion of Technological Innovations

Here the problem is at the same time much simpler and much more delicate. It is simpler because the fact that the urban environment is a more favorable milieu than the rural environment for the diffusion of technological innovations requires no demonstration: it is difficult to see how it could be otherwise. It is more delicate, however, by reason of this self-evidence, which has made empirical studies specifically devoted to this problem exceedingly rare: proving something that is already perfectly obvious is not very interesting. It is also more delicate because it is often easier to follow the subsequent progress of an innovation than to locate its place of origin. But there is no lack of studies on the general problems of the diffusion of innovation. In the bibliography to the second edition of Rogers's (1971) work on this subject, one finds 1,640 titles (of which 1,230 are empirical studies on diffusion), not counting 170 general references to subjects bordering on this question. (Rogers modestly says that his work is the distillation of more than 1,500 publications.) The appendix to Rogers's book—which presents, for a hundred or so different propositions, the number of studies on the given question, the relevant references, and the percentage of studies confirming or disproving the given thesis—constitutes a wonderful research tool. (It is true, however, that this reader at least was left wondering whether the fact that 95% of the studies devoted to the matter reject a given hypothesis necessarily means it is false.)

However important all of this may be, I must set such considerations aside, because absolute certainty is very rare. In any case, it does appear that at least as a general rule the city is more favorable to the diffusion of technological innovations than the countryside. Symptomatic of the lack of investigations on this matter is the fact that, of the hundred-odd headings under which Rogers classes the studies on diffusion analyzed in his book, none explicitly relates to the problem of differences in the amount of diffusion between cities and the countryside. In a way this problem invokes one of the most fundamental distinctions between urban and rural districts, that of the mentality and behavior of their populations. In his now classic study *The City*

(1921), the sociologist Max Weber distinguishes between the behavior of townspeople and country people on the basis of two basic oppositions: rational versus traditional, and contact versus custom. And though Weber's observations specifically relate to conditions at the time of his writing, the same distinction existed much earlier in history, for urban behavior has always had a character of its own.

Rationality and frequent contacts between people—clearly two important concepts with regard to innovation. To be sure, there is room for nuance. In a famous article "Urbanism as a Way of Life" (1938), Wirth notes that the very large number of people one has relations with in the city makes genuine contact impossible. But from my point of view here the number is the decisive thing: it is the possibility of seeing inventions or learning of them that counts. And I would be inclined to consider the development of a rational outlook as resulting from the enhanced possibilities of contacts with other people; or rather, putting it the other way around, I would regard the maintenance of a traditional outlook as resulting from the absence of such contacts. This is to say that the second of Weber's two distinctions between town and country seems somewhat more doubtful; but one should not disregard the social constraints which lead to a more traditional way of life in rural areas.

Modern analyses of the city's role in the diffusion of innovation have chiefly been carried out by American, British, and Swedish scholars. Hägerstrand (1967) has made one of the best-known contributions in this area. He insists on the importance of proximity and interpersonal contacts. It is worth noting the distinction Pederson (1970) draws between what he calls business-related innovations and household-related innovations. A good example illustrating this difference is television. In the United States and the other countries in which private television stations exist, the establishment of a TV station is the business of the entrepreneur; the diffusion of television sets, on the other hand, depends on decisions made in the home. But while this distinction is interesting, one ought to stress the fact that both of these processes of diffusion have an important role in economic development, and are, moreover, interdependent: the diffusion of new television stations is faster the more households in other regions buy television sets.

When all is said and done, there are few attributes of urban life that do not favor the diffusion of innovation. Following Hägerstrand, I have spoken of increased interpersonal contacts. But I shall take other aspects of urban living and see what Rogers's synthesis has to say. Education: 74% of the 275 studies Rogers analyzes conclude that people with higher levels of education adopt innovations more readily. Social mobility: all five of the relevant studies show that social mobility is everywhere correlated with the adoption of innovations. The same holds true for the upper social classes (68%), for a cosmopolitan population (76%), for exposure to the mass media (69%), and for the population of cities belonging to modern urban systems (70 %). Thus the studies prove what already seemed self-evident: the city promotes the diffusion of innovations more than the country.

Does the Size of Cities Affect the Diffusion of Technological Innovations?

As in the case of innovation itself, the role played by the size of cities brings additional evidence of an urban component. The studies in this area are no more numerous than those on the urban contribution generally: an exhaustive bibliography would certainly contain no more than about thirty titles. The great majority of existing studies were done in and concern the United States. There are two reasons for the dominance of the United States in the field: the amount of money available for this kind of research and the size of the country, which makes the findings of the research statistically more significant.

The earliest study is apparently that of Bowers (1937). It is in any case always cited as such, which by no means rules out the possibility of precursors, especially in languages other than English. Bowers's study is on the growth in the United States of the number of ham radios according to region and size of city. The analysis concerning the period 1914–1930 shows that this innovation first gained acceptance in cities with populations of 25,000–100,000, progressively diffusing to smaller towns thereafter. Cities with populations of more than 100,000, however, were always less affected than the others. The reason for this is easy to imagine: the diversions offered by larger cities were more abundant.

This type of analysis was started again after the Second World War by Crain (1966) in his investigation of the diffusion of the practice of fluoridating water. This study shows very clearly that there is a relation between the size of cities and their openness to this practice. More evidence of the positive relation between the size of cities and readiness to adopt innovations is found in Hägerstrand's (1967) work. The few other studies relating the diffusion of innovations to the size of cities all confirm the same conclusion. It should nevertheless be noted that the relevant studies practically always concern the contemporary United States.

Robson (1973), however, more recently reached the same conclusion after a detailed study of the diffusion of three innovations through the urban network in nineteenth-century England: the establishment of gas plants from 1820 to 1840, of house-building contractors in 1853 and from 1862 to 1894, and of telephone exchanges from 1881 to 1892. In addition to the size factor, however, Robson quite properly stresses the role of proximity: innovations diffuse from large towns to smaller ones as a function of their proximity to them.

For Robson, as also for Pred and most other students of these problems, the flow of innovations is an important factor in the growth of urban populations, and the slowdown in the growth of the larger English cities during the last quarter of the nineteenth century was due to the slowdown in the flow of innovations.

Thus the analyses once again prove that the larger the city, the more rapidly innovations are adopted. One must nevertheless regret the extreme rarity of analyses of this kind on technological innovations in the productive sector of the economy. This is another example of the necessary distinction between business-related innovations and household-related innovations. And it should be remembered that of the two, the former is the more decisive. To what extent, for example, did the nineteenth- or twentieth-century spinning mills in the large towns tend more readily to convert to more modern equipment than their counterparts in smaller towns? The chances are that industry follows the rule. The study by Törnqvist (1970) demonstrating the important role of contacts (already stressed by Hägerstrand) in industry lends indirect support to this assertion.

21 Urbanization and Economic Development in Countries Affected by the Industrial Revolution □

This chapter will be a general conclusion about the interactions between urbanization and the economy during a pivotal period in the history both of development and of urbanization. The fact that the same adjectives can be applied to the two phenomena and that both developed most rapidly as a result of the Industrial Revolution suggests the strength of the relations between them. But while part 3 has wholly confirmed the ties between the city and the economy brought out in parts 1 and 2, this does not mean that all of the problems have been solved and that no uncertainties remain. These uncertainties would indeed have been all the greater had I not left entirely aside the many problems linked with the other side of development: colonization and underdevelopment, the themes of part 4. As will be seen, these uncertainties chiefly concern the impact of urbanization on economic development, the inverse—development as a factor in urbanization—posing no particular problem.

A general conclusion cannot easily avoid being repetitious. But I have tried to limit the number of repetitions by giving some new analyses and by going over old ground only where absolutely necessary. Partly for ease of representation, but also for clarity, I shall follow chronological order. I begin, then, with the role of urbanization in the Industrial Revolution.

Levels of Urbanization and the Beginnings of the Industrial Revolution

Two questions arise here: what part did urbanization play in triggering the Industrial Revolution in England? And what part did it play in the subsequent international diffusion of the Industrial Revolution? I shall begin with the first question (see chapter 15).

Before the many economic and social transformations making up the Industrial Revolution began, England, the cradle of this revolution, was no more urbanized than the other advanced nations of Europe. Indeed, quite the opposite. It can be estimated that around

1700 the level of urbanization in England was lower than that of the Netherlands, Portugal, Italy, and probably Spain, and about the same as that of France. London shared with Paris the status of being one of the two largest cities in Europe. But London's contribution to the overall population of England was smaller than Lisbon's to Portugal or Amsterdam's to the Netherlands, to take only Western examples. All of this leads one to infer that urbanization was not the factor responsible for triggering the Industrial Revolution.

This conclusion is reinforced by the analysis of urban growth during the first stages of the Industrial Revolution. The old urban network did not provide the basis of industrialization. On the contrary, industrialization originally developed in very small towns and villages that became large cities afterwards, but were certainly nothing of the sort when the new industries were first established. Thus between 1700 and 1800 London grew at the rate of 0.4% per year. And the seven other large English cities whose populations in 1700 ranged between 11,000 and 30,000 grew by no more than 0.5% per year. By contrast, the seven small towns or villages that became major cities during the Industrial Revolution grew at the rate of 2.1% per year.

Further, it is significant that the analysis of studies of the causes of the Industrial Revolution in England discloses an almost general absence of the urban factor as a major explanatory element. Finally, when one examines the location of enterprises in the key industries of the early Industrial Revolution we see the overwhelming predominance, if not of purely rural locations, then at least of very small towns on the boundary between urban and rural. One finds an all-but-total absence of large, as well as medium-sized, traditional cities among the sites at which the new industrial concerns were founded.

The failure of the traditional urban network to contribute to the beginnings of industrialization is not, however, as paradoxical as it may at first appear. It can be easily explained by a great number of factors, starting with energy. Water mills were for a very long time the chief source of power for machines. And the profound technological change that took place in the iron and steel industry favored the use of coal; but during this period, the coalfields did not necessarily lie near existing urban centers. To this should further be added purely economic motives, such as lower wages in rural districts and even small towns, the lower cost of industrial sites and buildings, and the absence of regulatory restrictions that in many cities would have hindered the establishment of the new industrial enterprises.

It is interesting to note that in more or less pronounced fashion and for the same reasons the older cities are found to have played very little part in the developmental process in the other countries of the West. What makes the point all the more interesting is that one observes that the countries which developed first (England, France, Switzerland, Belgium, the United States) were almost all little urbanized, while heavily urbanized countries (notably Spain, Italy, the Netherlands, and Portugal) figure prominently among the late developers. Although I cannot conclude with absolute assurance that a high level of urbanization acted as a brake on development during the nineteenth century, the facts nevertheless compel me to observe that in the relation between growth rates and levels of urbanization, as well as in the relation between levels of industrialization and levels of urbanization, a high level of urbanization appears to have had a negative impact.

Can we go even further and say that the first stages of the Industrial Revolution owed nothing at all to the urban system? The fact that the Industrial Revolution first began in agriculture would seem to support such a view. In England what has been termed the agricultural revolution preceded industrial changes by forty to fifty years. But such an interpretation goes too far. As a socioeconomic phenomenon, urbanization certainly encouraged the origin and international diffusion of the Industrial Revolution. The city has always provided a ready outlet for manufactured goods, while technological innovations were born and spread in urban areas far more than in rural areas. I shall return later to the relationship between the city and technology.

A trickier problem is that of the city's contribution to the agricultural revolution. The case of the Netherlands and of many other examples where urban pressure did not lead to a genuine agricultural revolution makes the determining role of the city very uncertain in this regard. Nor does the example of England offer evidence to strengthen such a theory. It would be a mistake, however, to argue that the city made no contribution whatever to the development of agriculture just because its contribution was small. By virtue both of its size and of its rapid growth, London certainly stimulated demand for agricultural products. But one can find many similar precedents for the case of London, not only in Europe, but in other societies of the traditional world as well. And the case of the Netherlands in particular—where the pressure of a large urban population conspicuously failed to precipitate a genuine agricultural revolution—makes it very unclear whether the city could have played a decisive part in this regard. To this must be added other evidence tending to minimize London's role. Most notably there is the fact that demographic pressure chiefly encouraged the adoption of farming techniques tending to increase yields rather than productivity, whereas productivity was the essential component of the agricultural revolution.

I said earlier that the city has always promoted the creation and diffusion of technological innovations. How, then, is it possible to explain the negative impact of urbanization on the international diffusion of industrialization that empirical analysis reveals? Here, too, uncertainties remain. In all likelihood, however, the answer for this riddle lies in the too elevated levels of urbanization, requiring the introduction of such notions as that of overurbanization, hyperurbanization, and so on. During the eighteenth century and the first half of the nineteenth century, Spain, Italy, Portugal, and the Netherlands had levels of urbanization and numbers of large cities that no longer corresponded with the antecedent economic functions that had stimulated this degree of urbanization. When all is said and done, one finds oneself in the presence of overurbanization, of a case of urban hypertrophy somewhat similar to what has existed for several decades now in the Third World (see part 4). And while the causes of this hypertrophy may have been different, the consequences were roughly the same. There is no doubt that this excessively high level of urbanization impeded the flow of investments into the productive sectors of the economy, owing precisely to the cities' need for food and sometimes for equipment as well. This overdeveloped urban sector also implied urban underemployment and thus a lowering of the productivity of the economy as a whole. Underemployment must also have been partly responsible for increasing the amount of employment in services, eventually resulting in inflexibility in the supply of labor and a lack of mobility.

Economic Development and Urbanization: Some Close and Obvious Links

The links between the enormous strides made in agricultural productivity after the Industrial Revolution and the rapid increase in the level of urbanization are obvious. Despite the improvements successively introduced by the cultures of antiquity and by the other cultures of Europe and Asia, the most advanced agricultural techniques in use in the seventeenth century still required, for the production of food and agricultural raw materials (essentially textiles) alone, the efforts of some 70–75% of the entire work force. In other words, no more than 25–30% of the working population was free to engage in nonagricultural forms of labor. In the absence of substantial imports of food (as was the rule in the larger economic units), this implied the impossibility of having a level of urbanization greater than about 20% if the limit defining urban populations is fixed at a population of 2,000. And if, as here, where the analysis gives particular emphasis to the period following the Industrial Revolution, the limit defining urban populations is set at 5,000, the maximum attainable level of urbanization drops to 15%.

I just said that in the larger economic units the absence of significant food imports was the rule. I would in fact do better to speak of the impossibility of such imports. For given the modest degree of agricultural productivity, surpluses of food available for export were very restricted, and only small countries with exceptional resources were able, by purchasing the surplus produced over vast regions, to support their cities by means of imports. This was notably the case of the Netherlands, which had a level of urbanization on the order of 40%. But, during this period the Netherlands imported enough grain to support around 50% of its total population. This grain came from regions with a population some 20–30 times greater than that of the Netherlands itself, which around 1700 had a population of some two million, representing 1.4% of the population of Europe, Russia included. Thanks to these imports the Netherlands was able to maintain some 55–70% of its labor force in nonagricultural sectors of the economy.

In other countries of Europe, having an unexceptional commercial function (and, as will be seen in part 4, the same applies to countries of the other continents as well), the proportion of the work force engaged in nonagricultural activities prior to the Industrial Revolution never exceeded 22–27%. Nor did the level of urbanization ever exceed 12–15%. In Europe (including Russia) and in other very large regions with advanced cultures, the proportion of the working population engaged in nonagricultural labor never went beyond 17–22% and the level of urbanization never went beyond 10–12%. In England as early as 1820, and without substantial food imports, nonagricultural workers already represented some 70% of the working population, and the level of urbanization had risen slightly above 30% (32–33% if one applies the criterion of 2,000). In 1913 the developed world as a whole, namely Western Europe and countries outside it settled by Europeans, already had half of its population in cities, and this despite the fact that, as a whole, it did not depend on external sources of food, the deficit in most of the countries of Europe being made up for by surpluses from other European-settled countries.

Statistical analysis confirms the close link during the whole nineteenth century between levels of economic development and levels of urbanization. Thus if one computes the linear correlation coefficient between real per capita GNP (that is, per capita GNP expressed in constant values and corrected to allow for international differences in price levels) and levels of urbanization, one finds very high and statistically very significant coefficients for each of the five periods for which I calculated percentages of urban population in a number of countries (for the nineteenth century: 1800, 1850, 1880, 1900, and 1910).

Thus, confining myself for the moment to the fourteen European countries for which the estimates of urban population are relatively good, I find correlation coefficients varying from a minimum of 0.68 for 1800 to a maximum of 0.89 for 1900, with average coefficients of 0.83 for the other three periods. If one computes coefficients for all developed countries (including those outside Europe), the relation becomes less close, but remains highly significant. For a total of twenty-two countries, the correlation coefficient varies from a minimum of

0.46 (for 1850) to a maximum of 0.67 (for 1880), the average for the other three periods being 0.65. One may therefore conclude that in Europe from as early as the 1850s, differences in levels of development explain some 60–70% of the differences in levels of urbanization. The remaining 30–40% are accounted for by other factors, such as the level of industrialization, the nature of the relief, forms of government, the composition and scale of national exports, and so forth, as well as the important contribution made by history, the urban legacy of the past.

The relation between economic development and urbanization will of course appear even closer if one considers evolution over time: in other words, if one compares, either for one or more regions or for one or more countries, the level of urbanization and the degree of economic development over several periods. Simply to give a general idea (for these statistics are less significant than those given above), I would point out that at the level of individual countries over the same five periods of the nineteenth century, one obtains very high coefficients of correlation. If Portugal is left out, the mean of the coefficients for the remaining twenty-one developed countries is 0.97, with only a very modest dispersion: the coefficient of variation is only 2.6%.

After 1930, and even more so after 1960, the relation between levels of development and urbanization becomes less close, but remains highly significant. Thus for the twenty-eight developed countries of the twentieth century (to the original list of twenty-two countries analyzed earlier, adding from 1919 Japan and the new nations created after the First World War by the partition of the Austro-Hungarian Empire and Poland), one obtains coefficients of correlation of 0.67 for 1930, 0.57 for 1950, and 0.35 for 1980. A change of this sort is perfectly predictable given the absolute limit on the level of urbanization, a limit absent in the case of economic development. As of 1950, a large number of countries were near a certain threshold which, while below the absolute limit of 100%, nevertheless seems to be a real limit linked to a new mode of behavior vis-à-vis urbanism—a mode of behavior I shall return to later.

Urbanization and Economic Development in the Nineteenth and Twentieth Centuries: Some Certainties, but Some Unknowns as Well

From the influence of economic development on urbanization, I shall now go on to the influence of urbanization on development. And while there are some certainties in this area, there are also some unknowns. In fact the unknowns outnumber the certainties. The uncertainty is explained by the complexity and multiplicity of the factors involved, coupled with the relative scarcity of studies devoted to the question. I shall start with the certainties. A first and important certainty concerns the role of urbanization as a factor in technological innovation.

The City and Innovation

The conclusion of chapter 20 is very clear: the city unquestionably encourages both innovation itself in the broadest sense of the word and its diffusion from one place to another. The modalities of this innovative role are many and obvious. I shall briefly summarize them.

First, the higher population density in cities facilitates human contacts, thereby accelerating the flow of information. Second, the diversity of urban activities quite naturally encourages attempts to apply or adopt in one sector (or in one specific problem area) technological solutions adopted in another sector. Third, cities tend to concentrate educational activities that throughout history have combined teaching and, if not research in the modern sense of the term, at least a certain systematic reflection. Fourth, the urban milieu provides a natural refuge for original spirits ill at ease in rural areas, where the pressure to conform is as a rule stronger. Last but not least, the city is, par excellence, the point of contact with other cities by way of trade and through the migration of artisans, laborers, and clerical and administrative staff between different cities. (Migrations between different rural regions have always been much rarer.)

All of this, together with other, less important factors, explains why the city contributes to innovation in general and to technological innovation in particular. Empirical analysis has confirmed this contribution, just as it has confirmed the role of cities in the diffusion of innovation. And since the positive impact of innovation on economic development is in no doubt, the city is for this reason alone a contributor to development.

One last bit of evidence will further strengthen, if this is necessary, our certainty in this regard: the positive effect of the size of cities on economic development. All the empirical studies lead to the same conclusion, namely, that a city's size favorably influences both innovation and its diffusion from one place to another. The larger a city is, the greater the number of innovations per capita, and the more rapid the adoption of the innovations. To be sure, this has mainly been established in the technological domain, but the less numerous analyses of innovation in other areas lead to very similar conclusions.

Urban Technological Innovations and Agricultural Development

The certain role of the city in stimulating and disseminating innovation brings me to another certainty concerning part of a vast problem about which many unknowns remain, and which I have approached in several chapters of this book. Here, as in the case of technology, I have to deal with a key element in the problem of economic development: the impact of urbanization on agriculture. Agriculture has undoubtedly benefited from many technological innovations originating in the cities. On the one hand, there have been general innovations in technology that have had obvious applications in agriculture. On the other hand, there have been technological innovations specifically designed for agriculture which were elaborated in the city. I shall look at a few important examples of each of these two ways in which technological innovation in the city has led to progress in agriculture.

The history of the rural effects of urban technological innovations is very ancient. It can in fact be argued that this history dates back to the very earliest phases of urbanization, with among other things the invention of writing and metallurgy. I shall pass over traditional societies to the stage opening with the Industrial Revolution. The two chief technological breakthroughs marking the start of the industrial age had important agricultural effects. The first and most important was the manufacture of cast iron and especially an appreciable improvement in the terms of trade between agricultural products and products manufactured from iron. Thus in France, for example, if one follows the movement of wholesale prices for iron and wheat, one observes that for a kilogram of wheat one could purchase 0.6 kilogram of iron around 1790, 0.9 kilogram of iron around 1850, and 1.4 kilograms of iron around 1900.

The price reduction resulting from this and other technological innovations made possible the wider use of iron in traditional agricultural equipment and in the perfecting of new equipment. This in turn unquestionably led to perceptible gains in agricultural productivity, without, however, being the decisive factor in those gains in productivity to which new methods of cultivation (the continuous rotation of crops) and new methods of seed selection doubtless contributed to an even greater extent. The impact of the mechanization of spinning on agriculture was perhaps as important as that of cheap iron, but the explanation for it is less obvious and consequently more uncertain. In a study in which I tried to determine the mechanisms underlying the Industrial Revolution (Bairoch, 1963) without concerning myself with the problem of urbanization, the agricultural effects of the mechanization of spinning appeared important. From a somewhat simplifying perspective, the mechanization of spinning led to the disappearance of rural textile manufacturing. The consequences of this differed depending on the dominant characteristics of the farms on which textile manufacturing had been carried out. On farms on which the quality of the land was marginal, textile manufacturing led in many cases to the complete abandonment of farming. By contrast, on farms with more fertile land, the time previously used for textile manufacturing went back to agriculture. All of this induced an increase in the average level of productivity in the agricultural sector.

Before moving on to what has been described as the second agricultural revolution, one should certainly also ask, without being able to arrive at any definite conclusion, about the influence of cities on the important innovations of the first agricultural revolution. To what extent did the new methods of selecting seeds and breeding stock take their cue from methodological considerations resulting from the general growth of scientific knowledge in which the city played so important a part? The same question arises about the improvements in the continuous rotation of crops, a practice that implies a general knowledge of soil science. All of this lies in the area of probability, not certainty, since here as in the case of industrial techniques the gropings of empiricists proceeding by trial and error made a significant contribution.

With the innovations of the second agricultural revolution it is already possible to be more certain. It may be recalled that the second agricultural revolution, which began about 1840–1870, was essentially characterized by two groups of innovations: those in agricultural machinery and those in artificial fertilizers. I shall look at each type of innovation separately, beginning with agricultural machinery.

During the first phases of the mechanization of farming, the urban component was not especially important. At least until the end of the nineteenth century the new machines did not involve principles so complex as to lie beyond the grasp of untutored practitioners. As a result, rural people were able to play a determining part. Thus McCormick, for instance, was raised on a farm where his father tried (often successfully) to perfect various machines; among them was the harvester that his son, remaining on the farm, eventually made truly operational. And it was also McCormick who founded the first factory manufacturing those machines. And further examples could be cited. Before very long, however, the production and also the improvement of farming equipment began to take place in urban settings. Moreover, had it not been for previous progress in mechanics and the manufacture of iron and steel, these inventions would probably not have been made, or would have encountered greater obstacles and delays.

In the case of artificial fertilizers, the city's contribution was decisive. This does not mean, however, that there was no empirical and therefore largely rural component of technological development of fertilizers. The practice of marling (mixing clay in sandy soil), for instance, was very ancient. But there is no doubt that artificial fertilizers, used from the second half of the nineteenth century and contributing substantially to the increase in European agricultural yields, resulted directly from breakthroughs in chemistry. Practically all of the great names in this field belong to scientists (generally university professors) thoroughly integrated into urban life. And this applies as much to the precursors who paved the way (along with Bernard Palissy, Lavoisier, Cavendish, Hermbstadt, and Thaer) as to the more direct contributors to the understanding of the needs of soils and to the perfecting of chemical fertilizers (Boussingault, Lawes, Liebig, and Ville).

Chemistry's influence on agriculture leads me to the twentieth century, and even to the second half of the twentieth century. Indeed, in the rapid progress recorded in yield and agricultural productivity over the last thirty to forty years, pesticides and herbicides have been a determining factor. And the whole development of these compounds has unquestionably been the fruit of research, even pure research. Also of urban origin were the motivation for and the perfecting of the internal combustion engine, an invention that substantially promoted the use of agricultural machinery. Tractors owe much of their efficiency, flexibility, and reliability to the enormous improvements in automobile design and construction. And while in the beginning, notably in the United States, the automobile was used more in rural areas than in urban areas, it was nevertheless a technological breakthrough inconceivable outside the urban framework. It suffices to mention the names of the most important innovators associated with the development of the automobile to reveal the importance of the city. Among the pioneers of the automotive industry, both in North America and in Europe, city residents greatly outnumber rural residents. And while it was not until the age of sixteen that Ford left the farm on which he was born to seek work in Detroit as an apprentice mechanic, mechanics was his ruling passion, a passion only the city could satisfy. (Nor should it be forgotten that vanadium steel, an urban invention, was the basis of the famous Model T.)

Besides the automobile, an important contribution was made to progress in agriculture by another urban innovation in transportation: the railroads. Even though in some regions the railroads unquestionably caused serious problems in the agricultural sector, in the last analysis the benefits distinctly outweighed the disadvantages. The first effect (as in the case of the mechanization of spinning) was the concentration of production in regions better suited to cultivation. This concentration made itself felt in two ways. There was first the transfer to the wide open spaces of the countries settled by Europeans overseas of a sizable fraction of the production of grain and livestock. Second, there was increasing regional specialization in the cultivation of crops, a specialization that, though often creating serious social problems, nevertheless further enhanced yields and productivity. On a more general level, the railroads enlarged the markets for agricultural products, and also the possibility of providing equipment and especially fertilizer to rural regions. In France, for instance, which made only moderate use of artificial fertilizers, the consumption of these products and other chemicals used for agriculture had risen by 1913 to 2.8 million metric tons. Assuming an average railroad journey of three hundred kilometers, this would have required (had horses been used for transport) the mobilization throughout the entire year of some 400,000 horses and 200,000 drivers; and this assuming the most favorable conditions: a daily capacity of 7 ton-kilometers per horse, or 2,100 ton-kilometers per year.

The City and the Demand for Agricultural Products

I shall now turn to one last important effect of cities on the rural world following the initial phases of the Industrial Revolution: the impact of urbanization through increasing demand for agricultural products, especially food. There is no question that increasing urban demand favored a high sale of agricultural commodities. But while the overall consumption of agricultural products may have grown, there is no reason to think that average per capita consumption was higher in cities than in the country. The opposite may even have been the case. And since until the start of the twentieth century, and even later, the city acted as something of a brake on demographic growth (fertility being lower, while mortality was higher), the city constituted for this reason a brake on demand. Finally, from the 1860s, the pronounced liberalization of tariff policies for the importation of food encouraged buyers to satisfy demand by turning to the open lands overseas, which in Europe diminished the incentives for more progress in agricultural yield and productivity.

Nevertheless an entirely new phenomenon in demographic history has to be taken into account. Beginning around 1880–1900 (and much earlier in England), the population of the developed world began to grow as it never had before. For dating from this period, despite the fact that total population increased at the fastest rate ever recorded (1.1% per year) and despite the fact that the natural growth rate in rural areas also reached unprecedented heights (1.2% per year), the number of people living in rural areas remained stable. Through migrations, the process of urbanization was able to absorb the entire surplus rural population. This meant that there was no increase in the rural work force. The important point here is that an increase in the demand for agricultural products occurred without an increase in the density of population on the land. As a result, the chances for gains in productivity improved. Dating from the 1920s, moreover, growth in total population was accompanied by a decrease in the number of workers engaged in farming.

In short, it seems that beginning in the final quarter of the nineteenth century urbanization contributed more powerfully to progress in agriculture and, most decisively, to progress in agricultural productivity than it had ever done before. From this time, the impact of urban demand was added to the consequences of the flow of technological innovations originating in the cities.

In a way the impact of urban demand must have been still greater after 1910–1920 than before. After this time, the rise in the standard of living stimulated a rapid increase in the consumption of a greater variety of agricultural products such as milk, meat, vegetables, and fruit. This in turn encouraged changes in the structure of agricultural production in developed countries. But by this stage agriculture, once the dominant sector, had become merely one sector among many in the economies of developed nations (in 1930 the agricultural work force accounted for only 30% of the total working population in Western Europe and only 23% in North America).

The City and Money

To the extent that one believes the monetarization of the economy favored economic development, the city unquestionably played a positive role in this domain too. The rural world is par excellence a world based on subsistence farming and barter. The urban world, on the other hand, is the world of the market and for this reason of monetary forms of payment. The part played by industrialization in this connection has been as important as that of urbanism. Indeed, so long as industry retained its original craft character, three sets of factors considerably reduced the need to use money. First of all, there was the limited consumption of manufactured goods. Second, a substantial part of production was done by farmers for their own consumption. Finally, even urban craftsmen bartered a fraction of their output. Obviously the situation completely changed with industrialization, where trade involves middlemen and leads to the almost complete disappearance of the rural artisan and of barter.

The City and Social Mobility

To the old proverb, "city air makes you free," could be added another just as true, especially for the period following the Industrial Revolution. This one involves a pun of sorts: "City air facilitates upward mobility." Without question, the urban world is much more amenable than life in the countryside to social mobility, whether horizontal or vertical.

As for horizontal mobility, the simple fact of moving to the city implies in almost every instance a change in economic activity. But this is not the most important point. The important thing is the opportunity to move through innumerable sectors of urban economic life, both in industry and in services. And there is the opportunity to move around within a given sector, something much more difficult in the rural world, whether one is a farm owner or a mere hired hand.

As for vertical mobility, this too occurs in many different ways in the city. Within a given sector or firm the chances of promotion are greater than in the country. The transition from hired hand to salaried employee, even within a single sector, also constitutes a promotion of sorts, more subjective than real, but no less important for that. The world of teaching plays a dual role in this context: as a factor in social promotion by virtue of the education it dispenses and as a factor in economic promotion by reason of the growing number of teachers. Social promotion, moreover, has often preceded migration. For the sons and daughters of farmers, becoming a schoolteacher has often meant moving to the city.

Social mobility of this sort has unquestionably worked in favor of economic development, notably by permitting a better match between the supply and demand of qualified personnel. These positive aspects should not obscure the reverse side of the coin, which, it is true, chiefly applies to the first stages of the Industrial Revolution (until around 1860–1880). During this early period the standard of living had risen very little relative to what it had been in traditional economies; and this was combined with the absence of organized trade unions. During the first phases of the Industrial Revolution, then, the move from the rural environment to the urban environment usually implied—owing to the status of the worker in industry—a loss of individual freedom on the job, a rise in the number of working hours, and terrible housing conditions. All of this in large part explains the disproportionately high urban mortality rate. For indeed, as has been shown, migrating to the city meant increasing by about 50% the mortality rate for babies and young children and shortening by some eight to twelve years the life expectancy of adolescents. And this excess mortality rate persisted until the last years of the nineteenth century.

The City and the Size of the Market for Industrial Goods

The generally accepted viewpoint is that over the course of the nineteenth century, by concentrating an ever larger population in one place, the cities gradually became major markets. The emergence of very great cities in particular suggests such a situation. By 1850 the five cities with populations of more than 500,000 in the developed world had a greater population than the total population of the four Scandinavian countries, Portugal, and Switzerland combined in 1700. And by 1900 the nine cities with populations of more than a million in the developed world had a population greater than that of the countries just cited plus Belgium, the Netherlands, Scotland, Ireland, and the five Balkan states combined in 1700. This means that in 1900 nine cities had more people than sixteen countries did two hundred years earlier.

As I noted earlier, during the urban growth of the sixteenth and seventeenth centuries the increasing size of cities favored the division of labor within the cities. For they came to constitute in themselves sufficient markets for a vast array of goods, luxury goods in particular. But can one be sure that the same process was at work during the nineteenth century for manufactured goods? I am not at all convinced, for there is a tendency to overlook another phenomenon serving to increase the size of the market needed for industries. I have in mind, quite simply, the sharp rise in the productive capacity of the enterprises themselves resulting from both technological progress and commercial concentration. Thus to take one example, the average European iron manufacturer at the start of the eighteenth century had a productive capacity roughly equal to the amount of iron used by some 100,000–200,000 people. By the end of the nineteenth century, despite the fact that, in the interval, per capita consumption of iron had increased forty- or fiftyfold, the average firm satisfied the needs of some 600,000–800,000 people, five times more than at the start of the eighteenth century. During this time, however, the average size of European cities had only doubled at most (increasing by a factor of two if the limit defining urban populations is set at 2,000 and by 1.4 if the limit is set at 5,000). This example from the iron industry is not necessarily representative of the average situation in all industrial sectors, and in the absence of studies specifically devoted to this question it is difficult to be certain of the extent to which it departed from the general norm. But judging from the summary analyses I have been able to carry out, it appears likely that an analogous state of affairs existed in most other sectors.

The analysis of the optimal size of industrial enterprises provides an interesting indirect approach to the problem. With the exception of a few sectors like iron and steel and the automotive industry, the optimal size of industrial concerns in the contemporary period in developed countries lies at what appears to be a relatively low level. It should be noted that this level appears low only when viewed in the perspective of modern notions of scale, in which giant corporations seem, quite mistakenly, to be the rule. When compared with what was the optimal size in traditional societies, the current optimal level will appear much higher.

In any event, according to the data I have collected (Bairoch, 1977a), the dominant optimal size stands at around 600–800 workers (and the mean optimum size of the 50% of the sectors where the optimum is higher is around 800–1,000 workers.) When allowance is made for a large set of additional factors, one can conclude that in contemporary developed countries, a city with a population of 50,000–70,000 will support an adequate number of businesses (around ten) of a size close to the optimum. These parameters would obviously be different from the point of view of markets for goods. Assuming a consumption of manufactured goods amounting to 35% of overall consumption, I find that a city with a population of about 150,000–200,000 will provide a sufficient market for around ten firms near the optimal size. It is true that in practice, given the necessity of offering a wide range of options to consumers, it does not make sense to suppose that a city is supplied only by its own businesses. But here it is a question of comparing two different theoretical situations in different historical periods.

Naturally in the context of traditional societies it is difficult to find any valid basis for estimating what would have been the average optimal size of manufacturing firms. Basing my calculations chiefly on the predominant size of industrial concerns in traditional societies, however, I find that the optimal size was very likely below 20–30 workers. Taking this as a base, and assuming a consumption of manufactured goods amounting to 10–12% of overall consumption, and making allowance as above for additional parameters, ten concerns of a size approaching the optimum would have required for a market a population of something like 10,000–15,000. This market is one-tenth the size of the one required by the same number of concerns of corresponding size in the 1970s, while the average size of cities in the developed world has in the interval increased only by a factor of three if the limit defining urban populations is set at 5,000, or a factor of four if the limit is set at 2,000. It is, however, much more significant to note that the proportion of the urban population of Europe living in cities with populations of more than 15,000 around 1700 and the proportion living in cities with populations of more than 200,000 in 1970 were identical (by chance, my calculations give exactly the same figure in each case, 66%).

Looking at the problem from this angle, we find the same paradox as in the case of development in the iron and steel industry. As the result of progress in technology the size of the required market for an industrial concern has increased at a much faster rate than the average size of cities, and at a rate about equal to that of the predominant size of cities. Thus, except for the upper fringe of very large cities (say, those with populations of more than 500,000 in the nineteenth century and more than one million in the twentieth century), it seems unlikely that the city any more than before provided a market sufficient in itself to support industrial development and therefore economic development. Indeed, it even seems possible, if not probable, that the opposite is the case, since by applying our modern notions of scale scholars have tended to overestimate the optimal size of enterprises in the framework of traditional economies. Finally, it is significant to observe that when Pred (1962) sought to test empirically the hypothesis that industrialization leads to a widening of the geographic zone of a city's external relations he did not obtain the results he had hoped for—and this despite the fact that his research was on the period 1868–1890 in the city of Göteborg, which is in a region for which information is very abundant for the period studied. The only domain in which there was any broadening of the city's external relations was in the zone from which immigrants were recruited.

It appears, then, that growth in the size of cities has not in itself been an important factor in creating the markets needed for industrial enterprises to expand and develop. Certainly in the absence of such growth the rationalization of production would have run up against serious commercial obstacles: in the absence of expanding markets, there would be few incentives for improving industrial techniques in order to enhance productivity. But it seems difficult to conclude that the increase in the size of cities was in this case the driving force, though this does not in the least diminish the importance of the fact that industry found most of its markets in urban settings.

The Overall Balance Sheet

I shall now draw up the overall balance sheet for the relations between urbanization and economic development after the first phases of the Industrial Revolution. These relations were certainly positive: even though closer empirical scrutiny has obliged me to qualify rather heavily certain of my presumptions in this regard, urbanization has indeed favored the development of the Western World. As I have shown over the course of this and preceding chapters, urbanization was a factor in economic development in many ways: by favoring innovations and their diffusion; by inducing the monetarization of society; by facilitating social mobility and a closer match between the supply of and the demand for skilled labor; and by widening the markets for agricultural and industrial goods. But unknowns still remain, work enough for generations of historians of urbanism.

By contrast, the margin of uncertainty is much smaller for the impact of development on urbanization in the West. It was the development resulting from the Industrial Revolution that made it possible to break the many barriers to urban growth in former centuries.

Before going on to examine the other aspect of economic development, that of the Third World of today, it is necessary to recall the recent change that has taken place in the process of urbanization. The slowdown in the growth of the cities of the developed world (see chapter 19) unmistakably reflects a new mistrustful attitude toward the city. Does this indicate a transient phenomenon or an enduring trend? And to what extent will the changes in urban policies, aiming at the revitalization of the inner cities, the creation of pedestrian streets, the introduction of electric cars (in the future), and so forth, precipitate a return of the ancient preference for city life? On the other hand, is there not a chance that the decentralization both at the level of employment and at the level of entertainment, education, and the flow of information made possible by the new breakthroughs in data processing will lead to a great dispersion of all nonagricultural households? Clearly the number of variables involved is too great and their influences too difficult to gauge and too contradictory for me to be able to make any valid predictions of what the future may bring.

Part Four
Urbanism in the Third World

Between the beginning of the sixteenth century and the years 2010–2020, the spatial distribution of the world's urban population will have completed a full cycle. Around 1500 the regions that make up today's Third World accounted for three-quarters of the world's urban population. By the 1930s their share had fallen to one-quarter. Since then, however, it has begun to grow once more, and was one-half by 1980. And assuming that in the interval no major change of direction occurs in current demographic trends, by 2010–2020 these regions will once again have three-quarters of the world's urban population. It is on the Third World component of this cycle that part 4 will focus.

Over the next nine chapters I shall tackle three entirely separate problems. The first problem concerns non-European societies before the sixteenth century, that is, before colonization by the West. To begin with, the whole notion of a Third World is an anachronism. Moreover, the questions one may ask about urban life in the precolonial societies of Asia, Africa, and the New World are related to those of the cities of traditional Europe. Indeed this analysis will serve to highlight the special character of urbanism in Europe as much as that of the cities of the various non-European worlds. The non-European worlds have very heterogeneous urban features and are for that reason sharply distinct from each other. The second problem, focusing on the impact of colonization on urban life outside Europe from the start of the sixteenth century to the 1930s, will concern the Third World as we know it today. The third problem is the crucial problem of the urban explosion with which the Third World has had to contend since 1920–1940.

The history of urbanization in the various non-European societies before the nineteenth century will be the main theme of chapters 22 and 23. But since this involves at least two separate urban systems (those of Asia and the Islamic cultures), the analysis cannot be as detailed as that of urbanism in traditional Europe. Moreover, uncertainties continue to be abundant in this area, making exhaustive treatment impossible. As for the cultures of the pre-Columbian New World and Black Africa, I refer the reader to what I have already had to say on this score in chapter 4.

The impact of colonization on urbanism outside of Europe has had many forms, from the foundation of Batavia in Java by the Dutch in the seventeenth century to the foundation of Leopoldville in the Congo by the Belgians in the twentieth century; or from Mexico City rising from the ruins of Tenochtitlan, one of the largest cities, if not the single largest city, of the pre-Columbian New World, to Calcutta, once a small village that, beginning with the establishment of a trading post by the East India Company, eventually became the largest city in the Indian peninsula. Chapters 24, 25, and 26 will therefore cover a whole array of distinctive socioeconomic conditions. These three chapters should also be regarded as an introduction to the problem of urbanization in the Third World. This problem will be examined in greater detail than any other dealt with in this part of the book, four chapters being reserved for it (chapters 27, 28, 29, and 30). These last four chapters will show that the ever more rapid urbanization of the Third World has created a situation never before met with in the history of humanity, and that it raises serious problems, not only for the present, but above all for the future.

22 The Cities of Asia: Socioeconomic Systems Different from Those of Europe □

Were the socioeconomic systems of Asia different from those of Europe? This question has fueled many controversies since Marx suggested that Asia had a specific mode of production: a mode of production which implies a type of relation between town and country distinct from that found in Europe. Needless to say, I too shall tackle this question. But faithful to the method followed in the rest of the book, I shall do so only after trying to analyze the links between the city and the economy in the principal cultures of Asia. I shall, moreover, adopt a historical perspective, taking up the evolution of the urban societies of Asia from the point at which I left it in chapter 3, namely, during the first stages of urbanization. This analysis will be more or less successful depending on the availability (or rather unavailability) of data for the various societies concerned. In order to assure some uniformity of treatment, I shall follow the same order as in chapter 3. Thus I shall begin with India, moving on from there to concentrate in somewhat greater detail on China, bringing the chapter to a close with a brief discussion of Japan and Southeast Asia.

India: An Apogee of Urban Life under the Mogul Empire

Given the enormous number of unknowns, even a summary history of urbanization in India during this period is out of the question. I shall therefore have to content myself with highlighting a few salient points.

Up until the ninth and tenth centuries India had relatively few cities, and what cities there were remained small. With his customary shrewdness and courage and armed with the detailed account left by a Chinese Buddhist of his travels through India, Russell (1972a) has attempted to estimate the population of the principal Indian cities around the years A.D. 629–645. Even if we accept the upper limit Russell places on the density of the sites described (a limit that is far from excessive: 100 inhabitants per hectare), there would only have been about seven cities with populations of more than 50,000 (none of them with populations of as much as 100,000) and perhaps another thirty or forty cities with populations of 20,000–50,000.

This finding, together with other, still more pertinent arguments, induces Russell to cast doubt on the traditional image of India as being overpopulated for nearly two millennia. It has generally been thought, particularly on the basis of written accounts left by travelling Buddhist monks, that between the last few centuries B.C. and the end of the eighteenth century the population of India was around 100–140 million. For Russell, on the other hand, especially around A.D. 650—when (chiefly owing to plagues) India apparently reached a demographic low watermark—the population was less than 50 million and probably even less than 30 million (a figure accepted by most demographers today).

It was apparently not until the eleventh century that the population of Indian cities surpassed 100,000 for the first time. By 1300, probably five cities, and perhaps six to ten, had surpassed this size. It may be recalled that during this same period, with a population of some 80–100 million, just about the same as India's, Europe also had five cities with populations of more than 100,000. On the basis of this rough criterion for determining the approximate size of the population of all Indian cities taken together, India in 1300 apparently had a level of urbanization comparable to that of Europe for the same period. The population of Indian cities appears to have continued to grow during the fourteenth and fifteenth centuries, but only at a fairly modest rate, except for Vijayanagar, whose role as capital enabled it to reach a population of 500,000 in the early sixteenth century. At this time Vijayanagar figured among the three largest cities in the world and was probably surpassed by Peking alone. Paris, the largest city in Europe, had a population of only 200,000–250,000 at this stage.

This highlights a feature peculiar to urbanism in Asia, one in evidence as early as the year 100 B.C.: the existence of one or more cities of great size. Between 100 B.C. and A.D. 1200 there were always one or two Asian cities among the three largest in the world. And between 1200 and 1820 there were invariably six or seven Asian cities (even excluding the Middle East) among the ten largest in the world. By contrast, there were only three around 1875, and none at all in 1900.

But to return to precolonial India, the unification brought about by the Mogul conquest (dating from 1526) had substantial consequences for urban and economic life. Between the reign of Akbar (beginning in 1556) and the reign of Aurangzeb (ending in 1707) came a period marked by pronounced economic development, although within the limits of a traditional economy. All of the available evidence suggests that there was perceptible progress in both agriculture and industry. And since the Mogul conquest involved the imposition of an administration foreign in cultural, religious, and geographic terms, it led to the creation of a certain number of new cities and to the integration of existing urban centers as a mechanism of political control over the country as a whole.

In practical terms, this induced a surge of urbanization whose extent, given the current state of research, it is impossible to measure accurately, but that unquestionably raised the level of urbanization in India to a point close to, if not slightly greater than, that reached in Western Europe during the same period. In any event, as I noted earlier, the larger Indian cities were larger than the larger European cities. Agra, founded only in 1506 and remaining the seat of the central government until 1638, very likely had a population of 500,000, perhaps even 650,000, by the time the seat of government was transferred to Delhi. And by around 1700 Delhi itself had probably reached the half-million mark. India as a whole had at least ten to twelve and perhaps as many as twenty other cities with populations of more than 100,000, the largest of which was Ahmedabad, with (at its height) a population of 400,000. As far as the level of urbanization is concerned, the historian I. Habib (1982) put it at 15% around 1600 (but he apparently includes very small cities).

But more important than these figures for the probable level of urbanization and the population of the cities is the fact that, taking all of the cities of this period, one is unquestionably dealing here with industrial and commercial centers whose sphere of economic influence was far from purely local. As Naqvi (1968) showed with reference to the cities of northern India, and which Gokhale (1972) confirmed: "the economy of seventeenth-century India can no longer be held to be static and fragmented into self-contained small regional units but was rapidly becoming quasi-continental," with cities "highly localized and specialized manufacturing centers." And while Russell's work in this area indicates that Indian cities of the sixth century were smaller than had been supposed, recent research on the seventeenth and eighteenth centuries rather suggests raising the previous figures for many cities.

In his cogent reflections on relations between town and country in Mogul India, moreover, Chaudhuri (1978) sharply underscores one particular aspect of the situation that has led Western writers to underestimate the extent of urbanism in precolonial India: the ecological aspect. When comparing the cities of their own countries with those of India, Europeans failed, among other things, to take differences in climate into account. While recognizing the substantial gaps in the urban history of India, especially where the links between the city and the economy are concerned, Chaudhuri insists on the similarity between urbanization in the subcontinent and in other parts of the world with respect to the close interdependence between cities, on the one hand, and both the economy and politics, on the other.

But things began to change in the eighteenth century. The death of Aurangzeb in 1707 meant the end of Indian unity and the fragmentation of the empire. The economy also apparently went into decline, further weakening Indian society which from 1757 on progressively succumbed to British domination. It is at this point, then, that European colonization genuinely got under way. But though very limited before this date, penetration by Europe had nevertheless already left its mark on urban life, promoting the creation of a few new cities dominated by Europeans. I shall examine the principal features of these new cities in chapter 24.

China from 200 B.C. to A.D. 1850: An Urban and Economic History Full of Contrasts

Whatever the population of the cities of ancient China may have been, the unification of the empire (in 221 B.C.) brought about regression in a great number of them. Almost all of the ancient capital cities were turned into the administrative seats of provincial prefects, and their regression may be easily explained in terms of the loss of function suffered in this way. What is more, it seems that the cities left out of the new administrative network declined even more. The number of prefectural seats varied around 1,400. And until the onset of what Elvin (1973) has called "the medieval revolution in market structure and urbanization," the Chinese urban system was closely determined by the administrative functions of the various types of cities. To cite one especially important example, each administrative region was allowed only one market, located in the regional capital or prefectural seat. This in no way precluded unequal development, some of these cities becoming commercial centers with spheres of influence larger than the regions of which they were the administrative capitals by a wide margin. But it did encourage a degree of uniformity, setting certain absolute limits on the range of differences.

Another characteristic of the first phase of urbanization after the unification of the empire was the rapid growth of the cities which were successively the imperial capital. One century after unification (100 B.C.) the population of Loyang (Honan) probably surpassed 300,000; the population of Sian (Changan), the capital between 583 and 906, probably reached one million around 700. Kaifeng, capital between 960 and 1127, did not have time enough to reach a very great size; but by around 1120 its population had nevertheless grown to about 400,000–450,000. But by this stage the capital had long stopped being the only great city in the Empire. According to Elvin's estimates, in the twelfth century cities with populations of more than 100,000 accounted for 6.0–7.5% of the total population. By contrast, cities with populations of more than 100,000 did not account for 6% of the total population of Europe until after the Industrial Revolution (for Europe except Russia around 1820; when Russia is included around 1865).

But in the twelfth century the "medieval urban revolution," which essentially concerned the trade system, was already two centuries old. This revolution introduced a pronounced relaxation of the regulations permitting only one market town per region and the collapse of the rigid system of laws regulating commercial exchange. This induced (or was itself induced by) an increasing monetarization of the economy, a more important role for merchants, and an intensification of long-distance trade—in short, the emergence of cities with well-developed economic and commercial bases. Though this illustrates the synchronicity of events in China (and perhaps in parts of Asia less well known than China) and in Europe, I must nevertheless emphasize that even during this period Chinese cities were far less independent than their European counterparts. But I leave this question until later. Now I shall look into the relative size of the urban population of China and the factors that may explain the level of urbanization reached.

A High Level of Urbanization by the Twelfth Century

According to Elvin, the level of urbanization in China had by the twelfth century reached at least 10%—say 10–12%. This would have implied an urban size structure very different from that of Europe, marking a substantial deviation from Davis's Law. For in Europe 6–7% of the total population came to be concentrated in cities with populations of more than 100,000 only when the overall level of urbanization (calculated using the criterion of 5,000) had reached 14%. In arriving at his figures, Elvin probably included cities with populations of even less than 5,000. By contrast, fixing the limit at 3,000, Rozman (1973) calculates a perceptibly lower level of urbanization, on the order of 6–7%. And even adding towns with populations of less than 3,000 and with a market to Rozman's roster, one still obtains a level of urbanization of no more than 7–9%. This difference is all the more striking in that Rozman's analyses seem to indicate that the urban size structure in China was not far from the European pattern. But the wonder expressed by Marco Polo, coming from Italy where the level of urbanization was something like 15–21%, and other quantitative as well as qualitative evidence suggests a spread closer to Elvin's than Rozman's. In my view 10–13% of the population of China lived in cities with populations of more than 5,000, making a level of urbanization 1–2 points higher than that in Europe (except Russia) during the same period and close to the maximum reached in Europe (minus Russia) at any time before the Industrial Revolution.

It is not difficult to account for so high a level of urbanization if one considers the economic environment of China during this period. There is no doubt that by the ninth century, and even more by the thirteenth century, agriculture had reached a level that even the most agriculturally advanced parts of Europe did not reach until the seventeenth century and even, in certain respects, until after the agricultural revolution of the eighteenth century. By the thirteenth century China had already adopted the rotation of crops, more highly developed plows, seed selection, and so forth, and many agricultural treatises were in circulation. In the South farmers cultivated at least thirty-three varieties of rice; and in some southern regions, a judicious choice of strains made possible two and sometimes even three harvests per year. Chinese advances in industrial techniques and money are well known. It does not seem superfluous to mention, however, that the age of canals began in China by the fifth century, and that the construction of new canals continued through the following centuries. As a result, the network of Chinese canals was already very extensive by the twelfth and thirteenth centuries. It is thought that during this period, by means of the canals connecting them, the various river basins formed an integrated national system of waterways. There was also transportation along the coasts, for which ships with a capacity of around one hundred metric tons had been specially designed for transporting cereals.

It was not only domestic trade that prospered: for a time foreign trade also flourished. As Ma (1971) shows, under the Sung dynasty (960–1279), maritime trade increased greatly and provided the basis for the very substantial growth of some coastal cities. The image of a China closed in on itself, greeting foreign traders with distrust, as seen by Europeans beginning in the sixteenth century when they came into direct contact with the Celestial Empire, has no bearing whatever on the centuries of interest here. Commercial relations with the outside world were not only tolerated, but actively sought and encouraged. Thus the edict of 1137 issued by the Emperor Kao Tsung declared, among other things: "The profits from maritime trade are very great. If they are managed adequately, they can bring in a million [monetary units of the period]. Is this not better than to tax the people?" Foreign merchants were not only welcomed, but were sometimes feted and were authorized to establish themselves in many cities. Moreover China itself dispatched trade missions abroad and participated directly in international exchange.

As early as 971 Canton had a customs house, and beginning in 1064, customs houses were set up in nine other cities. Chuanchow founded its own in 1087 and became the chief port in China, its renown under the name of Zaiton spreading throughout the whole medieval world in the twelfth century. Though of little importance before taking on this commercial role, Chuanchow grew rapidly, reaching a population of perhaps 500,000 at its height during the thirteenth and fourteenth centuries (after the fifteenth and sixteenth centuries it dwindled to merely average size, practically vanishing by the mid-nineteenth century). According to the great Arab traveller and writer Ibn Batuta, who by the end of his life had traveled some 120,000 kilometers, Chuanchow was the largest port in the world. China imported chiefly luxury agricultural products, exporting manufactured goods, mainly textiles.

All of these factors (advanced agriculture and industry, and flourishing foreign trade) explain the high level of urbanization and also the great size of the larger Chinese cities. Around 1300 at least four cities had populations between 200,000 and 500,000, the population of the capital, Hang-chou, being perhaps considerably larger. Indeed, in addition to the large quantities of rice paid in taxes and private rents to urban landowners, Hang-chou received on the average, through the trade of its merchants, some 116,000 metric tons of rice per year. If it is assumed that total supplies amounted to only 200,000 metric tons and that annual per capita consumption was 250 kilograms, this gives a population of 800,000.

Rice: A Factor in Urbanization?

The difference between rice and wheat is crucial. Like the potatoes and maize of the pre-Columbian societies, rice is more favorable to urbanization than wheat. Rice supplies around 3,600 calories per kilogram, as against 3,400 for wheat, which eases transport problems. But the great advantage of rice is the higher yield. I may very roughly estimate that in the framework of traditional societies, and basing my calculations on the average situation in advanced macroregions, one hectare of land yielded 1,600 kilograms of rice, as opposed to only 600 of wheat. In both cases, about 100 kilograms would have to be reserved to sow one hectare of land in the following year. Therefore in terms of usable output, the ratio in favor of rice is 1,500 to 500, or 3 to 1; and if caloric value is taken into account the ratio rises to 3.2 to 1. Furthermore, as was shown earlier, in many parts of China farmers could produce two harvests per year. This means that, if we assume identical levels of productivity and possibilities for a surplus per agricultural worker, the area needed to provision a city in a rice-producing region would have been three to six times smaller than that for a city in a wheat-producing region. This is probably part of the explanation for the large size of Asian cities. But only a part. For on the one hand, the contribution of other factors should not be overlooked; and on the other, the proposition as set forth above contains an important qualification: the assumption of identical levels of productivity and surplus. But to my knowledge, there has been no serious analysis of the relative rates of productivity for these two types of cultivation within the framework of traditional societies. Nor should it be forgotten that the earliest urbanized region in China, the North, produced wheat (first, millet). But agriculture was very early in this part of China, and soybeans played an important role (see chapter 3).

The period between 1300–1350 and 1450–1500 is considered to

have been a negative phase from the economic point of view. The explanation generally given invokes the classic mechanism of a growing population running up against a brake in food resources—often referred to as a Malthusian brake. Then again, this was also the era of the Mongol invasions, accompanied by the massacres, famines, and epidemics usually associated with periods of strife. As for epidemics, it should be remembered that the Black Death appears to have struck China too, and earlier than Europe, beginning in the 1330s, a period further marked in China by numerous natural catastrophes exacting a heavy toll of human life.

Around 1300, a large proportion of the land suitable for farming was already under cultivation. Population had probably grown from 50–80 million around the year 1000 to 120–130 million around 1200. It seems then to have stagnated during the thirteenth century, and reached a low of some 65–80 million around 1400 before renewed population growth got under way in the early fifteenth century. It is illusory to try to determine the change in the level of urbanization during this troubled period. After analyzing the fragmentary data available, I came to the very tentative conclusion that the level of urbanization in China followed a course similar to that recorded in Europe over the same period, meaning that the level reached at the start of the fourteenth century was maintained.

At the beginning of the sixteenth century, by which time China had been ruled by the Ming dynasty for a century and a half and had a population of some 110–140 million, the level of urbanization seems to have risen to a point slightly higher than that of the beginning of the fourteenth century, say around 11–14%. This represented a level of urbanization a little higher than that of Europe during the same period; but as before, China had a few very great cities. At this time Peking, which had become the capital once more in 1421 (as it had been between 1267 and 1368), certainly had a population of more than 600,000; and there were at least four other cities with populations of more than 300,000.

A Population Explosion and a Decline in Urbanization: The Absence of an Agricultural Revolution

Beginning in the sixteenth century and particularly at the start of the seventeenth century, there was strong growth in population, which continued until the middle of the nineteenth century, with a brief halt or decline (depending on the estimates) in the first half of the seventeenth century. The population rose from 110–140 million around 1500 to 140–160 million around 1600 (and also around 1700) before rising to 310–330 million about 1800 and to 420–440 million about 1850. This amounts to an annual growth rate of 0.3–0.4% between 1500 and 1850, and 0.6–0.8% for the period from 1700 to 1850 alone. This veritable explosion in population beginning at the start of the eighteenth century (and which gave birth to a Chinese Malthus) is unique in the history of the major regions of the world during the preindustrial age. Even in Europe, already in the initial phases of modern development, population grew during this period by only 0.4–0.6% per year, the growth rate in the rest of the world, Europe and China excluded, being a mere 0.1–0.3%. In the long term this rapid population growth seems to have been due less to improved economic conditions than to the absence of wars and to various social factors, chief among them being the progressive disappearance of serfdom which, still extremely strict and widespread in the sixteenth century, had already become very marginal by the middle of the eighteenth century. Another important factor was the adoption of food crops from the New World, especially maize, potatoes and peanuts. Around the mid-nineteenth century, a population three times greater than that of the sixteenth century had at its disposal only about two to three times more land, much of it of marginal value. This goes a long way toward explaining the Malthusian blockage already noticeable at the end of the eighteenth century but very marked by the mid-nineteenth century. But by the middle of the nineteenth century China was already subjected to the heavy constraints of colonial domination (see chapter 25). For now I shall look back on the centuries preceding the nineteenth, which were probably characterized by unfavorable economic development, especially during the second half of the eighteenth century.

These negative developments are indirectly confirmed by the changes in urban population. It is certain that urban population did not grow as rapidly as overall population. According to my own calculations, based on the surveys of Chandler and Fox (1974), between 1500 and 1850 the population of the larger cities grew by a factor of 2.0–2.1, and total population grew by a factor of 3.8–4.5. Between 1700 and 1850 the population of these same cities roughly doubled, while total population tripled. This would imply a decline in the level of urbanization, even though the population of the smaller cities may have grown at a faster rate. This decline is confirmed by Skinner (1977), who calculates for 1843 a level of urbanization of 4.1–4.6% using the criterion of 5,000 to define urban centers, and 4.9–5.3% using the criterion of 2,000. These figures seem, however, to indicate that the proportion of very small cities was much lower than in Europe (in my view, too low). In order to determine more accurately the rest of the urban population of China, I have made some calculations of my own based on cities with populations of more than 100,000 and adapting to the "Chinese model" estimates of likely omissions and the ratios of large to small cities used to establish urban population under similar circumstances in the case of Europe. According to these calculations, the level of urbanization seems to have been 6.0–7.5%

(using the criterion of 5,000), pointing to a pronounced decline in the relative size of the urban population, though not so pronounced as Skinner's figures would lead one to believe.

This decline in the level of urbanization does not mean that the urban network remained unchanged. On the contrary, as Sen-dou Chang (1963) remarks, more cities were created under the Ching dynasty (1644–1911) than under any other dynasty before it. But it was also under this dynasty that overall population grew most rapidly, whence the pronounced decline in the level of urbanization, a decline which in no way implies a diminution in total population, but quite the opposite. As Elvin (1978) notes, the growth in total population brought about a rise in overall population density that led to a great reduction in the former contrast between town and country. In this context Elvin seconds the observation made by Baron von Richtofen in the 1870s: "The difference between villages and cities is generally more in size than in character, and the smallest hamlet has a tinge of the city." But this observation may apply to a great many European villages as well.

One of the Limits of Traditional Societies

The decline in the level of urbanization in China may be related to my observations concerning the limits on urbanization in Europe within the framework of traditional economies. In China, given its growing population and an already densely inhabited territory, additional expansion or even simply the maintenance of the level of urbanization reached at the start of the eighteenth century would not have been possible without rapid and substantial change in agricultural productivity. What would have been needed, in short, was an agricultural and industrial revolution of the sort that occurred in eighteenth-century England. The question of the causes of the absence of such a revolution remains open, and will continue to remain open for a long time to come. As I see it, however, one explanation, and an important one at that, lies in the high population density on agricultural land in China in the early eighteenth century. By around 1600, according to the estimates of Perkins (1969), there must have been some 4–6 people per hectare of cultivated land. By 1700, there appear to have been 5–7. This means that China was three to five times more densely populated than England, where on the eve of the Industrial Revolution there were certainly fewer than 2 and probably fewer than 1.5 people per hectare of cultivated land. To be sure, as was just seen, rice makes it possible to support three times as many people per hectare as wheat. But quite apart from the fact that a good deal of arable land was given over to the cultivation of wheat in China too, rice alone would not have eliminated the obstacles population density put in the way of a genuine agricultural and industrial revolution.

On the other hand, and this is a very important point, whatever the real reasons for the absence of an agricultural revolution, the case of China provides a powerful argument for those who believe that demographic pressure does not constitute a factor sufficient to bring about industrial revolution. This would appear to hold true, moreover, even when this pressure—where it does not lead, as so often happens, to catastrophic collapse—compels a society to effect a profound reorganization, a compulsion reflected in the case of China by the decline in urbanization among other things. A decline in urbanization of this sort could have postponed the catastrophe by leaving a greater proportion of the production of food for rural districts at a time when, as all the available evidence suggests, food production decreased in terms of quantity per capita.

Thus is found also in the case of China the agricultural determinism that was at work in the context of traditional Europe. Those periods likely to have been marked by an increase in agricultural productivity were also those registering a rise in the level of urbanization. On the other hand, whenever agricultural productivity entered a negative phase, or perhaps a decline, the level of urbanization also fell. Certainly, given the unreliability of the available data, the case of China cannot be said to prove that such a link existed between the level of agricultural productivity and the level of urbanization. But coupled with examples met with in other parts of the book, it reinforces the likelihood that such a link existed.

Before passing on to specific problems of the cities of Asia, I shall review the major features of the urban history of traditional Japan, the country with the third largest population in Asia, and survey the main features of the urban history of Southeast Asia.

Japan: An Urbanized Society

Moving from India and China to Japan involves a complete change of scale even though Japan had the third largest population in Asia. As has been seen, India and China each had a human mass roughly comparable to that of Europe. Japan, on the other hand, stood on a par with one of the larger European countries and had a population equal to no more than one-eighth that of either India or China. The available figures are too unreliable to establish the relevant orders of magnitude. Probably Japan had some 10–14 million inhabitants around 1500 and somewhere near 25 million by the start of the eighteenth century.

Although true cities emerged very late in Japan (around 650–700), the process of urbanization proved rapid (see chapter 3). And as elsewhere in Asia, large cities appeared very early on. By the twelfth and thirteenth centuries, there was a fairly dense urban network of fairly substantial cities. This phase continued until the end of the sixteenth century, when the central authority reinforced once more its hold over the country.

The period from the late sixteenth century to the early eighteenth century was marked by renewed urban growth. The population of the larger cities increased and the urban network as a whole was enriched by the addition of new members. Rozman (1973) estimates that around 1700 Japan was the most heavily urbanized country in the world, a view shared by Hanley and Yamamura (1977), and also implicitly by Takeo (1968). This is also the opinion of Kornhauser (1976), who argues that Japan must have been the most heavily urbanized country in the world in the seventeenth century as well as the eighteenth century. Certainly this position is mistaken, for like almost all researchers in the field Razman and Kornhauser assume, following Davis (see the methodological appendix), that the rest of the world had attained only a very modest level of urbanization. It nevertheless remains the case that, applying the criterion of 5,000 to define urban population, Japan at the start of the eighteenth century had probably reached a level of urbanization on the order of 11–14%. This represented a level close to that of Europe (except Russia) at this time, but lower than that of certain European countries such as Italy and Spain, not to mention Portugal and the Netherlands (see table 11.2).

At the start of the eighteenth century, with a population of some 500,000 (or perhaps even one million), Edo (the future Tokyo) figured among the six largest cities in the world; and during this same period, Kyoto and Osaka each had populations of 350,000–450,000. To these very large metropolises should be added two cities with populations of around 100,000 and some six to ten cities with populations of 40,000–80,000. The growth of these cities, especially the largest of them, slowed down a little between 1700 and the middle of the nineteenth century; but, on the whole, urban population seems to have grown more rapidly than total population. As a result, the level of urbanization increased once more, reaching about 14–15% around 1800 and was perhaps even higher around 1850.

This urban expansion cannot be explained, like that in Europe during the sixteenth and seventeenth centuries, by international trade, Japan having remained isolated throughout the period. One must therefore seek the explanation in the Japanese economy. According to Hanley and Yamamura (1977), agricultural output, and probably agricultural productivity as well, seems to have increased perceptibly during the period. This view of the matter is not shared by earlier studies, none of which, however, were very thorough. In any event, a positive evolution of this sort in agriculture is the only factor capable of providing a valid explanation of growth on this scale in the level of urbanization; and that the level of urbanization did indeed grow rapidly at this time is accepted by all concerned.

After 1850 the destiny of Japan was to follow a course altogether different from that of the rest of Asia, which quite naturally leads me to incorporate Japan, from the end of the nineteenth century, into the developed world, and thus also into the preceding part of the book (chapter 19).

Southeast Asia: The Mediterranean of Asia?

The maritime space of Southeast Asia, among other parts of the world, was destined by geography to play the role of an international exchange zone. Not only is it the most vast archipelago on the planet, traversed through and through by rivers and by the sea, but it is also one of the most important networks of international routes, linking the Indian Ocean and the Mediterranean with China on one side and Japan on the other. These features have from the beginning determined the maritime space of Southeast Asia to fulfill a function very close to that fulfilled by the Mediterranean world, in which maritime trade was the backbone of urban growth and political power. What is more, it was from Southeast Asia that the most sought-after goods on the world market of the fifteenth and sixteenth centuries came—pepper, cloves, nutmeg, camphor. (Reid, 1979)

There is no doubt that, thanks to the commercial expansion of China and the Muslim world, this region saw the development of a fairly substantial number of large cities oriented toward international trade as early as the fourteenth century. By the fifteenth and sixteenth centuries, around fifteen cities chiefly given over to long-distance trading had emerged with populations of betwen 50,000 and 100,000, a few of them perhaps having even larger populations. The existence of fairly large port towns devoted to international trade does not, however, seem to have been a constant as early here as in the Mediterranean.

The phase sometimes called that of the "Angkorian cities," lasting from the ninth century to the fifteenth century (see chapter 3), was characterized by cities located deep within the interior. Nor should one forget that the commercial expansion of China did not reach appreciable proportions until the eleventh century. But one must also recognize that many unknowns continue to surround the history of the cities of Southeast Asia. These unknowns, moreover, tend to undermine McGee's (1967) assertion that the earliest cities in the region, those of the second to ninth centuries, were clearly associated with international trade.

I would give even greater stress, on the other hand, to what Lombard (1970) qualifies as being merely a "preliminary conclusion not

without interest." Lombard draws this conclusion from a brief historical chronology of the cities of Southeast Asia:

> We meet in this region with a great deal of instability
> among its urban sites. There are no large cities that,
> like Rome or Paris, Canton, Xian, or Zheng Zhou,
> trace their origins back to a high, indeed a very high
> antiquity. Of the five largest metropolises in exis-
> tence today . . . none dates from before the six-
> teenth century. Conversely, the region affords the
> archaeologist a fairly large number of deserted
> cities, empty and, as it were, fossilized shells: Angkor
> of course, with its multiple surrounding walls, but
> also Pagan, Sukhotai, Sri Sacchanalai, Modjopahit,
> and Ayuthia, which still, in the seventeenth century,
> inspired the admiration of the ambassador of Louis
> XIV. Only a few scattered sites dating back before
> the fifteenth century are still occupied today by ag-
> glomerations of any importance.

This region thus constitutes an exception to the general rule of the
persistence of urban systems down through the ages. Almost all of the
other instances of the eradication of urban networks were due to catastrophes linked with invasions. Mention should be made, however,
of the way in which the disappearance of the early urban cultures of
Southeast Asia resembles that of the various pre-Columbian cultures
that vanished before penetration by Europe. The fact that there were
in the two cases closely similar climates and ecological conditions is
most certainly not the effect of chance. It would seem, then, that the
instability of these urban cultures was probably related to the fact that
in very humid, subtropical zones, minor changes in climatic conditions and in the balance of forces between human systems and the environment have more serious consequences than elsewhere.

The Asiatic Mode of Production and the Cities of Asia

One cannot approach the problem of the nature of the cities
of Asia without introducing the notion of the Asiatic mode of production. For to the extent that the hypothesis of a specifically Asian mode
of production proves valid, the existence of such a mode would imply
a mode of relations between town and country very different from
that observed in Europe. I shall briefly recall what is at issue; and it
seems appropriate in this context to begin by defining what is meant
by "mode of production."

Mode of production is a highly fruitful notion developed by Marx.
I cite here the definition given in the *Dictionnaire économique et social*
published by the Centre d'études et de recherches marxistes (Center
for Marxist Studies and Research): "Mode of production: mode of ob-

taining the means of existence, the material goods indispensable for the satisfaction of social needs. It is the ensemble formed by productive forces and the relations of production that, at each stage of social evolution, expresses the state of the society." Still quoting from the same source:

> The mode of production indicates the manner in which such or such goods serving to satisfy a specific social need were created, that is, the objective bonds established between men on the occasion of the social production of their material life. Thus, wheat could have been produced by some small farmer working with his family . . . or by some capitalist entrepreneur of the Beauce region . . . employing agricultural laborers. . . . The mode of production is fundamentally social. It embraces both productive forces and relations of production. For without productive forces, there could be no production; but conversely it is the character of the relations of production that defines the manner in which goods are produced. It cannot therefore be reduced to its technical aspect alone.

According to the Marxist schema, different modes of production have succeeded one another in Western societies, corresponding to the following stages: primitive commune, slavery, feudalism, capitalism, and socialism. And in each case the contradictions between the economic and social aspects of a mode of production inevitably lead to a transition to a further stage characterized by a new mode of production.

Now the Asiatic model would seem, owing to its specific form, to have avoided this historical evolution. It is not part of my present task to report the numerous controversies surrounding the notion of a uniquely Asian mode of production; nor above all do I intend to discuss the various debates concerning the alleged socioeconomic stagnation of Asia and the causes thereof. Instead, I shall essentially confine myself to analyzing one aspect of the Asiatic mode of production directly related to our problem here. I shall begin by recalling the three characteristics generally attributed to the Asiatic mode of production:

1. The absence of the private ownership of the land, or at any rate its very limited extension
2. The existence of a central authority controlling, or at least strongly influencing, economic life
3. The tendency of agriculture and crafts to form a self-contained unit in each community, or to put it another way, the tendency of villages to become self-sufficient units.

It is obviously this last feature that is of interest here. To what extent do recent studies make it possible to confirm this view? It is certainly impossible to generalize. Not only were the urban systems of Japan, India, and China, for example, totally different, but, as has been shown, the urban history of each of these three countries followed a path entirely its own. And had I been able to broaden the scope of my analysis, I should undoubtedly have revealed even greater variety. It is true that the lack of historical studies has until recently encouraged the belief that there was no Asian urban history at all. For many Asian societies, however, over fairly long periods, the hypothesis of rural autonomy has already been ruled out. For a situation of this sort would have made the levels of urbanization reached impossible. It should be recalled in any case that both China and Japan went through phases during which their levels of urbanization exceeded that of Europe, despite the higher spatial specialization of economic activities in Europe.

But this clearly does not mean that the cities of traditional Asia were not on the average different from those of traditional Europe. True enough, they were much less different than was once thought during a whole era in which researchers implicitly compared the cities of nineteenth-century Asia with those of nineteenth-century Europe, too readily overlooking the impact both of Western development and of colonization. But differences did exist, the most important unquestionably being the greater central authority in Asia and the correspondingly lesser degree of independence of Asian cities. But it has to be remembered once again that Europe is more peculiar than Asia.

The question of the uniqueness of the Asian division of labor is more delicate. Which phase of which urban culture in Asia should be compared with which phase of European cultures? This is a crucial matter, for both cases offer a wide variety of situations. Taking a very hypothetical average, assuming such a thing were possible, we might find in Asia a larger crafts sector in rural areas and thus a less pronounced differentiation between the cities and the countryside. But any conclusions would be highly conditional. As has been seen, however, there is a good deal of certainty concerning the predominance of large cities, and this even in a country like Japan, comparable in size to the larger European countries. For there is obviously no comparison in the sixteenth century, for instance, between China, with its population of 110–140 million, or India, with its 80–140 million, and England, with some 3–5 million, Italy with some 9–12 million, or even France, with some 15–18 million—the whole of Europe, Russia included, having at that time a population of only some 80–110 million, and Japan some 15–20 million.

Certainly Asian cities had other peculiarities linked to many aspects of urban life more distantly connected with the economy, such as civil or religious administration, education, urban planning, and so on. Mark Elvin, that great specialist in Chinese history, writes (1978) that "Chinese air made nobody free." Speaking of freedom one should also note that Asian cities were in general less autonomous than their European counterparts; however, it was the European situation that was peculiar.

But there is also that other question so often asked, about the causes of what David Landes (1983) calls "a magnificent dead end." Why did Chinese technology, so much more advanced than that of Europe (around the fourteenth century), not lead to a technological and scientific revolution like that of Europe on the eve of the Industrial Revolution? I am inclined to think that the peculiarity lies much less in the dead end of the Chinese civilisation, or in the dead ends of the Indian or Arabic civilisations, than in the *breakthrough* of the European civilisation. However, my own lack of competence in these fields and the framework of this study oblige me to set aside all such problems as these, however interesting they may be.

23 Urbanism in the Middle East and the Maghreb before the Nineteenth Century □

The two religions engendered by Judaism have strongly affected the urban history of the Mediterranean world. In the preceding parts of the book, devoted to Europe, I have dealt with the northern region of the Mediterranean, with the Christian world. In this chapter I shall chiefly focus on the South and the various Muslim worlds. But the split between North and South is far from total. While commercial relations tended mostly to follow a horizontal axis (East-West), one should not overlook the axis running from North to South. Further, in Spain and the Balkans the Muslim world succeeded in implanting itself for more or less long periods in the North; and in Byzantium the Christian world managed to implant itself in the South where Christianity was born and developed before the coming of Islam.

Constantinople: A Transition between Christian Europe and the Muslim Middle East

Before moving on to the cities of the various Muslim cultures, it is worth recalling the history of Constantinople. This metropolis of the Byzantine Empire was for about three centuries (roughly 360–650) the largest city in the world, and still figured among the two or three largest for a further six centuries (until about 1250). The Byzantine Empire, whose beginnings may be said to date from the year 395, with the dividing up of the Roman Empire of which it formed the eastern half, reached its height around the eleventh century, and disappeared completely in 1453 when it captured by the Turks. Constantinople was probably founded in 324 with the enlargement and reconstruction of the ancient city of Byzantium. Constantinople was "already at its birth a costly venture; an urban complex of exceptional size, a capital built in order to serve as the political center of the Empire and as the privileged meeting ground of Hellenism and Romanism" (Dagron, 1974).

By 390 the population of the metropolis had probably risen to some

250,000–350,000, reaching some 300,000–400,000 about the year 450, and fluctuating around 400,000 to 600,000 until the 1070s. Constantinople was simultaneously the empire's chief port, royal seat, administrative capital (headquarters of a highly bureaucratized and thus heavily manned administration), religious capital, and industrial and commercial center. It was to the combination of all of these functions and also to the key role the city played in trade around the Mediterranean that Constantinople owed its prodigious size. But although the Byzantine Empire unquestionably had an urban structure of the primate type, it is still necessary to mention the existence of other cities of average size. There were probably some four to seven cities with populations of 30,000–50,000 and perhaps ten or more with populations of 20,000–30,000. Almost all of these cities resulted from waves of urbanization occurring prior to the founding of Byzantium.

Probably, perhaps, almost all. These admissions of vagueness do not in fact bear sufficient witness to the degree of uncertainty surrounding the history of the cities of Byzantium other than Constantinople: Ephesus, Antioch, Edessa, and Jerusalem, to cite only the most important of them. In 1957 Ostrogorsky (1959) noted that "among the fundamental problems of Byzantine history it would be hard to name one that has been studied less than that of cities." This observation remains largely valid today. But despite its promising title, "Byzantine Cities in the Early Middle Ages," Ostrogorsky's study, as the author himself confessed, was only an outline "to indicate in what way and by what methods such an investigation might be carried out."

But the fact that the history of the other cities of Byzantium is full of uncertainty does not mean that it is a blank page. Certainly Constantinople was a primate city, but the other cities formed an integral part of the system. I may cite Hélène Ahrweiler (1977) in this regard:

> Constantinople, as capital of a highly structured and excessively centralized state, a state that, despite the many compromises made in its structures, survived without fundamental change for over a thousand years, was called upon to become the City par excellence: not merely "the first of cities" as Rome had been before it, but the node, the spring of the urban network it dominated and controlled. From this point of view, one understands why the size of each Byzantine city, why the number, activities, and prosperity of its inhabitants, depended to a large extent on its position and role relative to Constantinople. So, too, one understands why formerly modest agglomerations experienced a particular surge of growth, acquiring the status and rank of official cities and benefiting from imperial grants and construction, simply owing to the fact that they marked stages on the roads linking the capital with its prov-

inces and more especially with its frontiers, while
other cities, once prosperous, were jeopardized because they became distant from Constantinople's
zone of interest. The fact nevertheless remains that
the Byzantine city continued to be at the heart of a
form of "political" life and, moreover, became at this
time the magnetic pole for the population of the surrounding countryside who found in it not only a refuge in times of danger, but an active market and,
above all, an administrative center covering more or
less extensive regions while remaining in contact
with the capital.

As further proof of the importance of Byzantine cities other than
Constantinople, I shall cite another of Ahrweiler's observations: "The
ecclesiastical organization, which, like the state administration, covered the whole of the imperial territory, adopted the formula created
by the provincial regime, each city, in accordance with a law of the
fifth century, being decreed an episcopal see."

It appears almost certain that globally, that is, for the whole of the
Byzantine Empire, urbanization reached a level higher than ever before. It is not to be excluded that this was true as well for a number
of its provinces. According to Gutwein (1981), the third Palestine
(southern part of the country and period A.D. 300–636) had a total
population and probably also an urban population higher than that of
any previous period.

But with the upheavals provoked by the Arab conquests both in Africa and in Asia and by Slavic penetration in the Balkans, a phase of
deurbanization took place, followed by a

reorganization of the urban network dictated by the
imperatives of the historical situation of the period:
the cities making up the Empire were larger but less
numerous than before; a great number of cities destroyed or abandoned during the disturbances, especially those cities situated in regions now near the
imperial frontiers, never rose again. In addition, the
cities presented a new aspect, marked by a pronounced military character. (Ahrweiler, 1977)

But apparently Constantinople itself was not much affected by this
first hammer blow delivered by the new forces established in the region, since, as we saw earlier, its population remained high—around
400,000–600,000 until the 1070s. From this date on, however, the political and economic decline of the Byzantine Empire, which began to
accelerate, brought about the decline of the metropolis as well.

Around 1200 the population of Constantinople had fallen to somewhere around 200,000. The Fourth Crusade (1202–1204) inflicted a

terrible blow on the empire and above all on the capital, which the Crusaders sacked and largely destroyed. The empire was even split in two, and its "reunification" did not take place until 1261. But by this stage the term Empire no longer corresponded to the geographical reality; for the territory of the empire had in fact dwindled to the region immediately surrounding Constantinople. After that time the population was less than 200,000, and this even during positive phases. And when the Turks finally seized the city, it no longer had more than 40,000–50,000 inhabitants. Apparently, as the systematic analysis of the data available for twenty Byzantine cities shows, the contraction also affected the rest of the urban network, but not in so pronounced a fashion (Foss, 1977).

But even with a population of a little more or less than 200,000, Constantinople remained in the thirteenth and fourteenth centuries a great Christian metropolis. After all, around the year 1200, despite more than two centuries of growth, the largest Christian city after Constantinople, namely Paris, only had a population of 120,000, a very large population for the time, but still much smaller than Constantinople's. No other city in Christian Europe had more than 70,000 to 80,000 people. Even Palermo and Seville, the two largest cities in Muslim Europe, had only 150,000 people.

Constantinople preserved, moreover, its splendid monuments, which explains the wonder of Western visitors during the Middle Ages. But many dwellings and some public edifices fell into disrepair, and large portions of some neighborhoods were turned into gardens (Foss, 1980).

Byzantium: Subsistence and the Urban Economy

Before passing on to the cities of the Muslim world, I shall pause to consider the problems of supplying food to what was for several centuries the largest city in the world. During a first phase (Teall, 1959), Constantinople imported a large proportion of its food supplies from Egypt; the secondary cities, on the other hand, obtained their food from neighboring regions. It may be recalled that (see chapter 5), at the time of Justinian (527–565), Constantinople's imports of wheat amounted to at least 170,000 metric tons per year.

In fact, as Dagron (1974) notes, these imports began with a rerouting of part of the Egyptian wheat destined for Rome, a rerouting that very soon became a transfer of rights, but one limited to supplying Constantinople itself. There also was soon established in Constantinople a vast system for the free distribution of wheat (to 80,000 beneficiaries), a system which seems to have been intended for assistance even less than Rome's, though poor people were among the beneficiaries. Water was also a problem. The size of the city combined with its negative environment made water supply a very serious problem, which was solved by means of the construction of an extensive and costly system (Mango, 1985).

Arab domination of the Nile led both to the geographic diversification of Constantinople's cereal imports (a portion of which came from Bulgaria), and to an increase in local agricultural production, chiefly by means of an expansion of the amount of land under cultivation, but with very little technical progress. In exchange for grain, Byzantium mainly offered manufactured goods, which was possible because Byzantium was until the tenth century one of the most dynamic regions in the world from an economic point of view. This dynamism was only relative, however, for according to the title of an article by Lopez (1953–55), Byzantium was something of a "One-eyed Man in the Kingdom of the Blind." This relative dynamism nevertheless implies a fairly high level of urbanization, certainly more than 8–9%, and probably around 10–13%.

The limits on the dynamism of the Byzantine economy and in particular on urbanism in Byzantium are delineated very clearly in a book by Evelyne Patlagean (1977) about economic and social poverty in Byzantium:

> The period beginning in the fourth century was characterized by a phenomenon that, without being wholly new, nevertheless came henceforth to exercise considerable pressure on the urban equilibrium of the times: an influx of workers very little or not at all qualified for the kinds of activities peculiar to cities: indeed of individuals who, owing to various sorts of handicaps, were totally incapable of productive work.

This influx inevitably led to a marked increase in urban unemployment. Unemployment seems, moreover, to be a characteristic of urban societies that draw excessively on the surrounding countryside, a characteristic which will be further discussed in this part of the book.

The Cities of the Muslim Worlds

In discussing Muslim cities, one must speak of cities in the Muslim worlds. The use of the plural in this case proves doubly necessary. In the first place, there is history, the simple duration of Muslim urbanism. Between the Muslim world of the year 632 (the date of the death of Muhammad) and that of 1830 (the time of the capture of Algiers and the start of the earliest major domination of a Muslim society by a European state) lies a history rich in religious and social developments as much as in political and economic developments. Between the Muslim world of the caliphates of the ninth century (each practically autonomous) and the Ottoman Empire of the sixteenth century very substantial differences existed. But perhaps deeper still were the differences between regions, especially in those geographic and socioeconomic conditions that help shape urban life. In the eleventh century the Maghreb, Egypt, Persia, and Spain, for example, were all societies ruled in accordance with the Koran; yet in each case, history and geographical context produced a unique type of culture.

Islam and the Diffusion of Urbanism

Contrary to what happens in the case of the civilizations of India and China, the question of the originality of urbanism does not arise where the Muslim cultures are concerned. The Muslim cultures lie in regions in which urbanism was earliest. Islam was implanted in preexisting urban worlds. And if the Arabs who were the spearhead of the spread of Islam were nomads, Muhammad was born in a commercial city.

What is more, recent research has shown that the extent to which the Arab conquerors created new cities in the Middle East has been overestimated. As Lapidus (1973) notes, the Arabs only rarely founded new cities; they tended instead to settle in existing towns and villages, the most notable exceptions being Baghdad, Basra, Kufa, and Fostat. These cities trace their origins back either to military encampments or, as in the case of Baghdad, to administrative decree. The history of Baghdad was a stormy one. Based on plans drawn up in the year 758, work on the construction of the city began in 762 and by 765 the caliph was installed in the new capital, which very soon had a population of some 400,000. Baghdad became the largest city in the world around the year 850, reaching its first apogee around 930, with a population on the order of one million. But trade routes have often turned into invasion routes, and this was the reason for both the success and the various eclipses of Baghdad. The city was destroyed on numerous occasions, sometimes partially, sometimes completely.

But on the whole, such new cities as the Arabs did create in the Middle East failed to alter the urban structure of the region to any appreciable extent. In other regions, however, and especially in the Maghreb and in part of Black Africa, Arab conquests and the spread of Islam did in fact significantly contribute to urbanization. According to my own survey of the available data, roughly half of the larger cities in the Maghreb in the eleventh century had been founded as a result of the spread of Islam in the region. Such was in particular the case for Algiers (ca. 940), Biskra (ca. 680), Fez (ca. 810), Kairouan (ca. 670), Mahdia (ca. 920), Marrakesh (ca. 1070), and Meknes (ca. 940). In the Maghreb, then, some 50% of the cities owed their existence to Islam, while in the Middle East Islamization accounted for only some 10% of the total.

Given the current state of research, it is difficult to establish the exact role played by the spread of Islam in urbanization in Black Africa. There is no doubt, however, that it contributed significantly in this part of the world both through the creation of new cities and in particular through enlargement of the existing urban network. But to what extent was it a matter of the establishment of new cities and to what extent a matter of the expansion of small towns already in existence? Though I reviewed a few of the main elements in chapter 4, this page of the urban history of the region remains to be written.

By contrast, developments in Spain closely resembled those in the Middle East: in other words, very few new cities were created. According to my own review of the available data, of the twenty largest cities of twelfth-century Spain, only two can (with many reservations) be considered to have been founded owing to the Muslim presence: Granada (the doubts are enormous) and Valladolid (with greater probability). However, it is likely that future research will bring a further reduction of Islam's role in creating new cities, not only in Spain, but also in the Middle East, the Maghreb, and Black Africa. Indeed, one of the most stable trends of recent archaeological research is to push backwards the dates for the birth of cities. It is very likely that a sizable fraction of the cities whose foundation is traced to the Arab expansion existed before that expansion. Every colonization tends to obliterate local history.

On the other hand, there is no question that Muslim culture induced a surge of economic development leading in its turn to very substantial urban growth. It may be recalled (see the chapters devoted to Europe) that Muslim Spain was among the most heavily urbanized regions of that continent. At the start of the eleventh century Cordoba, with its population of 400,000–500,000, was the largest city in Europe; and the second largest, Venice, had a population of only about 40,000–60,000. Accounting for about 19–25% of the total population of Europe (except Russia), Spain at this time had 30–40% of the European population living in cities with populations of more than 20,000.

Ultimately Islam created more new cities along its trade routes, whether maritime (with Asia and East Africa) or overland (in particular with Black Africa) (see chapter 4). With regard to maritime trade, research over the last twenty years has enabled us to learn more about four of the many cities that owed their existence to the expansion of the Muslim world: Siraf and Banbhore in the Indus delta and Kilwa and Manda in East Africa.

Siraf and Banbhore were both located in regions fairly unfavorable in ecological terms (Whitehouse, 1980). This has surprised some researchers. But it should be remembered that settlement in a more hospitable area would have involved already established ports and a populous hinterland. This would have made it necessary for the newcomers to fight in order to settle in the region, and it would above all have necessitated the setting up of permanent defences for them to remain there. These genuinely Islamic cities essentially lived off trade and as a result failed to survive the dwindling of commercial relations.

Kilwa, in present-day Tanzania, was founded in the ninth or tenth century and had become the chief commercial port in East Africa by the start of the sixteenth century, that is, by the time the Portuguese, having rounded the Cape of Good Hope, had begun to record information about this part of the world, hitherto unknown to Westerners. The city center covered one hundred hectares; other stone buildings, and perhaps a shantytown of sorts as well, were located in its outskirts. It is thus possible that some estimates that have been thought excessive, giving the city a population of 10,000, have in fact been underestimations; a population of 30,000–40,000 is plausible.

Manda (in modern-day Kenya) was much smaller, with only a few thousand people. This seaport seems to have principally served in the exportation of masts. From this period dates the introduction of bananas from Asia into Africa, which was probably a secondary effect of Muslim trade, just as the introduction of cassava into Africa was a secondary effect of European trade. The banana was to play in Africa a role close to that played in Europe by the potato. In tropical countries the banana is more a staple food than a fruit.

Islam exerted an urbanizing influence in another way (see chapter 4): the migration of dissident Muslim sects. Sometimes places chosen by reason of their inaccessibility nevertheless became genuine cities. This was notably the case of the city of Ghardaïa.

In the eleventh century, followers of the Kharidji movement, combated as heretics by other Muslims, decided after several successive settlements to take refuge in the Sahara, and in an area (the Mzab) whose environment was particularly hostile and which lay apart from the caravan routes. Thanks to waterworks, a

> rural oasis life grew up. During the first centuries of their settlement at M'zab, the Mzabites drew most of their resources from the cultivation of their gardens in the various scattered palm groves near the Pentapolis itself. To this was added a little livestock raising, limiting as far as possible contacts with the outside world, these contacts being confined to a few exchanges with the Arab nomads living in the surrounding desert (Josse, 1970).

But gradually the very persistence of an agricultural community brought about a change in the currents of exchange, and a genuine urban commercial center was born, connecting to a system of commercial traffic whose geographic limits grew in time. This development led to the creation of a small urban network: four other towns were joined to Ghardaïa, making in all five cities with a total population of 19,000 before the end of the nineteenth century, 8,000 of them living in Ghardaïa itself, which remained the largest of the five towns. At the time of the census of 1966, the population of Ghardaïa was 28,000, and that of the four other towns together was 19,000. And in 1977 the population of Ghardaïa had risen to 70,000. It is true that in the meantime oil had been discovered in the region, and while the wells are quite distant from the town, Ghardaïa serves as a service center for the industry.

Islam: Economy, Technology, and Urbanization

While Arab conquests and other contributions of the new Islamic culture did not lead to the creation of a great many new centers of urban growth, they did most certainly favor urban expansion. As was later the case for European colonization in the future Third World, Muslim domination brought about, along with the diffusion of a new religion, a large transfer of innovations in various sectors of technological, scientific, and economic life—though a sizable number of these innovations originated in Asia rather than in the Muslim world itself. And as would also happen again later in the case of European colonization, the spread of the new religion (and way of life) was itself furthered by political and economic pressures, with Jews and Christians having to pay taxes Muslims were excused from paying and adherents to nonbiblical religions faring even worse. But even though the conversion of the inhabitants of the conquered lands theoretically made full citizens of them, in practice a series of discriminations remained which made a privileged class of the conquerors. There is no colonization without colonized people, even in the context of the societies of the preindustrial age.

On the economic plane, agriculture and industry made great progress. In those places in which comparisons are easy, particularly in Spain, agriculture reached levels of yield and probably of productivity perceptibly higher than those achieved in the rest of Europe. Much more than any urbanizing character supposedly peculiar to the Muslim religion, this economic growth stimulated the urban growth experienced in the various Muslim worlds. Recent research tends to reduce very considerably the specifically religious component. Inasmuch as Islam, even more than Christianity, took deepest root in regions already urbanized since ancient times, one could almost say that it played a more limited role than Christianity in the spread of urbanism.

Around the year 1000 the Muslim world must have had approximately forty to fifty cities with populations of more than 20,000, six to eight of which had populations of more than 100,000. During the same period, Europe (except Russia and Spain) counted about thirty cities with populations of more than 20,000, but none with populations of 100,000. Further, it should be stressed that around this period the Muslim world probably had some 22 to 30 million people, as against 27 to 35 million in Europe (except Russia and Spain). We may deduce from this, making all due allowances, that the level of urbanization in the Muslim world was something like 10–13% as opposed to only 8–9% in Europe (except Russia and Spain). This estimate takes account of the specific structure of the urban network, which was most likely characterized by a much smaller number of small towns than in Europe. For instance, cities of the Muslim world subsisted by means of long-distance trade more than their European counterparts of the same era.

The cities of the various Muslim cultures seem not to have experienced the same growth as European cities from the eleventh century to the fourteenth century. On the basis of highly fragmentary data, and overlooking regional differences, it can be concluded that urban population remained relatively stable. The growth recorded in the Maghreb, for example, was offset by decline in the Middle East proper. These centuries represented for this part of the world the real transition from singular to plural, for the Muslim world fragmented more and more after this period. This fragmentation was both cause and effect, the various Muslim societies undergoing a series of invasions. But as in the case of Europe, the urban history of the Muslim world as a whole is also the history of individual cities, each city undergoing a combination of circumstances and events all its own.

Taking advantage of the crumbling of the various other Muslim societies and of the weakening of Byzantium, a new empire gradually emerged beginning at the end of the thirteenth century: the Ottoman Empire. By the close of the fifteenth century this empire extended over the whole of Turkey and a large part of the Balkans; and during the sixteenth century it absorbed the Middle East and most of the Maghreb. Before passing on to the effects of the emergence of this new imperial power on the urban development of the various regions involved, it is worth pausing to consider the unique features of Muslim cities before the rise of the Ottoman Empire.

The Specific Features of Muslim Cities

I have already drawn attention to some of the special features of urbanism in the various Muslim worlds, among them a higher level of urbanization than in Europe during the same period and a more marked predominance of larger cities. In this section, however, I shall focus more on the sociopolitical and topographical aspects of Muslim cities. It should also be recalled what was noted earlier concerning the multiplicity of Muslim worlds; for the adoption of the Muslim way of life could never completely eradicate local peculiarities, much less geographic differences. Consequently in this brief and highly compressed synthesis of the current state of the problem I shall confine myself to the dominant urban models found among the various Muslim cultures before the Ottoman Empire.

To begin with, as in the case of the societies of Asia and of Africa and the New World as well, it should be noted that Muslim cities were less independent than those of Europe. In this instance, however, the sense of peculiarity derives wholly from Eurocentrism. Apparently the relative autonomy characteristic of the cities of traditional Europe (and only a part of Europe at that) was unique to the European urban experience.

The cities of the various societies absorbed into the Muslim world had to reflect the fact that their expansion was the result of Arab military conquest. This implied, notably, the existence of a dominant immigrant class monopolizing political and often economic power as well. This and other migratory movements also resulted in very homogeneous ethnic and religious quarters, as would happen again later, beginning in the second half of the nineteenth century, in the cities of countries settled by Europeans, particularly the United States. This does not mean that traditional European cities were not divided into well-defined quarters, each with a clearly defined population of its own. But the phenomenon was much more pronounced in Muslim cities.

Recent research appears to have completely ruled out the existence of craft guilds similar to those characteristic of medieval Europe. According to recent findings, as Bonine (1977) shows in his review of the problem, what were once taken for genuine guilds—organizations formed and effectively acting to promote the interests of the crafts concerned—were in fact supervisory bodies run by the political authorities. This explains, moreover, the less extensive independence of Muslim cities; for in Europe as in Japan, it was in part (though not exclusively) due to the guilds that the amount of freedom cities enjoyed increased.

One last unmistakable peculiarity of Muslim cities deserving mention here is urban planning, or rather the lack of it. Muslim cities were in general characterized by a maze of narrow streets, and private initiative seems to have been the rule in construction. If I speak of urban planning here while omitting it in the rest of the book, it is because it led to, or resulted from, two features of the mode of transport unique to Muslim societies: the use of camels and the absence of wheeled vehicles.

The Camel: A Technological Advance over the Wheel?

In Europe the use of wheeled vehicles for human transportation was strictly regulated inside cities. But in Muslim societies the use of wheeled vehicles was exceptionally limited, not to say unknown, even in transporting merchandise from city to city or in rural areas. In a work devoted to Muslim Spain, Lévi-Provençal expressed perplexity on this score as early as 1953. Describing the outfitting of troops, he writes: "It is curious to observe that no mention is ever made of carts." And he adds in a note: "At least throughout the Middle Ages, there seems to have been a sort of prohibition in the Muslim West outlawing the use of wheeled vehicles, a prohibition for which it would be worth finding a plausible explanation." A similar observation has been made with respect to all of the Muslim societies of the Middle East. As additional confirmation, there is the fact that in an analysis of the very rich documentation found in the Genizah of Cairo (a repository for ancient manuscripts and ritual objects) concerning the life of the Jewish community chiefly during the Middle Ages, Goitein (1967) finds no mention of wagons or carts (except in India, where they would have been drawn by oxen). What makes the search for some sort of explanation all the more intriguing is the fact that carts or wagons and other wheeled vehicles were used in the Middle East for at least a few millenia before the advent of Islam. It appears, however, that the use of the wheel had already disappeared before the Arab conquest.

The most plausible explanation may be the introduction and eventual predominance of the camel as a beast of burden in Muslim societies. And it should be noted in this connection that, as Bulliet (1975) has clearly demonstrated, the replacement of the cart by the camel in traditional societies, especially in semidesert regions, constituted technological progress and not a step backward. In comparison to the traditional ox-drawn cart before the invention of the harness collar, the camel offered many advantages. In the first place, a camel can carry at least as much as a cart harnessed to a pair of oxen. In the second place, a camel can cover on the average 25 to 30 kilometers a day, as against 10 to 15 for a cart. And one man can drive three to six camels, whereas he can manage only one cart. A further by no means insignificant point is that a cart requires roads, while the camel does not. Finally, while camels can eat anything oxen can eat, they are also able to assimilate semidesert vegetation that oxen are incapable of eating. Thus Bulliet is probably not overstating the case when he calls the use of the camel a technological advance.

But though the use of camels marked progress at one stage of development, it also led to a neglect of the wheel that unquestionably had negative consequences at later stages. This neglect left traces right up to the beginning of the twentieth century and even until our own time. Litters borne by two camels were still to be seen in Cairo as late as the 1920s; wheelbarrows are still used very little, if at all, on the work sites of present-day Teheran; and carts are as a rule rare in rural districts in the Middle East. But this brings us to the delicate and as yet imprecise question of the likely consequences of certain technological choices analyzed in the light of a single model. It may perhaps be necessary to draw upon the rich literature of science fiction to grasp the set of virtualities for all technological alternatives. And given the ravages wrought in urban areas by the wheel in combination with the internal combustion engine, there is reason to dream of urban transportation systems without wheels, of which the still tentative experiments with pedestrian streets offer a promising foretaste.

The Ottoman Empire: An Expanding Metropolis with Cities in Decline at the Periphery?

It will undoubtedly take several generations of historians before all of the causes accounting for the divergent evolution of the Ottoman Empire can be determined. There is no question, however, but that mechanisms associated with colonization were largely responsible both for the growth of the cities of Turkey, especially Istanbul (the new name for Constantinople), and for the decline of most of the cities located in the rest of the empire, that is, at the periphery.

While the population of Constantinople had fallen below 200,000 after 1204, and was no more than some 40,000 to 50,000 at the time of the capture of the city by the Turks in 1453, the population of Istanbul had reached 300,000 to 500,000 by 1530–1540. It became the largest city in the world once more between 1560–1600 and 1700–1730, with a population of some 650,000 to one million. The seventeenth century appears to have been marked by a decline in population, but the population in all likelihood never fell below 550,000. I have been able to find little information regarding long-term developments in other Turkish cities apart from Adrianople, whose population increased from less than 30,000 around 1400 to nearly 200,000 by 1600. But the long-term growth of these two cities should not give one the impression of linear and positive growth of either the total population or the urban population. Recent research by Erder and Faroqhi (1979) confirms the pioneering work done by Omer Barkan, giving evidence of a fall in population in several urban centers at the end of the sixteenth century, a fall apparently preceded by a sharp expansion in the middle of the same century. But despite all these fluctuations, typical of any traditional society, with respect to Turkey proper, the Ottoman Empire had during its first centuries of existence, if not growth in all of its urban centers, at least growth in the total number of city dwellers, in view of the growth of the population of Istanbul. And even more than during the era of Byzantium, the urban system of the Ottoman Anatolian plateau was of the primate type. Thus around 1560–1580, when Istanbul had a population of 700,000–900,000, the two other largest cities (Bursa and Kayseri) each had probably 25,000–40,000 people.

This urban expansion was certainly furthered by levies drawn on the empire. The empire included the following territories (given their present-day names): Greece, Albania, almost all of Yugoslavia, Hungary, and Rumania, parts of southern Russia and Iran, most of Syria, Iraq, Lebanon, and Israel, parts of Jordan and Saudi Arabia, and all or nearly all of Egypt, Libya, Tunisia, Algeria, and Cyprus. In the case of those eighteen cities for which, on the basis of the data of Chandler and Fox (1974), it is possible to trace the approximate growth of population between 1500 and 1700, one observes either decline or stagnation. Taking all eighteen cities together, the population fell from 1.2 million in 1500 to 950,000 in 1700, falling to 800,000 by around 1800. Of these eighteen cities, only five seem likely to have experienced growth, generally modest, between 1500 and 1700, ten declining, while the remaining three maintained a relative status quo.

A change of this sort conforms with conventional wisdom, but how often has conventional wisdom been subject to revision. This may be a case in point. Raymond (1979) has thrown doubt on the reality of the decline, if not in urbanization as a whole, at least in the population of the principal cities of the Arab provinces, and this during the first decades of Ottoman colonization. He writes in the conclusion to his article:

> The reality of vigorous urban growth in the larger
> Arab cities of the empire during the decades follow-
> ing the Ottoman conquest seems to us largely un-
> questionable. This urban growth is revealed by a
> certain number of features (modifications in urban
> structure, events in urban history) and it is equally
> visible in the three major cities of the Arab prov-
> inces, Cairo, Damascus, and Aleppo. This surge of
> urban growth was linked to the expansion of trade
> that followed the establishment of the empire—
> though this expansion of trade remains to be stud-
> ied in detail. This surge of urban growth also doubt-
> less reflected an upsurge in population whose
> existence has been firmly established in the Balkan
> and Anatolian provinces of the empire.

Raymond adds, however, that:

> Our knowledge of the economic history of the Arab
> provinces of the Ottoman Empire is not sufficiently
> precise to enable us to conclude that generalized
> economic development occurred in these provinces
> during the decades following on the establishment
> of the empire or that, on the contrary, the cities
> constituted a sector of growth within a zone of
> stagnation.

Nor, according to Raymond, would the development of the cities be in contradiction to "the cultural apathy which unquestionably characterized the Arab world of the times."

But Raymond tends to overestimate the differences in development in traditional societies. Thus in comparing per capita export values, for example, around the close of the eighteenth century in Egypt and France (24 and 44 livres respectively), he concludes that "we have to deal here with two quite comparable figures, especially when one takes into account the relatively high level of economic development in France as compared with Egypt at this time. One must then conclude that Egypt had a very active foreign trade." In fact, it is more likely that during its positive phases Egypt had a standard of living closer to that of late eighteenth-century France than Raymond postulates.

On the other hand, and in this case Raymond himself is very conscious of the problem, nothing rules out the possibility that, owing to more intensive levies on rural districts, certain large cities grew at the expense of the rest of the urban network. In the light of the current state of research in this area, one would have to say that it appears likely that the cities of the Ottoman Empire outside Turkey did not have an especially favorable growth rate at this time, but that it was not as negative as has traditionally been thought.

While this evolution certainly owed a great deal to the type of economic relations imposed by the Turkish metropolis, one cannot exclude the possible intervention of other factors. In this context it is worth recalling that classical accounts of the decline of the Arab provinces of the Ottoman Empire include among its causes indirect penetration by Europe. For beginning with the sixteenth century, Europe regained at least partial mastery of the Mediterranean, and European traders began to compete with Arab merchants along the African coasts. On the other hand, it is symptomatic that the principal cities of those countries that managed to remain aloof from Ottoman domination experienced population growth. Thus in the six Persian cities for which it is possible to trace the relevant trends, the combined population rose from 420,000 to 920,000 between 1500 and 1700. For Morocco (four cities), the growth was more moderate (from 225,000 to 335,000), but in this case the increase was entirely due to the rapid growth of a single city, Meknes.

It seems likely, then, that Ottoman colonization exerted a rather negative influence. The fragmentary indications available with respect to the economic life of the various colonized regions converge in such a way as to suggest a negative evolution that would explain, if not the decline, at least the stagnation of the urban population of these regions. The decline in the population of some of the existing cities appears not to have been accompanied by the creation of new colonial cities, as was the case under European colonization in many parts of the world. And incidentally, European colonization got under way during nearly the same period in which the most dynamic phase of Ottoman expansion outside Turkey occurred. It is true, though, that the cities created by the Europeans were chiefly located in regions of low urban density whereas the Ottoman Empire almost exclusively occupied regions heavily urbanized since ancient times.

24 Traditional Colonization and Urbanization: From 1490–1530 to 1780–1815 □

The history of European colonization unquestionably began at the start of the sixteenth century with the arrival of the conquistadores in the New World and did not come to a close until the 1960s with the independence of the countries of Africa. But it is very arbitrary to treat these four and a half centuries as a single entity. Here, too, the Industrial Revolution precipitated a profound break in the course of historical events.

The Break with the Past Brought About by the Industrial Revolution

Over nearly three centuries, until around 1780–1815, European colonization was still of a traditional type. It followed in the wake of numerous other colonizations. Nor was Europe the only colonial power during these three centuries; in relative importance, Europe was far from being first. Around 1750 European colonies probably had a population of some twenty-two million, equivalent to roughly 18% of Europe's own population (except Russia, itself a colonial power ruling in Asia over a population equal to some 15% of its European population). These twenty-two million people represented about 3–4% of the total population of the regions later to become the Third World. The Ottoman Empire, on the other hand (see chapter 23) most likely had at this time a population of some thirteen to twenty million, as against some fifteen to eighteen million in Turkey proper, making a colonial population equal to anywhere from 70 to 130% of the population of Turkey. With the Industrial Revolution, however, things changed dramatically. By 1830 Europe's colonial empire had a population roughly equal to its own; and by 1860 or thereabouts, if China—which may be regarded as a virtual colony—is included, the colonial population had already risen to a level equal to 230% of the population of Europe. This percentage reaches 240% if we include Latin America, politically independent, but in economic terms largely surbordinate to the European economy.

The quantity of primary products (both agricultural products and raw materials) exported by the future Third World to the emerging developed nations was very modest before the upheavals brought about by the Industrial Revolution. I have been able to estimate, albeit very roughly, that these exports reached a volume of about 100,000 to 120,000 metric tons per year around the start of the eighteenth century (Bairoch, 1986). During the seventeenth century the quantities involved annually must on the average have been even smaller, increasing only moderately until 1750. By 1830, on the other hand, the volume had reached 700,000 metric tons per year, rising to 28 million around 1911, to 69 million around 1936, and to over 1.2 billion around 1980. Certainly population also increased during this period, but not to anything like the same extent. Translated into annual quantity per capita, exports of raw materials rose in the Third World from 0.2 kilogram around 1700 to 0.8 kilogram around 1830, 49 kilograms around 1936, and 380 kilograms around 1980. In developed countries, imports rose from 0.8 kilogram per capita per year around 1700 to 3 kilograms around 1830 and 87 kilograms around 1936—reaching more than 1,000 kilograms around 1980.

Before 1780–1815 the nature of economic relations between the future Third World countries and future developed countries was very different from one continent to the next. Indeed, one can speak of genuine colonial domination only in the case of the New World. In the New World, most of the territory and population had been colonized. Moreover, in terms of population, the New World represented roughly three quarters of all European colonial dominions around 1750. In Africa and Asia, taken globally, only some five to seven million people inhabited the as-yet-small European enclaves. These enclaves accounted, then, for only about 1% of the population of the continents involved. This is why I shall concentrate in this chapter chiefly, though not exclusively, on Latin America.

From the Pre-Columbian New World to Latin America: A Radical Modification in the Ethnic Composition of the Population

Around 1520, less than thirty years after Christopher Columbus had for the first time landed in the Americas believing he had reached the Indies, the era of the conquistadores began. Over the course of about twenty years, some thousands of Spaniards—among whom mingled adventurers from other countries: Portuguese, Frenchmen, Flemings—succeeded with relatively limited means in conquering cultures that had attained a high degree of development, thereby giving the Emperor Charles V "more kingdoms than he had provinces." Paladins in a new Christian crusade according to some, noble cadets in search of glory or bloodthirsty plunderers in search of personal fortunes according to others; God or glory or riches, or most likely riches plus glory plus God—the motives matter little. What remains certain is that this fantastic epic brought about the death of the pre-Columbian cultures and was largely responsible for the collapse of the populations that composed them.

And it was indeed a collapse, even if one considers excessive the population figure given by demographers of what is called the Berkeley school for the start of the sixteenth century: 80–100 million. One may reasonably accept a population of more than 40 million, and it is certain that by around 1650 the population had fallen to somewhere on the order of 10 million. This collapse was due to the combined effects of the massacres accompanying and following the conquest, the deadly epidemics caused by viruses and microbes introduced by the Europeans and unknown in the New World before that time (smallpox especially, but also, among others, typhus, leprosy, the plague, dysentery, and even yellow fever, probably imported from Africa), the excesses of the colonial system of exploitation both in mining and agriculture, and finally by the effects of the economic disorganization resulting from the collapse of the pre-Columbian states and empires. Thus the collapse was real enough in quantitative terms, but there was collapse in qualitative terms as well, for the populations of the high cultures suffered the most from the effects of colonization. This meant in practice the nearly complete disappearance of the population of the urban centers whose size and diversity were seen in chapter 4.

Until 1570 or thereabouts, the colonization of the New World was based on precious metals. To begin with it consisted of the simple confiscation of wealth accumulated over the centuries. Afterwards this gave way to mineral exploitation with the perfecting of a more economical method of separating silver ore that made the mines of Mexico and Peru profitable. The need for labor in these mines was one of the causes for the vast transfer of slaves from Africa that would indirectly draw the New World into the network of European colonial expansion. But very early on, the difference in climate between Latin America and Europe encouraged the cultivation of tropical products with a view to exporting them to Europe. This difference in climate was, indeed, an essential factor; for owing to the high cost of transport, it was impossible to export any agricultural goods other than those that could not be produced in Europe itself and which were therefore able to bring a high price.

Sugar came first, followed somewhat later by coffee. The need for labor on the plantations considerably accelerated the slave trade, some 7 million slaves being brought to Latin America, under unspeakable conditions, during the eighteenth century alone, and some 10–15 million in all to the New World as a whole by the time of the total abolition of slavery around the 1880s (though a slave ship was seized as late as 1901). It should be noted, however, that at the international level the slave trade was outlawed by the start of the nineteenth century (see below). Around 1825, of some 24 million inhabitants in Latin America, only a little more than 8 million were native-Americans, Europeans accounting for 4.9 million, blacks for 4.1 million, and half-breeds for some 6.4 million.

A Colonization with an Urbanizing Character

It is symptomatic that the first attempt to create a colonial city was undertaken by Christopher Columbus himself. But as Socolow and Johnson (1981) note: "Columbus proved himself to be a far better navigator than city planner, and both of his efforts to found settlements, Navidad (1492) and Isabela (1493), failed." It has been calculated that between the creation of Navidad and the start of the twentieth century the Spanish alone founded, if not thousands, as some have estimated, at least hundreds of towns—not far short of a thousand.

Certainly many of these towns were nothing more than small military outposts, and, like the two founded by Columbus, many of them disappeared. But Spanish colonization, and to a lesser extent that of the Portuguese and the other European powers, brought about the establishment of a whole new urban network. "The Iberian Conquest and Colonization: An Urban Venture" is the title of the section of their book devoted to this period by Butterworth and Chance (1981).

Most of the cities created by the Spanish were already founded in the sixteenth century, in particular between 1530 and 1560. The Portuguese cities, on the other hand, were founded two centuries later. As for the French and English, present above all in the Antilles, the creation of their cities began either in the second half of the seventeenth century or the first half of the eighteenth.

A noteworthy fact is that in many cases the colonial cities of America were relocated several times, the initial choice proving unsuitable, notably owing to climatic phenomena specific to certain regions and unknown to Europeans, such as the hurricanes of the Caribbean.

An Urban Network without Strong Links to the Past

Around 1750 Latin America probably had 28–32 cities with populations of more than 20,000, 4 or 5 with more than 50,000, making altogether a situation close to that of the pre-Columbian New World at the start of the sixteenth century (see table 24.1). But in the great majority of cases, these were cities populated by the descendants of immigrants from outside the New World, and they were often located on new sites. In short, an almost complete break with the past had been made, even though two of the three principal urbanized regions around 1750 had been superimposed on formerly urbanized areas: Mexico and the northern Andes (Bolivia, Colombia, Equador, Peru). The third urbanized region at the time was Brazil.

But although these cities were generally located on new sites, this was not always the case, for it can be estimated that of the 28–32 cities with populations of more than 20,000 in Latin America around 1750, 10–12 occupied the sites of ancient pre-Columbian cities. The most significant example is Mexico City, erected on the site of the Aztec city of Tenochtitlan. But mention should also be made of a certain number of other capitals, such as La Paz (Chuquiapu), Bogota (Teusquillo), Guatemala City (Iximche), Quito (Quito), and so forth. This list would be considerably larger if smaller towns were also included. But with the urban expansion of the temperate regions of Latin America, the relative proportion of cities built on new sites increased markedly. Furthermore, continuity of site does not necessarily imply continuity of the topography of the city, still less that of the people living there.

Towns Based on Mining and the Export of Tropical Products

The small degree of continuity between the cities of Latin America and those of the pre-Columbian New World essentially reflects economic factors related to colonization. The new cities founded and largely populated by Europeans responded to two fundamental stimuli: the mining of precious metals and the exportation of tropical products. Clearly this excludes neither the administrative component nor above all the military factor. Thus, in Chile (Guarda, 1978), half of the 204 settlements established between the first years of the Conquest and independence were fortified. And many of the cities of this region began as a military forts. Chile must, however, be looked upon as an extreme case, given the "bellicose nature" of the native Araucanian Indians, who were not "pacified" until our own times. But analysis of the dominant functions around 1750 of the twenty-two cities with populations of 20,000 or more that can be identified with any certainty reveals nine mining towns and six ports. Moreover, a certain number of nonmining towns depended economically on the exploitation of minerals. This was equally true of some port towns. As a result, the mining sector (gold and silver chiefly) may be considered the fundamental driving force behind the urbanization of Latin America until the second half of the eighteenth century. Were it possible to draw up a complete list of all mining towns, including those with populations of less than 20,000, it would prove very long indeed. The determining role played by mining and the cultivation of crops for export was all the more decisive insofar as the colonizers attempted to impose limits on industrial development. This meant in general that there were few jobs in manufacturing industries in the colonial cities of

Latin America—though it ought to be remembered that, while such jobs were in short supply, they were by no means totally absent.

The fate of the principal mining towns depended on the mineral deposits, which explains the main trends in urbanization in Latin America. As a general rule, nonmining towns, even when indirectly dependent on the mining industry, tended to resist more successfully the economic decline resulting from the exhaustion of deposits, presumably because the nonbasic sector (see chapter 9) was much larger than in mining towns. The fact that mining towns were generally located in relatively infertile regions added to their vulnerability. Potosi and Ouro Preto are the most striking examples, illustrating particularly well the rapid rise but precariousness of cities based on the extraction of precious metals.

The Bolivian city of Potosi was founded in 1547, two years after the first silver deposits were discovered. It was situated 3,960 meters above sea level on a plateau without agricultural potential. To supply it with water, the city required costly waterworks, which were justified solely by the richness of the deposits. By 1555 the city already had a population of 45,000; in 1585, 120,000; and in 1610, some 160,000. These figures are perhaps excessive, for they probably include the mining districts themselves. A rich city, "city of silver madness," as Vilar (1974) calls it, Potosi generated heavy demand both for local goods (but brought in from relatively distant parts of Latin America) and for luxury goods imported from Spain. One of the bases of its wealth was the Indian labor requisitioned through the system of the *Mita*, a system inspired by the Inca practice of requiring communities to pay collectively tribute in the form of work, in this case to the mine. The deposits were becoming exhausted from 1700–1730 on, and the cities began to decline, the population falling to 40,000 by around 1750 and to a mere 8,000 by about 1820, after the disturbances following independence. But exploitation continued throughout the nineteenth century. There was even a fresh rise in population, which reached 20,000 once more by the turn of the century.

Ouro Preto, "Black Gold," is today a small Brazilian town (declared a national museum) of some 10,000 people. But at its height around 1750 its population probably reached 60,000–100,000. The city dates from 1701, when gold deposits were discovered in the area. Named, for good reason, Vila Rica, it continued to prosper until around 1760–1780, when the deposits began to be exhausted. This precipitated the city's decline, its population falling to no more than 20,000–25,000 by the start of the nineteenth century. In 1889 it was decided to transfer the seat of the provincial capital to a more favorable site, Belo Horizonte, thus accelerating the city's decline. At the start of the twentieth century Ouro Preto had no more than 11,000 inhabitants.

The history of Potosi and Ouro Preto should not overshadow that of the chief mining region, namely Mexico, whose output of precious metals, principally silver, accounted around 1740–1760 for roughly a third of the world total and for 55% of the total for Latin America as a whole. And in this region too, many mining towns suffered declines once their mineral deposits had been exhausted.

While mining deposits are generally located in regions largely unfavorable to the establishment of cities, this is not always the case. One of the exceptions is Chile. Thus is it that, in the colorful language of the early nineteenth century, the *Dictionnaire géographique universel* (1823–33) says with reference to Chile: "In this country, sterile soil is not the lot of districts rich with mines. The rivers . . . roll grains of gold through reaches of countryside bedecked with all the luxury vegetation can bestow and the miner mines successfully in the same earth from which the farmer reaps an abundant harvest" (vol. 2, 1825). But things would no longer be the same after the first years of the nineteenth century, for the mines yielding nonprecious metals, whose exploitation intensified from this point on, were located in less hospitable regions.

This brings us to another factor in urbanization in Latin America, namely export crops, and especially sugar, which accounted for most of the volume and value of all Latin American exports other than precious metals. As late as around 1830, when competition from European beet sugar already was felt, sugar accounted for a little more than 40% of all Latin American exports, as against 13% for coffee, 6% for leather and hides, 5% for textile fibers, 2% for tobacco, and less than 1% for cacao (Bairoch and Etemad, 1985).

These agricultural exports were responsible for the emergence of two new urban regions: Brazil and the Antilles. In around 1600 none of the twelve cities with populations of more than twenty thousand in Latin America lay in these regions (see table 24.1). In around 1750, on the other hand, 6 out of 29 cities with populations of more than twenty thousand, representing 21% of the total, were found there, and 11 out of 41 (or 27%) in 1800.

In fact, between 1550 and 1800 urbanization occurred in two distinct phases. The first, chiefly linked with precious metals, unfolded between 1550 and 1700–1730. During this phase urban development was for the most part concentrated in three countries, Peru, Mexico, and Bolivia, which accounted for more than half of all of the larger cities of Latin America. The second phase, linked with the exportation of agricultural products, began between 1680 and 1720 and centered on Brazil and the Antilles. This phase continued in the nineteenth century with the emergence of large cities, beginning in the 1860s, in the temperate regions of the continent.

The outward-looking character of the Latin American economy led to a relatively high level of urbanization. According to my estimates, in around 1800 the level of urbanization in this part of the world was

TABLE 24.1   Regional Distribution of the Number of Latin
American Cities with Populations of 20,000 or More
(1500–1920)

	1500[a]	1600	1700	1750	1800	1920
Northern Andes	20	7	11	13	10	33
Bolivia	—	3	3	3	2	6
Colombia	—	—	1	3	2	16
Equador	—	1	2	2	2	4
Peru	—	3	5	5	4	7
Mexico	10	3	4	6	8	27
Brazil	—	—	3	4	7	47
Temperate Regions	—	—	—	1	2	46
Argentina	—	—	—	—	1	30
Chile	—	—	—	1	1	13
Uruguay	—	—	—	—	—	3
Antilles	—	—	1	2	4	25
Latin America as a whole[b]	32	12	21	29	41	207
Urban population (in millions)	—	—	1.5	1.9	2.9	23.2
Total population (in millions)	—	10.0	12.0	15.0	20.0	91.0
Level of urbanization (%)	—	—	12.5	13.0	14.5	25.5

Sources: Calculations and estimates by the author; see the methodological appendix.
Note: The fact that these figures have been only slightly rounded off does not imply a correspondingly small margin of error.
[a] Very approximate figures.
[b] Including regions and countries not indicated above.

on the order of 13–16%, that is, some 2–3 points higher than that of Europe (except Russia) during the same period, making a difference of 15–25%. Compared to Europe as a whole, Latin America had a level of urbanization higher by some 30–40%. Indeed, it was at this time the most heavily urbanized part of the world.

Before moving on to the other parts of the world, it may not be amiss to recall that, until the start of the nineteenth century, Latin America contained by far the largest part of the urban population of America, North and South. Around 1700, at a time when Latin America had twenty to twenty-two cities with populations of more than 20,000 (three of them with more than 50,000: Mexico City with 100,000, Potosí with 95,000, and Oruro with 70,000), the three largest American and Canadian cities were Boston with a population of 7,000, Quebec with 6,000, and New York with 5,000. Even as late as 1800, beside the forty-odd cities with populations of 20,000 and the total urban population of 2,900,000 in Latin America, northern North America could only muster four cities with populations of

20,000 and some 300,000 city dwellers overall. By contrast, in 1900 there were only 8 million city dwellers in Latin America as against almost 30 million in the United States and Canada.

Black Africa: Small European Enclaves

Black Africa was not affected by European colonization in a direct and substantial way until the end of the nineteenth century. But one cannot overlook the dramatic slave trade which, from the start of the sixteenth until the first years of the nineteenth century, bled the continent of some ten to fifteen million people. And the discovery of the maritime route to Asia eventually resulted in a need for supply posts, also generating a heavier flow of trade than before.

To what extent did these two phenomena, both related to European colonization, influence the urban life of Black Africa? It is not easy to answer this question because, given the current state of research, the impact of the slave trade is difficult to determine. It appears very likely, however, that during the four centuries involved the urban life of the continent was influenced more by the autonomous evolution of local cultures and by Muslim penetration than by European interference.

Historians have attributed two contradictory consequences to the impact of the slave trade on urbanization in Black Africa. For some, the insecurity caused by the slave raids led to economic disorganization and thence to decline in urbanization, a decline accelerated in many instances by the flight of certain urban populations into the bush. For others, however, the need for defence against the slave raids encouraged the creation of fortified towns and led to the growth of the populations of the urban centers made secure in this way. Furthermore, not the least important effect of the slave trade—and this is a certainty—was that it fostered the establishment of African cities themselves based on the slave trade. On which side does the reality ultimately lie? It seems likely that both outcomes materialized, depending on the region. But in my opinion the negative component was probably more important.

Thus as far as urbanization is concerned, the most certain, but least significant, outgrowth of the slave trade was the creation or enlargement of a certain number of European urban centers or enclaves in African urban centers as places to buy and sell slaves. Added to or combined with centers more focused on trade proper, these urban centers were ultimately fairly numerous, but were not especially populous. Many were merely forts intended to provide havens for ships or lodge the personnel of the relatively limited military and civil administration. The Portuguese founded one of the earliest establishments, erecting in 1486, to the west of Accra, the fort of Saint George of the Mine, which eventually became the city of Elmina. The site was explored as early as 1481; Christopher Columbus apparently participated in this expedition as one of its officers. In all, about fifty forts and "towns" had thus been established by the end of the nineteenth century. One of the most important was (Sao Paulo de) Luanda, founded in 1576, a city having at its height during the seventeenth and eighteenth centuries a population of some 20,000, 3,000 of them Europeans. Among the other relatively early settlements were Saint Louis (founded by the French in 1626); Gorée (founded by the Dutch in 1619); Benguela (founded by the Portuguese in 1647); Sekondi (Fort Orange; founded by the Dutch in about 1640); Cape Coast (Cabo Corso; founded by the Portuguese in 1610); and Accra, an urban center that grew up around three forts established very near each other—one British, one Danish, and one Dutch. On the east coast the Portuguese played a major role. Among the "cities" they founded were Mozambique (1507), Quelimane (1544), Sofala (1505; but already a sizable Muslim town before its capture at this time), Sena (1531), and Ibo (beginning of the seventeenth century).

Mention should also be made of the special case of Freetown, in Sierra Leone, the result, in a sense, of the abolition of slavery. It was originally founded in 1787 as a settlement for black soldiers who had served in the English army in North America and for black slaves who had taken refuge in London—some 400 people in all. These were joined by 1,100 former slaves who had sought asylum in Canada and were sent to Freetown in 1792.

One may add to this list of colonial urban centers the city of San Salvador, the new name given to his capital, Mbanza Congo, by the Congolese sovereign after his conversion to Christianity. And just as on coming under Islamic influence other African cities came to be covered with mosques, so San Salvador came to be covered with churches, to such an extent, indeed, that it was eventually called "Ekongo dia ngungo," the city of church bells. But San Salvador remained an isolated case; it was not until the twentieth century that acculturation of this sort became widespread.

These fifty-odd small urban centers, many of which were the starting point for the calvary of millions of black slaves, were also very often the end point in the career of many white overseers in Africa. Owing to climatic conditions and above all epidemics, the life expectancy of the Europeans who settled in these towns was extremely short. According to the available data, life expectancy was only three to four years. This too may perhaps help to explain the delay in the creation of true European urban centers in Black Africa.

The Other Flow of Slaves

Before turning to the exceptional case, which was the creation of real European colonial cities on two small African islands, it would not be superfluous to mention briefly the second important flow of slaves.

It has been noted that the extension of Islam contributed to the urbanization of a large part of Black Africa, especially through the intensification of trade, in which black slaves destined for the Maghreb and the Middle East occupied an important place (see chapter 4). This trade began before the eleventh century and kept its importance until the end of the nineteenth century.

This slave trade with the Muslim world had the same sort of consequences as that with America: cultures and probably cities suffered from slave raids as cultures and cities added the slave trade to their basic economic activities. The history of the cities which profited, more or less, from this trade is generally better known than the history of the cities which suffered from it. And among those which profited were the city-states of the Hausa culture: Kano, Katsena, and Zaira. These city-states, although converted to Islam, kept their independence until the European colonization, to which I now return.

An Exception: Two Small Islands Both Colonized and Urbanized by Europe

It was really not until the eighteenth century that on two small islands, each less than three thousand square kilometers in area, off the southeast coast of Africa, "European" cities were created which were based on economic exploitation proper. The fate of these two islands would come to play, despite their small size, an important part in the history of European colonization in Africa, first in the eighteenth century and then again in the nineteenth century. It is with the first phase of this saga that I shall be concerned here (for the second see chapter 25).

These two islands, deserted at the time of their discovery, changed hands many times before Franco-British rivalry definitely rendered one of them, Réunion, French (in 1642) and the other, Mauritius, British (in 1810). On Réunion (successively named Mascareigne, Bourbon, Réunion, Bonaparte, and then Bourbon once more before becoming Réunion once and for all), plantations were established (chiefly for growing coffee) on which slaves imported either from Asia or from the African mainland were used. During the first decades of the eighteenth century, these plantations spawned a string of six or seven towns, all given saints' names. While they grew especially rapidly during the first half of the nineteenth century, these towns already had a combined population of some 40,000 around 1800, nearly 10,000 in the capital, Saint Denis. Mauritius (successively known as do Cerno, Mauritius, île de France, and finally Mauritius once again) had during the eighteenth century only one genuine town, Port Louis, with a population on the order of 2,000 around 1800 (the population grew greatly during the nineteenth century, however, rising to 50,000 by around 1850). In both cases Europeans represented a large, but not dominant part of the urban population. In around 1800 some 10,000–15,000 Europeans lived in all of the cities of the two islands taken together.

Colonization in Black Africa as a Whole: Little Influence on Urbanization

What was the population of the fifty-odd European towns, forts, or enclaves, in Africa? Unfortunately there exists as yet no general history of these settlements. But in any event the European population was decidedly small. For the start of the seventeenth century in southeast Africa, Axelson (1960) estimates that the number of Portuguese permanently established there did not exceed 400. The figure must have been higher at the start of the nineteenth century, taking all of Africa and all Europeans into account. But even postulating 100 or 200 Europeans per geographic location (though these numbers are probably too high) and including the Europeans on Réunion and Mauritius, the figure arrived at is only some 15,000–25,000 people, more than half of them on the two islands. What of the total population of those towns, African and Asian as well as European? Excluding the two islands, it could not have been more than five or at most ten times greater than the European population, making an absolute upper limit of some 120,000 people (which is not very many) and a minimum of some 30,000 (which is very few). This can be compared to the three to four million which is the likely total urban population of Black Africa around 1800.

But one cannot leave the history of relations between Europe and Black Africa before the onset of colonization proper without recalling one last, very important consequence of these relations: the introduction of plants domesticated in the New World. The introduction of these plants must undoubtedly have led, if not to a general increase in agricultural productivity, then at least to an increase in average yields in terms of calories relative to the amount of land under cultivation, an increase without which it would be impossible to account for their rapid diffusion. Once the Portuguese had initiated the process, the diffusion was generally spontaneous, but it was also sometimes the result of deliberate policy on the part of local leaders. This was notably the case with Shamba Bologongo, who at the start of the seventeenth century usurped the throne of the kingdom of Kuba (in contemporary Zaire). Shamba Bologongo, who had lived in regions in which these plants were already grown, introduced in particular maize, peanuts, and tomatoes into his kingdom. The relative prosperity of his kingdom, and also the craft activities Shamba Bologongo fostered, were certainly not unrelated to the introduction of these crops.

Asia: A Very Marginal European Presence

Before the nineteenth century the impact of European colonization on the urban world of Asia was even more marginal than its impact on the urban world of Africa. The cities created, transformed, or enlarged by Europeans were very few and far between. The two most important cases were Batavia and Goa. In Batavia (present-day Djakarta) the Dutch had by 1610 established a "factory" (trading establishment) in what was then a small town. By 1619 a veritable Dutch city had been founded, with a population of 50,000 around 1700 and 100,000 around 1760–1780. Europeans, however, were in the minority.

The case of Goa was different in that, when Europeans arrived, the Indian city of Goa was already large and wealthy, with some 40,000–50,000 inhabitants. The city was taken by the Portuguese in 1510 and a large part of the population was massacred. But a policy of intermarriage with local women and an influx of immigrants from Portugal enabled Goa to grow once more, and it became a very wealthy Portuguese city, reaching its height between 1575 and 1625. The resplendent architecture of the city gave rise to a Portuguese proverb: "Who has seen Goa need no longer see Lisbon." According to some estimates, moreover, during its apogee Goa had a population of 200,000. While this is certainly an exaggeration, it nevertheless seems likely that the city had a population of 100,000, a population approaching, if not greater than, that of Lisbon. A century and a half later, however, around 1770, Goa no longer even had a population of 2,000. And fifty years later only a few priests, monks, and nuns would remain in what during the era of its splendor had been called the "Rome of India," owing to the great number of religious establishments it contained. Here again is an instance of the fragility of certain cities. The loss of maritime supremacy by the Portuguese explains the start of the process of decline, which accelerated, beginning in 1759, after the transfer of the seat of government to Panjin.

Less glorious but more stable was the fate of the other Portuguese city of Asia, Macao. Macao was also less independent, for although the Chinese authorized the establishment of "factories" and thus of a town in 1557, the city was until the nineteenth century, if not directly governed, at least controlled by the Chinese authorities. Moreover, Europeans never made up the majority of its population.

Without drawing up an exhaustive list, one should further mention the Indian cities of Pondicherry, founded by the French in 1683 on the site of a native village, and Calcutta, founded by the East India Company in 1690, also on the site of a native village. The European presence in Pondicherry remained very small. Calcutta meanwhile, owing to its favorable location for foreign trade, grew very rapidly, its population rising from 12,000 in 1710 to 120,000 by around 1750. But here, too, the European presence was never significant; even in 1900 Europeans represented less than 3% of the population. The impact these few Europeans had was great, however, and prefigured the colonization to come.

Before summing up the situation, I ought to evoke once more Indochina and the Philippines, regions whose fates contrasted sharply. Indochina, a "large peninsula situated in Southeast Asia, between India and China, was divided in the eighteenth century as today into multiple states." But, as Devèze (1970) continues, "The Europeans did not, however, take advantage of this fragmentation, essentially due to geographic factors. The Portuguese, it is true, established themselves very early on at Malacca (1511), where the Dutch supplanted them in 1641. But by that time Malacca had lost much of its economic activity and population to the benefit of Batavia." It was not, in fact, until French colonization during the last quarter of the nineteenth century that there was a significant European presence in this part of the world.

Very different was the fate in store for the Philippines, which in a way constituted the extension of Spanish colonization in Latin America. While the Spanish language has almost completely disappeared (the archipelago was a colony of the United States from 1898 to 1946), Catholicism has remained preponderant. And Manila, founded in 1571 on the site of a native town destroyed by the Spanish, was a genuine colonial city, whose population reached 30,000 fairly quickly (remaining at this level until the start of the eighteenth century). About a tenth of the inhabitants were Spanish; but this proportion decreased afterwards with the rapid growth of the population, which surpassed 100,000 around 1810–1820. In fact the first European city was Cebu (first called Villa de Santisimo Nombre de Jesus). Founded in 1565, Cebu was far from being as large as Manila, which was true of the few other Europeanized cities as well.

While seen from Europe these cities may have seemed numerous and sometimes large, it should be remembered that around the same period (around 1700), Asia (not counting the Middle East) contained some fifty-five cities with populations of more than 100,000 and most likely more than a hundred with populations of 50,000 to 100,000. All of the colonial cities of Asia combined, then, constituted a very marginal phenomenon. At no time before the second half of the eighteenth century did these cities, including their non-European population, have more than 1% of the total urban population of Asia, the exact figure in all likelihood being some 0.3–0.6%.

Since I discussed Asia without dealing with the Middle East, it is perhaps worth stressing that the omission of the urban worlds of the various Muslim cultures is explained by the fact that European colonization in this part of the world did not begin until 1830, with the capture of Algiers. In addition, there were no European urban enclaves resembling those in Asia and Africa. As a result, Europeans did not directly interfere with the urban life of the Middle East and the Maghreb before the second third of the nineteenth century.

Before leaving the history of traditional European colonization, I should pause to reflect on the impact of traditional colonization (non-European included) on urbanization. The fundamental question is whether traditional colonization was an urbanizing or a deurbanizing factor. And as is very often true in the human sciences, the answer is not unequivocal. Simplifying somewhat, one may advance the two following rules. The first concerns colonized territories: in this case colonization was an urbanizing factor in thinly urbanized regions and a deurbanizing factor in heavily urbanized regions. The second concerns colonial powers: in this case the colonial adventure was almost always an urbanizing factor. The simplicity of these two rules is obviously disturbed not only by the many forms of the process of traditional colonization, but also by the vast range of situations in the relative levels of the forms of urbanization of the two societies brought into closer contact in this way: the colonizing power and the colony.

If we regard the colonizing powers and their colonies as single geographical entities, traditional colonization was as a general rule an urbanizing factor, because of the intensified trade brought by colonization. But here too, exceptions were possible, as for example in the case of a small colonizing power whose colonization destroyed large urban cultures. This was the case in the sixteenth century where Europe and the New World were concerned, the scale of the decline in the urban population of the New World surpassing the scale of urban growth inspired in Europe by that colonization.

25 Modern Colonization and Urbanization in Asia and the Maghreb from 1780/1815 to 1930/40 □

The years 1780 to 1815 mark a profound break in the history of the parts of the world that gradually came to form the Third World of today. This break was occasioned by a series of phenomena affecting sometimes all of the future Third World, sometimes specific parts of it.

The most important change, one already hinted at, was that brought about by the Industrial Revolution. Already by the 1790s, because of mechanization, a worker in an English textile mill could produce 120 to 160 times as much cotton thread as an Indian or European traditional craftsman. During the same period, because of the use of coke, with a population of eight million, England turned out some 100,000 metric tons of cast iron, or probably as much as, if not more than, all of India with a population of nearly 200 million. Within about twenty years (around 1810–20) this industrial change brought about a complete reversal in the flow of trade between Europe and those regions in other parts of the world with advanced traditional technological cultures, particularly Asia. Asia, which during the first years of the nineteenth century still exported manufactured goods especially to Europe, was to be inundated with European industrial products, thereby engendering a process of deindustrialization to which I shall return later. This new form of trade would, moreover, spell the death of the system of "companies" that had in each country monopolized trade with the East and West Indies. These companies were to be replaced by genuine colonization which by 1815–1820 already affected a large part of Asia.

The start of the nineteenth century also witnessed the emergence of three major phenomena that would subsequently shape the history of Latin America. The first was independence. Between 1804 and 1822 almost all of Latin America succeeded in shaking off the colonial yoke.

At the same time Europe itself began to produce the chief export commodity of Latin America, sugar, the production of sugar from beets beginning early in the nineteenth century, but not assuming substantial proportions until after 1840. By the beginning of the 1880s the world's production of beet sugar became as important as that of cane sugar, and around 1900 it exceeded that of cane sugar by 60 percent. By that period the production of beet sugar was more than six million metric tons, that is, twenty times greater than the total for cane sugar at the beginning of the nineteenth century.

Finally, still in the early nineteenth century, the banning of the slave trade became increasingly effective; and even though the slave trade did not totally disappear during the first half of the nineteenth century, it was significantly curtailed, leading to a substantial reduction in the number of new slaves arriving in Latin America. It should be remembered, however, that slavery was abolished at this point in those countries in which it played no important economic role; in other countries slavery was not abolished until 1860–1880. The prohibition of the slave trade, needless to say, had consequences in Black Africa, which between 1800–1810 and 1880–1890 had a period of relative nonintervention on the part of Europe.

The point of departure for the present discussion having been largely established, a few words are called for concerning its terminal point. The latter coincides with the beginning of the acceleration of the process of the explosive growth of urbanization that furnishes the theme of the last chapters of this part of the book, a process that constitutes one of the major aspects of the general problem of the Third World. In the present chapter, I can only bring out a few salient features of developments over the century and a half between 1780 and 1940 in Asia and the Maghreb, regions whose urban history still contains many shadowy areas. Chapter 26 will be devoted to events in Black Africa and Latin America.

Asia: The Impact of Deindustrialization and Colonization

In June 1812, the young republic of the United States of America declared war on its former colonizer. The causes of this conflict, which lasted until December 1814, were chiefly local, concerning the Indians and Canada. But it would subsequently have profound consequences for the daily life of millions of inhabitants of India. Between 1784, when English customs officials seized the first bales of cotton imported from the United States (their motive, amazingly, being doubt as to its origins), and 1809–1811, by which time the United States exported on the average 32,000 metric tons of cotton per year, the new republic had become not only the chief exporter of this raw material to the world, but also far and away the main source supplying the English cotton industry. The abrupt diminution of this source caused by the war of 1812 provided fresh arguments for the lobby on behalf of English industrialists demanding the liberty to export cotton textiles to the vast Indian market and thereby the abrogation of the monopoly exercised by the East India Company, which had hitherto prevented all imports of cotton textiles into India. In the eyes of these industrialists, it was a mistake not to bring in raw cotton from India to process in England, where technological advances made it possible to produce fabrics at a considerably lower cost.

In 1813 the monopoly over trade with India held by the East India Company was abolished. And what might have been expected happened: from nothing in 1812, imports of cotton fabrics into India rose by 1814 to half a million meters, by around 1820 to twelve million meters, reaching 900 million meters around 1870 and then stabilizing at around 1.9 billion meters for several decades beginning in the 1880s. This massive flow is explained by two factors. The first is obviously the enormous increase in productivity of the English spinning industry owing to mechanization. The second is related to colonialism. While European countries had customs duties on these products of 30–60%, these same products entered India freely. And when, for fiscal reasons, the British government in India was finally obliged to impose modest duties on textile imports from Britain, the "legitimate" protests of English manufacturers led to the imposition of a similar tax on local production in order to place British and Indian producers on an "equal footing."

Under conditions such as these, can there be any surprise at the rapid disappearance of the Indian textile industry? Whatever uncertainty may surround this point concerns disputes between specialists over matters of detail. By the 1860s, had the Indian textile industry vanished completely, or did artisan spinners still hold on in isolated regions? And if some did hold on, did they supply 5–10% or 15–25% of the national needs? The degree of uncertainty is even smaller where the other important sector of industry, iron and steel, is concerned. In 1890 did the indigenous iron and steel industry supply 1 or 5% of local consumption? To put these questions in perspective, it should be remembered that during the seventeenth and eighteenth centuries, India's chief export goods were not its spices, nor even its tea, but articles made of cotton: the famous calico prints that Europe sought (and eventually managed) to imitate.

A Decline in Traditional Cities Offset by the Rapid Growth of Export Towns: The Case of India

The process of deindustrialization in India must clearly have had important effects on employment and thus on urban life. According to my calculations, there was in India a decline in the population of traditional cities. Thus for the seventy-three cities whose growth between 1800 and 1850 it was possible for me to trace there was a fall of 8%, from 4,560,000 to 4,190,000. This decline does not, however, seem sufficient to reflect the impact of deindustrialization, for the figures available chiefly concern fairly large cities (more than 30,000 people). It appears likely that the decline was sharper still in smaller cities: the larger cities recouped through foreign trade some of the jobs lost in industry.

But while the traditional network of Indian cities was suffering the consequences of deindustrialization, the increased activity in the field of foreign trade brought about the rapid growth of the population of a small number of cities, particularly Bombay, Calcutta, and Madras, whose combined population rose sharply, rising from 500,000 around 1800 to 1,300,000 by around 1850. These were the cities in which the activities of the East India Company were concentrated. On this score, it will be noted that a similar turn of events seems already to have taken place in the eighteenth century. But according to my calculations, although the data in this case are less complete, if exception is made for the "company towns," the population of the the other large urban centers fell by roughly 35–40% between 1700 and 1800. But if I add Bombay, Calcutta, and Madras, the decline was only about 20%, a figure suggesting a decline on the order of 10–18% in total urban population. This decline during the eighteenth century may be imputed to the political and economic disorganization following the death of Aurangzeb (see chapter 22).

The decline (or stagnation) of traditional cities, which began as early as the beginning of the eighteenth century, appears to have continued until 1860–1870. Afterwards a period of accelerated growth was already under way, with the result that, between 1850 and 1900, based on the growth of eighty-five large cities there was an increase of 36%, while the three great commercial cities grew by more than 100%. This would have meant a rise of 46% (from 6.1 to 8.9 million) for those eighty-eight cities taken together. At this later point (1901), 9.2% of the 294 million people living in India lived in towns with populations of more than five thousand. These fairly reliable data, derived from the third complete census taken by the British authorities, enable me, on the basis of the developments described above, to give probable figures for the level of urbanization in India. This level would seem to have evolved as follows:

1700	11.0–13.0%
1800	9.0–11.5%
1850	7.5– 9.5%
1900	9.0–10.0%
1940	14.0–16.0%

The renewal of urban growth can be accounted for by the combined effects of the rise in the export trade fostered by colonization and the reindustrialization that took place despite colonization. Of great interest is the fact that the creation of new industries (to start with mainly in textiles) was the work of native entrepreneurs. These were for the most part Parsis (a small religious minority connected to the cult of Zarathustra and established in India since the eighth century). The most dynamic of these entrepreneurs, Tata, founded an industrial dynasty whose enterprises today represent the largest conglomerate in the country. The first mechanized spinning mill had been established by 1853, but it was not until the 1870s that the number of spindles in India exceeded one million. There would be 4.9 million in 1900 and 10.1 million in 1939. At this time (the late 1930s), the Indian textile industry supplied more than 80% of local needs. And alongside it other modern sectors had emerged: iron and steel, a chemical industry, manufacturing in metals, and others.

Even though the level of industrialization remained modest—the same as that of continental Europe at the start of the nineteenth century—this nevertheless represented enough industrial jobs to employ some two million people in modern sectors in urban areas alone. As a result, beginning in the 1930s, India surpassed the highest level of urbanization reached formerly. Around 1940 city dwellers made up 14–16% of the total population; and since total population had more than doubled since 1700, this meant an urban population nearly three times greater than in the early eighteenth century. But while city dwellers were three times as numerous as before, they were also three times as poor.

A Steep Decline in the Standard of Living for City Residents

Deindustrialization and the likely cornering of the profits from the export trade by nonnative intermediaries brought about a catastrophic fall in the standard of living of the great mass of the urban population of India. Data are available making it possible to compare levels of urban wages. According to the calculations of R. Mukerjee (1967), real wages in the second half of the nineteenth century and the early twentieth century were only a quarter of what they had been in the second half of the sixteenth century, the unusually favorable era of the reign of Akbar.

This estimate probably exaggerates the extent of the fall, for it seems unlikely, though not impossible, that during the reign of Akbar real wages were four times higher than the minimum required to sustain life, a level below which wages could clearly not have fallen during the nineteenth century or at any other time. But other calculations (Desai, 1972) comparing the purchasing power of urban wages in Akbar's time and the middle of the twentieth century also come up with very negative results: real wages about two times lower. In any case, there is little doubt concerning the wretched plight of Indian city dwellers during the second half of the nineteenth century and the first decades of the twentieth century: contemporary observers bear witness to it, as do the available data on infant mortality. In Bombay from 1900 to 1909 records show that for each 1,000 births 603 infants died in their first year. It is true that for Calcutta the corresponding figure was "only" 358, and that in Bombay itself over the preceding two decades (1880–1899), infant mortality did not exceed 450 per 1,000. But even these lower rates bespeak a highly unfavorable situation, especially when one considers the extent to which Western medicine, already capable of partially offsetting the effects of all this misery, had penetrated Indian society.

To be sure, India was an extreme case, the model par excellence of the total colonization of a large country which, in the context of traditional societies, had formerly been heavily industrialized. This indeed made the impact of colonization on the urban system all the more dramatic. In other parts of the world, the modalities were sometimes different. I shall turn now to what happened in the chief among them.

China: A Process of Semicolonization Engrafted upon a Negative Phase of Urbanization

In China the flood of European manufactured goods began later than in India—in fact nearly a half century later. Though the Treaty of Nanking (1842)—which brought to an end the Opium War, the first defeat suffered by the Celestial Empire at Western hands— opened five ports to English traders, many obstacles still stood in the way of penetration by European manufactures (and Indian opium). It was not until the treaty of 1858, imposed following a second military expedition and ratified only in October 1860, thanks to further military intervention by both Britain and France this time, that China finally lost all autonomy in matters of foreign trade and that the intensification of imports truly began. European gunboats even had the right to navigate on Chinese rivers in order to enforce "free trade," which meant among other things "freedom" to ship Indian opium to China under the supervision of the English East India Company. Although China was not after this date a genuine colony, it nevertheless formed part of what is sometimes described as an "informal empire." This dependence lasted a long time. Despite the revolution of 1911, it was not until the Special Conference of 1925–26 in Peking dealing with customs matters that the major powers recognized China's right, as of January 1, 1929, to fix its own customs tariffs.

The fate of the Chinese economy differed, however, from that of India inasmuch as local industry put up stiffer resistance, a resistance made possible because the flood of European goods began later, because a certain local autonomy persisted, and because of China's enormous size. The resistance may also have been sustained by the ancient tradition of rejection of the outside world, of mistrust toward foreigners. But the stiffer resistance did not spare China a process of deindustrialization. In the case of China, debate among specialists revolves around the figure of 60%. Around 1890, for instance, did the local textile industry meet 50 or 70% of the country's needs?

Despite the great unreliability of the available data, one may reasonably estimate that the first decades of intense economic relations with the West brought about no decline in the level of urbanization. To be sure (see chapter 22), when China opened to European trade it was already undergoing a negative phase of urban growth; the level of urbanization had fallen by around 1850 to 6.0–7.5%, as against 11–14% in the sixteenth century. According to the fragmentary indications available, it appears that as early as the second half of the nineteenth century cases of urban expansion outnumbered those of urban decline. Most of the cities forced open to foreign trade—some of which, like Shanghai, were Europeanized—saw their populations grow rapidly. Shanghai, with a population of just over 200,000 in the mid-nineteenth century, had 800,000 by the end of the century, and exceeded one million between 1910 and 1920. During this same period the more traditional cities experienced more moderate growth, in some cases (fewer than in India, it is true) even suffering decline. It seems likely, therefore, that around 1900 the level of urbanization was higher than a half century earlier. According to my own estimates, during this half century urban population rose by 15–20%, rural population having remained practically stable, thus yielding a level of urbanization of 7.0–8.5%.

Developments accelerated between 1900 and 1937, bringing the proportion of city dwellers to 11–14%. Around 1938 Shanghai had a population of more than 3.5 million, Peking 1.5 million, and Canton and T'ien-tsin 1 million. Around 1840, on the other hand, the populations of Shanghai and T'ien-tsin were only on the order of 200,000, and that of Canton 700,000.

This growth is largely explained by the intensification of trade. Exports, for example, which must have stood at a value of some $20–30 million around 1840, rose to a value of $190 million in 1913 and $700 million in 1928. In addition, since, beginning from the 1870s and 1880s, reindustrialization began to outstrip deindustrialization, and since the new industries tended to be established in urban areas more often than those disappearing at this time, the cities had a net increase in jobs. In 1937 China had 5.1 million cotton spindles and produced 800,000 metric tons of cast iron. On the other hand, it is true that between 1910–1914 and 1930–1940, agricultural yield and perhaps productivity as well increased only moderately; but even this moderate growth contrasted with the stagnation or decline recorded in the nineteenth century.

As elsewhere, the railroads also contributed to the growth of certain Chinese cities. Thus, T'ien-tsin, just mentioned, owed a part of its rapid expansion to the railroads, which added a further asset to this river port that had already become the seat of the viceregency and a site for textile manufacturing. In China, despite the exceedingly dense network of traditional cities, new cities emerged thanks to the railroads. Such was notably the case for Harbin, a small village in Manchuria, where at the start of the nineteenth century the accidents of geography and human choice caused two railroad lines to cross. By 1940 the city had a population of 470,000.

Harbin affords an excellent transition to another form of colonization that northern China, and in particular Manchuria, owed to Russia and Japan. This form of colonization was essentially based on the exploitation of the region's mineral resources. While Harbin became in part a Russian colonial town, another city, with a prestigious past, Mukden (present-day Shenyang), became the chief colonial town of Japan. Thanks to the railroads and more particularly to the neighboring coalfields, Mukden became an industrial center with a population of 770,000 in 1938, as against 200,000 around 1920. And among these 770,000 inhabitants at least 91,000 were Japanese. Meanwhile, in 1938, after passing under Japanese domination, Harbin still had 27,000 Russians from a much larger Russian community at the end of the Tsarist era.

The presence of so many foreigners was, however, the exception rather than the rule. The only other cities with a fairly large number of foreigners were Macao, Hong Kong, and above all, Shanghai. In Macao around 1940 there were some 9,000 Portuguese, many half-breeds figuring among them for a great many years, out of a total population of 370,000. Hong Kong at that time had 22,000 foreigners, 15,000 of them from the West, out of a total population of 1.6 million. Around 1935 some 62,000 foreigners, 47,000 of them from the West, lived in Shanghai, out of a population of more than 3 million. But this was a mere drop in the ocean: at most 300,000 foreigners out of a total urban population of nearly 50 million.

And What of the Rest of Asia?

What of the rest of Asia? Many regions had already succumbed to colonization more completely than the vast Chinese Empire. This was especially true of the group of islands forming contemporary Indonesia. This part of the world had been open to international trade for a great many years (see chapter 22), the Dutch having established a colonial enclave there—Batavia—as early as the seventeenth century. By the first years of the nineteenth century, and more intensely after 1830, these regions were forced by the Dutch to become major producers of sugar, coffee, and so forth, and they lost all of their craft industries. Beginning in the 1860s, it was the turn of the Indochinese peninsula to suffer more or less the same fate. Only Siam (contemporary Thailand) escaped colonization, by playing skillfully on the rivalry between the British established to the west (in Burma) and the French to the east (in Indochina). In fact, with Japan, Siam would be the only region outside Muslim Asia to be spared colonization. But unlike Japan, and like Muslim Asia, Siam would not escape deindustrialization, for under the influence of the "liberal spirit," it opened its ports to manufactured goods coming from Europe, though these goods were, it is true, very cheap.

Before European intrusion these other regions were both less urbanized and less industrialized than India and China. This being the case, it is natural that colonization should have influenced urbanization differently. Colonization proved more urbanizing in these regions than elsewhere: the new urban jobs created owing to the effects of colonization usually outnumbered those lost due to deindustrialization.

Indonesia and Southeast Asia

I shall pause first of all with the largest region of Southeast Asia, corresponding to present-day Indonesia. The exceptionally brutal, but efficient Dutch colonization made this group of islands—whose 24–28 million people around 1860 equalled one-ninth the population of India—an economic entity whose exports equalled one-quarter of India's. During the first half of the nineteenth century colonization had brought about no real urban expansion. It is true that the policy of the governor, Van den Bosch (in force between 1830 and 1860), by forbidding Europeans to own land and by other measures, managed directly or indirectly to put a brake on the rural exodus and thus on urban growth. It should be pointed out that before returning to Indonesia as governor Van den Bosch had studied economics. He considered himself a disciple of the socialist Owen and had in a sense a tendency to think of urban life as negative. Thus his plan for solving the problem of urban poverty and unemployment in the Netherlands prescribed installing the poor in rural areas.

After 1860–1870 urban population grew rapidly. According to my estimates, between 1850 and 1910 urban population doubled. But total population just about kept pace with it. As a result, the Indonesia of 1910 was no more urbanized than that of 1850. In spatial terms, however, this rise in urban population created a denser network of cities. From 1910 to 1930 urban growth proceeded more rapidly than growth in total population, the respective rates being 3.7–4.6% and 1.0–1.4% per year. While before colonization there were one or two cities with populations of more than 100,000, there were seven or eight around 1930. Batavia, which had grown little between 1750 and 1900, went from 115,000 people in 1910 to 440,000 in 1930. The population of Surabaya reached 340,000. We find here the beginnings of the urban explosion to be examined in chapter 27.

But while these are the beginnings, they are not yet the kind of urban hypertrophy that will be seen later. For Indonesia in 1930 remained relatively little urbanized: the cities most likely contained no more than 8–10% of the total population. Certainly there was no industry whatever; practically 100% of all manufactured goods consumed were imported. But the comparatively modest level of urban growth helped fend off the sort of misery that was to be the lot of Third World cities after the Second World War.

The European presence was greater than in India or China. In 1930 there were 37,000 Europeans and Eurasians in Batavia and 26,000 in Surabaya. It is likely that, taken all together, Europeans represented 2–4% of the urban population, as against a proportion distinctly lower than 1% in India and China.

Despite the existence of a few industries, French Indochina was even less urbanized than Indonesia, and its cities were smaller as well. Around 1930 Saigon had a population of around 100,000, and Hanoi of around 140,000. At this time Indochina was probably the least urbanized of the great cultures of Asia, perhaps only 6–9% of its population living in cities. To be sure, certain rural areas were nearly as densely populated as some cities.

Very different was the situation in the Philippines. Should this be seen as the reflection of cultural differences tending in general to bestow a more urban character on the colonies of Mediterranean countries than on those of European countries lying further to the north? Something of the sort has been noted with reference to the preceding phase of the history of colonization in the New World. To this factor should certainly be added the early date of the beginnings of colonization in the region. But whatever the cause, the fact remains that, based on the data provided by the census of 1887, the urban population accounted for some 12–16% of the total population of the Philippines, and perhaps even more. Manila, moreover, already had a population of 150,000, making it large for a country of seven million people at this stage in its urban development.

The Colonization of Asia: A Factor in Its Urbanization?

Before leaving Asia, it is worth asking some questions about the overall impact of modern colonization on the urbanization of this vast continent with its advanced cultures, a continent whose population accounted for nearly two-thirds of the population of the world as a whole and four-fifths of that of the future Third World. Looking no further than around 1930–1940, if one confines oneself to considering levels of urbanization one may be tempted to say that colonization induced no dramatic change in this continent. Around 1700, as well as around 1930, 10–12% of the population of Asia lived in cities. Owing to the decline recorded in China, a decline in no way imput-

TABLE 25.1   Levels of Urbanization of the Principal Countries
of Asia according to their Political Status
(1900–1930)

	1900	1930
Colonized or semi-colonized countries		
China	7–9	10–12
India	9–11	10–12
Indonesia	5–8	8–10
Philippines	14–16	16–19
Vietnam	6–9	6–9
Relatively independent countries		
Iran	12–15	14–17
Korea[a]	8–11	10–13
Thailand	8–10	9–11
Turkey	15–18	14–17
Asia as a whole	8–10	10–12

Sources: Calculations and estimates by the author; see the methodological appendix.
[a] Independent around 1900, but colonized by Japan in 1930.

able to colonization, the level of urbanization had dropped to 8–10%
by the start of the nineteenth century. Around 1930, on the other
hand, it stood again at 10–12%. The deurbanizing effects of deindustrialization were more or less offset (and even a little more than
that) by the urbanizing impact of increased trade and the outward-
looking character of the new economies fostered by colonization.
Thus, superficially, no radical changes occurred (see table 25.1).

Colonized countries were not, indeed, systematically characterized
by higher levels of urbanization than other countries. The high level
reached in Turkey, for instance, especially in 1900, has to be interpreted as reflecting the fact that Turkey was itself the mother state of
an empire. Though this empire was much smaller than in earlier centuries, Turkey nevertheless retained a potent urban vestige of its former glory, in the form especially of the size of Istanbul, which around
the turn of the century had a population of 800,000, representing
4–5% of the country's total population.

But though around 1930 the levels of urbanization in colonized
countries showed no signs of dramatic change, this does not mean
that these were the same cities as before with the same urban structure. Not only had the hierarchy of cities been changed from top to
bottom, but the cities themselves exhibited a completely different economic structure, and the relations between town and country and between social classes within the cities had taken on a new form. More
serious still was the fact that the people living in these cities were most
likely more wretched than their ancestors had been, a fate probably

shared by rural residents. This fall in the standard of living, moreover, poses a problem: how can it be reconciled with the maintenance and even the growth of the level of urbanization? I shall return to this important question at the end of chapter 26, after tracing the history of colonization and the cities in the other continents forming today's Third World.

The Maghreb: Colonization by Settlement

The Maghreb, of which Morocco alone had escaped colonization by the Ottoman Empire, was colonized by Europe in its entirety. I shall review the stages of this process of colonization.

The process began in 1830 with the capture of Algiers by the French. But it was not until the end of the century that the other countries of the region succumbed. The first to fall was Tunisia, where, as the *Petit Larousse** of 1952 notes: "In 1881, desirous of bringing an end to the threat posed to Algeria by the anarchy in neighboring countries, France set about establishing our protectorate over the regency of Tunis." The term "protectorate" is justified in this instance, for Tunisia did in fact retain, if not complete independence, at least a definite margin of local autonomy. The Algésiras conference of 1906 marked the true beginnings of the colonization of Morocco, which was first subjected to a sort of European protectorate. In 1912 it became a protectorate of France. It was at this time that Italy began its occupation of Libya. But this last case was of more marginal importance; the total population of Libya was around 1930 less than 1 million, as against 15–16 million in the parts of the Maghreb controlled by France.

Unlike Ottoman colonization, in which the presence of Turks remained fairly restricted (some 20,000 of them were in the Maghreb at the end of the eighteenth century), the European colonization of the Maghreb was characterized by a massive influx of colonials. By 1900 there were nearly 600,000 Europeans in Algeria, the French themselves representing only some 60% of this number. Around 1920 there were a little over a million Europeans in the Maghreb, and in 1936, 1.6 million, representing 9% of the overall population. Of these 1.6 million, in round figures, 990,000 had settled in Algeria, 240,000 in French Morocco, 110,000 in Spanish Morocco and in Tangiers, 210,000 in Tunisia, and some 50,000 in Libya. This influx is all the more significant in the context of the problem dealt with in this book, inasmuch as a very high proportion of these Europeans settled in the cities.

The period leading up to colonization was marked by a decline in

*This is the most widely used popular dictionary—TRANS.

urbanization very likely reflecting worsening economic conditions. Although the available data are not very numerous, they all converge on the same point: during the nineteenth century before the onset of colonization the population of the cities of the Maghreb had fallen well below that registered in former centuries. The peak before the rapid growth of the twentieth century was probably either in the thirteenth century or in the sixteenth and seventeenth centuries. Given that the available figures for total population are even more dubious than those for urban population, it would be foolish to try to estimate the scale of the decline in urbanization. It must nevertheless have been substantial, given the extent of the decrease in urban population. Thus in Algeria it can be estimated that on the eve of the French conquest the population of the larger cities was lower by at least 50% than that reached during the most positive phases of urban life before this date. The corresponding decrease in Morocco was less pronounced, but probably amounted to some 30–40%.

Colonization with Urban Growth

Thanks to the development of export crops on the one hand and the massive influx of European colonials, many of them settling in the cities, on the other hand, colonization had a very distinct urbanizing influence in the Maghreb. But few new urban centers were created. The exceptions (which were only relative, for these new cities were generally erected next to smaller towns already in existence) were first and foremost Casablanca, and then Kenitra and Boufarik (Medina Clausel). But in most cases the dual economic system was expressed by a dual urban system. The European city would develop alongside the former urban center, which progressively became the city's Arab quarter, or Medina, a quarter characterized, like all traditional Muslim cities, by high population density. In some instances, under pressure from the growth of the European part of the city, the Arab quarter was demolished. In Morocco, on the other hand, there was (on the part of Lyautey) even a deliberate policy of preserving the traditional city, the new city developing at a certain distance from it.

The port towns and administrative capitals underwent the most rapid development. Casablanca, a small port to begin with, had been chosen by 1907 as the site for the construction of a modern harbor to facilitate the exportation of agricultural products from the rich hinterlands. Point of departure (or destination) for one of the first Moroccan railroads, Casablanca had a population of 102,000 in 1921, of 260,000 in 1936, and of 680,000 in 1950, thereby becoming the largest city in North Africa (excluding Egypt). But over the course of the nineteenth century the intensification of trade had already stimulated the development of this city. A small hamlet around 1830–1840,

Casablanca had a population of nearly 20,000 at the turn of the century. For the same reasons Oran, with a population of only a few thousand at the time of the French conquest, surpassed 100,000 by 1900.

It would be easy to multiply the instances of rapid urban growth in the Maghreb. Overall urban population also grew rapidly. By 1900, total urban population in Algeria was already two to three times greater than around 1830–40, and was to double once again between 1900 and 1935. Having risen to somewhere on the order of 14–16% by the turn of the century, the level of urbanization reached 20–22% around 1930. While urban growth in the rest of the Maghreb proved more modest, the urban population of the region as a whole increased between 1900 and 1930 at the rate of 1.9% per year.

But this expansion was far from uniform. The widest disparity lay between coastal towns and the cities of the interior. The former grew much more rapidly because of expanding export activities. The cities of the interior, on the other hand, stagnated in some cases or even declined. The cities of the interior were also those with the largest native population, because urban growth in the Maghreb was in large measure the doing of Europeans. While around 1830 Europeans certainly represented less than 1% of the urban population of the Maghreb, by 1936 the proportion had increased to something like 45% (60% in Algeria, 25% in Tunisia, and 15% in Morocco). As a general rule, the larger the city, the greater the proportion of Europeans. Looking at these figures in another way every bit as meaningful, it emerges that nearly 90% of the Europeans living in the Maghreb were city residents, as against 7% for the native population. This difference well illustrates the unique character of the urbanizing influence of colonization in this part of the world.

Cotton and Urbanization in Egypt

Before moving on to Black Africa, it is worth evoking, if only briefly, the evolution of urbanism in Egypt, where colonization (under way by 1882) was not accompanied by a migratory influx of the sort witnessed in the rest of North Africa. It is true that at this time the population density was already very high. But the change in Egyptian agriculture—Egypt becoming as of the 1860s a major exporter of cotton (15,000 metric tons around 1850, 310,000 metric tons around 1910)—had a substantial impact on demographic and urban trends.

The terms of trade of cotton vis-à-vis grain came to favor cotton, and the ensuing agricultural specialization made possible very rapid growth in population, which rose from 4.5–5.5 million in 1850 to 11.7 million in 1910, representing an annual rate of increase of about 1.4%. Having formerly been an exporter of grain, Egypt developed a deficit in this domain, imports of grain (and flour of various sorts) rising for the period 1908–1912 to some 210,000 metric tons yearly,

representing just about 17 kilograms per capita or, even more significantly, roughly 120 kilograms per capita in cities with populations of
over 20,000.

Combined with the opening of the Suez Canal, which further fostered trade, this trend in foreign relations marked the chief factor
underlying the very rapid growth of the urban population of Egypt
that began around 1850–60. In around 1850 the population of cities
with populations of more than 20,000 grew to some 550,000; in 1910
it reached 1,700,000. The population of Cairo grew from about
260,000 in 1850 to 690,000 in 1910, and Cairo was the first African
city to surpass the one-million mark (sometime around 1924–1927).
The population of once glorious Alexandria, which had fallen to some
4,000 by around 1800, reached 140,000 around 1850 and 380,000 in
1910. Alexandria was, moreover, around 1950 to be the second African city to exceed the one-million mark.

In attempting to determine the level of urbanization, one runs up
against the problem posed by the exceptionally dense occupation of
land in the Nile valley, amounting to 350 people per square kilometer
at the turn of the century. This engendered highly concentrated settlements of essentially agrarian populations whose population often surpassed 5,000, thereby undermining the criterion of 5,000 inhabitants
used throughout this book to define urban populations. The application of more realistic standards adapted to the specific case of Egypt
yields a level of urbanization of something like 18–20% at the turn of
the century, and 25–28% around 1930. This made Egypt the most
heavily urbanized region in the whole of underdeveloped Africa;
around 1930 it accounted for some 31% of the total urban population
and nearly 60% of the population of all cities with more than 100,000.

26 Modern Colonization and Urbanization in Black Africa and Latin America from 1780/1815 to 1930/40 □

During this period there were diametrically opposed trends in political status for Black Africa and Latin-America. Black Africa, which up to this time had enjoyed relative, but often very wide autonomy, passed under a regime of intense colonial exploitation. On the other hand, almost all of Latin America acquired political independence—a political independence, however, that had the paradoxical effect of increasing interference on the part of the advanced economic powers, notably Britain. Being colonies of Spain or Portugal had in a sense protected Latin American countries against the influx of manufactured goods resulting from the Industrial Revolution. This form of intrusion on the part of the advanced industrial powers, coupled with the region's colonial past, justifies Latin America's inclusion in this chapter devoted to problems stemming from colonization.

Black Africa: From the End of the Slave Trade to Colonial Exploitation

Between the end of the legal slave trade, which had begun by 1800–1810, and the effective start of colonization around 1880–1890, Black Africa had enjoyed a respite. This respite was, to be sure, only relative, for commercial relations continued and even intensified during these years. And though the flow of slaves to the New World was considerably reduced, slaves continued to be sent to the Middle East. The years of respite, which thus concerned the interior of the continent more than coastal regions, was also the age of European exploration of the interior. This exploration was chiefly carried out by men of science who brought back reports of the cultures they found, and especially of life in the many populous cities they discovered. The best known and most important of the African urban cultures of the nineteenth century was that of the Yorubas. Yoruba culture makes it possible to reformulate the problem of the definition of cities.

I shall leave aside here the long history of this culture, concerning which many unknowns persist, notably regarding relations with the urban cultures of the Muslim Sudan during the Middle Ages (see chapter 4). According to the surveys of Mabogunje (1968), in the mid-nineteenth century the Yoruba culture—whose settlements extended over a zone corresponding to present-day southwest Nigeria and a part of Dahomey—contained some 27–30 "cities" of more than five thousand people. What is more interesting, most of these cities were very populous. One of them, Ibadan, had a population of around 100,000, three others of 50,000–70,000, and a further dozen of 20,000–50,000. This meant that the 27–30 cities Mabogunje speaks of had a combined population of some 750,000.

These settlements merit the name of cities on many accounts. First of all, there is size; but there are economic criteria as well: the presence of a relatively advanced industry, long-distance trade, and the use of money. They also qualify on sociological grounds: a scornful attitude toward rural people, the formation of distinct socioeconomic groups, and a high density of population. A problem arises, however, owing to the very high proportion of farmers in the urban population, a proportion that has never been exactly determined but that may have amounted to more than 50%. In any event, even a century later at the time of the census of 1952, the cities of the western part of Nigeria were still very agricultural. Whereas in the region as a whole 37% of the male working population worked in farming (a percentage, it is true, that seems very small), the proportion in cities of 5,000–20,000 people was the same, falling to 33% in cities with populations of 20,000–40,000, to 31% in cities with populations of 40,000–80,000, and to 22% in cities with populations of more than 80,000. To the high proportion of farmers among city dwellers should be added the absence of any true form of writing. Under such circumstances, can one really speak of cities? Yes and no. Yes, because this was unquestionably not a rural world. But no, if one confines oneself to a Eurocentric view of cities. Once again, urbanism in Europe appears to have been the special case, even if, as has been seen elsewhere, agriculture was far from completely absent in European cities.

But although Black Africa unmistakably had important urban centers, was it really an urbanized continent? I was able to estimate the probable level of urbanization in this part of the world in 1900 (see table 26.1). The figures I arrived at are certainly dubious. The margin of error surrounding the number of city dwellers must be something like 25%, with the likelihood of bias on the side of underestimation. Moreover, the figure for total population is still too approximate, with a margin of error on the order of 30%. As a result, in table 26.1, the level of urbanization for 1900, for example, should read 2.0–5.0% rather than 3.2%. But even here, the upper limit denotes a very low

Size of Cities	1900	1910	1920	1930	1950
	Number of Cities				
20–50	36	39	41	45	(70)
50–100	9	9	9	11	33
100–200	1	1	1	3	13
200–500	—	—	1	1	5
500 or more	—	—	—	—	—
Total	46	49	52	60	121
	Urban Population				
20–50	990	1,070	1,200	1,370	(2,200)
50–100	530	560	560	730	2,280
100–200	150	150	100	390	1,660
200–500	—	—	230	380	1,560
500 or more	—	—	—	—	—
Total	1,670	1,780	2,090	2,870	7,700
Urban population[a]	3,500	3,700	4,200	5,300	11,400
Total population	110,000	110,000	110,000	120,000	163,000
Level of urbanization (%)	3.2	3.3	3.9	4.3	7.0

Sources: Calculations and estimates by the author; see the methodological appendix.
Note: The fact that these figures have been only slightly rounded off does not imply a
correspondingly small margin of error.
[a] A criterion of 5,000 is used for urban population.

level of urbanization, and this despite the fact that in 1900 the initial
stages of the surge of urban growth spawned by European colonization were already under way.

Although it may very well have precipitated major upheavals in
some parts of Black Africa before 1900, this surge of urban growth
was nevertheless still in its initial stages at this time so far as the impact
of colonization on Black Africa as a whole is concerned. Since in chapter 24 I brought the urban history of this region to a halt in 1800 before going on to look at the data relating to the twentieth century, I
shall review the main features of the impact of colonization on the urban life of Black Africa during the nineteenth century.

A First Local Outbreak of the General Colonization
Process: The Sugar-Producing Islands

During the first half of the nineteenth century, a minuscule
local outbreak of the general colonization to come took place on the
islands of Réunion and Mauritius. With a combined area of 4,400

square kilometers, these two islands together represent 0.02% of the total area of Black Africa, the Sahara desert not included. Around 1860, however, this tiny fraction of the continent exported more goods to the developed world than all of the rest of Black Africa (excluding South Africa, as throughout this analysis, which solely concerns those parts of the continent today underdeveloped). And whereas in the rest of Black Africa, oilseeds predominated among exports, sugar represented about 99% of the exports of Réunion and Mauritius.

The loss of Santo Domingo, a major supplier of sugar to France, in a sense provided the spark that set off an out-and-out explosion. Within a few decades all existing arable land was planted with sugar-cane and new lands were cleared for more. From practically nothing around 1800, sugar exports increased to some 17,000 metric tons around 1825, reaching a first maximum of 200,000 metric tons in 1860. This volume represented roughly one-fifth of total European imports at this time, and in all likelihood as much as Europe had imported yearly around 1770–80. It was made possible by an influx of laborers from Asia and the African mainland, in the form of slaves, and also by the use of guano as fertilizer. The total population of the islands rose from 120,000 in 1800 to 490,000 in 1860. At this time exports amounted, in current values, to $34.00 per capita, as against $.10 to $.20 in the rest of Black Africa, $9.00 in Latin America, $.50 in Asia, and $7.00 in Europe. Réunion and Mauritius probably had at that time the largest per capita export volume in the world.

The rapid growth of the islands' exports brought about a steep rise in the population of their cities, already in existence since the eighteenth century (see chapter 24). On Mauritius most of the urban population was concentrated in Port Louis, which had a population of more than 50,000 in 1860. During the same period on Réunion, the capital, Saint Denis, had a population of about 20,000; the six other cities together had some 60,000–70,000 more. As a result the average level of urbanization for the two islands must have been on the order of 29%.

Out of a total of 140,000 people living in the cities, there appear to have been 30,000–40,000 Europeans, the very great majority of them, naturally, being Creoles. While a significant proportion of these Creoles enjoyed a very high standard of living, this was not true for the population of European origin as a whole, subject as it was to increasing pauperization. Indigent whites were numerous in rural as well as in urban districts. But the urban centers were in the main wealthy, and whites especially enjoyed a high level of education. The lycée on Réunion had 500 students in around 1860, a total which, in relation to overall population, represented 29 high school students for every 10,000 people, a proportion practically identical to that in France during the same period. But if one takes into account the very low level of schooling of non-Europeans, it implies that the proportion of European children attending high school was seven to nine times higher than in France (if the comparison is limited to the urban sector, it was probably four to five times higher than in France).

The decline in sugar prices, the opening of the Suez Canal, and manpower problems reversed the economic fortunes of the islands, leading to stagnation in exports: export revenues in 1910 were about the same as in 1860. The result was a corresponding stagnation in total population, and above all only a very small increase in urban population.

Black Africa: Colonization and Urbanization

In Black Africa proper, European colonization did not perceptibly influence urban life during the nineteenth century. The sharp reduction in the slave trade led to decline in population in many of the fifty-odd small towns, or rather supply posts, distributed along the region's 16,000 kilometers of coastline. Some of these towns almost completely vanished. However, the slow rise of what was called the legal trade, in order to distinguish it from the proscribed traffic in slaves, eventually led to the development of a few urban centers. Such was notably the case for Saint Louis and Dakar for the French trade, Lagos for the British trade, and a few other small towns.

This nevertheless amounted to almost nothing until the very end of the nineteenth century, for colonization and even simple trade with the region remained slow. Around 1860, exports from Black Africa (excluding Réunion and Mauritius) amounted, according to my calculations, to perhaps $7–10 million, but certainly less than $15 million. By around 1880, exports were only $18–20 million, a figure which did not even equal 0.2% of the total for the Third World as a whole. And even around 1890, exports amounted to less than $25 million, probably $23 million. But in 1885 in Berlin, the colonial powers set about dividing up Africa, the continent having become attractive owing to the discovery of diamonds and gold in South Africa. Africa was also made attractive by technological developments in the West fostering the consumption of vegetable oils, both as lubricants for machines and as ingredients in the manufacture of candles, soap, and, beginning in the 1860s, margarine. In addition the rise in the Western standard of living brought about increased demand for tropical food products. So why not grow them in Africa? Quinine made it possible for white men to penetrate more easily into the African interior. As a result of all these things, between 1890 and 1900 exports more than doubled, and this was only the beginning.

These developments were bound to affect the process of urbanization in the region. Indeed by the last years of the nineteenth century many new urban settlements were created to meet the needs of colonial exploitation, and a few existing ones were enlarged. By 1900

Black Africa had 4,500 kilometers of railroad lines, as against a mere 200 in 1880, and exports had risen from a value of $19 million in 1880 to $50 million in 1900. In relative terms, however, foreign trade remained at a very low level: $50 million represented roughly $.50 per capita, as compared with $10.10 in Latin America, $2.10 in Asia, and $11.80 in North Africa (the Maghreb and Egypt).

But things changed rapidly, especially after 1900. In 1934 the rail network extended over 30,000 kilometers, and in 1937 Black African exports reached $340 million, representing 6% of the total for the Third World as a whole. This constituted the key element in the changes that took place in the interval in the process of urbanization. Whereas there had been fewer than fifty cities with populations of more than 20,000 around 1900, there were more than sixty in 1930. More important still, where there had been only one city with a population of more than 100,000 at the turn of the century, there were now four. To be sure, as I have already noted, this surge of urban growth was chiefly accomplished through the creation of many new cities. One should not, however, overlook the growth of some of the traditional urban centers. Thus all four of the cities with populations of more than 100,000 in 1930—Ibadan (385,000), Addis Ababa (160,000), Lagos (125,000), and Khartoum (100,000)—were traditional cities undergoing rapid population growth; their populations together rose from 310,000 to 770,000 between 1900 and 1930.

But one should not conclude from this that all traditional urban centers grew. This was far from the case. Even during the nineteenth century some traditional cities, for internal and external reasons, and some Europeanized cities had suffered declines. The declines were especially the case, as has been seen, of cities specializing in the slave trade. For some of them decline continued from 1900 to 1920, and sometimes even longer. This explains the as yet only moderate growth registered by the urban population of Africa between 1900 and 1920: a mere 0.9% per year, despite the upheavals caused by colonization. Beginning in 1920, however, the urban explosion already looms: between 1920 and 1930 the urban population grew at the rate of 2.4% per year, rising to 3.9% between 1930 and 1950. Nevertheless, given the low level of urban population at the start, one cannot properly speak of hyperurbanization even for 1950, by which time the level of urbanization in Black Africa had barely reached 7%, a level lower than that of Europe before the Middle Ages. By 1970, on the other hand, the level of urbanization in Black Africa had already reached 15%.

In closing this section devoted to Africa, I shall move on to an aspect of the question that forms a good transition from the Maghreb, as described in chapter 25, to Latin America, as I shall describe it in the next section of this chapter: the link between European population and urbanization. Unlike what happened in the Maghreb and in Latin America, the European population did not directly play an important role in the growth of the cities of Black Africa. A comparison of the relative sizes of the European populations of these three regions will easily suffice to show the difference. We have seen that around 1936 Europeans represented 9% of the population of the Maghreb. In Latin America during the same period, Europeans accounted for 43%—though a fraction of this percentage was made up of the descendants of Europeans settled in Latin America since the sixteenth and seventeenth centuries. In Black Africa, by contrast (and bearing in mind that I omit South Africa from this analysis because it figures among the developed nations), it can be estimated that around 1936 there were some 240,000–300,000 Europeans, making up only 0.3% of the total population, the 70,000-odd Europeans living on Réunion Island included, even though Réunion did not really belong to Black Africa. At the level of urban population the share of Europeans was much higher: it can be roughly estimated that at least half, and perhaps as many as three-quarters, of all Europeans lived in cities, which suggests that they accounted for about 2–3% of the urban population of Black Africa. This is only an average percentage, however, resulting from a very broad spread. To cite only two examples, neither extreme, in around 1938, out of a total population of 65,000, Nairobi (Kenya) had 6,500 Europeans (or 10 % of the total) and 18,500 people of Asian origin. In Ibadan (Nigeria), by contrast, of the 386,907 people registered in the census of 1931, only 226 (or 0.06% of the total) were non-Africans.

Latin America: The Time of Catastrophes and the Time of Growth

"The Time of Catastrophes" is the title of the chapter Pierre Chaunu (1964) devoted to Iberian America from 1800 to 1860–80 in his synthesis of research on the history of America and the Americas. The catastrophes referred to were mainly those due to the disorganization and disturbances that followed independence and that probably caused a decline, or at least stagnation, in the economies of many of the countries of Latin America, especially those in the northern Andean regions. This decline was reinforced, moreover, by the exhaustion of the mineral deposits. The production of silver in Latin America, which had reached an annual rate of some 810 metric tons around 1800–1810, fell to 370 metric tons around 1821–1830, the production of gold falling from fifteen to eight metric tons per year. Production did increase again later, but it did not return to the level reached in 1800 until about 1870, and this in part thanks to the rise in output in Chile.

To these problems were added those mentioned both in the introduction to this chapter and in the introduction to chapter 25, namely, the competition from beet sugar and the drying up of the supply of slaves from Africa. The combination of these factors made Latin America's traditional agricultural exports less profitable, a state of affairs rendered still worse by the fact that, dating from the start of the nineteenth century, Latin America had to compete with new suppliers of tropical products, certain Asian countries being notable among them. Moreover, political independence reinforced the influence of the developed nations by removing the trade barriers formerly imposed by Spain and Portugal.

These difficulties led to slower growth in urban population than in total population, and as a result the level of urbanization was a little lower around 1850 than in 1800. This trend was particularly negative in mining districts, beginning as early as the second half of the eighteenth century. The population of most of the cities in this region decreased. Thus in the northern Andes there were fewer cities with populations of more than 20,000 around 1850 than in 1750 (see table 26.2). Peru stopped being *pérou* (French for "very wealthy"), and its share in the urban population of Latin America living in cities with populations of more than 20,000, from about 20% in 1700 fell to only 3% by the start of the twentieth century.

What growth there was took place mostly in Brazil, where expansion continued even through the first half of the nineteenth century, and in the temperate regions, in Argentina, Chile, and Uruguay, where there was economic expansion in the second half of the nineteenth century. These two regions were responsible for 50% of the increase in the number of cities with populations of more than 20,000 in Latin America between 1800 and 1920. Like that of earlier centuries, this phase of urban growth was linked to foreign trade; and during the nineteenth century, European demand for luxury tropical products (coffee in particular) and for grain provided the driving force. The value of exports from Brazil and the temperate countries rose between 1800 and 1913 from $35 million to $1.04 billion, representing an increase from 29 to 60% in their share of total exports from Latin America.

The scale of the contribution made to urbanization by this volume of exports can be estimated approximately. If one supposes that the added value resulting from export activities (transportation, conditioning, storing and handling, insurance, etc.) amounted to 10%, and that the annual income per working person was $250, the $1.04 billion earned from exports would have meant 420,000 urban jobs— enough to provide directly for roughly a million people in the two regions concerned. And if one takes into account the jobs indirectly created by these export activities the figure doubles. Thus around 1913, roughly 2 million people, or about 28% of the total urban population of the two regions involved, would have been able to live off

TABLE 26.2   Regional Distribution of the Number of Latin
American Cities with Populations of 20,000 or More
(1750–1920)

	1750	1800	1850	1900	1910	1920
Northern Andes	13	10	9	22	30	33
Bolivia	3	2	2	4	6	6
Colombia	3	2	1	10	16	16
Equador	2	2	3	3	4	4
Peru	5	4	3	5	4	7
Mexico	6	8	11	26	29	27
Brazil	4	7	11	35	43	47
Temperate regions	1	2	3	17	27	46
Argentina	—	1	1	10	17	30
Chile	1	1	2	6	9	13
Uruguay	—	—	—	1	1	3
Antilles	2	4	7	16	18	25
Latin America as a whole[a]	29	41	51	138	173	207

Sources: Calculations and estimates by the author; see the methodological appendix.
[a] Including regions and countries not mentioned above.

these exports. And this reflects the impact of exports alone which, it should be remembered, were accompanied by a flow of imports of comparable proportions.

Industrialization and Urbanization

Alongside the contribution made by foreign trade to urbanization, one should not overlook that attributable to industrialization dating from the 1830s and especially from the 1880s. Commercial policies took a protectionist turn intended to foster industrialization. This brought about substantial development in the manufacturing sector, chiefly in Mexico and Brazil, but development was not totally absent from Argentina and other Latin American countries. Moreover, the traditional image of a Latin America collapsing over the course of the first half of the nineteenth century under the weight of a catastrophic economic situation calls for some revision: there has been too great a tendency to look solely on the mining side of the equation, overlooking the start made by industry.

In Mexico above all we encounter, as early as the 1830s, a policy of industrialization, inaugurated in 1829 by the "manifesto to my compatriots" issued by President Guerrero. In this manifesto Guerrero declared: "The policy of blindly applying liberal measures has brought about the decline of industry. In order that the country may prosper, it is essential that workers be allocated to all branches of industry; and in particular that manufactured goods be protected by protective tariffs calculated in an intelligent manner." To customs measures was added (in 1830) the creation of a State Bank "for the development of national industry." This array of measures unquestionably bore fruit, for around 1850 Mexico was not only the most industrialized of all of the countries of Latin America, but was also more industrialized than many European countries. In textile manufacturing Mexico supplied most of its own needs and, according to my own calculations, had sixteen to eighteen spindles for spinning cotton for every thousand people—that is, almost as much as Austria-Hungary, and more than Italy, Spain, and Russia, not to mention the small nonindustrialized European states. And alongside textile manufacturing was an iron and steel industry producing roughly ten thousand metric tons of cast iron per year, a glass industry, a paper industry, and so on. This industrialization certainly accounts for a large part of the urban growth highlighted in table 26.2.

The travellers who visited Mexico between 1820 and 1875 had noted the role of manufacturing in the prosperous cities of that country. "Each had a manufacturing base that travelers recognized to be a vital component of urban size and relative stability" (Arreola, 1982).

In the other Latin American countries, and particularly in Brazil, Colombia, and Paraguay, the history of industrialization during the first fifty to seventy years of the nineteenth century was a series of disappointments rather than successes. But beginning in the 1880s, especially in Brazil and Argentina, tariff policies aimed at protecting local manufacturing fostered the establishment of a Latin American industry reinforced even more by a fresh surge of industrialization in Mexico during the less troubled era of Diaz (1877–1910). And while the various revolutions in Mexico slowed down the process of industrialization in that country, the First World War helped accelerate industrial development in the others.

In 1929 Latin America had around 3.8 million cotton-spinning spindles. It is true that they represented only 2.3% of the world total, while the population of Latin America represented 5.2% of world population; but Asia (except Japan), ten times as populous, had only three times as many spindles, and Black Africa, with a population about the same as that of Latin America, had practically none at all. This would show, were there any need for it, that even though political independence did not lead to genuine economic independence, it did nevertheless foster the adoption of a series of measures furthering the beginnings of industrialization and thus a "healthier" form of urbanization.

Latin America at the End of the Nineteenth Century: A Prefiguration of the Third World in the Second Half of the Twentieth Century

Even at the end of the nineteenth century, however, signs appeared foreshadowing the coming urban explosion and especially the future heavy concentration of population in the larger cities (see chapter 27). As early as the turn of the century, the level of urbanization reached 20% (see table 26.3). In Argentina, Uruguay, and Cuba, indeed, it surpassed 30%. At the same time, moreover, two cities already had populations of more than 500,000: Rio de Janeiro, with 690,000, and Buenos Aires, with 830,000. Twenty years later the population of these two cities exceeded one million, and four others surpassed the half-million mark: Santiago, with 510,000; Sao Paulo, with 580,000; Mexico City, with 600,000; and Montevideo, with 700,000. Moreover, the level of urbanization for the continent as a whole had already surpassed 25%. Things got even worse after 1920, after which it becomes possible to speak of hyperurbanization. But this too is a problem I shall discuss in the following chapters; the urban history of Latin America prefigures in this respect that of the rest of the Third World.

Another area in which Latin America gave a prefiguration of events in the rest of the Third World was the exportation of minerals other than precious metals; this began as early as the mid-nineteenth century, while the same phase did not get under way elsewhere until some sixty to eighty years later. Chile and later Bolivia played leading roles in this domain, and this too had an impact on urban life. In 1930, 78,000 people worked in Chilean mines, a figure representing 5.8% of all jobs. This was and remains an extremely large proportion, one of the largest ever recorded in any country. Today in the Third World, the average proportion is 0.6–0.8%; in countries exporting the largest quantities of minerals, the mining industry accounts on the average for only 3–4% of all jobs; and in the chief oil-producing nations, the corresponding figure is a mere 1–2%. Sodium nitrate (a fertilizer) and copper were at that time Chile's main exports. As the *Encyclopédie Larousse méthodique* of 1936 puts it: "Vast deposits of sodium nitrate exploited in the latter half of the nineteenth century caused cities and factories to spring from the desert."

Not only were mining towns created, but also ports from which the raw materials could be exported. Thus sodium nitrate, for instance, was first exported from Iquique, an insignificant fishing port until the 1830s, when the exportation of sodium nitrate began. In 1900 the city had a population of 42,000. Iquique was then succeeded by Antofagasta, a port created around 1870 to help expedite the export of the silver deposits discovered in the region. Antofagasta grew rapidly in its turn: from 16,000 people in 1900 to 52,000 in 1920.

TABLE 26.3 Growth of Latin American Cities according to Population (in Thousands) (1750–1920)

Size of Cities	1750	1800	1850	1900	1920
	Number of Cities				
20–50	23	35	40	102	131
50–100	5	5	6	22	46
100–200	1	1	5	6	17
200–500	—	—	—	6	7
500 or more	—	—	—	2	6
Total	29	41	51	138	207
	Urban Population				
20–50	580	940	1,220	2,960	4,020
50–100	270	450	420	1,420	3,180
100–200	110	130	760	710	2,250
200–500	—	—	—	1,600	1,940
500 or more	—	—	—	1,520	5,310
Total	960	1,520	2,400	8,210	16,700
Urban population[a]	1,940	2,900	4,300	13,400	23,200
Total population	15,000	20,000	33,000	66,000	91,000
Level of urbanization (%)	13.0	14.5	13.0	20.3	25.5

Sources: Calculations and estimates by the author; see the methodological appendix.
Note: The fact that these figures have been only slightly rounded off does not imply a correspondingly small margin of error.
[a] A criterion of 5,000 is used for urban population.

In Bolivia it was tin. Bolivia and its urban network had already been heavily affected by mining as early as the second half of the sixteenth century (see chapter 24), but in that case the deposits exploited had contained precious metals. The famous city of Potosi was located in Bolivia. In the nineteenth century, however, Bolivia had become only a very marginal producer of precious metals, with an output equal to a mere 2% of world production around 1860, as against 10% in the eighteenth century. The era of tin began in the 1890s, and by the eve of the First World War Bolivia had emerged as the second largest producer in the world. Tin gave a new life to two cities already connected with mining: Potosi and Oruro. Its population having fallen from a maximum of 150,000 around 1600 to a mere 8,000, Potosi rose to 35,000 once more by around 1936, while the population of Oruro, having fallen from 70,000 around 1700 to 5,000 around 1850, reached 45,000 in 1936.

Was the expansion of mining production an urbanizing factor? There is no doubt that it was. But it must be observed that it did not constitute in these cases, as it had in the developed world during the nineteenth century, a factor stimulating economic development. For not only were these minerals exported abroad, thereby considerably reducing the secondary effects, but often the profits were as well. The exportation of profits, indeed, represents another way in which Chile and Bolivia foreshadowed a situation that would arise in many parts of the Third World half a century later: almost all of the mining companies, especially the largest among them, were founded by and belonged to foreign capitalists. And where there is no economic development, there is also less impact on urban life, and above all there is urbanization without the kind of industrial base it had in the developed world during the nineteenth century. This leads to a risk of urban hypertrophy, that is, a level of urbanization exceeding the economic potential—in short, the crucial problem faced in the Third World today.

But did nineteenth-century Latin America in fact prefigure the Third World of the latter half of the twentieth century? This is unquestionably the case in many areas, the most important of which have already been mentioned above. One must, however, avoid two fairly widespread errors of interpretation. The first consists of forgetting that Latin America represented only a very small fraction of the future Third World, its population amounting to only 3% of the Third World's around 1800 and only 7 % in around 1913. The second error consists of thinking that the problems faced in various parts of the future Third World posed themselves in precisely the same terms. The preceding pages have already revealed many differences, but there is one very important difference I have omitted: the lack of similarity in standards of living. Thus taken as a whole Latin America had at the end of the nineteenth century an average per capita income twice as high as that of the rest of the Third World. It should be remembered, for instance, that in the years before the First World War, Argentina, the richest country in the region, figured among the ten to fifteen nations enjoying the highest average per capita income in the world. This suggests that, although it was not absent, urban poverty was not as acute here as elsewhere. And since I have cited figures for infant mortality in the larger cities of Asia and of Egypt, it may be worth comparing them with those for the larger cities of Latin America for which data are available. Taking the average for five large cities of Asia, I obtain a rate of 338 infant deaths per 1,000 for 1900–1909; and during this same period the rate was 286 per 1,000 in Alexandria and 321 per 1,000 in Cairo. The average for five of the larger cities of Latin America, on the other hand, was only 196 per 1,000—but with a fairly wide dispersion (99 per 1,000 in Buenos Aires, 199 in Havana, 111 in Montevideo, 190 in Rio de Janeiro, and 382 in Santiago). I shall discuss urban demography in the various societies of the Third World in chapter 28.

I had to formulate these reservations before moving on to a matter which concerns the Third World as a whole, which has regions much poorer than Latin America.

Can the Urban Expansion of the Third World during the Nineteenth Century Be Explained by a More Equal Income Distribution?

The question of whether the urban expansion of the Third World during the nineteenth century can be explained by a more equal income distribution may seem paradoxical when one considers the large incomes enjoyed by the Europeans settled in colonial cities and the extent to which resources were exported abroad. Nevertheless, at the conclusion of the analysis of the interactions between urbanization and colonization given in these pages, I came away with a sense that the factors invoked to explain both the growing size of some cities and the slight decline recorded in others did not suffice in themselves. At the end of my analysis of the situation in Asia, for instance, I found it necessary to ask how the fall in the standard of living characterizing this period could be reconciled with the maintenance, and even the rise, of the level of urbanization.

I believe that it is not at all unreasonable to advance the following hypothesis: owing to the loss of power on the part of traditional elites, colonization promoted a more equal distribution of income among native populations in urban and rural districts alike. The loss of power in rural areas quite naturally favored a greater drain on agricultural surpluses; these surpluses were no longer absorbed by rural elites consuming them in the countryside but were instead absorbed by the cities. Thus by distributing agricultural surpluses at the expense of traditional rural elites, but to the benefit of the general population of the cities, colonization made possible a larger proportion of city dwellers. By contrast, the loss of power on the part of traditional urban elites must in its turn have led to a reduction of the quantity of resources transferred from the countryside to the cities. But this was certainly more than offset by another aspect of the changes brought about by colonization. The new European elites and the new native elites quite naturally tended to prefer to settle in the cities. As a result, the reduction in the standard of living in rural areas, combined with a more equal distribution of income, made possible a greater transfer of resources to the cities. Meanwhile, in the cities themselves the reduction in the standard of living made it possible for more people to share this greater surplus, a process made easier still by the new outward-looking character of the economies and by the attendant rise in the number of intermediary activities in urban districts at the expense of rural districts.

It goes without saying that this was neither the sole nor the most important factor contributing to urban growth in colonized societies. We have seen, indeed, that such urban growth was everywhere conditioned by increases in the volume of agricultural and mineral exports and in some countries by urban-centered reindustrialization as well. But the greater paradox may well be that the real problems facing the cities of the colonized world did not emerge until after colonization had ended. It is to the situation in the postcolonial Third World that I shall turn in the following chapters. But before that, I have to make an important comment.

It appears, in fact, that the effects of modern colonization on levels of urbanization in the colonized territories were fairly close to those in evidence in the case of traditional colonization (see the end of chapter 24). In the absence of a massive European settlement, the same general rule held in the present case: modern colonization tended on the whole to be an urbanizing factor in thinly urbanized societies and a deurbanizing factor in heavily urbanized societies (thinly or heavily urbanized in the context of traditional societies). But, here again, as in traditional colonization, exceptions exist; each case has always and everywhere been unique. And to mention one last reservation, all of this holds before that phase of urban expansion whose history I shall now examine, beginning in chapter 27.

27 The Urban Explosion in the Third World during the Twentieth Century □

By the first years of the twentieth century an entirely new phenomenon in the urban history of the world had begun to emerge: for the first time there was a genuine urban explosion. Unprecedented in scale, this explosive urban growth was also unprecedented in its causes and in its effects. Between 1900 and 1920 the urban population of what we may henceforth without reservation call the Third World increased by more than one-quarter, growing at the rate of some 1.3–1.4% per year (see table 27.1). Certainly this did not in itself constitute an explosive growth rate, but growth on this scale can no longer be considered consonant with traditional societies. It may be recalled that even during the most positive phases of preindustrial Europe urban population increased at a maximum of 0.3–0.4% per year, and that over periods of a century. And if we confine ourselves to the most positive periods of one-third of a century, the rate certainly never rose above 0.6–0.8% per year. Nor does the history of other large traditional societies reveal growth rates any higher than this.

From 1920 to 1930 urban population growth accelerated even more, reaching a rate of 1.9–2.1% per year. It is necessary to be careful in this instance, however, because of the margins of error surrounding the relevant data; the rate cited here may well be an overestimation. Moreover, roughly 30% of the increase in urban population was accounted for by Latin America alone. The level of urbanization in other parts of the Third World did not progress much more rapidly than before, the faster growth of urban population essentially stemming from accelerated demographic growth generally. But by the end of the Second World War a real urban explosion was under way. During the third of a century between 1950 and 1985, the population of the cities of the Third World increased fourfold, making an annual growth rate of 4.1%. Meanwhile the level of urbanization rose at the rate of 2% per year. To put this in perspective, following the Industrial Revolution the thirty- to forty-year period marked by the strongest urban growth in the developed world was between 1860 and 1900.

TABLE 27.1 Growth of the Urban Population and Levels
of Urbanization in the Third World as a Whole
(1800–1985)

	Total Population (millions)	Urban Population		Level of Urbanization	
		Millions	Annual Variation (%)	% of Total Population	Annual Variation (%)
1800	(727)	(61)	—	(8.3)	—
1900	1,089	99	0.5	9.1	0.1
1910	1,137	109	1.0	9.6	0.5
1920	1,198	129	1.6	10.8	1.2
1930	1,325	157	2.0	11.8	0.9
1950	1,651	259	2.5	15.7	1.4
1960	2,049	414	4.8	20.2	2.6
1970	2,589	627	4.2	23.9	1.7
1980	3,282	905	3.7	27.6	1.4
1985[a]	3,624	1,072	3.4	29.6	1.4

Sources: Calculations and estimates by the author; see the methodological appendix.
For recent data see United Nations (1986a) with adjustments.
Note: The fact that these figures have been only slightly rounded off does not imply a
correspondingly small margin of error. The figures in parentheses have a much wider
margin of error than the other data.
A criterion of 5,000 is used for urban population.
[a] Preliminary figures; in part projections.

During these years urban population increased at a rate of only 2.4%
per year and the level of urbanization at a rate of only 1.3% per year.
In the developed world, moreover, it took about one hundred years
for the level of urbanization to rise from 12 to 32%. In the Third
World the same increase took fifty years.

There can be no question, then, that this was indeed an urban explosion, and a phenomenon, moreover, unique in the history of cities.
This was all the more true in that this exceptionally rapid rise in the
level of urbanization was accompanied by a general demographic explosion every bit as unprecedented, whence an enormous increase in
the population of the cities of the Third World in absolute as well as in
relative terms. Between 1950 and 1985, the cities of the Third World
as a whole (including China) increased their population by more than
800 million, an increase greater than the urban population of the entire world in 1950, which was the result of an urbanization process
extending over several centuries.

As I noted at the outset, the urban growth of the Third World since
the twenties and thirties was unprecedented in both its causes and its
effects. This was indeed the first time in world history that there had
been urban growth on this scale which was not rooted in a corresponding phase of economic development. This is one of the many
unique features of the causes of the urban explosion in the Third

World. And one of the unique features of the effects of the urban explosion (closely related to this aspect of its causes) is the terrible chronic underemployment suffered by nearly all Third World cities.

In this chapter I shall examine the general characteristics of the urban explosion (regional aspects and distribution according to size of cities). Chapter 28 will be devoted to its causes and chapters 29 and 30 to its effects. Chapters 27–30 deliberately overlap chapters 25–26 on the period from 1780–1815 to 1930–40. In order to get a better grasp of contemporary developments, I have decided to include the period 1900 to 1930–40 in the following analyses. So this chapter, as well as the three following ones, will cover the years from 1900 to 1985.

Different Starting Points, but a Convergent Evolution

I must stress from the outset that I shall often speak of the "Third World except China" or of "Asia except China." The exclusion of China has no political motive whatever, but springs simply from statistical considerations. Chinese statistics both for 1900 and for the contemporary era are either unreliable or nonexistent. I shall furnish some evidence later regarding the course of urban events in China, but it will only offer a broad indication of how things have evolved there.

The urban explosion in the Third World began from different starting points. Indeed, at the turn of the century levels of urbanization varied widely from continent to continent (see table 27.2). With an urban population representing some 20% of overall population, Latin America stood at a level two and a half times higher than the rest of the Third World. It should be noted from the start, however, that the inclusion of the temperate regions of Latin America in the Third World is highly misleading, especially for the early period. Argentina, for example, as mentioned before, was at that time one of the ten to fifteen richest countries in the world in terms of the standard of living. But since most classifications include these regions in the Third World (which is justified by events after 1950), I decided that it was preferable to conform to this practice. It should also be borne in mind that, as was seen in chapter 26, the levels of urbanization in the various Latin American countries at the beginning of the twentieth century were highly unequal, the least urbanized countries having levels of only 10 to 12%, the most urbanized 33 to 35%.

At the other end of the spectrum stands Africa, where the level of urbanization reached was extremely low: 5.5%. Africa was even more heterogeneous than Latin America, encompassing as it did two major types of society: the Maghreb and Egypt, urbanized since ancient times, on the one hand and Black Africa, some parts but not all of which had very low levels of urbanization, on the other. North of the Sahara, the cities at the turn of the century must have had some 16%

TABLE 27.2   Growth of the Urban Population and Levels of
Urbanization in the Third World by Region
1900–1985

	1900[a]	1920[a]	1930	1950	1960	1970	1980	1985[b]
	Urban population (in millions)							
Africa	7	10	12	22	38	65	106	136
Latin America	13	23	30	66	104	159	231	273
Asia[c]	43	49	59	101	152	235	356	433
Third World[c]	64	82	101	189	294	458	695	842
China[d]	(35)	(47)	(56)	(70)	(121)	(169)	(210)	(230)
Total for Third World	99	129	157	259	414	627	905	1,072
	Level of Urbanization (in percentages)							
Africa	5.5	7.1	8.0	10.5	15.5	19.3	23.5	26.0
Latin America	20.3	25.5	27.6	40.0	48.0	56.2	64.0	67.4
Asia[c]	9.9	10.3	11.0	14.5	17.5	20.8	25.2	27.6
Third World[c]	10.0	11.6	12.6	17.6	21.9	26.2	31.1	33.6
China[d]	(7.9)	(9.5)	(10.6)	(12.0)	(17.0)	(19.4)	(20.0)	(20.5)
Total for Third World as a whole	9.1	10.8	11.8	15.7	20.3	23.9	27.6	29.6

Sources: Calculations and estimates by the author; see the methodological appendix.
For recent data, United Nations (1986a) with adjustments.
Note: The fact that these figures have been only slightly rounded off does not imply a
correspondingly small margin of error. The figures in parentheses have a much wider
margin of error than the other data.
A criterion of 5,000 is used for urban population.
[a] Approximate figures.
[b] Preliminary figures (in part projections).
[c] Market economies.
[d] And other Asian countries with planned economies.

of total population, while in Black Africa the proportion was probably
on the order of 3%.

Asia, most of whose societies had a long urban history, around 1900
had a relatively low level of urbanization: about 9%, placing this continent at a level 2 to 3 points lower than that in Europe on the eve of the
Industrial Revolution. But Asia's level of urbanization was higher in
the eighteenth century before colonization. There was in 1900 greater
homogeneity among the levels in different Asian countries than was
the case in the other continents. Thus the difference between the respective levels of urbanization of India and China, for instance, was
barely greater than the margin of error surrounding the relevant
data. The same applies when one compares these two great civilizations with the cultures of Southeast Asia. The early diffusion of the

Chinese, Indian and Muslim cultures over almost the whole of Asia explains this relative homogeneity.

Despite the different starting points, however, the various parts of the Third World underwent a convergent evolution, since each of these regions experienced very rapid increase in their respective levels of urbanization and urban growth has accelerated throughout the Third World since 1930–1950. There was also convergence in the sense that the levels of urbanization reached in different regions have tended to harmonize. This means that as a general rule the regions least urbanized to begin with have grown more rapidly than the most urbanized. This has proved especially true in Africa. In Asia, on the other hand, growth has been even slower (or, rather, less rapid) than in Latin America. I shall trace the course of events in each region in more detail.

In Africa, between 1930 and 1970 alone urban population increased fivefold, making an annual growth rate of 4.2%. This led to a rapid rise in the level of urbanization as well, which climbed from 8.0 to 19.5%, reaching a level approximately equal to that of Asia. The increase was particularly rapid in Black Africa, which had been very little urbanized at the turn of the century. At this stage Black Africa had only one city with a population of more than 100,000 (Ibadan) and in 1930 there were only four (Addis Ababa, Lagos, Khartoum, and Ibadan). By 1970, however, the region had reached a level of urbanization of 15% and contained some thirty-four cities with populations of 100,000 or more, seven surpassing half a million. And in 1980 the number of cities with populations of more than 100,000 appears to have surpassed fifty.

North Africa, on the other hand, had relatively many large cities after its long urban history. In 1900 six cities had populations of more than 100,000: Cairo had a population on the order of 650,000; Alexandria, 350,000; Algiers and Tunis around 150,000; and Fez and Oran a little over 100,000. Until 1930 few new cities of comparable size had emerged (three in all). But growth accelerated thereafter: in 1950 seventeen cities had populations in excess of 100,000.

The combination of rapid population growth and a rapid rise in the level of urbanization led to a greater urban explosion in Latin America than anywhere else. The urban population of this region, which was around 13 million in 1900 (and under 4 million in 1850), had reached 30 million by 1930, 160 million in 1970, and probably 270 million in 1985. Since 1920 annual growth in urban population has surpassed 4%. Between 1900 and 1960, although making up only 13% of the urban population of the Third World as a whole, Latin America accounted for 30% of the increase in overall urban population. By the start of the fifties the level of urbanization in Latin America was very near that of Europe; and today the levels in the two parts of the world are almost identical, despite the great disparity in standards of living. In the temperate regions of Latin America the level of urbanization has even exceeded that of the developed world, currently standing at 80% as against 66% in developed nations. All of this illustrates particularly well the exceptional character of the urban explosion in Latin America, a problem to which I shall return in chapter 28.

In Asia (except China), urban population grew fairly slowly up to the thirties. Taking margins of error into account, the level of urbanization in 1930 seems to have been about the same as in 1900. Things changed, however, after the Second World War. In the thirty-five years from 1950 to 1985, urban population grew by a factor of 4.3 or thereabouts, as against a factor of 1.5 during the preceding forty-five-year period.

China: A Succession of Urban Policies

China at the turn of the century was less urban than the average of the rest of the Third World. Thus around 1900 the level of urbanization in China was on the order of 7.0–8.5% as against 9–10% in the rest of the Third World. Certainly, as I noted earlier, the margins of error in this case are very wide. But it is practically certain that India in particular had a level of urbanization higher than China's by about one point. Between 1920 and 1950, however, China apparently caught up with the other Asian countries.

Since the early fifties and the coming to power of the Communist Party, "China's efforts in dealing with her urban problems have been constantly marked by the marriage between ideologically oriented considerations and pragmatic solutions, between political concepts and down-to-earth decisions." This conclusion reached by N. You (1980) sums up very nicely the many changes that have characterized the last three decades of government action in Chinese urban affairs. From 1949 to the present one can distinguish four main phases, whose guiding thread has been "to urbanize the countryside and ruralize the city."

Beginning with the Liberation, the Chinese government first sought to reduce the influence of Shanghai, which, as was seen in chapter 26, had become the economic penetration point for the West and as a result was the largest city in China, probably having around 1950 a population of 10.4 million (as against 6.7 million in Peking). Taken in the main, Chinese urban policy until about 1957 consisted of an attempt to restructure the spatial distribution of the urban population more than to put a general brake on the process of urbanization itself. This policy led to the attempt to restrict migration toward the coastal towns by locating or relocating industries and services in two types of cities: small towns in the interior and new towns created in thinly populated and above all largely unurbanized parts of the country.

Since 1957 a change of policy has taken place. To begin with, some twenty million young city residents, most of them considered as being unemployed, were sent out into rural areas, and an effort was made to decongest the larger cities by creating satellite towns. It is true that the growth in urban population and in the larger cities had been very rapid. Between 1949 and 1957 the number of city residents increased by some 70–80%, and most large cities (except Shanghai) also grew rapidly.

Then ensued the Great Leap Forward, which had profound consequences in the area of policy relating to the spatial distribution of the urban population. The new policy aimed at neither more nor less than creating an entirely new urban system; one might even say that it aimed at realizing the quip of Alphonse Allais: "construct the cities in the country." More specifically, the policy consisted of transforming the communes into basic units of economic organization, incorporating industrial activities in rural communes and agricultural activities in urban ones.

The failure, or semifailure, of the Great Leap Forward, and in particular the poor harvests of those years, led to a further effort to disperse the urban population, which apparently continued to grow. So city residents were sent out into the countryside. This transfer affected young people most of all, and received fresh impetus in 1968 when it was given the official blessing of Mao Tse-Tung. The number of young people transferred in this way is thought to have reached forty million by 1964 and perhaps twice that by around 1975 (though this is probably an exaggeration).

> Initially, the transfer of urban youths to the border
> regions and to the rural areas was probably re-
> garded as a temporary measure, an improvisation by
> the authorities to cope with some short-term, urgent
> needs (i.e., the agricultural crisis). As time went on,
> some top officials advocated the rustication program
> as an effective way to solve the problems of over-
> population and youth employment in the cities.
> (P. H. Chang, 1979)

Chinese policy from 1964 to 1977 may be summarized as consisting of the wish to bring a better balance to the spatial distribution of the population in favor of rural areas, especially by creating numerous small centers of industrial development in the countryside.

Military considerations appear not to have been absent from this policy of dispersing urban population and thus industry as well. In China's quarrel with the Soviet Union, a very wide dispersal of economic targets represents a substantial asset, making it possible to offset, at least partially, China's disadvantage in the field of long-distance missiles and nuclear arms.

In summary, it appears that the sole constant feature in the government policy during the 1949–1977 period was its clear preference for small cities. From 1961 to 1965 and from 1969 to 1976, the government has even acted in favor of the expansion of those small cities (Buck, 1981).

China After Mao: A New Urban Policy?

How have things changed since Mao's death (in September 1976), and more especially since the overthrow of the "Gang of Four" (in July 1977) and the extremely radical change of direction in Chinese policies this brought about, a change of direction affecting both politics and above all the economy? In practical terms, the basic principles underlying the new aim of modernizing the economy should lead to a certain acceleration in the process of urbanization. But it is clearly too soon to know what the real consequences will be. In any event, the urban policy currently in force differs fundamentally in practice from the one pursued before 1977. I say "in practice" because, to my knowledge, there has been no official declaration of principle concerning urban policy. But it is symptomatic that the authorities recommend that young, educated, unemployed workers in the cities set up collective enterprises, both in community services and in activities resembling what in the West is called the informal sector, that is (see chapter 29), activities often marginal in character, using chiefly traditional technologies.

More significant still is the publicity given the fact that during 1979, which may be considered the first year of "normalization" and of the new economic policy, a large number of urban jobs were created to absorb part of the residue of unemployment accumulated over the years of the "erroneous policy" pursued by the Gang of Four. Thus in an interview published in the *Beijing Review* for 11 February 1980, the Director of the State Bureau of Labor made it clear not only that efforts to create jobs would in part focus on urban areas, but that no further attempts would be made to solve the problem of urban unemployment (thus expressly recognized) by sending young people out into the countryside, attention being especially directed toward catching up in the service sector. In "the ten years of turmoil starting in 1966," the director stated,

> the national economy was brought to the brink of
> collapse and many avenues of employment were
> blocked. The unbalanced development between vari-
> ous economic sectors, particularly between agricul-
> ture and industry, was another major factor. Light
> industry, commerce, catering, and service trades in
> cities could not develop as they should. Though
> the urban population increased sharply in the last
> twenty years, the proportion of workers and staff

members in commerce and service trades in relation to all the workers and staff members decreased by approximately one-third. This alone reduced opportunities for employment for several million.

Unemployment was recognized as a reality even if the expression was used only by oversight, since unemployment theoretically cannot exist in a socialist regime, which even the China of today claims hers to be. Thus a press review of the French edition of *Beijing Review* (*Beijing Information*) of 15 February 1982 reproduces an article that begins as follows:

> In China there are now young people without work who are called "young people waiting for employment" instead of being called "unemployed," because there is a difference in substance between those two terms. First of all, in a capitalist regime unemployment is due to overpopulation. "Waiting for employment" in China means that temporarily a fraction of the young people living in cities have no work; this is not due to a relative surplus of population, but is a temporary phenomenon due to the disequilibrium between the increase of population and the production of material goods.

And the level of unemployment in the early 1980s was very high (see chapter 27).

And what in practical terms was the impact of these three decades of contrasting policies on the growth of the urban population of China? As in all other areas where statistics are concerned, it is necessary to be content with non-Chinese estimates which seek to grasp the reality behind the available data using information that is at best incomplete and at worst either nonexistent or contradictory. The publication of the preliminary results of the 1982 census has not solved the problems: "The study of urban population trends continues to be plagued by definitional problems; indeed, the actual size of China's urban population remains a demographic mystery" (Chan and Xu, 1985). The most likely figure for 1982 is an urban population of some 207 million and a rate of urbanization of 21% (excluding, as in the rest of this book, the population of Taiwan). In my opinion these data appear credible and close to what I had estimated before the publication of these data. These figures show a more moderate increase in urbanization than in the rest of Asia, but an increase nevertheless significant (see table 27.2).

The United Nations (1986b) estimates that in 1985 the population of China's largest city, Shanghai, was 11.8 million, which means a very modest increase over the preceding thirty-five years, since in 1950 its population was estimated at 10.4 million. But Beijing has increased during the same period from 6.7 to 9.1 million, and many small cities increased even more rapidly. Moreover, since 1977 the level of urbanization has increased much more rapidly than before. Between 1977 and 1985 it is probable that the increase was on the order of 3.2% per year, compared to an average 1.7% between 1950 and 1977 (but total population also increased much more slowly during recent years). This difference implies that migration to the cities has increased, since the analysis of demographic data shows that urban fertility is low (M. Cartier, 1986).

The Concentration of Population in Very Large Cities in the Third World

Even during the period before the Industrial Revolution, the most advanced societies of the future Third World characteristically contained larger cities than their European counterparts. The analysis in previous chapters already suggested as much. Table 27.3, however, makes it possible to highlight the differences involved. It should be born in mind that the ratio between the total population of developed countries and that of the countries of the Third World was on the order of 1 to 3.0–3.3 until 1700, 1 to 3.0 in 1800, 1 to 2.0 in 1900, and 1 to 2.8 in 1980.

Around 1500 the world appears to have had some fifty to sixty cities with populations of more than 100,000, and all but four lay in the regions destined to become the Third World of today. Asia had the most: forty to forty-five of those cities belonged to the great cultures of that vast continent. The pre-Columbian cultures had perhaps two or three, and Africa three or four, almost all of them in the Islamic north. By about 1700 the situation had changed a little. The future Third World now accounted for only 85% of the largest cities, as against 90–95 % in 1500. A further significant indicator providing a preview of the upheavals to come is the fact that Europe had two of the seven cities with populations of more than 500,000 in the world around 1700.

The Industrial Revolution, of course, by stimulating rapid urban growth and the emergence of very great cities in developed nations, had within a little more than half a century brought about a situation in which the largest cities were chiefly located in the developed world. On this score it will be recalled that by 1820–1830 London had replaced Peking as the largest city in the world. This was the first time since the decline of ancient Rome that the greatest metropolis in the world was in Europe. Muslim Granada may perhaps have been for a fairly brief period at the start of the eleventh century the largest city in the world. But this would have been at a time when the largest cities in the world had populations of less than 500,000, which was exceptional.

TABLE 27.3   Distribution of the Number of Cities according to
Population and Economic Region
(1500–1980)

| | Population of Cities (in thousands) | | | | | |
	100–200	200–300	300–500	500–1,000	1,000 or more	Total
1500[a]						
Developed countries	3	1	—	—	—	4
Third World	38	8	2	2	—	50
1700[a]						
Developed countries	9	1	—	2	—	12
Third World	45	8	6	5	—	64
1800[a]						
Developed countries	16	5	1	1	1	24
Third World	41	12	4	4	1	62
1900[a]						
Developed countries	97	33	23	24	8	185
Third World	56	21	13	14	3	107
1900[b]						
Developed countries	101	33	28	24	9	195
Third World	52	21	8	14	2	97
1980[b]						
Developed countries	490	220	160	120	110	1,100
Third World	590	210	160	130	115	1,200

Sources: Bairoch (1977a), with additional figures for 1980.
Note: Cities according to the definition of "metropolitan areas" for 1900 and 1980.
The figures for the period 1500–1800 for the Third World have been sharply revised upwards. The underestimation forecasted in the 1977 text was verified by subsequent research.
[a] In this series Japan is included in the Third World.
[b] In this series Japan is included among developed countries.

In the near future, certainly in the 1990s, the largest city in the world, if not the several largest, will be in the Third World. The prospects for the year 2000 are even more heavily laden with implications. In their first forecast (1975b), the United Nations had predicted that Mexico City would be the largest city in the world and in the year 2000 would reach a population of thirty-two million; and that altogether the Third World would have nineteen cities with populations of over ten million. The estimated population of these nineteen cities would reach 320 million, or more people than inhabited all the cities of the world around 1900. These projections are probably excessive. I had at the same time made projections of my own based on slightly different assumptions, and arrived at a total of only fourteen cities with populations of more than ten million, none greater than twenty-five million, with a combined population of 200 million (Bairoch,

TABLE 27.4 Growth of Cities of Third World Market Economies according to Population (1900–1980)

Size of Cities (in thousands)	1900	1930	1950	1980
	Number of cities[a]			
100–200	40	44	134	449
200–500	22	39	79	274
500–1,000	7	8	23	99
1,000–5,000	1	6	18	63
5,000 or more	—	—	2	14
Total	70	97	256	899
	Urban Population[a] (in millions)			
100–200	5.4	6.2	17.3	64.9
200–500	5.4	12.1	22.3	86.6
500–1,000	5.4	6.3	16.2	68.5
1,000–5,000	1.2	9.6	30.9	129.0
5,000 or more	—	—	10.4	100.0
Total	17.5	34.2	97.2	449.0
Urban population[b]	64.0	101.0	189.0	695.0
Total population	631.0	800.0	1,072.0	2,232.0

Sources: Bairoch (1977a), p. 80, with revised data and new estimates for 1980.
Note: The fact that these figures have been only slightly rounded off does not imply a correspondingly small margin of error.
Third World market economies include all Third World countries except Asian countries with nonliberal economies, that is, essentially China.
[a] Cities according to the definition of metropolitan areas.
[b] A criterion of 5,000 is used for urban population.

1977a). The United Nations' projections published in 1986 reduced the figure for Mexico City to twenty-six million (United Nations, 1986b), and altogether there would be seventeen cities with populations of over ten million in the Third World, totalling 240 million. But even these projections reflect what is in fact a highly negative trend, the first signs of which were visible as early as the thirties: the heavy concentration of the urban population of the Third World in very large cities (see table 27.4).

Around 1930, there were some fourteen large cities (cities with populations of more than 500,000) in the Third World, and of these fourteen cities, six had populations of more than a million. These six cities were, in approximately descending order, Buenos Aires, Rio de Janeiro, Calcutta, Bombay, and Mexico City. (If China is taken into account, five other cities, one of them the largest in the Third World, join the list.) These fourteen large cities already had a population of

TABLE 27.5   Proportion of the Third World Urban Population
Living in Large Cities
(1900–1980)

Population of Cities	1900	1930	1950	1980
500,000 or more				
Africa	10	17	25	45
Asia				
(market economy)	10	10	32	44
Latin America	11	28	30	38
Third World				
(market economy)	10	16	30	43
1,000,000 or more				
Africa	—	12	16	30
Asia				
(market economy)	3	5	22	35
Latin America	—	17	23	31
Third World				
(market economy)	2	10	22	33

Sources: Bairoch (1977a) with additional figures for 1980.

sixteen million between them, representing nearly 16% of overall urban population. So high a concentration of urban population in large cities was only attained in the developed world around 1880, that is, at a time when the process of urbanization was much further advanced than in the Third World around 1930; the relevant levels of urbanization were 24 and 12%, respectively. The number of very large cities in the Third World, having risen from eight to fourteen between 1900 and 1930, increased very rapidly thereafter, rising to 112 in 1970, and probably to 178 in 1980. The size of the population living in these cities grew even more rapidly, rising from sixteen million in 1930 to 191 million in 1970, and some 300 million in 1980. In 1980 these cities had 43% of the total urban population, that is, a proportion similar to that in the developed world at the same date. It goes without saying that a concentration this high poses serious economic problems (see chapter 29).

In spite of the fact that governments have for more than two decades been aware of the necessity for better urban planning, which they have shown mainly by encouraging intermediate-sized cities, the rapid growth of large cities, especially the capitals, has continued. As Rondinelli (1982) notes, "the concentration of national government investments and expenditures in national capitals seems to be a common cause of the large disparities between the major metropolitan area and middle-sized cities in developing countries."

At the start of the twentieth century, the concentration of urban population in large cities (those with populations of more than 500,000) was chiefly in Latin America (see table 27.5). In 1900, 16%

of the urban population of Latin America lived in great cities, and this proportion grew very rapidly thereafter, to the point where in 1930 it reached 28%. The situation was similar in the other regions of the Third World only after 1930. After this date a certain equalization of the situation in different regions took place, but only at a very high level of concentration in great and even very great cities. In 1980 one-third of the urban population of the Third World as a whole lived in cities with populations of more than a million. On the basis of the available data it can be estimated that in 2000 the proportion will reach about 50%. By contrast, in the developed world the proportion has never surpassed 33%.

I just said that the concentration of urban population in large cities of the Third World poses serious economic problems. But it also poses serious human problems—and that, of course, is the important thing. Mention the large cities of the Third World, and immediately there springs to mind the terrible image of the shantytowns. This and other consequences of the urban explosion in the Third World will be discussed in chapter 29.

Very Little Evolution against the Trend

By the twenties demographic growth, and particularly growth in urban population, had reached such proportions that only very few cities managed to escape it. Certainly urban history remains individual: we sometimes meet with enormous differences in growth rates from one city to the next. But whereas in all earlier phases of urban expansion in traditional societies a large number of cities would be found to have declined, now rare indeed were those cities in which population fell.

We have analyzed and completed the data gathered by Johannot (1977) on population trends in the cities of the Third World between 1900 and 1950. In this analysis, I looked at all the cities of the Third World (less China) that at some point during this period had populations of more than twenty thousand. Of the 650-odd cities studied, I found only some twenty whose populations remained stable between 1920 and 1950, and only ten or so that declined. Thus decline affected less than 2% of all Third World cities that had populations in excess of twenty thousand at one time or another over the thirty-year period from 1920 to 1950. To put this in perspective, it should be recalled that in the case of sixteenth-century Europe I have estimated that some 20% of the cities declined in population.

Those Third World cities registering declines were almost all concentrated in Central America, including three of the five largest cities of El Salvador. The most heavily affected was San Vicente, which owed part of its wealth to indigo plantations (one of the first dyes completely superseded by a chemical product developed at the end of

URBANISM IN THE THIRD WORLD

the nineteenth century). There were also two cities in Guatemala, one of which, Totonicapan, was badly damaged by an earthquake. The vicissitudes of the mining industry account for the decline of Zacatecas and Guanajuato in Mexico, while more complex factors, both economic and political in character, explain the fall in population (still between 1920 and 1950) in the second largest cities of Nicaragua (Leon) and Paraguay (Villa Rica). The only significant case of decline outside Central America was that of the millenary city of Istanbul. The transfer of the capital of the "New Turkey" to Ankara and the loss of the colonial empire brought about the decline of Istanbul's population. This decline did not, however, exceed the margin of error surrounding the data on the city's population. Finally, among the cities whose populations stagnated during this period were the large traditional cities of Nigeria, especially the ancient city of Kano.

These cases of stagnation and decline, however, did not as a rule continue beyond 1945–1955. After this period demographic growth and the increase in urban population reached such dimensions that there were practically no more significant cases, in terms of the number of cities involved, of Third World cities either declining or stagnating. The explosion affected the entire urban system—more or less greatly, to be sure, but virtually without exception.

Thus there was an urban explosion that was not only without historical precedent and entailing an equally unprecedented concentration of population in very great cities, but was generalized to the entire Third World. It is to the causes and effects of this explosion that I shall now turn.

28 The Causes of the Urban Explosion in the Third World □

The rapid growth of the cities of the Third World did not escape what seems to be a constant of urban development: any urban system experiencing rapid growth in population will owe a large part of this growth to an influx of rural people. It can be estimated that migrations have been responsible for 40–50% of the increase in the population of the cities of the Third World. This is a very general average, and substantial differences exist at regional and national levels as well as at the level of individual cities. But it nevertheless points to a significant aspect of the problem we are dealing with here.

Seeking the causes of the urban explosion in the Third World also entails seeking the causes of the migratory flood of country people into the cities. Nor are guilty parties hard to find. I shall begin by looking at four main causes, to which I shall later add some accessory, but by no means minor, causes.

An Extremely High Density of Agricultural Population

Classical theories of the causes of migrations have always insisted on the effects of factors of repulsion and attraction, of push and pull. Among the factors pushing people off the land and into the cities, the excessively high density of agricultural population figures prominently. If the density of occupation of the land has constituted one of the causes explaining internal and international migrations in industrialized countries, it is undeniable that, given the scale of demographic pressure in developing nations, this factor must play an infinitely more decisive role in the Third World. The very dense occupation of the land obviously reflects one of the most important aspects of underdevelopment—demographic expansion. These things are, of course, well known. But it is worth recalling that by 1910–1920, and certainly by 1940, population growth in the Third World proceeded at a pace without precedent in human history. From 1920 to 1940, it reached a rate of 1.1% per year; from 1940 to 1950, 1.2%;

and from 1950 to 1980, 2.2%. In the industrialized world during the first half century of development, the rate was only 0.7%, the highest rate reached during any thirty-year period being 1.2 percent (between 1880–1910). And even this was possible only because of the expansion of the territory of non-European countries populated by Europeans (chiefly North America). In western Europe, for instance, the highest recorded growth rate was 0.8%.

It should also be remembered that this demographic explosion essentially resulted from the introduction of medical technology permitting a very rapid decrease in mortality rates, and infant mortality rates in particular. In the space of thirty years (from 1920 to 1950) infant mortality was divided in half in the Third World, falling from 200–220 deaths per 1,000 live births to around 100 deaths per 1,000 live births. In Europe, by contrast, it took one hundred years (from 1820 to 1920) to achieve the same result. And for those who may be surprised to find that the birth rate failed to follow closely the curve of the mortality rate, it should be recalled that in Western societies it was not until nearly a century after the fall in the mortality rate had begun that birth rates started to fall.

An even more fundamental difference between the evolution of underdeveloped and developed countries lies in the fact that in the Third World rapid population growth was not accompanied by industrial development. In the West, as has been seen in earlier chapters, industrial development made it possible to absorb the surplus rural work force, thereby sharply reducing the increase in the number of agricultural laborers and thus the density of occupation of the land as well. As a result, in Europe (except Russia) between 1800 and 1880, the total number of agricultural workers rose by no more than about 35%, while total population increased by 60%. During the same period, moreover, the amount of land under cultivation increased, probably by 10–15%. Between 1880 and 1910 the number of agricultural workers grew very little; and after the twenties it went into decline, thereby making more land available per farm worker.

In the Third World, on the other hand, in the six decades between 1920 and 1980 the number of farm workers practically doubled. The exceptional character of this trend is highlighted even more by the fact that this was not a process of catching up following a decrease in the density of occupation of the land, a decrease that might have been caused by demographic catastrophes caused by great epidemics, famines, or wars, or by all three combined, as had frequently been the case in traditional economies in the past. Without moving too far ahead in time, one may note that the working agricultural population in developing countries in 1920 was probably greater by some 60–70% than in 1800. Even Latin America had regained by around 1900–1920 the population it had before the sharp decline of the sixteenth century.

Thus globally the number of agricultural workers in developing countries more than tripled between 1800 and 1980, most of this increase occurring, as I have already indicated, between 1920 and 1980.

The sharp rise in the number of agricultural workers brought about increasingly dense occupation of the land. Indeed, according to the incomplete figures available, it seems unlikely that between 1800 and 1980 the amount of land under cultivation in the Third World grew by more than 40%. Thus around 1980 the density of agricultural population was nearly three times as great as in 1800, when it was already high. Today (or rather around 1985), each agricultural worker in the Third World has at his disposal an average of 1.4 hectares of farmland (pasture not included), although this average covers a wide range. The figures for various parts of the Third World are 4.4 in Latin America, 1.4 in Africa, and only 0.9 in the Far East. In Europe (except Russia), by contrast, when the density of agricultural population was at its height around 1920, each agricultural worker had at his disposal an average of 2.3 hectares of farmland. And since then the figure has gone up steadily to around 4 hectares today. Meanwhile, in 1920 in the United States and Canada, from which Europe at that time imported some of its grain, each agricultural worker had at his disposal 14.5 hectares of farmland, a figure that has reached 80 today. It is true that in many parts of the Third World two harvests per year are possible, which colors this comparison somewhat. But it does not diminish or obscure the catastrophic nature of the situation on the land.

This means that after 1940–1950, given the speed of demographic growth, within the space of one generation it became necessary on the average either to divide each agricultural holding in two or to make two households live on each holding. This being the case, it is easy to understand why the rural exodus reached such proportions—why so many young people left the land to seek jobs in the city, which became not only a place to which people escaped but, at around this same period, a source of many attractions, often more illusory than real. And among these attractions one of the most powerful was higher wages.

A Large Difference between Urban and Rural Income

Just as the high density of agricultural population is the most important factor pushing people off the land, so high urban wage levels figure prominently among the factors pulling them into the cities. Indeed it appears that, contrary to what took place in the West during the nineteenth century, a wide gap opened in the Third World between urban and rural income as early as 1950–1960.

Before examining the indicators pointing to the greater wealth of city dwellers, I must insist that this situation is of recent date. In chapters 25 and 26, I showed that during the nineteenth century and much of the first half of the twentieth century the standard of living of city dwellers in the Third World, and in colonial Asia in particular, was very low, much lower than in traditional societies before colonization. It was in fact so low that it could not have been much higher than that of rural people. The situation may have been different in Latin America. Nevertheless, even in this case the gap between average urban and average rural income remained relatively narrow.

All of this changed rapidly after the Second World War. A systematic analysis of the available data (Bairoch, 1973) leads to the following conclusions. At the start of the seventies the average difference between agricultural wages and wages paid industrial laborers was roughly 80–150%. If one compares average wages for all workers in agriculture and industry, the difference widens to 100–200%. For income, however, the difference narrows to only about 60–120%. It should be noted that these averages do not reflect the recorded extremes, especially where the upper limit is concerned, but rather the approximate orders of magnitude of average differences. It should also be noted that between the start of the seventies and today there has been no noticeable change in this domain.

In interpreting the data, one must take care to allow for a number of factors introducing bias into the comparisons. These notably involve differences in the cost of living in rural and urban areas. What is more, urban workers must often devote an appreciable portion of their incomes to paying for services, transportation in particular, that are either free or unnecessary in rural districts. Moreover, one has to take into account the fairly widespread transfer of income between urban and rural regions, a transfer operating in both directions. This generally involves either country people subsidizing family members living in the city while they look for work, or city residents sending money home to help support family members (in the broad sense) who have remained in the countryside. And the incidence of direct and/or indirect taxation may vary widely. Finally, it should also be possible to allow for the numerous cases of city people taking on additional jobs and raising their income levels. Nor should one forget income derived from extralegal activities—theft, prostitution, and so forth. Insufficient data exist on differences in the cost of living in most developing countries. But by way of indicating their approximate order or magnitude, I would say that the difference probably lies somewhere between 10 and 60%. It is practically impossible to quantify the other contributing factors.

But while the analysis of real income would require integrating all of these factors, it should be stressed that in the decision to immigrate to the city differences in nominal earnings (or income) have always proved decisive. For the potential immigrant either knows nothing about these additional factors or tends to overlook them. Further, only the success stories filter back to rural areas, and very often those stories are embellished.

I shall now look at the extent to which the situation in developing countries thus described differs from that in industrialized countries during the initial phase of development. I shall confine myself to wages, the data relating to income not only being harder to come by, but having for this period a wider margin or error.

In chapter 17 I showed that the difference between the average wage for an agricultural worker and that for an unskilled urban laborer was extremely small in Western countries. In many cases, indeed, there was no difference at all. Were one to try to fix a very rough average, this would lie around 15–30% in the first half of the nineteenth century and around 25–30% until the First World War. It is true that the range of wages within the industrial sector was very broad, and that the wages paid a qualified worker exceeded those paid an unskilled laborer by about 50%.

It needs to be emphasized, however, that in the industrial sector with the largest increase in jobs and which absorbed a large proportion of immigrants, namely the textile and garment industries, wages were very low. Indeed, the difference between wages in this sector and in agriculture was extremely small, or even nonexistent. Finally, it is likely that before the Industrial Revolution the difference between urban and rural wages was even smaller. And this was true in both the traditional societies of Europe and those of the future Third World.

The Third World today, then, confronts us with a new kind of situation. And Michael Lipton (1977) may be right when he writes that: "The most important class conflict in the poor countries of the world today is not between labor and capital. Nor is it between foreign and national interest. It is between the rural class and the urban class."

What are the main causes of this large income gap? First, it is obvious that the dual character of the economies of most Third World countries constitutes the chief cause of the situation. One of the dominant aspects of this duality lies in the difference between agricultural and industrial productivity. Agricultural productivity, to which I shall return later, has declined in many regions. As a result, it stands (or, rather, stood around 1960–1970) at a lower level than in the nineteenth century or even the seventeenth century. The industries established in the Third World, on the other hand, generally use technologies very close to those used in developed nations today, whence a high level of industrial productivity. The widespread adoption of legislation prescribing minimum wages also seems to have made a significant contribution to this situation. For this legislation has fixed mandatory minimum wages at levels that fail to take the economic context into account, political motivation prevailing over a sense of reality.

The enforcement of this legislation, moreover, has practically everywhere been more complete in urban than in rural areas, without allowing for the fact that wage earners are proportionally much less numerous in rural districts than in the city. This applies only in general terms, of course, for the dividing line between the traditional and the modern runs through the city itself as well, owing to the importance of the informal sector (see chapter 29).

Get an Education and Move to the City

The inappropriateness of education for the real needs of the economy, both in quantitative and in qualitative terms, has always and everywhere been a problem. This problem is all the more acute in the societies of the Third World, however, owing to the triple constraints of the advanced level of contemporary technologies, the high level of illiteracy, and the legacy of an educational system too faithfully modelled on that of the former colonial powers.

The failure of education to adapt to economic conditions has played a major role in speeding up rural emigration. Investigation has confirmed the observations of René Dumont (1966), who writes that "the number of children who spend more than three or four years in school and return to the fields afterward is very small." Tibor Mende has also very aptly remarked at a conference devoted to these matters that "by teaching Racine to the children of the Third World, we have deracinated them."

The link between the level of education and the propensity to emigrate, particularly to the city, has emerged in most of the studies investigating the causes of migration in the Third world. Nor is this factor unique to developing nations. What we have to determine here, then, is the extent to which the growth of education has been rapid enough to constitute a major factor in the increasing tide of rural migrants moving into the cities of the Third World.

Education has in fact developed exceedingly quickly, owing to the emphasis, since the end of the Second World War, on the need for and right to schooling. Despite the extremely sharp rise in the number of young people, crude figures on school enrollment in the Third World have gone up very rapidly. Thus at the level of primary education, while in 1939 fewer than one-sixth of all children went to school, by 1960 the total approached 50%, and was more than 85% at the start of the eighties. At the secondary and university levels, education rates had by the early eighties become the same as in Western Europe in the early fifties.

This quantitative success story of education can largely be explained by the fact that teaching is one of the few areas where the production process has no risk of a bottleneck due to a shortage of qualified labor.

If one uses strictly economic terms one can say that in this case the same plant produces both the consumer goods and the equipment needed for the plant.

The rapidity of the rise in school attendance has contributed, especially in rural areas, to creating a generation gap. Many young people in the Third World have received an education, have illiterate parents, and, rightly or wrongly, believe that knowing how to read and write compels them to leave the countryside. In this context the fact that education has failed to adapt to economic realities plays a substantial role. In the West during the nineteenth century, not only was the diffusion of education more gradual—whence a smaller generation gap—but education did not include urban values alone: rural life was frequently depicted in reading manuals, for instance, in texts for dictation, and in literature and poetry. Even arithmetic exercises were more rural. And given that urbanization was more recent and had as yet affected only a part of humanity, the traditional rural world was closer in spirit.

The City in the Third World: From High Mortality Rates to Rapid Natural Growth

In order to deal with the fourth explanatory factor in the urban explosion, it is necessary to make a digression about an important aspect of urban life. In preceding chapters I have not raised the problem of the specific urban demography of the traditional societies of the future Third World. There was good reason for avoiding it, moreover: the available data are too fragmentary. What few indications are available, however, point to the existence of disproportionately high mortality rates in the cities. Everything suggests that these indications do in fact reflect, if not the general situation, at least the dominant one, for there is little reason to think that the traditional cities of the non-European world before the nineteenth century were very different in this respect from those of Europe.

Death in the City

It is certain that at the end of the nineteenth century the cities of the Third World were still marked by disproportionately high death rates. Thus for the period 1880–1900 in the larger Asian cities, infant mortality was on the order of 350–450 per 1,000 live births, while in rural regions it was on the order of 210–250 per 1,000. During the same period, the difference was not so large in Latin America: 210–260 in the larger cities, as against 180–200 in rural areas. For other parts of the Third World the data are too fragmentary to make any valid conclusions possible.

Given the high infant mortality rates in Asian cities, the question immediately arises as to the extent to which colonization had a hand in them. It is difficult, in view of the lack of data, to draw any definite conclusions on this score. There is, however, a strong presumption that the negative aspects of colonization did indeed influence mortality. It is worth citing in this connection the results of a systematic examination of parish records for the nineteenth century in the Philippines (Smith, 1978). These findings attest to a pronounced rise in mortality rates. After eliminating fluctuations due to epidemiological causes, the author of this study concluded that the most plausible scenario accounting for this rise

> seems to be one which places major stress upon the
> shifting relationship between subsistence and com-
> mercial agriculture within the colony. If generally
> deteriorating levels of livelihood and temporary
> food shortages—both induced by the commercializa-
> tion of agriculture and accompanying changes in
> land tenure—contributed to a growing susceptibility
> to disease, this process could explain the rise in mor-
> tality levels during the century.

But prudence remains necessary. It will probably be impossible to establish any certainties. Nevertheless, in those cases characterized, like that of India, by a fall in the standard of living for city residents, it is just about certain that until the end of the nineteenth century the negative effects of the deterioration of living conditions could not have been offset by Western medicine. But what has happened in the area of urban mortality and fertility rates since the close of the nineteenth century?

The efficiency of the British civil service gave India a statistical apparatus very early. The first census had been taken by 1872, that is, earlier than in some European countries (for example, Russia, whose first census was taken in 1897, and Bulgaria, whose first was taken in 1887). Making allowance for the inevitable margins of error, one can make profitable use of these censuses and especially those of the beginning of the twentieth century. The census of 1911, for example, gives a precious indication of the decisive role of immigration in urban growth. The proportion of city residents born in rural districts was very high: 80% in Bombay, 70% in Calcutta, 34% in Madras, and 36% in Delhi. The proportion for all cities with populations of more than 100,000 was 46%. Taking the case of Bombay, extreme since it was the largest industrial city in India, I have calculated that between 1881 and 1911, when the population of the city rose from 822,000 to 979,000, there was a natural population deficit of 590,000. This means that the gain through migration must have been 750,000 people during this period, a situation recalling that of seventeenth-century London (see chapter 12).

Epidemics, especially of cholera, were responsible for some of these

TABLE 28.1   Infant Mortality Rates in Third World Countries
and Larger Cities
(1890–1959)

	1890–99	1900–1909	1911–14	1921–25	1930–39	1940–49	1950–59
Africa							
Egypt[a]	—	—	—	144	164	153	166
Egypt[b]	—	—	—	224	205	—	—
Cairo	315	321	289	228	199	233	166
Alexandria	291	286	246	207	212[c]	177[d]	—
Asia							
Ceylon	—	—	—	190	174	123	74
Colombo	430[e]	361	—	—	172	134	83
India	—	—	205	182	169	150	110
Bombay	505	603	370	410	247	190	122
Malaysia	—	—	—	178	157	101	83
Singapore	406[e]	366[f]	—	224[g]	186	146	58
Philippines	—	—	—	157	148	96	100
Manila	—	—	—	—	146	143	66
Thailand	—	—	—	—	96	91	62
Bangkok	—	—	—	—	164	126	83
Latin America							
Argentina	—	—	—	116	98	80	64
Buenos Aires	142	99	92	80	56	40	33
Colombia	—	—	—	—	141	147	110
Bogota	—	—	—	—	192	163	104
El Salvador	—	—	—	—	132	108	80
San Salvador	—	—	—	—	197	136	90
Mexico	—	—	—	116	131	112	86
Mexico City	—	—	—	—	152	142	85
Uruguay	—	101[h]	104	105	97	81	64
Montevideo	131	111	126	118	100	64	43

Sources: Data for cities for 1880–1909: Bureau Municipal de Statistique d'Amsterdam (1912), pp. 44–49; for 1911–27: Office permanent de l'Institut international de Statistique (1927), pp. 275–83 and 327–30; (1931), pp. 104 and 130; for 1937–48: Institut international de statistique (1954), pp. 91, 92; for 1930–59: Robinson (1963), pp. 291–308; except for Alexandria, see above.

National data: League of Nations (various issues); United Nations, *Demographic Yearbook* (various issues); Robinson (1963); and national sources.

[a] Country as a whole.
[b] Only localities with hygiene stations, implying a more complete registration.
[c] 1937–38.
[d] 1947–48.
[e] 1893–99.
[f] 1900–1907.
[g] 1925–27.
[h] Average for 1903 and 1908.

deaths. Thus in three years (1899–1901) 195,000 people died in Bombay, nearly one-fourth of the total population. Epidemics and other scourges were the daily companions of city dwellers for many years. The most tragic decade was 1897–1906, during which (taking the case of Bombay again) deaths outnumbered births by 405,000. This means that without the influx of population from the neighboring countryside Bombay would have lost more than half of its inhabitants. Similarly, between 1895 and 1904, had it not been for immigration, Singapore would have lost about a third of its population. These data prove, if proof were needed, that the high mortality rates in Third World cities affected adults as well as infants.

The situation had already begun to improve between the two world wars, as attested by the change in infant mortality rates in the few cities for which data are available (see table 28.1). Obviously one has to allow for the unreliability of these figures. This is especially true for the data at the national level, underregistration of deaths being as a rule more pronounced in rural than in urban districts. Taking this into account, it can still be estimated that as early as the eve of the Second World War, the disproportionately high infant mortality rates in the cities had begun to disappear in most regions, a change inaugurated one or two decades earlier in Latin America.

During the interwar period even the larger Asian cities began to record a positive natural balance, that is, natural population growth. In one of the most negative cases, for instance, that of Bombay, births began to outnumber deaths sometime around the thirties, a trend accelerating thereafter. In Latin America, except for the wealthiest nations, like Argentina, where Buenos Aires, for example, already had natural growth by the 1880s and perhaps even earlier, this phase got under way around 1900–1910.

In the first years after the Second World War, Western technology made possible a rapid fall in mortality rates by means of antibiotics and DDT. This affected rural areas as well as cities, with the result that equalization slowed down a little. It can still be concluded that at the start of the fifties, mortality rates for the population at large—and not only for infants—were no longer higher in the cities than in the countryside. Western medicine had succeeded in offsetting the negative effects of the high density of urban population. Despite the acceleration of the urban explosion and the many negative consequences in the form of shantytowns, unemployment, and so forth, urban mortality rates have not increased relative to those in rural areas since the fifties. The opposite even seems to be the case, modernization having had a greater impact in the cities than in the countryside. Thus it is that I have been able to assemble recent infant mortality data distinguishing between urban and rural districts for eighteen Third World countries. Although there is bias due to underregistration in rural areas, ten countries had lower infant mortality rates in the cities than in the countryside, a similar but very small difference being found in three other countries. A synthesis of various specific studies on this topic (United Nations, 1982a) confirms and even reinforces the probability that there was equalization not only of infant mortality rates, but also of general mortality rates. This largely explains why since the fifties natural population growth in the cities would become a significant factor in urban expansion. But before looking into this further, I should pause to examine the second contributor to natural population growth: birth rates.

Births in the City

To what extent was there even as early as the end of the nineteenth century a specific urban behavior with respect to fertility? To what extent, in other words, do disproportionately low urban birth rates contribute to the negative balance in the natural growth of cities during the first decades of the twentieth century? The data are not sufficient to make it possible to pronounce on this question without reservations. It should be noted, however, that in his analysis of the population of India, Davis (1951) concludes that urban fertility had fallen below rural fertility by the 1930s. It is even possible that this had taken place as early as the 1880s. Indeed, for the decade from 1881 to 1890, despite the fact that young people were probably proportionately more numerous in the cities than in the countryside, while crude birth rates for India as a whole were on the order of 44–46 per 1,000, the fertility rates were 20 per 1,000 in Bombay, 18 in Calcutta, and 16 in Colombo. Madras, on the other hand, had 40 births per 1,000. But Madras had an unusually rural character. As the 1911 edition of the *Encyclopaedia Britannica* puts it: "The city presents a disappointing appearance, . . . it is spread over a very wide area, and many parts of it are almost rural in character." Other words to describe the Madras of this period are those of a scholar of today, in *A City of Villages* (Neild, 1979).

The harvest of data for the fifties is much more abundant and points to lower fertility rates in the cities than in the countryside; the differences are small, however (United Nations, 1965). The same holds true for the early '60s. Thus using the study of Kuznets (1974), already used for developed nations (see chapter 14), and applying the same crude index of fertility (which, though crude, is the most readily available), namely, the number of children under five years of age per 1,000 women aged fifteen to forty-nine, I find that birth rates in the Third World were on the average 20% higher in rural areas than in the cities, as compared with 31% in developed countries. This average derives from a wide variety of contrasting situations, not only at the international level, but at the intercontinental level as well. While the difference was a very substantial 42% in Latin America, for example, it was only about 10% in Asia and Africa. The very fragmentary information now available suggests that these differences have narrowed little since then (United Nations, 1977a), despite the fact that as a rule fertility seems to have declined a little in rural areas as well as in the cities.

One of the Causes of the Urban Explosion: The Natural Growth of Population

Despite modernization, the cities of the Third World have not avoided the catastrophic consequences of the time required for adaptations in human behavior. As was the case in developed countries, the process whereby fertility rates adapt to new mortality rates is very slow, for it requires deep-rooted changes in mentality. As has been seen, the essential difference between the Third World and the developed world has been the rapidity with which mortality rates have fallen, and the resulting quite natural major population growth. The cities of the Third World have consequently suffered severe demographic imbalance. The earlier shift in behavior in urban areas induced by modernization has not sufficed to cancel out the effects of the fall in death rates, with the result that natural population growth has been very great over the last three decades. This growth has been all the greater in that, by lowering the average age of the urban population, the influx of migrants tips the scale more on the side of births than of deaths. According to the data I have assembled, natural population growth in the cities has been nearly on a par with that in rural areas, varying between 2 and 4 % from one country to another. This has produced natural growth rates without precedent in human history.

Thus, unlike in the West, where the city acted as a brake on its own growth from the time modern urbanization set in and throughout the first 150 years of its evolution, in the Third World, 10–20 years after accelerated urbanization got under way, the city tends to stimulate its own growth. Therefore natural population growth has accounted by itself for more than half of the urban explosion.

More Factors Contributing to the Urban Explosion

The causes for the urban explosion accumulate: pressure on the available farmland, differences in wages and income, the impact of extending educational opportunities without adapting them to objective conditions in developing nations, and now natural population growth. But this is not all. Still other factors have to be added to the list.

And foremost among these factors is the process of decolonization, which has made a decisive contribution to accelerating urbanization in five particularly significant ways:

1. Decolonization has been accompanied practically everywhere by an excessive growth in the ranks of the civil service.

2. Industrial policies, especially in the area of substituting local products for imported goods, have brought about a much more rapid development of urban industrial employment than in the past.

3. In nearly every case in which colonial authorities had adopted administrative measures aimed at restricting migration to certain urban centers, these measures have been either rescinded or loosened since independence.

4. The Balkanization of some colonial empires or of parts of some colonial empires has furthered urbanization in some regions by creating new political or administrative capitals. It will be noted in this connection that, in certain former capitals whose zone of influence was reduced following independence, decolonization engendered additional unemployment.

5. In a great many regions political disturbances have led to movements of refugees, greatly increasing the population of some cities.

The diverse social constraints inherent in rural life have certainly helped motivate an appreciable fraction of the migration into the cities. I do not think, however, that one can consider this factor as unique to the Third World, and it cannot therefore be seen as a significant cause of the urban explosion. But I did not want to overlook it completely, especially since many students of the question insist, wrongly in my view, on the uniqueness of a great number of traditional rural societies, contrasting them with contemporary societies in developed nations. Comparison should properly be made between traditional societies as such and not between traditional and industrial societies. But these remarks do not suggest that certain of the social constraints characteristic of rural life have failed to contribute to the exodus of country people. Tribalism, in particular, by inhibiting migration from one rural region to another, has indeed indirectly fostered migration to the city, the detribalized world par excellence.

In a similar vein, mention should also be made of the extent to which certain aspects of the urban way of life are themselves inherently attractive. Many students of urbanization have rightly stressed the important part played by this factor. From the Greek city-states to the megalopolises of today (omitting the cities of the Middle Ages), the urban way of life has always exerted a strong pull on all social classes, each of them finding in the city various sorts of services either nonexistent or relatively undeveloped in rural parts. But what distinguishes the current situation in the Third World, and in developed nations as well, is that, thanks to the prodigious development of the means of communication, the existence of these services is far better advertised than ever before, thereby amplifying their power of attraction. And by means of communication I mean here both the mass media and modes of transportation. Until the mid-nineteenth century, for example, it took more than a week to make a round trip of one hundred kilometers or so. Today the same journey can be made in a single day at low cost. And the mass media have made the city a constant presence in the daily lives of country people, generally emphasizing, moreover, its most positive features.

In this connection, the conclusions of Brisseau-Loaiza (1972) concerning the key role played by trucks in a region of Peru may be generalized to most of the rural populations living at a distance from rail networks, that is to say, to the great majority of these populations:

> In the region of Cuzco, where its use was introduced about thirty years ago and has intensified over the last ten years in particular, its impact has been considerable both on economic activites and on the population. Most often, it directly supplants the llama and the mule as a means of communication. . . . Intensifying links between the city and the surrounding region, it has become an instrument of domination at the city's service. By giving them the means of exerting a regional influence, it has conferred on cities an importance that they have never had before despite their age and their permanence.

Thus the truck has broken down "geographic and cultural isolation and stimulates migration to the cities."

Another aspect of these problems is the mass media, which make the city so present, and which generally show the positive aspects of urban life. Without mentioning motion pictures or the radio whose invasive presence is felt throughout the Third World (by 1965 already, an average of one to every household), it may be noted that the diffusion of television has been very rapid. By 1965 in the Third World market economies, there were eight million television sets in service, making on the average nearly 1 for every 37 households. In 1985 there were some 110 million sets, or 1 for every 6 households.

I examined the effects of the first phases of colonization in chapters 24 through 26, and those of the more contemporary period are implicitly reflected in practically all of the factors dealt with in this chapter. But I have not gone at all deeply into the problem of the influence of the extension of the plantations. An econometric study by Firebaugh (1979) has recently confirmed that (so far as Asia and Latin America are concerned, at any rate) plantations have indeed been responsible for a perceptible increase in the level of urbanization. This study also confirms the impact of another factor, discussed toward the start of this chapter: the density of the occupation of farmland. Firebaugh has also found that the greater the density, the higher the level of urbanization.

Finally, one should not overlook the role played in the decision to migrate to the city by the aspiration—justified or not—to be more modern. In leaving their homes for the city, country people frequently hope to move from the underdeveloped world, associated in their minds (often mistakenly) with an inferior stage of culture, to the developed world, wrongly regarded as constituting a superior stage.

If So Many Faults, Why No Greater Damage?

In trying to draw conclusions from the foregoing discussion, I find it difficult to identify the one factor most responsible for the rapid urbanization of developing countries. The attempt to construct theoretical models determining the respective contributions of each of the many factors involved strikes me as illusory. What can be said, however, is that the rapidity with which education has spread and the difference between urban and rural income levels, coupled with the population explosion and its direct consequences, constitute the chief contributors to the rural exodus. To these highly important factors, unique to the Third World, may be added those others just examined.

It goes without saying that the order of importance of these factors differs as one moves from region to region, and even more so as one moves from one country to the next. The scale of the migration is conditioned not only by the extent to which the other factors are found, but also by deep-seated differences in the social and political structures determined by history, religion, culture, and even the environment.

In fact the causes of the rural exodus to the cities are so numerous and powerful that I am almost tempted in these final lines to ask why it has not been even more rapid than I have found it to be. The scale of urban unemployment must doubtless be an important part of the answer to this question. And it is indeed to this phenomenon, and to other consequences of the urban explosion in the Third World, that I shall turn in the next chapter.

29 The Consequences of the Urban Explosion in the Third World □

To what extent has the extremely rapid increase in urban population over the last fifty years corresponded to a process of accelerated economic development? For if the Third World were undergoing rapid economic growth, the urban explosion would, in the end, seem almost natural. But then are these not, as Barbara Ward (1969) calls them, "cities that came too soon," cities unjustified by their economic environment?

By the fifties this question had become heavy with economic and social implications, for it was at that point that people began to realize that the levels of urbanization in the Third World had perceptibly surpassed those of traditional societies of the past. It may be recalled that before the Industrial Revolution the level of urbanization in Europe never exceeded 13% even when Russia is excluded. By 1950, however, the level in Asia had exceeded 13%, in North Africa 26%, and in Latin America it had even reached 40%—and, needless to say, some countries had levels much higher than these regional averages. It was during this period that students of the Third World's urbanization began to speak of "hyperurbanization," "urban hypertrophy," and "overurbanization." This notion was notably at the center of discussions during a joint symposium of the United Nations and UNESCO held in Bangkok in 1956 (Hauser, 1959). It was already present in a study of Davis and Hertz (1954), who claim to have encountered the notion of overurbanization in a paper delivered by P. Parker to a meeting of the Eastern Sociological Society in 1954.

Urbanization without Economic Development

I have made a comparison of levels of development and levels of urbanization (table 29.1). As an index of levels of development, I have used the least inadequate single indicator available, namely real per capita gross national product (GNP). I have made the figures as comparable as possible, mainly by eliminating international differences in prices and purchasing power. I also corrected, of course, for price variations over time (thus GNP is expressed as a volume). It is obvious, however, that comparisons covering so long a period and concerning societies so different from each other involve a distortion of many aspects of the reality. It goes without saying that GNP is an imperfect measure of economic levels and an even more imperfect measure of living conditions. Estimates of GNP clearly do not account for the external costs of growth. Similarly, they reflect certain aspects of living conditions such as the environment (climate, the character of the urban or rural site, historical monuments, etc.) very inadequately, and often not at all. Even though I am more and more convinced that an approach based on physical indicators is probably the most appropriate way to tackle these problems, it has to be recognized that, given the current state of research, real per capita GNP remains—and will most likely remain for a long time to come—the least inadequate of the global indicators of economic development, especially for purposes of historical comparison. To enhance comparability, all the data are expressed in 1960 dollars.

For the Third World as a whole, it may be considered that, until the twenties, the situation remained relatively normal inasmuch as levels of urbanization were roughly in line with levels of development. At this date, with a per capita GNP of $200, a little less than 11% of the population of the Third World lived in cities, a level practically identical to that recorded for the developed world when it had a similar per capita GNP around 1800. From 1920 to 1930, on the other hand, although growth in per capita GNP was negligible, the level of urbanization increased by some 8%. But given the more outward-looking character of the economy of the Third World, this trend was more or less normal.

But things were already very different by around 1950. Between 1930 and 1950, while per capita GNP increased by only 10%, the level of urbanization increased by 50%, rising from 11.7 to 17.6%. By contrast, in developed countries an increase of 10% in per capita GNP was on the average accompanied by a rise of only 8% in the level of urbanization, and during phases of accelerated urban growth, by 24–28% at most. Thus for the 1920–50 period, one may already legitimately speak of urban inflation, a situation destined to worsen. If one takes the relation between levels of development and levels of urbanization in developed nations as being the norm, the Third World in 1950 already had a level of urbanization exceeding the normal by 50–60%: in other words, instead of a level of urbanization of 17.6%, it ought normally to have had one of 11.0–11.5%. Between 1920 and 1980 per capita GNP increased by only 95% while the level of urbanization grew by 160%, leading to a level of urbanization some 60–70% above normal.

The fact remains that the postulate set forth above—that evolutions

	Developed countries[a]		Third World[b]		Africa		Latin America		Asia[b] (market economies)	
	GNP[c]	Levels[d]	GNP[c]	Levels[d]	GNP[c]	Levels[d]	GNP[c]	Levels[d]	GNP[c]	Levels[d]
1800	200	10	170	9	135	4	245	14	180	10
1850	300	16	160	9	130	4	255	13	170	10
1880	425	24	165	9	130	4	290	17	160	10
1900	475	31	170	10	130	5	310	20	160	10
1910	650	34	185	10	135	6	360	22	180	10
1920	625	37	190	12	145	7	370	25	180	10
1930	835	40	200	13	150	8	380	28	180	11
1950	1,125	47	220	18	185	11	465	40	180	15
1960	1,515	54	260	22	220	15	520	48	210	18
1970	2,240	61	310	26	270	19	620	56	245	21
1980	2,920	64	375	31	285	24	775	64	300	25

Sources: Levels of urban population: Calculations and estimates by the author; GNP: Bairoch (1979b); Bairoch (1980), Bairoch (forthcoming).

Note: The data for the nineteenth century, especially for the Third World, merely indicate orders of magnitude.

[a] Except Japan.
[b] Market economies.
[c] Per capita GNP in 1960 U.S. prices and dollars.
[d] Percentage of urban population (criterion of 5,000) in relation to total population.

in developed countries and in the Third World can be compared— needs important emendation to be capable of explaining in part, but in part only, the higher level of urbanization in the Third World. I must introduce two essential factors. The first, already mentioned, is the more outward-looking character of Third World economies. It can be estimated that around 1970 (for 1980 the data are too exceptional, due to oil prices), exports from Third World market economies represented some 14% of their GNP. For developed countries, on the other hand, the level was only 6–7% for those with a comparable level of per capita GNP. A difference of this size can account for 1–3% of the additional urban population.

The second factor slightly mitigating overurbanization in the Third World is the larger proportion of agricultural workers among the urban population. Existing analyses of this matter, both for developed countries in the nineteenth century and for the Third World today, do not make it possible to quantify the relevant differences with even a modicum of precision. As a suggestion of how matters stood, however, and bearing in mind that regional differences are substantial, it can be estimated that on the average, taking all of the cities of the contemporary Third World together, some 7–9% of the working population works in farming. By contrast, toward the end of the nineteenth century the corresponding figure in developed countries was perhaps 3–5%. This would account for some 1–2% of the additional urban population in the Third World.

Correcting in this way the level of urbanization in the Third World in 1970 to make it more comparable with that in developed countries in the nineteenth century, I find that it falls from 26 to 22–23%. This still leaves a degree of overurbanization amounting to 30–50%.

The degree of overurbanization is not uniform, however, from one region to the next. Without correcting the figures to reflect structural differences, in 1970 overurbanization was on the order of 30% in Africa, 120% in Latin America and 55% in Asia. As this shows, the problem is especially serious in Latin America. Today (or rather 1980), the level of urbanization in Latin America is practically identical to that in developed nations, despite the fact that its level of development is four times lower. Overurbanization in Latin America had, moreover, already reached major proportions as early as the thirties (see table 29.1).

Before going any further I must voice a significant reservation. To say that urbanization in the Third World has taken place without economic development (or, as will be seen later, without industrialization) clearly does not mean that economic development (or industrialization) has not, in the Third World as everywhere else, been a factor in urbanization. All other things being equal, the more highly developed (or the more industrialized) a Third World country is, the more heavily urbanized it will be. But these two factors, which played a decisive role in the surge of urban growth in the West during the nineteenth century, explain only a very small part of the urbanization in the Third World over the last eight decades.

Urbanization without Industrialization

The surge of urban growth in developed countries took place largely owing to industrialization (see chapter 17). Until 1900–1910 the increase in urban population was chiefly accounted for by the jobs created in industry. During the first half of the nineteenth century an almost exact parallel links the rise in the number of industrial jobs (manufacturing and mining) with the growth in urban population in developed countries (see table 29.2). Moreover, if changes in the spatial distribution of industrial jobs are taken into account, the parallel becomes closer still and extends over practically the entire nineteenth century. It should be remembered that at the dawn of the industrial age a substantial fraction of all industrial jobs were located in rural districts, but that the further modernization progressed, the smaller this fraction became. It can be estimated that in 1800, in the developed world, the number of industrial jobs in the cities represented

TABLE 29.2   Percentages of Industrial Employment
and Levels of Urbanization
(1800–1980)

	Developed Countries[a]		Third World[b]	
	Employment[c]	Urbanization	Employment[c]	Urbanization
1800	10	10	10	9
1850	15	16	9	9
1880	17	24	8	9
1900	19	31	9	10
1910	20	34	9	10
1920	21	37	9	12
1930	21	40	9	13
1950	24	47	8	18
1960	27	54	9	22
1970	29	61	11	26
1980	29	64	13	31

Sources: Industrial employment: Bairoch (1971) and supplementary estimates by the author; levels of urbanization: Calculations and estimates by the author; see the methodological appendix.
[a] Except Japan.
[b] Market economies.
[c] Manufacturing industries and mines.

only 6–7% of total employment; and since urban population represented 10% of overall population, the gap between the level of urbanization and the proportion of the total number of industrial jobs located in the cities was 45–65%. Around 1880, 14–16% of all industrial jobs were in the cities and the level of urbanization stood at 24%. Thus the gap between the two remained practically unchanged: 50–70%. Owing to the growing number of jobs in the tertiary sector, however, the gap progressively widened thereafter. By 1920 it had reached 90%, and stabilized at around 100% until 1950. Since then the phenomenon has pursued its course, the gap reaching 110% around 1960 and 140% around 1980.

In the Third World, on the other hand, events have followed an entirely different course. The first half century of urban growth (from 1900–1910 to 1950–60) unfolded without change in the relative dimensions of industrial employment and even without change in the relative dimensions of urban industrial employment, for by the start of the twentieth century almost all industry was located in the cities. While at a comparable stage of urbanization in developed nations (i.e., from 1860 to 1870), the gap between the percentage of industrial jobs in the cities and the level of urbanization had been only 50%, in the Third World in 1950 it was 130%. And despite the accelerated industrialization occurring in the Third World beginning in 1948–1955, the gap remained at just about the same level. This was thus unquestionably a form of urbanization very different from that of the West: not merely urbanization without economic development, but urbanization without industrialization as well.

Urbanization without industrial growth implies one of two possibilities: either a high level of unemployment or the existence of other types of jobs. In the Third World both of these things were united. It will be seen later how great unemployment is in Third World cities. It will also be seen that some of the slack has been taken up by the tertiary sector, but that the tertiary sector is out of step with existing economic possibilities. If one further takes into account the more massive presence of agricultural workers in Third World cities, it will become clear how very small is the position occupied by industry. On the average only some 26–28% of the jobs available in Third World cities are in industry, a percentage as small as that in European cities in the early nineteenth century.

But urbanization in the Third World differs from that in Europe in yet another respect. For not only has it been achieved without economic development and without industrialization; it has also been unaccompanied by progress in agricultural productivity.

A Paradox: Urban Expansion without an Increase in Agricultural Productivity

Already standing at a fairly low level in 1910–1920, productivity in subsistence agriculture in the Third World suffered a slight decline thereafter, especially during the period from 1920–25 to 1946–50 (Bairoch, 1975). Despite the very modest advances realized since the early fifties, agricultural productivity probably remains lower today than 1910–1920. Even putting the best face on things, then, no progress has been made. But even more serious than the lack of progress is the very low level of productivity, which currently stands at a point roughly equal to that of Europe in the late eighteenth century before the agricultural revolution.

Given a situation of this sort, coupled with the lack of progress, the problem immediately arises of how substantial urban growth could have been possible. In the light of the observations made earlier concerning the close link between agricultural productivity and urbanization, the urban explosion of the Third World assumes the aura of a paradox. But this seeming paradox finds a counterpart in the urban growth in the Netherlands in the seventeenth century. Just as urban growth in the Netherlands during the seventeenth century depended on increasing food imports, so too the urban expansion of the Third World has been made possible, despite the low agricultural productivity, by similar imports, particularly of grain. Before the Second World War, the Third World was still a net exporter of grain. But since the fifties, there has been a deficit that has grown ever larger. Thus taking the Third World market economies together (excluding Argentina, which in this respect is not part of the Third World), the trade balance for grain has developed as follows:

1934-38: annual surplus of 4 million metric tons
1948-52: annual deficit of 6 million metric tons
1958-62: annual deficit of 15 million metric tons
1968-72: annual deficit of 24 million metric tons
1973-77: annual deficit of 40 million metric tons
1978-82: annual deficit of 66 million metric tons
1983-87: annual deficit of 77 million metric tons

To these massive grain imports should be added appreciable quantities of meat and dairy products. If one carries out a rough calculation based on an annual rate of consumption of 210 kilograms of grain per capita (the average for the Third World at large during the last decades, which represents some 60–65% of total food consumption), it can be seen that by around 1950, net grain imports already represented enough to support some thirty million people, or nearly 16% of the total urban population. For 1960 and 1970 this proportion was on the order of 37%. And in 1985 these imports could support some 370 million people, or roughly 45% of the urban population of the Third World market economies.

Until recent years the trade surplus of tropical food products (and sugar in particular) reduced somewhat the overall food deficit. But today (around 1985), the surplus eight million metric tons of sugar is offset by a deficit of over one million metric tons of meat, to which is further added a deficit of more than three million metric tons of dairy products. The surplus in the exchange of oil-yielding products in existence since the start of the nineteenth century has also recently turned into a deficit of some three to four million metric tons, owing to heavy imports of soybeans and rapeseed. In short, today overall trade of food other than cereals yields for Third World market economies a deficit of one to two million metric tons, which has to be added to the enormous deficit in cereals.

Another element further accentuating the dramatic character of these food deficits is the fact that the reconversion of land used for the cultivation of export products will not solve the problem. Indeed, if all of the land used for nonstaple export crops had around 1985 been reconverted for growing cereals, this land would have produced only about one-third of the cereal deficit.

Thus yet another vicious circle has been added to the list of problems associated with underdevelopment. The strong demographic pressure on the available agricultural land encourages the exodus of the rural population to the cities and explains the low level of agricultural productivity; but the growing concentration of population in the cities encourages further food imports, thereby reducing the incentive to increase agricultural productivity. Resorting to imports of food is encouraged even more by the facts that most of the urban population happens to be concentrated near the coasts and that imported cereals usually cost less than those that are locally produced.

An Inescapable Consequence: A Dramatic Shortfall in Urban Employment

In the early fifties, when the problem of underdevelopment began to occupy the attention of some economists and political leaders, employment problems chiefly centered on rural underemployment. Things started to change in the mid-sixties, however, and the exceptional character of urban growth and the severity of the problem of urban unemployment were gradually discovered at the same time. Before examining the scale of urban unemployment, I must stress the arbitrariness of applying this concept to societies very different from those for which it was originally formulated.

For one thing, in a large number of Third World societies extended family ties and the scale of certain marginal activities perceptibly improve the socioeconomic situation of the unemployed worker. One must also take into account the income derived from extralegal sources in some urban centers by a substantial fraction of the population. On the other hand, the lack or low level of unemployment benefits has a negative impact on the economic situation of unemployed workers.

Furthermore, and this is a very important reservation, in many, if not all, of the traditional societies of the Third World, the lack of a job is not necessarily looked on as an unfortunate circumstance. Thus in the Maghreb, "the notions of unemployment or underemployment are totally absent from the consciousness of individuals and unknown in the collective awareness" (Stambouli, 1971). As Berque (1959) notes, "it is the eruption of Western values that has created a situation in which the leisurely life of the former peasant has become the unemployment of the Third World farmer." One should not, however, idealize living conditions in traditional societies, periodically marked as they are by food shortages taking a heavy toll of human life, and in which only a minority are able to live in abundance. But it is nevertheless true that in many instances colonization brought about a fall in the standard of living of a large segment of the population, owing particularly to the many evictions from the land or the forced introduction of export crops.

Moreover, even in the West the notion of unemployment as understood today is of relatively recent date. In French, for example, the word for unemployment, *chômage*, comes from the verb *chômer*, which derives from the Low Latin *caumare* (from the Greek *kauma*, "burning heat") and meant, to begin with, "to rest during the heat of the day," becoming later a synonym for holiday. The term *chômeur* (unemployed worker) did not come to be used with its current meaning until 1876. The English term "unemployment" came into use even more recently, its first appearance dating from 1888.

Once these reservations have been registered, it must still be emphasized that in the urban centers of the Third World the notions of unemployment, full employment, and underemployment have real meaning and content, which increase every day. And in any case, even though unemployment and underemployment may not be perceived in the same way as in the West, they do nevertheless, for the Third World as a whole, have roughly the same consequences.

From a study of Turnham (1970), supplemented by my own research (Bairoch, 1973a), one can get a fairly clear idea of the scale of urban unemployment around the middle of the sixties in the Third World market economies. The data on unemployment nevertheless remain relative, owing to variation in the quality of the research on which it is based or of the census records from which the data were derived. One should also allow for variations due to differences (none fundamental) in definitions of unemployed worker. In the main these definitions are close to that adopted at the Eighth International Conference of Labor Statisticians held in Geneva in 1954, which can be summed up in this way: any person of working age who is able to work, is *without a job* and *actively seeks* remunerated work. The last part of this definition (actively seeks work) has often been criticized, for there are a certain number of people without jobs who, though available for work, do not actively seek employment. The failure to look for a job does not necessarily imply unwillingness to work, but often simply reflects the realization that it is useless to seek work. It seems likely that, if "available" workers were included among the urban unemployed, unemployment levels would rise sharply. According to Turnham, in such a hypothetical case the increase might even reach 100%.

Unemployment in the strict sense, then, has already reached major proportions. If, despite the wide dispersion, one attempts to establish an average that eliminates the effects of certain biases, it can be concluded that urban unemployment amounts to 12 %, a percentage one and one-half to two times higher than that in rural areas. Urban unemployment affects the young most of all, for whom it is on the order of 30% (as against 10% for the rest of the population). And among the young, those with an average level of education, that is, having six to eleven years of schooling, are especially vulnerable. The unemployment rate among university graduates and illiterates, on the other hand, is lower. In the case of illiterates this is explained by a lower level of expectations regarding the type of work that will be acceptable. In the case of university graduates it is accounted for by the as-yet small number of people with so much education and by political considerations: unemployment in the intellectual class entails grave political risks. It is significant, moreover, that unemployment is generally lower in capital cities than in other cities of similar size.

During the seventies the level of unemployment apparently did not increase greatly. But the first half of the eighties, which saw a slowing down of industrial growth, saw a strong rise in unemployment, especially in the cities of Latin America and Africa. Apparently levels of underemployment also increased, but data for this are more ambiguous.

Romes without Empires

To unemployment proper should be added partial unemployment and underemployment. All together it can be estimated that total inactivity is on the order of 30–40% of potential working man-hours. This situation has no historical precedent, except perhaps in the case of ancient Rome. If one compares the current situation in the Third World with that in developed countries over the course of the nineteenth century, two fundamental differences emerge. On the one hand, the average unemployment rate in the cities of developed countries during the nineteenth century was much lower, on the order of 4–6%. But above all there is the fact that whereas in developed nations urban unemployment was cyclical, that is, essentially concentrated in years marked by economic depression, in the Third World it is structural. In the Third World urban unemployment, for which I have coined the term "overunemployment," is the natural outcome of the rural exodus caused by excess rural population. While in the nineteenth century the young European who migrated to the city was drawn chiefly by the available jobs, in the Third World today young people migrate to the city either because they cannot live on the land or because they do not want to.

I just said that the sole historical precedent for the employment problem in the cities of the Third World is perhaps ancient Rome, the "perhaps" reflecting the uncertainty surrounding the level of underemployment in Rome (see chapter 5). But in addition to the high level of unemployment itself, there is a second similarity: the fact that the food needed to support the inhabitants of the cities of the Third World comes from abroad. Further, as in ancient Rome, though in a less generalized fashion, food is distributed gratis. And yet obviously there are enormous differences. First of all, there is the sheer scale of the contemporary phenomenon. In the ancient world Rome was practically the only city to be in such a position, while today there are already some eighty cities involved with populations of more than a million. Furthermore, while the population of Rome was around one million, the population of the cities of the Third World taken together amounts to more than seven hundred million in the market economies alone. And there is above all the fundamental difference that, although the cities of the Third World may resemble Rome, they do not have her empire and are thus obliged to import food from countries technologically and militarily more advanced than they are. The only cities to have established empires of a sort, albeit informal ones, are the cities of the oil-producing nations, for whom the quasi monopoly over sources of energy plays a part akin to that played for Rome by her quasi monopoly over military might in the ancient world. It is interesting to note in this context that, thanks to the steep rise in real oil prices since 1973, the large oil-exporting countries have become major importers of grain and other food. Between 1953 and 1973, a metric ton of crude oil bought on the average 0.2 metric ton of grain. For 1974–1978, however, the figure rose to 0.6 metric ton, reaching 1.4 metric tons in 1980–1982. But even in this case, like almost any others where supply and demand interact, the favorable situation cannot be taken for granted. The recent sharp decline in oil prices means that in 1986 a metric ton of oil bought 0.5 metric ton of grain.

Urban Unemployment in China

Before moving on to other consequences of the urban explosion in Third World market economies, it is worth pausing for the case of China. The new authorities recognize the reality of urban unemployment (and also of rural unemployment) even if the terms "unemployed" or "unemployment" are not used (see chapter 27). And according to those authorities, the unemployment has existed since the Cultural Revolution of 1966, which was the source of all, or at least most of the evils of contemporary China. To a certain extent the economic policies of the new regime have made unemployment more visible and more real. Before it was rather disguised unemployment or underemployment. At the beginning of the seventies, some Japanese visitors "found factories staffed by several times the number of workers they thought were actually needed to perform the existing jobs. They observed that each employee was responsible for a mere fraction of what a worker might normally be expected to accomplish" (Nihei, 1982).

The real size of urban unemployment in China in recent years is very difficult to determine. Even official figures vary considerably. On the basis of data assembled by Nihei (1982) and Emerson (1983), the published figures for the end of the seventies vary between 10 and 25 million, or between 8.5 and 22.5 % of the urban labor force. And it is even probable that the reality for 1977–1980 exceeded 25 million. Since then the massive effort made to create urban jobs has reduced the level of unemployment (and may also have increased the level of underemployment). But it seems impossible to evaluate the real level of urban unemployment.

As is the case in the less developed market economies most of the unemployed are young people, and among those most left school after their secondary education.

Hypertrophy in the Tertiary Sector

The urban explosion has not only led to substantial under-employment; it has also brought about excessive growth in the service sector (or tertiary sector), that is, in areas other than agriculture and industry. This excessive growth has been especially pronounced in the commercial sector and in administration. By 1970, roughly 21% of all employment in Third World market economies was in services. So high a level was not reached in developed nations until around 1913, that is, until a time when per capita income in the West was more than twice as great (120%), as in the Third World in 1970. Another significant point of comparison is that in developed nations, by the time 21% of the working population were employed in services, there were already some 24% employed in industrial manufacturing, leaving only 55% in agriculture. In the Third World, on the other hand, 10% were in industrial manufacturing and 70% in agriculture. As was to be expected, this hypertrophy in services has proved especially prevalent in Latin America, where by 1960, 30% of all workers were employed in the tertiary sector, a proportion that must be on the order of 43% today (as against 20% in the rest of the Third World).

It can be estimated that by around 1960–1970 the low standard of living in underdeveloped countries notwithstanding, there was a greater proportion of jobs in the tertiary sector in the cities of the Third World than in those of developed countries: 60–65% as against 55–60%. If levels of development (with all the crude simplifications that implies) are taken into account, when developed countries were at the level reached by developing countries today, only 32–37% of all urban jobs were in the tertiary sector. The hypertrophy is especially pronounced in services proper, but there is considerable overemployment in trade and transportation as well.

Though economic factors, and unemployment in particular, go a long way toward explaining overemployment in the tertiary sector, the political aspect of the problem should not be overlooked, accounting as it does for the overemployment in the civil service. Traditionally, owing to the concentration of political and economic power in the cities and the urban character of the major revolutions, great significance has been attached to urban discontent, itself practically synonymous with discontent in the working class. It could almost be argued that between rural and urban discontent lies the difference between a peasants' revolt and a revolution. The Chinese and Cuban revolutions have notably disturbed this classic schema, however, and have extended a greater political dimension to the rural world. But recently the urban terrorism raging in certain countries, the numerous student uprisings, and the sheer scale of urban unemployment have once more turned the focus of political interest and attention onto the cities.

Furthermore, as Gugler (1982) writes: "Revolutionary movements have seized power in four countries since the establishment of the People's Republic of China on October 1, 1949. A brief look at the cases of Bolivia, Iran, and Nicaragua will show that these were essentially urban struggles. The case of Cuba is more ambiguous." And in this context, jobs in the public sector serve as a safety valve in the Third World. There are many cases in which the hiring of university graduates in the civil service depends not on any real public need, but rather on supply. An unemployed university graduate is a potential political revolutionary; and it scarcely matters what the political complexion of the regime may be—any sudden change in government is called revolutionary by those who bring it about.

What impact have overemployment in services and urban unemployment had on economic development in the Third World? This is one of the aspects of the vast problem of underdevelopment, which I shall address in chapter 30, which is devoted principally to the question of the links between urbanization and development. But before moving on to this question, and without pretending to exhaust the entire list of contributing factors, I will discuss one more component of the employment problem, the informal sector, and one more consequence of the urban explosion, the shantytowns.

The Informal Sector: The Shadowy Frontiers of a Vast Domain

The first stumbling block met with in studying the informal sector of the economy is its definition. What makes a definition so difficult is that one of the characteristics of the informal sector is precisely the vagueness of its boundaries. The informal sector ranges from the urchin with laughing eyes who shines your shoes, to the white-bearded old man who sells lottery tickets; from the dynamic entrepreneur who with a handful of workers and rudimentary equipment manufactures sandals with soles cut from old tires, to the artisan who with movements in use since time immemorial carves statuettes for tourists. It also embraces the segment of the population living on the margins of legality, from the man you have to bribe to gain access to public services, and whose favors have value only because of your ignorance of the modern "rites" of public service, to the genuine underworld present in any city.

The notion of an informal sector is recent, emerging for the first time in the early seventies. Its emergence marked the break with the notion of the dual economy as it was conceived in the late fifties. In the dual economy the frontier, or dividing line, essentially ran between the rural and the urban: on one side lay the country, with its traditional and therefore largely unproductive agriculture; on the other side lay the cities, with their industries based on technologies borrowed from the West, enabling them to reach levels of productivity close to those achieved in Western economies. With the intensification of research on what is also sometimes called the unstructured sector, carried out chiefly by the ILO (International Labor Office), this dividing line has been found to cross the city, which has a vast range of activities, some of them even industrial, closely resembling what may be very roughly described as traditional industries. And with the introduction of this new notion has emerged a new problem, at least in terms of its scale. Although the presence of informal economic activities may be traced back to the beginning of industrialization in the Third World, and even in European cities, the phenomenon did not assume major proportions until the urban explosion and the unemployment that followed in its wake.

One of the first definitions of the informal sector was proposed in the report submitted to the government of Kenya by the ILO, published in 1972:

> informal activities are not confined to employment
> on the periphery of the main towns, to particular oc-
> cupations, or even to economic activities. Rather,
> informal activities are the way of doing things, char-
> acterized by: (a) ease of entry; (b) reliance on indige-
> nous resources; (c) family ownership of enterprises;
> (d) small scale of operation; (e) labor-intensive and
> adapted technology; (f) skills acquired outside the
> formal school system; and (g) unregulated and com-
> petitive markets.

But even before 1972, that is, even before the term "informal sector" had begun to obtain wide acceptance (and before the informal sector had, thanks to the work done by the ILO, been properly identified), the break with the traditional notion of the dual economy had already been consummated. By 1963, in his book *Peddlers and Princes*, Geertz was already talking about the "firm-based economy" and the "bazaar economy." Among the many researchers who have helped move the study of this question forward, I shall cite in particular McGee (1973) for Asia, Weeks (1973) for Africa, and Santos (1972) for Latin America. In "L'espace partagé" (1975), Santos again takes up in depth his notion of the two circuits in the urban economy:

> One of the two circuits is the direct result of tech-
> nological modernization; it embraces the activities
> created as a function of technological progress and
> the people who benefit thereby. The other is also the
> result of technological modernization, but an indi-

rect result relating to individuals who benefit only partially or not at all from recent technological progress and the activities associated with it.

In a way, the dynamism, and even the "imperialism," of researchers in this area has progressively enlarged the field of the informal sector, perhaps beyond the point required. Thus in a recent synthesis of research on the informal sector, Sethuraman (1981), one of the people who has applied himself most pertinaciously to the problem of defining this sector, has ultimately reached the conclusion that "it consists of small-scale units engaged in the production and distribution of goods and services with the primary objective of generating employment and income to their participants, notwithstanding the constraints on capital, both physical and human, and know-how."

The research findings collected by Sethuraman present the image of an informal sector including most economic activities. In few of the cities studied does this sector account for less than 30% of overall economic activity. In the dominant situation, the informal sector accounts for about 40–50% of overall economic activity in all cities of some size (say with populations of over 100,000). In some countries, even when all cities of whatever size are taken together, the informal sector would seem to account for as much as 60% of all economic activity, if not more. Such is notably the case in Pakistan and in Peru. As always, there are differences stemming from the particular characteristics of the cities concerned and their respective histories. As a rule the informal sector gains in importance in larger cities and in cities experiencing particularly rapid growth in population.

Is the informal sector an economic asset or merely disguised unemployment? This question is of fundamental importance and obviously claims the attention of those responsible for formulating development policies for the Third World, local leaders and international experts alike. I shall return to this fundamentally important, yet also highly delicate, question in the next chapter. But before closing the present discussion, I shall take a brief look at one last consequence of the urban explosion, related to the informal sector in many respects, namely the shantytowns. As McGee (1979) observes: "the illegal character of the settlements means that all types of activities can be carried out here that would be subject to legal restrictions in the formal sector."

Shantytowns: A Major Form of Habitat

Shantytowns, or "spontaneous settlements," as specialists rather primly put it, are neither a new phenomenon nor one unique to urban life in the Third World, for they also exist in developed countries. But while they may also exist in developed countries, they affect only a very small fraction of Western cities, and in those cities in which they have appeared, they represent only a very marginal habitat. They have, moreover, increasingly dwindled in importance in the West, and were chiefly a feature of the immediate postwar years. In recent years, as Lacoste (1968) remarks, they have shrunk to the point of being nothing more than "very limited pockets in relation to the urban mass as a whole: they are marginal phenomena. They are chiefly inhabited by foreign workers, temporary immigrants only rarely entitled to benefit from certain social programs."

In the Third World, by contrast, the phenomenon is characterized both by its unprecedented scale and by its generality. Practically no large city in the Third World has managed to avoid this lamentable "solution" to the apparently insoluble problem of rapidly providing housing for the great mass of newcomers to the city, newcomers whose economic resources are practically nonexistent. As Dwyer (1975) remarks, "shantytowns are a major form of habitat." He cites a few verse lines from Carolina Maria de Jesus in an epigraph to his book: "Oh Sao Paulo! . . . All dressed up in velvet and silk but with cheap stockings underneath—the favela." Favela, shantytown, spontaneous settlement—there is no lack of terms for describing this type of habitat. The names for it are especially numerous in Latin America, where the imaginativeness of the writers—coupled with the fact that the phenomenon emerged sooner there than elsewhere and, because of the intensity of the urban (and demographic) explosion, is more important there—has spawned an exuberant abundance of terms. Without pretending to provide a complete list, I shall cite some of the more colorful coinages, beginning, as etiquette would seem to dictate, with Latin America: *azotea, barriada, barrio* and *barrio pirata, callampa, colonia proletaria, carralone, rancho, vacindare* and *villa de emergencia*. In Iran: *halabi abad* (canned-foods town), *alatchir* (peasant huts), and *gode* (hole, quarry). In Turkey: *gecekodular* (erected in a single night). In Iraq: *serifas* (hut). In Indonesia: *kampong* (little village). In India: *bustee* (just a place to live). In countries in which the predominant language is English: squatter settlements, shantytown (from the French *chantier* for "worksite"), and slum. This last is more ambiguous, inasmuch as most slums are not shantytowns. In French-speaking countries, the term "bidonville" (*bidon* meaning a can or drum) is almost universal, and was first used in Morocco between the two world wars. Bidonville has, moreover, entered other languages, in particular German, Italian, and Russian.

Technically, according to the recommendations issued by the Statistics Commission of the United Nations, among the different non-classic types of housing are units of improvised habitation, that is, "an independent makeshift shelter or structure built of waste materials and without a predetermined plan, for the purpose of habitation by one household and that is being utilized as living quarters at the time of the census. This type of housing unit is usually found in urban and suburban areas, particularly at the peripheries of the principal cities." But even the United Nations returns to the term "squatter settlements," whereas earlier, as the United Nations inquiry on housing (1976) notes, "the terms 'uncontrolled,' 'transitional,' and 'marginal' have been used in an attempt to eliminate the pejorative implications of 'slums' and 'squatter settlements.'"

Even though one can cite many examples proving that shantytowns began very early in a great many Third World cities, all historical analyses agree that they only became important in the sixties. In other words, the problem reached major proportions at a time when the urban explosion had already triggered enormous population growth in the cities, at a time when the flood of immigrants had become so massive that it overwhelmed traditional forms of urban housing. It is useless to describe the terrible living conditions usually associated with these shantytowns. And terrible they are, even if in affective sociocultural terms they confront the peasant newly arrived in the city with a milieu less traumatizing than the project housing of modern cities. It is true that one can find a parallel for these living conditions in those endured by European workers in the early nineteenth century (see chapter 17). But there are compelling differences, the most important being the scale of the phenomenon.

What exactly is the importance of these shantytowns? The data are fragmentary, but they are sufficient to confirm their overall significance. The "World Housing Survey" conducted by the United Nations (1976) has assembled data bearing on sixty-seven large cities in the early seventies. The average proportion of the population living in shantytowns is 44%; but in many cities the proportion exceeds 70%. Such is the case for Addis Ababa (90 %), Ibadan (75%), Douala (87%), Yaoundé (90%), Mogadishu (77%), Lomé (75%), Buenaventura (unfortunately named) (80 %), and Santo Domingo (72%).

Naturally the criteria of evaluation are not strictly comparable; and the few data available for the urban population as a whole indicate that the average proportion of shantytowns and slums must be lower than that for the larger cities alone. As a probable order of magnitude, it can be calculated that about 35–40% of the inhabitants of Third World cities lived in shantytowns around 1970. According to the fragmentary evidence available, the proportion was appreciably lower around 1960 and has continued to grow since 1970, though more slowly than before. It can be estimated that around 1980 some 40–45% of all city dwellers in the Third World were living in shantytowns (of which some have undergone considerable improvement). To be precise, however, it should be noted that this pertains only to Third World market economies. For there are no shantytowns in China, or at least there were none in Maoist China. In all Third World market economies, then, some 280–320 million people, including some 115–

135 million children under fifteen years of age, live in shantytowns. In short, to paraphrase the title of the book of Granotier (1980), a real "planet of shantytowns."

As in the case of the informal sector of the economy, however, the question arises whether the prospect is entirely bleak—whence the title of Lloyd's book, *Slums of Hope* (1979). This question fits perfectly into the framework of chapter 30, devoted to the relation between urbanization and economic development. Chapter 30 will serve as a conclusion to part 4, in which I have reviewed the history of what today is called the Third World, and sought to identify the distressing problems of its various urban domains.

30 Urbanization and Economic Development in the Third World □

To what extent does the hyperurbanization of the Third World constitute an asset from the point of view of its future economic development? And what was the city's influence on economic development before the onset of the urban explosion? These are two crucial aspects of the problem of the link between the city and the economy in the Third World. Three very different phases have to be distinguished in the history of this problem. The first concerns urbanization in what may be called the traditional framework of the various parts of the future Third World. This was before the nineteenth century. The second phase is that of colonization until the onset of the urban explosion. The period of the urban explosion itself (between 1920–30 and 1985) obviously forms the third and final phase.

Urbanization and Development in the Traditional Societies of the Future Third World: Some Uncertainties

I just noted that the first phase was mainly before the beginning of the nineteenth century. The approximate date for the end of this phase is thoroughly justified. This phase ended around 1810 to 1830 in most of Asia, and since Asia accounted in the early nineteenth century for roughly 75 to 80 percent of the total population of the future Third World, in most of the Third World as a whole as well. But it ended much sooner than this in Latin America (around 1520) and continued until the 1950s in those few countries, such as Afghanistan, that had remained apart from colonization or from the indirect effects of economic development.

It is extremely difficult to reach any even remotely definite conclusions concerning the relations between urbanization and development during this phase. The gaps in urban history, coupled with those in the history of development, are too great to allow one to pass judgement on empirical grounds. The only thing that can be said with any confidence is that in these societies economic development unquestionably conditioned both the level and the direction of urban growth.

Although few studies have yet been devoted to this question, the influence of economic development was both diverse and unmistakable, thereby confirming the close relations between the economy and the city evident throughout this book. I shall cite a few examples from the first chapters of part 4. Close links between the economy and the city are found at practically every stage of the long history of China. Progress in agriculture stimulated urban growth, and declines in agriculture prompted declines, if not in the cities themselves, at least in the level of urbanization. The expansion of trade from the tenth century to the fifteenth century engendered and promoted the prosperity of large coastal towns in China. Furthermore, the geographic spread of Islam, introducing in many regions alongside the Islamic faith a whole body of more advanced economic and technological knowledge, brought about in Spain, the Maghreb, and Black Africa urban growth sometimes of great magnitude. And in this case too, economic decline led to urban decline. Finally, the presumptions that can be made concerning the pre-Columbian New World point in the direction of an evolution similar to that observed in other parts of the world.

As for the problem specifically addressed in this chapter, namely, the impact of urbanization on development, given the current state of research the only thing I can do is reason by analogy with what took place in the traditional societies of Europe. And on the whole, the differences that emerge tend to indicate that the city played a less positive role in the Third World than in Europe. Certainly, the differences do not suggest that urbanization was a greater driving force in the Third World than in Europe. The reasons for this more limited contribution stem in particular from two characteristics of urbanism in the future Third World. One is the smaller margin of independence of cities and the other their lower degree of economic specialization. Both of these characteristics reduced the chances for innovation and, above all, the possibilities for the diffusion of innovations.

But generalization would be a mistake here as elsewhere. The various societies of the future Third World cannot be regarded as a single entity simply on the grounds that they all came by historical chance to be Third World societies. Even given the general lack of information, there is room to believe, albeit with many reservations, that the cities of the various Muslim cultures, especially before the fourteenth century, must have contributed more to economic growth than the cities of the great empires of Asia or those of the pre-Columbian New World. And here a further restriction is necessary, even crucial: although they remained throughout at a traditional stage of development, none of these societies were unchanged. It is true that things changed slowly in the traditional world; the economy could not progress beyond a certain threshold, a threshold the Industrial Revolution was to raise dramatically in the space of only two centuries (raising the maximum standard of living twenty times over). But even in the traditional world, historical events were capable of revolutionizing the economic and sociopolitical structures of society, sometimes gradually, sometimes violently. The China of the eleventh century is not the same as that of the sixteenth century, nor was fourteenth-century Japan the same as its seventeenth-century counterpart. Eleventh-century Constantinople did not resemble the city of the early fifteenth century and was even less like the Istanbul of the late fifteenth century. The Mayan empire collapsed practically overnight at about the same time as Constantinople fell into Turkish hands. And it seems likely that life in the pre-Columbian New World in the ninth century differed from what it was to become in the fifteenth. It would be too problematic, however, to try to go beyond such general reconstructions as these; I would prefer to avoid mere presumptions here, no matter how tempting they may be.

Colonial Cities and Development: A Reinforcement of the Negative Effects of Colonization

The second phase of the urban history of the Third World is relatively easier to deal with. The essential question arising here bears on the influence on economic development exerted by cities created (or considerably enlarged) as a result of colonization and by traditional cities. It is of course necessary to try to distinguish in this phase between the impact of colonization and the impact of urbanization, something it is not always easy or even possible to do.

On the whole, the impact of colonization was unquestionably very negative. Without going into superfluous detail, I may point out that colonization played a detrimental role through two types of interference in the life of the various societies of the Third World. The first consisted of more or less forced intensification of commercial exchange, while the second consisted of imposing regulations subordinating the economic affairs of the colonies to the interests of the colonizing country, a course of action which proved damaging even in those many cases where the intentions were of the best.

Owing to the massive influx of manufactured goods from Europe—an important consequence of the intensification of trade—a process of deindustrialization took place (see chapter 25). The other component of trade, the increasing exportation of nonstaple agricultural products, brought about excessive specialization (often imposed from outside), in the production of those commodities and thus deteriorating productivity for food crops. The most extreme (but by no means marginal) case was the cultivation of opium in India for export to other parts of the Third World, chiefly China. Between the 1820s and the 1880s, opium represented 13–16% of total Asian exports, or 6 to 8 percent of all exports from the Third World as a whole (Bairoch and Etémad, 1985).

The most detrimental of the economic regulations generally imposed on the colonies was the partial or total prohibition of industrial production. The measures taken with this end in view were mainly direct between the sixteenth and nineteenth centuries and mainly indirect, in the form of very low customs duties, during the nineteenth and twentieth centuries. The consequences of these two types of interference were probably a decline in the standard of living and, above all, the setting up of socioeconomic structures conducive to economic underdevelopment. The fundamental problem that needs to be raised here, then, is whether the creation of colonial cities accentuated or mitigated these harmful effects.

The answer generally seems to point to an accentuation of the harmful effects of colonization, the harmful effects outweighing any conceivable beneficial contribution of colonial cities. Indeed, even setting aside the fact that colonial cities were founded chiefly as a means of penetrating colonized regions, it must be remembered that by their very nature they encouraged the consumption of goods produced with technologies more advanced than those of the Third World, which therefore had to be imported from the West. In many cases, advantageous return shipping rates even tended to encourage the importation of agricultural products. Thus here, too, the impact of the cities was negative. Nor was this impact more than partially offset by the greater educational opportunities the cities offered the indigenous population. Leaving primary and secondary schools aside, the first three "European" universities in India (in Calcutta, Bombay, and Madras) dated from 1857. During the first decades of their existence, however, these universities essentially functioned as instruments of control over knowledge rather than as centers of learning. Except for Latin America, the establishment of schools and universities was generally rare before the twentieth century.

Furthermore, leaving aside the case of Latin America, to which I shall return later, colonial cities represented only a marginal fraction of the overall urban mass. The impact of traditional cities therefore has also to be considered. And these, too, probably reinforced the detrimental effects of colonization, inasmuch as the concentration of population within them further promoted the influx of manufactured goods from Europe. Existing studies show that in just about every case in which traditional industry is found to have managed to resist the flood of European imports, it was in rural regions distant from the cities or in small towns in peripheral regions.

One final point, more in the nature of a hypothesis than of a certainty (see chapter 26). It appears that as a result of colonization the city came increasingly to draw on the countryside for resources. Thus the city became more parasitic than before, owing to the loss of power suffered by traditional rural elites. These elites were replaced by new elites composed of Europeans and natives with a marked preference for city life.

It can be concluded, then, that not only colonial cities, but also urbanization as a whole, played a negative part in this phase of the evolution of the Third World. The cities tended more to amplify the deleterious impact of colonization than to help improve matters.

The Case of Latin America

It is now necessary to establish an important distinction regarding the case of Latin America. For one thing, the large European population of Latin American cities made the situation different. Moreover, almost all of Latin America had achieved political independence as early as the first decades of the nineteenth century. It should be borne in mind, however, that I am discussing here the phase preceding the urban explosion, that is, in Latin America the period before 1920; the consequences of this urban explosion will be considered later.

During the period before independence, and despite the regulations imposed by the various colonizing powers, the great numbers of Europeans living in Latin America had already fostered a degree of industrial development in most cities. What is more, Latin American cities could and did fulfill the function of centers of innovation and of the diffusion of innovation, since they had important intellectual institutions. There is a tendency to forget that before the nineteenth century there were certainly twenty-one, and perhaps as many as twenty-three, universities in Latin America, most of them founded in the sixteenth and seventeenth centuries; the four oldest were in Santo Domingo (1538), Lima (1551), Mexico City (1553), and Bogota (1580). This last city was known as the Athens of Latin America. For in addition to its universities, it housed three schools of advanced studies, an academy, an observatory, a botanical garden, a large public library, and other institutions. Among the other cities having a university before the nineteenth century were Cuzco (1598), Arequipa (1616), Queretar (1618), Cordoba (1621), Quito (1622), Sucre (1624), Ayacucho (1677), Caracas (1725), Havana (1728), Santiago (1747), Campeche (1756), Guatemala City (1792), Guadalajara (1792), and also Mendelin, Guayaquil, and Cuenca. Nor should one forget the important part played by the Jesuits in Latin American history, their presence and activity having a great deal to do with this situation.

If we assume that the population of Latin America around 1800 amounted to twenty million, then there was one university for every 900,000 people. This figure can be brought even lower, and that appreciably, if we limit ourselves to the population of European extraction alone (roughly four million people), that segment of the overall population for which these institutions were chiefly intended. In this case there was one university for every 200,000 people. In Europe, by contrast, there were at this time ninety-five universities, or one university for every 2.2 million people. (Around 1500 there had been one university for every 1.4 million.) It is true that this comparison is rather misleading in that it overlooks such factors as the size of the universities, the number of departments or faculties they contained, and the quality of the instruction they imparted, as well as the question of geographic dispersal. Europe (including European Russia) covered 10.5 million square kilometers and Latin America 20.6. It nevertheless bears witness to the wealth of intellectual life in Latin American cities. To be sure, the average standard of living in these cities was in all likelihood higher than in the European cities of the time. But this applies only to the average situation, it being just as likely that income distribution was far more unequal in Latin America than in Europe.

Paradoxically, over the next six to seven decades independence led to a reinforcement of the negative effects of colonization—and in this case the term "neocolonialism" is highly appropriate. The negative effects resulted from the greater possibility for commercial intervention by Great Britain, cut off from Latin American markets until that time. During this phase the cities probably enhanced the possibilities of commercial penetration. They were, however, also the decision centers for policy changes that from the 1880s engendered substantial industrialization. During these years an original school of economic thought emerged that was aware of the problems of unequal development. Moreover, to the twenty-odd universities in existence in 1800 were added between 1800 and 1914 nearly forty more, the only large country lagging behind in this domain being Brazil.

Thus until the era of the urban explosion, the cities of Latin America may largely be considered to have made something of a positive contribution. But Latin America is the exception rather than the rule, the rule being that in the wake of colonization, urbanization has had a negative impact on economic development.

Urbanization and Economic Development in the Third World

Although economic development has not had a decisive effect on urbanization in the Third World, one may nevertheless ask what influence urbanization has had on economic development. In this context, two separate ways of approaching the problem have to be distinguished. The first as a working hypothesis sets aside the phenomenon of overurbanization in order to address the ways in which economic underdevelopment has affected the positive influence normally exerted by urbanization on development, as seen in the Western world. The second analyzes the consequences of overurbanization with respect to development. In this second analysis I shall focus on the Third World market economies, leaving out—with good reason—the unique case of China.

Underdevelopment and the Traditionally Positive Aspects of Urbanization

To what extent has the current situation in the Third World distorted the positive aspects of urbanization as it unfolded in developed nations during the nineteenth century? To answer this question, I shall review each of the principal components, each of the principal ways in which urbanization has traditionally made a positive contribution to economic development.

The first component is unquestionably the role played by the city in technological innovation. The effect the city has in the diffusion of innovation is just as important as the effect it has in engendering it (see chapter 20). The fact remains that in the Third World, owing to the lack of technological development, the city's role as the mother of invention has certainly been more restricted than in the West, and that this same lack of technological development has reduced the possibilities for diffusion. In the absence of specific corrective measures—an assumption obviously underlying this analysis—one may even conclude that the city tends to impede the diffusion of technological innovation, inasmuch as it fosters the consumption of products that are difficult to produce locally. Indeed, available studies show that cities in general, and especially large cities (of which the Third World has a great many), bring about a pattern of consumption favoring sophisticated products. In the Third World this tends to encourage imports more than local production.

By concentrating the population, the city provides a market promoting the division of labor, as well as the formation of manufacturing concerns of a size approaching the optimum. In this case as well, particularly given the location of the larger Third World cities, it is more than likely that foreign concerns have profited from the market these cities constitute: of the fifty-two Third World cities with populations of more than a million in 1970, thirty-six were located on the coast or at the mouth of a river.

In my book on the size of cities (Bairoch, 1977a), I studied the impact of urbanism on imports. Econometric analysis led me to conclude that urban structure probably influences the level of per capita imports appreciably. The urban variables explained some 45 percent of the variation in the level of total per capita imports not explained by the level of development and the size of the countries involved. The increase in the propensity to import imputable to urbanization affects the importation not only of manufactured consumer goods and auto-mobiles, but of food products as well. Furthermore, statistical analysis suggests that the size of cities is a factor in the increase in imports, especially in the case of cities with populations of more than 300,000.

On the whole, the same consequences result from the monetariza-tion of the economy which urbanism favors, and which contributed to economic development in the Western world. In the case of the Third World, monetarization has encouraged the increasing importation of manufactured goods and even agricultural products.

Social mobility, on the other hand, whether horizontal or vertical, which the urban environment favors, may play a more positive role in the Third World than it did in Western countries. This is because the social constraints associated with rural life are probably greater in Third World societies than they were in Western societies during the nineteenth century. From this point of view, social mobility resembles education. It is likely that in the cities of the Third World education has also played a positive role, one at least as important as the one it played in the cities of the West, if not more important.

And what of the city's impact on agriculture? I have already cited on several occasions the thesis of Boserup (1965) to see how far it can be applied outside the context for which it was originally formulated. The time has come to see how it performs in its natural habitat. I do not wish to question the fact that, in certain regions and during cer-tain periods, demographic pressure (and in particular urban demand) has served as a powerful stimulus for the adoption of new, more pro-ductive agricultural techniques. I nevertheless feel compelled to ob-serve that over larger regions and the long term, it does not appear to have been enough to bring about any marked rise in agricultural pro-ductivity (see chapter 29). In fact it is dismaying to note that the green revolution on which so many hopes were based has even been inca-pable of accelerating growth in agricultural output.

And what has in fact become of the green revolution? I shall begin by recalling what is meant by the term. The term green revolution simply refers to the gains resulting from the development of certain high-yield cereal seed strains adapted to the climates of underdevel-oped countries. Among these were in particular a strain of wheat se-lected in Mexico and a strain of rice selected in the Philippines. The practical use of these seeds, begun around 1956 in the case of wheat and around 1966 in the case of rice, has led to sharp rises in yields, sometimes surpassing 100 percent. At first sight, then, the use of these seed strains would seem to constitute a decisive advance genu-inely deserving the name revolution. The name was given it all the more readily in that in 1967–1968 a combination of circumstances, chiefly climatological in nature, led to an overestimation of the poten-tial of these seed strains.

Today we are at a sufficient distance from the facts to draw up a balance sheet. The balance is positive so far as the dissemination of the seed strains goes. At the present time, roughly three quarters of the land sown with wheat in Third World market economies has been planted with the new strains, the corresponding area planted with the new strains of rice amounting to roughly half. This led to a rapid increase in yields. Between 1960–66 and 1981–87, rice yields went up from 1,620 to 2,300 kg per hectare, and wheat yields from 950 to 1,670 kg per hectare. The balance is negative, however, where total output is concerned. Taking data for seven-year averages in order to eliminate distortions due to climate fluctuations, it will be found that, having progressed at the rate of 2.9–3.1% per year between 1948–54 and 1960–66, agricultural food production rose by only 2.8–3.0% per year between 1960–66 and 1980–86. It is possible that a part of this minor slowdown can be imputed to improvements in statistics, which may formerly have overestimated growth. But the elimination of this potential bias will not make an improvement appear, only an absence of deterioration at most. Thus, even at best, the introduction of these new seed strains has only prevented a slowing down of the increase in production, thereby masking other negative aspects in the social domain (unequal distribution of the gains from the new seed stock) and in the ecological domain (increased need for fertilizers and excessive reliance on a single seed strain). The possibility of importing grain may perhaps be responsible for the absence of positive effects. Perhaps. But these imports may also have been the only way to prevent famine. On the whole, then, I find it at least difficult to argue that urbanization has had an especially beneficial impact on agriculture.

With this I have completed my review of the chief urban factors traditionally favoring economic development. The conclusion that can be drawn from this examination is that, owing to the local and international context, the cities of the Third World have on the whole been less conducive to economic development than those of the West during early phases of development.

Before I move on to the consequences of overurbanization, an aspect of the situation omitted from the preceding analysis, I should mention one last area in which urbanization in the Third World has in fact made a positive contribution to development: the reduction of fertility. To the extent that any reduction in the pace of demographic growth would unquestionably constitute, if not a precondition for, then at least a factor favoring genuine development, the city has truly helped to improve the situation. There is no doubt that the urban way of life brings about a reduction in fertility among city residents and encourages the spread of this form of behavior to society as a whole. However, (see chapter 28) the city also brings about a reduction in mortality, thereby increasing natural population growth, which has been very rapid in the cities, as rapid since the early fifties in cities as in rural areas.

Hyperurbanization and Development

Most of the consequences of the urban explosion (outlined in chapter 29) have created a highly unfavorable situation for economic development. I shall examine these consequences once again.

First I shall look at unemployment and underemployment in the cities. Some 30 to 40 percent of all potential man-hours go unused, an enormous waste of human resources. This waste is even more serious than that brought about by rural underemployment, in that, whereas rural underemployment reflects insufficient production on the part of workers, in the cities there is generally no production whatever. Another factor aggravating the negative effects of urban underemployment is the fact that the population involved has generally attained a higher level of education than its rural counterpart. But one also has to allow here, as in the case of overemployment in services, for the informal sector, a source of employment that has not been taken sufficiently into account in calculations of the extent of urban underemployment. But though it has not been taken sufficiently into account, its contribution is not large enough to alter to any substantial degree the measures of underemployment, still less the measures of effective unemployment. I shall discuss the potential of the informal sector later in this chapter.

Overemployment in services is highly prejudicial to the economy as a whole. Since the studies of Colin Clark (1939) and Fourastié (1949) placing in evidence the way in which, following economic development, the work force gravitates toward employment in services, there has occasionally been a tendency to underestimate the inertial weight that abnormally high employment rates in the tertiary sector place on the economy. It is obvious that as productivity rises in agriculture and industry and as the general level of consumption increases, the tertiary sector must also grow. This is necessary to ensure the distribution of the enlarged volume of goods produced thanks to increased productivity and to provide for the wider consumption of services made possible by the rising standard of living. It is just as obvious, however, that any increase in employment in services in the framework of an economy in which agricultural and industrial productivity remains relatively low will impede development. In such cases, owing to the additional distribution costs it entails, overemployment in services will exert pressure on the standard of living and also, more importantly, on prices in the productive sectors of the economy. This pressure reduces profit margins and consequently the level of productive investment. Furthermore, while the capital accumulated in services will be directed toward fresh investment, it will tend to return to the sector from which it originated, if only owing to the need in any sector of the economy for self-financing. For these reasons alone, even without taking into account the underemployment associated with it, over-employment in services constitutes an obstacle to development.

As a result of the wide gap between urban and rural income (a gap less wide during the early phases of development in the West), the cities of the Third World absorb a disproportionate fraction of overall economic resources. As a reasonable hypothesis, it can be estimated that per capita income in urban areas exceeds per capita income in rural areas by some 80–100 %, which means that the cities absorb a share of national resources exceeding their share of the total population by 80–100%. In other words, the urban share of total national income in Third World market economies currently stands at some 50–55%. This monopolization of national resources is reflected both in high rates of urban consumption and by investments in real estate. Urban construction (housing and urban infrastructures) absorbs a high proportion of total investments, probably as much as half, particularly when the overall transportation infrastructure for city needs is taken into account.

Another serious consequence of excessive urban growth has been urban giantism. It has been seen that as early as 1970 a third of the urban population was concentrated in cities with populations of more than a million. If no corrective measures are taken, the proportion will reach 45 percent by the year 2000, and the year 2000 is just around the corner. Cities of this size not only have a detrimental impact on living conditions (pollution, poor housing, increased crime rates, etc.), but their negative effects outweigh whatever positive contribution they may make to the process of economic development (Bairoch, 1977a). As a result, although industrial productivity may in general rise as a function of the size of cities, the progress stops once a population of 500,000 to a million has been reached. The same applies to the productivity of the distribution system and to the chances of making optimal use of labor. And to the absence of positive effects must be added the negative consequences: the per capita cost of the urban infrastructure goes up as soon as the population exceeds 100,000–200,000; the level of savings and consequently of investment capital drops; the cost of transportation rises perceptibly as soon as population exceeds 700,000–900,000; and as has been seen, patterns of consumption emerge that tend to increase imports from developed nations.

One final aspect of the situation, already discussed in chapter 29 and above, is the detrimental impact of hyperurbanization on subsistence agriculture. Rapid urban growth is probably the chief cause of the increasing food deficit in the Third World. In the case of grain, the Third World went from an annual surplus of four million metric tons in 1934–38 to an annual deficit of seventy-seven million metric tons for 1983–87. Nor has this growing deficit been accompanied by a perceptible improvement in the level of food consumption. In fact, based on data issued by the FAO (Food and Agriculture Organization), it can be estimated that around 1948–1952 average daily food consumption in Third World market economies reached 2,050–2,100 calories per person. For the very period 1981–85 it stood at 2,360 calories per person. Thus only minimal progress has been made; and even this may overstate the reality, inasmuch as the figures for the recent period are probably somewhat overestimated and those for the previous period somewhat underestimated.

Thus not only has urbanization in the Third World lost most of its positive components from the point of view of economic development, but hyperurbanization has added many new and substantial obstacles to those already in existence. Rapid urbanization without economic development leads to hyperurbanization, which acts in turn as a powerful brake on subsequent development, thereby creating a further vicious circle in the difficult problem of underdevelopment.

Are the Handicaps Also Opportunities?

Is the informal sector of the economy an economic asset or disguised unemployment? May the shantytowns legitimately be regarded as "slums of hope"? Are they stages in a transition toward development or tumors to be removed? Such questions as these, evoked at the end of the preceding chapter, reflect an almost complete reversal of the terms in which the problem of Third World cities has traditionally been posed. The main thing is not to go too far, to remember that although there may be some truth to the proverb, "every cloud has a silver lining," walking in the rain may not be the best way of getting where we want to go. I shall try to find something positive in each of these two handicaps.

The Informal Sector: An Economic Asset or Disguised Unemployment?

In the informal sector there is unquestionably a good side. The view that these marginal economic activities are merely a form of disguised unemployment is undoubtedly out of date. In many aspects of the production of goods and services, informal economic activities provide an adequate solution to the problem of maximizing the available resources, whether human or capital, technology or raw materials. As Santos (1975) observes: "The lower circuit increasingly provides the structure welcoming people driven from the countryside. It assumes, therefore, an undeniable social and economic function." Without this lower circuit—this informal sector of the economy—unemployment rates would unquestionably be much higher than they already are. But the jobs furnished by this sector, poorly paid though they may often be, also help increase the flood of immigrants leaving the land. The choice, then, is not merely between unemployment and the informal sector, a choice in which the informal sector clearly wins hands down, but also between the informal sector and finding some way of holding a larger number of young people in the countryside. And in the latter case, it is not at all certain that the informal sector is the lesser of the two evils. With this, moreover, I suggest one of the chief conclusions of this part of the book: the solution to the urban problem in the Third World must also, and perhaps above all, be sought in the country.

What is more, even taken on their own terms, the advantages offered by the informal sector are by no means unalloyed. As Santos further remarks: "If the lower circuit must change, it is because its chief function is not so much to provide jobs and furnish a means of survival as to perpetuate poverty while collecting the people's savings and channeling them into the upper circuit through intermediaries of every sort." Among the other drawbacks of the informal sector is of course its low level of productivity. It is true that the efforts of the ILO and other national and international organizations concerned with this problem have been in a sense aimed at modernizing this sector of the economy—at eliminating as many of the handicaps as possible in order that it may make a more positive contribution to economic development. But is this possible?

Within the ILO itself, Georges Nihan (1979), tragically taken from us in a "banal" road accident, concluded his reflections on these matters by remarking that

> the chief problem remains that of the potential contribution of the "modern" unstructured sector to development: as it exists today, does this sector represent a reservoir of economic growth, jobs, and the formation of human capital—the basis for the differential-structures thesis—or is it simply a transitory phase in the process of development . . . That the large modern sector is a multifarious phenomenon . . . is scarcely to be questioned and it is clearly perceived as such by the countries concerned. . . . For this reason the unstructured sector could therefore have a relative advantage at least in the production of goods and services meeting the essential needs of the population, so long as policies based on self-sufficiency are developed. Something of this sort would make it possible to maintain a national economic sector, mediating between traditional activity and large-scale industry, adapted to the socioeconomic constraints of each country, a sector acting as a stopgap helping both to alleviate the employment situation and to provide the national economy with

some room for maneuver. It would still be necessary for this "modern" unstructured sector to have a dynamic potential for growth enabling it over the long run to adapt its modes of production in order that this base economy, making use of an original process of production, might remain competitive.

Remaining competitive is obviously the crucial thing. For the key problem in the Third World is the race between population and the economy. What I wrote in 1963 as an introduction to my first study on underdevelopment is even more true today:

> The problem of growth, or if one prefers, of development, has become all the more distressing in that it no longer takes the form of an option, but rather of a necessity. Choice was possible in the eighteenth century and partially in the nineteenth; traditional societies had a relatively stable balance, a balance that was costly, to be sure, in terms of the human suffering involved in the decreases in population due to periodic famines and frequent epidemics, but a balance just the same. Today, however, the introduction of medical technology—the fruit of development in Western societies—has upset the balance in underdeveloped countries. Maintaining stable food production can no longer be considered a realistic objective. In combination with the tempting, even tantalizing, presence of examples of massive success in development, the upsetting of this balance leaves Third World nations no choice. Development is no longer an option in these cases, but a vital necessity.

And it is not at all certain that the informal sector provides sufficient impetus to help solve this problem in any reasonable way. It is therefore necessary to weigh all of the alternatives. The fact that the present Chinese authorities have also encouraged the emergence of an informal sector gives additional evidence in any case that this option should not be overlooked.

The Shantytowns: Slums of Hope or Tumors to Be Removed?

"From the point of view of the urban dweller, the squatter settlement is a community of misery offering only the very lowest level of urban services. For the migrant, however, the squatter settlement constitutes an important first achievement in his participation in the process of urbanization. In this sense, the squatter settlement is a community in transition to a markedly greater degree than the urban region to which it pertains." It is in these terms that the United Nations inquiry into the worldwide housing situation (1976) approaches the problem of the shantytowns.

This clarification is necessary to the extent that, until the mid sixties, the nearly unanimous view was that the shantytowns were a totally negative manifestation, which it was indispensable to eradicate completely, if possible. There is no doubt that the shantytowns are less negative than the "tourist expert" might deduce from a visit or a brief study. One should not compare housing conditions in the shantytowns with those in the cities, still less with those in the wealthier cities, but rather with conditions in the rural districts from which the immigrants have come. The relative number of "dwellings" equipped with running water or electricity or containing toilet facilities is larger in most shantytowns than in rural regions. Moreover, in chapter 29, I mentioned the traumatic character of the shift from a traditional rural environment to a habitat too closely based on the Western model. It is true, on the other hand, that here too things have changed, and that the spread of education and the mass media have made modern forms of habitat not only acceptable, but often desirable.

If these things are taken into consideration, then as a transition the shantytowns unquestionably have a more positive function than used to be supposed, all the more so in that it is in the shantytowns that the activities of the informal sector are pursued. But it is hard to regard this form of habitat as an asset from the point of view of economic development. The shantytowns have changed the terms in which the problems of the housing deficit and thus of investment needs in this sector are posed, thereby easing the constraints, but without producing a solution. And here I should repeat what I said earlier: "Every cloud has a silver lining"; but you still get wet if you walk out in the rain.

Furthermore, in September 1983 the first shantytown revolts occurred. In both Mexico and Brazil residents of certain shantytowns plundered food from stores and supermarkets. Witnesses indicated that this was an act of starving people: their food supply had been drastically reduced because of price increases and higher unemployment. The future will decide whether these were exceptional events, chance occurrences, or the first signs of periodic revolts. If the revolts continue they will, of course, provoke defensive reactions, one of which will be measures to reduce the size of shantytowns.

The City a Handicap? Agriculture a Solution?

How should I conclude this analysis of the cities of the Third World? What should I say about the city's impact on development? We shall be very brief for the traditional period, for which the unknowns by far outnumber the certainties. The most probable generalization is that the cities of the future Third World usually had a more limited impact than their Western counterparts. This generalization, however, overlooks pronounced spatial and historical differences.

It is easier to determine the city's contribution during the colonial era. Here urbanism was unquestionably an unwitting allay of colonialism and was an important factor intensifying the detrimental consequences of colonization. This was particularly true during the phase of modern colonization following the Industrial Revolution. Here, too, however, regional differences have to be taken into account, and in particular the more positive role of Latin American cities. As early as the close of the nineteenth century, on the other hand, Latin America anticipated many of the phenomena that would appear in the rest of the Third World only after 1920–30, the most notable among these being exceptionally rapid urban growth and the massive exportation of minerals. It should not be forgotten, however, that Latin America accounted at this time for only a very small fraction of the future Third World—6 percent of its overall population at the turn of the century.

The past matters insofar as it explains the present. So, too, the present matters in part because it is the seed of the future. What is the impact of the city on the Third World today?

Even setting aside the consequences of the urban explosion (which may perhaps have been too hastily judged negative), it still cannot be shown to have made Third World cities a factor contributing to economic development. The evident handicaps are numerous and substantial, the assets rare and slight. It is true that weighing the advantages and disadvantages and drawing up a balance sheet does not have the simplicity, much less the rigor, of classical accounting techniques. Nevertheless, in this case what doubts remain after the negative balance has been established are highly marginal. Urbanization as it has unfolded in the Third World for nearly a half century now has certainly not helped development. One may even say that the city has in a way contributed to underdevelopment. When placed in the context of existing national and international socioeconomic structures, the current level of urbanization in the Third World constitutes a handicap much more than an asset for economic development.

Political independence has not had sufficient influence to modify the problem. On the contrary, it seems rather to have accelerated the urban explosion. Moreover, the colonial legacy has weighed very heavily on the Third World's socioeconomic structure, and in many countries neocolonialism has continued to have the impact of colonialism. In many other cases, however, colonialism and neocolonialism are convenient scapegoats for errors of local policy makers. But art is as difficult as criticism is easy. And the art of leading Third World countries out of the morass of underdevelopment they have largely inherited from colonization is a most difficult one indeed.

More serious still, the problems of the cities—those of today and, even more so, those of tomorrow—cannot be solved within the urban framework alone; the countryside will have to have a large place in the solution. As always and everywhere, there is here an underlying relationship between economic and social life, and in particular between town and country.

If over the next decades no catastrophes intervene and population goes on growing at an explosive rate, it is certain that, in the absence of measures to improve agriculture, the flood of rural migrants will continue to increase the population of the cities. The cities, meanwhile, will continue to experience rapid natural population growth. Agriculture is today the most important sector of economic life in the Third World, and will remain so for several decades to come. Though my position regarding the problems of underdevelopment may have changed in many respects since the late fifties, when I first became interested in the matter, I have found nothing to alter my opinion about the primordial place of the agricultural sector. Quite the opposite. When in 1972, at the request of the ILO, I studied the problem of urban unemployment, I came to the conclusion that this problem could not be solved without some changes in the rural world. Today, in the light of all evidence I have collected for this book, I am as certain as before that this is the correct conclusion—a conclusion that may easily seem trivial since it is so obvious even without a long investigation.

The key to the problem of development (and thus to the problem of cities as well) lies chiefly in agriculture. In a recent report on development (1982), the World Bank, despite its pronounced "technical" and "proindustrial" bias, in a sense supported the conclusions of my first book on Third World development (Bairoch, 1963): "The vitally important position of agriculture should not be forgotten, and measures aimed at industrial development must seek to create favorable interactions between industry and farming." The World Bank put it this way: "Discussion of agriculture stresses a key factor of development experience—the strong association between agriculture and overall economic growth."

To be sure, as in any multifaceted socioeconomic problem, one must avoid overemphasizing any one component. For some Third World societies, and in particular for smaller countries able to derive from foreign trade a base for their economic life, industrialization may indeed offer the solution for the urban problem. This seems to have been especially true of certain Asian countries in which, since the early seventies, the relocation of many Western industries has provided an economic base for many urban systems (McGee, 1980). But such solutions suit only a very modest fraction of Third World cities. Indeed, if all Third World cities exported to the developed countries of the West as many manufactured goods as Hong Kong exports,

Western imports would have to increase eighty times over. This volume of imports would exceed by a very wide margin the total consumption of manufactured goods in developed Western countries.

But what measures should be taken in the rural world? What measures should be taken in order to solve the urban problem at the same time as the problem of development? This is not the place to discuss the measures in detail. I would simply say for the moment that this would first of all involve, everywhere in the Third World, increasing the yield and more especially the productivity of agriculture. Moreover, wherever necessary, agrarian reform must be undertaken: reform designed to enable the mass of the peasantry to benefit from advances in productivity but also, at a deeper level, reform that avoids compromising productivity—no easy task. Alongside these two fundamental measures, others must be taken to improve social facilities in rural areas, to reduce the gap between urban and rural wages, to improve the urban habitat, and to change the content of education in such a way as to enhance the popular image of rural life. The urban problem, the problem of agriculture, and all the other problems besetting the developing world would, of course, be helped by a slowdown in demographic growth. But even with such a slowdown, things will be far from simple.

Is the city a handicap? Is agriculture a solution? As the reader will have realized, the answer to both questions is yes. In fact it is necessary to put the matter even more emphatically: the city is a serious handicap, and agriculture offers just about the only solution.

31 Conclusions □

The appearance of cities was early, multiple, and simultaneous; this is one of the chief conclusions of part 1 of the book, devoted to the beginnings of urbanism. Another important conclusion was that agriculture not only constituted an absolute precondition for the emergence of genuine urban systems, but that there was also an inverse causal relationship: wherever agriculture appeared, the appearance of cities was all but inevitable. Almost everywhere, in the Old World as well as the New World, two to three thousand years after agriculture was established, the city emerged. Thus emerged that revolutionary form of socioeconomic organization uniquely associated with humankind. On the one side was the town, on the other the country. On the one side was the production of manufactured goods, commercial and intellectual pursuits, and in almost every case the center of political power as well; on the other side was the countryside, supplying not merely the food and raw materials the city needed to survive, but also the people; for one of the constants of the history of traditional cultures is that the city was never able by itself to maintain a stable population, still less to assure demographic growth.

I shall provide a few reference points, for all of these observations have to be placed in a very long historical perspective. To do this, I shall review the course of events in those parts of the world in which most of the world's population (roughly 80%) and in particular most of the world's urban population (roughly 90%) was concentrated in 1500: namely, southern and eastern Asia, the Middle East, North Africa, western and southern Europe, and Central and South America.

Depending on the region, agriculture first appeared between 8500 and 5000 B.C., that is, very recently, or if you prefer, very late, given that several million years had already elapsed since the emergence of the first human beings on the earth. Real cities, depending on the region, appeared between 3500 and 500 B.C.; and if preurban "cities" are taken into account, the date has to be pushed back a further two to three thousand years.

Thus an early emergence of cities, but also a world much more heavily urbanized than had been supposed. Indeed, my comparative analysis, supported by my elaboration of many new data sets, has radically revised my image of the world: the traditional world, the world before the Industrial Revolution, was far more urban in character than had generally been thought.

A World Highly Urbanized Very Early

Ancient Rome, the most highly urbanized society in the traditional world; or seventeenth-century Japan, or thirteenth-century China, or Western Europe, or one or another of the pre-Columbian cultures, and so forth. One could add even further examples to this list drawn from recent studies. The mistake the writers make does not lie in their assessments of the levels of urbanization in the societies they describe, but in the reference point they have chosen to establish the level of urbanization in the world at large before the Industrial Revolution. The reference point almost always explicitly used (and sometimes implicitly used) is the estimate of Davis and Hertz (1957). Davis and Hertz concluded that roughly 3% of the world's population lived in cities with populations of 5,000 or more around 1800. The reader will remember that a population of 5,000 is the criterion I have used to define urban population: a criterion that may be questionable in certain respects but which nevertheless remains for all that the most adequate and especially the most operational.

In fact, around 1800 the number of people living in cities in the world as a whole stood at some 78–97 million out of a total population of some 940 million to 1 billion, making a level of urbanization as high as 8–10%, at a time when the world had as yet been very little affected by industry. Moreover, since Europe was no less urbanized in 1700 than in 1800, and since China and India were even more urbanized in 1700 than in 1800, the world at large was still more heavily urbanized in 1700 than in 1800. And all things considered, the world had reached a level of urbanization in 1500, and even in 1300, close to that achieved in 1800. Finally, the world may easily have reached a level of urbanization on the order of 7–10% as early as the year 200.

I compared my estimates with those of earlier students of urban history and found that my estimates lead to a very substantial revision of levels of urbanization (see table 31.1). Compare the data for 1700, since the eighteenth century was the last to be unaffected by industrialization and the various consequences it brought in its wake. While Davis and Hertz (authors of the most widely used estimate) put the level of the world's urbanization a little below 3%, and while other estimates put it at 5–6%, I estimate a level on the order of 10%. Despite this considerable gap, I believe it possible that my findings may even fall a little short of the reality—not very far short, of course, but while

494

TABLE 31.1   Levels of Urbanization in the World as a Whole (1300–1980)

	1300	1500	1700	1800	1900	1950	1980
Previous world estimates							
Davis & Hertz	—	—	—	3.0	13.6	29.8	—
Doxiadis &							
Papaioannou[a]	—	7.6	5.0	6.2	18.0	31.5	—
Grauman:							
Low hypothesis	4.1	4.6	5.0	5.0	13.2	28.0	—
Average hypothesis	4.7	5.1	5.4	5.3	13.6	28.6	—
High hypothesis	5.3	5.6	5.8	5.5	14.0	29.2	—
Bairoch (1977) estimates	—	—	—	7.9	17.2	27.2	—
Current estimates,							
Bairoch							
World as a whole	9.0	9.4	9.8	9.0	16.0	25.6	37.6
Africa	4.0	5.0	3.9	4.0	5.5	12.0	25.2
America	8.2	8.4	11.4	12.3	28.5	47.9	63.8
Asia	10.2	10.7	10.9	9.1	9.3	14.9	25.6
Europe	9.5	9.6	10.8	10.4	30.2	42.9	64.2
Future Third World	9.0	9.5	9.5	8.3	9.1	15.7	27.6
Future Developed World	9.0	9.2	10.8	10.8	29.7	46.1	65.4

Sources: Davis & Hertz (1957), p. 56; Doxiadis & Papaioannou (1974), p. 405; Grauman (1977), p. 29; Bairoch (1977a), and calculations and estimates by the author; see the methodological appendix; Hoyt (1963), p. 170.

Note: Hoyt (1963) estimates that around 1800 the population of cities with more than 2,000 inhabitants represented 5% of world population.

A criterion of 5,000 is used for urban population.

The fact that these figures have been only slightly rounded off does not imply a correspondingly small margin of error.

[a] Around the year 1000: 11.4%. The figure for 1700 is interpolated from those for 1650 and 1750.

I suggest a spread of 9–11% for 1700, a level of urbanization of 11 or even 12% seems plausible to me in the light of the large body of data I have collected.

Thus one may without too much trepidation formulate the following rule: in any society with normal geographic characteristics, some 1,000 to 1,500 years after the appearance of the first city urbanization reached a level close to the maximum possible in the framework of traditional societies, a maximum somewhere around 10 to 15%. The exceptions lie in regions subject to climatic extremes, especially of cold, and in very mountainous areas. And since such regions are as a rule thinly populated, the level of urbanization in the world as a whole approached the maximum possible in the framework of traditional societies very early in its history.

An Urban World: Sources of Instability and Sources of Stability

Although the world reached the limit of urban growth very early in its history, urbanization was neither stable over time nor uniform in space. Nineteenth-century China was less urbanized than twelfth-century China, despite the larger number of city residents, for overall population had in the interval grown even more rapidly than urban population. Similarly, second-century Italy was more urbanized than seventh-century Italy. Black Africa, on the other hand, was less urbanized than the rest of the ancient world; but in the eighteenth century, Latin America was more urbanized than Europe as a whole, and twice as urbanized as Russia. And many more examples could be cited to the same effect.

This instability, however, rarely led to the complete disappearance of urban networks. There is a sort of inertia in urban systems, as well as at the level of individual cities, even if one of the conclusions drawn from the analysis of the evolution of cities is the individual character of urban history. Each city has a history all its own and faces a unique combination of circumstances that is often different from that of the network of which it is a part. Whether at the level of systems or of individual cities, fluctuations, sometimes cutting very deep, and divergent long-term trends form the fabric of which urban history is made. But beyond a certain size, once a certain threshold has been crossed, cities rarely die. And even where death does occur, a new city or network will often fill the void left by its predecessor: the conditions which led to the birth of an original city or network disappear only rarely.

The City, for Better or for Worse

In adopting agriculture humanity adopted the city as well. And the city very rapidly became important. The city, for better or for worse. This is one way of formulating the fundamental problem addressed in this book: what are the relations between the city and the economy, between the city and what today is called economic development? Born of a change in the economy, the city continues to be determined by its economic environment. This much is self-evident, and the problems it raises are simple in comparison with those raised by the other types of influence, those originating in the city itself. For the city has in turn had substantial consequences for both the economic and social life of the societies of which it was a part.

Moreover, the history of these reciprocal relations cannot neglect the fundamental break precipitated by the Industrial Revolution, which radically changed the whole relation of the city with the economy, as well as the rest of social life. It is necessary to make a clear distinction between these two very different worlds: the world of traditional societies and the world of change. The world of traditional societies has many different cultures, yet all of them are united by the limits of the traditional economy. The world of change, on the other hand, is divided into two radically different groups owing precisely to the break brought about by modern economic development and colonialism. On the one side are the so-called developed nations; on the other, nations which, though undeveloped, have nevertheless undergone irreversible change owing to the very fact of the development of the first group. On one side, then, are the rich, on the other the poor. Thus it is necessary to deal with three different types of world. In this concluding chapter I shall review the relations in these three worlds between the city and the economy since the beginnings of urbanization.

Obviously, I cannot take up all of the evidence given in the conclusions to each of the four parts of the book. The reader interested solely in my conclusions may consult chapters 6, 12, 21, and 30. In the following pages I shall try to synthesize the material presented in these conclusions. Setting aside certain special aspects of the problem discussed in greater detail in the conclusions in the main body of the book, this synthesis will inevitably overlook many points of detail. What I offer here is merely a digest, and any digest will perforce leave out some nuances brought out in the foregoing discussions. Furthermore, I shall leave almost completely aside here the history of urbanization, despite its importance in the rest of the book. This does not mean, however, that I shall be able entirely to avoid repeating myself.

Traditional Cities and the Limits of Agriculture

Engendered by agriculture, the city has remained completely tributary to it. The proportion of city residents among the total population is determined by the relative size of the food surplus that country people, voluntarily or not, are able to allocate them. This fact is obvious, but it should not be forgotten. The surplus was never truly substantial until the Industrial Revolution.

What was the upper limit on this surplus? What was the maximum proportion of the food yield that could be extracted from the peasantry to support the cities? Despite the improvements successively achieved by the cultures of antiquity and by the later cultures of Europe and Asia, the most advanced agricultural technology of traditional societies still needed, for the production of food and agricultural raw materials (essentially textiles) alone, the use of 70–75% of the entire work force. This meant that the proportion of the overall work force engaged in nonagricultural pursuits could not exceed 25–30%. Urban population was even less able to exceed this level since there was as a rule a higher proportion of nonfarmers in the countryside than of farmers in the cities. It is true that if I set the limit defining urban population arbitrarily at 5,000, the limit adopted in the rest of this book as well as in almost all comparative studies, this meant that the ceiling on urban growth stood at around 15%, or 20% if one adopts the criterion of 2,000 to define urban population.

Does this mean that no traditional society exceeded this ceiling? Yes and no. No, if one considers larger economic entities like the Roman and Persian empires of antiquity or traditional Europe and China. Such entities could not exceed this ceiling. But yes, if one considers smaller societies specializing in international trade, like ancient Phoenicia and Greece, medieval Italy, and the Netherlands of the seventeenth century. But these smaller societies achieved a higher level of urbanization only thanks to agricultural surpluses in other regions for which they performed economic functions.

But does this in turn mean that within the larger economic unit the level of urbanization was strictly determined by the size of the agricultural surplus—that to a surplus of such a size corresponded such a level of urbanization? No, for many other factors could, and still can, modify the size of an urban network. First of all, there is the degree of specialization in the economy. If farmers live in the city while artisans and traders are absent from the countryside, then levels of urbanization will be higher than in intermediate situations. There are also differences in the density of the occupation of agricultural land, differences largely determined not only by the quality of the land, the climate and the level of technology, but also by the dominant type of food crop: rice, maize, and potatoes, for example, permit more people per hectare than wheat. It is at this point, moreover, that the tyranny of distance intervenes. For it remains necessary to transport the agricultural surplus to the city; and beyond a certain distance, varying as a function of geographic and technological conditions, the surplus ceases to have any value. Finally, to limit this list to the essentials, there are the rules dictating the division of the pie. Depending on the society, more or less of the surplus may be left for the peasantry—and the city resident is often better fed than the rural resident.

This limit, together with the numerous factors affecting it, engendered a variety of strategies societies could follow whenever urban growth ran up against the limit. An urban system driven to the limit, especially by generalized population growth and/or when handicapped by agricultural decline, could pursue one or more of the five following courses—assuming that in the interim the problem had not already been "settled" by a catastrophe like the Black Death of the fourteenth century: (1) change nothing in the various modalities of the relations between town and country, in which case the relative share of the city would fluctuate accordingly; (2) relocate into rural districts some of the economic activities normally pursued in the city, thereby reducing the drain on agriculture, not only by lowering transport costs, but also by enabling agriculture to make use of a fraction of the artisan's time; (3) limit the urban standard of living; (4) limit the rural standard of living; (5) ruralize the city, this last option coming into play whenever the level of urbanization tended to decline.

In a way these adaptations help explain the stability or only modest decline of many urban networks that had lost some of their economic functions. I think it necessary in this case to introduce another factor as well: a declining or stagnating urban population may help economize on a substantial part of construction costs (housing and urban infrastructure). This means that the urban population could adjust to a fall of 3–5% in the level of resources without a reduction in the standard of living. In sum, though to a much lesser extent, these consequences resemble those resulting from a fall in rural population leading to a rise in the ratio of land to people. Needless to say, however, this hypothesis can explain only a part of the paradox, and it does not rule out the intervention of other factors.

Traditional Cities and Economic Development

While it may be legitimate to speak of the city in the singular with respect to the limits of agriculture in traditional societies, this is no longer admissible with respect to economic growth. The European city, the Chinese city, the Muslim city, and the African city were so many separate universes in the ways in which they acted upon the economy. But despite the differences, there were similarities as well. I shall begin by looking at the similarities.

To begin with there was the close relation between the city and civilization. While civilizations may exist without cities, it has to be admitted (contrary to certain wholly groundless prejudices) that many aspects of civilization owe their existence to cities, just as cities, once they are established, already imply a certain level of civilization. It is extremely unlikely, for instance, that writing and the major technological innovations could have emerged or been maintained in a purely rural setting. In this context, the city has always brought together the conditions favoring significant innovation. And prominent among these conditions are the real demand for such innovations (and thus their usefulness), increased chances of social contacts fostering the circulation of information, and the existence of a labor pool entirely given over to nonagricultural pursuits.

Another similarity, or rather generalization, is that if cities could and occasionally did become parasitic, it was only after a certain stage had been reached and only under specific conditions. Before this stage had been reached, cities always acted as a leaven stimulating economic development (the term is used to simplify the discussion although it is an anachronism). The city was able to play this positive role with respect to economic development because of the way it promoted foreign trade, progress in industrial technology, and—up to a point—progress in agricultural technology.

But what of the differences? To begin with, these lay in the intensity of the city's positive impact on the rest of the economy. And in this case the frontiers cut across time as well as space. What were the spatial divisions? To simplify matters greatly, European cities can be said to have had a more positive influence than the cities of other cultures. Moreover, among these other cultures, the Muslim cities may perhaps have had a more favorable influence. But even here, it depends on which Muslim cities we mean: those of Spain or those of Iraq; those of the Maghreb or those of Black Africa. Above all, one has to specify the period.

This brings us to the temporal boundaries. What were the divisions in time? In this case no simplification is possible. Caesar's Rome was no longer what it had been two centuries earlier. Fifth-century Europe was unlike twelfth-century Europe. And twelfth-century China did not resemble eighteenth-century China. To this multitude of contrasting situations has to be added the absence of studies and also the lack of the sort of information needed to conduct valid research. Among the chief causes modifying the positive effects of the cities, I should mention their degree of independence, their geographic location, their size, and, above all, the socioeconomic and political structures of the societies of which they formed an integral part.

There were still other differences. For while, as has been seen, almost all cities had at some stage been positive, some became parasitic. A whole series of conditions, economic as well as social and political, were capable of turning the city not only into an obstacle in the path toward development, but into a factor inducing economic regression. And before moving on to the Industrial Revolution (with which this feature of the urban phenomenon faded somewhat), I should mention once more the individual character of each city's history. Above and beyond the trends peculiar to each society and to each period, instances of divergent evolutions abound. These divergences can be explained by many factors, most of which have already been mentioned. But a place has to be made for chance, in the form of the strengths or weaknesses of the leaders responsible for the destinies of their cities and for the choices that are made. And one should not forget what some call "acts of God" and others "fate": earthquakes, floods, and so on.

The Break with the Past Caused by the Industrial Revolution

In the field of history, as in many other disciplines, the great explanations, the great schemata, are generally those marked by the movement of a pendulum: arguments swing from one extreme to the other, and then back again. In the case of the Industrial Revolution, ten to twenty years ago the pendulum had swung to the side arguing for the radical character of the Industrial Revolution, to the side arguing that it constituted a fundamental break with the past. Then others sought to prove what those studying the Industrial Revolution had never denied, namely, that the two to three centuries in Europe before the Industrial Revolution had already witnessed economic, technological, and cultural changes that served as foundations for the changes occurring in the eighteenth and nineteenth centuries. As a result, for some historians, and especially for historians of traditional societies, the notion of a sharp break with the past, of a revolution, was replaced by that of an evolution.

This shift from one explanatory schema to another was all the easier in that the proponents of the view that the Industrial Revolution marked a decisive break with the past had themselves always insisted on its gradual character. None of them had ever sought to present the caricature of a Europe going to sleep one night a traditional society to learn on awakening the next morning that an industrial revolution had just broken out. The revolutionary character of this event consisted rather in the combination of two facts: that a profound upheaval took place and that the time span involved was in historical terms very brief. What, after all, does less than a century mean, given the several thousand years of the history of civilization (not to mention the millions of years of human history)? Of course the Sophists succeeded in demonstrating that Achilles would never be able to overtake the tortoise, and one can also demonstrate that practically any break with the past is simply a sharp acceleration of a continuous process already at work. But is this really what the argument is about?

Although I shall not enter here into a discussion of the scale of the break with the past (or of the acceleration in the rate of evolution) in the various areas of socioeconomic life, there is no doubt that, where urbanization is concerned, the Industrial Revolution was a break (or acceleration) without precedent since the birth of urbanism. I shall look no further back than the last two thousand years, and I shall confine myself to data for the world at large, a procedure that will have the effect of perceptibly attenuating upheavals, inasmuch as the contemporary Third World has been affected only over the last fifty to sixty years.

From the year 0 to A.D. 1300, the number of city residents in the world at large doubled at most, and the level of urbanization increased by perhaps one or two points. From 1300 to 1800, a period for which data are more reliable, the level of urbanization remained approximately stable, which, since the total population of the world had doubled, means that the number of city residents doubled. But in less than two centuries—from 1800 to 1980—the number of city resi-

TABLE 31.2   Urban Population and the Number of
Large Cities in the World
(1300–1980)

	1300[a]	1500[a]	1700	1800	1900	1980
Urban population						
(in millions)	41	45	68	87	260	1,670
Level of urbanization						
(in percentage)	9.0	9.4	9.8	9.0	16.0	37.6
Number of large cities						
by population						
(in thousands)						
100–200	35	41	54	57	153	1,080
200–500	11	11	15	22	90	740
500–1,000	1	2	7	5	38	250
1,000–5,000	—	—	—	2	10	200
5,000–10,000	—	—	—	—	1	22
10,000 or more	—	—	—	—	—	5
Total of more than 100						
(thousands)	47	54	76	86	292	2,290

Sources: Calculations and estimates by the author; see the methodological appendix.
Note: The fact that these figures have been only slightly rounded off does not imply a
correspondingly small margin of error.
[a] Very approximate figures.

dents grew roughly twenty times and the level of urbanization rose
from 9% to 38%. The number of what in the context of traditional
societies may justly be considered large cities, namely those with
populations of more than 100,000, probably only doubled between
1300 and 1800, rising from 40–50 in 1300 to 80–90 in 1800. On the
other hand, the number of large cities increased by a factor of 30 between 1800 and 1985, reaching some 2,600 by about 1985.

During the millennia between the birth of urbanism and the onset
of the Industrial Revolution, there was from time to time in the world
a city that, over a few decades or centuries, had a population of more
than a million. By 1900, however, the world contained a dozen such
cities, and around 1980 there were more than 230 with a collective
population slightly higher than or close to that of the total world
population around 1700. With the upheavals that the Third World
will experience (and has been experiencing since 1950), matters will
change even more rapidly in the future. Around the year 2000 the
world will have some 430 cities with populations of more than one
million. But I shall leave the future for now, to return to it in the last
few pages of this concluding chapter. I shall look now more closely
into the break with the past caused by the Industrial Revolution.

A Break with the Past That Began in England

In the context of Western Europe, England in 1700 had only an average level of urbanization, city residents accounting for some 12% of the total population. By around 1840, on the other hand, the proportion was on the order of 40%, despite the absence of significant food imports. In the developed world as a whole (which can be considered a self-sufficient entity in terms of food production), urban population was one-third by around 1913 and one-half by around 1950. All of this was made possible by progress in agricultural productivity leading to enormous growth in the available surplus per agricultural worker. Evidence to this effect abounds. But there is no need for empirical analyses to prove the decisive part played by agriculture in this regard; the purest deductive reasoning will suffice. Assuming stability in agricultural productivity, progress in the industrial sphere alone could have increased the quantity of industrial products consumed per capita, but they could not have reduced the proportion of the work force required to provide food. And while they might have reduced the number of farm laborers needed to produce raw materials for industry, the extent of such production was marginal, representing only 4 to 7 percent of overall agricultural output. The only thing that might conceivably have changed this situation would have been the discovery—only recently emerging from the realm of science fiction—of techniques for manufacturing food from nonagricultural raw materials.

Paradoxically, the city does not seem to have played an important part either in unleashing the Industrial Revolution in England or in the first stages of its diffusion to the rest of the future developed world. A surprising fact in this early phase of the Industrial Revolution was that there were no traditional cities, especially large traditional cities, among those in which the Revolution developed. Apparently each great period in economic history creates its cities in the same way that it creates its entrepreneurs. To be sure, it is not true that the city had no hand whatever in the emergence of the major technological breakthroughs associated with the Industrial Revolution; but a look at the location of concerns in the sectors providing the driving force behind the initial phases of the Revolution reveals the overwhelming preponderance, if not of entirely rural districts, at least of regions with very small towns, on the borderline between the rural and the urban. Virtually no large traditional cities, and virtually no medium-cities either, figured among the sites in which the most important enterprises were located.

The fact that the traditional urban network contributed so little to the beginnings of the Industrial Revolution does not, however, prove as paradoxical as it may seem at first glance. A large number of factors readily account for it, first and foremost being energy. For a great many years, water mills provided the chief source of power for operating machines, and water was in most plentiful supply in the countryside. Furthermore, the fundamental technological innovation in the iron and steel industry—the shift to coal as the main source of energy—likewise encouraged the establishment of industrial plants in rural areas where they would be nearer the coalfields. To this factor should be added purely economic motives, such as the lower wage levels in rural districts and even in smaller towns, the lower cost of plant sites and buildings, and the absence of the sort of regulations that in many cities would have hindered the establishment of industrial concerns.

Even more interesting is the fact that those countries in which industrialization was soonest under way were almost all, to begin with, little urbanized, while those countries that lagged behind in industrialization were for the most part heavily urbanized. Though it may be impossible to conclude with absolute certainty that a high level of urbanization necessarily acted as a brake on economic development during the nineteenth century, I am nevertheless compelled to observe that a high level of urbanization generally tended to constitute a disadvantage.

An Increased Role for the City in Development

While cities may to begin with have gained more from the Industrial Revolution than they contributed to it, things soon changed. By gradually becoming a more independent variable in the developmental equation, technology reinforced the city's role as a center of the creation and diffusion of technological innovations. The transition took place sometime after 1810 and sometime before 1860. But this was not the only factor responsible for turning the cities of the West into a force for development. Among the others, mention should chiefly be made of the fact that the city promoted the monetarization of the economy, facilitated social mobility and a better match between the supply of and demand for skilled labor, and enlarged the market for industrial and agricultural production.

This last point in particular merits close attention. If during the first phase of the Industrial Revolution the city contributed little to agriculture, this changed during the next phases, especially beginning in the second half of the nineteenth century, when a whole host of technological innovations were developed which increased agricultural productivity. And in the great majority of cases these innovations originated in the cities. What is sometimes called the second agricultural revolution (the diffusion, beginning in the latter half of the nineteenth century, of mechanization and artificial fertilizers), owed a great deal to the cities. And one may speak of a third agricultural revolution, under way in the United States since 1940 and in Europe since 1950. This third agricultural revolution involved the more intensive use of pesticides and herbicides and the introduction of other technological advances leading to a complete reversal in the relative growth rates of agricultural and industrial productivity. While between the start of the Industrial Revolution and the period 1940–1950 industrial productivity increased on the average twice as fast as agricultural productivity, the opposite has been the case since. This increase resulted from the great growth in agricultural productivity rather than from a slower pace of growth in industrial productivity. (It should be noted in passing, however, that in some developed nations, notably the United States, a slowdown in growth in industrial productivity has in fact taken place over the last few years.)

The City, the Country, and Death: An Industrial Revolution That for a Long Time Did Not Change the Essentials

In the complex marriage between town and country, the flow of exchange has not involved merchandise alone, but people as well. The wealth of available evidence proves that, so far as Europe since the end of the Middle Ages is concerned, death struck city residents more than rural residents, especially the citizens of the larger cities. In the urban tribute to death, moreover, infants figured prominently. The more fragmentary information available about other times and other parts of the world indicate that this was a constant of traditional societies. This being the case, in order to grow, and often simply to maintain a stable population, the city had from the dawn of time to draw on the rural young.

Over nearly two centuries the Industrial Revolution brought no fundamental change in this domain. It was not until 1900–1930 that the gap between urban and rural mortality rates in developed nations was finally negligible. Moreover, the cities had anticipated by several decades the second demographic revolution (or if one prefers, the demographic transition), that is, simplifying somewhat, the voluntary and perceptible decline in fertility. This meant that despite the general decline in mortality, urban growth in the Western world continued to be provisioned to a considerable extent by people from the country—especially since, coupled with the absolute limit set by nature on per capita food consumption, advances in agricultural productivity reduced each year the number of people required to produce the West's daily bread. Among the causes for the persistence of disproportionate mortality rates in the cities, particular mention should be made of the living conditions of urban workers. During its initial stages the Industrial Revolution involved not only an unprecedented rise in output and productivity, but also an intensified exploitation of working people, who were compelled to work longer hours in a more oppressive and unwholesome environment and often to live in terrible slums, where the high housing density favored the spread of diseases.

European Colonization and the City

Before industrialization Western colonization was a factor of urbanization not only in Europe, where many commercial cities on the Atlantic coast owed much of their growth to direct or indirect relations with the colonies, but in the colonies themselves as well. The colonial domain was at this time limited to the New World, where on the ruins of the pre-Columbian cultures a new, Latin American society was erected that was more urbanized than its predecessors, owing to its highly outward-looking character. The production and exportation of precious metals and tropical products left sufficient revenues in Latin America to sustain an urban population greater and, on the average, probably richer than in Europe. By the start of the eighteenth century, 11 to 14 percent of the total population of Latin America lived in cities. This high level of urbanization was also favored by the sharp decline in the population, which enabled the new Latin American society to concentrate its crops on the most productive land. But we already meet here with an important feature of later forms of urbanization due to colonization after the Industrial Revolution, namely cities having very little industry, the colonizing countries reserving for themselves this source of exchange revenues.

The distinctly Western form of colonization truly began, however, only with the consequences of the Industrial Revolution. Before this Europe took its place in the long line of traditional colonial empires from Rome to China, from Persia to Ottoman Turkey. Moreover, in the context of the traditional world Europe was itself colonized for a longer time than it ever succeeded in colonizing other regions. In 1700 the population of Europe's colonial empire was only 10% of its own population, and the volume of its imports from these colonies, even including imports from future colonies, amounted to about 0.1 million metric tons. By contrast, on the eve of the Second World War the population of the colonial empire, both formal and informal, was 200% of the population of the West, and the volume of imports from colonial or semicolonial sources reached 70 million metric tons.

What was the impact of all of these traditional colonizations? Simplifying matters somewhat, one may suggest the following two rules. The first concerns colonized territories: in this case, colonization was an urbanizing factor in thinly urbanized regions and a deurbanizing factor in heavily urbanized regions. The second rule concerns colonizing powers: in this case the colonial adventure was almost always an urbanizing factor. The simplicity of these two rules is obviously disturbed by an array of specific conditions relating to both colonizing powers and their colonies.

In its initial phases, between 1800–1820 and 1850–80, modern colonization had two effects with opposing consequences from the point of view of cities. On the one hand, the process of deindustrialization brought about by the massive dumping of European manufactured products in the colonies prompted deurbanization. But on the other hand, by stimulating activity in trade and transportation the development of export crops induced urban growth. In the main, these two forces offset each other, but there were pronounced differences from one country to the next. In general, older societies—being both more urbanized and, within the limits of traditional economies, more industrialized—experienced a decline in urbanization, while the others tended instead to experience urban expansion. In the next phase of modern colonization, however, from 1850–80 to 1920–30, the urbanizing component won out. It did so all the more in that in some countries—chiefly India, China, Mexico, and Brazil—a process of reindustrialization got under way, only tentative as yet, but nevertheless creating jobs in urban areas. As a general rule, then, the lower the level of urbanization before colonial domination, the greater the extent to which colonization encouraged urban growth.

Then came the point at which events really took off: the phase of the urban explosion. But before discussing this last phase, I shall consider the paradoxical fact that in the nineteenth century, despite a declining standard of living, the level of urbanization remained stable and often even rose sharply. I shall also discuss the role of the city in reinforcing the negative effects of colonization.

In my view the paradox of the contradictory changes in the standard of living and in the level of urbanization during the first century of colonization may largely be explained by the more equal distribution of income among indigenous populations brought about in urban and rural areas alike by the loss of the power of traditional elites—an equalization at a lower level. The loss of power on the part of rural elites naturally favored a greater drain on agricultural surpluses by the cities; these surpluses stopped being absorbed by rural elites, who in the past had essentially consumed them at their place of origin. Here, then, is one way in which equalizing income levels made a higher level of urban population possible. The loss of power suffered by traditional urban elites, on the other hand, led to a reduction in the transfer of resources from rural areas to the cities. But this was more than offset by another aspect of the changes induced by colonization. The new European and indigenous elites quite naturally tended to prefer living in the cities. This meant that the combination of the diminishing standard of living in rural areas and the more equal distribution of income made possible an increased transfer of resources to the cities. Meanwhile, the falling standard of living in the cities made it possible for more people to share the growing surplus drawn from the countryside. This became all the easier because the colonial economies became more outward-looking, a larger proportion of the intermediary activities engendered by growing trade relations with the outside world being pursued in urban areas to the detriment of rural regions.

The City: An Ally of Colonization?

The city was unquestionably an objective ally of colonization, although it may have been an unwitting ally. It furnished the ideal penetration point for colonization and helped accentuate the negative impact of colonization on the economic and social structures of the future Third World countries. On the one side stood the city, child of colonialism; on the other, the traditional cities already in existence. I shall start with the former.

Colonial cities either were expressly conceived to further the economic exploitation of the territory or resulted from this exploitation. In each case, the cities were almost always located on the seaboard and became both the exit point for agricultural products and minerals exported from the interior and the entry point for manufactures from Europe. These cities also quickly became starting points for the network of railroads set up to facilitate the integration of the colonized territory into the world economy, that is, into the economy of the developed world. As geographers have observed, whereas rail networks in developed countries take the form of a spiderweb radiating outward from the capital city at the center, in the Third World they have the form of a funnel ending in a port. Colonial cities were also those registering the largest population growth and their growing population consumed manufactured goods and often agricultural products imported from the developed world. For since, in terms of weight and space, the volume of the Third World's exports was greater than that of its imports, there resulted what specialists call a return freight advantage—lower transport costs for imports. And the population of the new colonial cities also lived on the resources derived from the exportation of primary products.

I insist, however, that these were primary rather than raw materials. For one must take care not to perpetuate the myth that the colonies supplied a substantial proportion of the raw materials needed for the industrialization of developed nations. Until the eve of the Second World War, the developed world was self-sufficient in energy (even exporting more energy than it imported until the beginning of the thirties), and produced roughly 95 percent of the other raw materials it required. Dependence came only after 1946, even if Latin America began exporting raw materials very early. But exporting large amounts of raw materials does not necessarily mean having a considerable impact on the developed world. A country might export 100 percent of its mineral output to developed nations, and yet those materials might only represent 1 percent of the consumption of these developed nations.

Having closed this necessary digression, I shall return to the question of the negative effects of the city in colonized countries, considering now the part played by noncolonial cities. The traditional urban network of Third World countries also reinforced the negative impact of colonization, essentially through deindustrialization and the adoption of forms of consumption favoring imports. Whenever traditional industry succeeded in surviving fairly well, it was almost always in rural regions, far from urban centers. Certainly traditional cities did not adopt as rapidly as colonial cities patterns of consumption modelled on those in the West. But the lag time was not great; the city provided the ideal medium for the transmission of new patterns of consumption.

An Urban Explosion Unprecedented in Both Its Scale and Its Modalities

Since 1920–1930, the Third World has recorded a rise in urban population whose speed is without precedent in world history. Around 1930 some 150–160 million people lived in cities in the Third World; in 1985, there were 1 to 1.2 bllion. And despite the unparalleled increase in overall population, the level of urbanization went up from 12% to 30%.

The term explosion (or inflation) is thus entirely justified both by the scale of the phenomenon and above all by its nature. For this rapid increase in the number of city dwellers and in the proportion of the total population concentrated in urban centers has taken place virtually without economic development, without industrialization. More serious still, it has been accompanied by no increase in agricultural productivity. All of this completely justifies the expressions coined to describe this form of urbanization: cities before their time, hyperurbanization, overurbanization, urban hypertrophy, and so on.

But how do we explain this urban growth? It is essentially one of the elements of underdevelopment. I just said that the level of urbanization has increased despite the unprecedented rise in total population. Has this rise in total population been responsible? Although it is not the only guilty party, it is certainly the principal one. The unparallelled increase in population, the demographic explosion stemming from the intrusion of Western medical and paramedical technologies, has led to a rise in the density of occupation of agricultural land. Every thirty years the number of people on the land doubles. Rural young people are not only attracted by the city, they are also rejected by the land. To this potent cause of rural exodus, others have been added. The chief among them is the large disparity in wage levels in favor of the cities. This disparity is considerably wider now than it was in the West during the first stages of its urbanization; it results from the dual character of Third World economies and from inequality in the application of social regulations. There is also the rapid extension of education in rural areas, which creates a pronounced generation gap and instills values closely modeled on those of a society altogether unlike the Third World, and even more unlike rural life in the Third World. Finally, whereas in the nineteenth century the cities of the West, owing to the disproportionately high mortality rates in urban areas, acted as a brake on their own growth, Third World cities, owing to the introduction of Western medicine, sanitation, and so forth, have experienced rapid natural population growth since the early fifties. I shall close the list of contributing factors here, since it already more than suffices to explain the causes of the urban explosion.

The Consequences of the Urban Explosion

While man does not live by bread (or rice or manioc) alone, this does not mean he can live without it. Today, owing to the fact that agriculture has stagnated at a very low level of productivity, developing market economies (the barbarous term used by the United Nations to designate all Third World countries other than China and three other countries with planned economies) suffer from an enormous food deficit amounting, in the case of grain, to around 77 million metric tons, that is, enough to supply two-thirds of the total number of calories needed to feed almost one-half of all city dwellers. This grain originates in the West and could be replaced only in part by a reconversion of the land currently devoted to export crops in the Third World—land that in any case brings in more financial receipts now than it would were it sown with grain. On the eve of the Second World War, on the other hand, the Third World still produced a food surplus. This by itself suggests that the sharp surge in urban population growth has not sufficed to bring about a sufficient change in the technology for producing food crops.

As I shall show, the fact that the urban explosion has failed to have a positive influence on agriculture is not the sole change caused by underdevelopment in the relations between the city and the countryside. Indeed the food deficit is far from being the only negative result of the urban explosion. One inevitable consequence of urbanization without development is the deficit in urban jobs. During the sixties, urban unemployment reached critical proportions because of the high levels registered and because it affected so many young people, and in many cases educated young people. Another serious consequence has been excessive growth in the tertiary (or service) sector, a phenomenon weighing heavily on the efficiency of the economy as a whole. Finally, there are the shantytowns. Even though there is currently a tendency to downplay their negative aspects, one cannot really regard them as positive. This same revision of the problem of development has induced some to attribute a more positive role to the informal sector, a sector resulting from underdevelopment. A more positive role, or a less negative one. But as I suggested earlier, while every cloud may have a silver lining, walking in the rain is not the best way of solving the problem.

The City in the Third World: The Loss of Its Functions as a Factor in Development

Practically all of the qualities that made the cities of the West in the nineteenth century (and in traditional societies in general) a factor in economic development do not play that role in the Third World. We have already seen that the city has failed to have any significant beneficial effects on agricultural technology. Let's now see what has happened in the other principal sectors of the economy.

Owing to the extent to which population is now concentrated in urban areas, Third World cities favor imports over local production, whether manufactured products or agricultural products. Roughly the same thing has happened where the monetarization of the economy is concerned: a factor in development in the Western world, it encourages imports in the Third World. Likewise, the complexity of present-day technology and the enormous gap between developed countries and the Third World in terms of the available supply of information, scientists, and technicians have considerably reduced the city's function as an agent of innovation and the diffusion of innovation.

To these reversals of the traditionally positive effects of the city should further be added the unfavorable impact of the negative consequences of overurbanization. I have already drawn attention to the most important of these, in particular unemployment and over-employment in services. Another direct consequence of the urban explosion is the great size of Third World cities. Today too great a proportion of the urban population lives in cities of excessive size—cities in which the advantages, especially the economic advantages, of large size have vanished, but in which the disadvantages (pollution, crime, congestion, noise, social isolation, poor housing, etc.) have reached dramatic proportions.

By contrast, the greater social mobility that goes with city life makes a positive contribution in Third World cities as well as in Western ones. The same applies to education, to which the city's contribution has always been fundamental, and this despite the fact that, owing to both its modalities and its pace, education has had more negative than positive effects in rural areas. There is, finally, one other field in which, in the Third World, urbanization constitutes a positive factor tending to promote development: the reduction of fertility. To the extent that slowing down the rate of demographic growth represents, if not a precondition, at least a contribution to genuine economic development, the city has a part to play. For there is no doubt that the urban way of life induces a reduction in fertility among city dwellers and stimulates the diffusion of this behavior throughout society as a whole.

As I said at the end of the preceding chapter, even setting aside those of its consequences that have perhaps been too hastily judged negative, the urban explosion has not made Third World cities a factor favoring development. The disadvantages are many and powerful, the advantages few and slight. It is true that adding the debits and credits and drawing up a balance sheet has not here the simplicity, much less the rigor, of classical accounting procedures. In this case, however, what doubts remain once the negative balance has been established are highly marginal. Urbanization in the Third World has certainly not facilitated development. Placed in the context of existing national and international structures, the current level of urbanization constitutes a severe handicap much more than an asset for the economic development the Third World so badly needs.

And What Will Tomorrow Bring?

Tomorrow the urban problem will be one of the major preoccupations of humanity and will be a tragic problem in the Third World. Assuming no ecological catastrophe (and nobody wants one), and no important policy change (and many have recommended one)—neither event seeming at all likely—within the next generation there will be a massive increase in the number of city dwellers in the Third World. Over the next thirty years, some 1.0–1.5 billion city dwellers will join the 1.1 billion in the Third World around 1985. This increase represents an urban population two to three times greater than that of the entire world at the end of World War II, when the urban population was the result of a process of urbanization extending over several centuries.

I shall examine the figures in table 31.3 in a little more detail with regard to the regional aspect and the possibility of bias. Concerning the regional aspect, the future urban explosion will be strongest in Africa. The number of city dwellers will increase by almost a factor of three between 1980 and 2000 and by a factor of seven between 1980 and 2025. By contrast, the explosion will be most moderate in Latin America: urban population there will grow by a factor of three between 1980 and 2025. This difference largely results from existing levels of urbanization, only 26% of the population of Africa living in cities around 1980 as against 63% in Latin America. But the different levels of urbanization do not explain everything, for although its level of urbanization is near that of Africa, Asia will have a much more

TABLE 31.3   Projections of the Urban Population
and Levels of Urbanization of the World
(1980–2025)

	Urban Population (in millions)			Level of Urbanization (%)		
	1980	2000	2025	1980	2000	2025
Third World	905	1,781	3,621	28	36	52
Africa	106	288	609	24	35	38
Latin America	231	410	640	64	75	82
Asia (market economy)	356	745	1,669	25	34	57
Third World (market economy)	695	1,445	2,923	31	41	55
Asia (planned economy)	210	336	698	20	25	44
Developed Countries	762	917	1,067	65	66	71
Europe	321	363	393	66	71	75
USSR	161	214	262	61	66	71
North America	162	194	232	64	65	67
Japan	91	102	108	78	79	82
Others[a]	27	44	72	59	64	70
World	1,667	2,698	4,688	38	44	57

Sources: Derived from United Nations (1986a). Figures have been adjusted in order to make them comparable with those presented elsewhere in this book.
Note: The fact that these figures have been only slightly rounded off does not imply a correspondingly small margin of error.
[a] Australia, New Zealand, and South Africa.

modest urban explosion: between 1980 and 2000 the number of city dwellers in Asia will increase by a factor of 2.1 (as against 2.7 in Africa). This is accounted for chiefly by the likelihood of slower total population growth in Asia.

And what of the possibility of bias? It goes without saying that every projection contains an element of uncertainty, and the further the projection's horizon reaches, the greater this element becomes. This is why I insisted at the start on using a scale of one generation. Granting this, what would be the likely direction of the bias in these figures, which are based on the most recent projections of the United Nations? In all likelihood these figures (at any rate those for the year 2000) contain a bias on the side of underestimation. The reality risks being even more dramatic than the projections suggest, urban growth proving even more rapid than table 31.3 indicates. These forecasts postulate a perceptible slowdown in the growth of the level of urbanization as early as the first decades after 1980, and this at a time when the level of urbanization for most of the Third World will still be under 35%. Even though the comparison is very delicate and in part arbitrary, it may be noted that in the Western world a slowdown of this sort has in general taken place only when the level of urbanization has reached 40–50%. Thus between 1980 and 2000, there will be 1.1 billion more city dwellers rather than 1 billion more, and between 2000 and 2025, 2 billion more rather than 1.9 billion more. But in this case the degree of uncertainty is too great.

How are the problems of jobs, food, and housing for so vast a number of additional city people going to be solved when the solutions for these problems today are so imperfect? The essential solutions are a slowdown in demographic growth and a rise in agricultural productivity. But this is easier said than done, particularly given the sociopolitical factors in the situation.

There is another important facet contributing to the seriousness of the urban problems looming on the horizon of the year 2000 in the Third World: the heavy concentration of city residents in large cities and the emergence of many very large cities, of giant cities. I shall take a look at this horizon. And in order to reduce the margin of uncertainty, I shall not go beyond the year 2000, and I shall exclude China, whose contemporary data are less reliable and whose future is more uncertain despite (or rather because of) the more voluntary character of its urban policies.

There are two projections on the growth of Third World cities between now and the year 2000: one done by the Population Division of the Secretariat of the United Nations and the other by me (see table 31.4). It may be noted that the two do not completely agree. Even though my projection was inevitably less complex, I believe it has a good chance of coming closer to the truth. Most of the differences stem from different postulates concerning the slowdown in the growth of urban population once a certain size has been reached. My hypotheses forecast a sharp slowdown, even stagnation, in urban growth beyond a certain threshold (in particular beyond a population of ten million) while the United Nations forecasts few inflections in the curve of population growth as a function of the size of cities. (This was even more true in previous United Nations forecasts.)

Even if one accepts my projections, one observes a perceptible reinforcement of the already-excessive concentration of urban population in very great cities. In 1980, cities with populations of more than a million represented 33% of overall urban population. Around the year 2000 the proportion will be 49 percent. In absolute terms, the population of this urban size class will grow from 300 to 870 million. As for cities with populations of more than 5 million, their number will increase from 17 to around 46 and their population from 120 to 400 million (whereas around 1950 it was only 16 million).

Now it appears fairly clear that cities of this size involve negative conditions from the point of view both of general living conditions and of employment or economic development. The current modalities of this serious problem were discussed earlier (see chapters 21 and

TABLE 31.4   Projections by Population (in Millions) of Large Cities
of Third World Market Economies
(1980–2000)

	Population of Cities			
	1 to 5	5 to 10	10 or more	Total
Number of cities				
in 1980	90	14	3	107
in 2000				
Author's estimates				
(1977)	223	32	14	269
United Nations				
estimates				
(1975)	221	24	19	264
(1980)	229	22	20	271
(1986)	—	20	17	—
Population of cities				
in 1980	177	91	33	301
in 2000				
Author's estimates				
(1977)	472	203	199	874
United Nations				
estimates				
(1975)	451	143	320	914
(1980)	451	138	314	903
(1986)	—	127	242	—

Sources: Bairoch (1977a); United Nations (1975a, 1980, 1986b).
Note: The fact that these figures have been only slightly rounded off does not imply a correspondingly small margin of error.

30). There is little chance that over the coming years the negative features of these large cities will improve at all perceptibly. These large cities (cities of more than one to two million people) will continue to be more unfavorable for economic development than smaller ones, and the lives of people in them will continue to be much worse.

To this will be further added the problem of giant cities. Even using my estimates, the number of cities with populations of more than 10 million in the Third World will grow from 3 in 1980 to 14 in 2000 (to 17 according to the United Nations). And while I do not believe that in the year 2000 Mexico City, which will then be the largest city in the Third World (and in the world generally), will reach the population of 26–28 million forecast by the United Nations, even with a population of, say, 23 to 25 million one may expect problems of unprecedented scale. In developed countries cities reached populations on the order of 10 million at a very advanced stage of development. Thus New York, the first city to have a population of 10 million, passed this stage around 1927–29, at a time when the per capita GNP of the United States was on the order of $1,700 (in U.S. prices and dollars); London reached this size around 1949–50 at a time when United Kingdom's per capita GNP was around $1,400. When Tokyo reached this size around 1966–68, per capita GNP was $1,600. The cities of the Third World have reached or will reach this stage with a per capita GNP on the order of $250 to $500, which considerably restricts the chances of correcting the negative factors resulting from their size.

Thus the expansion of these giant cities will add a new dimension to the almost inextricable problems mentioned earlier. How will the problems of employment, food, housing, transportation, sanitation, and education for this enormous additional mass of city dwellers be solved?

The developed world, on the other hand, will face the sort of problems that go with wealth. Owing to the high levels of urbanization, however, these problems will affect three-quarters of the developed world's population. In fact, there is only one essential problem, as well as a question. The question is related to the solution of the problem, and is simple: what form will the city of the future take? The rapid technological changes of the end of the seventies (especially in electronics), the growing importance of multinationals, the accelerating decline of industrial employment, the rapid increase in employment in the service sector, the new attitude toward the city on the part of a large number of city residents: all this (and much more) will have consequences for the city of tomorrow.

What is certain is that the city of tomorrow, like that of yesterday, will keep a large reserve of individuality for no other reason than that of its history, which people seek everywhere to preserve; but also individuality because of regional factors. Let me cite two recent articles. When two researchers from an old industrial region were asked about the future of their cities, they noted with some anguish that "new industries tend to avoid for environmental reasons this type of city from an old industrial region" (Bruyelle and Dezert, 1983). When an American researcher was asked that same question, he argued that "spatial hierarchies of cities in advanced countries are a function of the location of the parts of organizational hierarchies. These latter are increasingly dominated by multinational, multilocational conglomerates, which constitute an economic and political configuration which may be defined as a corporation." He also argues that, paradoxically, advanced countries are "moving towards a self-service rather than a service economy" (Simmie, 1983).

How can the city be made more habitable? This is the essential problem facing the West. The solution has been delayed by the automobile, which has so largely contributed to undermining urban life. But these are the kinds of problems that go with wealth, that is, these are problems that can be solved if one takes the trouble to analyze them correctly. The technologies available today and certainly those that will be available tomorrow could solve all of the West's difficulties, provided the will is there. Let me give an example I take particularly to heart. It would suffice to prohibit in five to ten years the use of all but electric vehicles and to impose a speed limit of twenty to thirty kilometers per hour to make the city street once again what it should never have stopped being: a meeting place rather than the danger zone it is today. Each year, in the developed world alone, more than ten thousand children lose their lives crossing the street. The number of those injured is ten times that figure. And the corresponding numbers for the elderly are twice as high again. Yet even this is the sort of problem only the rich have to deal with, trivial beside the drama in which the Third World is engaged.

Appendix:
Methodology and Sources

Some of the data series used in the present study have never been discussed in publications. It is therefore necessary to give here at least a minimal explanation of the methodology and sources.

1. General Approach

The processing of data on urban population, with regard to both the number of cities and their population, was conducted in two very distinct stages, depending on the period and the regions involved. For recent data, I obviously relied on the statistics given in census records and, in some cases indicated in the text, on syntheses done under the auspices of the United Nations. My use of these data requires no methodological justification. But this approach is only possible for the period beginning in the 1850s in Europe and other developed regions and for the period beginning in the 1950s in the rest of the world.

It was therefore necessary to turn to other sources and methods. I decided to assemble what may be described as a data bank on the population of cities. In other words, I tried to gather together, for as many cities as possible, all available estimates relating to their population at a certain number of selected dates. I had already done this for Europe from 1600 on (see Bairoch 1976c). For Third World market economies between 1900 and 1950, a similar study was conducted under my direction by a student in the Department of Economic History at the University of Geneva (see Johannot 1977).

But I hasten to render unto Caesar that which is Caesar's. Indeed, had it not been for the publication of the investigations of Chandler and Fox (1974), I would never have done the research reported here, at least not in its present audacious form. Even though the urban universe with which they deal proved in practice to be incomplete in many cases, I wish to express here my admiration and thanks for the pioneering work they have done in this field. Given, moreover, that their work represents the first study of its kind, assembling the available population estimates for 1,800 cities throughout the world between 1360 B.C. and A.D. 1850, supplemented in many instances by estimates done by the authors themselves, based on indirect evidence, the gaps in Chandler and Fox's work were scarcely to be avoided.

The basic task of the two studies mentioned above was, starting from the data provided by Chandler and Fox, to enlarge the list of cities, supplementing and where necessary revising some of their estimates using sources more recent than those available to Chandler and Fox or sources they overlooked. For the purposes of this book, I decided to revise my data completely on the basis of additional investigations intended to enlarge further still the number of cities included and to supplement the data for them. This project was conducted relatively in depth for the following regions and periods: Europe from 800 to 1800 (ten periods), Latin America from 1600 to 1950 (nine periods), Africa from 1900 to 1950 (five periods), and the larger countries of Asia from 1500 to 1950 (nine periods).

But given the current state of data and research, it is impossible in the case of most countries to assemble figures on urban population sufficiently complete to give a valid indication of the population of all cities with populations of more than five thousand, the standard of definition used here (see chapters 8 and 13). I believe that after the minor adjustments described below, my data bank provides enough accurate information for a valid assessment of the population of cities with populations of more than twenty thousand for most of the countries. (Work currently in progress will enable me within a few years to lower this population limit to eight thousand, at least for Europe.) Consequently, to establish the population of cities of five to twenty thousand people another approach was needed. With all of this in view, I give below the relevant supplementary information regarding my data bank (the number of cities and their populations), the methods used to estimate total urban population, and the figures I have used for total populations. I shall then offer assessments of the margins of error surrounding my data.

2. Cities: Their Number and Population

Even though the starting point for collecting data on each part of the world was the same, the degree to which each set of data had to be treated and the form this treatment took varied from case to case. I shall therefore present the information relevant to each region separately. Most of the emphasis will, however, fall on Europe and Latin America.

2.1 Europe

For Europe the basic aim was to assemble data for all cities with populations of five thousand or more around 1800 and, further, for all cities reaching a size of five thousand people or more during any preceding period. In order to avoid duplications due to changes in name, geographical location (longitude and latitude) was also noted. I drew up this list of cities by systematically consulting the various sources likely to furnish the requisite information: census records, urban studies (and in particular studies in urban history), encyclopedias, geographical dictionaries, and so forth, and of course, the book by Chandler and Fox. To the same end, another approach was to look into lists relating to what may be regarded as specifically urban functions: for instance, the list of all university towns from the twelfth century to the fourteenth century, the list of bishoprics and other religious institutions indicating the existence of a city, the list of fairs, and so on. The rule here was to sin rather by excess than by omission.

The next step (though these tasks were, of course, carried out in conjunction with each other) consisted of supplementing the population figures I came up with. This necessitated the consultation of a very wide range of documents, among which, for obvious reasons, urban histories predominated. These sources may be grouped under three headings according to the amount of information they yielded. First and foremost, I repeat, came the book by Chandler and Fox, followed by a certain number of works providing figures for a fairly large number of cities. Here is the list of works furnishing data for at least eight cities:

Bickel, W. *Bevölkerungsgeschichte und Bevölkerungspolitik der Schweiz seit dem Ausgang des Mittelalters.* Zurich, 1947.

Biraben, J.-N. *Les hommes et la peste en France et dans les pays européens et méditerranéens.* Vol. 1, Paris, 1975; vol. 2, Paris, 1976.

Carter, F. W. "Urban Development in the Western Balkans: 1200–1800." In Carter, F. W., ed., *An Historical Geography of the Balkans.* London, 1977, pp. 148–95.

Centre Aixois d'Etudes et de Recherches sur le XVIIIe Siècle. *La ville au XVIIIe siècle.* Colloquium held in Aix-en-Provence, 29 April to 1 May 1973. Aix-en-Provence, 1975.

Dictionnaire géographique universel. 10 volumes. Paris, 1823–33.

Encyclopaedia Britannica. 13th ed. London, 1926.

Fedor, T. S. *Patterns of Urban Growth in the Russian Empire during the Nineteenth Century.* Chicago, 1975.

Helin, E. *La démographie de Liège aux XVIIe et XVIIIe siècles.* Brussels, 1963.

Historisk Statistik för Sverige. Vol. 1. 2d ed. Stockholm, 1969.

Hoffmann, A. *Österreichisches Städtebuch.* 4 vols. Vienna, 1968–76.

Keyser, E. *Deutsches Städtebuch.* 5 vols. Stuttgart, 1939–74.

Lot, F. *Recherches sur la population et la superficie des cités remontant à la période gallo-romaine.* 3 vols. Paris, 1945–53.

Mitchell, B. R. *Abstract of British Historical Statistics.* Cambridge, 1962.

Mols, R. *Introduction à la démographie historique des villes d'Europe du XIVe au XVIIIe siècle.* 3 vols. Gembloux-Louvain, 1954–56.

Patten, J. *English Towns, 1500–1700.* London, 1978.

Pouthas, C. H. *La population française pendant la première moitié du XIXe siècle.* Paris, 1956.

Russell, J. C. "Late Ancient and Medieval Population," *Transactions of the American Philosophical Society* n.s. vol. 48, part 3, June 1958, pp. 1–152.

———*Medieval Regions and Their Cities.* Newton Abbot, 1972.

Schaml, H., ed. *Patterns of European Urbanisation since 1500.* London, 1981.

Schowers, V. V. *World Facts and Figures.* New York, 1979.

Vincent, B. "Récents travaux de démographie historique en Espagne (XIVe–XVIIe siècles)," *Annales de démographie historique 1977.* Paris, 1977, pp. 463–91.

Vries, J. de. "Patterns of Urbanization in Pre-Industrial Europe, 1500–1800." Schmal, H., ed., *Patterns of European Urbanisation since 1500.* London, 1981, pp. 77–109.

Wolff, P., ed. *Guide international d'histoire urbaine.* Vol. 1: Europe. Paris, 1977.

Finally, a few hundred other texts relating to individual cities (or a very small number of cities) were consulted in order to verify or supplement the data.

By the time I began the statistical analysis serving as the basis for the data for the original French version of this book, the data bank for Europe contained about nine hundred cities. For cities with populations of more than twenty thousand (the only ones surveyed by Chandler and Fox), I generally increased the number by more than 15%, and by a much larger percentage even than that for cities for which population figures were available. I have continued my research, and at the time of the revision of the text and figures for this translation (the middle of 1986) the data bank contained close to two thousand cities. It seems probable that the larger data bank will confirm what I have said in this book about the likelihood that the levels of urbanization are actually closer to the upper limits of the brackets presented than to the middle of those brackets.

2.2 Latin America

For the period 1900–1950 the basic source for Latin America was the study of Johannot (1977); for earlier periods it was the study of Chandler and Fox. As was the case for Europe, however, I had to do supplementary research to enlarge both the number of cities and the body of demographic information relating to them. For much of this research I used the same sources as for Europe (historical and geographic dictionaries, encyclopedias). But mention should also be made of the two following works: P. A. Gerhard, *A Guide to the Historical Geography of New Spain*, Cambridge, 1972; and R. M. Morse, ed., *The Urban Development of Latin America, 1750–1920*, Stanford, 1971. Finally, I consulted some studies on the economic history of Latin American countries.

The omissions in Chandler and Fox's book are more substantial for Latin America than for Europe. Thus for 1850 Chandler and Fox's estimate of the number of cities with populations of more than twenty thousand represents only around 50% of the cities of this size probably in existence during the periods covered by their study. Most of their omissions, however, are in the lower fringe of urban sizes.

2.3 Other Regions

For other regions the research I did to supplement the basic sources (Johannot, and Chandler and Fox) was on the whole less thorough for other regions than for Latin America. It still enabled me to get a better grasp of the reality, since the gaps in my basic sources were probably fairly close to those for Latin America. It is worth noting in this connection that these omissions largely account for Grauman's underestimation of the level of urban population (see table 31.1), for Grauman essentially relied on Chandler and Fox for larger cities.

3. Estimates of Urban Populations

I considered, then, that after minor adjustments, my data bank provided statistics that could be regarded as valid for cities with populations of more than twenty thousand. The minor adjustment consisted of estimating, at the level of each country or region, the probable number of cities with populations of more than twenty thousand that were omitted. Obviously this correction is largely arbitrary, being based on a personal assessment of the likely scale of these omissions, an assessment rooted in the repeated experience of successive improvements in my data bank. But these corrections were fairly minor. For example, in the case of Europe except Russia, I added seven cities (3.7%) for 1800, an addition confirmed by a more complete treatment of the data, give or take one city. Similarly, I added five cities (4.3%) for 1600, and so forth.

The problem was greater in estimating the number and population of cities of five to twenty thousand people on the basis of data relating to cities of more than twenty thousand people. As is currently done in the field, I applied Davis's Law (see chapter 9), but did calculations designed to adapt this law to the urban structures likely to have existed in the periods and societies concerned. I tested the hypothesis that the ratio of overall urban population in cities of 5,000–20,000 people to that in cities of more than 20,000 people was more stable than that to cities of 20,000–50,000 people. The results of this test were negative: in statistical terms, there is a closer relation between the ratio of overall urban population in cities of 5,000–20,000 people to that in cities of 20,000–50,000 people, the coefficients of variation in the ratios being perceptibly lower in this case for all periods for which such calculations were possible. I postulated that in addition to growth over time one would find at the start of any period of urban expansion a pyramid with a wider base. For Europe I ultimately found the following ratios (the relation between the population of cities of 5,000–20,000 people to that of cities of 20,000–50,000 people): for the year 800, 2.1; for 1000, 2.2; for 1300, 2.1; for 1500 and 1600, 2.2; for 1700 and 1750, 2.1; and for 1800, 2.15. I adapted these ratios for other regions, taking into account their socioeconomic and geographic situations.

For this English edition I was also able to use revised figures for the developed countries in the nineteenth century (Bairoch and Goertz, 1986).

4. Total Population

For non-European countries, as a general rule I used the most recent estimates available (see below), making some minor adjustments in a few cases. For Europe, on the other hand, for which my research on urban population was more elaborate, I tried to prepare a more plausible data series.

Concerning data for periods after 1750, which served as my starting point, see P. Bairoch, *Commerce extérieur et développement économique de l'Europe au XIXe siècle*, Paris and the Hague, 1976b (see especially section F of the methodological appendix, "Population de l'Europe par décennie," pp. 327–28, and p. 24 for the data).

For the data for the period 1500 to 1750, I have for years now systemati-

	Clark	Russell	Mols	Durand	McEvedy & Jones	Biraben	Bairoch
200	(40)	—	—	(45)	33	44	48
500	(18)	23	—	—	—	30	36
800	23	(27)	—	—	25	25	32
1000	32	32	—	35	33	30	38
1300	—	(59)	—	—	67	70	75
1340	77	63	—	—	—	74	79
1400	—	(43)	—	—	48	52	55
1500	60	—	69	65	65	67	75
1600	70	—	84	—	80	89	95
1700	86	—	92	—	94	95	102
1750	98	—	—	127	107	111	120

Sources: Clark (1977), p. 64; Russell (1972b), p. 36; Mols (1974), p. 28; Durand (1977), p. 259; McEvedy and Jones (1978), pp. 18, 75, and 79; Biraben (1979), p. 16. For author's estimates, see text.

Note: The figures in parentheses are interpolations based on data provided by the same author, but for different periods.

Russia is defined here within its frontiers in the nineteenth century.

cally collected all new estimates as they have been published. I wish to thank here my colleague and friend, A. Perrenoud, for the many sources he has drawn to my attention that might otherwise have escaped me. The results I have obtained differ from the global estimates made recently for Europe. It should be noted, however, that these estimates do come close to my own figures when compared with the global estimates formerly available. (See table A.1, where the series are presented according to the chronological order of their publication.) The fact that my own estimates were systematically higher than the others (by about 10%) did not surprise me. I have observed, indeed, that almost all figures for population levels in individual countries, when subjected to serious revision, have increased.

For population growth before 1500 I adopted the general trends shown by the data series of Biraben and Russell. I have modified these figures, however, based partly on the difference observed for later periods and partly on my own estimates of urban population and general information on the growth in levels of urbanization. I believe that I have reduced a little in this way the margin of error surrounding the data. But this does not mean that these margins have become negligible. (See table 8.1 for my estimate of the margins of error involved.) A great deal of work done by many researchers concentrating on each country is needed here. It seems likely that several decades will pass before somewhat better figures will become available, especially for the periods before 1700.

5. Margins of Error in the Figures for Urban Population

Obviously the margins of error given here are only estimates. For them to be complete it would be necessary in each case not only to distinguish the margin of error surrounding data on the number of cities from that surrounding data on their population, but also to distinguish between the margins of error for each of the different urban population categories. That would take me too far and would give a false impression of precision. That is why I shall only indicate the general situation.

As a rule the margin of error surrounding population must be considered greater than that surrounding the number of cities. And the larger the cities, the narrower the margin of error surrounding their number. At the level of population, the differences in margins of error according to population category are smaller. This is because, although the data for larger cities are more reliable, the larger number of small towns probably compensates for the greater margins of error. Finally, the margins of error for developed countries are narrower than those for Third World countries; and within the Third World, the margins of error are narrower for Latin America than for the other regions.

I shall leave aside the data I did not calculate (developed countries since 1850, the Third World since 1950). At the level of the population of cities with populations of more than 20,000, treatment of the data by successive stages has enabled me to verify that the margin of error surrounding global figures is relatively narrow. This is easily explained. While the margin of error may be very great at the level of individual cities, the large number of cities and the fact that the estimates are in the great majority of cases independent of each other make it probable that there is a statistical compensation for the margins of error. For data for developed countries in 1800 and the Third World in 1930, I estimate that the margin of error surrounding the population of cities with populations of more than 20,000 is very small: probably less than 5%. By contrast, for cities with populations of 5,000–20,000, where estimates chiefly rely on Davis's Law (in amended form), the margin should be on the order of 8–10%, leading to a margin of error of 6–8% for urban population as a whole. For developed countries and Latin American countries in 1700 (and this probably holds for the rest of the Third World for 1850–1900), the margin of error for cities with populations of more than 20,000 seems to be a little more than 5%, and for other cities on the order of 10–15%, making for urban population as a whole a margin of error of not more than 10%. The margin of error for cities with populations of 5,000–20,000 in earlier periods is scarcely larger. For larger cities, on the other hand, it was probably larger, owing to the nature of the data and the smaller number of cities involved. Globally the following very approximate margins of error may be proposed: for Europe around 1300 and 1500, about 10 %; and for the rest of the world, 15–20%; for Europe in the year 1000, 15%, and in the year 800, 20%; for the rest of the world before 1300, 20–25%.

Classified Bibliography

In this bibliography I present, in separate sections for the specific problems dealt with in the book, the principal titles likely to help readers wishing to enlarge their knowledge of these problems. For a list of all works cited in the text and tables, see References (p. 541).

Even though the bibliography contains a large number of titles (including some published after the completion of this book), it must not be regarded as exhaustive. An exhaustive bibliography would contain tens of thousands of titles, owing to the enormous number of studies devoted to individual cities or to specific urban questions.

The sections are as follows:
1. General History of Urbanization and Its Links with the economy
2. From the Birth of Urbanism to the Beginnings of the Great Civilizations
3. Traditional Europe from the Fifth Century to the Eighteenth Century
4. The City and Development in the Western World
5. Non-European Societies before Colonization
6. Urbanism and the Third World

Sections 2 through 5 correspond to the first three parts of this book and sections 5 and 6 to the fourth part.

1. General History of Urbanization and Its Links with the Economy

Abrams, P., and Wrigley, E. A., eds. *Towns in Societies: Essays in Economic History and Historical Sociology*. Cambridge, 1978.

Bairoch, P. *Taille des villes, conditions de vie et développement économique*. Paris, 1977.

Berry, B. J. L. "City Size Distribution and Economic Development." *Economic Development and Cultural Change* 9, no. 4, part 1 (July 1961): pp. 573–87.

Braudel, F. *The Structures of Everyday Life*. London, 1982.

Castells, M. *The Urban Question: A Marxist Approach*. London, 1977.

Chandler, T., and Fox, G. *3,000 Years of Urban Growth*. New York, 1974.

Childe, V. G. "The Urban Revolution." *The Town Planning Review* 21, no. 1 (1950): 3–17.

Collins, W., ed. *Cities in a Larger Context*. Athens, Ga., 1980.

Davis, K. *World Urbanization, 1950–1970*. Vol. 1, Berkeley, 1969; vol. 2, Berkeley, 1972.

Duby, G. (under the direction of). *Histoire de la France urbaine*. 5 vols. Paris, 1980–83.

Dyos, H. J., ed. *The Study of Urban History*. London, 1968.

Finley, M. I. "The Ancient City: From Fustel de Coulanges to Max Weber and Beyond." *Comparative Studies in Society and History* 19 (1977): 305–27.

Galantay, E. Y. *New Towns: Antiquity to the Present*. New York, 1975.

Gappert, G., and Knight, R. V., eds. *Cities in the 21st Century*. Beverly Hills, Calif., 1982.

Golden, H. H. *Urbanization and Cities*. Lexington, Ky., 1981.

Griffeth, R., and Thomas, C. G., eds. *The City-State in Five Cultures*. Santa Barbara, Calif., 1981.

Gutkind, E. A. *International History of City Development*. 8 vols. New York, 1964–72.

Handlin, O., and Burchard, J., eds. *The Historian and the City*. Cambridge, Mass., 1963.

Harvey, D. *The Urbanization of Capital: Studies in the History and Theory of Capitalism and Urbanization*. Baltimore, 1985.

"Histoire et urbanisation." *Annales, E.S.C.*. Special issue, 25th year, no. 4. July–August 1970.

Holton, R. J. *Cities, Capitalism and Civilization*. London, 1986.

Hoselitz, B. F. "Generative and Parasitic Cities." *Economic Development and Cultural Change* 3, no. 3 (April 1955): 278–94.

Jacobs, J. *The Economy of Cities*. New York, 1969. Harmondsworth, 1970.

———. *Cities and the Wealth of Nations: Principles of Economic Life*. Harmondsworth, 1984.

Jefferson, M. "The Law of Primate City." *Geographical Review* 29 (1939): 226–36.

Jones, E. *Towns and Cities*. London, 1966.

Mumford, L. *The City in History*. London, 1961.

Sjoberg, G. *The Preindustrial City, Past and Present*. Glencoe, Ill., 1960.

Toynbee, A. *Cities on the Move*. London, 1970.

United Nations. *Growth of the World's Urban and Rural Population, 1920–2000*. New York, 1969.

———. *Patterns of Urban and Rural Population Growth*. New York, 1980.

Weber, A. F. *The Growth of Cities in the Nineteenth Century: A Study in Statistics*. New York and London, 1899.

Weber, M. *The City*. Glencoe, Ill., 1958. (First edition in German, 1921.)

Wirth, L. "Urbanism as a Way of Life." *American Journal of Sociology* 44 (July 1938): 1–24.

Wolff, P., ed. *Guide international d'histoire urbaine*, vol. 1: Europe. Paris, 1977.

2. From the Birth of Urbanism to the Beginnings of the Great Civilizations

Adams, R. E. W. "Swamps, Canals, and the Locations of Ancient Maya Cities." *Antiquity* 54, no. 212 (November 1980):206–14.

Adams, R. McC. *Land behind Baghdad: A History of Settlement on the Diyala Plain*. Chicago, 1965.

———. *The Evolution of Urban Society: Early Mesopotamia and Prehispanic Mexico*. Chicago, 1966.

————. "Urban Revolution: Introduction." *International Encyclopedia of Social Sciences*, vol. 16, pp. 201–7. N.Y., 1967.

————. *Heartland of Cities: Surveys of Ancient Settlements and Land Use on the Great Central Floodplain of the Euphrates*. Chicago, 1981.

Alexander, J. "The Beginning of Urban Life in Europe." In Ucko, P. J., Tringham, R., and Dimbleby, G. W., eds., *Man, Settlement and Urbanism*, pp. 843–50. London, 1972.

Amiran, R. "The Beginning of Urbanization in Canaan." In Sanders, J. A., ed., *Near Eastern Archaeology in the Twentieth Century: Essays in Honor of Nelson Glueck*, pp. 83–100. Garden City, N.Y., 1970.

Andrew, G. F. *Maya Cities, Placemaking and Urbanization*. Oklahoma City, 1975.

Balard, M. "Amalfi et Byzance (Xe-XIIe siècle)." Centre de Recherche d'Histoire et Civilisation de Byzance. *Travaux et Mémoires* 6 (1976): 85–95.

Barley, M. W., ed. *European Towns: Their Archaeology and Early History*. London, 1977.

Bonine, M. E. "From Uruk to Casablanca: Perspectives on the Urban Experience of the Middle East." *Journal of Urban History* 3 (February 1977): 141–80.

Braidwood, R. J., and Braidwood, L. "The Earliest Village Communities of Southwest Asia." *Journal of World History*, no. 2 (October 1953): 278–310.

Braidwood, R. J., and Willey, G. R., eds. *Courses toward Urban Life*. Chicago, 1962.

Buccellati, G. *Cities and Nations of Ancient Syria: An Essay on Political Institutions with Special Reference to the Israelite Kingdom*. University of Rome, 1967.

————. "The 'Urban Revolution' in Socio-Political Perspective." *Mesopotamia Revista di Archeologia Epigrafia e Storia Orientale Antica*, vol. 12, pp. 19–39. 1977.

Bunnens, G. *L'expansion phénicienne en Méditerranée*. Brussels and Rome, 1979.

Calnek, E. E. "The Internal Structure of Cities in America: Pre-Columbian Cities; the Case of Tenochtitlan." In Schaedel, R. P., Hardoy, J. E., and Kinzer, N. S., eds., *Urbanization in the Americas from the Beginning to the Present*, pp. 315–26. The Hague and Paris, 1978.

Chang, Kwang-chih. *The Archaeology of Ancient China*. New Haven, 1963. 3d ed., revised, 1977.

Chêng, Tè-k'un. "The Beginning of Chinese Civilization." *Antiquity*, 47, no. 186 (June 1973): 197–209.

Clark, G. *World Prehistory in New Perspective*. Cambridge, 1961. 3rd ed., 1977.

Cohen, M. N. *The Food Crisis in Prehistory: Overpopulation and the Origins of Agriculture*. New Haven, 1977.

Dagron, G. *Naissance d'une capitale: Constantinople et ses institutions*. Paris, 1974.

Davidson, B. *The Lost Cities of Africa*. Boston, 1959.

Duby, G., ed. *La ville antique*. Vol. 1 of *l'Histoire de la France urbaine* (under the direction of Duby, G.). Paris, 1980.

Effenterre, H., van. *Le palais de Mallia et la cité minoenne*. 2 vols. Rome, 1980.

Elvin, M. *The Pattern of the Chinese Past*. London, 1973.

Finley, M. I. *The Ancient Economy*. Berkeley, 1973.

Hammond, M. *The City in the Ancient World*. Cambridge, Mass., 1972.

Hassan, F. A. *Demographic Archaeology*. New York, 1981.

Helms, S. W. *Jawa: Lost City of the Black Desert*. London, 1981.

Hopkins, I. W. J. "The City Region in Roman Palestine." *Palestine Exploration Quarterly*, 112th year, January–June 1980, pp. 19–32.

Hopkins, K. "Economic Growth and Towns in Classical Antiquity." In Abrams, P., and Wrigley, E. A., eds., *Towns in Societies: Essays in Economic History and Historical Sociology*, pp. 35–77. Cambridge, 1978.

Huot, J.-L. "Des villes existent-elles en Orient dès l'époque néolithique?." *Annales, E.S.C*, special issue, 25th year, no. 4, July–August 1970, pp. 1091–1101.

Jawad, A. J. *The Advent of the Era of Townships in Northern Mesopotamia*. Leiden, 1966.

Jones, A. H. M. *The Greek City from Alexander to Justinian*. Oxford, 1940.

———. *Cities of the Eastern Roman Province*, 2d ed. Oxford, 1971.

Kemp, B. J. "The Early Development of Towns in Egypt." *Antiquity* 51, no. 203 (November 1977): 185–200.

Lampl, P. *Cities and Planning in the Ancient Near East*. New York, 1968.

Leman, P. "Les villes romaines de la région Nord/Pas-de-Calais à la lumière des fouilles récentes." *Revue archéologique*, no. 1 (1979): 168–76.

Lepelley, C. *Les cités de l'Afrique romaine au Bas-Empire*. 2 vols. Paris, 1979–81.

Lot, F. *Recherches sur la population et la superficie des cités remontant à la période gallo-romaine*. 3 vols. Paris, 1945–53.

McIntosh, S. K., and McIntosh, R. J. *Prehistoric Excavations at Jenne, Mali*. Oxford, 1980.

Millon, R. "Urban Revolution: Early Civilizations of the New World." *International Encyclopedia of Social Sciences*, vol. 16, pp. 207–16. New York, 1967.

Morris, J. *Londinium: London in the Roman Empire*. London, 1982.

Piggott, S. *Some Ancient Cities of India*. Oxford, 1945.

Pounds, N. J. G. "The Urbanization of the Classical World." *Annals of the Association of American Geographers* 59 (March 1969): 135–56.

Puri, B. N. *Cities of Ancient India*. Meerut, New Delhi, and Calcutta, 1966.

Randles, W. G. L. *Pre-Colonial Urbanization in Africa South of the Equator*. In Ucko, P. J., Tringham, R., and Dimbleby, G. W., eds., *Man, Settlement, and Urbanism*, pp. 891–97. London, 1972.

Reed, C. A., ed. *Origins of Agriculture*. The Hague and Paris, 1977.

Rivet, A. L. F. *Town and Country in Roman Britain*, 2d ed. London, 1964.

Sabloff, J. A., ed. *Archaeology: Supplement to the Handbook of Middle American Indians*, vol. 1. Austin, Tex., 1981.

Schaedel, R. P. "The City and the Origin of the States in America." In Schaedel, R. P., Hardoy, J. E., and Kinzer, N. S., eds. *Urbanization in the Americas from the Beginning to the Present*, pp. 31–49. The Hague and Paris, 1978.

Schaedel, R. P., Hardoy, J. E., and Kinzer, N. S., eds. *Urbanization in the Americas from the Beginning to the Present*. The Hague and Paris, 1978.

Schofield, J., and Palliser, D., eds., *Recent Archaeological Research in English Towns*. London, 1981.

Scullard, H. *The Etruscan Cities and Rome*. London, 1967.

Sherratt, A., ed. *The Cambridge Encyclopedia of Archaeology*. Cambridge, 1980.

Stillwell, R., ed. *The Princeton Encyclopedia of Classical Sites*. Princeton, 1976.

Thakur, V. K. *Urbanisation in Ancient India*. Abhinav, 1981.

Ucko, P. J., Tringham, R., and Dimbleby, G. W., eds. *Man, Settlement and Urbanism*. London, 1972.

UNESCO, ed. *Histoire générale de l'Afrique*. Vol. 1, *Méthodologie et préhistoire africaine* (directeur Ki-Zerbo, J.); vol. 2, *Afrique ancienne* (directeur Mokhtar, G.). Paris, 1980.

Veyne, P. *Le pain et le cirque: Sociologie historique d'un pluralisme politique*. Paris, 1976.

Watson, W. "Neolithic Settlement in East Asia." In Ucko, P. J., Tringham, R., and Dimbleby, G. W., eds. *Man, Settlement and Urbanism*, pp. 329–41. London, 1972.

Wellard, J. *The Search for Lost Cities*. London, 1980.

Wheatley, P. *The Pivot of the Four Quarters: A Preliminary Enquiry into the Origins and Character of the Ancient Chinese City*. Edinburgh and Chicago, 1971.

Wheatley, P., and See, T. *From Court to Capital: A Tentative Interpretation of the Origins of the Japanese Urban Tradition*. Chicago, 1978.

3. Traditional Europe from the Fifth Century to the Eighteenth Century

Bardet, J.-P. "La démographie des villes de la modernité (XVIe–XVIIIe siècles): Mythes et réalités." *Annales de démographie historique, 1974*, pp. 101–26. Paris, 1974.

Barel, Y. *La ville médiévale: Système social, système urbain*. Grenoble, 1977.

Bergier, J.-F. *Genève et l'économie européenne de la Renaissance*. Paris, 1963.

Butlin, R. A., ed. *The Development of the Irish Town*. London, 1977.

Carter, F. W. "Urban Development in the Western Balkans: 1200–1800." In Carter, F. W., ed., *An Historical Geography of the Balkans*, pp. 148–95. London, 1977.

Centre Aixois d'études et de recherches sur le XVIIIe siècle. *La ville au XVIIIe siècle*. Colloque d'Aix-en-Provence, 29 avril–1er mai 1973. Aix-en-Provence, 1975.

Chalklin, C. W., and Havinden, M. A., eds. *Rural Change and Urban Growth 1500–1800*. London, 1974.

Chevalier, B. *Les bonnes villes de France du XIVe au XVIe siècle*. Paris, 1982.

Clark, P., ed. *Country Towns in Pre-Industrial England*. Leicester, 1981.

———, ed. *The Transformation of English Provincial Towns 1600–1800*. London, 1984.

Clark, P., and Slack, P. *English Towns in Transition, 1500–1700*. Oxford, 1976.

Démographie urbaine XVe–XXe siècles, (IIIe Rencontres Franco-Suisses), Centre d'histoire économique et sociale de la région lyonnaise, no. 8. Lyon, 1977.

Dollinger-Léonard, Y. "De la cité romaine à la ville médiévale dans la région de la Moselle et de la Haute-Meuse." In *Studien zu den Anfängen des Europäischen Städtewesens*, 1958, reprinted, pp. 195–226. Sigmaringen, 1970.

Duby, G. "Les villes du Sud-Est de la Gaule du VIIIe au XIe siècle." In Settimane di Studio del Centro Italiano di Studi sull'alto Medioevo, VI, ed. *La Città nell'alto medioevo*, pp. 231–58. Spoleto, 1959.

Dyos, H. J., and Wolff, M., eds. *The Victorian City: Image and Realities*. 2 vols. London, 1973. Reprinted, 4 vols. London, 1976–78.

Everitt, A., ed. *Perspectives in English Urban History*. London, 1973.

Fritz, P., and Williams, D., eds. *City and Society in the 18th Century*. Toronto, 1973.

Garden, M. *Lyon et les Lyonnais au XVIIIe siècle*. Paris, 1975.

Glick, T. F. *Islamic and Christian Spain in the Early Middle Ages.* Princeton, 1979.

Guidoni, E. *La ville européenne: formation et signification du IVe au XIe siècle.* Paris, 1981.

Hamm, M. F. *The City in Late Imperial Russia.* Bloomington, Ind., 1986.

Hammarström, I. "Urban History in Scandinavia: A Survey of Recent Trends." *Urban History Yearbook, 1978*, pp. 46–55. Leicester.

Haslam, J. *Early Medieval Towns in Britain.* Santa Cruz, 1985.

Hensel, W. "The Origins of Western and Eastern European Slav Towns." In Barley, M. W., ed., *European Towns: Their Archaeology and Early History*, pp. 373–90. London, 1977.

Higounet-Nadal, A. "La démographie des villes françaises au Moyen-Age." In *Annales de démographie historique, 1980.* Paris, 1980.

Hohenberg, P. M., and Lees, L. H. *The Making of Urban Europe, 1000–1800.* Cambridge, Mass., 1985.

Langer, L. N. "The Medieval Russian Town." In Hamm, M. F., ed., *The City in Russian History*, pp. 11–33. Lexington, Ky., 1976.

Le Goff, "The Town as an Agent of Civilisation, 1200–1500." In Cipolla, C. M., ed., *The Fontana Economic History of Europe*, vol. 1, pp. 71–106. London, 1972.

————, ed. *La ville médiévale.* Vol. 2 of *l'Histoire de la France urbaine* (under the direction of Duby, G.). Paris, 1980.

Le Roy Ladurie, E., ed. *La ville classique.* Vol. 3 of *l'Histoire de la France urbaine* (under the direction of Duby, G.). Paris, 1981.

Martines, L. *Power and Imagination: City-States in Renaissance Italy.* London, 1983.

Miskimin, H. A., et al., eds. *The Medieval City.* New Haven, 1977.

Mols, R. *Introduction à la démographie historique des villes d'Europe du XIVe au XVIIIe siècle.* 3 vols. Gembloux-Louvain, 1954–56.

Nicolas, D. "Le développement urbain dans la Flandre médiévale: Structures du peuplement, fonctions urbaines et formation de capital." *Annales, E.S.C.*, 33d year, no. 3 (May–June 1978): 501–27.

Patten, J. *English Towns, 1500–1700.* London, 1978.

Perrenoud, A. *La population de Genève, XVIe–XIXe siècles.* Geneva, 1979.

Perrot, J.-C. *Genèse d'une ville moderne: Caen au XVIIIe siècle.* 2 vols. Paris, 1975.

Phythian-Adams, C. *Desolation of a City: Coventry and the Urban Crisis of the Late Middle Ages.* Cambridge, 1979.

Pirenne, H. *Les villes du Moyen-Age: Essai d'histoire économique et sociale.* Brussels, 1927.

Piuz, A.-M. *Les relations économiques entre les villes et les campagnes dans les sociétés pré-industrielles.* In *Villes et campagnes XVe–XXe siècle* (IIIe Rencontres Franco-Suisses). Centre d'histoire économique et sociale de la région lyonnaise, no. 9, pp. 1–53. Lyon, 1977.

Poussou, J. P., et al., *Etudes sur les villes en Europe occidentale (milieu du XVIIe siècle à la veille de la Révolution française).* Vol. 2, *Angleterre, Pays-Bas, Provinces-Unies, Allemagne rhénane.* Paris, 1983.

Renouard, Y. *Les villes d'Italie de la fin du Xe siècle au début du XIVe siècle.* Paris, 1969.

Rorig, F. *The Medieval City.* London, 1967.

Rozman, G. *Urban Networks in Russia, 1750–1800 and Pre-Modern Periodization.* Princeton, 1976.

Russell, J. C. *Medieval Regions and Their Cities*. Newton Abbot, 1972.

Schmal, H., ed. *Patterns of European Urbanisation since 1500*. London, 1981.

Sharlin, A. "Natural Decrease in Early Modern Cities: A Reconsideration." *Past and Present*, no. 79 (May 1978): 126–38.

Tikhomirov, M. *The Towns of Ancient Rus*. Moscow, 1959.

Todorov, N. *The Balkan City, Fourteen Hundred to Nineteen Hundred*. Washington, 1983.

Trigger, B. G. "Determinants of Urban Growth in Pre-Industrial Societies." In Ucko, P. J., Tringham, R., and Dimbleby, G. W., eds., *Man, Settlement and Urbanism*, pp. 575–99. London, 1972.

Vercauteren, F. "La vie urbaine entre Meuse et Loire du VIe au IXe siècle." In Settimane di Studio del Centro Italiano di Studio sull'alto Medioevo, VI, ed., *La Città nell'alto Medioevo*, pp. 453–84. Spoleto, 1959.

Villes du passé. In *Annales de démographie historique, 1982*. Paris, 1982.

Villes et campagnes. XVe–XXe siècle. IIIe Rencontres Franco-Suisses, Centre d'histoire économique et sociale de la région lyonnaise, no. 9. Lyon, 1977.

Vries, J. de. *European Urbanization, 1500–1800*. Cambridge, Mass., 1984.

Wolff, P. *Commerce et marchands de Toulouse (vers 1350–vers 1450)*. Paris, 1954.

Wrigley, E. A. "Parasite or Stimulus: The Town in a Pre-Industrial Economy." In Abrams, P., and Wrigley, E. A., eds., *Towns in Societies: Essays in Economic History and Historical Sociology*, pp. 295–309. Cambridge, 1978.

4. The City and Development in the Western World

Abrams, P. "Towns and Economic Growth: Some Theories and Problems." In Abrams, P., and Wrigley, E. A., eds., *Towns in Societies: Essays in Economic History and Historical Sociology*, pp. 9–33. Cambridge, 1978.

Agulhon, M., ed. *La ville de l'âge industriel*. Vol. 4 of *Histoire de la France urbaine* (under the direction of Duby, G.). Paris, 1983.

Alexander, J. W. "The Basic-Nonbasic Concept of Urban Economic Functions." *Economic Geography* 30 (July 1954): 246–61.

Barker, T. C., and Robbins, M. *A History of London Transport: Passenger Travel and the Development of the Metropolis*, vol. 1: *The Nineteenth Century*. London, 1963.

Bauer, G., and Roux, J.-M. *La rurbanisation ou la ville éparpillée*. Paris, 1976.

Bradbury, K., Downs, A., and Small, K. A. *Urban Decline and the Future of American Cities*. Washington, 1982.

Burnley, I. H. *The Australian Urban System: Growth, Change and Differentiation*. Melbourne, 1980.

Chombart de Lauwe, P.-H. *La fin des villes: Mythe ou réalité*. Paris, 1982.

Christaller, W. *Die Zentralen Orte in Süddeutschland*. Jena, 1933.

Corfield, P. J. *The Impact of English Towns, 1700–1800*. Oxford, 1982.

Dennis, R. J. *English Industrial Cities in the Nineteenth Century: A Social History*. Cambridge, 1984.

Derycke, P. H. *L'économie urbaine*. Paris, 1970.

Dyckinson, R. E. *The West European City: A Geographical Interpretation*. London, 1951.

Dyos, H. J. *Exploring the Urban Past*. A collection of papers of H. J. Dyos, edited by Camadine, D., and Reeder, D. Cambridge, 1982.

Fedor, T. S. *Patterns of Urban Growth in the Russian Empire during the Nineteenth Century*. Chicago, 1975.

Feller, I. "The Urban Location of United States Invention, 1860–1913." *Exploration in Economic History* 8 (Spring 1971): 285–303.

———. "Determinants of the Composition of Urban Invention." *Economic Geography* 49, no. 1 (January 1973): 48–58.

French, R. A., and Hamilton, F. E. I., eds. *The Socialist City: Spatial Structure and Urban Policy*. New York, 1979.

Friedmann, J. *Urbanization, Planning, and National Development*. New York, 1973.

Glaab, C. N. *A History of Urban America*. 3d ed. New York, 1983.

Gottmann, J. *Megalopolis: The Urbanized Northeastern Seaboard of the United States*. New York, 1961.

Gurr, T. R. *Rogues, Rebels, and Reformers: A Political History of Urban Crime and Conflict*. London, 1977.

Guyot, F. *Essai d'économie urbaine*. Paris, 1968.

Hagerstrand, T. *Innovation Diffusion as a Spatial Process*. Chicago, 1967.

Harris, C. D. *Cities of the Soviet Union*. Chicago, 1970.

Kellett, J. R. *The Impact of Railways on Victorian Cities*. London, 1969.

Kornhauser, D. *Urban Japan: Its Foundations and Growth*. London and New York, 1976.

Lee, J. J. "Aspects of Urbanization and Economic Development in Germany 1815–1914." In Abrams, P., and Wrigley, E. A., eds., *Towns in Societies: Essays in Economic History and Historical Sociology*, pp. 279–93. Cambridge, 1978.

Lequin, Y. (under the direction of). *Ouvriers dans la ville*, special issue, *Le Mouvement social*, no. 118 (January–March 1982).

Lingeman, R. *Small Town America, a Narrative History, 1620 to the Present*. Boston, 1980.

McCarty, J. W., and Scheduin, C. B., eds. *Australian Capital Cities: Historical Essays*. Sydney, 1978.

McKay, J. P. *Tramways and Trolleys: The Rise of Urban Mass Transport in Europe*. Princeton, 1977.

Martin, I. *Inventions techniques et urbanisation en Europe au XIXe siècle: Allemagne, France et Royaume-Uni*. Master's thesis, Department of Economic History, University of Geneva). Geneva. 1977.

Meuriot, P. *Des agglomérations urbaines dans l'Europe contemporaine*. Paris, 1897.

Mohl, R. A. *The New City: Urban America in the Industrial Age, 1860–1920*. Arlington Heights, Ill., 1985.

Ogburn, W. F., and Duncan, O. D. "City Size as a Sociological Variable." In Burgess, E. W., and Bogue, D. J., eds., *Contributions to Urban Sociology*, pp. 129–47. Chicago, 1964.

Pedersen, P. O. "Innovation Diffusion within and between National Urban Systems." *Geographical Analysis* 2 (1970): 203–54.

Pred, A. R. *The External Relations of Cities during the "Industrial Revolution."* Chicago, 1962.

———. *The Spatial Dynamics of U.S. Urban Industrial Growth, 1800–1914*. Cambridge, Mass., 1966.

———. *Urban Growth and City Systems in the United States, 1840–1860*. Cambridge, Mass., 1981.

Pumain, D. "Chemins de fer et croissance urbaine en France au XIXe siècle." *Annales de géographie*, no. 507, 91st year (September–October 1982): 529–50.

Rémy, J. *La ville: phénomène économique*. Brussels, 1966.

Rémy, J., and Voyé, L. *Ville, ordre et violence*. Paris, 1981.

Riefler, R. F. "Nineteenth-Century Urbanization Patterns in the U.S." *Journal of Economic History* 39, no. 4 (December 1979): 961–74.

Robson, B. T. *Urban Growth: An Approach*. London, 1973.

Rozman, G. *Urban Networks in Ch'ing China and Tokugawa Japan*. Princeton, 1973.

Stave, B. M., ed. *Modern Industrial Cities: History, Policy and Survival*. Beverly Hills, Calif., 1982.

St. Clair, D. J. *The Motorization of American Cities*. New York, 1986.

Takeo, Y. *Social Change and the City in Japan: From Earliest Time through the Industrial Revolution*. Tokyo, 1968.

Thernstrom, S., and Sennett, R., eds. *Nineteenth-Century Cities: Essays in the New Urban History*. New Haven, 1969.

Thomlinson, R. "The Nature and Rise of Cities." In Ficker, V. B., and Graves, H. S., eds., *Social Science and the Urban Crisis*, pp. 4–11. New York, 1971.

Thompson, W. R. *Preface to Urban Economics*. Baltimore, 1965.

Wakstein, A. M., ed. *The Urbanization of America: An Historical Anthology*. Boston, 1970.

Williamson, J. G. "Antebellum Urbanization in the American Northeast." *Journal of Economic History* 25, no. 4 (December 1965): 592–608.

Wrigley, E. A. "A Simple Model of London's Importance in Changing English Society and Economy 1650–1750." *Past and Present* 37 (July 1967): 44–70.

Yeates, M. H., and Garner, B. J. *The North American City*. New York, 1971.

Zipf, G. K. *Human Behaviour and the Principle of the Least Effort*. Cambridge, 1949.

5. Non-European Societies before Colonization

Ahrweiler, H. "La ville byzantine." In Wolff, P. (under the direction of). *Guide international d'histoire urbaine*. Vol. 1: *Europe*, pp. 21–31. Paris, 1977.

Amanat, A., ed. *Cities and Trade in Nineteenth Century Iran*. Oxford, 1983.

Basu, D. K., ed. *The Rise and Growth of Colonial Port Cities in Asia*. Boston, 1985.

Beach, D. N. *The Shona and Zimbabwe 900–1850*. London, 1980.

Bemont, F. *Les villes de l'Iran: Des cités d'autrefois à l'urbanisme contemporain*. 2 vols. Paris, 1969–73.

Bhattacharya, B. *Urban Development in India (since Prehistoric Times)*. Delhi, 1979.

Brown, L. C., ed. *From Medina to Metropolis*. Princeton, 1973.

Chang, Sen-dou. "The Historical Trend of Chinese Urbanization." *Annals of the Association of American Geographers* 53, no. 2 (June 1963): 109–43.

Chaudhuri, K. N. "Some Reflections on the Town and Country in Mughai India." *Modern Asian Studies* 12 (1978): 77–96.

Doeppers, D. F. "The Development of Philippine Cities before 1900." *Journal of Asian Studies* 31, no. 4 (August 1972): 769–92.

Elvin, M. "Chinese Cities since the Sung Dynasty." In Abrams, P., and Wrigley,

E. A., eds., *Towns in Societies: Essays in Economic History and Historical Sociology*, pp. 79–89. Cambridge, 1978.

Elvin, M., and Skinner, G. W., eds. *The Chinese City between Two Worlds*. Stanford, 1974.

Erder, L. T., and Faroqhi, S. "The Development of the Anatolian Urban Network during the Sixteenth Century." *Journal of the Economic and Social History of the Orient* 23, part 3 (October 1980): 265–303.

Faroqhi, S. *Towns and Townsmen of Ottoman Anatolia: Trade Crafts and Food Production in an Urban Setting, 1520–1650*. Cambridge, 1984.

Foss, C. "Archaeology and the 'Twenty Cities' of Byzantine Asia." *American Journal of Archaeology* 81, no. 4 (fall 1977): 467–86.

Gokhale, B. G. "Burhanpur: Notes on the History of an Indian City in the XVIIth Century." *Journal of the Economic and Social History of the Orient* 15, part 3 (December 1972): 316–23.

Griffeth, R. "The Hausa City-States from 1450 to 1804." In Griffeth, R., and Thomas, C. G., eds., *The City-States in Five Cultures*, pp. 143–80. Santa Barbara, Calif., 1981.

Grove, D. *The Towns of Ghana*. Accra, 1964.

Guarda, G. "Military Influence in the Cities of the Kingdom of Chile." In Schaedel, R. P., Hardoy, J. E., and Kinzer, N. S., eds., *Urbanization in the Americas from the Beginning to the Present*, pp. 343–82. The Hague and Paris, 1978.

Gutwein, K. C. *Third Palestine: A Regional Study in Byzantine Urbanization*. Washington, 1981.

Hitti, P. C. *Capital Cities of Arab Islam*. Minneapolis, 1973.

Hourani, A. H., and Stern, S. M., eds. *The Islamic City: A Colloquium*. Oxford, 1970.

Hull, R. W. *African Cities and Towns before the European Conquest*. New York, 1976.

Kraeling, C. H., and Adams, R. M., eds. *City Invincible: A Symposium on Urbanization and Cultural Development in the Ancient Near East*. Chicago, 1960.

Krapf-Askari, E. *Yoruba Towns and Cities*. Oxford, 1969.

Lapidus, I. M., ed. *Middle Eastern Cities: A Symposium in Ancient, Islamic, and Contemporary Middle Eastern Urbanism*. Berkeley, 1969.

———. "The Evolution of Muslim Urban Society." *Comparative Studies in Society and History* 15, no. 1 (January 1973): 21–50.

———. *Muslim Cities in the Later Middle Ages*. Cambridge, 1984.

Lombard, D. "Pour une histoire des villes du Sud-Est asiatique." *Annales, E.S.C.*, 25th year, no. 4 (July–August 1970): 842–56.

Ma, L. J. C. *Commercial Development and Urban Change in Sung China*. Ann Arbor, 1971.

Mango, C. *Le développement urbain de Constantinople (IVe–VIIe siècles)*. Paris, 1985.

Naqvi, H. K. *Urban Centres and Industries in Upper India, 1556–1803*. London, 1968.

Ostrogorsky, G. "Byzantine Cities in the Early Middle Ages." *Dumbarton Oaks Papers, No. 13*, pp. 45–66. Washington, 1959.

Patlagean, E. *Pauvreté économique et pauvreté sociale à Byzance, 4–7 siècles*. Paris and The Hague, 1977.

Prins, J. "Les villes indonésiennes." In *Recueil de la Société Jean Bodin*, vol. 7, *La Ville*, pp. 195–206. Brussels, 1955.

Raymond, A. "La conquête ottomane et le développement des grandes villes arabes: Le cas du Caire, de Damas et d'Alep." *Revue de l'Occident musulman et de la Méditerranée*, no. 27 (1st trimester 1979): 115–34.

———. *The Great Arab Cities in the 16th–18th Centuries: An Introduction*. New York, 1984.

Reid, A. "La structure des villes du Sud-Est asiatique (XVe–XVIIe siècles)." *Urbi*, no. 1 (September 1979): 82–94.

Skinner, G. W., ed. *The City in Late Imperial China*. Stanford, 1977.

Spodek, H. "Studying the History of Urbanization of India." *Journal of Urban History* 6, no. 3 (May 1980): 251–95.

Timberlake, M. *Urbanization in the World Economy*. New York, 1985.

Wheatley, P. *Nāgara and Commandery: Origins of the Southeast Asian Urban Tradition*. Research paper no. 207–208. Chicago, 1983.

6. Urbanism and the Third World

Abu-Lughod, J., and Hay, R. *Third World Urbanization*. Chicago, 1977.

Ankerl, G. *Overurbanization in Tropical Africa, 1970–2000*. Bristol, Ind., 1984.

Bairoch, P. *Urban Unemployment in Developing Countries*. ILO, Geneva, 1973.

Blardone, G. *Progrès économiques dans le Tiers-Monde: Environnement sociopolitique, croissance démographique et urbanisation*. Paris, 1972.

Bose, A., *India's Urbanization, 1901–2001*, 2d ed. New Delhi, 1978.

Breese, G. *Urbanization in Newly Developing Countries*. Englewood Cliffs, 1966.

———., ed. *The City in Newly Developing Countries: Reading on Urbanism and Urbanization*. Englewood Cliffs, 1969.

Butterworth, D., and Chance, J. K. *Latin American Urbanization*. Cambridge, 1981.

Chang, P. H. "Control of Urbanization, the Chinese Approach." *Asia Quarterly*, no. 3 (1979): 215–28.

Chang, Sen-dou. "Modernization and China's Urban Development." *Annals of the Association of American Geographers* 71 (June 1981): 202–19.

Chatterjee, L., and Nijkamp, P., eds. *Urban Problems and Economic Development*. The Hague, 1981.

Costello, V. F. *Urbanization in the Middle East*. London, 1977.

Davis, K., and Hertz, H. "Urbanization and the Development of Pre-Industrial Areas." *Economic Development and Cultural Change* 111, no. 1 (October 1954): 6–26.

Drakakis-Smith, D. *Urbanization, Housing and the Development Process*. London, 1981.

Dwyer, D. J., ed. *The City in the Third World*. London, 1974.

———. *People and Housing in Third World Cities: Perspectives on the Problem of Spontaneous Settlements*. London, 1975.

Field, A. J., ed. *City and Country in the Third World: Issues in the Modernization of Latin America*. Cambridge, Mass., 1970.

Firebaugh, G. "Structural Determinants of Urbanization in Asia and Latin America, 1950–1970." *American Sociological Review* 44, no. 2 (April 1979): 199–215.

Friedmann, J., and Wulff, R. *The Urban Transition: Comparative Studies of Newly Industrializing Societies.* London, 1976.

Gilbert, A., ed. *Urbanization in Contemporary Latin America.* Chichester, 1982.

Gilbert, A., and Gugler, J. *Cities, Poverty, and Development: Urbanization in the Third World.* Oxford, 1982.

Gosh, P. K., ed. *Urban Development in the Third World.* New York, 1984.

Granotier, B. *La planète des bidonvilles: Perspectives de l'explosion urbaine dans le Tiers-Monde.* Paris, 1980.

Guibbert, J. J. (under the direction of). *Transports en sursis? Quelle politique des "petits transports" urbains dans le Tiers-Monde?*, Enda, Dakar, *Document Tiers-Monde*, no. 13–81. March 1981.

Gwynne, R. E. *Industrialization and Urbanization in Latin America.* Baltimore, 1986.

"Habitat sous-intégré." *Hérodote*, no. 19, special issue, September–October 1980.

Hardoy, J. E., ed. *Urbanization in Latin America: Approaches and Issues.* New York, 1975.

Hauser, P. M., ed. *Le phénomène d'urbanisation en Asie et en Extrême-Orient.* Calcutta, 1959.

———, ed. *L'urbanisation en Amérique latine.* Paris, 1962.

Herbert, J. D. *Urban Development in the Third World.* New York, 1979.

Hugon, P. (under the direction of). "Secteur informel et petite production marchande dans les villes du Tiers-Monde." *Revue Tiers-Monde* 21, no. 82 (April–June 1980).

Johannot, C. *Etude de l'évolution de la structure par taille des villes du Tiers-Monde entre 1900 et 1950*, Master's thesis, Department of Economic History, University of Geneva. Geneva, 1977.

Kelly, A. C., and Williamson, J. G. *What Drives Third World City Growth.* New York, 1984.

King, A. D. *Colonial Urban Development: Culture, Social Power, and Environment.* London, 1976.

Linn, J. F. *Cities in the Developing World.* Oxford, 1983.

Lipton, M. *Why People Stay Poor: Urban Bias in World Development.* Cambridge, Mass., 1977.

Lloyd, P. *Slums of Hope? Shanty Towns of the Third World.* Harmondsworth, 1979.

Ma, J. C., and Hanten, E. W., eds. *Urban Development in Modern China.* Boulder, Colo., 1981.

Mabogunje, A. L. *Yoruba Towns.* Ibadan, 1962.

———. *Urbanization in Nigeria.* London, 1968.

McGee, T. G. *The Southeast Asian City.* London, 1967 (reprinted in 1969).

———. *The Urbanization Process in the Third World.* London, 1971.

———. "The Urbanization Process and Industrialization in the Market Economies of Asia." *Regional Development Dialogue* 1, no. 2 (August 1980): 131–43.

Morse, R. M., ed. *The Urban Development of Latin America, 1750–1920.* Stanford, 1971.

Murison, H. S., and Lea, J. P., eds. *Housing in Third World Countries: Perspectives on Policy and Practice.* London, 1979.

Neild, S. M. "Colonial Urbanism: The Development of Madras City in the Eighteenth and Nineteenth Centuries." *Modern Asian Studies* 13. no. 2 (1979): 217–46.

Portes, A., and Walton, J. *Urban Latin America*. Austin, Tex., 1976.

Roberts, B. *Cities of Peasants: The Political Economy of Urbanization in the Third World*. London, 1978.

Santos, M. *L'espace partagé: Les deux circuits de l'économie urbaine des pays sous-développés*. Paris, 1975.

Sethuraman, S. V., ed. *The Urban Informal Sector in Developing Countries: Employment, Poverty and Environment*. ILO, Geneva, 1981.

Socolow, S. M., and Johnson, L. L. "Urbanization in Colonial Latin America." *Journal of Urban History* 8, no. 1 (November 1981): 27–59.

Todaro, M. P. *Internal Migration in Developing Countries*. ILO, Geneva, 1976.

"Villes éclatées." *Herodotes*, special issue, no. 17. January–March, 1980.

References

Adams, R. E. W. "Swamps, Canals, and the Locations of Ancient Maya Cities." *Antiquity* 54, no. 212 (November 1980): 206–14.

Adams, R. Mc C. *Land behind Baghdad: A History of Settlement on the Diyala Plain.* Chicago, 1965.

Aharoni, Y. *The Land of the Bible: A Historical Geography.* London, 1967.

Ahrweiler, H. "La ville byzantine." In Wolff, P. (under the direction of). *Guide international d'histoire urbaine.* Vol. 1, *Europe,* pp. 21–31. Paris, 1977.

Alexander, J. "The Beginning of Urban Life in Europe." In Ucko, P. J., Tringham, R., and Dimbleby, G. W., eds., *Man, Settlement, and Urbanism,* pp. 843–50. London, 1972.

Alexander, J. W. "The Basic-Nonbasic Concept of Urban Economic Functions." *Economic Geography* 30 (July 1954): 246–61.

Alimen, M.-H. "Présence humaine et paléoclimats au Sahara nord-occidental." In Roubet, C., Hugot, H.-J., and Souville, G., eds., *Préhistoire africaine: Mélanges offerts au Doyen Lionel Balout,* pp. 105–12. Paris, 1981.

Allchin, F. R. "How Old is the City of Taxila?." *Antiquity* 56, no. 216 (March 1982): 8–14.

Ambrosiani, B. "Urban Archaeology in Sweden." In Barley, M. W., ed., *European Towns: Their Archaeology and Early History,* pp. 103–26. London, 1977.

Anderson, D., and Leiserson, M. W. "Rural Nonfarm Employment in Developing Countries." *Economic Development and Cultural Change* 28, no. 2 (January 1980): 227–48.

Anderson, O. "Did Suicide Increase with Industrialization in Victorian England?" *Past and Present,* no. 86 (February 1980): 147–73.

Andrews, G. F. *Maya Cities, Placemaking and Urbanization.* Oklahoma City, 1975.

Aristote. *La politique* (new translation by J. Tricot). Paris, 1970.

Arreola, D. D. "Nineteenth-Century Townscapes of Eastern Mexico." *Geographical Review* 72, no. 1 (January 1982): 1–19.

Auerbach, F. "Das Gesetz der Bevölkerungskonzentration." *Peter Mann's Mitteilungen,* no. 59 (1913): 74–76.

Aurenche, O., et al. "Chronologie et organisation de l'espace dans le Proche-Orient de 12000 à 5600 av. J.-C." In *Préhistoire du Levant,* Colloques internationaux du C.N.R.S., pp. 571–78. Paris, 1981.

Aurousseau, M. "The Distribution of Population: A Constructive Problem." *Geographical Review* 11, no. 4 (October 1921): 563–92.

Austin, M., and Vidal-Naquet, P. *Economies et sociétés en Grèce ancienne*. Paris, 1972.

Axelson, E. *The Portuguese in South East Africa, 1600–1700*. Johannesburg, 1960.

Bailey, W. B. *Modern Social Conditions*. New York, 1906.

Bairoch, P. *Révolution industrielle et sous-développement*. Paris, 1963.

——. "Niveaux de développement économique au XIXe siècle." *Annales, E.S.C.*, 20th year, no. 6 (November–December 1965): 1091–117.

——. "Structure de la population active mondiale de 1700 à 1970." *Annales, E.S.C.*, 26th year, no. 5 (September–October): 960–76.

——. *Urban Unemployment in Developing Countries*. ILO, Geneva, 1973a.

——. "Commerce international et genèse de la révolution industrielle anglaise." *Annales, E.S.C.*, 28th year, no. 2 (March–April 1973b): 541–71.

——. *The Economic Development of the Third World since 1900*. London, 1975.

——. *Emploi et taille des villes*. Working Papers WEP 2-19/WP 15, ILO, Geneva, 1976a.

——. *Commerce extérieur et développement économique de l'Europe au XIXe siècle*. Paris, 1976b.

——. "Population urbaine et taille des villes en Europe de 1600 à 1970." *Revue d'histoire économique et sociale* 54, no. 3 (1976c): 304–35.

——. *Taille des villes, conditions de vie et développement économique*. Paris, 1977a.

——. "Estimation du revenu national dans les sociétés occidentales pré-industrielles et au XIXe siècle." *Revue Economique* 28 (March 1977b): 177–208.

——. "Ecarts internationaux des niveaux de vie avant la révolution industrielle." *Annales, E.S.C.*, 34th year, no. 1 (January–February 1979a): 145–71.

——. "Le volume des productions et du produit national dans le Tiers-Monde (1900–1977)." *Revue Tiers-Monde* 20, no. 80 (October–December 1979b): 669–91.

——. "The Main Trends in National Economic Disparities since the Industrial Revolution." In Bairoch, P., and Lévy-Leboyer, M., eds., *Disparities in Economic Development since the Industrial Revolution*, pp. 3–25. London, 1980.

——. "International Industrialization Levels from 1750 to 1980." *Journal of Economic History* 11, no. 2 (Fall 1982): 269–333.

——. *La place de l'énergie hydraulique dans les sociétés traditionelles et au cours des XIXe et XXe siècles*. Communication à la Decima Settimana di Studio: *Le Acque Interne (sec. XII–XVIII)*, Prato, April 1983.

Bairoch, P. "Historical Roots of Economic Underdevelopment: Myths and Realities." In Mommsen, W. J., and Osterhammel, J., *Imperialism and After: Continuities and Discontinuities*, pp. 191–216. London, 1986.

Bairoch, P. *La consommation d'énergie: des sociétés traditionnelles du XVIIIe siècle au monde actuel*. To appear in 1988.

Bairoch, P. "World Gross National Product, 1750–1985." To appear.

Bairoch, P., and Etemad, B. *Commodity Structure of Third World Exports, 1830–1937*. Centre of International Economic History, University of Geneva, 1985.

Bairoch, P., and Goertz, G. "Factors of Urbanization in the Nineteenth Century Developed Countries: A Descriptive and Econometric Analysis." *Urban Studies* 23, no. 4 (August 1986): 285–305.

Balard, M. "Amalfi et Byzance (Xe–XIIe siècle)." Centre de Recherche d'histoire et civilisation de Byzance, *Travaux et Mémoires*, no. 6 (1976): 85–95.

Bardet, J.-P. "La démographie des villes de la modernité (XVIe–XVIIIe siècles): Mythes et réalités." *Annales de démographie historique, 1974*, pp. 101–26. Paris, 1974.

Barel, Y. *La ville médiévale: Système social, système urbain.* Grenoble, 1977.

Barker, T. C., and Robbins, M. *A History of London Transport: Passenger Travel and the Development of the Metropolis.* Vol. 1, *The Nineteenth Century.* London, 1963.

Barley, M. W., ed. *European Towns: Their Archaeology and Early History.* London, 1977.

Baron, S. W. B. "Population." In *Encyclopedia Judaica*, vol. 13, pp. 866–903. Jerusalem, 1972.

Bauer, G., and Roux, J.-M. *La rurbanisation ou la ville éparpillée.* Paris, 1976.

Beach, D. N. *The Shona and Zimbabwe 900–1850.* London, 1980.

Beckmann, M. "City Hierarchies and the Distribution of City Size." *Economic Development and Cultural Change*, 6, no. 3 (April 1958): 243–48.

Beckwith, C. I. "The Introduction of Greek Medicine into Tibet in the Seventh and Eighth Centuries." *Journal of the American Oriental Society* 99, no. 2 (April–June 1979): 297–312.

Bender, B. *Farming in Prehistory. From Hunter-Gatherer to Food-Producer.* London, 1975.

Beresford, M. *New Towns of the Middle Ages.* London, 1967.

Berque, J. *Le village.* Paris, 1959.

Berry, B. J. L. "Notes on Central Place Theory and the Range of a Good." *Economic Geography*, no. 34 (October 1958): 304–11.

———. "City Size Distribution and Economic Development." *Economic Development and Cultural Change* 9, no. 4, part 1 (July 1961): 573–87.

Bible. King James translation.

Bickel, W. *Bevölkerungsgeschichte und Bevölkerungspolitik der Schweiz seit dem Ausgang des Mittelalters.* Zurich, 1947.

Binz, L. "Le Moyen-Age genevois (VIe-XVe siècles)." In Guichonnet, P., ed., *Histoire de Genève*, pp. 61–128. Lausanne and Toulouse, 1974.

Biraben, J.-N. *Les hommes et la peste en France et dans les pays européens et méditerranéens.* Vol. 1. Paris, 1975. Vol. 2. Paris, 1976.

———. "Essai sur l'évolution du nombre des hommes." *Population*, 34th year, no. 1 (January–February 1979): 13–24.

Bogaert, R. *Banques et banquiers dans les cités grecques.* Leyden, 1968.

Bonine, M. E. "From Uruk to Casablanca: Perspectives on the Urban Experience of the Middle East." *Journal of Urban History* 3, no. 2 (February 1977): 141–80.

Borsay, P. "The English Urban Renaissance: The Development of Provincial Urban Culture ca. 1680–ca. 1760." *Social History*, no. 5 (May 1977): 581–98.

Boserup, E. *The Conditions of Agricultural Growth.* London, 1965.

Bovill, E. W. *The Golden Trade of the Moors.* London, 1958.

Bowers, R. V. "The Direction of Intra-Social Diffusion." *American Sociological Review* 2, no. 6 (December 1937): 826–36.

Braudel, F. *La Méditerranée et le monde méditerranéen à l'époque de Philippe II.* 2 vols. 2d ed. Paris, 1966.

———. *Civilisation matérielle et capitalisme.* Paris, 1967.

————. *Civilisation matérielle, économie et capitalisme, XVe–XVIIIe siècle.* Vol. 3, *Le Temps du Monde.* Paris, 1979.

————. *Structures of Everyday Life.* London, 1982.

Brisseau-Loaiza, J. "Le rôle du camion dans les relations ville-campagne dans la région du Cuzco (Pérou)." *Cahiers d'Outre-Mer*, 25A, no. 97 (January–March 1972): 27–56.

Bruyelle, P., and Dezert, B. "Les relations entre la ville et l'industrie: formes anciennes et formes nouvelles." *Hommes et Terres du Nord*, 1983-1:7–11.

Buccellati, G. "The 'Urban Revolution' in Socio-Political Perspective." *Mesopotamia Revista di Archaeologia Epigrafia e Storia Orientale Antica* 12 (1977): 19–39.

Buck, D. D. "Policies Favoring the Growth of Smaller Urban Places in the People's Republic of China, 1949–1979." In Ma, J. C., and Hanten, E. W., eds., *Urban Development in Modern China*, pp. 114–46. Boulder, Colo., 1981.

Bulliet, R. W. *The Camel and the Wheel.* Cambridge, Mass., 1975.

Bunnens, G. *L'expansion phénicienne en méditerranée.* Brussels and Rome, 1979.

Bureau Municipal de Statistique d'Amsterdam. *Annuaire statistique de la ville d'Amsterdam*, various issues.

————. *Annuaire statistique de la ville d'Amsterdam jusqu'à 1921*, no. 67. Amsterdam, 1923.

————. *Quarterly Bulletin*, vol. 66, part 4. Amsterdam, October–December 1960, supplement; and vol. 86, part 4. Amsterdam, October–December 1962, supplement.

————. *Statistiques démographiques des grandes villes du monde pendant les années 1880–1909*, no. 33. Amsterdam, 1911.

————. *Statistiques démographiques des grandes villes du monde pendant les années 1880–1909*, no. 40, part 2. Amsterdam, 1912.

Busino, G. *Vilfredo Pareto e l'industria del ferro nel Valdarno.* Milan, 1971.

Butterworth, D., and Chance, J. K. *Latin American Urbanization.* Cambridge, 1981.

Calnek, E. E. "The Internal Structure of Cities in America: Pre-Columbian Cities: the Case of Tenochtitlan." In Schaedel, R. P., Hardoy, J. E., and Kinzer, N. S., eds., *Urbanization in the Americas from the Beginning to the Present*, pp. 315–26. The Hague and Paris, 1978.

Canada Year Book, 1922–1923. Ottawa, 1924.

Carothers, J., and McDonald, W. A. "Size and Distribution of the Population in Late Bronze Age Messenia: Some Statistical Approaches." *Journal of Field Archaeology* 6, no. 4 (Winter 1979): 433–54.

Carter, F. W. "Urban Development in the Western Balkans: 1200–1800." In Carter, F. W., ed., *An Historical Geography of the Balkans*, pp. 148–95. London, 1977.

Carter, G. F. "A Hypothesis Suggesting a Single Origin of Agriculture." In Reed, C. A., ed., *Origins of Agriculture*, pp. 89–133. The Hague and Paris, 1977.

Cartier, M. *Les villes chinoises en transition, Caractéristiques démographiques.* Seminar on urbanization and population dynamics in history. Tokyo, 22–25 January 1986.

Centre Aixois d'études et de recherches sur le XVIIIe siècle. *La ville au XVIIIe siècle* (Colloque d'Aix-en-Provence, 29 April–1 May 1973). Aix-en-Provence, 1975.

Centre d'études et de recherches Marxistes. *Dictionnaire économique et social.* Paris, 1975.

Chakrabarti, D. K. "The Beginning of Iron in India." *Antiquity* 50, no. 198 (June 1976): 114–24.

Chan, Kam Wing, and Xu, Xueqiang. "Urban Population Growth and Urbanization in China since 1949: Reconstructing a Baseline." *The China Quarterly* 104 (December 1985): 583–613.

Chandler, T., and Fox, G. *3000 Years of Urban Growth.* New York, 1974.

Chang, Kwang-chih. *The Archaeology of Ancient China.* New Haven, 1963. 3rd revised ed., 1977.

Chang, P. H. "Control of Urbanization: The Chinese Approach." *Asia Quarterly*, no. 3 (1979): 215–28.

Chang, Sen-dou. "The Historical Trend of Chinese Urbanization." *Annals of the Association of American Geographers* 53 (June 1963): 109–43.

Charanis, P. "Observations on the Demography of the Byzantine Empire." In *Proceedings of the XIIIth International Congress of Byzantan Studies*, pp. 445–63. Oxford, 1967.

Chartiers, R., and Neveux, H. "La ville dominante." In Le Roy Ladurie, E., ed., *La ville classique*, vol. 3 of *Histoire de la France urbaine* (under the direction of Duby, G.), pp. 15–285. Paris, 1981.

Chaudhuri, K. N. "Some Reflections on the Town and Country in Mughal India." *Modern Asian Studies* 12, no. 1 (1978): 77–96.

Chaunu, P. *L'Amérique et les Amériques.* Paris, 1964.

Chedeville, A. "De la cité à la ville, 1000–1150." In Le Goff, J., ed., *La ville médiévale*, vol. 2 of *Histoire de la France urbaine* (under the direction of Duby, G.), pp. 29–181. Paris, 1980.

Chêng, Tè-k'un. "The Beginning of Chinese Civilization." *Antiquity* 47, no. 186 (June 1973): 197–209.

Childe, V. G. *The Most Ancient East.* New York, 1928.

———. "The Urban Revolution." *The Town Planning Review* 21, no. 1 (1950): 3–17.

Chittick, N. "Indian Relations with East Africa before the Arrival of the Portuguese." *Journal of the Royal Asiatic Society of Great Britain and Ireland*, no. 2 (1980): 117–27.

Choe, Chong-Pil. "The Diffusion Route and Chronology of Korean Plant Domestication." *Journal of Asian Studies* 41, no. 3 (May 1982): 519–29.

Chombart de Lauwe, P.-H. "Périphérie des villes et crise de civilisation." *Cahiers internationaux de Sociologie* 72 (1982): 5–16.

Christaller, W. *Die Zentralen Orte in Süddeutschland.* Jena, 1933.

Clark, C. *The Conditions of Economic Progress.* London, 1939.

———. *Population Growth and Land Use.* 2d ed. London, 1977.

Clark, C., and Haswell, M. *The Economics of Subsistence Agriculture.* London, 1970.

Clark, G. *World Prehistory in New Perspective.* Cambridge, 1961. 3d ed., 1977.

Cohen, M. N. *The Food Crisis in Prehistory Overpopulation and the Origins of Agriculture.* New Haven, 1977.

Condran, G. A., and Crimmins, E. "Mortality Differentials between Rural and Urban Areas of States in the Northeastern United States 1890–1900." *Journal of Historical Geography* 6 (1980): 179–202.

Cooley, C. H. *The Theory of Transportation.* Publications of the American Economic Association, no. 9 (1894): 1–148.

Corfield, P. J. *The Impact of English Towns, 1700–1800.* Oxford, 1982.

Crain, R. L. "Fluoridation: The Diffusion of an Innovation among Cities." *Social Forces* 44 (1966): 467–76.

Crisler, J. "Caesarea World Monument." *Biblical Archaeology Review* 8, no. 3 (May–June 1982): 4.

Dagron, G. *Naissance d'une capitale: Constantinople et ses institutions.* Paris, 1974.

Dark, P. J. C. *An Introduction to Benin Art and Technology.* Oxford, 1973.

Darnhofer-Demar, E. "Colombia's Lost City Revealed." *New Scientist* (20 May 1982): 513–15.

Daumas, M., ed. *Histoire générale des techniques.* 5 vols. Paris, 1962–79.

Daunton, M. J. "Towns and Economic Growth in Eighteenth-Century England." In Abrams, P., and Wrigley, E. A., eds., *Towns in Societies: Essays in Economic History and Historical Sociology,* pp. 245–77. Cambridge, 1978.

Davidson, J. "The Prehistory of Western Polynesia." *Journal de la Société des Océanistes* 37, 70–71, (March–June 1981): 100–10.

Davis, K. *The Population of India and Pakistan.* Princeton, 1951.

———. *World Urbanization, 1950–1970.* Vol. 1. Berkeley, 1969. Vol. 2. Berkeley, 1972.

Davis, K., and Hertz, H. "Urbanization and the Development of Pre-Industrial Areas." *Economic Development and Cultural Change* 3, no. 1 (October 1954): 6–26.

———. Unpublished estimates of the size of urban population, cited in Hauser, P. M., ed., *Urbanization in Asia and the Far East.* Calcutta, 1957.

Deane, P. *The First Industrial Revolution.* Cambridge, 1967.

Dejevsky, N., "The Urbanization of Eastern Europe." In Sherratt, A., ed., *The Cambridge Encyclopedia of Archaeology,* pp. 314–18. Cambridge, 1980.

Delbos, G. "A l'ombre des usines, comme si de rien n'était . . . , L'industrialisation et le maintien d'une communauté paysanne en Lorraine." *Etudes rurales,* no. 76 (October–December 1979): 83–96.

Della-Pina, M. "L'évolution démographique des villes toscanes à l'époque de la naissance et de l'affirmation de l'état régional (XVe–XVIIe siècles)." *Villes du passé, Annales de démographie historique, 1982,* pp. 43–53. Paris, 1982.

Desai, A. V. "Population and Standard of Living in Akbar's Time." *Indian Economic and Social History Review* 9 (March 1972): 43–62.

Deschamps, H. *Histoire générale de l'Afrique Noire.* Vol. 1, *Des origines à 1800.* Paris, 1970.

Deshayes, J. "Les techniques des Grecs." In Daumas, M., ed., *Histoire générale des techniques,* vol. 1, pp. 183–217. Paris, 1962.

Desplanques, G. "La ville ou la campagne." *Economie et statistique,* no. 107 (January 1979): 17–29.

Devèze, M. *L'Europe et le monde à la fin du XVIIIe siècle.* Paris, 1970.

Diaz de Castillo, B. *La conquête de la Nouvelle Espagne.* Editions Rencontre (collection *Sommets de la littérature espagnole,* vol. 4). Lausanne, 1962.

Dickinson, O. T. P. K. *The Origins of Mycenaean Civilisation.* Göteborg, 1977.

Dictionnaire Géographique Universel. 10 vols. Paris, 1823–1833.

Doehaerd, R. *Le Haut Moyen Age occidental.* Paris, 1971.

Doeppers, D. F. "The Development of Philippine Cities before 1900." *Journal of Asian Studies* 31, no. 4 (August 1972): 769–92.

Dollinger-Léonard, Y. "De la cité romaine à la ville médiévale dans la région de la Moselle et de la Haute Meuse." In *Studien zu den Anfängen des Europäischen Städtewesens*. 1958, reprint, pp. 195–226. Sigmaringen, 1970.

Doxiadis, C. A., and Papaioannou, J.-G. *Ecumenopolis, the Inevitable City of the Future*. Athens, 1974.

Dublin, L. I, and Lotka, A. L. *Length of Life: A Study of the Life Tables*. New York, 1936.

Duby, G. "La révolution agricole médiévale." *Revue de géographie de Lyon* 29 (1954):361–66.

———. "Les villes du Sud-Est de la Gaule du VIIIe au XIe siècle." In Settimane di Studio del Centro Italiano di Studi sull'alto Medioevo, VI (ed.): *La Città nell'alto medioevo*, pp. 231–58. Spoleto, 1959.

Dumont, R. *False Start in Africa*. London, 1966.

Duncan-Jones, R. *The Economy of the Roman Empire: Quantitative Studies*. Cambridge, 1974.

Durand, J. D. "Historical Estimates of World Population: An Evaluation." *Population and Development Review* 3, no. 3 (September 1977): 253–96.

During Caspers, E. C. L. "Sumer, Coastal Arabia, and the Indus Valley in the Protoliterate and Early Dynastic Eras Supporting Evidence for a Cultural Linkage." *Journal of the Economic and Social History of the Orient* 22, part 2 (May 1979): 121–35.

Duval, P.-M. "L'apport technique des Romains." In Daumas, M., ed., *Histoire générale des techniques*, vol. 1, pp. 218–54. Paris, 1962.

Dwyer, D. J. *People and Housing in Third World Cities: Perspectives on the Problem of Spontaneous Settlements*. London, 1975.

Dyhouse, C. "Working-Class Mothers and Infant Mortality in England, 1895–1914." *Journal of Social History* 12 (1978–9): 248–62.

Dyos, H. J. "Workmen's Fares in South London, 1860–1914." *Journal of Transport History* 1 (1953): 3–19.

Earle, T. K., and Ericson, J. E., eds. *Exchange Systems in Prehistory*. New York, 1977.

Edelstein, G., and Gibson, S. "Ancient Jerusalem's Rural Food Basket." *Biblical Archaeology Review* 8, no. 4 (July–August 1982): 46–54.

Effenterre, H. van. *Le palais de Mallia et la cité minoenne*. 2 vols. Rome, 1980.

Ehret, C. "On the Antiquity of Agriculture in Ethiopia." *Journal of African History* 20, no. 2 (1979): 161–77.

Elvin, M. *The Pattern of the Chinese Past*. London, 1973.

———. "Chinese Cities since the Sung Dynasty." In Abrams, P., and Wrigley, E. A., eds., *Towns in Societies: Essays in Economic History and Historical Sociology*, pp. 79–89. Cambridge, 1978.

Emerson, J. P. "Urban School-Leavers and Unemployment in China." *The China Quarterly* 93 (March 1983): 1–16.

Encyclopaedia Britannica. 13th ed. London, 1926.

Erder, L., and Faroqhi, S. "Population Rise and Fall in Anatolia, 1550–1620." *Middle East Studies* 15, no. 3 (October 1979): 328–45.

Falkus, M. E. "The Early Development of the British Gas Industry, 1790–1815." *Economic History Review*, 2d ser., vol. 35, no. 2 (May 1982): 217–34.

Fedor, T. S. *Patterns of Urban Growth in the Russian Empire during the Nineteenth Century*. Chicago, 1975.

Feller, I. "The Urban Location of United States Invention, 1860–1913." *Exploration in Economic History* 8 (Spring 1971): 285–303.

———. "Determinant of the Composition of Urban Invention." *Economic Geography* 49, no. 1 (January 1973): 48–58.

Filesi, T. *China and Africa in the Middle Ages*. London, 1972.

Finlay, R. "Debate: Natural Decrease in Early Modern Cities." *Past and Present*, no. 92 (August 1981): 169–74.

Finley, M. I. *The Ancient Economy*. Berkeley, 1973.

———. "The Ancient City: From Fustel de Coulanges to Max Weber and Beyond." *Comparative Studies in Society and History* 19 (1977): 305–27.

Firebaugh, G. "Structural Determinants of Urbanization in Asia and Latin America, 1950–1970." *American Sociological Review* 44, no. 2 (April 1979): 199–215.

Fisher, F. J. "The Development of the London Food Market, 1540–1640." *Economic History Review* 5, no. 2 (1935): 46–64.

Fixot, M. "Une idéale, une réalité difficile: les villes du VIIe au IXe siècle." In Duby, G., ed., *La ville antique*, vol. 1 of *Histoire de la France urbaine* (under the direction of Duby, G.), pp. 495–563. Paris, 1980.

Flinn, M. W. *Origins of the Industrial Revolution*. London, 1966 (3d edition, 1969).

Floud, R., and McCloskey, D., eds. *The Economic History of Britain since 1700*. Vol. 1, *1700–1860*. Cambridge, 1981.

Foss, C. "Archaeology and the 'Twenty Cities' of Byzantine Asia." *American Journal of Archaeology* 81, no. 4 (Fall 1977): 467–86.

———. "Byzantium: An Empire under Stress." In Sherratt, A., ed., *The Cambridge Encyclopedia of Archaeology*, pp. 284–88. Cambridge, 1980.

Foster, M. S. *From Streetcar to Superhighway: American City Planners and Urban Transportation, 1900–1940*. Philadelphia, 1981.

Fourastié, J. *Le grand espoir du XXe siècle*. Paris, 1949.

Fourquin, G. "La Chrétienté latine occidentale désenclavante." In Leon, P., ed. *Histoire économique et sociale du monde*. Vol. 1, *L'ouverture du monde, XIVe–XVIe siècle*, pp. 175–391. Paris, 1977.

François, E. "La mortalité urbaine en Allemagne au XVIIIe siècle." *Annales de démographie historique, 1978*, "La mortalité du passé," pp. 135–65. Paris, 1978.

Galantay, E. Y. *New Towns: Antiquity to the Present*. New York, 1975.

Gallaway, L. E., and Vedder, R. K. "The Increasing Urbanization Thesis: Did 'New Immigrants' to the United States Have a Particular Fondness for Urban Life?" *Explorations in Economic History* 8, no. 3 (Spring 1971): 305–19.

Garden, M. *Lyon et les Lyonnais au XVIIIe siècle*. Paris, 1975.

Garelli, P. *Le Proche-Orient asiatique, des origines aux invasions des peuples de la mer*. Paris, 1969.

Garlake, P. S. *Great Zimbabwe*. London, 1973.

Garnick, D. H. "Shifting Patterns in the Growth of Metropolitan and Non-metropolitan Areas." *Survey of Current Business* (May 1983): 39–44.

Geertz, C. *Peddlers and Princes: Social Change and Economic Modernization in Two Indonesian Towns*. Chicago, 1963.

Gerhard, P. A. *A Guide to the Historical Geography of New Spain*. Cambridge, 1972.

Gilbrat, R. *Les inégalités économiques*. Paris, 1931.

Gilman, A. "Neolithic of Northwest Africa." *Antiquity* 48, no. 191 (September 1974): 273–82.

Gleichmann, P. R. "Des villes propres et sans odeur. La vidange du corps humain: équipements et domestication." *Urbi*, no. 5 (April 1982): 88–100.

Glick, T. F. *Islamic and Christian Spain in the Early Middle Ages*. Princeton, 1979.

Goitein, S. D. *A Mediterranean Society*. Vol. 1, *Economic Foundations*. Berkeley, 1967.

Gokhale, B. G. "Burhanpur. Notes on the History of an Indian City in the XVIIth Century." *Journal of the Economic and Social History of the Orient* 15, part 3 (December 1972): 316–23.

Golson, J., and Hugues, P. J. "The Appearance of Plant and Animal Domestication in New Guinea." *Journal de la Société des Océanistes* 36, no. 69 (December 1980): 294–303.

Gottmann, J. "Office Work and the Evolution of Cities." *Ekistics* 46, no. 274 (January–February 1979): 4–7.

Goudineau, Ch., and Kruta, V. "Les antécédents: y a-t-il une ville protohistorique?" In Duby, G., ed., *La ville antique*, vol. 1 of *Histoire de la France urbaine* (under the direction of Duby, G.), pp. 139–231. Paris, 1980.

Gran Aymerich, J. M. J. "Prospections archéologiques au Sahara atlantique." *Antiquités Africaines* 13 (1979): 7–21.

Granotier, B. *La planète des bidonvilles: Perspectives de l'explosion urbaine dans le Tiers-Monde*. Paris, 1980.

Grauman, J. V. "Orders of Magnitude of the World's Urban Population in History." In United Nations, *Population Bulletin of the United Nations, no. 8— 1976*, pp. 16–33. New York, 1977.

Graunt, Captain John. *Observations upon the Bills of Mortality*. London, 1662 (edited by C. H. Hull, Cambridge, 1899).

Grenier, A. *Manuel d'archéologie gallo-romaine*, vol. II-2. Paris, 1931–34.

Grenier, L., and Wieser-Benedetti, H. *Les châteaux de l'industrie: Recherches sur l'architecture de la région lilloise de 1830 à 1930*. Vol. 2. Paris, 1979.

Griffeth, R. "The Hausa City: States from 1450 to 1804." In Griffeth, R., and Thomas, C. G., eds., *The City-States in Five Cultures*, pp. 143–80. Santa Barbara, Calif., 1981.

Griffin, J. B. "Agricultural Groups in North America." In Sherratt, A., ed., *The Cambridge Encyclopedia of Archaeology*, pp. 375–81. Cambridge, 1980.

Grigg, D. B. *Population Growth and Agrarian Change: An Historical Perspective*. Cambridge, 1980.

Guarda, G. "Military Influence in the Cities of the Kingdom of Chile." In Schaedel, R. P., Hardoy, J. E., and Kinzer, N. S., eds. *Urbanization in the Americas from the Beginning to the Present*, pp. 343–82. The Hague and Paris, 1978.

Gugler, J. "The Urban Character of Contemporary Revolutions." *Studies in Comparative International Development* 17, no. 2 (Summer 1982): 60–73.

Gutton, J. P. *Domestiques et serviteurs dans la France de l'Ancien Régime*. Paris, 1981.

Gutwein, K. C. *Third Palestine: A Regional Study in Byzantine Urbanization*. Washington, D.C., 1981.

Habib, I. "Population." In Raychaudhuri, T., and Habib, I., eds., *The Cambridge Economic History of India*, vol. 1, *ca. 1200–ca. 1750*, pp. 163–71. London, 1982.

Hägerstrand, T. *Innovation Diffusion as a Spatial Process.* Chicago, 1967.
Hammarström, I. "Urban History in Scandinavia: A Survey of Recent Trends." In *Urban History Yearbook 1978*, pp. 46–55. Leicester.
Hammond, M. *The City in the Ancient World.* Cambridge, Mass., 1972.
Hammond, P. C. "New Lights on the Nabataeans." *Biblical Archaeology Review* 7, no. 2 (March–April 1981): 23–41.
Hanley, S. B., and Yamamura, K. *Economic and Demographic Change in Pre-industrial Japan, 1600–1868.* Princeton, 1977.
Harlan, J. R., de Wet, J. M. J., and Stemler, A. B. L., eds. *Origins of African Plant Domestication.* The Hague and Paris, 1976.
Hartung, H. "Pre-Columbian Settlements in Mesoamerica." *Ekistics* 45, no. 271 (July–August 1978): 326–30.
Hartwell, R. M. *The Causes of the Industrial Revolution in England.* London, 1967.
Hassan, F. A. *Demographic Archaeology.* New York, 1981.
Hauser, P. M., ed. *Le phénomène d'urbanisation en Asie et en Extrême-Orient.* Calcutta, 1959.
Helin, E. *La démographie de Liège aux XVIIe et XVIIIe siècles.* Brussels, 1963.
Hensel, W. "The Origins of Western and Eastern European Slav Towns." In Barley, M. W., ed., *European Towns: Their Archaeology and Early History*, pp. 373–90. London, 1977.
Herm, G. *Les Phéniciens, 'L'antique royaume de la pourpre'.* Paris, 1976.
Herrmann, J. *Research into the Early History of the Town in the Territory of the German Democratic Republic.* In Barley, M. W., ed. *European Towns: Their Archaeology and Early History*, pp. 243–59. London, 1977.
Hewitt, M. *Wives and Mothers in Victorian Industry.* London, 1958 (reprint Westpoint, Conn., 1975).
Higgs, R. "American Inventiveness, 1870–1920." *Journal of Political Economy* 79 (May–June 1971): 661–67.
Higounet-Nadal, A. "La démographie des villes françaises au Moyen-Age." In *Annales de démographie historique, 1980.* Paris, 1980.
Historisk Statistik för Sverige. Vol. 1, 2d ed. Stockholm, 1969.
Ho, Ping-Ti. *The Cradle of the East.* Hong Kong and Chicago, 1975.
———. "The Indigenous Origins of Chinese Agriculture." In Reed, C. A., ed., *Origins of Agriculture*, pp. 413–84. The Hague and Paris, 1977.
Hobsbawm, E. J. "The Nineteenth Century London Labour Market." In Centre for Urban Studies., *London, Aspects of Change*, pp. 3–28. London, 1964.
Hoffmann, A. *Oesterreichisches Städtebuch.* 4 vols. Vienna, 1968–76.
Hofsten, E., and Lundström, H. *Swedish Population History: Main Trends from 1750 to 1970.* Urval no. 8. Stockholm, 1976.
Hohenberg, P. M., and Lees, L. H. *The Making of Urban Europe 1000–1950.* Cambridge, Mass., 1985.
Hopkins, I. W. J. "The City Region in Roman Palestine." *Palestine Exploration Quarterly*, 112d year (January–June 1980): 19–32.
Hopkins, K. "Economic Growth and Towns in Classical Antiquity." In Abrams, P., and Wrigley, E. A., eds., *Towns in Societies: Essays in Economic History and Historical Sociology*, pp. 35–77. Cambridge, 1978.
Howard, E. *Garden Cities of Tomorrow.* London, 1898.
Hoyt, H. "The Growth of Cities from 1800 to 1960 and Forecast to the Year 2000." *Land Economics* 39, no. 2 (May 1973): 167–73.

Hull, R. W. *African Cities and Towns before the European Conquest.* New York, 1976.

Huot, J.-L. "Des villes existent-elles en Orient dès l'époque néolithique?" *Annales, E.S.C.,* 25th year special issue, no. 4 (July–August 1970): 1091–101.

ILO. *Employment Incomes and Equality: A Strategy for Increasing Productive Employment in Kenya.* Geneva, 1972.

Institut international de statistique. *Statistiques démographiques des grandes villes, 1946–51,* A1, The Hague, 1954; and *1946–53,* A2, The Hague, 1957.

Jacobs, J. *The Economy of Cities.* New York, 1969.

Jacobson, J. "Recent Developments in South Asian Prehistory and Protohistory." *Annual Review of Anthropology* 8 (1979): 467–502.

Jacquart, J. "Les paysanneries à l'épreuve." In Leon, P., ed. *Histoire économique et sociale du monde.* Vol. 2: *Les hésitations de la croissance, 1580–1740,* pp. 345–494. Paris, 1978.

Jaffe, A. J. "Urbanization and Fertility." *American Journal of Sociology* 47, no. 1 (July 1942): 48–60.

Jefferson, M. "The Law of Primate City." *Geographical Review* 29 (1939): 226–36.

Johannot, C. *Etude de l'évolution de la structure par taille des villes du Tiers-Monde entre 1900 et 1950.* Master's thesis, Department of Economic History, University of Geneva. Geneva, 1977.

Johnson, G. Z. "Differential Fertility in European Countries." In National Bureau of Economic Research, *Demographic and Economic Change in Developed Countries,* pp. 36–72. Princeton, 1960.

Johnson, R. E. *Peasant and Proletarian: The Working Class of Moscow at the End of the Nineteenth Century.* Brunswick, N.J., 1979.

Jones, A. H. M. *The Greek City from Alexander to Justinian.* Oxford, 1940.

———. *The Later Roman Empire, 284–602.* 3 vols. Oxford, 1964.

———. *Cities of the Eastern Roman Provinces.* 2d ed. Oxford, 1971.

———. *The Roman Economy.* Oxford, 1974.

Jones, R. "The Fifth Continent: Problems Concerning the Human Colonization of Australia." *Annual Review of Anthropology* 8 (1979): 445–66.

Josse, R. "Croissance urbaine au Sahara: Ghardaïa." *Cahiers d'Outre-Mer,* 23A, no. 89 (January–March 1970): 46–57.

Kan Hla. "Ancient Cities in Burma." *Journal of the Society of Architectural Historians* 38, no. 2 (May 1979): 95–102.

Kemp. B. J. "The Early Development of Towns in Egypt." *Antiquity* 51, no. 203 (November 1977): 185–200.

Keyser, E. *Deutsches Städtebuch.* 5 vols. Stuttgart, 1939–74.

Kim, Won-Yong. "Discoveries of Rice in Prehistoric Sites in Korea." *Journal of Asian Studies* 41, no. 3 (May 1982): 513–18.

Knodel, J. *The Decline of Fertility in Germany, 1871–1939.* Princeton, 1974.

———. "Town and Country in Nineteenth-Century Germany: A Review of Urban-Rural Differentials in Demographic Behavior." *Social Science History* 1, no. 3 (Spring 1977): 356–82.

Kohl, J. G. *Der Verkehr und die Ansiedlungen der Menschen in ihrer Abhängigkeit von der Gestaltung der Erdoberfläche.* Leipzig, 1841.

Kohl, P. L. "The Balance of Trade in Southwestern Asia in the Mid-Third Millennium B.C.." *Current Anthropology* 19, no. 3 (September 1978): 463–75.

Kopp, A. *Changer la vie, changer la ville.* Paris, 1975.

Kornhauser, D. *Urban Japan: Its Foundations and Growth*. London and New York, 1976.

Krautheimer, R. *Rome, Profiles of a City, 312–1308*. Princeton, 1980.

Krzyzaniak, L. "New Light on Early Food-Production in the Central Sudan." *Journal of African History* 19, no. 2 (1978): 159–72.

Kuznets, S. "Rural-Urban Differences in Fertility: An International Comparison." In American Philosophical Society, *Proceedings of the American Philosophical Society* 118 (1974): 1–29. Philadelphia, 1974.

Lacelle, C. "Les domestiques dans les villes canadiennes au XIXe siècle: effectif et conditions de vie." *Histoire Sociale* 15, no. 2 (May 1982): 181–207.

Lacoste, Y. "Bidonville." In *Encyclopaedia Universalis*, vol. 3, pp. 258–60. Paris, 1968.

Lampert, R. J. "Trends in Australian Prehistoric Research." *Antiquity* 49, no. 195 (September 1975): 197–205.

Landes, D. "Technological Change and Development in Western Europe, 1750–1914." In Habakkuk, H. J., and Postan, M., eds., *The Cambridge Economic History of Europe*, vol. 6, part 1, pp. 274–601. Cambridge, 1965.

———. *Revolution in Time*. Cambridge, Mass., 1983.

Langer, L. N. "The Medieval Russian Town." In Hamm, M. F., ed., *The City in Russian History*, pp. 11–33. Lexington, Ky., 1976.

Lapidus, I. M. "The Evolution of Muslim Urban Society." *Comparative Studies in Society and History* 15, no. 2 (January 1973): 21–50.

Law, R. C. C. "North Africa in the Period of Phoenician and Greek Colonisation, c. 800 to 323 B.C.." In Fage, J. D., ed., *The Cambridge History of Africa*, vol. 2, pp. 87–147. Cambridge, 1978.

League of Nations. *Statistical Year-Book of the League of Nations*. Geneva, various issues.

Le Goff, J. "The Town as an Agent of Civilisation, 1200–1500." In Cipolla, C. M., ed., *The Fontana Economic History of Europe*, vol. 1, pp. 71–106. London, 1972.

———, ed. *La ville médiévale*. Vol 2 of *Histoire de la France urbaine* (under the direction of Duby, G.). Paris, 1980.

Leman, P. "Les villes romaines de la région Nord/Pas-de-Calais à la lumière des fouilles récentes." *Revue Archéologique* (1979), no. 1: 168–76.

Lepelley, C. *Les cités de l'Afrique romaine au Bas-Empire*. 2 vols. Paris, 1979–81.

Lepetit, B. "L'évolution de la notion de ville d'après les tableaux et descriptions géographiques de la France (1650–1850)." *Urbi* 2 (December 1979): 99–107.

Lequin, Y. "Ouvriers dans la ville (XIXe et XXe siècles)." *Le Mouvement social*, no. 118 (January–March 1982): 3–7.

Lesthaeghe, R. J. *The Decline of Belgian Fertility 1800–1970*. Princeton, 1977.

Levasseur, E. *La population française*. Vol. 2. Paris, 1891.

Lévi-Provençal, E. *Histoire de l'Espagne musulmane*. Vol. 1, *La conquête et l'Emirat hispano-umaiyade (710–912)*. Paris, 1950. Vol. 2, *Le califat umaiyade de Cordoue (912–1031)*. Paris, 1950. Vol. 3, *Le siècle du califat de Cordoue*. Paris, 1953.

Levtzion, N. *Ancient Ghana and Mali*. London, 1973.

Lipton, M. *Why People Stay Poor: Urban Bias in World Development*. Cambridge, Mass., 1977.

Livi-Bacci, M. *A History of Italian Fertility during the Past Two Centuries*. Princeton, 1977.

Lloyd, P. *Slums of Hope? Shanty Towns of the Third World*. Harmondsworth, 1979.

Lombard, D. "Pour une histoire des villes du Sud-Est asiatique." *Annales, E.S.C.*, 25th year, no. 4 (July–August 1970): 842–56.

Loofs-Wissowa, H. H. E. "The Development and Spread of Metallurgy in Southeast Asia: A Review of the Present Evidence." *Journal of Southeast Asian Studies* 14 (March 1983):1–11.

Lopez, R. S. "Un borgne au royaume des aveugles: la position de Byzance dans l'économie européenne du haut Moyen Age." *Bulletin de l'Association Marc Bloch de Toulouse* 5–6 (1953–55): 25–31.

Losch, A. *Die Räumliche Ordnung der Wirtschaft*. Jena, 1940.

Lot, F. *Recherches sur la population et la superficie des cités remontant à période gallo-romaine*. 3 vols. Paris, 1945–53.

Lotka, A. J. *Elements of Natural Biology*. New York, 1925.

Ma, L. J. C. *Commercial Development and Urban Change in Sung China*. Ann Arbor, 1971.

———. "Preliminary Results of the Census in China." *The Geographical Review* 73, no. 2 (1983): 198–210.

Mabogunje, A. L. *Urbanization in Nigeria*. London, 1968.

———. *Géographie historique: Aspects économiques*. In UNESCO, ed., *Histoire générale de l'Afrique*. Vol. 1, *Méthodologie et préhistoire africaine* (under the direction of Ki-Zerbo, J.), pp. 365–81. Paris, 1980.

McEvedy, C., and Jones, R. *Atlas of World Population History*. Harmondsworth, 1978.

McGee, T. G. *The Southeast Asian City*. London, 1967 (reprinted in 1969).

———. "Peasants in the Cities: A Paradox, a Paradox, a Most Ingenious Paradox." *Human Organisation* 32 (Summer 1973): 135–42.

———. "Conservation and Dissolution in the Third World City: The 'Shanty Town' as an Element of Conservation." *Development and Change* 10, no. 1 (January 1979): 1–22.

———. "The Urbanization Process and Industrialization in the Market Economies of Asia." *Regional Development Dialogue* 1, no. 2 (August 1980): 131–43.

McIntosh, R. J., and McIntosh, S. K. "The Inland Niger Delta before the Empire of Mali: Evidence from Jenne-Jeno." *Journal of African History* 22, no. 1 (1981): 1–22.

Maitre, J. P. "Contributions à la préhistoire récente de l'Ahaggar dans son contexte saharien." *Bulletin de l'Institut fondamental d'Afrique Noire* 38, Série B, no. 4 (1976): 715–89.

Mango, C. *Le développement urbain de Constantinople (IVe–VIIe siècle)*. Paris, 1985.

Mantoux, P. *The Industrial Revolution in the Eighteenth Century*. London, 1928.

Maret, P. de. "New Survey of Archaeological Research and Dates for West-Central and North-Central Africa." *Journal of African History* 23, no. 1 (1982): 1–15.

Martin, I. *Inventions techniques et urbanisation en Europe au XIXe siècle: Allemagne, France et Royaume-Uni*. Master's thesis, Department of Economic History, University of Geneva. Geneva, 1977.

Massu, C. "Pullman City: une 'ville modèle' du capitalisme sauvage américain." *Urbi* 7 (March 1983): 91–100.

Mathias, P. *The First Industrial Nation: An Economic History of Britain, 1700–1914*. London, 1969.

Mendels, F. F. *Industrialization and Population Pressure in XVIIIth Century Flanders*. Wisconsin, 1969.

Mestier du Bourg, H. de "La première moitié du XIe siècle au Cambodge: Suryavarman 1er, sa vie et quelques aspects des institutions à son époque." *Journal asiatique* 258, nos. 3–4 (1970): 281–314.

Mgomezulu, G. G. Y. "Recent Archaeological Research and Radiocarbon Dates from Eastern Africa." *Journal of African History* 22, no. 4 (1981): 435–56.

Millon, R. "Urban Revolution: Early Civilizations of the New World." In *International Encyclopedia of Social Sciences* 16: 207–16. New York, 1967.

———. "Teotihuacan: City, State and Civilization." In Sabloff, J. A., ed., *Archaeology. Supplement to the Handbook of Middle American Indians*. Vol. 1, pp. 198–243. Austin, Tx., 1981.

Milov, L. V. "On the So-Called Agrarian Towns of Eighteenth-Century Russia." *Soviet Studies in History* 21 (Summer 1982): 10–31.

Mitchell, B. R. *Abstract of British Historical Statistics*. Cambridge, 1962.

Mitchell, S. "The Hellenistic World." In Sherratt, A., ed., *The Cambridge Encyclopedia of Archaeology*, pp. 216–21. Cambridge, 1980.

Mols, R. *Introduction à la démographie historique des villes d'Europe du XIVe au XVIIIe siècle*. 3 vols. Gembloux-Louvain, 1954–56.

———. "Population in Europe 1500–1700." In Cipolla, C. M., ed., *The Fontana Economic History of Europe*. Vol.2, pp. 15–82. London, 1974.

Morel, J. P. "L'expansion phocéenne en Occident: dix années de recherches (1966–1975)." *Bulletin de correspondance hellénique*, no. 109 (1975), part 2: Chronique et Rapports, pp. 853–96.

Morris, J. *Londinium: London in the Roman Empire*. London, 1982.

Morse, R. E., ed. *The Urban Development of Latin America, 1750–1920*. Stanford, 1971.

Mosk, C. "Rural-Urban Fertility Differences and the Fertility Transition." *Population Studies* 34, no. 1 (March 1980): 77–90.

Muckelroy, K. "Two Bronze Age Cargoes in British Waters." *Antiquity* 54, no. 211 (July 1980): 100–109.

Mukerjee, R. *The Economic History of India, 1600–1800*. Allahabad, 1967.

Mulhall, M. G. *The Dictionary of Statistics*. 4th ed. London, 1898.

Mumford, L. *The City in History*. London, 1961.

Munson, P. J. "Archaeology and the Prehistoric Origins of the Ghana Empire." *Journal of African History* 21, no. 4 (1980): 457–66.

Naqvi, H. K. *Urban Centres and Industries in Upper India, 1556–1803*. London, 1968.

Naudou, J. "L'Inde." In *Histoire universelle*. Vol. 1, *Encyclopédie de la Pléiade*, pp. 1411–1518. Paris, 1956.

Neild, S. M. "Colonial Urbanism: The Development of Madras City in the Eighteenth and Nineteenth Centuries." *Modern Asian Studies* 13 (1979): 217–46.

Nelson, S. M. "The Effects of Rice Agriculture on Prehistoric Korea." *Journal of Asian Studies* 41, no. 3 (May 1982): 531–43.

Nenci, G. "Chômeurs et manoeuvres dans la Grèce classique." *Dialogues d'histoire ancienne* 7 (1981): 333–43.

Nicolas, D. "Le développement urbain dans la Flandres médiévale: Structures du peuplement, fonctions urbaines et formation de capital." *Annales, E.S.C.*, 33d year, no. 3 (May–June 1978): 501–27.

Nihan, G. *Le secteur non structuré: Signification, aire d'extension du concept et application expérimentale.* Working Papers, WEP 2-33/Doc. 7, ILO. Geneva, 1979.

Nihei, Y. A. "Unemployment in China: Policies, Problems and Prospects." *China Newsletters,* no. 38 (May–June 1982):14–20.

Oates, J. "The Emergence of Cities in the Near East." In Sherratt, A., ed., *The Cambridge Encyclopedia of Archaeology*, pp. 112–19. Cambridge, 1980.

O'Brien, P. "European Economic Development: The Contribution of the Periphery." *Economic History Review* 35, no. 1 (February 1981): 1–18.

Office Permanent de l'Institut International de Statistique. *Annuaire statistique des grandes villes.* The Hague, 1927.

———. *Annuaire statistique des grandes villes.* The Hague, 1931.

Ogburn, W. F., and Duncan, O. D. "City Size as a Sociological Variable." In Burgess, E. W., and Bogue, D. J., eds., *Contributions to Urban Sociology*, pp. 129–47. Chicago, 1964.

Oliver, R., and Fagan, B. M. *Africa in the Iron Age c. 500 B.C. to A.D.1400.* Cambridge, 1975.

Oliver, R., and Fage, J. D. *A Short History of Africa.* New edition. Harmondsworth, 1975.

Ostrogorsky, G. "Byzantine Cities in the Early Middle Ages." *Dumbarton Oaks Papers No. 13*, pp. 45–66. Washington, D.C., 1959.

Parrot, A. *L'aventure archéologique.* Paris, 1979.

Patlagean, E. *Pauvreté économique et pauvreté sociale à Byzance, 4e–7e siècles.* Paris and the Hague, 1977.

Patten, J. *English Towns, 1500–1700.* London, 1978.

Pawson, E. *The Early Industrial Revolution.* London, 1979.

Peacock, D. P. S., ed. *Pottery and Early Commerce: Characterization and Trade in Roman and Later Ceramics.* London, 1977.

Pedersen, P. O. "Innovation Diffusion within and between National Urban Systems." *Geographical Analysis* 2 (1970): 203–54.

Perkins, D. H. *Agricultural Development in China, 1368–1968.* Edinburgh, 1969.

Perrenoud, A. *La population de Genève, XVIe–XIXe siècles.* Geneva, 1979.

———. "La transition démographique et ses conséquences sur le renouvellement d'une population urbaine." In Bairoch, P., and Piuz, A.-M., eds., *Des économies traditionelles aux sociétés industrielles*, pp. 81–117. Geneva, 1985.

Perrot, J.-C. *Genèse d'une ville moderne: Caen au XVIIIe siècle.* 2 vols. Paris, 1975.

Perroux, F. *L'économie du XXe siècle.* Paris, 1961.

Petersen, W. "A Demographer's View of Prehistoric Demography." *Current Anthropology* 16, no. 2 (June 1975): 227–37.

Petit, P. "Phénicien: L'activité économique et la colonisation." In *Encyclopaedia Universalis*, vol. 12, pp. 928–29. Paris, 1972.

Philbrick, A. K. "Principles of Areal Functional Organisation in Regional Human Geography." *Economic Geography*, no. 3 (1957): 299–336.

Phythian-Adams, C. *Desolation of a City: Coventry and the Urban Crisis of the Late Middle Ages.* Cambridge, 1979.

Pirenne, H. *Histoire économique et sociale du Moyen Age*. Paris, 1914 (reprinted 1933 and 1963).

Piuz, A.-M. "Pouvoirs et subsistances à Genève vers 1650–1750." In Livet, G., and Vogler, B., eds., *Pouvoir, ville et société en Europe, 1650–1750*, pp. 337–45. Paris, 1983.

Poinsotte, J.-M. "Les Romains et la Chine: Réalités et mythes." *Mélanges de l'Ecole française de Rome* 91 (1979): 431–79.

Pounds, N. J. G. "The Urbanization of the Classical World." *Annals of the Association of American Geographers* 59 (March 1969): 135–56.

Pouthas, C. H. *La population française pendant la première moitié du XIXe siècle*. Paris, 1956.

Pred, A. R. *The External Relations of Cities during the "Industrial Revolution"*. Chicago, 1962.

———. *The Spatial Dynamics of U.S. Urban Industrial Growth, 1800–1914*. Cambridge, Mass., 1966.

Price, R. *Observations on Reversionary Payments: On Schemes for Providing Annuities for Widows, and for Persons in Old Age*, etc. London, 1772.

Prins, J. "Les villes indonésiennes." In *Recueil de la Société Jean Bodin*. Vol. 7, *La ville*, pp. 195–206. Brussels, 1955.

Pumain, D. "Chemins de fer et croissance urbaine en France au XIXe siècle." *Annales de géographie*, no. 507, 91st year (September–October 1982): 529–50.

Randles, W. G. L. "Pre-Colonial Urbanization in Africa South of the Equator." In Ucko, P. J., Tringham, R., and Dimbleby, G. W., eds., *Man, Settlement and Urbanism*, pp. 891–97. London, 1972.

Rathbone, D. W. "The Development of Agriculture in the 'Ager Cosanus' during the Roman Republic: Problems of Evidence and Interpretations." *Journal of Roman Studies* 71 (1981): 1–23.

Ratzel, F. *Anthropogeographie*. Vol. 1, Stuttgart, 1882. Vol. 2, Stuttgart, 1891.

Raymond, A. "La conquête ottomane et le développement des grandes villes arabes: Le cas du Caire, de Damas et d'Alep." *Revue de l'Occident musulman et de la Méditerranée*, no. 27, first trimester (1979): 115–34.

Redfield, R. *The Primitive World and Its Transformations*. Ithaca, N.Y., 1953.

Reed, C. A. "Origins of Agriculture: Discussion and some Conclusions." In Reed, C. A., ed., *Origins of Agriculture*, pp. 879–953. The Hague and Paris, 1977.

Reid, A. "La structure des villes du Sud-Est asiatique (XVe–XVIIe siècles)." *Urbi*, no. 1 (September 1979): 82–94.

Reilly, W. J. "Methods for the Study of Retail Relationships." *University of Texas Bulletin*, no. 2944. 1929.

Renfrew, C. *Problems in European Prehistory*. Edinburgh, 1979.

Reviv, H. "Trade and Commerce in the Bible." In *Encyclopaedia Judaica*, vol. 15, pp. 1293–96. Jerusalem, 1971.

Riché, P. *Ecoles et enseignements dans le Haut Moyen Age*. Paris, 1979.

Rickman, G. *The Corn Supply of Ancient Rome*. Oxford, 1980.

Ridgley, D. C. "Geographical Principles in the Study of the Cities." *Journal of Geography* 24 (February 1925): 66–78.

Riefler, R. F. "Nineteenth-Century Urbanization Patterns in the U.S." *Journal of Economic History* 39, no. 4 (December 1979): 961–74.

Roberts, B. *Cities of Peasants: The Political Economy of Urbanization in the Third World.* London, 1978.

Roberts, E. "Working-Class Standards of Living in Three Lancashire Towns, 1890–1914." *International Review of Social History* 28, part 1 (1982): 42–65.

Robinson, W. C. "Urbanization and Fertility: The Non-Western Experience." *The Milbank Memorial Fund* 41, no. 3 (July 1963): 291–308.

Robson, B. T. *Urban Growth: An Approach.* London, 1973.

Rogers, E. M., with Shoemaker, F. F. *Communication of Innovations: A Cross-Cultural Approach.* 2d ed. New York and London, 1971.

Rondinelli, D. A. "Intermediate Cities in Developing Countries." *Third World Planning Review* 4, no. 4 (November 1982): 337–86.

Rose, E. "Innovation in American Culture." *Social Forces* 26, no. 3 (March 1948): 255–72.

Rossiaud, J. "Crises et consolidations, 1330–1530." In Le Goff, J., ed., *La ville médiévale.* Vol. 2 of *Histoire de la France urbaine* (under the direction of Duby, G.), pp. 408–613. Paris, 1980.

Roubet, C. "Une économie pastorale pré-agricole en Algérie orientale: le néolithique de tradition capsienne." *L'Anthropologie* 82, no. 4 (1978): 583–86.

Rozman, G. *Urban Networks in Ch'ing China and Tokugawa Japan.* Princeton, 1973.

Russell, J. C. "Late Ancient and Medieval Population." *Transactions of the American Philosophical Society,* n.s., vol. 48, part 3 (June 1958): 1–152.

———. *Medieval Regions and Their Cities.* Newton Abbot, 1972a.

———. "Population in Europe 500–1500." In Cipolla, C. M., ed., *The Fontana Economic History of Europe,* vol. 1, pp. 25–70. London, 1972b.

Rybakov, B. "Kiev à l'aube de son histoire." *Sciences sociales* 53, no. 3 (1983): 10–25.

Santos, M. "Los dos circuitos de la economia urbana de los paises subdesarollados." In Funes, J., ed., *La ciudad y la region para el desarollo,* pp. 67–99. Caracas, 1972.

———. *L'espace partagé: Les deux circuits de l'économie urbaine des pays sous-développés.* Paris, 1975.

Schaedel, R. P., Hardoy, J. E., and Kinzer, N. S., eds. *Urbanization in the Americas from the Beginning to the Present.* The Hague and Paris, 1978.

Schmal, H., ed. *Patterns of European Urbanisation since 1500.* London, 1981.

Schmitthenner, W. "Rome and India: Aspects of Universal History during the Principate." *The Journal of Roman Studies* 69 (1979): 90–106.

Schmookler, J. *Invention and Economic Growth.* Harvard, 1966.

Schowers, V. V. *World Facts and Figures: A Unique Authoritative Collection of Comparative Information about Cities, Countries, and Geographic Features of the World.* New York, 1979.

Scullard, H. *The Etruscan Cities and Rome.* London, 1967.

Sella, D. "European Industries, 1500–1700." In Cipolla, C. M., ed., *The Fontana Economic History of Europe,* vol. 2, pp. 354–426. London, 1974.

Sethuraman, S. V., ed. *The Urban Informal Sector in Developing Countries: Employment, Poverty, and Environment,* ILO. Geneva, 1981.

Sharlin, A. "Natural Decrease in Early Modern Cities: A Reconsideration." *Past and Present,* no. 79 (May 1978): 126–38.

Sherratt, A., ed. *The Cambridge Encyclopedia of Archaeology.* Cambridge, 1980.

Shinnie, M. *Ancient African Kingdoms*. London, 1965.

Simmie, J. M. "Beyond the Industrial City?" *Journal of the American Planning Association* 49, no. 1 (Winter 1983): 59–76.

Singer, H. W. "The 'Courbe des Populations': A Parallel to Pareto's Law." *Economic Journal* 46, no. 182 (June 1936): 254–63.

Sjoberg, G. *The Preindustrial City: Past and Present*. Glencoe, Ill., 1960.

Skinner, G. W., ed. *The City in Late Imperial China*. Stanford, 1977.

Slicher van Bath, B. H. *The Agrarian History of Western Europe* A.D. 500–1850. London, 1963.

Smith, P. C. "Crisis in Mortality in Nineteenth Century Philippines: Data from Parish Records." *Journal of Asian Studies* 38, no. 1 (November 1978): 51–76.

Socolow, S. M., and Johnson, L. L. "Urbanization in Colonial Latin America." *Journal of Urban History* 8 (November 1981): 27–59.

Sombart, W. *Der moderne Kapitalismus*. Leipzig, 1902.

Sosson, J.-P. *Les travaux publics de la ville de Bruges, XIVe–XVe siècles: Les matériaux, Les hommes*. Brussels, 1977.

Sponner, B. *Population Growth: Anthropological Implications*. Cambridge, Mass., 1972.

Stadelmann, R. "La ville de pyramide à l'ancien Empire." *Revue d'égyptologie* 33 (1981): 67–77.

Stambouli, F. "Chômage et espace urbain: les bidonvilles du Maghreb." Conférence sur le chômage urbain en Afrique. September 1971.

Starr, C. G. *The Economic and Social Growth of Early Greece: 800–500* B.C.. Oxford and New York, 1979.

Statistiques générales de la France. Statistique internationale du mouvement de la population. 2 vols. Paris, 1907–14.

Stillwell, R., ed. *The Princeton Encyclopedia of Classical Sites*. Princeton, 1976.

Summers, R. *Zimbabwe: A Rhodesian Mystery*. Johannesburg, 1963.

Sundbarg, G. *Aperçus statistiques internationaux*. Stockholm, 1908.

Szilagyi, J. "Beiträge zur Statistik der Sterblichkeit in der Illyrischen Provinzgruppe und in Norditalien." *Acta Arch. Acad. Sc. Hung* (1962): 297–396.

Takeo, Y. *Social Change and the City in Japan: From Earliest Time through the Industrial Revolution*. Tokyo, 1968.

Tauber, I. B. *The Population of Japan*. Princeton, 1958.

Teall, J. L. "The Grain Supply of the Byzantine Empire, 330–1025." *Dumbarton Oaks Papers, no. 13*, pp. 87–139. Washington, D.C., 1959.

Thakur, V. K. *Urbanisation in Ancient India*. Abhinav, 1981.

Thirring, G. *Annuaire statistique des grandes villes européennes*. Budapest, 1913.

Thomlinson, R. "The Nature and Rise of Cities." In Ficker, V. B., and Graves, H. S., eds., *Social Science and the Urban Crisis*, pp. 4–11. New York, 1971.

Thunen, J. H. von *Der isolierte Staat in Beziehung auf Landwirtschaft und Nationalökonomie*. Hamburg, 1826.

Tikhomirov, M. *The Towns of Ancient Rus*. Moscow, 1959.

Timberlake, M. *Urbanization in the World Economy*. New York, 1985.

Tits-Dieuaide, M.-J. *La formation des prix des céréales en Brabant et en Flandres au XVe siècle*. Brussels, 1975.

Törnqvist, G. *Contact Systems and Regional Development*. Lund, 1970.

Toynbee, A. *Cities on the Move*. London, 1970.

Trigger, B. G. "Determinants of Urban Growth in Pre-Industrial Societies."

In Ucko, P. J., Tringham, R., and Dimbleby, G. W., eds., *Man, Settlement and Urbanism*, pp. 575–99. London, 1972.

Turnham, D., with Jaeger, I. *The Employment Problem in Less Developed Countries*, OECD. Paris, 1970.

Ullman, E. "A Theory of Location for Cities." *American Journal of Sociology* 46 (1941): 853–64.

United Nations. *Demographic Yearbook*. New York, various issues.

——. *Population Bulletin of the United Nations, no. 7, 1963. Condition and Trends of Fertility in the World*. New York, 1965.

——. *Growth of the World's Urban and Rural Population, 1920–2000*. New York, 1970.

——. *The Determinants and Consequences of Population Trends*. Vol. 1. New York, 1973.

——. *Trends and Prospects in Urban and Rural Population, 1950–2000, as Assessed in 1973–1974*. New York, April 1975a.

——. *Trends and Prospects in the Population of Urban Agglomerations, 1950–2000, as Assessed in 1973–1975*. New York, November 1975b.

——. *World Housing Survey, 1974*. New York, 1976.

——. *Levels and Trends of Fertility throughout the World, 1950–1970*. New York, 1977a.

——. *Population Bulletin of the United Nations, no. 8, 1976*, pp. 16–33. New York, 1977b.

——. *Patterns of Urban and Rural Population Growth*. New York, 1980.

——. *Levels and Trends of Mortality since 1950*. New York, 1982a.

——. *Estimates and Projections of Urban, Rural and City Populations, 1950–2025: the 1980 Assessment*. New York, September 1982b.

——. *Urban and Rural Population Projections. 1984 Assessment*. New York, 1986a.

——. *Selected Characteristics of the Population of Urban, Rural, Capital City, and Urban Agglomeration in Countries with more than 2 Million in 1985. 1984 Assessment*. New York, 1986b.

Van Leuven, J. V. "Prehistoric Grain Explosions." *Antiquity* 53, no. 208 (July 1979): 138–40.

Vatin, C. "Jardins et services de voirie." *Bulletin de correspondance hellénique*, no. C, part 1, *Etudes* (1976): 555–64.

Veyne, P. *Le pain et le cirque: Sociologie historique d'un pluralisme politique*. Paris, 1976.

Vilar, P. *Or et Monnaie dans l'Histoire, 1450–1920*. Paris, 1974.

Villermé, M. *Tableau de l'état physique et moral des ouvriers employés dans les manufactures de coton, de laine et de soie*. 2 vols. Paris, 1840.

Vincent, B. "Récents travaux de démographie historique en Espagne (XIVe–XVIIe siècles)." *Annales de démographie historique, 1977*, pp. 463–91. Paris, 1977.

Vishnu-Mittre. "Changing Economy in Ancient India." In Reed, C. A., ed., *Origins of Agriculture*, pp. 569–88. The Hague and Paris.

Vries, J. (de). *The Dutch Rural Economy in the Golden Age, 1500–1700*. New Haven and London, 1974.

——. "Patterns of Urbanization in Pre-Industrial Europe, 1500–1800." In Schmal, H., ed., *Patterns of European Urbanisation since 1500*, pp. 77–109. London, 1981.

Ward, B. "The Poor World's Cities: The Cities that Came Too Soon." *The Economist*, pp. 56–70, 6 December 1969.

Warren, P. "The Aegean and Western Anatolia in the Bronze Age." In Sherrat, A., ed., *The Cambridge Encyclopedia of Archaeology*, pp. 136–43. Cambridge, 1980.

Watson, W. "Neolithic Settlement in East Asia." In Ucko, P. J., Tringham, R., and Dimbleby, G. W., eds., *Man, Settlement and Urbanism*, pp. 329–41. London, 1972.

Weber, A. F. *The Growth of Cities in the Nineteenth Century: A Study in Statistics*. New York and London, 1899.

Weber, M. *The City*. Glencoe, Ill., 1958. Originally published 1921.

Weeks, J. "An Exploration into the Nature of the Problem of Urban Imbalance in Africa." *Manpower and Unemployment Research in Africa* 6, no. 2 (November 1973): 9–36.

Weinstein, M. S. *Health in the City: Environmental and Behavioral Influences*. New York, 1980.

Wheatley, P. *The Pivot of the Four Quarters: A Preliminary Enquiry into the Origins and Character of the Ancient Chinese City*. Edinburgh and Chicago, 1971.

Wheatley, P., and See, T. *From Court to Capital: A Tentative Interpretation of the Origins of the Japanese Urban Tradition*. Chicago, 1978.

White, H. P., and Gleave, M. B. *An Economic Geography of West Africa*. London, 1971.

Whitehouse, D. "The Expansion of the Arabs." In Sherratt, A., ed., *The Cambridge Encyclopedia of Archaeology*, pp. 289–94. Cambridge, 1980.

Whiting, J. W. M., Sodergren, J. A., and Stigler, S. M. "Winter Temperature as a Constraint to the Migration of Preindustrial People." *American Anthropologist* 84, no. 2 (June 1982): 279–98.

Wilkinson, J. "Ancient Jerusalem: Its Water Supply and Population." *Palestine Exploration Quarterly*, 106th year (January–June 1974): 33–51.

Willey, G. R. "Recent Researches and Perspectives in Mesoamerican Archaeology: An Introductory Commentary." In Sabloff, J. A., ed., *Archaeology. Supplement to the Handbook of Middle American Indians*. Vol. 1, pp. 3–27. Austin, Tx., 1981.

Williamson, J. G. "Antebellum Urbanization in the American Northeast." *Journal of Economic History* 25 (December 1965): 592–608.

———. *Urban Disamenities, Dark Satanic Mills and the British Standard of Living Debate*. Discussion Paper Series, Economic History, University of Wisconsin. Madison, 1980.

Wilson, J. A. "Egypt through the New Kingdom: Civilization without Cities." In Kraeling, C. H., and Adams, R. Mc., eds., *City Invincible: A Symposium on Urbanization and Cultural Development in the Ancient Near East, December 1958*, pp. 124–64. Chicago, 1960.

Wirth, L. "Urbanism as a Way of Life." *American Journal of Sociology* 44 (July 1938): 1–24.

Wittfogel, K. A. *Oriental Despotism: A Comparative Study of Total Power*. New Haven, 1957.

Wolff, P., ed. *Guide international d'histoire urbaine*. Vol. 1, *Europe*. Paris, 1977.

World Bank. *World Development Report, 1982*. New York, 1982.

Wrigley, E. A. "A Simple Model of London's Importance in Changing English Society and Economy 1650–1750." *Past and Present* 37 (July 1967): 44–70.

————. *Société et population.* Collection l'Univers des Connaissances. Paris, 1969.

Wrigley, E. A., and Schofield, R. S. *The Population History of England, 1541–1871.* Cambridge, 1981.

Yen, D. E. "The Southeast Asian Foundations of Oceanic Agriculture: A Reassessment." *Journal de la Société des océanistes* 36, nos. 66–67 (March 1980): 141–47.

Yener, K. A. "A Review of International Exchanges in Southwest Asia: The Neolithic Obsidian Network" *Anatolica*, no. 9 (1982): 33–75.

You, N. *Alternative Strategies in Urban Development: Some Chinese Experiments in Quest for an Agropolitan Space.* Itinéraires, notes et travaux no. 4, Institut Universitaire d'Etudes du Développement. Geneva, 1980.

Zipf, G. K. *Human Behaviour and the Principle of the Least Effort.* Cambridge, 1949.

Zuiches, J. J., and Rieger, J. H. "Size of Place Preferences and Life Cycle Migration: A Cohort Comparison." *Rural Sociology* 43, no. 4 (1978): 618–33.

Index

Lagos, 416, 417, 431
Lampert, R. J., 69
Lancaster, 251
Landes, David, 251, 265
Langer, L. N., 171
Laon, 156
La Paz, 386
Lapidus, I. M., 371
Latin America, 397–98, 439–40, 457, 460, 475–76, 496; and colonialism, 382–90, 506; employment, 397–98, 468; fertility rate, 453; industrialization, 420–24, 431–32; population, 443; universities, 479–80; urbanization, 439–40, 457, 460, 475, 496, 512
Law, R. C. C., 79–80
Lebanon, 30, 31, 379
Lebon, Philippe, 286
Le Creusot, 263
Leeds, 251, 292
Leek, 256
Le Goff, J., 162–63, 189, 210
Leipzig, 135, 167, 196, 207
Leman, P., 90
Leningrad, 225, 303
Leon, 441
Leopoldville, 348
Leppeley, C., 87
Lequin, Yves, 317–18
Letchworth, 312–13
Levtzion, N., 62
Leyden, 168, 179
Libya, 37, 379, 408
Liège, 168, 263
Lille, 135, 263, 271–73, 275
Lima, 479
Lipton, Michael, 446
Lisbon, 63, 132, 168, 331; population, 140, 180, 183, 248, 267, 394
List, Friedrich, 296–97
Liverpool, 155, 236, 251, 292
Livi-Bacci, M., 239–40
Lloyd, P., 474
Locris, 79
Lombard, D., 361–62
Lomé, 473
London, 91, 132, 168, 190, 198, 284, 292; and agriculture, 248–50, 332; growth rate, 249, 253, 257; mortality rate, 210, 232, 240; population, 119, 136, 141, 180, 183, 184, 209, 225, 240, 246–48, 278, 285, 310, 319, 331, 515–16; public transport, 281–83
Longwy, 263, 317

Loofs-Wissowa, H. H. E., 51
Lopez, R. S., 370
Los Angeles, 298, 314
Lot, F., 113
Louvain, 190
Loyang, 352
Luanda, 391
Lübeck, 167
Lucca, 183, 267
Ludwigshafen, 263
Lugdunum Convenarum, 112–13
Lundt, 190
Lyautey, Louis, 409
Lydians, 36
Lyons, 127, 166, 167, 196, 263, 280

Ma, L. J. C., 354
Mabogunje, A. L., 53, 413
Macao, 394–95, 404
McCloskey, D., 251
McCormick, Cyrus, 338
McDonald, W. A., 148
McGee, T. G., 361, 470, 471, 491
McIntosh, S. K. and R. J., 57
MacNeish, R. S., 67
Madina al-Zahira, 119
Madina al-Zahra, 119
Madras, 400, 449, 452, 478
Madrid, 155, 183, 190, 267, 282
Maghreb, the, 36–37, 53, 398, 408–10, 416–18; employment, 464; and Greece, 79–80; and Islam, 60–62, 119, 371, 372, 375, 476, 500; urbanization, 429–30, 457
Magyars, 110, 120
Mahdia, 371
Maitre, J. P., 53
Malacca, 395
Malaga, 156
Malay archipelago, 48–49
Mali, 57
Mallia, 73
Malmö, 263
Malthus, Thomas, 356, 357
Manchester, 250, 251, 256, 292
Manchuria, 404
Manda, 372, 373
Manila, 49, 395, 406
Mannheim, 155
Mantoux, P., 253, 255, 256
Mao Tse-Tung, 191, 433
Mari, 27
Marrakesh, 371
Marseilles, 80, 167, 172, 236

Oliver, R., 53, 56
Olmec culture, 64
Opole, 122
Oran, 410, 431
Oruro, 389, 423
Osaka, 282, 305, 313, 360
Oslo, 23, 136, 155
Ostrogorsky, G., 367
Otranto, 79
Ottoman Empire, 158–59, 186, 259, 371, 375, 378–81, 382, 408
Ouro Preto, 387
Oxford, 190

Pagan, 362
Pakistan, 471
Palembang, 48
Palermo, 120–21, 158, 160–61, 369
Palestine, 19, 35, 86, 368
Panjin, 394
Pannag, 32
Paraguay, 421, 441
Pareto, Vilfredo, 266
Paris, 27, 46, 90, 157, 168, 286, 313, 362; mortality rate, 232, 236; new towns, 313; population, 119, 136, 141, 183, 184, 225, 246, 247, 285, 309, 319, 331, 350, 369; public transportation, 280–82
Parker, P., 457
Parrot, André, 27
Pascal, Blaise, 280
Patlagean, Evelyne, 370
Pavia, 120
Pawson, E., 251–52
Pedersen, P. O., 327
Peikthano, 49
Peking, 226, 356, 402, 403, 432, 435–36
Pelusium, 111
Pereslavl, 171
Perkins, D. H., 358
Perrenoud, A., 16, 22–23, 203, 207, 209
Perrot, J.-C., 204
Persia, 380, 498. *See also* Iran
Persian Empire, 28, 30
Peru, 59, 62–64, 384, 386, 388, 419, 455
Perugia, 156
Petersen, W., 7
Petit, P., 33
Petra, 35–36
Philadelphia, 222, 282, 298
Philip II, 155
Philip of Macedon, 73
Philippines, 48, 223, 395, 406, 449, 482
Philistine cities, 25

Phoenicians, 10, 25, 29–34, 37, 97, 176, 498
Pirenne, H., 129, 162–63, 193, 256–57
Pisa, 156, 160, 166
Piuz, A.-M., 134
Plato, 74–75
Pliny, 31
Pliska, 123
Poland, 122, 187, 240, 335
Polo, Marco, 353
Polotsk, 171
Polynesia, 70
Pondicherry, 395
Pont-à-Mousson, 263
Port Louis, 393, 415
Portugal, 130, 175, 181, 259, 261; colonies, 200, 385, 390–94, 412; industry, 262, 265; urbanization, 199, 215, 222, 247, 248, 267, 331–33
Potosi, 59, 387, 389, 423
Pounds, N. J., 88
Poznan, 122
Prague, 122, 182, 313
Pre-Columbian civilizations, 35, 38, 62–69, 348, 362, 383–85, 506; preurban cities, 10, 436, 476, 477
Pred, A. R., 323, 329
Preslav, 123, 156
Preston, 253–54
Price, Richard, 236–37
Prins, Jan, 47–48
Provins, 156, 167
Prussia, 230
Pskov, 171
Puglia, 8
Pullman City, 313–14
Pumain, Denise, 278

Quebec, 222, 300, 389
Quelimane, 391
Queretar, 479
Quito, 386, 479

Randles, W. G. L., 58
Rathbone, D. W., 104
Ratzel, F., 142–43
Raymond, A., 379–80
Reed, C. A., 7, 13
Reid, A., 361
Reilly, W. J., 144–45
Reims, 46, 165
Renfrew, C., 88
Réunion, 392, 416, 418
Reviv, H., 31
Ricardo, David, 192

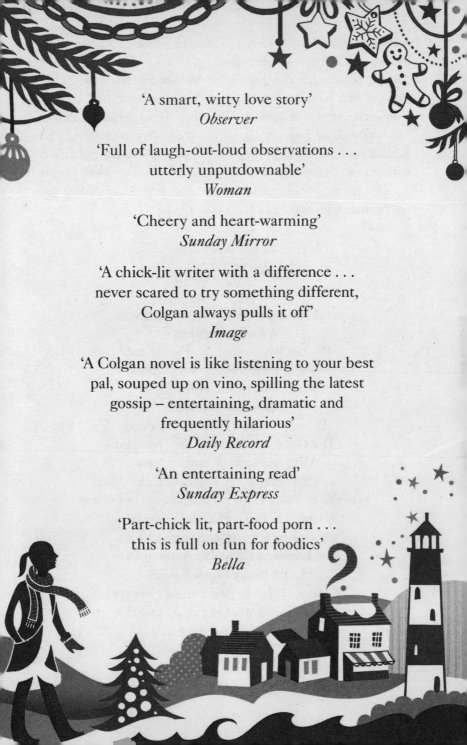

'A smart, witty love story'
Observer

'Full of laugh-out-loud observations . . .
utterly unputdownable'
Woman

'Cheery and heart-warming'
Sunday Mirror

'A chick-lit writer with a difference . . .
never scared to try something different,
Colgan always pulls it off'
Image

'A Colgan novel is like listening to your best
pal, souped up on vino, spilling the latest
gossip – entertaining, dramatic and
frequently hilarious'
Daily Record

'An entertaining read'
Sunday Express

'Part-chick lit, part-food porn . . .
this is full on fun for foodies'
Bella

Jenny Colgan is the author of numerous bestselling novels, including *Christmas at the Cupcake Café* and *Little Beach Street Bakery*, which are also published by Sphere. *Meet Me at the Cupcake Café* won the 2012 Melissa Nathan Award for Comedy Romance and was a *Sunday Times* Top Ten bestseller, as was *Welcome to Rosie Hopkins' Sweetshop of Dreams*, which won the RNA Romantic Novel of the Year Award 2013. Jenny is married with three children and lives in Scotland. For more about Jenny, visit her website and her Facebook page, or follow her on Twitter: @jennycolgan.

To the dreamers, and your dreams, big or small.
Like, even if they're puffin-sized small.

'You'll never find peace by hating, lad. It only shuts ye off more from the world. And this town is only a cursed place if ye make it so. To the rest of us, 'tis a blessed place!'

– Brigadoon

Dear Reader,

Thank you so much for picking up this, the last in the Little Beach trilogy (probably). I have loved writing the adventures of Polly, Huckle, and a very naughty puffin called Neil so very much.

If you are new to these stories, honestly you don't need to know very much: Polly moved to the tidal island of Mount Polbearne when her business failed, and has built a new life there.

She lives in a lighthouse because she thought it sounded romantic (it is a MASSIVE pain in the neck, NB), with her laid-back American boyfriend Huckle and a puffin, obviously. She bakes every day for Mount Polbearnites and their guests. Right, you're all ready to go!

A note on the setting:

Cornwall to me is a place of the imagination as much as a real home to lots of people, because I spent so much time there as a child.

To me, it is like a version of Narnia or any of the other

imaginary lands I liked to visit – I was absolutely obsessed with Over Sea, Under Stone, and of course the Famous Five and Malory Towers.

We used to stay in old tin miners cottages near Polperro. My mother was a great Daphne du Maurier fan, and she used to put me and my two brothers to sleep in the little narrow beds, and tell us bloodcurdling stories of shipwrecks and pirates and gold and wreckers and we would be utterly thrilled and chilled and one of us, probably my littlest brother – although he would probably say, me – would be up half the night with nightmares.

Compared to chilly Scotland, sunny Cornwall was like paradise to me. Every year, we were bought as a special treat those big foam body surf boards and we would get in to the water first thing in the morning and body surf body surf body surf until physically hauled out, sunburnt along the crossed strap lines on my swimming costume, to eat a gritty sandwich wrapped in clearseal.

Later my dad would barbecue fish over the little home-built barbie he constructed every year from bricks and a grill, and I would sit in the high sweet grass and read books, and get bitten by insects.

And after that, (because you get to stay up very late on your holidays), we'd drive down to Mousehole or St Ives; eat ice cream strolling along the harbour walk looking at the art galleries; or hot salty fried potatoes, or fudge, the flavours of which I was constantly obsessed with, even though fudge invariably makes me feel sick.

They were blissful times, and it was such a joy to revisit them when I started writing my Mount Polbearne series. We went on a day trip – as required by law, I think, of anyone visiting Cornwall – to St Michael's Mount and I remember being gripped and fascinated by the old stone road disappearing under the waves. It was the most romantic and magical thing I could possibly imagine, and it has been such a joy setting my books there. If I can convey even a fraction of the happiness Cornwall has brought to me in my life through my books – well, I'd be absolutely delighted.

Jenny xxx

Chapter One

This story is about one particular Christmas, but it actually starts with a very Bad Thing happening the previous spring.

It's a bit of a shame that the Bad Thing happens in the spring and we're only going to look at it for a bit, because the Cornish tidal island of Mount Polbearne in the spring is an extraordinarily beautiful place.

There is a causeway leading to the ancient settlement, which used to be connected to the mainland until the seas rose up. Now the tides cover the old cobbled road twice a day, which makes it both a very romantic and an extremely inconvenient place to live.

There are a jumble of cottages and shops alongside the harbour and beach, including Polly's Little Beach Street Bakery, to distinguish it from the original bakery. You might wonder how such a tiny village sustains two bakeries, but then you obviously haven't eaten there, because Polly is to baking what Phil Collins is to playing the drums. Hang on, that might not be the best example.

Anyway, rest assured: she is very, very good at baking. Her sourdough bread is nutty and firm and has the chewiest of crusts; her baguettes are lighter and fluffier than air. She makes the densest, most delicious olive oil focaccia and delicate, sharp cheese scones. The scent of her baking – she tests things out in the kitchen at home in the lighthouse, then there are the big industrial ovens in the bakery itself, plus an amazing woodburner – floats across the town and brings the hungry and the curious from miles around.

As well as the bakery along the harbour, there's Andy's pub, the Red Lion, which plays fairly fast and loose with licensing laws, particularly if it's a warm evening in the beer garden, which is strung with fairy lights and scented with the sea. Andy also runs a fantastic and mind-numbingly expensive fish-and-chip shop next door, so he's a busy man. In the harbour itself, the fishing boats rattle and chime; fishing, once the backbone of Mount Polbearne, is now the second most popular job in the tiny community, after tourism.

Up the hill ramble various little cobbled streets, where the same families have been living for generations. There were fears that the community was dying out, but Polly arriving to take over the bakery, after the graphic design business she used to run failed miserably, coincided with – some people say brought about – a new influx;

there's even a posh fish restaurant now. Babies are being born and there's a sense that things are definitely on the up.

The trick now is to keep it on the up without all the lovely tumbledown houses being bought as second homes by rich people from London and Exeter who never show up during the week and who make it too expensive for local people to live there. But with one or two exceptions, the lack of reliable Wi-Fi and the constantly shifting tides have kept the place more or less cut off from invasion – as it has been for hundreds and hundreds of years – so it could be worse.

Summer in Mount Polbearne is always mobbed and busy and a bit nuts, as everyone tries to make enough money to get them through the long, cold winter. But in the spring, the tourists haven't quite started yet – or at least, there's normally a bit of a rush at Easter, when everyone turns up and hopes for the best and pretends that they aren't remotely disappointed when the wind that used to wreck ships on that treacherous stretch of southern Cornish coastline blows their candyfloss right back in their faces; that the picturesque bounce of the fishing boats that line the little harbour isn't done just to look nice in holiday videos but is actually the white-tipped waves hurling the boats about, with red-fingered fishermen mending nets or, more commonly these days, frowning at computer printouts showing shoals and movements and tallying up just how much they can take from the sea.

But once the slightly disappointed Easter holidaymakers (and the incredibly smug ones, I should say, who hang on until the second Tuesday and are rewarded with a golden day so exquisitely perfect and beautiful that they annoy their friends immeasurably for the next five years by reminiscing about it) have gone, Mount Polbearne has a short respite before the summer floods arrive: children with crabbing nets; adults dreaming of the kind of holidays they had as children, with wide golden beaches and the freedom to run around (until they realise that the causeway doesn't have any sides and the tide rushes in astonishingly fast, and what was perfectly okay for their parents to let them do in 1985 is now a bit horrifying; and, well, obviously they'll need good Wi-Fi too, something Mount Polbearne can't provide but they'll just have to make the best of it).

In April, then, Mount Polbearne takes a breath. Looking towards the mainland, you can see the trees starting to blossom out in great big garlands of pink and white. Days that start chilly and unpredictable suddenly get a darting bolt of sunlight; and the early-morning mist burns off, and the heat rises and releases that gorgeous aroma of everything growing and birds building nests and chattering to one another, and the light bright green of trees in bud and a particular buzzing, gentle loveliness that is England in early spring, at its very best.

Our story does not stay there.

But it begins there. And it should be a time of new

beginnings; of cheery emerging from winter fleeces and television and blinking into the fresh light of the morning.

Mostly, though, it has Polly Waterford's best friend, the blonde and sophisticated Kerensa, wife of Huckle's best friend, swearing wildly down the telephone.

'Stop swearing,' said Polly sensibly, rubbing her eyes. 'I can't make out a word you're saying.'

As it so often did, the connection cut out between Polbearne and the mainland, where Kerensa lived in a huge and ridiculously opulent mansion with her wunderkind (and quite noisy) American husband Reuben.

'Who was that?' said Huckle, waiting for toast to pop up in the sunny kitchen of the lighthouse they shared, a faded grey T-shirt pulled on over his boxers. It wasn't really warm enough for just that, but Polly absolutely wasn't complaining. It was a Sunday morning, her only day off; there was salted local butter waiting to be spread, or a squeeze of Huckle's own honey, sweet orange blossom to go with the gentle morning weather.

'Kerensa,' said Polly. 'She had some very busy swearing to do.'

'That sounds like her. What about?'

Polly tried to ring her back, without success.

'Could be anything with Kerensa. Reuben's probably being a putz again.'

'Well I'd take that as a certainty,' said Huckle gravely, standing over the toaster, watching it fiercely. 'Oh, someone needs to invent a speedy toaster,' he complained.

5

'A speedy toaster?' said Polly. 'What?'

'Toast takes too long,' said Huckle.

'What on earth are you talking about?'

'I really want some toast, and I put your sourdough in the toaster – which makes the best toast in the world by the way . . . '

'I knew there was a reason you were with me,' said Polly.

'. . . and then OMG, it just smells so good, it's like you can't wait, you have to eat the amazing sourdough toast straight away.'

He pressed the button, and two not-quite-toasted pieces of light golden bread popped out.

'See?' he said, attacking them crossly with a butter knife. The butter was still hard from the fridge and tore a hole in the soft crumb. Huckle looked down gloomily at his plate. 'Every time. I panic and take it out too early and really regret it, and that's my toast experience totally spoiled.'

'Make more.'

'It doesn't work, I've tried it.'

Regardless, Huckle popped another couple of slices in.

'The problem is, I'll have eaten the first lot before the second lot is ready. It's a vicious circle. Exactly the same thing will happen all over again.'

'Maybe,' said Polly, 'you should just stand over the toaster with your mouth open when it's about to pop up.'

'Yeah, I thought of that,' said Huckle. 'Possibly with a

kind of butter spray gun so it's all ready to go and you don't have to hack it on in a hurry because you need to eat all the delicious toast so quickly.'

'I didn't think it was possible to meet someone more bread-obsessed than me,' said Polly. 'But – and I can't quite believe I'm saying this – I think it's possible you overthink toast.'

'If I could just invent the Speed-E-Toaster,' said Huckle, 'we'd be richer than Reuben.'

The toast popped up.

'QUICK! QUICK! QUICK!!!!'

And after that, they simply went back to bed, because Polly, being a baker, had to go to bed incredibly early every other day of the week, and Huckle, being a honey seller, didn't particularly, so their hours didn't always match up. And Polly sent a text to Kerensa saying not to worry, everything would be fine, she'd call her later, and then she turned off her phone.

This was to prove a terrible, terrible mistake.

Chapter Two

So let us be clear: none of what happened was truly Polly's fault, or Huckle's fault. It was obviously Kerensa's fault, as you'll see, and a bit Selina's, who wouldn't admit it in a million years but absolutely liked encouraging these things along (because some people are just a bit like that, aren't they? Stirrers).

But it was also a tiny bit Reuben's fault, because – and I can't stress this highly enough – even by *his* standards he was being the most unbelievable putz that day.

He had forgotten it was their wedding anniversary – their first wedding anniversary – and when Kerensa had pointed this out to him, he'd said yeah, well, he'd done a lot of that lovey-dovey stuff in the past and they were married now, so that was all kind of fine, right? Like, he'd done it and now they were all awesome, and anyway, she had a dozen handbags, right, and by the way, he had to be on a plane to San Francisco to talk to his massive IPO base, and Kerensa had said she hadn't known that and he'd said well she should read the schedule his PA emailed her, he was leaving in two hours, and she said could she come too, having heard that San Francisco in the spring was a magnificent place to be, and he said not really, sweetie, he'd be super-busy. Then he'd kissed her goodbye and suggested that seeing as they'd had a gym put in the house, why didn't she use it?

So. You see what I mean. He didn't mean it unkindly, that's just what Reuben is like: when he's working, he kind of turns into Steve Jobs and doesn't really think about anyone but himself, which is why he's pretty much as rich as Steve Jobs, more or less. It's a big number anyway.

So Kerensa stood in the completely empty huge luxurious hallway of their massive amazing house with its own beach on the northern coast of Cornwall and wondered about crying a little bit. Then she decided to be angry instead, because this had been happening more and more often, and Reuben never seemed to see that actually she didn't really like being contacted by his PA, who was cool and American and dressed very expensively and who Kerensa was slightly intimidated by, even though nothing much intimidated her, and ever since he'd kick-started his career last year, after a near-bankruptcy, she'd barely seen him at all; he'd never been off a flight.

So she'd decided to get angry and in a frenzy called Polly, who was busy as it turned out guffing on about toast with Huckle on her only day off, and absolutely was not as sympathetic as a friend should be in those circumstances, which Polly regretted bitterly afterwards.

So *then* Kerensa called their other friend Selina, who had been through a terrible time being widowed two years before and could still be a little emotional on occasion, and Selina, who had lived on the mainland and always had a fashionable career before she'd accidentally fallen for a fisherman, said she had a great idea: she was bored out of her mind, why didn't they go into Plymouth, go to the smartest restaurant they could find and drink the most expensive thing on the menu, then charge it to Reuben and say thanks for the lovely anniversary gift the next time she saw him?

And Kerensa liked this idea very much, so that was what they did. And what started out as lunch – and a lot, and I mean a *lot* of complaining about the men in their lives, or that had been in their lives – got a little out of hand, and they ended up meeting a bunch of other girls there on a hen night who immediately incorporated them into their gang, and they went to see a 'dance show' with those girls and I will leave it totally up to your imagination what the dance show entailed, but there was quite a lot of baby oil on display, and some very tall men with Brazilian accents, and flaming sambucas, and then Kerensa's memory gets a bit hazy after that, but when she woke up in the morning in an incredibly posh hotel she dimly recalled waltzing into brandishing a platinum credit card at some ungodly hour, she remembered enough to know that if she could possibly have it surgically removed from her brain, she absolutely would.

He'd already left. Although there was a long black hair in the shower.

I know. I did say it was a Bad Thing.

And oh, it gets worse. Think of something slightly regrettable you've done on a night out, then multiply it by a factor of about a million.

Kerensa got home – with a sniggering, only mildly hung-over Selina, who thought the entire thing was unutterably hilarious and had been careful to drink lots of water at the same time, as she is also that kind of a friend – to discover that Polly had felt so guilty about not seeing her that Huckle had phoned Reuben and basically ordered him to go home and be nice to his wife.

So Reuben had postponed his business in SF and flown all the way back, laden with every perfume in the duty-free shop because he couldn't remember what she liked. He'd marched back in the door – where a miserable Kerensa had been throwing up all morning and crawling along the tiles writhing with hung-over guilt and misery – grabbed her in his arms and declared his undying love for her, then attempted to dramatically carry her upstairs, which he couldn't manage as he'd been on a plane all night and Kerensa was two inches taller than him and also wanted to die; but they did their best together regardless, the early April light glowing through the huge floor-to-ceiling windows in their enormous circular bedroom,

11

with its ridiculous/ spectacular (delete according to taste) circular bed, and after that, he promptly whisked Kerensa away everywhere he went for the next six months.

So that is the terrible thing that happened in the spring.

And if this was a film, right, we would have reached the point where the ominous music crashes in and the credits start ...

Chapter Three

Five weeks before Christmas

'This year,' Polly was saying boldly, sitting up under the duvet, 'I am making a LIST. A PLAN. This year everything will not be a disaster.'

'When has Christmas ever been a disaster?' said Huckle, turning over, still sleepy and utterly unwilling to relinquish the duvet. Polly was getting up in the pitch dark, as she did for months on end in the winter, and their last heating bill had scared them both rigid, even though the house was almost never warm.

Polly had thought – and hoped – that heating the lighthouse would be like heating a gigantic chimney; that she could light the Aga at the bottom and the heat would permeate up the entire place. This was not the case at all. This was very far from the case. The kitchen was warm, but unless – and even after – they turned on the ancient clanky and very reluctant heating system for about five hours and tried to ignore the fact that they were living in a Grade I listed, non-insulated, not-meant-for-human-habitation building, running up and down the stairs was torture, a sport that took dares and bribery for anyone to accomplish.

Huckle did occasionally think longingly of the little beekeeper's cottage he'd once rented on the mainland, just across the causeway, which was a lot warmer simply by virtue of not being perched more or less in the middle of the sea. The beekeeper's cottage had had low ceilings and tiny windows and soft throws and cushions and curtains and two small bedrooms and had been cosy all winter long with one log burner and about four radiators.

And even further back, he thought of his childhood home in Virginia in the US, which was warm most of the year anyway – sometimes uncomfortably so – but when the cold weather did come in, his father would simply fire up the vast furnace in the basement and the whole house would heat up straight away. The first thing his father had said to him when he found out he was moving to England full time was, 'You know they don't heat their houses?'

At the time, Huckle had thought this was a quaint and outdated expression, like the British not knowing how to drink cold beer or go to a dentist. But now he was beginning to have a great deal of sympathy with his pa and wondering what other advice he should take from him whilst he still had the chance, before hypothermia set in and robbed him of brain stem function.

Polly was pulling a third sweater over her head.

'That's my favourite sweater,' said Huckle. 'It's kind of even more shapeless than the rest and gives you a sexy Marshmallow Man silhouette.'

She hurled a sock at him.

'Still more attractive than the goose bumps,' she said. 'Anyway, I don't think you're listening to my excellent plans for a list.'

'It's five a.m.,' said Huckle. 'You shouldn't even have woken me. It was vicious and cruel and I shall get my deadly revenge.'

And he grabbed her ankle and pulled her closer, trying to get her under the warm covers, where he liked, in fact, having to burrow beneath the layers of heavy clothing, knowing that somewhere in there, deep underneath, were Polly's soft creamy curves, waiting to be discovered like buried treasure; visible, in general, to nobody else but him. He could already anticipate the shiver of his cold hand on her warm skin.

Polly giggled and shrieked.

'No! NO way! I have a million things to do and all anyone wants to order is gingerbread.'

'You smell of gingerbread,' said Huckle, sticking his head up her sweater. 'It's awesome. It makes me horny and hungry all at the same time. They're going to ban me from supermarkets. I'm going to turn into Fru T. Bunn, the pervy baker.'

Polly scrunched up her face.

15

'Oh God, Huck, I can't. I can't. Now that I'm up and have momentum ... if I don't get going now, I'll get back into bed and never leave.'

'Get back into my bed and never leave. That's an order.'

'And we'll starve to death.'

'Neh, we'll live on nothing but gingerbread.'

'And die early.'

'So worth it. Where's Neil?'

Neil was the puffin Polly had inadvertently adopted when she'd nursed him back to health after he had broken his wing as a puffling. By all accounts he would soon fly off home to join his flock. It hadn't happened yet.

'Outside.'

They looked at one another. As ever, Huckle had that slow-burning, amused look in his eyes, as if the world was a funny game; that eternal sunny side of him that made him always think that everything would turn out for the best. His dark blonde hair was scruffy. He slept in his old college T-shirt and smelt like warm hay and honey mixed together.

Polly glanced at the alarm clock, which Huckle covered up with his hand. She had deliveries, invoicing, paperwork, baking, serving ...

'What happens one day,' said Polly, getting dressed again in a tearing rush, trying to text Jayden her assistant to tell

16

him she was running late, 'after we've been together for ages and everything, and sex kind of tails off?'

'That won't happen.'

'Well, it does.'

'Not to us.' Huckle gave her a warning look. They had got engaged in the summer, and every time he mentioned the future, Polly changed the subject or fretted about being too busy. He knew he had to sit down and properly talk to her about it; he knew she was busy, but he didn't understand why it seemed to be a problem. To Huckle it couldn't be simpler – they loved each other, they wanted to be together for ever, they wanted to raise a family. Of course, he sometimes reflected, he loved Polly because she wasn't like other girls. But he couldn't help thinking that most other girls, surely, would have been happy with that.

He decided, once again, that this wasn't the time. He grinned at her.

'Can't you enjoy just one thing for five minutes?'

Polly smiled back. 'Yes,' she said. 'And I think it was longer than five minutes.' She frowned. 'Mind you, I kind of lost track of time.'

'Fine. Deal with it. Be happy. Everything lasts for ever. I'm going back to sleep.'

And he did, even as Polly pulled on her thick woolly socks, his face completely smooth and relaxed in sleep, and Polly loved him so much she thought her heart would explode; she was terrified by how much she loved him.

It was just everything that came next that scared the life out of her.

Downstairs, she stoked up the Aga for Huckle later, grabbed a quick coffee and ran out of the lighthouse door. The rain threw itself violently at her face. She could always tell by the wind whistling through the windows how bad the weather was, but you had to steel yourself for it when it truly arrived, and now that it was nearly December, it was definitely here, with no end in sight.

That was what you got, Polly supposed, when you lived on a lump of rock in the middle of the sea, with houses built on steeply winding streets in grey slate, the same colour as the stone itself, leading upwards towards the great ruined church at the very top. The ancient causeway that led to the mainland was dangerous to navigate, although possible, but mostly the many tourists parked at the car park on the other side and walked the cobbled road, squealing if they mistimed it and the tide rushed in closer and closer. The fishermen who made their living on Mount Polbearne had a handy sideline in rescuing the stranded and acting as a highly expensive taxi service.

There had been a movement a year or so ago to build a permanent road to the island, but it had been defeated by the villagers, who liked its unique character; who didn't want Polbearne to change from the way it had been for hundreds of years, regardless of how inconvenient it was.

The sandwich shop Polly also ran up the road was closed for the winter, but the bakery continued, as busy as ever, as villagers and off-season tourists queued to get the freshest, warmest bread from the oven, not to mention the hot tasty pasties for the fishermen to take out in their boats; the flaky croissants that Patrick the vet would devour in his sunny office, waiting on his barking clients; the cream cheese brownies adored by Muriel, who worked in the little grocer's that sold every single thing you could possibly want; the doughnuts for the construction workers doing up the posh new second-home extensions, with their glass-walled balconies and steel wires; and the jam tarts for the old ladies who had lived here all their lives, whose voices had the low hum and musical cadence local to the region, whose own grandparents had spoken Cornish and who remembered Mount Polbearne without electricity or television.

Polly braved the incredibly high winds on the shell-embedded steps that led down from the lighthouse – then battled her way across the promenade, with its low stone wall, crumbling slightly from the years of pounding waves, and down the seafront to Beach Street, the cobbled road that faced out to sea.

Buying the lighthouse had been an act of temporary madness, she knew, triggered by the astonishing fact of it coming up for sale. There was far too much work that needed to be done, and they absolutely couldn't afford to, but still, she couldn't get over how much she loved it, or the great feeling of pride she experienced when she saw it beaming out through the darkness (the top, working segment still belonged to the government), its red and white stripes a cheerful bulwark at the very edge of the village. The light didn't reflect back into the house – it was the only place on Mount Polbearne where you couldn't see it shining – and from the seaward side there was a completely unbroken view out across the Channel. In Polly's eyes, the ever-changing panorama – sometimes angry and dramatic, sometimes stunningly restful, and sometimes, when the sunset hit, the most radiantly beautiful thing on earth – was worth every penny of the horrifying mortgage, and the freezing early starts.

The only lights on this early, apart from one or two lanterns along the seafront, were, of course, in the bakery. Polly ran round to the back door and slammed inside.

The kitchen was gorgeously, ravishingly warm, and she took off her gigantic parka with a sigh of relief. Jayden looked up enquiringly. Polly went pink, and it wasn't just from the heat in the kitchen; she was remembering with a smile what had made her so late.

'Um, hi!'

'The cheese twists are in,' said Jayden self-importantly. He'd grown a moustache for Movember the year before, and it had suited him so much he'd ended up keeping it. That, combined with his white apron and a rapidly increasing girth through stock sampling and eating far more from the bakery than Polly would recommend anyone to do, gave him the look of a jolly tradesman from about 1935, and it suited him rather well. Jayden was madly in love with Flora, a local girl who had an incredibly light hand with pastry, and she was feeding him up too, despite being very thin herself. They looked like a couple from a nursery rhyme.

At the moment, though, during the winter closure, Flora was at college on the mainland – the first time she'd ever spent much time there – studying at a patisserie school in Devon. Jayden was absolutely miserable about it; he couldn't bear her being away and humped around like a sad walrus. Polly thought their romance was very touching, but wished he wouldn't be quite so miserable with the customers. He used to flirt with them and cheer them up no end.

'Thanks, Jayden,' she said, topping up her coffee cup from the machine.

They'd recently started selling hot beverages, and Polly had spent a very long and over-caffeinated day at a trade fair trying to find a machine that could dispense drinks that weren't absolutely disgusting and tasted all the same. She'd found one eventually – you could tell it straight off by the way everyone was clustering around the stand trying out the freebies, even people who were trying to sell other coffee machines – but of course it was by absolutely miles the most expensive one there. She'd be lucky to make her money back on it if she kept it for thirty years. There was a limit to how much you could charge a freezing fisherman who'd been on the water for eighteen hours for a hot Bovril, and it only just covered their costs. But it was nice to have it.

Except for the hot chocolate. Nobody could make hot chocolate properly in a machine. After it had arrived, Reuben, their loud American friend (some might say pain in the neck, but Polly had grown quite tolerant in the last couple of years), had marched in shouting, 'I make the best hot chocolate ever. Don't even think of doing it in a machine, otherwise this friendship is totally at an end,' and brought her several tins of his specially imported Swiss chocolate.

No slouch in the kitchen himself, he'd shown her how to make it, with gently warmed milk and whisked cream and the chocolate folded in until it became a thick, warming syrup that tasted like liquid joy, finished off with special small American marshmallows, a touch of whipped cream and a Flake.

Polly charged for those separately and only served them in the winter, but there was absolutely nobody in town – and for a long way around – who didn't think they were absolutely worth it, much to Reuben's complacent happiness. In fact, the start of the Little Beach Street Bakery's hot chocolate season was, as far as many local inhabitants were concerned, the first bell of Christmas.

'There's a sou'wester out there,' observed Jayden sadly. 'I hope Flora's all right.'

'She's in a centrally heated hall of residence, on a

campus, on the mainland, and will still be in bed for another three hours,' said Polly. 'I think she'll be fine.'

Jayden sighed. 'I miss that lass.'

'She misses you too! That's why you get so much post.'

As if worried he wasn't getting enough baked goods, Flora was sending Jayden the results of her efforts through the post every couple of days. Some made it in fairly good shape – the French cakes were a particular highlight – but others, like the croquembouche, were something of a disaster. Dawson, the postman, was threatening to sue them for ruining his trousers, repeatedly. He was already furious because he was always either missing the tide or getting caught in it. Mount Polbearne wasn't the jewel in a postman's round, to be honest. On the plus side, they'd all agreed that he could bin the junk mail at the recycling centre on the mainland, so that helped everyone. Until Flora's cakes had come along. Jayden had offered to share the results with him, but Dawson had declined the first time and was too proud to change his mind now. If they came out particularly nicely – the cream horns had been surprisingly unspoiled – Polly put them on sale and posted the proceeds back to Flora. This made Dawson annoyed too, especially if she put coins in the envelope.

'Morning, Dawson,' said Polly now, answering the back door and taking the pile of bills and one slightly soggy jiffy bag off him. 'Want a cup of coffee?'

Dawson muttered to himself – he'd obviously had to come extremely early this morning, on his bicycle, in the pitch black, to catch the tide, and he really wasn't happy about it. The post delivery tended to vary between six a.m. and two o'clock in the afternoon.

'On the house?' added Polly. She worried that if Dawson ever got too cold and miserable he'd simply stop coming altogether and throw all their post into the sea. Mind you, she thought, leafing through the usual pile of endless bills, some days that wouldn't necessarily be the worst idea.

Dawson muttered some more and retreated into the inky darkness. Polly shrugged and shut the back door.

'It's amazing how well I've integrated into the community after a mere two years here. Accepted everywhere.'

Jayden sniffed. 'Oh, Dawson's always been like that. I was at school with him and he used to cry if they made him eat gravy. So we used to always give him our gravy, like. That seems wrong now, looking back on it, I suppose. We used to call him Ravy Davy Eat Your Gravy. Yeah, I think that might definitely have been wrong.'

'Oh!' said Polly, pulling out a letter from a plain brown envelope postmarked Mount Polbearne, which meant Dawson would have had to pick it up from the old-fashioned red pillar box on the town's little main street, cart it over to Looe, then bring it all the way back out with him again. 'Well, it's funny you were talking about schools ... '

Jayden and his contemporaries – now in their mid-twenties – had been the last generation of children educated on Mount Polbearne, in the little schoolhouse on the lee of the island that was now used for village get-togethers and parties. The tables and wooden desks were still stored there, rather forlornly, and the old signs carved into the lintels on each side of the tiny building, marking the entrances for 'BOYS' and 'GIRLS', were still visible, even though, like everything else on the tiny island, they were gradually being eroded by time and tides and heavy weather.

But here now was a letter from Samantha, who, despite only having a holiday home on Mount Polbearne with her husband, Henry, always liked to get her fingers into as many pies as possible. She'd also had a baby last year and had started making worrying noises about schools in London and nursery prices and children being too jaded and sophisticated in the big city (even though Polly and Kerensa had thought that being jaded and sophisticated was absolutely Samantha's favourite thing). The letter was a typed circular, announcing a meeting to discuss the possibility of appealing to the council to reopen the village school, seeing as there were now upwards of a dozen children being bussed to the mainland every day – expensive – and lots more babies on the way.

Jayden smiled when he saw it.

'Ah, school was fun here,' he said. 'You know, except for Dawson, prob'ly.'

'It would certainly improve the children's attendance in the winter,' said Polly, who had noticed how often they couldn't go because of bad weather making the crossing too difficult.

'Well go to the meeting then,' said Jayden.

'No way!' said Polly, for whom the idea of giving up a winter's evening wrapped round the fire and Huckle before falling asleep at 8.30 was sacrilege.

'You should,' said Jayden. 'You'll be having babies one day. One day soon, I reckon.'

Polly glanced down at the fourth finger of her left hand – it was still awaiting the ring Huckle was having made for her, the seaweed engagement ring he had put there the previous summer not having proved as long-lasting as they hoped their union was going to be.

'Hmm,' she said, feeling a slightly familiar wobble of panic that came over her whenever she thought about the future.

It was true, she wasn't getting any younger. But she was so crazy busy holding both the businesses together, and she couldn't possibly afford to employ someone else and take maternity leave. And that ridiculous lighthouse they'd thought was such a hilarious idea at the time … How on earth could she look after a child? How on earth did anybody do it? She had absolutely no idea. And Huckle would probably want to get married first, and truly, she had enough on her plate …

Even though it was still almost pitch dark outside, the first customers were lining up expectantly. The older people still started work early, after lifetimes of toil at the very edge of the British Isles, and the fishing boats came in to hit the fish markets so that the restaurants and chippies could get the very best and freshest from the cold, salty water. In the summer, Polly would head out and watch the sun coming up and sit out in the dawn in a jumper, chatting with the fishermen. In deepest, darkest winter, they all simply had to charge in at the speed of light, closing the door behind them as quickly as possible.

The old ladies bustled in with their dogs, and Archie, captain of the fishing boat *Trochilus*, turned up looking utterly freezing. There was a local saying that there was no such thing as bad weather, simply bad clothes, but all the fishermen had the best high-quality gear there was and even then it was a tough old life out there, particularly when sometimes you needed to use your stiff, freezing fingers to untie knots, or gut fish, or open the freezer compartment. Archie's were mottled red and white and took a while to unfurl as Polly handed him his incredibly strong tea in the special mug she kept for him in the back kitchen.

'Good catch?' said Jayden, who used to work with Archie and had never got over how grateful he was not to have to do it any more.

'Aye, not so bad,' said Archie, head down, inhaling the steam from the tea. That, from Archie, meant things were definitely looking up.

Old Mrs Corning, one of Polly's regulars, marched up to the counter.

'Where's your calendar?' she said, pointing with her walking stick. Brandy, her tiny dog, yapped as if to back her up.

'My what?' said Polly, confused.

'Your Advent calendar! Advent starts today. Or weren't you raised in a Christian society?'

'I haven't seen her at church,' said another of the old ladies, who was busy chatting to Jayden.

Polly rolled her eyes. She'd slightly hoped that everyone's opinion on her comings and goings and what she did and didn't do might have died down since she'd got engaged to Huckle, but if anything it appeared to have got worse. Polly had grown up in Exeter, quite a large city, and had found village living agreeable but certainly different.

'Mattie and I get along very well,' she pointed out. Mattie was the vicar who came over from the mainland every couple of weeks to hold a service. Polly tended to skip the service – in season she was working; out of season she was fast asleep – but Mattie often popped down for a coffee, since she and Polly were roughly the same age and had quite similar outlooks on things.

Polly paused, and froze. No wonder she'd been so funny with Huckle this morning. No wonder.

'Is it really the first of December today?' she said.

'Yes. First day of Advent. You know. To celebrate the birth of Our Lord, Christ the King. That's what Christmas is supposed to be about.' Mrs Corning, who was a kind old stick really but rather felt the world was running away from her – even in rural Cornwall – peered at Polly through her thick glasses. 'Are you all right there, me lover?'

Polly blinked. 'Sorry. I didn't realise the date. November was so grey and endless, it all felt as if it were sliding into one another . . . all the days . . . ' She wrung out her tea towel. 'I'm not making sense. Sorry, Mrs Corning. Well. Anyway. It's . . . it's my dad's birthday.'

It didn't feel right calling him that. He wasn't her dad; dads were people who turned up.

'Ah,' said Mrs Corning, who lived in a world where almost all the men had died, and she and her small battalion of ladies, with their thin permed hair and their sensible beige BHS anoraks bought on irregular trips to Looe, stuck close to one another and looked out for each other and spent far longer discussing the ailments of their small dogs than they did looking back on the past, and their handsome sixties Teddy boys, back from their National Service, grinning over their John Players. 'Has he been gone long?'

'Oh yes,' said Polly.

Even then she didn't want to tell the truth: that he'd never been there to leave in the first place. The only reason she knew his date of birth was because she'd written it on her passport application form. That had been literally all she'd ever had from him, according to her mother, apart from some basic maintenance. A ne'er-do-well. Someone

29

whose presence wasn't missed. You couldn't miss what you'd never had, after all, her mother had pointed out to her.

Polly wasn't sure about that, not at all.

The cold of the day brought punters in in shedloads, relieved to get out of the wind and pick up some warm pecan and cinnamon buns. The hot chocolate stayed simmering in its pot, getting richer and thicker with every new cup that was poured, and the till dinged satisfyingly all morning.

Huckle wandered down about three o'clock, as Polly swept up the mail ready to take back to the lighthouse. She would do her paperwork by the Aga as she tested out a new Christmas cake recipe, even though the idea that she was making different types of Christmas cakes had raised eyebrows throughout the village.

'Hey,' she said, pleased to see him.

Huckle looked at her, still a little concerned after what she'd said that morning.

'You all right?'

She nestled reassuringly into his arm as he leafed through the post, stroking her hair gently.

'I'm okay really,' she said, muffled. 'I just needed a quick cuddle. Mrs Corning wanted to give me one, but I was worried she'd break a hip.'

'Did you call your mom?'

They exchanged a look.

'The usual?'

'Yeah.'

Huckle sighed. Polly's mum wasn't really one for answering the phone. Or going out. Polly had never noticed until she'd left home how reclusive her mother actually was; she never invited friends over, never had people in, very rarely went out, only socialised with her own parents, both now gone. Because that was how Polly was raised, it hadn't even occurred to her to question it, until she'd gone out into the world and discovered loads of other people actually having fun.

'Just tell her to come down here! Breathe some fresh air, take some walks, get some colour in her cheeks. It'll do wonders for her.'

'She can't,' said Polly. This was not the first time they'd had this discussion. 'Seriously. It's impossible. Last time I tried to get her out, she told me she couldn't because she'd miss *Doctors*. *Doctors*,' she went on to an uncomprehending Huckle, 'runs on BBC One five days a week and has done for about seventy-two years. You can watch *Doctors* or you can actually have a life, but it's tricky to do both.'

'She should see an actual doctor,' said Huckle, and Polly grimaced. They'd been there before, too. Her mother wasn't sick, she was just ... introverted. That was all. It was all right to be quiet in a world full of shouting social-media extroverts, wasn't it?

'Well, call her again when you get home,' said Huckle. 'Hey ho,' he added, picking up Samantha's letter. 'What's this?'

'Meeting for a possible school,' said Polly. 'Have you seen Neil?'

Huckle snorted. 'Have I *seen* him? He's practically sitting in the Aga. I have never known a bird so fond of his home comforts. If he isn't careful, we're going to end up roasting him for supper.'

'That's not funny,' said Polly, who had a total blind spot as far as the cheeky puffin was concerned. 'Still no sign of Celeste?'

Celeste was Neil's girlfriend; or rather, he had mated with another puffin and they had been nesting round the back of the lighthouse. Their first egg, to Polly's absolute dismay, had not hatched. Celeste had been fairly grumpy with them to begin with, so this tragedy hadn't necessarily changed her attitude that much, and then one day she had simply upped and left. Polly had been so heartbroken, Huckle had had to put her to bed. It had taken all his powers of persuasion to convince her that birds couldn't actually imagine the future and therefore Neil had absolutely no idea what he was missing out on, though even now she didn't exactly quite believe him.

It was true, though, that as the weather had turned colder, Neil was quite happy to *eep* until the door was opened, then march in and settle himself down cosily in front of the stove for a snooze. He seemed more or less entirely unfussed about his longer-term prospects.

'Puffins shouldn't even be this hot!' Huckle had said, looking at the bird stretched out contentedly in front of the oven. 'They're going to die out as a species!'

Polly had skritched Neil behind the ears fondly, and he had fixed Huckle with a beady eye.

'Okay, okay,' said Huckle, who was mostly pretty good at hiding his feelings about sharing his life with a small black and white seabird.

They locked up the bakery and headed out into the already darkening afternoon. As they rushed across the pebbled esplanade and up the steps to the lighthouse door, the clouds scudded across the sky and handfuls of rain and seawater hit them in the face.

'Guh,' said Polly. 'Seriously. Why couldn't we have opened the Little Caribbean Beach Street Bakery?'

Huckle smiled.

'We still could,' said Polly. 'We could get Neil a very, very small straw hat.'

They shut the door behind them, and Polly took off her wet boots and put the kettle on.

'Oof. Right. I am not moving out of here tonight.'

Huckle was standing by the door, still studying the letter he'd grabbed from the counter.

'Are you *sure* we shouldn't be going to this?'

Polly frowned. 'A town meeting?'

'Yes, well, *our* town meeting.'

They looked at each other.

'What's this about?' said Polly suddenly.

'Well,' said Huckle. On the small kitchen table was a large ledger book. 'The honey . . . I mean, the honey thing isn't going too well . . . '

'That's all right,' said Polly. 'I'm not taking off this coat till spring. You can also sew me into my underwear if you think that would help.'

Huckle poured tea for them both and indicated she should sit down.

'Listen, I've been thinking.'

'Uh oh,' said Polly, her heart starting to beat a little faster. 'I've been thinking' was one of those phrases, like 'we need to talk' or 'you'd better sit down', that brought about a modicum of panic. It reminded her of her horrible break-up with her ex, Chris, and the loss of the business they'd built up together. She hated those kinds of conversations.

Huckle took her hand in what was clearly intended to be a reassuring manner but that unfortunately had completely the opposite effect.

'What is it?' she said in alarm.

'Oh. Well . . . '

There was never any rushing Huckle. He was a slow-talking, laid-back boy from the American South who could normally calm Polly down in any circumstances, no matter how frenetic she got. She hoped he would manage it now.

'I was just thinking 'bout our wedding.'

After Reuben and Kerensa had had the most over-the-top

crazy themed wedding ever a couple of years back, Polly and Huck had vowed never to do that, telling each other that they'd have something small and intimate. But small and intimate was proving harder and harder, seeing as how literally everybody in the village thought they would be invited, plus Polly's family and all her old friends from home, who complained they never saw her these days since she'd moved away to the back end of beyond. She could have pointed out it was only two hours away but didn't need to, as quite often people turned up with a carload of buckets and spades to spend their summer holidays at her house, which was lovely but could get a little tiring when she had to get up at five a.m. and her guests were carousing till all hours and begging her to join them.

She told herself that was why she didn't like to plan ahead. She didn't really want to think about what else it might be: that her own mother and father . . . that they'd never been a family. The only families she knew had failed so badly.

'Uh, yeah?'

Huckle cast his eyes down as he thought about what he wanted to say. He'd given up a good corporate job to move to the UK, almost on a whim, after a long-term relationship had fallen apart due to their crazy working habits. His initial idea had been to destress, downsize for a little bit, get himself some breathing space somewhere far away from home – he loved working with his bees – and his father's British nationality had made it a cinch.

Then he'd accidentally fallen madly in love with this strawberry-blonde whirlwind of baking powder and capability, and that had been that.

Except he was stuck in an extremely remote, if utterly beautiful, corner of Cornwall, far away from reliable broadband and transportation and normal jobs. Last year, when Polly had lost her job temporarily, he'd tried commuting back to work in the States, but it had nearly torn them apart. He couldn't be a management consultant again, he just couldn't. It felt like it ate his soul from the inside. Even if Polly had been willing to move to America, which she wasn't. There wasn't much for her to do in Savannah, he knew; there probably wasn't room for another artisan bakery in the beautiful old-fashioned town.

And anyway, Mount Polbearne was where she belonged, however much she complained about the weather. They'd both become part of this community through good times, as businesses thrived and the town was a happy place, and bad, like the previous year, when a fishing boat and its young captain, Tarnie, had been lost, breaking the hearts of everyone in the area. They were a part of it now.

But oh my goodness, he couldn't make any money. A few jars here and there of his exquisite honey, which he sold to wholefood shops and beauty salons, wasn't enough. It wasn't nearly enough to pay for a wedding, even one a million times less flash than Reuben's.

He held Polly's small hand, muscular from kneading

bread, with white crescents of flour beneath the tidy unpolished nails, and she looked up at him, concern in her eyes. He cursed himself for simultaneously thinking that money did and didn't matter. It shouldn't when it came to how you spent your days – free and creative, out in the fresh air or experimenting in a kitchen, as opposed to shut up in some ghastly air-conditioned office listening to boring managers and filling in spreadsheets for ten hours a day.

'You know, about the wedding?'

Polly winced. It seemed like it didn't matter what they did, this wedding was going to be a big deal regardless.

'Don't wince!' said Huckle. 'Seriously, that is not a good look for talking about, you know, marrying me.'

'I know,' said Polly. 'It's just . . . you know. Getting your family to come all that way, and it'll have to be something really nice and special, and my family too, and it's just so much and we're so . . . '

She didn't want to say 'skint', but she didn't know how to avoid it. She never, ever wanted Huckle to go back to that high-paying job that made him so miserable. It wasn't worth it, not at all, ever. They got by. They got by absolutely fine, they needed so little. Well, the lighthouse needed a lot, but it had stood for nearly two hundred years so far; it could survive a couple of winters more.

'Okay,' she said. 'I'm listening.'

'Well, I was thinking,' said Huckle. 'You know, you are thirty-three . . . '

'Thanks.'

'...and, well, I figure we seem to be giving ourselves a ton of stress with thinking about a wedding. And cash and other stupid things that we don't really want to think about.'

He held her close to him.

'You know,' he said softly, 'I couldn't love you any more than I do. I couldn't.'

Polly looked up at him, blinking.

'I love you too,' she said. 'So much.'

'Good!' said Huckle. 'Okay, this feels like a good start. Okay, listen. Without me ever under any circumstances not wanting to marry you, all right?'

'Uh huh.'

'What would you think if ...' He gripped the letter a little tighter. 'What would you think if we, like, maybe did it the wrong way round?'

Polly blinked, not sure she understood him straight away. Then gradually it dawned.

'You mean ...' she said, and her heart started to beat very fast. It wasn't that she hadn't thought about it; it was just she felt it was very far off. After the wedding, maybe, and everything, when the shop was stabilised and ... She felt suddenly panicked. Rushed.

She realised she'd been putting it off.

'I mean,' said Huckle, 'it's not like we've not been practising the stuff you need to do to kind of *make* a baby.'

'I know that,' said Polly. 'But ...'

38

Outside the sea crashed against the rocks, and spray flew upwards. But inside everything was warm and cosy, the fire lit and a candle burning in the window. She and Huck weren't superstitious, but the fishermen were, and Polly knew they liked to see the little light flickering as they returned to harbour, guiding them safely home.

She looked into Huckle's face: his blue eyes, which always had an amused look about them; the broad, generous lips, always so ready to break into a smile. He wasn't smiling now.

She reached out and took his hand.

'Do you think we're ready?' she asked.

'No,' said Huckle. 'You'll feed them on nothing but cake and make them obese and grumpy, like Celeste.'

'Oh,' said Polly.

He stroked her cheek. 'But I don't think anyone's ever ready. I don't think that's how it works.'

Polly swallowed down her fears and indecision. After all, she should be thrilled, shouldn't she? A man she loved dearly, to whom she was engaged to be married, had just asked her if she'd like to have a baby with him.

'You can think about it,' said Huckle, noting how anxious she was. He didn't want to rush her.

'Okay,' said Polly. 'Okay. Thanks.' She turned to him awkwardly. 'I mean, we could go upstairs now ...'

Huckle shook his head. 'I hope that isn't a ruse to get out of going to the town meeting.'

'Rumbled,' said Polly, though in fact she'd been trying

to change the topic of conversation as much as anything else. 'I thought maybe if I took you upstairs and did that thing you like, you might not make me leave the house again. Because I am never leaving the house again, like I told you. Once I'm in for the winter, I'm in. Summer we can stroll along the beach and eat outside and enjoy paradise. Winter time I am going to put on four stone and never change out of my sixty-denier tights and possibly not shave my legs, and you're just going to have to deal with it.'

'I *will* deal with it,' said Huckle, 'and I will deal with *you*, young lady, in absolutely no uncertain terms. After the town meeting.'

'Noooo!'

'Get your coat on.'

'My coat's wet!'

'I'll take you for chips afterwards.'

'I don't care.'

'Come on! And if you don't, I'll get Samantha to come round and sign you up for the committee.'

'I can't believe I'm supposed to be joining my life together with such a bad, bad man.'

Huckle grinned. 'It's my innate drive and decisiveness. Move your ass.'

Chapter Four

The village hall was surprisingly crowded – or rather not surprisingly when you considered how organised Samantha liked to be, and how relentless her pestering if she didn't get what she wanted.

It was vicious outside, rain seemingly dancing all ways in the sky, with a distinct promise of snow on the air. It didn't snow much on the island, simply because they were surrounded by too much salt water, but it wasn't unheard of, and the icy wind definitely seemed to make it feel like a possibility. Huckle put his arm around Polly, but it didn't help that much as they trudged up the hill to the old schoolhouse at the top, Huck clutching a box under his other arm. Polly had okayed Jayden to make some extra apple turnovers that afternoon and pretend they were leftover stock so they could donate them, though that only made lots of people tut at her and tell her about stock control and how she shouldn't be so wasteful if she was going to run a successful business, so she pretty much wished she hadn't bothered.

There was lots of chatter and some crying in the hall. Muriel from the grocer's was holding baby Cornelius, and Samantha had brought her daughter Marina, so the place sounded quite lively. Most of the village was there, it seemed to Polly, including lots of the older residents, who were out for a free cup of tea and a bit of excitement – nothing wrong with that; as well as Mattie, the part-time vicar, and a stern looking woman Polly didn't recognise, obviously the council worker from the mainland. She had a sour look to her.

Samantha cleared her throat, ready to call the room to order.

'Welcome, everyone, to the Mount Polbearne town meeting ... You will find agendas and minutes on your seats ...'

Everybody pretended to look at them.

'Now, tonight we're here to talk about the possibility of reopening the village school. As of the next calendar year, we'll have nine babies ready for nursery and a total of fourteen children up to the age of eleven. As this would be the largest school roll in Mount Polbearne in over twenty years, we feel the time is right for the county council to allocate us school services.'

She continued in this vein for rather longer than was possibly necessary, extolling the virtues of Mount Polbearne 'not as a monument of ancient Britain set in aspic, but as a living, breathing, growing community', and Polly, as she listened, rather found herself falling under her spell.

Mount Polbearne had grown and flourished for hundreds of years, the generations continuing through fathers and sons, mothers and daughters. It was only recently that the place had started to die, as holidaymakers travelled further afield and people began to favour convenience in their lives over all things. Was it possible, thought Polly, that now they could reverse the process? Keep alive their little corner of the world, with its inconvenient access, winding roads, inclement weather, terrible broadband and lack of home delivery services?

She had been up for a very long time, and it was warm in the hall. Samantha's soothing tones washed over her, and she found herself snuggling under Huckle's large arm, her eyelids drooping. Huckle nudged her and smiled.

'This is where ours will go one day,' he whispered in her ear, and she smiled sleepily.

Then, abruptly, Samantha stopped speaking, and after a short pause, another voice started up. This one was harsh and abrasive, and Polly jerked awake, blinking.

'We have a responsibility in our district to ensure the health and safety of all our customers,' said the annoyingly nasal voice. 'Now I can see here that two years ago Mount Polbearne fought very strongly against a new bridge to the mainland that would have enabled ambulances and other vehicles to get through in a timely fashion. I simply can't

43

see a situation in which anyone would allow a school to function in this place.'

And it's all your own fault, the voice implied, even if it didn't actually say it out loud.

There was a clamour of dissent, and a raft of questions, but the woman – whose name was Xanthe – simply closed her very thin lips and shrugged her shoulders. It was not going at all well.

Polly suddenly discovered that actually she did care, more than she'd realised, and she sat up straight and wondered how you would make a case for a child who fell over in the playground and couldn't get to a hospital on the mainland if the tide was in. One option would be to have the GP there more often, but the local doctor wasn't fond of the Polbearne beat either – that old timekeeping issue.

She sensed that Xanthe thought they were all totally ridiculous, clinging to a rock in the middle of the sea and refusing to move to modern identical boxes on the mainland, all neat and tidy and squared away for the convenience of the NHS and the local council and the postman and the people who picked up the bins. It made Polly quite determined to do the opposite. This was a free country, wasn't it? Why should they toe the line and conform just so some suit from the council could tick a bunch of boxes about health and safety? She sat up straighter.

'Couldn't we just have the school open when the tides are favourable?' she asked. Huckle glanced at her, grinning. Polly never could keep her natural enthusiasm down for long.

'I don't believe schools get to pick and choose their hours,' said Xanthe, smiling thinly.

'Course they do,' said Polly. 'It's not written on holy tablets that they're shut during August, is it? It's not, like, the law.'

'School hours *are* the law,' said Xanthe. She might as well have said '*I* am the law', and Polly started to bristle.

'Laws change,' she said.

'You think we should change the laws of England to accommodate Mount Polbearne?'

'Well that escalated quickly,' murmured Huckle. 'What is this, a *coup d'état*?'

Polly sat back, fuming. 'I just think that if you wanted to find a way, you could.'

'We have budget cuts to make and staff to keep safe,' said Xanthe. 'The world doesn't begin and end with Mount Polbearne. Even if the road does.'

'I hope she misses the crossing cut-off tonight,' muttered Jayden, sitting just behind them. There were small noises of agreement and the kind of shuffling that denotes a large group of people who are quite tired now and want to go home or to the pub.

Suddenly the door to the hall burst open, and everyone turned to look as Reuben and Kerensa marched in, Reuben looking as usual extremely bullish.

'Hey!' he shouted, as if everyone wasn't looking at him

45

already. Behind him, Kerensa looked uncharacteristically deflated and a little pale, Polly noticed. She hadn't seen her friend in a while – Kerensa worked sporadically and Polly on her own admission had very much gone into hibernation the last month or so. The idea of getting dressed up to go out somewhere when you first had to take off the seven layers of clothing you were already wearing didn't seem to appeal. They'd texted, of course, but the unpredictability of the Mount Polbearne signal meant they'd hardly spoken on the phone. Now Polly perked up to see her, but she couldn't help being slightly worried at the same time.

'Hey?' She waggled her eyebrows in Kerensa's direction, but got no response.

'Hey, everyone,' Reuben went on. 'Great news! Glad tidings and all that stuff! So, anyway, we're totally having a baby!'

Polly jumped up. Huckle rolled his eyes. Only his show-boat of a friend would use a public meeting to announce something like that. Nonetheless, everybody clapped and cheered, happy to hear good news. Reuben and Kerensa might live in a huge mansion on a private beach, but new babies were new babies and, right now, very welcome.

Polly ran up to hug her friend.

'I am going to kill you for not telling me,' she said fondly. 'Seriously. I am going to absolutely kill you.'

'I wasn't going to tell anyone,' said Kerensa, sounding horrified. 'I haven't got my head round it myself yet.'

'How far gone are you?'

'About eight months, apparently.'

'You're NOT!'

'I am. I know. Don't kill me.'

'But that's not even possible.' Polly was absolutely stung. 'Why didn't you tell me?'

Kernesa shrugged. 'I didn't know. I didn't realise.'

'You didn't *realise*? How thick are you? Didn't Reuben guess?'

'Not until tonight.'

There was something strange about Kerensa. Polly turned to look at her, then glanced over at Reuben.

'Is he handing out cigars?'

'I told him not to do that.'

'Are you feeling sick?'

'Sick, fat, everything.'

Polly stood back. This wasn't like Kerensa in the slightest.

'Seriously, Kez. Why ... why didn't you tell me?'

But Kerensa just shrugged, and Polly, hurt, made her promise to come over later, because Reuben was insisting on taking everyone to the pub and it looked like it was going to be quite a noisy night.

'So in conclusion,' said Xanthe, obviously annoyed that attention had been diverted away from her, 'I have to say that the case for a school in Mount Polbearne has not yet been successfully made.'

Reuben raised his hand to stop the hubbub and turned around.

'Oh yeah, you should have a school here,' he said. 'That's an excellent idea. I'll send my kids over. Nice. Brilliant. Okay, that's sorted.'

'Well, Health and Safety say the local council couldn't recommend a school facility on these premises,' said Xanthe thinly.

Reuben stared at her for a moment.

'Who cares?' he said eventually. 'I'll buy it and open my own school. No problem. Private school, we can do what we like. Free to local residents, of course. Then we'll charge a fortune to gullible Russians and I'll end up even richer than I am now. Which is very rich.'

The room applauded. Xanthe looked horrified.

'But the hours ... '

'My school, my hours,' said Reuben, and on this general wave of cheerfulness, the meeting broke up and the villagers swarmed out into the biting cold and down to the warmth of the pub, except for Jayden, who had to get the taxi boat out to take a furious Xanthe back to the mainland, where she had self-importantly parked her car on the forecourt rather than in the designated car park, and thus found it up to its axles in seawater.

'I can't believe how you can live out there,' she hissed, once she'd finally got it started.

Jayden looked at her, blinking, and to his credit didn't say, 'Because it's not full of people like you.'

Chapter Five

The next day, Polly left Jayden touting doughnuts to the blearily hung-over and headed straight out over the causeway to visit Kerensa.

Reuben and Kerensa's mansion had recently had a complete overhaul and was now freshly redecorated. Reuben had been going through something of a *Game of Thrones* phase, so the place had gone from frenzied gilt to a kind of peculiar medieval mishmash, full of tapestry and gigantic wooden throne-style chairs. Tartan curtains hung from wrought-iron poles and great oil paintings had been shipped in. There were also lots of candles. Polly thought it was spooky. Kerensa was just pleased she'd managed to talk Reuben out of getting a kestrel.

Polly rang the ridiculous deep clanging bell and was let in by Marta, the maid.

Kerensa was half lying on a dark purple chaise longue next to a huge roaring fire that looked like it should have a pig over it roasting on a spit. She still wasn't smiling; she still looked pale and wan.

'Last night was quite fun!' said Polly, who'd had two glasses of wine and considered herself almost ready to get in the Christmas spirit. 'How are you? Still feeling poorly?'

She hadn't even confessed to Huckle how hurt she felt at being left out of Kerensa's news. So they'd been away a lot, but ... eight months? Before she could think, she blurted out 'Who doesn't know they're having a baby for eight months?'

'Loads of people,' said Kerensa defensively, as Marta came in and set out the tea on a side table. Polly would never get used to this kind of thing. 'Some people don't know they're having a baby till they actually poo it down the toilet.'

'Okay,' said Polly. 'Okay, okay, okay. It just seemed ... Okay.' She looked at her dear friend. 'You just ... I mean, are you happy about it? Your mum must be over the moon.'

'She is,' said Kerensa. She stirred her tea.

'What's up?' said Polly, suddenly worried. Where was her mouthy, exuberant friend?

Kerensa let out a great sigh, and Polly moved forward on the huge overstuffed sofa she was sitting on.

'What?' she said. 'Weren't you ready, Kez? I mean, neither of us is getting any younger ... ' She was conscious that she was trying out some of Huckle's arguments on Kerensa. She was also curious as to whether her friend felt as ambivalent about the whole thing as she did.

To her horror, Kerensa suddenly dissolved in floods of tears.

'What?' said Polly, rushing to sit next to her. 'What is it? What's happened? Don't you want the baby? What is it?'

Kerensa could barely choke out the words.

'Do you remember in the spring . . . when Reuben was being such a putz?'

Polly cast her mind back. The problem was, Reuben was so often completely insufferable, it was hard to remember just one occasion.

'D'you mean that time when he booked that band to play in the garden for his birthday then insisted on getting up and singing all the songs, and he was terrible and started yelling at people for not enjoying it?'

Kerensa shook her head. 'No, not that.'

'Was it the time he fell out with the telephone company and hired ninety-five people to cut the wires into their building, and MI5 thought he was planning a terrorist atrocity and he had to get himself that incredibly expensive lawyer?'

'No, not that one either.'

Kerensa sighed.

'Remember our anniversary?'

'When he flew back from San Francisco because he felt guilty?'

'Yes,' said Kerensa, hanging her head.

'And took you to loads of places and whisked you off to the States with him and it was all lovely and romantic?'

'Yeah, all right,' said Kerensa. 'But leading up to that, he'd been totally awful.'

'And ...?' said Polly.

'Selina and I went out one night.'

Polly blinked, trying to remember.

'Oh yes, she said you were really drunk. I don't like people who tell other people that someone's been really drunk.'

'She didn't say anything else?'

Polly remembered there had been an excited gossipy look on Selina's face, but she hadn't wanted to know about other people's daft exploits – she had plenty of her own – and had just kept on working.

'No,' she said.

'Honestly?' said Kerensa. 'I was too ... Well. I didn't want to ...'

'Is this why you haven't been in touch?' said Polly. 'I thought it was because I was working too hard and didn't make enough time for you.'

'God, no,' said Kerensa. 'No. No. It wasn't that.'

There was a long pause.

'I sort of ... and it was only that one time, and I was really cross and a bit drunk and ... Well. I. Well. I maybe ... slept with someone else.' Kerensa hung her head.

Polly drew back, too shocked to speak.

'You did *what*?'

'I was really upset.'

'So upset you *fell on a willy*?' Polly immediately felt bad about saying that. 'Sorry. Sorry. Sorry. And also, sorry.'

Kerensa wasn't listening; her face was full of pain.

'I don't know what I was thinking. I was so annoyed and I went out to a bar and I had a couple of drinks and he happened to be there . . .'

Polly was shaking her head.

'Why didn't you just come and see me and vent?'

'Because exactly this!' said Kerensa. 'Because I tried and you were off being ooh blah blah blah the most loved-up person in the world, and also you would have been so judgy, so, like, oh Reuben bought you a new car and a big house, you should be completely grateful, 1950s house-wife style, that someone else is making all your decisions for you, instead of my perfect life where I'm running a business and have a devoted partner who respects me!'

The tears were coursing down her cheeks now. Polly shut her eyes.

'But it's okay now, though, right? It was a stupid mistake that came and then went away again. It doesn't mean anything. You managed to deal with it and forget about it and just not do anything stupid like that again, right? You're not here to tell me that . . .'

They both looked at the bump at the same time.

'Oh no,' said Polly.

'It was only once,' said Kerensa. 'Well. One night.'

'Yeah?'

'I've ... I mean, I woke up and felt awful and came back, and we made up straight away the next day. He flew back. We were fine. We ARE fine.'

She started to sob. Polly leant over to hug her.

'Oh for CHRIST'S sake,' said Polly. She was surprised how overwhelmed with sadness she was; how upset. Selfishly, she'd hoped Kerensa's joy – her presumed joy – would rub off on her, make her more ready.

'I know,' said Kerensa. 'Can we just handle the fact that I'm a terrible, horrible person and kind of move on?'

Polly swallowed hard. Kerensa had always been there for her; had provided her with a home, for God's sake, when she was bankrupt and had nowhere to go. She owed her everything. They were best friends. But this: this was so big. Huge.

'Tell me ...' she finally managed to say. 'Tell me he was short with red hair.'

Kerensa shook her head, tears spotted all down her cheeks.

'Nooo,' she said. 'He was Brazilian. Six foot four. Quite hairy. Very hairy. Dark hairy.'

'Fuck a duck,' said Polly. 'And can't you find out?'

'Not till he's born,' said Kerensa.

Silence fell.

'Did he look hairy on the scan?' asked Polly finally.

'It's actually quite hard to tell,' said Kerensa.

And they sat there letting their tea get cold.

'You're very quiet,' Huckle said later. 'How's Kerensa? We should have them over.'

'No we shouldn't,' said Polly. She was making stollen, and kneading it far more than it actually required, just for the happy thump of dough on wood, taking out her mood on it a little bit.

'What's wrong?' said Huckle. She hadn't seemed quite herself since he'd first mentioned this stupid wedding again, and the baby thing. He didn't normally rush anything in his life; he hadn't thought he was rushing this. He'd had a little vision of Polly pregnant, round and glowing like the moon; how beautiful she would look ... and now she was hammering the bread board like she wanted to karate-chop it in two.

'Nothing. Busy. Work,' she said.

She knew this was unfair, and not a nice way to talk to Huck, but she couldn't help it. Kerensa had sworn her to deepest darkest blood secrecy for ever, particularly from Huckle. It would be beyond awful if he felt he had to tell Reuben. It was the kind of black-and-white way men looked at things, Polly thought: that it would be too unfair if a man had to raise a child who might possibly not be his own, even though the statistics suggested that that was the case for quite a lot of babies.

On the other hand, the entire situation was just a disaster. And even though it wasn't Polly's direct disaster, it felt strangely somehow as though it was; that into their safe, cosy little world a wolf had come, quietly padding over the snow in the dark woods of winter and lying down just outside their door.

Chapter Six

After a week, Huckle was still worried about Polly's mood. She seemed withdrawn and a little strange about things. He hoped it wasn't him. She had hurled herself into work with abandon. Perhaps it was his suggestion that they try for a baby. He'd thought it was a great idea. After all, surely it was the natural next stage? He'd made his decision; he'd crossed the world and decided to make his home here – a bit cold and draughty, but they could handle that. He loved their life, and he would love a baby. To Huckle, life was pretty simple. He just couldn't understand why Polly was so confused.

Polly felt horrible, like her stomach had dropped out. She couldn't imagine what Kerensa must be going through. She wanted to call her, text her, but she couldn't think of the words. She was having trouble sleeping, which wasn't like her at all – Polly slept like the dead normally, as Huckle had had cause to point out. And she could understand, couldn't she? People made mistakes. Life was made up of loads of mistakes.

But she thought of Reuben, and his many, many kindnesses to her – he'd sent her the oven to start up in her first ever bakery; he'd supported her when she'd gone out on a limb and bought a van; even when he didn't have any money, he'd always been there for them, however annoying he might be sometimes.

How could she stand by and watch him care for a new baby that might not be his; that might not look anything like him? To be complicit in all that deception? And it could last for years. She wished in a way that Kerensa hadn't told her.

But then she'd told her because she'd needed a friend – really really needed one. This was a true test of friendship. And Polly was failing it, right here, not even picking up the phone.

'You look like you've lost a penny and found a farthing,' said Jayden, bagging up a large collection of Empire biscuits. 'I have no idea what that means, but my grandmother always says it and I don't think it's good.'

'Oh, just lots on my mind,' said Polly.

'Yeah, I know,' said Jayden. 'They've started on you already, haven't they? They've got to you.'

'What do you mean? Who's got to me?'

'For the Christmas fair.'

'What Christmas fair?'

Jayden stared at her.

'Where were you last year?'

'I went to my mum's. What are you talking about?'

'The Christmas fair,' intoned Jayden seriously. 'Highlight of the Mount Polbearne social calendar. Revived, as all these things are, by Samantha and her All-Cornwall Social Committee.'

'I should have guessed,' said Polly. 'What is it?'

The bell on the door rang and Samantha herself bustled in.

'Ah, Polly!' she said, beaming. 'I hoped I'd catch you.'

Polly didn't point out that there was absolutely nowhere else she was likely to be.

'Hi, Samantha,' she said. 'Hello, Marina.'

The toddler looked up from her buggy and grinned gummily. She had inherited Henry's high colour, but it rather suited her; she was a rosy-cheeked, bonny little thing.

'Now!' said Samantha. 'Here's the thing. We're reviving the Christmas fair.'

'So I hear,' said Polly.

'She's been miserable about it all morning,' chipped in Jayden.

'Excuse me, I have not!' said Polly. Jayden and Samantha exchanged looks.

'So I wondered if perhaps I can put you down for a stall?' said Samantha.

'Um, what would that entail?' said Polly.

'Well, just what you normally do, but up in the village hall.'

Polly looked at her. 'And I give you all the money?'

'Well, quite, that's the point.'

'And it's on a Saturday?'

Samantha nodded. 'Yes! Then we get lots of people visiting from the mainland and they can do their Christmas shopping, do you see? We're going to have all sorts – craft stalls and books and bric-a-brac!'

Polly nodded. The thing was, craft stalls and books and bric-a-brac were absolutely great and fine and everything, but this would be a whole day's profits she'd be expected to donate, and it was tough enough to stay afloat as it was.

'And what's the cause?' she said.

'Well, it was going to be the school development fund,' said Samantha. 'But that all seems to have been sorted by that wonderful friend of yours with the loud voice, isn't that magnif? So we'll have to think of a new one.'

She turned and was on her way out again before Polly had time to give her an answer.

'I'm guessing that's a yes,' said Jayden.

'Hmm,' said Polly. 'It looks that way.'

'You know, you could ask other people to bake cakes and have a competition,' said Jayden. 'On your stall. Without you in it, of course.'

Polly smiled. 'Or Flora. She'd wipe the floor with everyone.'

'She would,' said Jayden, looking moist around the eyes. 'But you know. Everyone else could get stuck in.'

'Wouldn't it cause the most terrible fights and bad feeling?' said Polly.

'Totally,' said Jayden. 'It'll be hilarious.'

Polly picked up her phone and checked it, regardless of whether she'd got a signal. There was nothing from Kerensa. She felt horrifically guilty whichever way she looked at the situation, but the longer she left it, the worse it got. Then something occurred to her.

Selina, who'd gone out with Kerensa on that fateful evening, lived upstairs in Polly's old flat. She was Tarnie's widow and helped Polly out in the bakery from time to time. She was new to the village – even newer than Polly herself – and didn't really know Polly's friends all that well. She'd had a tough time getting over the death of her husband at such a young age, but living in the village had seemed to bring her some of the peace she'd been searching for. Polly didn't think she'd be there for ever, but for now it seemed to comfort her to be near Tarnie's family and friends, even though she was a city girl born and bred. No wonder she'd jumped at the chance to take Kerensa out.

Selina tended to sleep late in the morning, so at about ten o'clock, Polly made a big fancy latteccino (the sort of drink most of the locals had absolutely no time for), put some hazelnut syrup in it and headed upstairs.

Selina was floating about in light loungewear. She'd done up the ratty old flat, with its uneven floors and holes in the roof that let the rain in. Now, instead of the cosy cushions and warm rugs Polly had strewn around the place, it was a calm oasis of white walls and stripped-back wood, with what to Polly's unpractised eye looked like quite expensive art on the walls. Selina's plump cat Lucas, whom Polly had distrusted ever since he'd mauled Neil the previous year, lay resplendently on a cushion.

Selina was all right for money, and was taking a kind of correspondence course in jewellery design on the mainland. Thankfully Tarnie had had a really good life insurance policy, and though it didn't make up for him not being there, not for a second, it was typical of his thoughtfulness that he had made sure she was looked after. Fishing was still one of the most dangerous professions in the world, even these days.

Polly still missed him terribly. She couldn't imagine what it was like for Selina.

'Hey,' said Selina. 'Is that for me! Oh wow, thanks!'

'And!' said Polly, producing a warm cheese twist from her apron pocket like a conjuror. 'Don't give any to Lucas; he looks fatter all the time.'

'No way!' said Selina. 'You know, I have to hold my nose every time I go past the shop to stop myself going in and just guzzling everything. I thought I'd get used to it, but no. Fresh bread, every morning. It's not fair!'

Selina was absolutely tiny and took being absolutely tiny extremely seriously. Polly's theory was that she gave all her cravings to Lucas.

'I should say that given your willpower, you're the best

person in the world to live here,' she said. 'Which is why you're allowed a cheese twist every now and again.'

Selina looked at it severely.

'I'll go halves with you.'

'You're on,' said Polly.

'Is there skimmed milk in the—'

'Yes!'

'So, what's up?' said Selina, as they sat down on the angular white sofa.

Polly bit her lip. 'Am I that obvious?'

Selina nodded. 'Yup. Otherwise you'd be up here all the time.'

'I'd like to come up more,' said Polly. 'I'm just . . . I'm so busy.'

'I know,' said Selina. 'I'm not.'

'I'd love you to work for us again in the summer, you know that,' said Polly.

Selina nodded. 'So, anyway. What is it? If it's the sodding Christmas fair, count me out.'

'But your jewellery . . . '

'I know,' said Selina. 'I was slightly hoping I could make myself sound tough enough to be convincing to Samantha, but it won't work, will it?'

Polly shook her head.

'You know she wants my entire profits for the day,' said Selina.

'Mine too,' said Polly.

'I mean, I wanted to do this for a job.'

'Exposure?' suggested Polly weakly.

'That's what she said,' scowled Selina. 'And *you* don't need the exposure. You're literally the only baker in town. What are people going to do, start getting their bread delivered by drone?'

'I quite like having someone bossy around,' admitted Polly. 'I even miss Mrs Manse.' Mrs Manse had been the original, rather dragonish, owner of the Little Beach Street Bakery. 'I just like the idea of someone else knowing exactly what's to be done, and insisting that it is. I only get really worried when I don't think anyone's in charge.'

Selina nodded. 'I know what you mean,' she said. 'What are you doing for Christmas?'

Polly rolled her eyes. 'Hopefully nothing.'

The previous year she and Huckle had gone to Polly's mum, in her small house in Exeter. Polly's mum was scared of anything out of the ordinary – Polly breaking up with her fiancé and moving to a tidal island to set up her own business had been quite a challenge for her – so it had been a quiet Christmas. Fortunately, though, she'd taken a shine to Huckle, who was very easy company and didn't mind not doing very much, which was just as well given Polly's mum's reclusive nature. Polly knew that she should persuade her to come down and spend a few days in Mount Polbearne, but she was aware how hard she'd find it, and she hated making her mum unhappy.

'What are you doing?' she asked Selina. 'Tarnie's family again?'

Selina nodded. The awkwardness of the arrangement was far outweighed by the pleasure it brought Tarnie's mother, having a connection to him in the house. They would drink too much at dinner, and then sit afterwards and watch old videos of him as a child, and then they'd watch the wedding video and everyone would cry for hours.

'Worst conceivable day of human existence,' said Selina. 'But I tell you what: if there is a heaven, I'm getting in.' She took another sip of coffee. 'Man, this is good. It's nice to drink real milk once in a while. Although I'm probably lactose intolerant.'

'Probably,' said Polly.

'Oh my God, you're agreeing with me even though you don't believe in it!' said Selina. 'How bad is this thing?'

'Right,' said Polly, steeling herself. 'I really need someone to talk to. And Kerensa's busy. I mean, I like you just as much… Um. Anyway. Listen. What do you think? I've got a friend back in Exeter. From school. You haven't met her; I don't see her very much. She's married and everything. And now she's pregnant. But. But she thinks it's somebody else's.'

'Oh my God,' said Selina, sitting up straight. 'Is it Kerensa? From that night? Oh my God, it is, isn't it? It's Kerensa. The dates totally work.'

'What?' said Polly. 'Of course it's not Kerensa. Don't be stupid. I just said someone you'd never met.'

'Yeah, but you're forgetting I was there!'

'What? No, it's not her! How could it be? She totally wouldn't. It isn't like her at all!'

Polly felt her face grow hot. Selina didn't say anything, just kept watching her for a while.

'Okay,' said Polly. 'Look, it's my cousin, okay. The family is falling apart. Please, could you not mention it? I know some families are all right about this kind of thing, but not mine ...' She looked down, but kept an eye on Selina to see if she was buying it. Thankfully it seemed like she was.

'Okay,' Selina said eventually. She paused. 'Is it you?'

'Of course it's not me!'

'Only you have form.'

'Don't bring that up,' said Polly, and she meant it. During a period of temporary estrangement from Selina, Tarnie had slept with Polly without telling her he was married. It had been awful for everybody. 'Look, this is a nasty family problem, but I can take it elsewhere if you don't want to treat it seriously ...'

'Okay. Sorry,' said Selina, who wasn't a bad stick really. 'I'm preparing myself for a month of being unbelievably thoughtful and lovely to everyone. Just getting the last of it out.'

'Okay,' said Polly. 'Look, it's just ... I mean, I feel really bad about it. Even though it's not officially my problem.'

'Do you know the husband?'

'Yes ... uh, a little bit.'

Selina looked at her shrewdly.

'And is he a dickhead?'

'Sometimes,' said Polly. 'Does that matter?'

'Does he have other women?'

'No! I don't think so.'

'Hmm,' said Selina. 'And are you good friends, you and your cousin?'

'Yes,' said Polly. 'I want to be. But this is ... it's so awful.'

Selina leaned forward. 'What do you think you have friends for?' she said softly. 'This is why. Have you the faintest idea how many people abandoned me when Tarnie died? I lost so many friends over it. How is that fair? People ... they didn't know what to say, blah blah blah. What's to say? You just say, it's a fucker. Then you maybe apologise in case you say the wrong thing in the future. It's not rocket bloody science. Then you start being friends again.'

Her jaw looked fixed.

'Some people stayed. Some people,' she looked at Polly when she said this, 'some people came. But some just vanished completely, as if by being miserable I would infect their cosy, perfect little worlds. Does that make sense?'

Polly nodded. It did. It made perfect sense.

'That's when friends need you more than ever. When something awful happens. And here's the crucial thing: even if the awful thing that's happened is your own fault. *Especially* when it's your own fault. Do you see?'

67

Chapter Seven

'Well get in then.'

Neil loved going in the van. Well, he preferred Huckle's sidecar, where he would perch and enjoy the wind ruffling his feathers, but he loved the van too.

The rain had cleared, leaving in its wake a bitter cold, but Nan the Van warmed up quite quickly and Polly wanted to get moving before, as normally happened, people started queuing up in front of it for a pasty or a Marmite twist.

When she'd lost her job at the bakery the previous year, she hadn't stopped baking; simply bought a van and moved her operation into that. It had worked far better than she'd expected, and she'd kept the van on, partly for transport and partly because she could use it in the summer for coffees and sandwiches and keep everything bustling over. People's faces lit up when they saw her out and about in it, and more than one person had asked if she'd consider a delivery service. But it was also her only mode of transportation when the rain came in.

She rocketed across the causeway – she'd done the crossing so often now, she no longer had the fear she used to have, that the van would swerve and she would simply drive off the side and down into the depths; you could still see, moving under the waves to their own current, the tops of the trees that had grown there when Mount Polbearne had been connected to the mainland all the time. Somebody had once sat under those trees; had thought and dreamed about their life. And now they were down deep beneath the sea, as one day Mount Polbearne itself would be, reclaimed by the ocean along with everything they now held dear.

It was a short drive across the thin end of the county to Cornwall's north coast. In the spring, summer and autumn, the beach Reuben and Kerensa owned was a perfect private surfing spot, coveted throughout the county. Reuben often let the local lads use it, in return for doing a bit of bouncing and keeping out the pushy weekend surfers, who drove down from the cities with their loud voices and stupid hipster vans and entitled manner.

But now, in the heart of winter, there was a touch of frost on the sand that had not rinsed away, and the entire beautiful, desolate beach was completely deserted. Reuben's beach hut – which had a full working kitchen and bar – was shuttered for the season; the turn-off to the private road was even harder to find than usual.

Polly drove along the bumpy track at the top of the dunes and on up to the house itself. She'd thought it was crazy the first time she'd been here, and time and circumstances hadn't changed it: this was a mad place.

The house was very contemporary in style, with a lot of steel and glass, overlooking the unbeatable views of the wild coastline. There was a round turret almost entirely glassed in, which Reuben had requested because he'd seen it in an *Iron Man* film. This pretty much summed up the madness of the project. Film companies were always asking to use the house, and Reuben generally said no, although he'd started saying yes if it was an actor Kerensa liked.

Polly was now starting to doubt the wisdom of being here. Then she got cross with herself for even thinking it. Oh God, what a mess. And it wasn't as if she'd never made a mistake herself. She'd slept with Tarnie without even knowing he was married. They'd been careful, but maybe she'd just been lucky. Maybe she'd have been raising Tarnie's baby right now ... Maybe, she thought, everyone was only ever two feet from disaster, and it was luck, not fundamental goodness, that made all the difference.

She'd stopped the van in the nearby town, which was full of chintzy gift shops selling driftwood with HOME written on it at highly inflated prices, and gone into the third one she saw. She'd chosen an incredibly overpriced, but very plain, cream cashmere blanket, then picked out all the wrapping bobbins, which seemed to cost just as much again, and handed over her credit card with her fingers crossed. Kerensa forgot sometimes that other people had to think about money, but this wasn't about that. This was about buying something lovely: and it was an apology, not a gift.

She rang the bell, not even sure if Kerensa would be in. It was often hard to tell, given how many cars they had parked on the gravel driveway around the peculiar fountain sculpture. She hadn't heard from her at all – normally they texted and spoke every day more or less – and she didn't blame her. She hadn't wanted to let Kerensa know she was coming, in case she told her not to. It wouldn't have surprised her; would have felt like what she deserved, really.

The vast door already had a thick wreath of holly hanging from it. They actually paid people to do the Christmas decorations in this house. Polly hadn't even known that was possible; that that was a job.

The maid didn't come to the door; instead, it was Kerensa herself.

She looked even worse than before, all her natural buoyancy gone. She was washed out and pale, with great dark circles under her eyes.

There was a silence between them. Kerensa looked sullen, like a dog waiting for a blow.

'Is Reuben in?' said Polly.

Kerensa shook her head. 'Why?' she said, looking terrified suddenly. 'Is that who you've come to see?'

'No,' said Polly. She handed over the present. 'Kerensa, can you forgive me? I'm so, so sorry.'

There was a roaring fire in the hallway and they sat beside it, underneath a Christmas tree that looked to be about thirty feet tall and filled the three-storey turret.

'That tree is mad,' said Polly.

'That's what I said,' said Kerensa. 'Then he ordered one that was about four times bigger on purpose.'

They both smiled ruefully. Kerensa stared at the floor as Marta brought them hot chocolate.

'I'm sorry,' said Polly. 'I'm sorry. I was just so shocked, that's all. The fact that you kept it from me all that time ...'

'YOU were shocked?' said Kerensa bitterly. She looked up at Polly, eyes full of pain. 'I didn't expect ... I didn't expect you to turn away.'

'I was wrong,' said Polly. 'I was so, so wrong. Kerensa, you're the best friend I've ever had. I shouldn't have ... I shouldn't have done anything except tell you it's going to be all right.'

'How can it be all right?'

'I don't know,' said Polly. 'Things work out. You love each other, right?'

'I think we'll find out when I have a six-foot olive-skinned baby with thick dark hair,' wept Kerensa.

'Don't be stupid, you'll drag up a relative from somewhere. Why don't I start seeding the conversation?'

'What, hey Kerensa, remember that Spanish grandfather you never mentioned before?'

'Exactly,' said Polly. 'That great-uncle who came back from sea very rarely.'

Kerensa perked up slightly. 'Well,' she said. 'There is that side of the family ... I mean, we hardly see them.' Her father had died four years ago, but her parents had been divorced for a long time before that.

'Exactly!' said Polly. 'Just don't bring it up when your mum's about.'

'I could say it was something of a scandal at the time ... marrying a foreigner.'

'Will he buy that?'

'Reuben thinks Spanish means Hispanic. He'll buy it.'

'That's incredibly racist.'

'Who's incredibly racist?' Reuben marched in, whistling cheerfully. 'Where's the gorgeous mother of my baby, huh? Huh?'

He chucked Kerensa under the chin, and she did her best to smile at him.

'She's been so sick,' said Reuben to Polly. 'Honestly. I thought she'd be, like, too awesome to be sick, but, huh, apparently not. She's sleeping in the spare room because she throws up every five minutes.'

'It's very common,' said Polly. 'Kerensa was just saying you're a big fat racist.'

'Did you bring me some hot chocolate?'

'No,' said Polly. 'But I did bring you some Sachertorte.'

Reuben's face brightened. 'That'll do. Yes, I am racist. I hate everyone.'

'Why?'

'Because at my school for advanced and gifted children I took a pounding on a regular basis by blacks, Chinese, Asians, Caucasians, Hispanics, Arabs, Jews, Catholics and Zoroastrians. So I just totally hate everybody.'

Polly looked at him.

'Are you absolutely a hundred per cent sure it wasn't, like, maybe possibly a tiny bit you?' she said.

'Don't be a putz,' said Reuben, eating all the Sachertorte without asking either Polly or Kerensa if they'd like any. 'It was them. Everyone. I hate everyone. Except you,' he added, speaking directly to Kerensa.

'Ahem,' said Polly.

'Yeah, whatevs,' said Reuben. 'Did you bring me anything else to eat?'

They followed him through into the vast, gleaming kitchen, which was flooded with light even on a cold grey day like today. It contained what appeared to be every single appliance in the history of kitchens, all of them shining and mysterious and mostly untouched. There was, incredibly, another kitchen downstairs where the chef cooked.

'You know about food: what should a pregnant woman be eating? To make her glow. I want one of those hot, glowing pregnant wives with utterly gigantic breasts.'

74

Polly smiled. 'I only know how to make toast, I'm afraid. Although it might help a bit.'

'I'm fine,' said Kerensa. 'I just need to juice some more.'

'That juicer cost four thousand bucks,' said Reuben. 'You totally should. But also you'd think at that price it would do it for you.'

'Gosh, Kez, I wonder if the baby will look like your dad's side of the family,' said Polly. It was out of the blue, but she was doing her best.

'No,' said Reuben shortly. 'It'll look exactly like me. I look exactly like my dad and he looks exactly like *his* dad. Finkels have been getting rich and marrying absolute knockouts for generations, but we still get short freckled redheads. Who can pull knockouts.'

Kerensa looked as if she was about to start crying again. 'Show me how the juicer works,' said Polly in a hurry, but Kerensa didn't know, so they had to leave it.

Reuben went upstairs to answer his emails, and Polly held Kerensa whilst she wept silent tears all over the cashmere blanket.

'It'll be okay,' promised Polly. 'It'll be okay. I'll be here every step of the way.'

'Good,' said Kerensa. 'Because I think I'll be raising this gigantic swarthy baby by myself.'

Reuben came charging back down the stairs.

'Crud!' he was shouting. 'CRUD CRUD CRUD CRUD CRUD.'

Kerensa blinked in alarm.

'What is it?'

Reuben sniffed. 'Oh, my entire family has just decided to come for Christmas. Man, they're going to hate my small paltry house.'

He sighed.

'This is going to *totally* suck.'

Chapter Eight

'You said what?' said Huckle.

'Ah,' said Polly.

'I mean it, seriously. You didn't want to check with me?'

'Ah,' said Polly.

'I mean, I have no say in this?'

'Yes, but—'

'Sheesh, I know you don't know these people, but let me tell you, I do. And.'

'And what? They aren't good people?'

'They're rich people,' said Huckle. 'Good or bad doesn't really come into it for them. They've all got lawyers for that kind of morality stuff anyway, so it's kind of beside the point.'

'What is the point?'

'The point is sitting around telling you how rich they are. My God, they make Reuben look like Mother fricking Teresa. With the witty conversation of Stephen Fry. Oh Polly, how could you?'

Polly knew she was in the wrong. But the look Kerensa had given her had been so full of yearning and sadness that she hadn't even considered not immediately offering. Actually, it hadn't even been a case of offering, not really; Reuben in his inimitable way had simply turned round and announced, 'Hey, you guys can come.'

'I think ... I think we have plans,' Polly had stuttered, even as Kerensa coughed loudly.

'What plans? Sitting in a freezing tower on your own watching a bird fly round and round,' said Reuben with some degree of accuracy. 'That will totally blow. I'll have a chef in and the biggest turkey, goose, whatever you people eat here ... you won't have to lift a finger. Except to talk to my pop, so I don't have to. That's it. That's the sole thing you'll have to do all Christmas.'

'Well,' said Polly.

'Great. It's settled. And also I'll need you to ... '

'What?' said Polly.

'Neh, I'll tell you later.'

'I'm so glad you're coming,' Kerensa had said, and she'd looked so happy and relieved that Polly hadn't had the heart to protest.

And now Huckle looked sad, which he rarely did, and Polly hated to see it. His crinkly blue eyes turned down at the corners.

'Only,' he said, 'I saw us ... '

Polly came and sat next to him, putting out a hand to reach him.

'Sleeping late, you know. For once. Not getting up till it's light.'

'Light!' said Polly.

'Yeah. And maybe not even then. No ovens, no dough, no baking.'

'No fresh bread on Christmas morning?'

'No,' said Huckle. 'Because we would have some of that coarse brown bread left over, you know? The squishy stuff? With fresh salty butter and loads of smoked salmon on the top ... and a bottle of champagne in bed. You and me.'

'And then what?' said Polly.

'What do you mean?' said Huckle. 'That's it. What on earth else do you need to do on Christmas Day? I'll give you a small present ...'

'Is it honey?'

Huckle grinned. 'It ... it maybe might be honey, yes. Of some type or another.'

'That's great,' said Polly. 'I love honey.'

'And maybe you could give me ...'

'A croissant?'

'Perfect. That's exactly what I wanted for a present.'

'Seriously, what *do* you want?'

'Seriously, I have everything I want,' said Huckle. 'Except ...'

He made a mischievous grab for her, and Polly giggled and pretended to shove him off, which didn't exactly work.

'Well, why can't we do all that stuff and *then* go over to Reuben's?'

'Because AFTER all of that,' said Huckle, rubbing her shoulders gently, 'we open those big bags of chocolate coins you do here and put the television on and then we watch movies all day eating candy.'

'What about Christmas dinner?'

'Can't I just have more smoked salmon? And some cheese? And then the rest of the chocolate coins?'

'Oh GOD, that sounds good,' said Polly, thinking about it. What with cooking for the Christmas fair, crossly, with Selina making jewellery downstairs in companionable fashion, and stocking up the freezer in case the weather turned bad, and having to think about dealing with Kerensa, and Reuben's family, and Christmas, everything had suddenly seemed to come at her like a freight train,

'I think we might need two bottles of champagne. For when we wake up from our nap in the afternoon ready for more champagne and more movies and more chocolate coins. And if we're feeling really, really energetic, a long, hot bath. And then another snooze.'

Polly, who'd never been a morning person in her life, let out a sigh.

'We couldn't turn up after that,' pointed out Huckle. 'I'd be too drunk to drive the bike and you'd be too drunk to get out of the bath. And we'd both be asleep. We have a really, really busy Christmas Day schedule. Tell him.'

'You tell him.'

'You started it.'

Polly closed her eyes.

'You know what he's like. He won't take no for an answer. He's so insistent.'

'You're pretty insistent,' said Huckle, moving closer to her. Polly turned her head and surrendered happily to him. Maybe they could put off making the decision for another day. Maybe she could put off all the decisions.

Chapter Nine

Polly looked at the printout and let out a groan. It was a full and packed schedule Reuben's PA had sent her for Christmas Day at the Finkels', including two hours of charades, some round singing, whatever the hell that was, a full ninety minutes of gift exchange, walking to church – which was ridiculous, as Reuben had never set foot in a church once in his entire life and had been married by a rabbi – plus various mysterious entries such as 'Finkel family pageant' and 'The bringing in of the beasts', which Polly didn't even want to speculate on.

It just looked like so much *work*. Also there was a present list of about sixteen people on the email, all of whom Polly knew were terribly rich. She wasn't sure of the protocol, though: did that mean they liked fancy presents, or did it mean they had everything and barely even noticed if they got a Christmas present or not? Well, regardless, she had a tiny budget for that kind of thing. In fact she was seriously considering simply making two dozen fruit cakes and handing those out instead. Everyone liked fruit cake, didn't they? Mind you, this being Reuben's family, someone would be allergic to something. She'd never met a more Piriton-dependent man.

She sighed and looked up from serving old Mrs Larson, who bought half a loaf every day, ate four slices for her tea with soup and sprinkled the rest for the birds, even though the local birds were tiger-sized seagulls who would eat a rabbit if they could get it to stay still long enough. Polly was worried that one day one of them would swoop down and do for Mrs Larson, who was tiny and frail and whose eyesight wasn't as great as it had been and who was entirely capable of mistaking a gigantic seagull for a beautiful lark that was closer than it looked. And just at that moment, Reuben banged through the door, looking cheerful.

'Hey!' he said. 'Right, so I've got this list.'

'What list?'

'A list of, you know. Stuff we want to eat at Christmas.'

Polly took the list and scanned down it. Warm baguettes ... gingerbread men ... a gingerbread house, full-sized ... 16 loaves of rye bread ... 14 loaves of wholemeal ... 60 latkes ...

She looked up.

'I thought we were invited to your house for Christmas?'

'Yeah, of course you are,' said Reuben, completely unabashed. 'It's going to be great!'

'But I don't want to be catering at Christmas time! I don't want to be working at all. It's Christmas. I want to take some time off and mostly stay in bed and not go to work!'

'But Polly,' said Reuben, his face creasing in incomprehension, 'we're going to need baked stuff. You do the best baked stuff. I don't know how to say it more clearly than that.'

His face lit up.

'Man, I wonder what you're going to charge me to bake at a really inconvenient time for you.'

'No, Reuben,' said Polly.

'I think it would be a really horrific amount of money. I mean, seeing as my only alternative would be to helicopter in supplies from Poilâne in Paris. So you guys would have to charge me something totally disgusting. Man, it's really going to hurt me in the wallet. I mean, ow. Ow, that is such a painful amount of money. Even to me. Oww.'

'Stop it, Reuben!' said Polly.

'Well of course if you don't really need the money ...'

'Stop it! I just want one quiet Christmas without being up to my eyeballs in flour!'

'I thought you liked baking.'

'I do like baking! As a JOB. As a JOB I like it.'

Reuben raised his eyebrows as he backed out of the shop.

'You know,' he said. 'They say people who love their jobs never work a day in their lives.'

'Shoo,' said Polly. 'Get out of here! I mean it!'

'Don't worry too much about the ninety-six bagels,' added Reuben. 'I think I'll just get them sent over from Katz. No offence, Polly, but your bagels pretty much suck.'

'GET OUT!'

The queue of old ladies looked at Polly with disapproval in their eyes.

'Isn't that the young man who's going to rebuild the school?' said one.

'Yeah, all right,' said Polly, cross and conflicted.

'*And* he's going to be a father,' said Mrs Larson, sniffing. 'You'd think he'd deserve a little kindness.'

Polly began to fill up bags slightly lighter on the doughnuts than they usually were.

How on earth would she break it to Huckle? On the other hand, there was absolutely no doubt about it: they were completely skint. His honey just didn't cut it. They didn't need much, but the lighthouse mortgage was big and . . .

She heaved a frustrated sigh. She knew that in the scheme of problems – Kerensa's, for example – this wasn't much. But she so longed for a quiet time this Christmas. Last year with her mother had been slightly awkward – not her mum's fault, she knew. And the year before that had been heartbreaking, with Huckle away in the States and her entire future hanging in the balance. All she wanted was a bit of a respite. Just the two of them, celebrating the huge next step they were about to take.

She knew she should be happy and grateful. That it was really selfish to wish for more than she had, when she had so much already. But she had imagined everything proceeding nice and relaxed, just as it was, for a little while. Then at some point in the future, when things weren't so hectic and mad, she'd enjoy the stage, and babies and things, but in a while.

This was, she knew, utterly ridiculous. They were engaged. He was committed. He was the love of her life beyond measure.

It was stupid to care about it. And she'd never really seen herself as a bride; it wasn't the kind of thing she dreamed about. Everything she dreamed about was here in the Little Beach Street Bakery: the tinkling of the bell as customers came in; the never-ending pleasure of the scent of fresh bread; the satisfaction of baking and feeding people. That was her dream.

Anyway, that was hardly the most pressing issue. First she had to break it to Huckle that she'd basically ruined his dream Christmas. Or else turn down Reuben's money. And she knew it would be a lot of money. Enough to pay to get the windows sealed up against the January storms, or ... No. She still didn't want to do it.

On the other hand, imagine having to spend Christmas at Reuben's with the entire conversation circling round how selfish she'd been for not making the bread and the cakes – basically for not having done all the catering.

To which Huckle would say, great, let's not go at all,

and Kerensa would give that tragic washed-out sigh and make those puppy-dog eyes again to show how horribly sad she was, and the wind would continue to blast through the bedroom windows.

The old ladies had left, and Selina snuck in tentatively through the back door.

'Have the biddies moved out? Man, they give me such a hard time about whether I've found a nice young man yet.'

Selina had had a brief torrid affair with Huckle's brother DuBose, but they tended not to mention it.

'They just want everyone to be happy,' said Polly weakly, given that she'd just fended them off herself.

'They don't,' said Selina darkly. 'They want stuff to happen so they can gossip about it and say it's awful.'

'That too,' admitted Polly. 'Oh Lord, what should I do?' She explained her dilemma about Christmas, skipping the Kerensa part.

'Don't go,' said Selina promptly. 'Are you nuts? Why would you do that? You're not starving. Okay, you bought a stupid house; that's your fault. Rent it out or something. But it's Christmas; for heaven's sake, just enjoy yourself. Somebody has to.'

The bell tinged, and a man burst through the door. He was broad and sandy-haired, with bright blue eyes. Selina immediately perked up.

'Ooh, did I just make a wish I didn't know about?'

She turned round and smiled.

'Hello, can I help you?'

'Selina!' said Polly. 'You don't actually work here at the moment.'

'This is more or less my house,' said Selina.

'Less,' said Polly firmly.

The man looked agitated.

'I'm looking for ... I'm looking for the lady with the puffin.'

'Ha,' said Polly. 'Um, sorry.' She wiped her floury hands on her apron. 'Hello. I'm Polly Waterford.'

The man shook her hand. He was about thirty-five; weather-beaten, but in an attractive way. His eyes crinkled a lot when he smiled. He had an Australian accent.

'Hi,' he said. 'Look. We need money.'

Polly looked at him for a long time.

'Well then,' she said, 'you've totally come to the wrong place.'

Chapter Ten

They made coffee and eventually calmed the man down a bit. He told them that his name was Bernard, and that he was the head of the puffin sanctuary up on the north coast, near Reuben's house. Polly had tried twice to release Neil into the wild up there; both times it had been an epic failure, much to her deep and profound relief. Neil, it turned out, was not at all a fan of the wild, although the last time he had at least returned with Celeste.

'We just heard,' he said, shaking his head despairingly. 'Kara told me.'

Kara was the capable New Zealand girl, Polly remembered, who'd taken Neil both times to release him.

'Heard what?'

'They're cutting our budget,' he said. 'Government cuts. Apparently puffins aren't a priority in our austerity culture.'

'What?' said Polly, shocked to the core.

'I know,' said Bernard. 'They're endangered, you know.'

'How are they endangered?' said Selina. 'I thought you had like two million or something.'

'Yeah,' said Bernard. 'But fewer and fewer all the time. The sea's getting too warm.'

'Didn't feel like that this morning,' said Selina, looking outside to where the wind was still blowing.

'Yeah, well, local weather isn't anything to do with it, is it?' he said, with a sudden flash of anger.

'Ooh,' said Selina. 'You're feisty. I like that.'

'But what about the school parties?' said Polly. 'I see them all the time.'

'Neh,' said Bernard. 'The schools have all had their budgets cut too, haven't they? No more of that kind of thing. And the kids aren't really interested any more. Either they're all off playing Laser Quest or ... '

He looked as if he was going to sob.

'They've got kestrels down the road,' he said, deeply wounded. 'A birds of prey exhibition. You can hold a hawk and launch a falcon.'

'Oooh,' said Polly. 'That sounds ... I mean, that doesn't sound anything like as interesting as what puffins do.'

'Puffins don't do anything,' said Bernard bitterly. 'They don't do tricks. Unless you count swimming at forty kilometres an hour and flying at twice that speed and having the best air-to-weight ratio of almost any living thing and mating for life and—'

'You know a lot about puffins,' said Selina. 'Watch out, Polly likes that in a man.'

Bernard didn't seem to hear her.

'I mean, just because I haven't got ... stunt puffins.'

The bell tinged and Huckle wandered in, wondering if Polly would be free to have lunch with him, a hope that faded as soon as he saw her face. Neil was with him; since Huckle had let the fire go out, he'd thought he might as well go for a bit of a hop. When the little bird saw Polly, he *eep*ed loudly and marched over to the counter, where he fluttered up in stages – he was getting rather too lazy and fat to fly – until he made it on to her shoulder, whereupon he leaned into her hair affection-ately until she gave in and absent-mindedly rubbed him behind the ears.

'Yes!' said Bernard. 'Like that! That's exactly what I need! How did you train him to do that?'

'I didn't,' said Polly, surprised. 'He just did it.'

Without thinking about it, she passed Neil a crumb of brioche that had fallen into her apron pocket. He chomped it up cheerfully and leaned against her hair again.

'There you go,' said Bernard. 'But how are we going to train up all those puffins?'

'What are you talking about?'

He turned his blue gaze on her.

'You don't want the puffin sanctuary to close, do you?' he said.

'Of course not,' said Polly.

'I mean, it would be the end, probably, of puffins in Cornwall.'

'That would be ... that would be awful,' said Polly, meaning it.

'We need a star attraction.'

'NO WAY,' said Polly.

'That's it!' said Huckle. 'That's what you have to start saying to people! Say it again!'

Polly barely glanced at him.

'I mean, he could turn things around,' said Bernard weakly.

'You're not having him,' said Polly in a warning voice. 'Don't even think about it.'

Neil *eep*ed and edged closer to her hair.

'C'mon, Polly, shall we take Neil out of here?' said Huckle.

'Yeah,' said Selina. 'I can stay and look after Bernard. It's no trouble.'

'Jayden will be back in a minute,' said Polly.

As she passed Bernard, she looked at him grimly.

'You can't have him,' she said again.

As if things couldn't get any worse, Jayden arrived just as she was on the point of leaving. He was blushing all the way down to his moustache.

'Um,' he said. 'Can I have a word?'

Polly looked at him.

'Of course.'

He rubbed the back of his neck.

'Um, I wanted to ask ... Can I have a raise?'

Polly blinked. Both of them took the absolute minimum out of the bakery. She was planning on raising prices a little during the summer; the holidaymakers who came over from the mainland had plenty of money and were inclined to spend it, and people who had tasted her delicious fresh offerings had assured her repeatedly that her wares would fetch much higher prices in London or Brighton or Cardiff.

The problem was that the local people were on fixed incomes or pensions or low wages – like the fishermen, who worked harder than anyone she had ever met and still found time to pull shifts for the RNLI. She couldn't have a two-tier pricing structure; it was against the law. And she absolutely wouldn't compromise on the 00 flour, or using local butter in the croissants and cakes. You got out what you put in, and Polly only put in the absolute best.

But it meant there was very little left over.

'Oh Jayden,' she said in disappointment.

Jayden nodded. 'I know, I know,' he said. When he'd started at the bakery, the wages had been more than he got for fishing, in much more agreeable conditions.

'What's changed?' Polly asked.

Jayden blushed even redder, if that were possible.

'Um,' he said. 'It's just ... Flora finishes college soon ... And I thought. I thought I might put a ring on it.'

He mumbled this last bit, as if embarrassed to say it out loud even just to Polly, whose eyebrows shot up.

'Oh my God! Jayden! But she's only twenty-one! And you're only twenty-three!'

Jayden looked confused at that.

'Happen,' he said. 'That's older than my parents when they got married. And Archie too.'

Polly reflected on the tired-looking captain of the *Trochilus*, whose three young children made him look considerably older than his years.

'I suppose so,' she said. 'But Jayden ... You see what we take through the till every day.'

Jayden nodded.

'I know. I just ... I wondered. Because Flora will be getting a job, you know, and I thought ... I thought it might be time we settled down.'

'Are you going to stay here?' said Polly.

'I'd like to, aye,' said Jayden. 'But we'll see. Getting a place to live ... '

Polly nodded. She understood completely. Jayden lived with his mum still, but of course he'd want to find a place of his own one day.

She had the oddest sense that everyone else seemed to be happily moving along with their lives, whereas she felt like she didn't want to move at all; that she was being carried forward against her will. She knew why on one level. But it didn't help her to feel much better.

'I just can't,' she said. 'Not at the moment. Can we see

if we have a good summer? Flora can run the other shop and we'll get the van open for ice cream and see how we do.'

Jayden shrugged.

'Sure,' he said, and deftly started clearing up the crumbs in the back kitchen, returning the room to pristine perfection. He was a brilliant member of staff. If Polly could, she'd have given him his raise and then some. She felt like a bad boss; like a mean person. The fact that Jayden wasn't even complaining made her feel even worse.

Polly was so frustrated by the time Huckle got her out of there, he frogmarched her down to the Red Lion and ordered her a hot toddy. There was a roaring fire in the grate and a few fishermen on night shift sitting sleepily beside it playing dominoes. There wasn't a jukebox in the pub, as most of the locals liked to sing a song or two after a night out, which meant the only sound was the ticking of the large ship's clock over the mantelpiece thick with local holly, and the occasional snuffling noises from Garbo, the pub's gigantic shaggy lurcher, who lived rather magnificently on a diet of fish and chips and the occasional spilled beer. He was less dog, more pony on the whole. That lunchtime he was stretched out in front of the fire, his paws twitching as he chased rabbits – or, more likely given the size of him, gazelles – across imaginary plains.

'What's up?' said Huckle.

'Oh God,' said Polly. 'I'm so, so sorry. Everything's kind of gone ... gone absolutely rubbish.'

She looked up at him and began to tell him about her day. Huckle tried to remember a time in his life when all that was important was whether the queen bee was fertilising the hive properly and whether he had enough boiled jars in stock.

'That's terrible, sweetie,' he said when she'd finished.

'Do you think Reuben would fund the puffin sanctuary?'

'What?'

'Do you think Reuben would fund the sanctuary?' Polly repeated. 'I mean, all those people will lose their jobs and nobody will look after the puffins and the sea will grow too warm and ALL THE PUFFINS WILL DIE.'

She looked a bit wobbly and as if she might burst into tears, and Huckle vowed not to buy her any more hot toddies.

'Look,' he said. 'You're doing too much. I said it all along. Just calm down. We're taking Christmas off and that's that.'

Chapter Eleven

That weekend, Huckle simply insisted that a walk was going to happen. Polly hadn't been outside properly in daylight for about four weeks. And there was nothing like a walk for clearing heads.

'And Neil needs the exercise,' Huckle added.

'So do I,' said Polly. She was happy to go, especially as there might be a tea shop at the end of it. Or a pub.

'No, you're fine, it's that puffin that's fat,' said Huckle, checking his phone. 'Can Reuben come?'

'No,' said Polly. 'I'm planning on bitching up him and his relations for several miles.'

There was a pause. Huckle tapped at his phone. Then he looked up.

'Ah,' he said. 'So, anyway, he's coming.'

'Don't tell him where we're going!'

'Ah,' said Huckle again.

'HUCKLE!'

She looked down.

'We've got our jumpers on now,' said Huckle.

'Hmm,' said Polly.

The sun was just about visible through a misty haze. Great pools of fog gathered in the fields, where birds swooped in hopeful fashion around newly planted seeds in the brown turned earth, and sheep tried to nibble the grass under heavy frost. The sky was a hazy pink, the days having the shortest possible attention span at this time of year; making the least effort. You had to get out and grab it while it was there, otherwise the wind and rain would tear in again and then you were stuck.

They were cutting through the north of Cornwall, the Tintagel path, which would take them out along the headland – it was hard where they lived to do anything really without a view of the sea – ending up just past the puffin sanctuary. Polly wanted to pop in and see how they were doing. Neil had his blue foot ribbon on just in case he decided to go off and play with his old friends, but showed no inclination to do anything except lie in his paper bag in Polly's backpack, which rather negated the purpose of the walk: getting a fat puffin some exercise.

But Polly didn't care as she walked along trying to match Huckle's long strides, breathing the cold, invigorating air. Winter had more to recommend it, she realised, than she remembered. Or rather, this part of winter. February she could more or less take or leave. Once Christmas was over, it just turned into a waiting game. But now, out here in the harsh air, the sun glistening off the frosted fields, the waves pounding into the cliffs far below, Huckle's dirty blonde hair dishevelled beneath his beanie hat, she could see why it was some people's favourite season.

'I like seeing roses in your cheeks,' said Huckle, smiling at her. 'I'd forgotten what you look like out of doors.'

'Me too,' said Polly. 'It's nice. I should come outside more often.'

Huckle smiled.

'I miss the summer, too,' he said. 'When the bees are buzzing again, rather than sleeping. I feel like a spare part kicking around.'

'A very sexy spare part,' grinned Polly.

'I need to earn more money,' said Huckle. 'I need to throw myself into that beauticians' circuit. I really do. There's lots to be made from organic products.'

'But who'd look after Neil?' said Polly. 'Who'd look after *me*?'

They walked on hand in hand, until a stray brown terrier ran up cheerfully to say hello and Huckle tousled its rough fur.

'Hello, buddy!' he said. 'How are you?'

The dog wagged its tail furiously, and Huckle gave Polly a look.

'No,' said Polly. 'Seriously. We're not getting a dog. Neil would pitch a fit.'

'How do you know?'

'Don't want to risk it,' said Polly.

From inside the rucksack came what seemed to be little bird snores. The dog started sniffing around it.

'Shoo,' said Polly. 'You do *seem* to be a nice dog, but Neil's already been in a fight or two and he doesn't come out of them terribly well. I think it might be quite easy to chomp him by accident.'

The dog scampered off to be with some children heading in the opposite direction. They laughed and jumped up and down with their pet, then the elder boy ran to a tree and started hanging off it upside down by the knees. Huckle went quiet again and watched them, and Polly looked at him in trepidation. He felt her eyes on him and looked away. He didn't know, truly, what her problem was, but he didn't want to press her on it. He didn't want to make it too much of an issue. Huckle didn't really like issues. On the other hand, some things were important.

Polly blinked as the children's shouting and laughter reached them.

'Nice place to bring up a family,' said Huckle softly.

Polly nodded. 'I suppose so,' she said stiffly. She was actually relieved to see Reuben and Kerensa appear, coming the other way on the path.

'HEY!' shouted Reuben. 'We're out to see if my pregnant-but-still-totally-hot wife can perk up a bit.'

Kerensa shot Polly a tight smile. Polly felt sick. This was awful. Such a horrible burden to be carrying around, and of course it was even worse for Kerensa.

'Hey, you guys!' she said, more cheerily than she felt, and linked arms with Kerensa. 'Come on. Only three miles and there's a pub that does the best cheese and ham toasted sandwich in Cornwall. And I know this because I have tried them all.'

'You're only trying to make me feel better because I can't have any hot cider,' grumbled Kerensa.

'You can have a tiny bit of hot cider,' said Polly.

'Nope,' said Reuben, overhearing. 'No way. You're not damaging this baby. This baby is going to be the most awesome kid ever. I'm not having him born with foetal alcohol syndrome. You shouldn't eat the cheese either.'

'Is he being like this the entire time?' said Polly. She could say it in Reuben's earshot; he was impenetrably thick-skinned.

'Yeah,' said Reuben. 'For our perfect baby.'

Kerensa didn't answer him back cheekily like she normally would. Instead she dug her hands in her pockets and trudged on. Reuben raised an eyebrow at Huckle.

Polly let the men get ahead and hung back with Kerensa. The ground was slippery and muddy from all the recent storms and wind. The two chaps made a funny combination ahead: Huckle so tall and broad with his slow nod; Reuben talking up to him nineteen to the dozen, arms flailing.

'How's it going?' said Polly, although she could see from the body language pretty much exactly how it was going.

Kerensa shook her head. 'It's like someone gave me a precious globe, made of glass or something, and told me to carry it safely. And I haven't. I dropped it and I broke it and it's shattered into a million pieces. There's absolutely no way I can put it together again. I've done something so awful. And one day – it could be any day, probably soon – he's going to walk in and he's going to find out; he'll look at the baby. And I'll have broken everything. Everything in my perfectly lovely life will be ruined and shot and I'll have to raise a baby on my own and my life will be over and I'll have lost this brilliant, clever, sexy, funny man I really, really love ... ' She collapsed into tears.

'You couldn't ... you couldn't explain?'

'How?' said Kerensa. 'How could I? God, Poll, I didn't even know I was pregnant for months, I was in such denial. He was the one that noticed my tits felt all different and brought me home a pregnancy test. He was so excited ... Oh God.'

The men turned round, but Polly waved them on. She put her arm round Kerensa's shoulders.

'You never know,' she said. 'I mean, it could be his, couldn't it?'

Kerensa nodded. 'Yes.' She sniffed.

'But why didn't you tell *me*?'

102

'What, with you all happy and loved up and living in a perfect fairy world?'

'I don't live in a perfect fairy world!' said Polly crossly. 'I work my tits off and I'm completely skint and . . . ' Her voice trailed off and she realised that she was going to cry too.

'What?' said Kerensa.

'. . . and I don't even know if we can afford a baby. With everything.'

'Oh no,' said Kerensa, for whom money was never a problem. 'Oh Poll. Don't be daft. You're doing all right.'

'We are doing just about all right,' said Polly. 'As long as we never buy anything. Or go out. Or try and have a baby that I have to give up work for. Or try and fix anything in that stupid too-big house I bought by mistake.'

'You wouldn't have to give up work,' said Kerensa. 'You could have a bakery baby. Just sit it up on the counter and give it a croissant to suck.'

'Is that how it works?'

'I dunno, do I? I don't know anything about babies.'

They looked at each other, and at Kerensa's huge bump.

'Oh GOD,' said Kerensa. 'How have we managed to fuck everything up so completely?'

Polly burst out laughing.

'God knows,' she said.

'At least you still get to drink cider,' said Kerensa darkly.

103

The little pub just off the trail was perfect: cosy and warm with firelight, old brasses gleaming on the walls. They used local cheese and home-made bread for perfect toasted sandwiches, just as Polly had said. The four of them flexed their chilly toes and sat in a cosy booth. Polly sat next to Reuben and decided, as Huckle had suggested, just to come out with it.

'Reuben,' she said. 'I need some money.'

'Well, cater the Finkel family Christmas,' said Reuben equably.

'I don't want to,' said Polly.

'Well then, we have a situation.'

'Listen, it's not for me. It's for the puffin sanctuary.'

'That stink hole?' said Reuben.

'What? What do you mean?'

'It's just up the coast from us. I can smell the fishy bastards when the wind's going in the wrong direction. Hey, why? Is it up for sale?'

'No,' said Polly in alarm. 'But they're having trouble keeping it open.'

'Well this is great news,' said Reuben.

'No, it's terrible news! They're an endangered species.'

'They can't be, there's millions of the pricks. Shitting all over my beach.'

'Reuben! You can't be serious. Neil can hear you.'

'He's all right. The rest of them can get eaten by cats

for all I care. Hey, I want another cheese melt. These things are awesome. Get me another one!'

'Two won't be more awesome than one,' said Polly, slightly horrified at his greed.

'Course they will,' said Reuben, rubbing his hands cheerfully.

'No, look. Can't you donate to keep it open?'

'No,' said Reuben. 'I'll make them an offer for it, though. Hey, I could build a nice summer house there.'

'A mile away from your actual house?'

'That would be just about right for my parents,' said Reuben. 'Although I could probably still hear them. Plus, I could have both beaches. Hell, yeah, I can see this coming together.'

'Nooo,' said Polly. 'Huckle, tell him.'

'I think I've known Reuben long enough to never try to tell him anything.'

'Well why don't you buy it and move the sanctuary and put all the puffins somewhere else?' said Polly.

'What, and ruin someone else's beach house? Yeah, good luck with that, taking ninety-five years to get through court and ruining everybody's lives.'

Reuben's second sandwich arrived and he fell on it with gusto.

'See,' he said. 'One is good, but more is better.'

'Reuben!' said Polly in total dismay.

'What?' said Reuben. 'I'm celebrating getting rid of those stinky puffins.'

By the time they'd finished lunch, the light was fading and absolutely nobody was talking to Reuben. They made their goodbyes in silence, Polly hugging Kerensa for a long time. As they headed back along the cliff path, Huckle looked at Polly with concern. They were approaching the puffin sanctuary, and as if by unspoken agreement, they both turned towards the entrance.

The place was just closing up as they got down there. Bernie and Kara were walking round checking water levels and fencing, to stop local wildlife getting at the birds.

'Hey,' said Bernard.

'Hey there, is that Neil?' said Kara. 'Hello, little fella!'

Neil, who'd seemed to sense where they were, had hopped out on to Polly's shoulder. Now he fluttered around the area cheerfully before returning to his perch, rubbing his head against her neck in case she was considering leaving him there again.

'Don't worry,' she said, patting him reassuringly. 'You're not going anywhere. You're staying here with me.'

'*Eep*,' said the little puffin.

'How's it going?' Polly asked Bernard.

Bernard looked glum.

'We tried to organise some Christmas parties here,' he said. 'We thought maybe offices would like to come down, you know.'

'Come down and look at birds in the cold?'

'Yeah,' said Bernard. 'For Christmas, like.'

'In the dark and the cold? Look at birds on the sea?'

'We've got a café.'

They had a horrible café, which sold cold greasy fish and chips to parties of schoolchildren under fluorescent lights. Polly looked at it.

'Hmm,' she said.

She looked at Huckle, and Huckle looked at her.

The room itself was actually rather nice: classically proportioned, with big windows overlooking the rocks and the ocean; birds flying everywhere. It had horrible formica tables and chairs. Polly wondered what it would look like with great big long traditional wooden tables and benches. And fresh baking and . . .

She shook her head. That was ridiculous. She didn't want to expand. She couldn't.

She thought about Flora, about to finish her patisserie course. She thought about the number of young unemployed there were in Cornwall. She heaved a sigh.

Huckle glanced at her. Polly mentally shook herself.

'How much money,' she said to Bernard, 'do you need to see you through? If we could look at it again, maybe in the summer.'

Bernard looked momentarily startled, then delighted. Polly worried in case he thought she was rich. People did when they saw the bakery. She bit her lip.

Bernard named a figure. 'It'd take us through to the summer,' he said weakly. 'And then, hopefully, it'll pick up again with the season. Especially if we maybe changed our caterers . . . '

Polly blinked. It was a lot. It really was a lot.

She looked around the empty facility. The moon had come up – low, still, given the time of year, but it was a clear, cold evening, and the moonlight shimmered on the waves. Under the stars, slowly popping out even at this hour, she could see the birds dancing, whirring and diving in the sea, crossing the sky, the cold nothing to them with their heavy oiled wings. Up on the cliff there were nests on every available surface, thousands of birds banding together, chattering, diving, heading out for fish; small pufflings stamping up and down in that funny way they had that reminded Polly of toddlers wearing wellington boots.

She heaved a sigh and pulled out her phone.

'What are you doing?' said Huckle.

'I'm invoicing Reuben in advance for catering his Christmas,' said Polly.

He read over her shoulder; it was the exact amount the puffin sanctuary needed. He took the phone off her and adjusted the total.

'What are you doing?' said Polly.

'It means we might get a holiday out of it,' said Huckle, kissing her. 'Cor, there's no messing about with you when you've got an idea in your head, is there?'

'Thanks for being so understanding,' said Polly, nuzzling into him. 'I don't deserve you.'

'You don't,' said Huckle. 'But hey, here I am anyway. Dealing with the fact that my very, very, very busy fiancée has just taken on a massive extra job.'

'Look on the bright side,' said Polly. 'If you sous-chef for me, you won't have to spend any time talking to Reuben's parents.'

Chapter Twelve

The next few days passed in a blur. Polly engaged Selina, who had a tendency to get distracted but when she applied herself was perfectly capable, and taught her, painstakingly, how to turn out perfect buns and rolls and croissants, doing most of the prep herself and leaving the selling to Jayden, who was desperate for any scrap of overtime he could get.

He was still planning on buying a ring for Flora when she got back from college. Polly still thought they were far too young, but didn't mention it. In fact she was slightly admiring. The idea of organising anything as complex as a wedding was far too much for her to consider at the moment; Jayden's confident attitude was impressive in its own way.

She knew she ought to buy Huckle a present, but she didn't know when or how. Online stores didn't really deliver to Mount Polbearne without a hefty surcharge, and even when they did, it was still something of an ordeal to deal with Dawson complaining about having to heave stuff across the causeway, so the best thing to do was to go to a big town. She managed finally to sneak an afternoon off with Kerensa. She was going to attempt some shopping in Exeter so she could go and see her mother, too.

Polly was aware that her family was strange. Kerensa had been raised by her mother, Jackie, entirely on her own, and it had all worked out fine. She knew the circumstances of why her dad had left, and she even saw him from time to time. It was tough, but it was how it was.

It wasn't like that in Polly's house. There, a mysterious shroud of silence covered everything. Her grandparents, with whom they had lived when Polly was little, had stiffened if Polly ever mentioned her father, so she had learned early not to ask questions, although she'd been extremely curious.

And unlike Jackie, who had dated and eventually married a lovely man called Nish, for whom Polly and Kerensa had been giggly, rather naughty bridesmaids, Doreen had never moved on, nursing her parents until they'd died within six months of each other, using them as an excuse not to have a social life really, or have any friends of Polly's round. The house was always quiet. Not much changed there: the same cross on the wall; the same school picture of Polly at six, with her strawberry-blonde hair and missing tooth, against a bright blue background;

her mother's circled *Radio Times* in the tidy magazine rack beside the floral sofa.

It was school that had saved her. There was a local school that had been founded for orphans hundreds of years ago. Now it was a posh private school, but it still had a mission to take in fifty or so children missing a parent every year on scholarships. Her primary school had suggested it, and she'd managed to pass the exam.

The school itself was academic, backbitey, a tough environment of lots of clever children jostling to take first place. And the gulf between the paying pupils and the parentless charity cases was absolutely huge; socially unbridgeable.

But Polly soon found she didn't care about that, because in the intake of scholarship children she made so many friends, among them Kerensa. They became an almost impenetrable group who bonded closer than glue. They felt affinity with the young motherless princes; as they became teenagers they got drunk on Mother's Day and Father's Day round each other's basements; they looked out for one another and stuck together, because they had all experienced something children shouldn't have to.

That was one of the reasons why it had been so shocking for everyone when Polly had upped and moved to Cornwall. Thankfully Kerensa had moved too and kept in touch. It was also why what was happening now was so awful. If Reuben found out, and if he decided to have nothing to do with the baby, then the cycle would start

again, and both Kerensa and Polly knew how much they
wanted to break it.

And it was why Polly was finding it so very difficult to
take the next step with Huckle.

The little red terrace was spotlessly clean as always.
Frosties, her mother's cat, who was pure black with cream
paws that looked like they'd been dipped in milk, was
sitting on the windowsill, behind the net, watching her
carefully. She was not an affectionate cat. Polly thought
her mum should get a little dog like the old ladies in
Mount Polbearne, something that would jump up and
down and yap and be happy to see her and give her enthu-
siastic licks and cuddles. But Frosties lived up to her name
and treated her mother with a casual disdain, like much
of the rest of the world.

Unlike Kerensa's mother, Doreen had never dated
again, despite looking perfectly presentable for her age
(and even if she hadn't, Polly thought, plenty of people
found other partners later in life). Her existence had
contracted to the local street, the church, the high street
shops. Polly didn't know if it was a bad life, but it was certainly a small one. Her mother was scared of everything:
the internet, public transport, people who weren't the
same colour as her; everything. In contrast, amongst
Polly's peer group, they dared each other, expanded their
horizons, travelled far. Because they knew life was fragile,

113

they embraced it rather than retreated from it. And that had opened up a great chasm between Polly and her mother. She couldn't even ask, really, what her father had been like, or her mother would start to cry.

Best not to, then, all things considered.

So she nipped in quickly whilst Kerensa was in John Lewis, and said hello, and invited her mother to Reuben's for Christmas, and Doreen of course immediately declined. Then they sat in near silence, and Polly felt, as ever, how much there was to say and how little ever actually got said. She wanted to ask her mother, 'Should I get married? Should I have a child? Is it worth it? What do you think? Would I manage it? Could I?'

But Doreen had nothing to say on the subject, and Polly didn't know how to ask.

Chapter Thirteen

The phone ringing at night was a horrible thing.

First of all it was so freezing, and only Polly would ever wake because Huckle was so used to her keeping weird hours late at night. So there was no point in her prodding him, even though statistically speaking it was far more likely to be his parents forgetting the time difference.

Also there was the panic factor. Already Polly could feel her heart beating far too fast. Phones shouldn't ring late at night unless you were expecting something nice, like your friend having a baby in Australia or something. Polly was not expecting anything like that.

She experimentally stretched her foot out of the bed. The cold air felt sharp, like a knife. She hoped they weren't going to get ice on the inside of the windows again. Neil had tried to sleep in the fireplace.

She made a grab for one of Huckle's enormous jumpers and leapt into some Ugg boots. She had a massive and, she felt, very valid objection to Ugg boots on aesthetic grounds – she had once seen a picture of a celebrity wearing them on what had looked like a really sweaty beach and had been opposed to them ever since – but the Cornish climate had somehow allowed them to worm their way in when Kerensa had given her a pair, seeing as she had six pairs and was feeling sorry for her poor relation. Kerensa looked fine in Ugg boots; she had legs like sticks. They did not suit, Polly felt, the more curvaceous lady.

However, they were very useful under the circumstances, she thought now as she ran down the cold stone stairs. One of these days she was going to miss a step and trip and slip all the way down, but for now she knew every inch of them; every missing lip and worn section where generations of lighthouse keepers' boots had marched patiently up and down.

The phone was not stopping. Probably not a wrong number then, she thought glumly. Her mum was all right, wasn't she? She'd seen her a couple of days ago, and it wouldn't be like her to be up after nine p.m., unless *Midsomer Murders* was on, a programme Polly thought entirely unsuitable for her nervous mother, though she wouldn't be told.

The phone was an old-fashioned thing they'd inherited when they'd bought the property, with big buttons that used to connect it to the RNLI. It looked quite excitingly cool, like a sixties retro piece of spy kit, and had a satisfyingly deep bell, which now thrummed through Polly's chest like a chime of doom.

She picked up the receiver anxiously.

'Hello?'

The voice on the other end sounded tremulous and nervous. Polly desperately hoped they were about to ask her for a minicab so she could go back to bed. They didn't.

'Hello ... is your name Polly Waterford?'

'Yes,' said Polly, feeling a horrible ominous cold shiver run through her. 'Who is this?'

'My name's Carmel.'

The voice was shaky, but deep. The name meant nothing to Polly.

'I'm ... I'm ... a friend of your father's.'

Her father. Polly flashed back to herself as a small child, asking her mother where her daddy was, drawing pictures of him at school, and being told that there was nothing to ask about; that they were a family and that was all that mattered, wasn't it?

And Polly would say of course, they were totally a family and it was all fine, anything to stop her mum from getting too upset, moving the subject on as quickly as she possibly could so as to keep things nice and calm and happy.

Then, as she got older, she would go into the kitchen and whip up yet another batch of bread, kneading the dough so furiously her knuckles went white.

She knew that her parents had been together very briefly and that her father had cut off contact before she'd been born; that he paid some money on the condition that he never saw her – something Polly found particularly difficult – and that Doreen often said she didn't want his stupid money but of course they needed it nonetheless.

And that was all she knew about him. She didn't know where he lived, she didn't know what he looked like or what his relationship with her mother had been like. She had never received a letter or a present from him. She assumed he was just some Jack the Lad who'd come to town, had his fun and probably never given it another thought.

As she'd grown older, she had wondered why her mother had never met someone else. Doreen had only been twenty-four when Polly had been born – plenty of time to start again. People did it all the time. She didn't think her father had been abusive, and she knew they hadn't been married. It was like her mum was stuck on this thing that had happened to her when she was very young – a man had got her pregnant and hadn't stayed – as if this was 1884, not 1984.

Throughout her schooldays Polly had seen absolutely loads of her friends' parents remarry or couple up again – some more than once – with occasionally hair-raising results. But it had never happened to her mother.

When she was in her teens, she'd kind of gone looking for her father online, but every time she found someone who might be him – Tony Stephenson wasn't an uncommon name, after all; Waterford was her mother's name – she'd panicked and hadn't dared take it any further.

She didn't know what was out there; she didn't know what she might uncover. What if he had an entire family who looked like her but who he'd stayed with, who he loved? How would she feel about that? Would they even want to know her? Did she mean anything to him other than a long-forgotten direct debit? Did he ever think about her? Or was she just a night of fun he barely recalled, now too busy with all his other children having happy loud Christmases round the fire while she sat with her mum, her nana and occasionally her awkward Uncle Brian watching BBC One, as Nana didn't trust the other channels.

School had helped so much – she could pretty much pretend he was dead, it didn't make much difference – and then first pouring herself into the business with her ex, Chris, and after that the amazing surprise of moving somewhere so out of the way and finding so much happiness doing something as basic as baking bread for a living, something she actually cared about: all of these things had changed her beyond recognition and she had been too busy living her own life and being an adult to care any more. Sometimes, when she saw a father tenderly pick up his daughter and carry her proudly on his shoulders, she might feel a tiny pang, but it had been going on too long now for it to hurt much. Some people got two parents, some started out with two and lost one; everyone was different. But you couldn't lose what you'd never had, and she wasn't going to let it get in the way of her happiness.

Well, that was what she'd thought, until now; until this telephone call.

'I'm so sorry,' came the voice again. 'It's just . . . I'm afraid he's not well. And he's been asking for you.'

Polly swallowed.

'Where are you?'

'Ivybridge.'

Devon. No distance away, not at all. Basically just up the road. All that time. He'd have seen her maybe; in the *South West Post*, where they'd run an article last year. Had he read it and thought about her? Or . . . well, who knew?

'Whereabouts?' she stuttered.

'In the hospital, darling,' said the tremulous voice. 'He's in the hospital in Plymouth.'

Polly blinked. She felt a rush of emotion that at first she couldn't quite work out. Then she realised. It was part worry and sadness, but a lot of it was anger. How dare he come into her life right now, making emotional demands on her like this? How dare he?

There was a pause at the other end of the line. Then the voice again, which was sweet, with a Welsh tinge.

'I would ... I'm sure he'd ... Polly, I'm sorry. I would totally understand if you weren't in the least bit interested.'

Polly's anger was growing.

'Who are you?' she asked, quite brusquely. Behind her she felt a touch on her shoulder. It was Huckle, groggy and confused-looking at the fierce expression on her face.

She pressed his hand with hers to let him know she appreciated it, then shooed him away with a serious look.

'I'm ... I'm his wife,' came the voice.

'Right,' said Polly. 'So he married you and you don't actually have a clue about him at all? He didn't bother to tell you any of this stuff when he finally grew up? That he already had a daughter? That didn't cross his mind?'

'No,' said the woman. 'No. We've been married ...' There was a sob in her voice. 'We've been married thirty-five years.'

Two years longer than Polly had been alive. And then she understood.

Chapter Fourteen

It was 4.30 a.m. Polly would have been getting up shortly in any case. She was in two minds. She hadn't phoned her mum. She hadn't phoned anyone. She was in Huckle's arms, wishing she could just stay there for ever and never have to move. His touch, his lovely smell tightly wrapped around her; it was the safest place in the world, the only place she wanted to be.

She laid her head against the golden hairs of his chest and sighed. Huckle knew about her dad, of course, or at least as much as she did, which wasn't much. His own family were noisy and affectionate, and apart from DuBose, his black sheep brother, they seemed nice and pretty normal, so she didn't know if he could possibly understand. It wasn't like losing a father, losing someone you loved. It was the weirdest sensation out there: that somebody, a person you didn't know, shared various things with you – Polly's unusual red-gold hair, for example, didn't come from her mother's side at all. You were half a person you'd never met.

Most of the time she never even thought about him. Sometimes she did. But she'd never gone looking for him; never been particularly interested in trying to make up the pieces of the puzzle. She knew friends from school who had, and in general they'd been severely disappointed, as well as upsetting the parent who'd actually brought them up. And it wasn't as if she had memories. He'd got her mother pregnant, that was all.

And now, somehow, he'd tracked her down – Huckle agreed with her that it was probably the piece in the paper they'd done last year; a nice journalist had come and asked all about the bread van Polly was running, and recommended it to everyone, and she had felt like quite the sensation for a week or so.

He must have seen it. That must have been it.

Polly blinked hard. She looked up into Huckle's eyes. 'What do you think? Should I go and see him?'

Huckle shrugged. 'It's up to you,' he said.

Neil had woken and had stalked across the kitchen counters as he usually did, leaving floury footprints behind him. He jumped up on to Polly's shoulder, knowing instinctively as he always seemed to that she needed him there for comfort.

'Don't tell me that!' said Polly. 'Tell me to do something one way or the other and that will help me decide!'

'Okay, well, I think you should go.'

'I don't want to go! He never knew me! He never cared for me! Not a Christmas card, nothing!'

'Okay, don't go.'

'But this might be my one chance to meet the only father I'm ever going to have!'

Huckle was still holding her tightly, even though Neil was breathing fish fumes in his face.

'Okay, so go.'

'But I don't owe him anything! You know, my mother never moved house her entire life. He'd have known where to find her. I think that's *why* she never moved. And he never once bothered ...'

Huckle nodded.

'No, you're right. Don't go.'

Polly stood back.

'You are absolutely no use at all.'

'I'm not, I know.'

Polly breathed deeply.

'Okay,' she said. 'I know what I'm going to do.'

'Toss a coin?'

'No,' she said. 'I'm going to get in the van and drive there. Then when I'm outside the hospital I'll see if I know what to do.'

'You're putting it off? How does that even work?'

'I don't know,' said Polly. 'I'll figure it out as I drive. I'll call Jayden and wake him; he can get Selina down to cover the basics.'

She grabbed her big parka and went to throw it on over her pyjamas.

'I'm just saying,' said Huckle carefully. 'I'm just saying that if you decided to go in, you probably wouldn't want to be in your pyjamas. But also if you want to, that is completely fine too.'

'Gah,' said Polly. 'No, you're right.'

While she ran upstairs to get changed, Huckle grabbed a clean shirt and washed in the sink.

'What?' she said when she came downstairs to find him dressed.

'I'll take you.'

'What do you mean? No, I'll be fine. What if I change my mind? You'll lose an entire day.'

'Yeah, right, for something that might actually be quite important. You can change your mind. But I don't like you thinking about it whilst also sitting in traffic. I don't like that at all.'

'You know if you're taking the bike . . . '

'I know, I know.'

Neil loved the sidecar.

'I still might change my mind.'

'Well if you aren't changing it now, you'll need to get a move on. The tide is turning.'

The tiniest glimmerings of dawn could be seen as they trundled across the treacherous causeway. It was strictly forbidden to cross it at night, but nobody paid the slightest bit of attention to that. Huckle steered the motorbike with its ancient burgundy sidecar carefully along the cobbles, the water lapping at the sides of the narrow ancient road.

It was freezing in the sidecar, even under the waterproof cover; Polly curled her fists into the sleeves of her jumper. Her hair was whipping out behind her underneath the old-fashioned helmet. Neil didn't mind the cold, of course, and Huckle was concentrating on the slippery, treacherous road beneath them. She shrugged down further in her layers and gazed out towards the dawn, enjoying the sense of motion beneath her and the quiet emptiness of the road ahead. Not quite empty, of course; this early in the morning there were tractors and farmers out and about; milkmen and postmen and of course bakers. The lighthouse flashed behind them – Polly hardly noticed it these days – then switched itself off as the pink spread across the sky and the morning was fully there.

It was too noisy to speak, but occasionally Huckle would turn his head to the left as if to check on how she was doing, and she would blink back to indicate that she was all right and he would power on.

But was she? She sat rigid in the sidecar, trying to examine herself to see what she actually thought. Was this all connected? she wondered. The way she kept brushing Huckle off whenever he tried to talk to her about children. She kept telling him they were too poor, or too busy ... but was that true? Or was it all down to the fact that she didn't know how to be part of a family? Not a full one anyway. She didn't know how a father should be.

She had a nasty memory, suddenly, from out of the blue. When she was very small, hardly older than Year 1, she had developed a huge pash for the school janitor and had to be told not to throw her arms around him or follow him about. Even at that tender age, she had been hopelessly humiliated as the headteacher had spoken gently but firmly to her mother, telling her to make sure it didn't happen again.

What had that been, she wondered now, but a sublimated desire to attach herself to a father figure?

And every dead end in her heart; every time she'd stopped thinking about it, or cut herself off. Had it changed things? Made them go away? Of course not. Just because she stopped herself spending a lot of time dwelling on things, that didn't mean they had disappeared. She was just putting off confronting them for another day, and then another.

And now that day was here.

She realised that part of her felt flattered, oddly vindicated. As if, yes, you *did* think about me. It *did* matter to you, whatever you said or didn't say, however much you didn't pay me any mind or make contact. I was there all the time. I did exist for you. I was real in your eyes.

Although did that matter in the end?

Her heart was beating dangerously fast.

She had to see him. Didn't she? But what kind of

a state would he even be in? Perhaps he was raving. Completely crazy.

And what would her mother say? This terrible thing, this elephant in the room, how would they move beyond it? Perhaps Polly wouldn't tell her. Yet would that not just add to the family secrets that bore down on them so heavily; that kept her mother's heart so sad even after all these years?

She sighed out loud, but Huckle didn't hear her. The sun was up properly now. It was going to be a ravishing English winter's day, the sun slowly rising over fields carpeted with frost; beasts turned out in the fields; a pause in the beat of the farming year as the world held its breath, waiting for Christmas, the darkest, quietest time – or at least it was meant to be – followed by the full bursting of spring. It was quite lovely.

They could go somewhere else: watch the cold crashing waves; find a deserted out-of-season hotel; eat scones in front of a roaring fire. Jayden already had the shop covered, and it didn't take much to persuade Huckle to bunk off. They could just have a lovely day, the two of them.

But how could she, when all she'd be thinking about was this?

Instead, they neared the busy outskirts of Plymouth, already clogged with angry-looking commuters – was it worse, Polly thought, commuting to work on a mucky day or a beautiful one? She hadn't ever thought about it when she used to drive to the graphic design office she ran with

Chris. It was traffic and parking and fuss. It was what it was. Nowadays she ran thirty metres along a cobbled promenade with trays of warm buns in her arms; that was her commute.

She looked at the angry drivers, most of whom turned to stare at the motorbike – it garnered attention wherever they went. They looked stressed, their shoulders and bodies tense over the steering wheel; groups of noisy, disruptive schoolchildren in the back; radios blaring.

It was funny, she reflected. When she thought about how tough it was working for yourself – the long hours, the paperwork, the worries that kept you up at night – she never considered that she no longer had to get to work, and how grateful she was for that.

They queued through the traffic and finally turned in to the hospital. There was nowhere to park, but Huckle popped them up on a grass verge: nobody minded a motorbike, even if it was as wide as a small car. He stilled the engine, and suddenly the world became a lot quieter.

Polly started to shake. She felt incredibly sick. She should have eaten before they left. Or maybe that would have been worse. Huckle blinked. Even his blinking, Polly thought sometimes, was kind.

'Well?' he said in that slow drawl she loved so much. 'Whadya reckon?'

She sat there, not moving. Huckle didn't feel the need to fill the silence, or indicate what he'd rather do either way. He was perfectly happy to wait, or to come, just as she needed him. Although if he'd heard her plan to take the day off and have a picnic, he'd probably have liked that the best.

Finally Polly turned to him, her face pale and anxious.

'We're . . . I mean. I suppose. We're here now,' she said.

Huckle shrugged. 'That doesn't matter.'

'But I don't . . . I don't know what I'm supposed to do. I don't know what I'm supposed to feel. Three hours ago I thought I didn't have a dad, or rather that it didn't matter. Three hours ago my life was totally happy.'

'Well that's good to hear,' said Huckle, politely not mentioning the snit she was in about Christmas, or the puffin sanctuary.

'But now . . . I mean, everything's been turned upside down.'

'*Eep*,' said Neil.

'Thanks,' said Polly. Huckle tried not to roll his eyes.

Stiffly Polly pulled herself out of the sidecar. It wasn't the easiest of manoeuvres. She stretched her legs.

'Well?' said Huckle.

'Well,' said Polly. 'Nothing ventured.'

'You're very brave.'

'I'm an idiot.'

'Do you want me to come?'

'Yes. No. Yes. No.'

'Don't start this again.'

Polly heaved a sigh.

'I feel this is something I need to find out by myself. Maybe. In case it all goes wrong.'

'Okay.' Huckle nodded. 'Oh,' he said. 'Look. I know this isn't exactly the time, but . . . I bought you something. Well, something I owed you. Selina made it for me. Well. For you. For us.'

Polly blinked.

'What do you mean?'

He handed her a little box.

'I was going to keep it for Christmas. But I decided I couldn't.'

'When did you decide this?' said Polly.

'Five minutes ago,' said Huckle. 'When you couldn't decide anything, I decided something.'

Polly took the box and opened it gently.

It was a beautiful engagement ring. Silver, the metal carved so that it looked like a tiny twist of seaweed; exactly what he'd proposed with in the first place. It was quirky and precious and entirely them, and suddenly Polly loved it more than anything in the world.

'Oh!' she said, slipping it on. It fitted perfectly. 'I love it,' she said.

'It goes very well with . . . whatever it is you're wearing.' Polly had got dressed in a hurry.

She kept staring at the ring, her eyes full of tears.

'You're part of my life,' she said, slowly. 'The most important part. Maybe you should come after all.'

'The thing I love most about you,' said Huckle, 'is your decisiveness.'

She didn't smile, just kept staring at the ring, shaking her head. Then, finally, 'Okay, stay,' she said. 'Look after Neil. I'll call you if I need you.'

Huckle pulled her forward, and she buried her face in his chest once more.

'Are you sure?'

She nodded and attempted a weak smile.

'And if I come out shouting GUN IT!, we break for the border, okay?'

'Okay,' said Huckle.

He watched her small frame disappear into the vast hospital, looking very alone. Her head was held high; you wouldn't have known from looking at her the turmoil she was in. That's my girl, he thought.

Neil *eep*ed enquiringly.

'I don't know either,' said Huckle. And he left the bike on the grass verge and went off in search of coffee.

Chapter Fifteen

It was slightly absurd, Polly thought as she looked out for Carmel, who'd said she'd be waiting for her by the entrance, that it had never crossed her mind that she might be black. Too long living out in the country, no doubt. It didn't matter, though, as the soft-voiced woman with the very short hair came directly towards her. Her face was drawn.

'Sorry. Sorry, are you ... are you Polly?'

That was it, Polly thought later. The final chance; her last opportunity. She could have lied, could have said no, sorry, you must have someone else in mind. She could simply have turned round, walked back out into the exquisite December morning.

The woman's hands were trembling, Polly noticed. Trembling almost as much as her own, which she'd jammed in her jeans pockets.

She cleared her throat.

'Yes,' she said quietly. 'Yes, I am.'

The hospital was vast. Endless pale, identically lit corridors. It reminded Polly oddly of a ship, crewed by men and women in green scrubs and white tops, sailing – well, where? From birth to death, she supposed. Travelling on. Pregnant women walked slowly up and down, interspersed with the elderly; people were wheeled around, some missing limbs, many pale and grey-faced. Carmel didn't seem to notice. But then she wasn't desperately trying to hang back as Polly was; wasn't trying to spin out time before some kind of reckoning had to be met.

'He saw you in the paper,' said Carmel. 'He stared at it for ages. I didn't know what was up with him.'

She looked at Polly, really looked at her. Then she laughed.

'What is it?' said Polly, thrown. She twiddled her new ring, a talisman to remind herself that things weren't so bad, no matter how strange the situation she found herself in.

'You ... I mean, it's undeniable. Do you remember when Boris Becker had a baby in a broom cupboard?'

Polly didn't say anything, and Carmel's face dropped.

'I'm so sorry, love. I'm just nervous.' She swallowed hard. 'I knew I'd say the wrong thing. I'm so sorry. I'm ...'

She looked at Polly again, then turned her face away, shaking her head.

'You see, until the paper ... and until he got sick the first time ... I had absolutely no idea you existed.'

Polly hadn't wanted to hear it, but there it was. She was invisible. She had been airbrushed out of his life completely, just as she had always thought. She came to a halt in the middle of the corridor.

'You didn't know?'

Carmel stopped beside her.

'No. Not until two weeks ago.'

'You never knew anything about me?'

Carmel shook her head. 'I thought he told me everything.' She paused. 'Turned out I was wrong.'

'What did he say?'

Carmel sighed. 'Oh Polly, I wouldn't want to ... I mean, your mum ... '

'Forget about my mum,' said Polly, shaking with anger. '*He* did. Tell me. What did he say?'

'He said it was a one-night stand,' said Carmel. 'He was a travelling sales rep. He said it had just happened ... ' She gave Polly a look. 'We were married very young. He travelled about. His family ... They didn't want him to marry me in the first place. Things were a bit different back then.'

Polly nodded.

'He calmed down, you know. After the children. He just got married young and he was a good-looking chap, and there was a lot of opportunity ... '

It sounded like she was trying to convince herself.

'My mum was not an *opportunity*,' said Polly, with barely concealed fury.

Healthcare workers and patients were having to move around them, standing stock still in the middle of the floor.

Carmel shrugged.

'No. No. I'm sorry. I'm saying the wrong thing again. You're right. It was just … I'm so sorry. I think it was just one of those things that happened.'

'*I'm* just one of those things that happened?'

'Oh dear,' said Carmel. 'I'm making things worse. I'm sorry. You have to realise this was as much of a shock to me as it is to you. And when he saw you in the paper … He'd been ill already, and he just gave the biggest sigh. Like it was a weight on his chest. I have never known a man apologise so much.'

Polly blinked in fury.

'I imagine there was probably more than an apology back then,' she spat. 'He probably offered to get rid of me.'

Carmel stared straight ahead.

'I don't know,' she said.

Polly thought back to her mother's face: so perpetually weary, disappointed in the world. She tried to imagine what must have happened when Doreen had realised she was pregnant. Did she go to the doctor? Twenty years old, but so sheltered, still living at home; she must have been terrified.

Did she turn up at his work when she found out? Did

she go round to his house, to be met by this gorgeous, immaculately groomed woman, and bottle it? Did she trail home afterwards, tears running down her face, all her hopes and dreams for the future gone, exploded in one night's madness; one night Polly's so-called father professed to barely remember? A night that meant exactly what she had always suspected: nothing. Nothing at all. *She* meant nothing.

'No,' she said suddenly, bile rising in her throat. 'No. I can't do this. I can't.'

And she turned around in the middle of the gleaming corridor and ran out against the flow of humanity pouring in; flew outside to the beautiful freezing winter's day.

Huckle had just got his cup of coffee, and was sitting feeding bits of a very poor croissant to Neil and enjoying the sunlight when he saw Polly, half blinded with tears, her red hair glinting, tearing down the hospital steps like a rushing wind, and stood up to catch her.

'Did you see him?' he said, and she shook her head mutely, dampening the shoulder of his jacket. He didn't mind.

'It's okay,' he said, over and over again. 'It's okay.'

He didn't say anything else at all, just calmly helped her into the sidecar, tucked her in and stuck Neil under the cover with her, where he curled up and went to sleep on her lap, which helped as much as anything anyone could ever say. Then he drove them back carefully all the way to Cornwall, and Polly stared out at the glorious frosty winter day, watching the leaves drift across the road and wishing with all her heart that this had never happened, that she could undo it all, that she didn't have to remember the look of awkward, terrified kindness on Carmel's face.

Chapter Sixteen

'Ooh, those are beautiful,' said old Mrs Larson a few days later. Polly was looking critically at her Christmas twists: little branches shaped like holly and made of raisin and cinnamon pastry, with a mincemeat filling. They were delicious; incredibly rich but very easy to make. She was going to make plenty for Reuben's family to keep them going, and a bunch more for the wretched Christmas fair that was coming up on Saturday, but for now she had gathered a little boxful together and was heading off to visit her mum. It had to be done.

She was going to take Kerensa with her; she'd be a good distraction. Well, normally she was a good distraction, talking nineteen to the dozen and cheering everybody up, though at the moment, of course, she was very turned in on herself and secretly googling things like 'intra DNA tests' and crying about Jeremy Kyle. Reuben, in his usual busy, distracted state, either didn't notice or insisted everything was going to be tremendous and fine, which didn't help matters in the slightest. Plus Kerensa was genuinely huge now, huffing around the place constantly uncomfortable.

They pulled up in front of Doreen's neat little council terrace, where Polly had grown up. The houses were a mixture of local authority and bought. You could always tell the bought, of course; they painted their front doors. Despite everything, it had been a happy place to grow up. Doreen hadn't minded Polly running in and out of the house; playing endless games of skipping at the neighbours' and watching *Top of the Pops* at her friends' on summer evenings; buying ice creams from the van and making toast. It was a happy place for Polly; it had taken a long time for her to realise it was a sad place for her mother, that she had had different hopes.

Doreen had been so proud of Polly for going to university – and so disappointed when she had downgraded her office job to work in a bakery, of all things. It didn't matter how much Polly explained that she was miles happier now, that she felt incredibly lucky to work in the lovely environment that she did, with the lovely people she knew. As far as Doreen was concerned, it was inexplicable; living in a lighthouse was a ridiculous idea, and all in all, given how much she had sacrificed to raise Polly all by herself, the fact that she would throw it all away on some cakes, an American without a proper job and a bird was a source of some sadness.

Polly sighed. Where she'd grown up didn't bring her down, but Doreen could.

'Let's get her drunk,' said Kerensa, who had admired Polly's ring, then got slightly upset. Reuben bought her lots of jewellery, and currently she couldn't bear to wear any of it. 'Seriously. Get her drunk. Then she'll talk.'

'You just want to infect people with the stuff you can't do,' said Polly.

Doreen very rarely drank. She didn't approve, and thought that Polly and Kerensa's cheerful Pinot Grigio habit (when Kerensa wasn't pregnant) was a sign of weak character.

'Pretend it's fruit juice or spritzer or something. It's the only way.' Kerensa looked sadly at the two bottles she'd insisted they buy. 'I wish *I* could get drunk. Get drunk and think about something bloody else.'

Polly patted her shoulder sympathetically.

'Listen,' she said. 'You don't know. Nobody knows. Don't worry about it. This baby will come out and everyone will love it and find things in it that look exactly like Reuben and you'll be overcome with love and everything will be totally fine and you'll be a family. Honestly. You have to think that.'

'What if it comes out with one of those big dark eyebrows that meet in the middle?' said Kerensa. 'Oh God. Oh God. What was I thinking? Seriously, if I ever have a stupid night of stupid pointless passion ever again – which I won't if I'm lucky enough to get away with this, which I don't deserve to, don't point it out, nobody is beating me up more than I'm beating myself up, believe me ... '

'Yes?' said Polly.

'Well, just make sure it's with a short ginger guy with freckles,' said Kerensa in despair.

'I'll keep a tight grip on you if we ever go to Scotland,' said Polly as they stood in front of the immaculate door. 'Okay, come on.'

'What's the game plan?' said Kerensa.

'Now you ask me,' said Polly. 'I don't know. You just pour the wine and we'll take it from there.'

'Nothing can go wrong,' said Kerensa.

Doreen opened the door in her usual cautious way, as if worried about who would be there, even though they were expected.

'Did you bring that bird?' she said nervously. Polly had introduced Doreen to Neil once. It hadn't gone well. Doreen had asked Polly where he pooed and Polly had said oh he wears a nappy and Doreen had believed her and then looked anxious when she realised he didn't.

'No, Mum,' said Polly, giving her a kiss on her dry cheek and handing over the box.

'What's this?'

'They're Christmas twists. I'm trying them out.'

'Also, we have wine!' said Kerensa, waving the bottle. 'Quick, Doreen, where are the glasses?'

Doreen was fond of Kerensa, if occasionally a bit intimidated.

'You look huge, Kerensa,' she said bluntly as Kerensa sidled over to get glasses.

'Uh, yeah, thanks,' said Kerensa shortly. She didn't like people pointing out how big her bump was. It just made her think even more that there was some six-foot hairy Brazilian in there. 'It's mostly water retention.'

'What did you do, swallow a swimming pool?' said Doreen. Polly and Kerensa exchanged glances. This wasn't like Doreen; she seemed very light-hearted.

'So, Pauline, how are things at the bakery?'

Polly resisted the temptation to roll her eyes. She hated the name Pauline. It made her sound thirty years older than she was. Or rather, there was nothing wrong with the name; it just didn't suit her. She felt like Doreen and Pauline were contemporaries, not mother and daughter. She longed for the pretty names her friends had: Daisy and Lily and Rosie. Even Kerensa was old and local and traditional. Pauline just sounded grey and dutiful. Doreen's father, Polly's grandfather, had been called Paul. So it seemed they'd picked her name with the least effort imaginable.

Polly knew this wasn't really the case. She knew her mum loved her. Just that she found it difficult to show.

The mince pie bites were delicious, but it was Kerensa who was truly wicked, topping up Doreen's glass whenever she so much as looked away.

Doreen got up to bring 'tea' – a reheated (but still frozen in the middle) shop-bought pie and some nasty plain salad with no dressing: large slices of droopy-looking tomato, over-thick cucumber and wilted lettuce that was all stalk. Kerensa looked at it in horror. Polly was used to it and didn't mind so much. There was a reason she'd rushed out to teach herself to bake as soon as she'd been old enough to turn on the oven.

Doreen, unaccustomed to drinking, loosened up after her second glass and got quite giggly by her third.

'Well of course when *I* was pregnant,' she said suddenly, and Polly stiffened. It wasn't a period of her life she ever spoke about. Kerensa squeezed Polly's knee in a kind of 'I told you so' excited way.

'Yes?'

Doreen pursed her lips as if to stop herself talking.

'Well, things were different then.'

'No, no, go on,' said Kerensa, wielding the wine bottle. 'Tell me. I want to know everything. Did you cry every day and feel like a heffalump?'

'Well, I was never as big as you,' said Doreen.

'Yeah, all right, thanks.'

'But yes,' she said. 'I cried every day. But it's different

for you. You've got a happy family and lots of money and you're going to live happily ever after. It was just me and my Pauline, wasn't it, love?'

'And Nana and Gramps,' said Polly awkwardly.

'Yes, yes. But you know,' Doreen sighed, 'I sat in that maternity ward – they used to keep you in for days then – and Nana and Gramps would visit, but my friends didn't, not really. Well, I didn't have a lot of friends really. Just a few people from school, and the women I knew at Dinnogs, and they disapproved, of course. Even though it was the 1980s, when you think things might have eased up a bit ... no, not at Dinnogs. I think they're trapped in the fifties even now. Not that I would ever shop there again. Never. Not in a million years.' She took another sip of wine, her face pink.

Polly looked around the room, immaculate from the net curtains to the identically matching floral three-piece suite. There on the mantelpiece was her Year 1 photo, one tooth missing, her hair a brighter red then before it had softened into strawberry blonde, freckles cheerfully scattered across her face. She looked like Pippi Longstocking. And there on the wall was her degree certificate from the University of Southampton – Polly hadn't wanted it particularly, so here it was, displayed, even though her mother received so few visitors. And she knew that upstairs, her old bedroom was still just as it had always been, her bed made up just in case she ever wanted to come home.

It didn't matter that sometimes they couldn't

communicate; that her mother had never, perhaps, been as naturally warm as she thought other families might be.

This was still home. It always had been.

Suddenly she didn't want to throw this bomb in here. Didn't want to disrupt her mother's careful, sheltered life any more than she had to. Yet she had to say something. Ever since Carmel's phone call, the only thing she'd been able to think about was the man dying in a hospital bed not too far from here. A man who was her biological father. Not her father in any meaningful sense, but a part of her nonetheless. And there was only one person on earth who could tell her the right thing to do.

Kerensa emptied yet more wine into Doreen's glass. She wouldn't have been this squiffy in years; she kept giggling and had gone very red in the face.

'Tell me what it's like,' said Kerensa. 'You know I don't have anyone. My mum says she can't remember and Polly is absolutely no use at all.'

'Oh, it was so long ago,' said Doreen.

'It wasn't *that* long ago,' said Polly.

'Tell us!' said Kerensa.

'Well . . . ' said Doreen.

Kerensa, with some lack of grace, got carefully to her feet.

'I'll just wash up,' she said, winking at Polly. 'I'm still listening!'

'No, no, I'll do that,' flapped Doreen, but without

making any real effort to get up. Kerensa gave Polly a stern look and another hefty wink.

'Now,' she hissed.

Polly refilled her own glass and leaned forward.

'Mum,' she said.

'Doesn't Kerensa look blooming!' her mother was saying. 'Oh, her mother is so lucky. How I'd have loved a grandchild. She's fallen right on her feet, hasn't she? Although I'd never have thought that little chap would have it in him!'

She giggled, then hiccuped. Polly realised she'd need to be quick, before her mother fell asleep at the table.

'Mum,' she said. 'Mum. I need to ask you about my dad.'

She'd said it before, of course. But this time she wasn't going to be fobbed off.

Doreen rolled her eyes and poured herself another glass. There was a long silence.

'That rat bastard,' she said finally.

Polly had never heard her mother swear in her life.

'Well?' she said. 'Please. Can you tell me a little more? Please? It's important.'

'Why?' said her mother. 'Why now?'

Polly thought for a moment.

'Well, if Huckle and I are going to get married . . . then we might have a baby . . .'

'Oh please,' said her mother. 'You've been engaged for months and haven't even bothered to book a date or tell

147

people what's happening. I don't think you can pin him down at all. He doesn't seem that fussed.'

This wasn't the time to tell her it was Polly who had cold feet, and that this was why.

'Just tell me about Tony,' she said. 'What was he like?'

Her mother sighed, staring into her glass.

'I don't feel very well,' she announced. This was a common tactic. Polly was meant to drop the subject now and start asking after her mother's health. Doreen could discuss her health issues for several hours at a time. One time they'd been walking down the high street and Polly was sure she had seen her GP hiding inside a shoe shop.

'You're fine,' said Polly. 'You can go to bed in just a minute. But first, please . . . You owe me, Mum. I can't . . . I don't feel I can take the next step in my life without knowing. Without knowing more.'

She felt bad lying like this. But she had to know.

Her mother blinked.

'Well,' she said. Then she sighed again. 'Your hair,' she said, setting down her glass. 'Your hair. That's exactly what his was like. And you know, lots of women, they don't like a sandy-haired man. I don't know why. I thought it was beautiful. Absolutely beautiful. It shone in the sunlight, and his freckles . . . they were like golden dots. I wanted to . . . I wanted to kiss them all.'

She laughed, harshly and suddenly. 'Listen to me.' She shook her head. 'Ridiculous.'

'No it's not,' said Polly. 'Really it isn't.'

'People think the eighties wasn't very long ago,' said Doreen. 'That things weren't that different. But I'll tell you, they were. Do you know, when Lady Diana Spencer got married, they sent her to see a doctor to see if she was a virgin or not. And they told people that; everybody knew. It was official. She went to see the official royal doctor and he said she was a virgin. In the eighties. SO.'

Polly stayed silent, willing her mother just to carry on talking.

'I was on hats,' said Doreen. 'Well, hats and gloves really, but it was the hats I liked. At Dinnogs. For weddings, mainly, and Christmas felts in winter. Men wore more hats then. People wore more hats then. Central heating ruined everything.'

This was obviously going off at a bit of a tangent, but Polly decided to ignore it and topped up her mother's glass again.

'So he used to come in . . . you'd always notice him. He was tall, like you. Thinner than you, though.' She smiled. 'He'd come in and look at the hats and chat to me . . . Well, he was a sales rep, he did a lot of business upstairs. Curtain material, that kind of thing. He'd always hover round the door. They put the pretty girls near the door, just to get the chaps in, you know.' She blushed. 'The young girls, anyway.'

'You were lovely, Mum,' said Polly loyally. In the very few photographs they had from that time, her mother had a Human League haircut and funny pointy shoulder pads.

149

'So he'd go upstairs, then he'd come down and talk about hats, and once ...' She went an even brighter red. 'Once he asked me to help him try on some leather gloves. He had ... he had the most beautiful hands.' She bit her lip. 'It was the most romantic thing that had ever happened to me. The boys round my way, all farm boys ... well, I wasn't interested, I really wasn't. I mean, he seemed so sophisticated. Well, he was twenty-three years old. Anyway, he asked me out and we went to a snug. That was the bit in a pub where women could go; they still had those in the eighties, you know.'

'It seems a million years ago.'

'It was! We smoked inside!'

Polly smiled. 'Whoa.'

'So we smoked Regal King Sizes, and I had half a cider and black and he drank a couple of pints, and he told me about life on the road and his car – he had a Ford Escort, he loved it.'

Polly nodded.

'It was ... it was the best night of my life. And he didn't try anything on, he really didn't. He gave me a lift home in his car. Then he came in the next week. And the next.'

Suddenly Doreen's face sagged and she looked terribly sad.

'He just seemed so nice. I was twenty. I thought this was it. You met a boy you liked, he liked you, that was it, you got married, that was how it was then. None of this wandering about until you're in your thirties thinking

150

you've got all the time in the world, then getting all panicky about it.'

Polly ignored this.

'And he met my mum and dad, you know, it was all
totally above board ... they thought he was charming. And
so handsome with that lovely hair. Of course you heard
jokes about travelling salesmen, but I didn't think it would
apply to Tony. More fool me.'

There was a pause.

'I walked in to Dimmogs one morning, and it was so
strange. As if I could feel something in the air. Lydia by
the perfume station, she barely looked up, and normally
you couldn't get five yards without her squirting something all over you. And Mrs Bradley was standing there
with a face like fizz. She had one of those monobosoms ...
you never see those any more, do you? I suppose she wore
a corset. They're a dying breed ...'

Polly held her breath. This was all new to her. She
leaned forward ever so slightly, desperate not to startle
her mother into clamming up again.

'And there she was.' Doreen shook her head. 'You
know,' she said, with a wondering tone, 'you know, she
was coloured! Sorry, black. Sorry. I don't know what to say
these days.' She paused. 'I wouldn't ... I mean, I wouldn't
have been surprised nowadays. But it was different then, it
really was. I mean, we weren't in London, or Birmingham.
This was the south-west of England. It was really white ...
I'm just making excuses now.'

She breathed out again.

'She had a big belly on her. So. That was a lot to take in right then. And one in me, although I didn't know it, of course. That damn Ford Escort. Anyway. At first I didn't take her seriously, her standing there saying Tony's her husband and to leave him alone. I really didn't. She was screaming and shouting and I just got the security guard to ask her to leave.'

She stared at the floor, bright red.

'Oh God, Polly. Oh God. I've never told anyone that. I never have. Things were different ... Oh Polly.'

The tears were coursing down her cheeks now, and Polly put her arm round her.

'It was just wrong that got wrong that got wrong. He did me wrong and I did her wrong, and then, well, you came along and I reckon we all did you wrong too.'

Polly shook her head.

'You didn't. You didn't, I promise.'

'I called him – no luck. No chance. There weren't mobile phones then, and I couldn't email him or Facebook. Then I tracked down his mam and dad; they were in the book.'

She shook her head.

'They were pleased to see me. It had been quite the family scandal when he'd met ... now what was her name ...'

Polly was half crying and trying to comfort her mother and feeling awful and slightly drunk as well, otherwise she wouldn't for a moment have said what she said.

'Carmel,' she supplied, without thinking.

Kerensa, who'd been shuffling unobtrusively in the kitchen, carefully listening in on absolutely everything, materialised like a bouncy ball in the middle of the floor.

'Coffee!' she bustled. 'I think we all need some coffee! Doreen, you need a coffee machine in there. Man cannot survive on granules alone, especially when you're up the duff and only allowed one cup a day. It might as well be decent.'

Doreen was staring at Polly in horror.

'You've seen her.'

Polly swallowed, desperately wishing there was a way out of this, but not knowing what it was.

'She just . . . she rang me,' she said. 'I'm sorry. I didn't do anything. I just . . . I just wanted to know a bit more.'

'So, what, are you friends?!' Doreen's eyes were wide with shock.

'No. She just . . . she said . . . '

Polly bit her lip with how much she didn't want to say what she was about to say.

'He's very ill. And he wanted to see me.'

The colour drained from Doreen's face. She was stone-cold sober now.

'And did you?'

'No,' said Polly. 'I wanted to talk to you first.'

'So that's reasonable, isn't it?' said Kerensa. 'That's the best thing to do in families, isn't it? Talk everything out?'

Polly shot her a look.

Doreen's hand was at her mouth.

'This is exactly why,' she said, 'I tried to keep this stuff away from you. All the horrible, bad stuff. I was just trying to protect you.'

'But he paid money all those years!' protested Polly.

'Oh, I let you think that, of course. Let you think he cared. It was his parents. They'd rather have had me than her. That's all it was. Their guilt money.' She practically spat.

Polly blinked, tears brimming at her eyes.

'So you walking in, dropping these bombs about reuniting with your father . . . '

'I wasn't! I'm not!'

'I haven't seen him since he got what he wanted and disappeared,' said Doreen. 'Didn't give a toss for the consequences. Not a toss. Knew where I lived. Didn't care.'

She stood up.

'But well done for raking everything up again. Well done for reminding me of how I messed up. Ruined my life.'

Polly jumped up and stepped towards her mother.

'Um, we should go, maybe?' said Kerensa.

'You should,' said Doreen.

'Are you going to be all right?' said Polly, reaching out, but her mother turned away and wouldn't look at her.

'Nobody asked me that then,' she said. 'I don't know why you're bothering to ask now.'

Chapter Seventeen

'So,' said Kerensa, after they'd driven some way in silence. It was getting late; the air was misting up and it was turning even colder. 'That went well.'

Polly winced through her sobs.

'Oh God,' she said. 'Oh God. Tell me that wasn't as awful as I think it was.'

'Well, it could have gone worse.'

'How? How could that have gone worse, Kerensa?'

'Um, a huge monster could have burst through the front window and wreaked bloody havoc everywhere. Zombie apocalypse? Nuclear bomb?'

There was a long silence.

'Oh Lord.'

Polly checked her phone. She'd texted her apologies immediately but didn't expect to hear back, and she hadn't.

'Well, look on the bright side. She wasn't coming for Christmas anyway.'

'Kerensa! How's that meant to cheer me up?'

'What do you want me to do?'

'I don't know.'

Polly leant her head against the cool glass of the window pane, a tear running down her face.

'Oh God, she really thought I'd been running around with my dad, playing happy families with Carmel.'

They drove on in silence.

'Can I say something?' said Kerensa.

'Something more? More than you would usually just say?'

'Yeah.'

'I can't imagine what it might be.'

'No, listen, right. I don't want to diss your mum, but honestly, if you wanted to see your dad, and she'd point-blank refused to talk about him but spent a lot of time being miserable about it and putting the misery kind of on to you ... I did ask permission to say this, by the way.'

'Yeah, right, I get that,' said Polly.

'Well. Honestly, I kind of think it's your business. It's your dad. He may have been an awful one ... he may not have told his wife he even had another kid, although she obviously knew something was going on ...'

'I bet it wasn't the first time,' said Polly.

'Or the last,' said Kerensa. 'Travelling bloody salesmen! Ha! That's probably where they get their reputation.'

Polly sighed.

'You see what I mean, though?' said Kerensa, as they

pushed on through the harsh winter night. 'You do know a little more now. But also, if you want to see him — if you want anything to do with him — well, it's up to you. You don't have to ask permission. Your mum ... she needs to get over it.'

'But she's so upset.'

'I've known you a long time,' said Kerensa. 'And you know what? I don't think I've ever known your mum not upset about *something*. I think that's why you're so cheery all the time.'

Polly was barely listening. She couldn't help thinking how happy her mother must have been when she got the job at Dimmogs; her mum, who'd left school without many qualifications; who'd been the pride of her family when she'd landed such a posh job.

She'd lost it of course when she'd got pregnant; Polly knew that much. They'd said it was because of cutbacks and that people were buying fewer hats, but Doreen had known the truth: even in the eighties, being an unmarried mother carried a certain stigma. She'd slunk home, defeated before she'd even begun. And Polly had been paying the price ever since.

'You remember Loraine Armstrong?' said Kerensa, apropos of nothing.

Polly nodded. Loraine's mum had been a young single mother too, and the pair had elicited snotty remarks and sidelong glances when they went clubbing together and to pubs, her mum often insisting to strangers after a couple of drinks that they looked more like sisters than mother and daughter. Doreen had always found them horrific.

'I reckon they had a better time than you guys did.'

Polly reflected on it.

'I do too,' she said finally. 'Oh Lord. Take me home.'

As they approached Mount Polbearne, Kerensa fell silent. Polly, roused from her own deep thoughts, glanced across at her.

'What's on your mind?'

Kerensa swallowed.

'Do you think that's what Reuben would be like? If . . . you know. If he found out.'

'You still don't know for sure,' said Polly. Kerensa stroked her huge bump, a sad look on her face. She could barely reach the steering wheel. She looked at Polly.

'Seriously. You don't know how badly I was ovulating that night. It was one of those times of the month where you'd fancy a tramp.'

Polly nodded. They sat in silence.

'Because if he found out . . . I mean, I don't know what he'd do.'

'You mean – God forbid – the baby would have to grow up like me?' said Polly.

'No!' said Kerensa. 'That's not what I meant at all. And anyway,' she added, 'that would be a good thing.'

Polly sighed crossly.

'It wouldn't be a good thing,' she said eventually. 'You're going to have to tough it out. You absolutely are.'

Kerensa looked at her.

'What if it's born with a thick black moustache?'

'Like we said before, invent an Italian grandfather or something. I mean it. Sort it out. Do it.'

'You can't tell Huckle. You can't.'

Polly was still in two minds about it. It felt such a horrible dilemma. She wanted to tell him everything. But he was Reuben's best friend. His best man. The only reason Kerensa had met Reuben in the first place. Yet he was also Polly's other half, her fiancé. It was horrible. She didn't know how he'd react – she didn't know if he would even know himself. Could she risk it? Sometimes she thought that of course she could, it would be fine, but there was always a chance that it might not be. And then where would they all be?

Deep down she suspected it might be something only another woman would understand. A mistake on this level, something that would affect your whole life.

Huckle understood things. He was amazing. But could anybody understand this happening to their best friend?

'I haven't,' she said.

'You can't, Pol. You can't. If I'm to have a shot at this, you absolutely can't.'

Polly bit her lip and thought of her mother's hollow life. She agreed with Kerensa, but she felt entirely conflicted; entirely awful about it. About everything.

They rumbled across the causeway. The harbour lamp posts were festooned with strings of plain white lights. Mount Polbearne didn't have much of a budget to compete with the fancier displays in the bigger towns, but the lights suited the cobbled streets, forming long dips and chains between the old-fashioned lamp posts built to withstand the spray and wind. There were red bows on the lamp posts too, and twinkling trees and candles in every window. The town looked extraordinarily lovely, filled with a deep peace; a lovely passing into the quietest season, of night and cosy beds and bright sharp stars glimmering overhead.

Kerensa drew up at the lighthouse door. The place was in darkness; Huckle must be sleeping. Polly kissed her gently on the cheek, then jumped down, wincing at the freezing air, as the Range Rover roared away.

The lighthouse was bitterly cold. She checked in on Neil underneath the kitchen table, but didn't even stop to make a cup of tea. Huckle grunted, rather sleepily, as she moved her frozen feet towards his lovely warm body, so she rolled over, staring out of the window, where they still hadn't got round to putting curtains up. The stars looked white and pale against the freezing air; she was blowing out steam when she breathed out, the house was so cold. She couldn't warm up at all; couldn't even take warmth from Huckle. Instead she just lay there, desperately wiggling her toes, trying to see a way through.

She could only think of one: carry on as normal.

Sometimes, if you pretended everything was normal, you had a chance of making it so. Keep buggering on, as the saying went. She couldn't think of anything else. Her mum would come round. They'd make it up. After all, she thought glumly, who else did they have but each other?

Work. Work would solve everything.

Chapter Eighteen

The next morning, Huckle was surprised and pleased to see Polly up and bustling about quite merrily, apart from a slight headache.

'Hey?' he said cautiously.

Polly turned round with her normal smile on her face.

'Hey,' she said.

'You okay?'

'I'm fine,' she said. 'Cheese scone?'

'YES! God, I like living with you.'

Polly popped a warm slice, covered in salty butter, into his mouth.

'Oh, heaven. So ...'

She shook her head to indicate she didn't really want to talk about it.

'My family's bananas,' she said. 'And it's the village fair on Saturday. So ...'

'All families are bananas,' said Huckle.

'Exactly. They're all nuts. Nuts and bananas.'

'An ice cream sundae.'

'Precisely. So I've decided. There's no point in dwelling on it for years and years and years. They're screwed up but it's not my fault, so I'm just going to get on with things and stop beating myself up about it. They did all the mad stuff, not me. I don't want anything to do with it. We are going to make a tremendous Christmas for Reuben, then pay off the puffin shelter so the puffins are safe, which will be more of a contribution to this earthly existence than I ever expected to make, then we are going to take the remainder of the money and go somewhere on holiday where they serve cocktails larger than my head – there's nothing larger than *your* head . . .'

'Thanks,' said Huckle.

'And we're going to lie on the sand and make love and go swimming and get drunk and think about absolutely nothing at all. How does that sound to you?'

'That sounds awesome.'

He came closer.

'Are you sure?'

'I am totally and utterly sure. Being unselfish is going to get me absolutely nowhere with Mum or with . . . with Tony. So I might as well be completely selfish.'

'Is saving a puffin sanctuary and cooking for someone else's Christmas and running the town fair your definition of selfish?'

'Yes,' said Polly. 'Because it will make me feel good.

Whereas none of the other stuff does. So I may as well stick to what I know will work.'

'Okay,' said Huckle. 'Well, that sounds fine by me. I am going out to sell honey to lots of stupid beauticians to pay for this holiday of ours. You've inspired me.'

'Good!' said Polly. 'Take some of these mini cheese scones as bribes.'

'I shall,' said Huckle.

'Are you going to eat them all before you get to your first client?'

But whatever Huckle's answer was, it was lost in a sea of crumbs.

Chapter Nineteen

Polly put out the tray.

'Free samples!' she said cheerily, and the old ladies gathered around, cooing happily. She was trying pigs in blankets with honey – she had a good supplier for the honey, which helped – and more of the mini scones.

'Not you, Jayden,' she said firmly to her second-in-command, who looked wounded and stroked the side of his moustache.

'But I need to test what I'm selling,' he said.

'I thought you wanted to get in shape for You Know What.'

Jayden coloured instantly.

'Go on then. One.'

Jayden grimaced. 'That barely touches the sides. I think you're getting mean in your old age.'

'Do you?' said Polly. Jayden was twenty-three, so of course he thought she was ancient for being over thirty.

'You'll be turning into Mrs Manse ... '

'Any more cheek from you,' said Polly, whipping him lightly with a tea towel, 'and you'll be scrubbing under the bread ovens for the next two weeks. Anyway, how are things going with Flora?'

'I'm just gearing up to it,' said Jayden solemnly. 'It's important to get these things right.'

'It is,' said Polly.

Patrick the vet came in, looking slightly harassed as usual. He liked Polly, although he disapproved mightily of her keeping a seabird as a pet. He'd long realised, though, that as in many other parts of his life, there wasn't actually that much he could do about it, so had learned to keep quiet.

'How's Neil?'

'He's good!' said Polly quickly. 'Perfect BMI for a puffin, probably. Free sample?'

'Thank you. That wasn't why I came in, though.'

'No?' said Polly.

Outside, it was absolutely freezing. The wind was blowing a gale sideways into the houses, whistling down the little alleyways that made up the bottom of Mount Polbearne; the houses became less frequent and the road steeper as you wound your way to the top, to the ruined church that stood there, ancient but magnificent.

No, today was a day for staying indoors with the fire on, watching the white-crested waves; or huddling some-where cosy and warm, whatever the weather. Hence the excellent trade at the bakery.

Polly thought about Neil.

'He really is fine,' she said. 'I was quite cross with him, actually, taking losing the egg so well.'

Patrick smiled. 'Male chauvinist puff, huh?'

'I like to think, when he's staring out to sea, that he's feeling bad for his little egg,' said Polly.

Patrick gave her a look.

'Instead of thinking about tasty fish?'

'Instead of thinking about tasty fish.'

'You really shouldn't anthropomorphise animals,' said Patrick. 'Seriously, it doesn't do them any good. Neil won't remember that egg. Neither will Celeste. They're instinct-driven creatures.'

As he said this, he helped himself to another sausage without even realising he was doing it, but Polly didn't mention it.

'Do you think he might ... find another girlfriend one day?'

'I don't know,' said Patrick. 'Puffins mate for life. They were just unlucky. Of course if you took him to the sanctuary ...'

Polly gave him a look.

'I think we already know that's not happening.'

'Well, quite. No, I think you're stuck with a bachelor puffin.'

'Good,' said Polly.

'You know they can live for twenty years?'

'Also good,' said Polly.

167

Patrick shook his head. 'Well then.'

'Did you hear they might be shutting the sanctuary?'

'Really?' said Patrick. 'Now that is a shame.'

He looked at her closely.

'You can't adopt them all,' he said.

'No,' said Polly. 'But I can do something.'

He looked at the spread in front of him.

'What's all this in aid of, then?'

'Well, it's partly getting ready for the Christmas fair . . . and partly to welcome Reuben's parents.'

'Oh,' said Patrick. 'Oh goodness. I wonder what they're like.'

'Exactly how you'd think,' said Polly. 'And then some.'

Chapter Twenty

The day of the Christmas fair dawned crisp and crackling. The village hall was absolutely heaving. People had come from miles around. Polly had been up for days on end making delicious gift baskets of gingerbread and clotted cream fudge and half a dozen small Christmas cakes that had been soaking in brandy for weeks now. Her stall was absolutely groaning, and, from the second the doors opened, totally mobbed. Selina was on her left-hand side with her lovely filigree jewellery that had taken hours upon hours of careful work.

'It's brilliant,' said Samantha, bustling around the many little stalls. 'This is going to raise so much money!'

'I'm getting all my Christmas shopping done!' said Mrs Corning. 'This is going to wrap it right up.' Polly and Selina tried not to think about how much money they would have made if people had done their Christmas shopping directly from them.

Flora was helping on the bakery stall, having brought a huge tray of her fabulous religieuses. Polly was paying her for being there. Well. At least Flora was a student. And it was Christmas. She should get into the spirit more.

'How's Jayden?' she said cheerfully. Flora as usual simply shrugged.

'He's all right,' she said.

'Polly, show this guy your ring,' called Selina from the next table, and she leaned over obediently and showed off her beautiful seaweed engagement ring.

'Oh yes,' said the man. 'Something like that would be lovely.'

Selina beamed. 'Ooh, maybe this exposure thing works after all,' she said, and Polly gave her a cross look.

'It is pretty,' ventured Flora, and Polly let her examine it, feeling proud.

'It'll be you next,' she said, remembering the conversation she had had with Jayden.

'Ha, no way,' said Flora. 'Don't think so.'

Polly winced and pulled her hand back. Maybe she would have to have another word with Jayden.

'Have you seen Kerensa?' said Selina. 'Only she's gone really weird on me. I haven't seen her for months.'

'Hmm,' said Polly, not quite trusting herself. 'She's just been really exhausted with the pregnancy and everything, I think. I've hardly seen her either.'

Selina gave her a penetrating look.

'When's the baby due again?'

Polly looked at Selina and decided that the best thing under the circumstances was to tell her a big fat lie.

'End of February,' she said.

Mid January was more like it. She could actually see Selina counting backwards in her head.

'Oh, right,' said Selina. 'She's enormous.'

Samantha was annoyingly tapping the mike at the front of the hall.

'Hello, everyone!' she said brightly. There was a large crowd milling around. 'Now, thank you so much to everyone who's contributed to make the fair such a success . . .'

Selina and Polly swapped rueful looks.

'And now, I'd like to ask our town's resident baker . . . the woman who feeds us all those naughty treats . . .'

Polly stiffened. She didn't really like being referred to like some kind of drug dealer.

'. . . to come forward and judge the baking competition! Jayden said it would be fine.'

Samantha grinned widely at Polly, as if she had no doubt that there was nothing Polly would like better. Polly blinked. She had no recollection of Samantha asking her to do this, but it was entirely possible it had been mentioned in one of the many emails she had never looked at.

'Um?' she said.

'To judge the baking competition!' Samantha repeated encouragingly.

Polly reluctantly made her way to the front of the hall. On the long table behind the microphone was a vast array of home-baked goodies, and standing behind each plate was an apprehensive-looking villager.

Polly knew every single person there. Every single one was a customer. Or ex-customer, once this went the wrong way, she thought.

She started at one end of the table and tried each of the various pies, cakes, breads and tarts, although she could hardly taste them for nerves. There were old Mrs Corning's rock buns ... Muriel had made a date tart ... and nine-year-old Sally Stephens, the vet's granddaughter, was standing proudly behind the most beautiful lemon meringue. All eyes followed Polly beadily as she moved from plate to plate.

'These are all wonderful,' she stammered. 'I really can't choose.'

Samantha's face was stern.

'Well you have to choose,' she said. 'I've donated first prize of a weekend at a spa.'

Polly groaned internally. There were very few people in Mount Polbearne who wouldn't fancy one of those in the middle of winter.

She looked around once more at the eager faces. Then she picked up old Florrie's dull, dry biscuit.

'Um, this one,' she said.

The elderly lady looked up with watery eyes.

'What?' she said in a quavering voice.

'You've won, love!' shouted Samantha cheerily.

'What?'

Polly had thought giving the prize to the neediest entrants was the best solution, but now she was feeling a bit unsure.

'You've won the baking competition! Congratulations, Florrie!'

Florrie blinked as someone from the local press took a photograph. Polly listened uneasily to the mutterings of the locals behind her. She'd probably lost about thirty per cent of the goodwill towards her business in one fell swoop. This was going great.

'It's a SPA!' Samantha was now hollering in Florrie's ear.

'A what, love?'

Polly was thrilled when Bernard from the puffin sanctuary walked in the door, as it gave her an excuse to escape from the baking table.

'Hello!' she said, waving at him frantically and heading over. 'Selina's over here!'

Selina shot her a look. Bernard looked anxious, as always.

'How are the puffins?' said Polly.

'Noisy,' said Bernard. He glanced around. 'This is a fund-raiser, is it?'

'For the village,' said Polly.

'We should do one for the sanctuary,' he said.

'Yes,' said Polly reluctantly.

'Can I sign you up?'

'Probably,' said Polly. 'But don't worry. I'm still doing Reuben's Christmas to raise money for you guys. And I was thinking, Flora. In the summer, you might fancy going in and helping Bernie with the catering.'

'Work on a bird farm?' said Flora, shuffling her feet.

'It's a job,' said Polly.

'I can get a job anywhere,' said Flora, and despite her sullen attitude, open-ended approach to timekeeping and total lack of initiative, you only had to taste her pastry to know that it was true; she could.

The one good thing about the stall, Polly supposed, was that they sold out early and could go. It took her a moment to compose herself enough to smile when she handed the money box over to Samantha, but she just about managed it.

Samantha, who lived in a big pile in London, as well as owning a second home in Mount Polbearne, just didn't have a handle on actual money, and that wasn't really her fault. So Polly smiled as widely as she could and said goodbye to everyone as she left.

'Aren't you coming to the pub?' said Selina. 'Everyone else is going to the pub. You're coming, aren't you?' she said to Bernard, who looked confused, and then cheerful.

'I can't,' said Polly, sighing. 'I need to get practising for Reuben's specialist bloody Christmas canapés. His parents arrive soon and I'm not sure I know what I'm doing.'

'Well say hi to Kerensa for me,' said Selina, and Polly vowed to do absolutely no such thing.

Chapter Twenty-One

It was nearly Christmas Eve, and Polly was still hard at work. She had started playing Christmas carols in the shop now; she refused to do it earlier, partly because it made it sound like a coffee shop and encouraged everyone to stay for absolutely ages, and partly because she couldn't listen to 'Mary's Boy Child' more than four hundred times per holiday season.

She hadn't heard from Kerensa, except a quick check to see if she was okay, which she insisted she was. She'd thrown herself into baking, trying out new types of gingerbread and mincemeat treats, and decorating – the bakery was overwhelmed with a little toy wooden village, with lights inside that she'd built up to look as much like Mount Polbearne as possible. The local children were absolutely obsessed with it, and clustered around, having to be torn away by their parents, often with a sticky bun or pain au raisins in their mittened hands. It didn't occur to Polly until much later how much her model village inspired the children of their austere little tidal island. For years afterwards they would come to look at it, and although as they grew older they could see how small and basic it actually was, they would be furious if she moved or changed the tiniest thing. Eventually they brought their own children, and the little ones would still gaze and exclaim in awe while the bigger ones shook their heads, absolutely astonished that their parents could have grown up in such entertainment-free surroundings.

But that was in the future. Now she was in a decorating frenzy, as if trying to make the whole world welcoming and cosy.

Inside the lighthouse, she'd wrapped miles of tinsel round the balustrade, was planning a vast tree and had hurled fairy lights at almost anything that moved. She'd also stocked up on Icelandic-pattern cushions and blankets for the sofa, so they could hunker down and watch Scandinavian box-set dramas whilst wearing more or less authentic Scandinavian jumpers.

Huckle just let her get on with it, a smile playing around his lips. He knew it was displacement activity and hoped it would burn itself out. He knew she needed distraction.

'Sweetie,' he said, late one night as they clung together in bed, bathed in the glow of eighty tiny penlights Polly had forgotten to switch off on her way upstairs, 'you know, if you want to get rid of all that excess zeal ... I mean, everything looks amazing, but I was just thinking you should channel it. I mean, we could ... We could think about bringing the baby forward? Or even think about organising a wedding? I mean, my parents were asking about it ... Obviously they'll have a long way to come and ... '

He could tell by the way she stiffened that he'd said the wrong thing.

'Well I thought it was nice,' he whispered gently in her ear. 'My dad said ... I mean, absolutely no offence to your mum or anything. And no offence to us, obviously, especially you, because you work your socks off ... '

Huckle had tried working his socks off and had hated it. Ironically, since he'd started working in a very sock-free fashion, his easy charm and natural nice looks had made him just as successful as he had been in the corporate world, with none of the early-morning starts Polly had.

But even being successful in a home-made honey business is very much not one of the more financially lucrative ways to be a success. Fortunately Huckle's wants were few; he had the same few well-made pieces of clothing in his wardrobe that only grew more faded and softer and thus rather more appealing with every passing year; he fixed up the motorbike himself if and when it needed it, and all the things he liked to do – walking, staying in, listening to unbelievably terrible MOR American rock music, drinking beer at the Red Lion, going to bed with Polly – were pretty inexpensive.

'Anyway, they have tons of money . . . God knows why, they don't deserve it. Polly, look. They've offered to pay for the wedding. Here. Apparently all their friends want to come to England, they think it's quaint. We could do anything you liked. Any way you wanted.'

There was a long silence.

'You're not insulted, are you? I mean, I didn't say we'd definitely take the money or anything . . . '

Polly shook her head.

'Oh love. No. It's not the money. It really isn't – that's so nice of them. Incredibly nice of them. I'm not proud, I'm really not remotely proud.'

'But . . . '

Polly shook her head.

'I can't . . . I just . . . Not now. Family stuff. I don't . . . I'm so busy. You know. I'm not . . . I'm so not ready . . . '

She meant to say, of course, *I'm not ready for marriage*, not *I'm not ready for you*.

But Huckle only heard one thing: that she didn't want to marry him.

'Okay,' he said. It was hard to hurt Huckle's feelings; he was genuinely good-natured and rarely got upset over anything. But it was certainly possible.

'I'm sorry,' said Polly. 'But you know how it is . . . and I'm so busy . . . '

'Yeah, yeah, I know.'

Polly thought about Carmel, spending years wondering if her husband was going to misbehave again. She thought of her mother, sitting alone in her kitchen eating soup night after night for the whole of the only life she was ever going to get.

She thought – briefly, glancingly – about the impossibly huge notion that she had half-brothers and sisters out there in the world. Of course it had always been a possibility, but one she hadn't had to dwell on particularly. But now she knew for a fact that it was definitely, absolutely true, and more than that, that one of them must be round about her own age.

Well. She was in no position to think about families just now. Even building one with Huckle. Surely he could understand that? She just couldn't, and that was an end to it.

The wind whistled around the lighthouse, although inside, lit gently with fairy lights, it was cosy and warm, the remnants of the evening's fire dampened down but still gently heating the way up the house for once. The fire had been wonderful that night, and the entire building felt warm.

Yes, thought Polly, trying to stop making lists in her head, and snuggling down. He would understand. He totally would. Huckle understood everything.

But if life teaches us anything, it's that what we assume someone should know about us – even someone we really, really love; *especially* someone we really, really love – can be completely misunderstood or overlooked, or that the silence we think contains so much is simply unobserved. We believe – or we would like to believe – that the people we're closest to can tell what our intentions are, the same way your mother knows when you are small whether you've been stealing biscuits out of the biscuit jar by the fact you have chocolate smeared around your mouth.

But nobody is psychic. And for once, it was Polly who drifted off to sleep to the sound of the crashing waves, whilst Huckle lay staring into the darkness, feeling unusually thoughtful; unusually sleepless; very unusually alone.

Chapter Twenty-Two

He might have understood more if he'd been at Reuben's the next day, when Reuben's parents showed up, but he wasn't.

The mansion had been decorated from top to bottom. Polly couldn't help sighing, just a little. It was a bit silly, having money, given that there were only so many buns one could eat in a day; only so far she could pretend she could tell the difference between a cheap and an expensive bottle of wine; and how much she couldn't see the point of a highly expensive handbag (Polly's bags invariably became full of bits of tissue, odd pencils, half-used lipsticks and a light scattering of powdered yeast; she couldn't imagine the horror of doing that to something worth more than a small car).

But the difference between her little fairy lights and Reuben's professional decorating job was obviously substantial. The tree in the driveway, at the circular turn in front of the door, was three storeys high. The theme was kind of diamonds and ice sculptures, which ought to be tacky but annoyingly looked utterly perfect against the metal frame and bright glass of the lovely modern house. Frost crackled on the ground outside, and on the beautiful spotlit path that led down to Reuben's private beach. Polly took her tasting trays into the massive professional kitchen. Reuben was a good cook, but obviously he kept someone on hand to do all this kind of stuff. Kerensa was nowhere to be seen. She'd told everyone she was doing lots of pampering and baby massage stuff, but Polly knew for a fact that she didn't give a toss for anything like that, which meant she must instead simply be lying low.

Polly sighed. Did nobody get a happy ending? Did it simply not work? This should be the happiest time of her best friend's life – married to a bloke who, whilst nobody would describe him as 'lovely', was fun and adored her and whom she adored back, and who suited her very well, expecting the birth of their first baby in their gorgeous mansion by the sea. It was like that girl who'd married the Prince of Monaco and had twins and always looked entirely furious about everything. Really, if Kerensa couldn't be happy, nobody could. And yet there she was, off with a Brazilian stripper. Well, briefly, but even so.

Polly sighed and dumped her two large trays of food, turning on the oven to heat everything up. She was officially catering just the Christmas party, Christmas Day and Boxing Day, but she'd agreed to put on a little taster session when Reuben's parents arrived, cold and presumably ravenous. She glanced around.

Marta, the maid, smiled at her politely, but they didn't speak. Polly made herself some coffee in Reuben's absurdly noisy and overcomplicated machine, which appeared to have enough technology to launch a Mars mission, then padded around the enormous room. It was far bigger than what she had at the bakery to feed the entire town. As well as the industrial-sized ovens, there was a huge grill wok, and a pizza oven ... you could run a fairly nice hotel from here. Which was, she supposed, what was happening.

The sun beamed in through the windows, adding to the warmth of the underfloor heating. As an American, Reuben liked his house boiling in the winter and freezing in the summer, and with the sun streaming in it was almost too warm. Polly wished she could stretch out on the floor like a cat and take a nap.

Suddenly she heard a noise, a loud flapping. It sounded ominous and weird. Marta didn't flinch, but Polly rushed out into the hall. As well as the vast tree filling the turret, she could see another, this one with carved wooden *Nutcracker* soldiers positioned all round it – in the sitting room, where a huge fire was crackling away despite the fact that the room was completely empty.

She opened the front door on to the sparkling driveway ahead and to her amazement saw a big black helicopter descending right in front of her. Of course she'd recognised the noise, but she hadn't seen a helicopter up close since ... since they'd had that great storm a year or so ago. She put that out of her mind and smiled anxiously, realising as she did so how much it made her feel even more like staff.

The helicopter made a tremendous noise as it teetered to a stop in a big H Polly hadn't even noticed in the driveway. Seriously, how did people get so much money? She knew Reuben did something with algorithms that drove big computer companies bananas, but she had no idea what an algorithm even was, though clearly it was something that allowed you to own a helicopter.

The blades finally came to a stop, and Reuben emerged, looking jolly as ever, taking off his headphones and jumping down. He waved heartily and Polly waved back obediently, still feeling like an indentured servant. Marta went forward and started collecting large amounts of heavy luggage, as Reuben helped down first his father, then his mother.

His father was so obviously future Reuben it was almost comical to see them together. He was bald, with only a hint of Reuben's ginger hair around the tops of his ears, and bushy pale eyebrows. The top of his head was covered with freckles. If you were a worse person than Polly, you might be tempted to connect some of them up and make a second face. His body was almost perfectly spherical, and he was wearing an extremely expensive-looking cashmere coat over an exquisitely tailored tweed suit – rather flamboyantly British – with a spotted hand-kerchief in the top pocket. His beautiful clothes did absolutely nothing to disguise the fact that he essentially looked like a snowman with tiny fat arms and legs sticking out the sides, or a cheerful baby.

Rhonda, Reuben's mother, was all hair. It was jet black, a colour unusual in nature for a woman of her age, which was, of course, completely indeterminate, and she was wearing – no she wasn't. Yes she was. Fur. A full-length mink coat, completely without shame. She was short, too, and it actually looked a bit like a scene from *The Revenant*.

Well. Polly did not like fur and that was that, but also she could imagine how much Rhonda would care about whether she liked it or not: not a whit.

Rhonda had also managed to keep her false eyelashes on through an eight-hour flight and a helicopter transfer, which was pretty impressive when you thought about it. She had hugely made-up eyes that reminded Polly of Liza Minelli, and a large lipsticky smile. The lipstick was bleeding slightly.

'Hey!' She waved, and Polly stepped forward. Rhonda kissed her hard on both cheeks. 'I remember you! You're the one that snuck out of Reuben's wedding to make out with that hunky groomsman!'

Polly smiled awkwardly.

'Ah,' she said. 'Yeah.'

'Is he still on the scene? Doubt it. Ha, that's never the

way to do it. You young ladies, you're always throwing yourselves about and—'

'Actually, we're engaged,' Polly said quickly. Rhonda frowned, or would have done if her skin could actually have stretched in any direction at all.

'Well there you are, it just goes to show.' She said it as if that was exactly what she'd thought all along. 'Now where's that daughter-in-law of mine?'

If there was ever, Polly reflected, a woman who could deal with having Rhonda as a mother-in-law, it was probably Kerensa.

'She . . . she's out and about,' said Polly, awkwardly.

Rhonda sniffed loudly.

'Hear that, Merv? Out and about. Too busy to be here to greet her in-laws. And what's she even doing gallivanting about the place when she's carrying our only grandchild? Huh? Huh?'

'Ma,' said Reuben in a conciliatory tone. 'She's not gone far. And it's not your only grandchild. Hayley has two kids.'

'Well, yes, *Hayley*,' said Rhonda, in a tone of voice that said absolutely everything about who was the more important of her two children. 'I mean Finkel children. Children that will be carrying on the family name. My adorable little Ruby-Woobie's children.'

She wobbled Reuben's chubby cheeks, and to his credit, Reuben didn't try in the least to shake her off; he seemed to totally accept that his mother would want to do this to him, in public.

Marta vanished with the bags and Rhonda swept into the house, trailing an extraordinarily powerful perfume behind her.

'Oh Rubes,' she said sadly. 'I mean ... You know.' She was looking round at the stunning lobby, with its huge tree and massive modern balustrade. 'I mean, it's so ... it's just so sparse! Couldn't you have gone for something a little bit more fancy? Now in our town house,' she said to Polly, 'we commissioned panelling top to bottom. Gives it a real classy look, you know what I mean? Properly done. They had to use some wood you can't even get any more. Completely rare. I think we were the last people allowed to chop it down.'

'Ha ha, yeah, she thinks that,' said Merv. 'She thinks we were allowed to knock it down. So adorably innocent.'

He chuckled benevolently and wandered into the kitchen.

'Hey, what you got to eat in this hellhole?'

Reuben trailed after his parents with a look of pleased terror on his face.

'I mean, would it hurt you to put a bit of gold here and there, huh? Show the world you're on the way to making it.'

'Round here most people think I *have* made it, Ma.'

'Yeah, round here.'

Polly deftly removed the trays of hot pastries from the oven: the rugelach and the chocolate matzos just as they'd asked for, and her speciality – which she'd had to make about nine times before Reuben finally declared himself satisfied – knishes from the old country, i.e. Europe about three generations before.

Merv tried to grab a handful when they hadn't yet cooled down. He stared at his fingers like a puzzled bear.

'Da-ad,' said Reuben, and Rhonda tutted and looked around.

'Where's the ice water?'

As it was December, Polly hadn't really considered iced water a necessity, but she rushed to Reuben's absurd industrial fridge and poured a glassful from the dispenser at the front.

'These are great,' said Merv, stuffing the pastries into his mouth as fast as he could. 'Of course, obviously I'm going to sue you for the burnt fingers . . . I'm kidding, I'm kidding. What are they anyway?'

Polly turned to Reuben. These were the special knishes she'd laboured over, refining a strange recipe she didn't know, sourcing ingredients that were incredibly hard to come by in rural Cornwall, and he didn't even know what he was eating?

Reuben didn't look remotely shame-faced.

'Hey, it's how *I* like them,' he said. 'And I'm paying.'

Polly sniffed.

Rhonda cast an eye over the pastries.

'Not for me, thank you. You know I have to keep myself trim.'

She waddled cheerfully over to the window and started

189

tut-tutting about the state of Reuben's butler sink –
'Seriously, it's so old-fashioned! You couldn't have got
anything with nice taps? This looks like something the
servants would use.'

Reuben smiled affectionately, then sidled up to Polly.

'Where's Kerensa?' he said through gritted teeth. 'I
can't stand this. I can't do it without her and she's not
answering her phone. What's up with her?'

Polly shrugged. 'I don't know . . . pregnancy stuff?' she
said hopefully, hoping the idea of it would be as weird to
Reuben as these things often were. Thankfully it worked.

'Guh,' said Reuben, shivering. 'Yuk. I heard the term
"mucus plug" once and that was quite enough for me,
thanks.'

'Are you not going to be there?'

'Not a chance! As someone said, it's like watching your
favourite pub burning down.'

'Oh Reuben, you have to be there.'

'I've booked the best obs/gynae in the country to be
on standby, plus a doula and a maternity nurse, and we're
going to get one of those Norland nannies that wear the
uniform and refuse to have sex with me . . . I'm kidding,
I'm kidding. About the sex, not the nanny.'

'Is this what Kerensa wants?'

'It's the best,' said Reuben mutinously. 'Everybody
knows it.'

'Okay,' said Polly.

Christmas was going to be fun, she thought. Just

concentrate on the money. Think about the money. Get the work done. It would be fine.

'It's a shame you didn't pay more attention to the decorations,' Rhonda was saying, looking around. 'Disappointing you didn't feel you could make the effort.'

'Okay, Ma,' said Reuben, for the first time looking shame-faced, like the naughty boy he must once have been. 'Do you guys want a nap or something?'

'Are we in that same room?' said Rhonda. 'Only, you know, it's so noisy.'

'It's the waves, Mom.'

'I'm just saying, they're incredibly noisy. Is there nothing you can do?'

'Yeah, Mom. I can go and stop the tide.'

Polly was feeling increasingly awkward. Rhonda didn't want to eat, and Merv and Reuben had finished everything else, so they were all just standing around looking uncomfortable in that cavernous kitchen.

Where the hell was Kerensa? If she was here, she could say something funny, break the ice. Instead she was doing something Polly considered quite dangerous: she was making Reuben look bad. Reuben was used to getting what he wanted; being the centre of attention. Standing him up in front of his parents was rude at best, potentially devastating at worst.

Polly glanced at Merv, who was dusting crumbs off his incredibly expensive coat. Looking up, he caught her eye.

'Yeah, come on, Rhonda,' he said. 'Let's take a snooze, let the kids get themselves sorted out, yeah?'

Rhonda sniffed.

'I won't sleep a goddam wink.'

'You always say that when you're tired. Then off you go, snoring like a freight train.'

'This is exactly why we're getting separate rooms. No, wings,' said Rhonda, folding her arms.

There was the noise of the motorbike pulling up outside. Huckle had popped by to say hello. Polly had rarely been more pleased to see him.

'Huck!' she yelled cheerfully as he slouched in.

'Um, hey?' he said, taking in the room gradually. 'Hi, Mrs Finkel. Mr Finkel.'

'Merv, please. You're Huckle, right?'

Huckle nodded.

'You know, I never get to meet any of Reuben's friends.'

'That's because he doesn't have any,' said Huckle smiling to show he was joking.

'I do! I have millions of friends! I have the best friends in the world and most of them are famous!' said Reuben.

'All right, Superman, I was only joking,' said Huckle. 'Hey, good to see you. How's Polly's amazing food?'

'Pretty good!' said Merv, patting his belly. 'Good hire, Reuben.'

'Actually I'm . . .'

But Polly decided not to pursue it.

'Thanks,' she said. Huckle beamed and put his arm round her shoulders. Rhonda sniffed again.

'So where's—' Huck started. Polly kicked him sharply on the shin.

'Ow! What?'

'Nothing,' said Polly. Huckle looked confused. Rhonda looked furious.

'She meant, don't ask about Reuben's wife, who didn't bother to turn up to greet us,' she said.

'Oh,' said Huckle, staring at Polly.

'Hello!' came a voice that echoed in the vast hallway, and Kerensa walked in – or rather, lumbered, because her bump was now absolutely enormous. Her roots were growing out and her face was bloated, the skin rough and spotty. Kerensa never looked anything other than perfect normally. Even Polly was shocked.

'Hey, Rhonda ... Merv.'

Merv patted her rather absent-mindedly, but Rhonda couldn't contain her shock.

'Oh. My. GAWD!!!!' she screamed theatrically. 'Reuben, she's a whale! Look at you! I have never known a Finkel woman blow up like that! Whatever's in there, it's bigger than Reuben!'

Kerensa attempted a wan smile, but she looked like she was about to burst into tears. Reuben scowled.

'She looks great, Ma.'

Rhonda would have raised an eyebrow if they weren't already painted on halfway up her forehead.

Kerensa just stared at them all blearily, as if she hardly knew they were there. Her entire face was sagging, and there was fear in her eyes. She could just about handle being with Polly, but all the Finkels in a row was simply too much for her.

'I'm going for a nap,' she said, dully, putting her expensive handbag down on the kitchen table. The gold clasps clattered horribly on the brushed concrete in the echoing room.

Chapter Twenty-Three

'Okay,' said Huckle, the second they got home. He looked riled. This was almost unheard of. He was the most unflappable of men, always. But now he stalked into the kitchen and put his hands heavily on the old scrubbed wooden table. Neil was nowhere to be seen. 'What the hell was that?'

'What do you mean?' said Polly nervously.

'You and Kerensa. Swapping glances. Looking all nervous. It's patently obvious something's up. What the hell is it?'

'Um,' said Polly. 'I think she was just anxious about Rhonda and Merv ... And you know, the baby coming. It's due in a month.'

Huckle shook his head. 'She can handle Rhonda and Merv. I've seen her do it before. That woman doesn't scare easily. No. It's something else.' He looked at her. 'And look at you! You're bright pink.'

Polly cursed her fair skin, which always showed when she was blushing, and the fact that Huckle knew her so well. He was staring at her now, those bright blue eyes not lazy and kind but hard-edged.

'What the hell is going on?'

'Nothing!'

'She's hardly been around, and you've been all tight-lipped about everything. What *is* it, Polly?'

He made them both a cup of tea. Polly didn't say anything. Her brain was working frantically. She couldn't . . . but on the other hand, this was *Huckle*. Her other half. Her love. She had to . . . she couldn't keep secrets from him. No lies. No dishonesty. That wasn't what they were about, was never what they had been about. When she was with Chris, he had lied about how the firm was doing fine, how everything was great, how she shouldn't worry. And the next thing that happened, they went bust and lost everything.

She couldn't bear to look at Huckle's wonderful, open, puzzled face. He was so straight. He told her the truth – always. He'd told the truth about how cut up he'd been about his ex-fiancée, that he needed a good year to get over her – and Polly had let him go, had let him do everything he needed to do, until he was ready. They'd always been upfront with each other.

But this. This cut right through the heart of their friendships, of the world they had built together, of the happiness they shared.

Or maybe he'd understand. He was reasonable, right? Maybe he'd see it was just a silly mistake, just a misunderstanding. Or maybe she could wait …

He was staring at her, and she realised she'd been quiet for far too long. The game was up.

'Polly?' he said, and the light tone in his deep voice was gone, and there was no mistaking the deadly seriousness of what he was saying. 'You have to tell me.'

Polly closed her eyes. Thought about it. Wished herself anywhere else than where she was. Thought about what she owed her best friend. And thought about truth, which she certainly owed her fiancé. Thought about her own life.

And then she told him the truth about Kerensa.

Chapter Twenty-Four

She had never seen him like this before. Of course they'd had rows; they were human. The previous year, when he'd been working away in the States, had been incredibly difficult for both of them.

But before when they'd argued it had been about a thing – the right way to plumb a bathroom, or what was the point of going all the way to the cinema (thirty miles) if Polly was going to sleep through the entire movie every single time?

They had been differences of opinion. This wasn't like that. Not at all. Huckle's normally placidly handsome face looked bizarrely almost amusing as it ran the gamut of emotions – shock, astonishment, fury and then, finally, deep hurt. He didn't say anything for a while. Then he started to say something and didn't quite manage to get it out. He stuttered, and stopped. He turned away. Then he turned back again, and Polly felt her heart sink right to the floor.

'How ... how long?' he managed to husk out eventually. 'How long have you known?'

Polly swallowed hard.

'Since ... well, a few weeks,' she said quietly.

'A few weeks?' Huckle blinked. He looked like he was going to cry. 'You knew about this and you didn't think to mention it to me? Ever? Not once?'

Polly shook her head.

'It wasn't ... it wasn't really my business to tell.'

'But Polly,' said Huckle. 'Polly, I'm ... I'm meant to be ... I'm meant to be your other half. Your ... your soulmate if you like.'

Polly couldn't bear him looking at her the way he was looking at her now: as if something he loved about her, or something he had thought about her, was somehow suddenly gone; as if she was not the person he thought she was. As if something precious and perfect they had had together had vanished. Tears sprang to her eyes.

'I mean ... we're meant to tell each other stuff.'

'But Kerensa swore me to secrecy!'

'Yes, to the rest of the world, not to me!'

'I couldn't,' said Polly. 'What if you'd told Reuben?'

'Well I think he has a right to know, don't you? That he's going to be raising a baby that's got nothing to do with him. You don't think that's his business either?'

'But we don't know. Nobody knows. And we won't know until the baby's born.'

Huckle shook his head.

'Reuben's my best friend, Polly! My best friend!'

'And Kerensa's mine,' said Polly gently.

'No. This is ... No. It's immoral. It's unethical. I can't take part in this, Polly. I can't ... I can't have anything to do with it.'

'Huckle, you know what Reuben's like! You know how awful he can be, how tricky! He drove her to distraction, he was never at home, kept treating her like a servant ...'

'Does that make it okay?'

'No,' said Polly. 'No, it doesn't. I think she went out to let off some steam and things got slightly out of hand. These things happen.'

Huckle nodded slowly.

'Do they? I mean ... is that the kind of thing you might do?'

'No!' said Polly, scandalised. 'Never in a million years!'

'But you think it's okay?'

'NO!' shouted Polly. 'How can you think that?'

'Because a friend of yours did it and you covered it up.'

'She made a mistake! She doesn't think it's remotely okay. Nobody thinks it's okay, Huckle. It was a terrible, horrible mistake.'

'Putting on odd socks is a mistake,' said Huckle bitterly. 'Voting for the wrong candidate. But this: they've only been married a year!'

Polly nodded. 'Don't ... don't think she hasn't been beating herself up about it ever since. She loves Reuben.

She really does. It was a slip. A silly slip that she'll never, ever forgive herself for.'

'How can she live with herself?' said Huckle. 'How?'

He looked at Polly as if she knew. Or as if he was asking how Polly could live with herself, keeping something so awful a secret.

'Are there . . . are there a lot of things you don't tell me?' said Huckle, painfully.

'No!' said Polly. 'No! The only reason I didn't tell you about this is because it isn't about me. It wasn't mine to tell. I wanted to, but she begged me, Huckle. She begged. For precisely this reason. Because it's nobody else's business.'

She suddenly found she was terrified. Everything was falling apart.

'Are you going to tell him?' she asked in a small voice.

Huckle pounded his fist on the kitchen table in frustration.

'Goddammit,' he said. 'GODDAMMIT, Polly.'

'I know,' said Polly. 'I know.'

'What if he finds out later? What if the kid is clearly not his? And then he comes asking us?'

'I don't know.'

Huckle shook his head.

'I trusted you,' he said. 'I thought we had something beautiful and real and kind of . . . kind of wonderful going on down here. In this beautiful place. With us. And them, and everything we had . . . everything lovely: friends, and family, and, well, everything I'd never been able to find in my life before ...'

He bit his lip.

'And now that's broken. It's ruined. It's shattered.'

'No!' said Polly, running to the door. 'No it isn't. You're being completely unreasonable. This has nothing to do with us.'

'But all four of us were an "us". All four of us were together. Were friends. Who trusted each other. Who did things together. And now ... three of us, what, have to watch this weird baby grow up? And not tell the other one? It's a conspiracy!'

Polly sighed.

'You can never put things back together how they were,' said Huckle glumly. 'You can't pretend this never happened. You can never unknow it.'

'Where are you going?' said Polly, her heart beating rapidly in terror. 'Where are you going? Are you going to Reuben's? Are you going to tell him?'

'No. Maybe. I don't know,' said Huckle. 'Just leave me alone.'

She heard the motorbike start up and roar off. She glanced at the tidal chart, which she knew mostly off by heart but it was still useful. The causeway would be flooded this time of the evening. He had nowhere to go; he certainly couldn't get to Reuben's. He'd probably go to the Red Lion and have a pint, cool off. Well, he'd have to; it was a freezing evening and there was literally nowhere else to go. Unless he had a change of heart and walked back through the door . . .

She spent a long time staring at the door, waiting for him. Her tea went cold. Dinner was unmade. She picked up her phone, but as usual the signal was non-existent, so there was nothing to do except stare at it as if it really might get a message. She didn't want to text in case she said the wrong thing. She felt absolutely awful.

She went upstairs, but the rest of the house was freezing and it made her sad to see all the Christmas decorations, so she just turned round and came back down to the kitchen again, huddling beside the log burner.

Neil hopped over and perched on her shoulder, and she rubbed the back of his neck mournfully as she ran the argument through in her head again. Even in the depths of her despair she could see the patterns of her life that had always made her smooth things over for her mother, try and make everything all right. She'd tried to do the same for Kerensa and it hadn't worked at all. You couldn't brush things under the carpet like that. Of course if she thought about it, it hadn't really worked for her mother either.

That habit she had of not facing up to things, of hoping for the best . . . Life wasn't butter icing. You couldn't just spread it over the cracks of the cake and make it look pretty and hope nobody would be any the wiser. It didn't work like that. Instead, the cracks got worse underneath, and then one day the wound was too deep to heal.

Polly burst into tears, horrible racking sobs, not pretty;

the kind of snotty crying that hurts your throat and makes your nose bright red and that you just can't seem to stop. It didn't feel cathartic at all; it just went on and on and on. And every time she caught sight of the lighthouse lamp reflected in a window, she thought perhaps it was the headlamp on Huckle's motorbike, and that he was coming home, but it wasn't, and he didn't. And all the time she was wrestling with the worst question of all: should she tell Kerensa she had betrayed her confidence? Should she put the fear of God into her that Huckle was going to ruin her entire life, had the power to do so at any moment and that it was entirely possible he would? Which wouldn't just ruin her life; it would ruin Reuben's too, and quite possibly the life of the tiny child whose life hadn't even started yet, and Polly felt she knew a bit about that.

Chapter Twenty-Five

Polly dozed off, still crying, about two a.m., then woke again with a start. The fire was nearly out and the kitchen was terribly cold. She looked around, horrified. She was still completely alone. Where was he? What had happened? Was something wrong?

She glanced down at her phone, which, as usual with the odd fluctuations of the signal, had popped on at some point, gathered her messages and now was gone again. She sighed and scrolled through. There it was, just a simple text from him.

Staying at friend's.

Oh well, at least nothing had happened to him. For one horrible instant earlier, she had thought he might have decided to drive through the water-covered causeway regardless of the consequences – she wouldn't put it past him. But he hadn't gone to Reuben's, because there were no missed calls or texts from Reuben or Kerensa. Unless they'd all been caught in a massive bloody shootout, of course.

She shook her head, then wrapped herself in a blanket off the back of the sofa and headed up the stairs to bed. The bedroom was icy. Her feet simply couldn't get warm, no matter what she did, and she lay on her back staring at the ceiling, her eyes too dry for tears. What was going to happen now? It was nearly Christmas, and it looked like it was going to be an absolute disaster. Would Huckle even come? And if he did, would he be able to stop himself saying something? What if everyone had a few glasses of champagne and things got a bit heated? That happened at Christmas. That happened all the time.

She couldn't sleep now. She had to get up and prep for the bakery, then she'd promised to go over and do an afternoon tea for Reuben's business partners and his parents.

This was the problem with work, which also made it a solution, she supposed: that it was relentless, that it was always there, however you were feeling, whether or not you were ready for it. So even though she was exhausted, and desperately worried about Huckle, she had no choice but to get up and carry on.

She was kneading bread and mainlining coffee at the kitchen table, having turned on the radio loud to try and cheer herself up, desperately trying to shake herself out of this awful torpor. She'd worked so hard to create this life for herself, to make a success of it. But now it felt like it was creaking, beginning to crash around her ears. Neil came in because he liked the music on the radio, but even seeing his little face didn't cheer her up the way it normally would. It all felt so empty and futile, but what else could she do other than carry on?

Outside, Huckle was drawing up on the motorbike, slightly hung-over after a night on Andy's sofa, having talked things through and realised that of course it wasn't his business, not really. He had no right to tell anyone anything. It was awful, of course it was, a terrible thing he would have to bear, watching his best friend raise another man's child. But it was what it was. He couldn't get upset with Polly about it; she hadn't done anything. And she must be utterly distraught after their fight. He shouldn't have stormed out like that. He would apologise and they would carry on, and he'd just avoid Kerensa.

Looking through the low, wide kitchen window, he could hear the music playing and could see Polly busying herself at the table, dancing away to the radio, getting on with doing what she always did; cheerfully carrying on with life as if nothing had happened. It stung him. He'd been in agony about this, and she'd been ... well.

Huckle had fallen for Polly with an absolute certitude that this was a girl who knew her own mind, her own heart; that was what he loved about her. That she was ballsy; that she grabbed hold of life with both hands, went for what she wanted. It was wonderful.

But with that went something else. Huckle had twice given up a high-powered career, knowing it wasn't for him, that it didn't make him happy. He much preferred pottering about with his bees, looking after them, making something lovely by hand. He didn't care about status, things like that. It didn't mean anything to him, much to his parents' occasional despair when they reflected on his expensive education.

He wasn't a go-getter, he wasn't a workaholic; none of those things. And as he looked at Polly, the thought that was uppermost in his mind was: she doesn't need me. She has Neil, and the bakery – look at her. I'm in agony, in despair about this, and she's just carrying on as if nothing is happening. She'll always be okay.

He blinked, his heart full of sadness, and missed Polly looking up and seeing him, and how her heart leapt and she wanted to run to him and throw her arms around him and beg forgiveness; promise that she would never, ever do anything like that, not ever again, that they would share everything, but please, please, *please* don't tell Reuben.

Then she saw his face – so grave – and her own face fell too, as he walked in through the kitchen door.

'Hey,' he said carefully.

'Hey,' she said.

'You're back at it?'

'Yeah, it's Reuben's big party this evening, plus I've got some afternoon buns . . .'

Her voice trailed away.

'Where were you?'

There was a tremor in it. It was fear. Huckle heard it as an accusation.

'Out. I don't have to tell you everything, do I?'

He regretted the words as soon as they came out of his mouth. Polly just looked so sad.

'No,' she said, and her eyes strayed back to her work surface and the flour dusted there. Neil stayed resolutely at Polly's side; he didn't even come to greet Huckle as he normally would.

'No,' said Polly again. 'I don't suppose you do.'

She sighed.

'Well, I'd better get on.'

Huckle had come back in the hope that ... What? he thought. What was he hoping for? For Polly to fall at his feet, promising anything to make him stay? But that wasn't the girl he knew. That wasn't the girl he loved. Nothing like.

Yet to see her like this, so unfazed by everything that had happened, when he was faced with the utter horror of his friend possibly having to spend the rest of his life raising a child who wasn't his; who wouldn't look like him or have anything in common with him ... It was just awful, and here she was, banging dough about like nothing had changed when everything had. Was this a female thing? Some secret conspiracy of girls against men? Huckle had always liked women, genuinely enjoyed their company.

But this felt like a place he just couldn't go; he couldn't understand it, not at all.

He cleared his throat.

'I was thinking,' he said. 'There's this beauty convention, they've been asking me to pop in, do some display samples ... maybe travel around a bit, visit a few buyers here and there.'

'Travelling salesman,' mumbled Polly quietly. This meant nothing to Huckle.

'So ... I'm going to take off for a few days.'

'But it's practically Christmas!'

'You're working, aren't you? You'll be busy,' he said, raising his voice.

Polly blinked several times.

'Oh,' she said. She didn't know what else to say. She didn't know what else there was to say.

'I'll get some things,' said Huckle, staring at the floor.

Polly's heart was beating incredibly fast in her chest.

'You aren't coming to Kerensa and Reuben's?' she said.

Huckle shook his head. 'Do you think that would be a good idea right now?'

'No,' said Polly.

'Well then,' said Huck. And he climbed the circular staircase to pack, and Polly watched him go.

Chapter Twenty-Six

Polly set off to Reuben's house in Nan the Van, doing her best to put everything out of her mind. Huckle would calm down, wouldn't he? Wouldn't he? It was a difference of opinion. Or rather, it wasn't a difference of opinion. They both knew Kerensa had made a terrible mistake. Where they differed was on what to do about it.

Polly wished he'd stated – utterly and categorically – that he wasn't going to tell Reuben. She should have got him to promise; to write it down and sign it or something.

Oh God. He was coming back, wasn't he? Of course he was. Of course. They'd fallen out, that was all. And he'd cool off and they'd sort it out and . . . well. Well. Things would happen. It would be okay.

But she didn't have time to dwell on it, as she picked Jayden up at the Little Beach Street Bakery. He was uncharacteristically quiet.

'What's up with you?' she said.

'So anyway,' said Jayden, looking awkward and staring at his knees. Polly shot him a sidelong glance.

'What?' she said, realising she'd been so caught up in her own problems, she'd hardly spoken to Jayden at all. He went even pinker.

'So I was thinking about what you said.'

Polly cast her mind back.

'About asking Flora to marry you?'

'Yeah. And you said I probably shouldn't do it because she's a student and everything and I'm only twenty-three.'

'Yes,' said Polly, remembering her brief conversation with Flora at the Christmas fair as she expertly manoeuvred Nan the Van across the causeway.

'Yeah, well, I thought about it and I've decided I'm going to totally ignore your advice.'

Polly looked at him.

'Oh good!' she said sarcastically. 'Well, everybody else does.'

'So. I'm going to ask her.'

Polly bit her lip. Flora was so nonchalant, it was hard to tell how this was going to go. And she was only twenty-one. Twenty-one! At that age Polly could barely find her keys, never mind get married.

Mind you, things didn't seem to have changed that much twelve years later.

'Well,' said Polly, resigning herself to picking up the pieces later, 'that's great news. No, it is. I'm really pleased.'

Jayden smiled.

'Well she hasn't said yes yet.'

'I'm sure she will,' said Polly, not in the least bit sure. 'And it will be lovely. How are you planning to ask her?'

'What do you mean?'

'Well, are you going to do a romantic gesture? Wrap it up or hide it or something?'

'Wrap what up?'

'The ring, Jayden!' She looked at him. Honestly, she really wasn't sure he was ready for marriage.

'Oh yeah,' said Jayden. 'My mum says she's got one somewhere I can have.'

Jayden's mother only had one son, amongst many girls in the family, and had possibly, in Polly's view, occasionally been a little overindulgent. She hoped Flora knew that Jayden's mum still squeezed toothpaste on to his brush for him in the morning and left it loaded in the bathroom.

'Are you sure Flora will like that? She wouldn't want a ring of her own?'

'A ring's a ring, right?' said Jayden, looking confused.

Polly took a very deep breath.

'I mean, you've only got some seaweedy stuff,' he added, looking even more confused.

'Yes,' said Polly. 'But it's very special to ... ' She was suddenly aware that she was about to cry, and swallowed it down hard.

'What's up, boss?' said Jayden.

Polly breathed out.

'Nothing,' she said, hitting the A road over to Reuben's house. It was the most glorious morning; good walking weather, and there were plenty of hikers out along the beautiful trails. Polly was suddenly very conscious of her horrible lack of sleep. 'Whatever you think will be best . . . '

'Do you think I should do something special?' said Jayden. 'I was just going to ask her. But there's still time to go to the jeweller's.'

'Is there really a rush?'

Jayden thought about it.

'Well it is Christmas,' he said.

He looked up as they turned in to the incredibly impressive drive towards Reuben's house.

'Wow,' he said. 'Wow. Is this all his?'

'It is.'

'It's amazing,' he said. 'I've never seen a house like it. It's incredible. Wow. This would . . . ' He trailed off. 'It's weird that some people are rich like this and some aren't,' he added. 'You'd think they'd spread it around more.'

'Then they wouldn't be rich, I suppose,' said Polly. 'But yes, I don't understand it either.'

'He must be so happy,' said Jayden, as they crunched over the gravel towards the house. 'He must be, like, the happiest guy in the world.'

Chapter Twenty-Seven

The happiest man in the world was marching up and down by the front door, shouting at someone on his mobile phone.

Polly didn't even bother pausing at the main entrance. She was happier round the back anyway. Marta was there and could help her out.

There were a lot of people turning up for Reuben's party: colleagues of Reuben's, as well as many of his friends and acquaintances (like many incredibly rich people, Reuben had the knack of attracting large crowds of people he didn't know particularly well). As she parked the van, Polly heard a massive roar start up next to her and popped her head out of the door. A huge machine was there, making fake snow.

'Seriously,' she said, 'that has to be the least environmentally friendly thing I have ever seen.'

'No,' said Reuben, wandering round the side of the

house, still shouting on his phone but pausing to put his hand on Polly's shoulder. He had, she never forgot, so few real friends. And what kind of a real friend was she being to him right now anyway? 'No, that'll be the full outdoor fires I've got coming later to heat you up from all the fake snow.'

'REUBS!'

'What? It's going to be an awesome party!'

He pointed over to where the tennis court usually was. In its place was a bar made of ice.

'Is that what I think it is?' said Polly. 'Oh my goodness, really?'

'Really,' said Reuben. 'Don't try the vodka luge until everyone's finished being served, okay?'

'Duh,' said Polly. 'But still. I mean. Incredible.'

'Thank you,' said Reuben. 'Have you seen Kerensa?'

Have you seen Kerensa? was becoming quite the refrain.

'I'm not sure she isn't too big to be in a party mood,' said Polly.

'Well tough,' said Reuben, jutting out his bottom lip and looking about six years old. 'She used to be fun and also not a whale.'

'Reuben, she's about a million months pregnant. Nobody's expected to be fun at this stage.'

'I thought she'd be one of those really cute bouncy pregnant women,' said Reuben mournfully, as someone carted what appeared to be blocks for an igloo across the garden. 'Not one of the gigantic elephant ones.'

'I don't think anyone chooses how they get to be when they're pregnant,' said Polly. 'I think it just happens and then you hope for the best.'

'I've been hoping for the best for months,' said Reuben.

Another person walked past with an ice sculpture of a bear. Polly glanced at it, then looked back to Reuben, slightly horrified.

'How big is this party?'

'Who knows? Who cares? I've got a planner. Listen. I wanted to talk to Huckle, but he's gone AWOL too. It's not like Huckle to actually do some work.'

'Excuse me,' said Polly crossly. 'He works a lot actually.'

'Yeah yeah, here are some bees, look at the bees, buzz buzz buzz. That's not work, is it.'

'He's actually doing a lot of sales . . .'

'Yeah, okay, whatever. But you know my wife, Polly. Tell me, is this normal? Huh? Is it normal for a pregnant woman to go batshit bananas and all weird and bizarre all the time?'

'Some women eat coal,' pointed out Polly.

'Yeah, but my wife isn't some women,' said Reuben, still pouting. 'I mean, my wife is totally the greatest, right? So. What's going on here? What's up? I think I have the best wife, but she's schlubbing around like Schlubby McSchlubberson. On holiday.'

'Listen, Kanye West,' said Polly, angry suddenly, even though she knew Reuben had a point. Actually, this made her angrier. 'It's her body. It's her pregnancy. It's not all about you.'

'Yeah it is!' said Reuben. 'This is my son! It is totally so about me!'

'It's about both of you.'

'Well, yeah, I realise that. But at the moment I'm not even in this picture. And man, normally I'm all over like everything.'

A bunch of surfy-looking guys, all ripped and handsome, wandered over and high-fived Reuben. As usual Reuben looked like he didn't have the faintest idea who any of them were, and tiredly returned the high-fives whilst totally ignoring the surfers' effusive greetings.

'It should be about me a little bit, right? Not just somebody mumbling past me and being tired all the time and ignoring me and disappearing on secret missi—'

Reuben closed his mouth as if he'd said something he shouldn't.

'What secret missions?' said Polly.

'Well I don't know, do I?' said Reuben crossly. 'If I did, they wouldn't be secret. It's ridiculous, she's never here.'

He sighed, and looked as deflated as Polly had ever seen him, all the bounce draining out of him even as the enormous DJ rig started sound-checking right behind him, the coloured lights bouncing off the fake snow.

'All right?' said Father Christmas – the most Father Christmassy Father Christmas Polly had ever seen, with a full white beard, a proper fat belly, kind creased eyes, the works. He was leading a real – no, surely not. But yes, it certainly smelled real – reindeer.

'Yeah, whatever, Santa,' said Reuben, and the round man wandered off.

'Look,' said Polly. 'Honestly. When the baby comes, everything will be different. I'm sure it will. It's just hard, pregnancy.'

'Good different?' said Reuben. 'What if it gets worse?'

'I don't know,' said Polly. 'But I'm sure it'll be fine.'

She wasn't in the least bit sure. But Reuben seemed a little cheered.

'Okay,' he said.

'Just the blues of being, like, fifteen stone,' said Polly.

'Yeah,' said Reuben. 'I can relate. Totally. I'm sure that's what it is too. Yeah. Thanks, Polly. You're a real pal.'

Polly felt awful.

Reuben turned round, his freckled face brightening up.

'Okay, everyone! Who's ready to PARRRRTAAA-AAYYYYYY?!'

'Yeah!' came back a plethora of voices from the people setting up. Everything was in position now, and guests were starting to arrive; they were nearly ready to begin.

'Not you, Polly,' reminded Reuben. 'You're working.'

'I KNOW, you putz,' groaned Polly, and she headed back into the kitchen with some relief, as the speakers cranked up, and 'It's CHRRRIIIIISSSSTTTTMAAAS' came rolling over the incredibly expensive stereo, and the doors were opened and the guests started to pour in and the party began.

Chapter Twenty-Eight

Polly rushed around with the other caterers, who were making great vats of mulled wine, even though the vodka luge was clearly much more popular, and huge winter stews that scented the air with cranberries and what Polly suspected was reindeer, though that hardly mattered, since none of the skinny-looking model girls – how did Reuben even know these people? – would eat a morsel. They were all too busy downing drinks and smoking on the pristine fake snow that now carpeted the stunning lawns at the back of the house, which was completely festooned with fairy lights of all colours.

It was beautiful, incredibly beautiful, and she felt a great sadness suddenly. Reuben threw wonderful parties. She shouldn't be here, slaving away over pastry, while Huckle and Kerensa were God knows where (Reuben himself was in the middle of a great crowd of people taking selfies, then studying them thoughtfully, deleting the pics they didn't like. This appeared to be what constituted socialising now). If it had been the four of them together, she thought wistfully, they'd have been having so much fun.

There was a cotton candy stand, with snow-white candyfloss being twirled. The models seemed to quite like that; it weighed even less than they did. And there was a big queue to sit on Santa's lap in his grotto, which was manned by rather foxy-looking elves. The DJ had stopped so that an incredibly cool retro swing band could play; they were doing ironic Christmas hits, with three girls in big circle skirts and bright red lipstick singing backing vocals, and people had started dancing. Huckle was a terrible dancer. It was strange; in bed, or on a surfboard, or in a beehive, he was completely graceful and natural and totally at ease, but ask him to move to a beat and he couldn't do it at all. By contrast, Reuben had taken classes and she always found it a true pleasure to dance with him, as he pushed and pulled her around on the dance floor whilst Kerensa watched and laughed at her technique. But that wouldn't be happening either.

Polly sighed, handing round more exquisite canapés filled with hot spiced-wine-flavoured pâté. She had somehow managed, she noticed, to overcome the food aversion of Reuben's guests; they were scarfing them down. Well at least one thing was going right. She refilled her tray in the kitchen as staff bustled about trying to keep up with the demand for champagne and mince-pie martinis. The hubbub of the room, the high-pitched squeals and laughter, was growing louder; the party was in absolutely full swing and going with a bang.

Suddenly the mike cut out and the band clattered to a halt. Polly thought Reuben was getting up to make a speech, which was just like him, but she didn't hear people applauding. She glanced around. Where the hell was Kerensa? This entire party was going on without her. Reuben must be fuming.

She moved forward to get a closer look and saw, to her horror, that it was Jayden who had climbed on to the stage. He looked fatter than ever in a shirt that was clearly too small for him, and his face was red and sweaty with nerves. He'd even shaved off his cute moustache, which made him look slightly featureless and awkward. The crowd of incredibly trendy London fashion and art types looked at him coolly. The room had gone very quiet, and Polly was suddenly intensely nervous for him.

He took the mike from the rather displeased-looking singer, and it immediately howled with feedback.

'Um, hello?' he boomed into it, far too loudly, holding it close to his mouth. The audience recoiled a little, and it was clear that his hand was trembling.

With a shock, Polly realised what he was about to do. Oh no. This was not the time or the place for a big proposal. This wasn't the crowd. She could see that Jayden would think that this incredibly posh do, awash with champagne, was quite the spectacular opportunity, but she couldn't imagine how quiet, shy Flora would react. She hadn't even known Flora was coming. If she had, she'd have got her to help.

'Um, Flora? I just want to ... Flora, are you there?' Jayden obviously couldn't see a thing, and was blinking carefully.

'Who are you?' said one wag cheekily, and the crowd laughed.

Polly glanced about. She spotted Flora, pale and rigid, cringing against the wall of the huge room. She wanted to go to her, but there was a thicket of people between them, all of them staring at Jayden, who looked incredibly uncomfortable and awkward now, up there in front of everyone, like a dream gone horribly wrong.

'Flora! Could you come up here, please?'

Flora was frantically shaking her head, but when it became apparent who she was, the crowd, hungry for what was going on, parted to make way for her. She slunk through, head down, her long carpet of hair covering her face.

Polly could not think of a worse place to get a proposal. She thought back, her heart aching, to Huckle asking, so quietly and gently that she hadn't quite understood to begin with what he meant, and then the gradual dawning realisation that he meant everything, and she wanted to cry. She fingered the seaweed ring; twisted it round and round on her hand, vowing to do whatever it took to get them back together.

Flora also looked like she was about to cry. She was helped awkwardly on to the stage, where she stood with her head bowed. Jayden, who was perspiring freely now, turned to face her and, with great clumsiness, got down on one knee.

'Rip!' shouted someone in the crowd, and Polly suddenly wanted to machine-gun them all. She was cross with Jayden, too; she'd told him not to do this, that it was too soon and Flora wouldn't like it, and here he was now, making an idiot out of himself. Some horribly scrawny model girl let out a high-pitched fake laugh of disbelief, and Polly only stopped herself sticking her with a fork by thinking about how many times the model girl would probably get divorced in the future. She sighed bad-temperedly.

'Flora, would you make me the happiest man in the world . . . ?'

There was silence in the room – an unpleasant silence, Polly could sense, as the huge gang of cool kids waited to laugh at the awkward chubby fellow with the shaking hands. She wondered if she'd lose Jayden, if the humiliation might make him give up or leave town altogether. And losing Flora for the holiday season would be a huge blow. The girl was a little divvy and distracted, but she had a natural gift for baking Polly could only dream of. Ugh. This was going so wrong.

But to Polly's amazement, Flora simply shrugged her shoulders.

'Yeah, whatevs,' she said, in a voice so low it was practically a whisper.

Polly blinked. What? The crowd stared too.

'YES!' shouted Jayden, raising both hands in the air, revealing very damp patches under his arms. 'Yes!'

He turned round to kiss Flora, but she'd already bolted from the stage. Jayden air-punched one more time, then jumped down after her.

'Hang on!' he shouted. 'I've got a ring!'

The band tittered politely.

'How charming,' said the singer into the mike, and Polly wanted to slap him. Then they struck up with 'I'm in the Mood for Love'.

As Polly went to find the happy couple to congratulate them – nobody else seemed to be – she walked slap-bang into Reuben.

'Your friends are all horrible,' she blurted.

'Yeah?' said Reuben, who was brandishing a gigantic cigar without actually smoking it. 'Well at least they're *here.*'

He had, Polly thought, a point.

She found Flora – looking furiously embarrassed – and a beaming Jayden by the downstairs cloakroom. Flora was putting on her coat.

'Um, congratulations, you two!' said Polly. Jayden gave her a not entirely friendly look.

'Yeah, well, you're the one who told me not to.'

'Well obviously I was wrong,' said Polly, trying to be breezy.

'You weren't wrong,' growled Flora. 'I was black affronted up there.'

'Oh my sweet pea,' sighed Jayden. 'I love you so much.'

'I'm going home,' said Flora.

'I'll come with you to talk you round,' said Jayden eagerly, and looked at Polly.

'Sure, you can go,' she said wearily. She'd stay and clear up. It was fine. She had nothing more pressing to do.

Chapter Twenty-Nine

Polly went outside. The sky was low and it was utterly freezing. She walked forward a little, just pleased to be out of the crush and the pressure and the noise inside, even though the party was starting to wind down. Even models and actresses had mums somewhere who needed them home for Christmas morning, she reflected. Sleek black cars were pulling up to the doorway; people were clutching the goody bags Santa had given everyone. Thankfully there were other people to help clean up, and she might leave a lot of it to them; Polly felt utterly exhausted.

She wandered across the busy driveway and round to the side of the house, with its path down to the private beach. It was so beautiful there, so calm and peaceful as the noise from the house receded and she could hear the heavy black waves pounding on the beach. She sighed. Christmas Eve. And this year had started out so promisingly . . .

'Hey.'

She turned round. Kerensa was walking along wrapped in a huge blanket, wearing a shapeless pair of black pregnancy trousers and a huge oversized hoody that did nothing to minimise her enormous bump.

'There you are!' said Polly. 'Everyone's been worried sick! Reuben didn't even do one of his speeches!'

'Well thank heavens for small mercies,' said Kerensa. Polly went closer. Kerensa was shivering with the cold.

'Come inside,' said Polly. 'You'll freeze. It's not good for you to be out here like this.'

'Are all those people gone?' said Kerensa. 'I just feel like I can't face it. That they'll all stare and judge me and ... Oh God, I don't know what's happened to me. I don't know.'

Polly grabbed her friend's arm.

'You're punishing yourself,' she said. 'And you don't even know if you have to.'

'Oh, I have to,' said Kerensa.

Polly took her hand. It was icy cold.

'Come on,' she said firmly. 'Inside. We'll go through the tradesmen's entrance. None of that lot will think to look there.'

'Thanks for opening up,' said the tall blonde man, sitting in the chilly puffin café.

'It's all right,' said Bernard. 'I didn't know where else to go either.'

They glanced around.

'You know, if your girlfriend can help,' said Bernard, 'it will make all the difference to us. All of it.'

Huckle nodded. He stared out of the window; there was a hint of snow in the heavy clouds above. It looked like it might unleash itself at any moment.

'I mean, she'll be a total hero,' said Bernard.

'Yeah, yeah, I know. She's a total hero. She helps everyone. Yeah, that's great. Thanks.'

'Are things all right between you two?'

Huckle picked up his beer and put it down again.

'Ah, well. You know. Life gets complicated.'

'You don't need to tell me,' said Bernard. 'I've got two million puffins to rehouse.'

They clinked glasses miserably.

'Happy Christmas,' said Bernard. 'Who knows where we'll be next year?'

'Surely it can't be worse than this,' said Huckle. Outside the puffins flew and danced in the sky. They all seemed to be having a great time.

'I've got some frozen chips in the freezer,' said Bernard. 'Want me to stick some on?'

'Sure,' said Huckle, sighing. He glanced at his phone. No messages.

But he didn't need to speak to her; he knew exactly what she'd be doing: bustling through the kitchen, her cheeks pink from the heat of the stove, a tendril of that lovely pale hair cascading down her face, sleeves rolled up, checking everything was coming out on time, arranging delicious morsels on plates, yelling at Jayden, ticking over, completely immersed, completely sure of herself. But never, ever too tired or busy not to look up at him in total delight every time he walked through the door.

He missed it so much it felt like a physical pain.

He thought back over the last evening. They had been strange and awful all at once. He drank some more beer. Even his parents had been out of reach, which wasn't like them. He sighed again.

'Something up?' said Bernard, coming back with the chips. Huckle wasn't hungry, but he took one listlessly. It was soggy. Bernard really, really needed someone to help with his catering.

'Nothing.'

'Seriously? Because, you know. It's late. And you're here.'

'Yeah,' said Huckle.

'You know,' said Bernard, 'anyone who wants to save a puffin sanctuary . . . I think they're a pretty good bet.'

Huckle smiled ruefully.

'She just . . . I mean, she just doesn't want to get married, I don't think.'

'Hmmm,' said Bernard. 'Maybe she's more like that fox Selina. Cunning. Treating you mean and reeling you in like a swordfish.'

'A swordfish?' said Huckle. 'Anyway, she's not like that.'

'Hmmm,' said Bernard again.

There was a pause.

'Bernard, could I ask you something?'

And he never told Polly afterwards that it had been Bernard, of all people, the puffin man, who'd confirmed what she'd been telling him all along: that it was absolutely none of his fucking business.

'You go back. Tail between your legs. And you smile and be really, really nice to the puffling. Baby. I mean baby.'

He paused.

'And that minxy girlfriend of yours ... I'd close that deal, if it's making you this crazy.'

'Hmmm,' said Huckle. 'That's one point of view. Or maybe ... maybe she just doesn't want to marry *me*. Maybe that's it. Maybe I should cut my losses now.'

Bernard shrugged as if he didn't care either way, which he didn't.

'Anyway, how are you?' said Huckle, changing the subject, because it was making him so sad.

'Not bad,' said Bernard. 'I own a failing puffin sanctuary and I'm in love with a beautiful jewellery designer who doesn't know I'm alive.'

They chinked beers again, Huckle deep in thought.

'Merry Christmas,' he said.

'And to you.'

Chapter Thirty

By the time Polly and Kerensa got back inside, everyone had left. There were still some people dismantling the stage, but otherwise it was as if the hundreds of beautiful people had appeared and dematerialised in a dream; everything had been swept up and put away and returned to how it was, and the magic of the house had gone.

Kerensa stood staring out of the window, like a bird in a cage desperate to be free.

The promised snow had not come down after all. It was bleak outside; not clear and cold but grey and solid, as if the clouds were blanketing the world, making everything heavy and sad.

Polly stood at her shoulder and gazed out too. There was little to see; just the occasional glimpse of a lighthouse. There was a ship a long way out to sea, a tanker, on its way to Plymouth perhaps, from who knew where – Sri Lanka? China? Italy? What was it carrying?

The men who crewed her would be missing their families tonight. Missing their loved ones. She raised her rapidly chilling cup of tea to them as the great blinking lights passed by.

The shadows under Kerensa's eyes were more pronounced than ever.

'What happened to Huckle?'

Polly shook her head.

'Never mind. Difference of opinion.'

'Tell me,' said Kerensa. 'Tell me what's happened. Is it to do with me? Please tell me.'

'It's fine,' said Polly, more harshly than she'd meant to. 'We're fine. He thinks I'm working too much.'

'Well tomorrow's going to be fun,' said Kerensa. 'When you're working again.'

'You can't have Christmas without a gigantic fight,' said Polly. 'Isn't that the law?'

'Oh God, and my lot are coming too,' said Kerensa. 'You know what my mum's going to be like with Rhonda.'

'They're very similar personalities,' said Polly without thinking. 'I mean . . . I don't mean that. I really don't.'

'And what about your mum?'

Polly sighed. 'Oh God. I texted her to say I'd come over after lunch.'

'And?'

'She didn't say yes. And she didn't say no either. It's been quite the silent treatment. She's relentless.'

'She's all right,' said Kerensa.

'Well I wish she'd tell me. I'm going over anyway, though I don't think she really wants me to come. And I'll be driving, so no booze. Yeah. And possibly no Huckle. Will be brilliant. I'm looking forward to sitting in total silence and watching *EastEnders*.'

Kerensa nodded.

'That sounds better than here.'

Polly thought self-pityingly of the plan she and Huckle had had originally – lying in bed in the lighthouse, drinking champagne. Why couldn't she have just done that? Why had everything got so mad and out of control? Why had she ended up saying yes to everything except the one thing she really wanted to do? Yes to everybody else, and no to them.

'Oh God,' she said. 'Next Christmas will be better, won't it? Won't it?'

Kerensa didn't say anything for a while.

'But Polly, what if . . . what if . . . '

Polly didn't say anything. She simply moved towards Kerensa and gave her a huge hug. She couldn't quite get her arms around her, but they stood there together, two friends in the dark.

Polly suddenly became conscious that she was standing in something. Had she spilled some of the leftover milk as she was taking it to the fridge? What had happened to the cup of tea she'd been continuously remaking and forgetting to drink for the last seven hours? She cast round, then glanced at the floor.

'Oh,' she said. Kerensa hadn't realised.

'Um,' Polly said. Kerensa still had her eyes closed and was leaning in, enjoying the hug.

'Kez,' she said. 'I don't want to alarm you. But I *think*...
I think your waters might have broken.'

Kerensa's eyes snapped open.

'What?' she said, and looked down. 'Oh Lord,' she said. 'Oh Lord. But it's WEEKS away.'

Polly sat Kerensa down on an expensive leather armchair. She thought briefly about the consequences of this, but put them out of her mind. Kerensa's eyes were wide open and she was breathing heavily. Polly found a cloth.

'OMG, what happens now?' she said.

'I don't know!' said Kerensa. She looked up at Polly. 'I didn't go to any of the antenatal classes.'

'What do you mean?' said Polly. 'That's where you were all those times you were out of the house! That and shopping for the baby.'

Kerensa shook her head.

'I couldn't,' she said. 'I went to one and it was all so vomitous, all those carey-sharey husbands, everyone showing off and pretending they were more in love than anyone else and that their birth was going to be the best. I couldn't do it. Reuben wouldn't come anyway, and I couldn't handle everyone else with their perfect lives. Couldn't handle it at all.'

'So what were you doing?' said Polly, grabbing the phone handset.

For a moment, Kerensa half smiled.

'Doesn't matter,' she said. 'Not now, anyway.'

Polly shot her a suspicious look, but this wasn't the time.

'So, who do I phone?'

'Actually,' said Kerensa, 'I feel okay. I don't . . . Polly, it's weeks to my due date. It must just be a mistake.'

'I don't think burst waters are a mistake. So that's all fine,' said Polly, trying to stay calm. 'You get to skip the boring hanging-about bit.'

There was a pause. Then Kerensa gasped as she thought of something.

'It means the baby's got too big,' she said, her eyes filling with tears. 'It's a gigantic big Brazilian stripper baby.'

'Stop it,' said Polly. 'There's nothing to be done about it now. Nothing. The baby is coming. Will I get Reuben?'

Kerensa blinked. Then suddenly her breathing hitched, and she bent over quickly.

'Ohhhhh!' she said, and her entire body tensed for what felt like a very long time to both of them. She was silent for a moment, then straightened up a little. She looked at Polly. 'I think . . . I think that might have been one,' she said.

'I agree,' said Polly. 'I'd better get Reuben.'

'As soon as he arrives, everything's going to go bananas,' said Kerensa, her breathing slowing gradually.

In the quiet unlit kitchen, surrounded by the scent

of Polly's bread that she'd put in so it would be fresh for breakfast, it was oddly peaceful and timeless. Both of them briefly wished they could just stay there for a little while longer. The Christmas tree glimmered and glistened in the hallway. The world stopped; breathed, waiting for Christmas morning. Waiting, Polly supposed, for a baby ...

Kerensa reached out her hand and Polly squeezed it.

'You know,' said Polly, 'everything is going to be all right.'

'Is it?' said Kerensa. Her face was full of fear.

'Yes,' said Polly. 'I'm here. It will be fine. Things end up fine.'

'Do they?' said Kerensa.

'Yes,' said Polly. 'That's the promise of Christmas. Believe it.'

They squeezed hands again. Then Kerensa lurched over once more.

'Okay,' said Polly. 'You're going to have to time your contractions.'

'How come you know this stuff?' grumbled Kerensa.

'I watch *Call the Midwife*,' said Polly. 'Your husband is going to come back from t'pit and not want to see it.'

'Yes, well, I wish,' said Kerensa.

Polly made sure she was sitting comfortably.

'Okay,' she said. 'I'm going. I'm going to get him, okay?'

They shared a look.

'Everything changes now,' said Kerensa.

'Everything always does,' said Polly.

She kissed Kerensa lightly on the head, then turned and left the silent, fragrant kitchen, as the great boat out on the horizon finally disappeared.

Chapter Thirty-One

Privately Polly couldn't believe it was in the least bit good for a new baby to be surrounded by so much fuss and fluster. Reuben had to be instantly persuaded out of calling for a helicopter, on the grounds that the baby was still probably a day or so away and that it would be the single most dangerous part of the entire birth.

Rhonda was running around – after emerging with a suspiciously full face of make-up for the time of day – trying to make everything about her and announcing what it had been like when Reuben was born (a feat of extraordinary pain and endurance that nearly killed her; she had lost eleven pints of blood, not something that anyone felt was particularly useful to say at the time). Reuben had of course instantly ignored/forgotten the fact that he'd been annoyed with Kerensa at the party.. Normally this was the most infuriating thing about him. But that night Kerensa was profoundly grateful for it as he stood in the middle of the kitchen barking orders and waking up his incredibly expensive gynaecologist, who tried to explain that he probably wouldn't be needed for quite a while, seeing as Kerensa's contractions were still a good fifteen minutes apart and, so far, not terribly debilitating, so perhaps they should call him in the . . .

Reuben gave this extremely short shrift, and sent the helicopter for him instead.

In an instant, a fleet of black cars had arrived at the door. Kerensa had at least packed a bag, but Reuben had packed two suitcases, and the entire boot of the car was soon filled.

'Come,' said Kerensa to Polly.

'Are you sure?' said Polly. Kerensa looked around at the others. 'Yes,' she said. 'Will you get my mum first?'

It was agreed that Polly would pick up Kerensa's mum and meet them at the hospital.

'Wait!' shouted Reuben as she left. 'Don't take that deathtrap van, you'll kill everyone.'

And he hurled her the keys to Kerensa's Range Rover.

Polly drove like the wind down completely deserted roads, revelling in the smooth automatic car that didn't let in draughts. She had to phone Huckle. It was her first instinct in everything: phone him, tell him.

But she hadn't told him everything, had she? And if she

told him about this, well, it would hurl them straight back into that incredibly knotty problem.

Reuben would call him. Of course he would. Reuben would call him and then . . . well. Then they'd see.

Kerensa's mum Jackie was standing on the kerb, her own suitcase completely packed, the joy and nerves and excitement plain to see on her face, all mixed in together.

'Baby Express?' said Polly cheerfully, leaning out of the window.

'This is totally the best Christmas present ever,' said Jackie, and Polly was suddenly so pleased and relieved to be with someone who was a hundred per cent straight-forwardly delighted about everything that was going on that she too relaxed and enjoyed the drive to the hospital, through little towns with jolly pubs where revellers had celebrated Christmas Eve; where old school friends, long scattered, came back together just for the night; students came home; everyone was at home to be with their families for Christmas, just as it should be, even though tomorrow there would be disappointments: batteries that didn't work, unsuitable gifts, arguments about politics, dry turkey and too much drink taken, who's looking after Granny, ancient unearthed sibling rivalries replayed around the table and overexcited children vomiting and crying.

But all of those were for tomorrow. Tonight there was a lovely sense of anticipation, almost nicer, as lights on in houses and cottages showed children bouncing up and down on beds and mothers trying to get them settled; people pulling mysterious shapes out of garages, marching with holly and wrapping paper; fairy lights flickering; the cars they passed piled high with bundles.

Polly remembered the old story about how at midnight on Christmas Eve all the animals fell silent in memory of the waiting baby and the creatures in the stall at Bethlehem and the sheep on the hillsides. When she'd been little, she'd always wanted to stay up till midnight to see if next door's Pomeranian would stop its usual yapping.

Had her mother told her that story? she wondered. Was that where it had come from?

They sped on through the night towards Plymouth. Polly glanced at Jackie.

'Are you all right?' she asked gently.

Jackie half smiled.

'It's so strange,' she said. 'It only feels like yesterday that Kez was a baby. My baby. having a baby. Well. Her dad wasn't half so calm as you, driving me to the hospital. Mind you, she wasn't for hanging about, that one. Always in a rush. Nearly had her in the car park.'

Jackie smiled.

'She was ... she was the sunniest child, Polly. The light of our lives, truly, even when the boys came along. There's something special about your first child, there really is. Always.'

Polly just nodded.

'And recently . . . I don't know. I've been worried about her. It's like the spark has gone out of her. Have you noticed? Do you feel that?'

Polly shrugged. 'I think . . . I think maybe she's had a tough pregnancy.'

'Maybe,' frowned Jackie. 'She's certainly looked enormous.'

'I wouldn't say that to her.'

'Ha! No!'

Jackie glanced at her phone.

'Nothing. She knows we're on the way, doesn't she?'

'She does,' said Polly. 'Also she'll be surrounded by everybody fussing. They probably won't let her do much. There's probably a special way of having babies rich people do, where it doesn't hurt and there isn't any mess or anything.'

'Hmm,' said Jackie.

Polly thought of a poem: all the way to the hospital, the lights were green as peppermints, the roads finally emptying out. It was time now; everyone it seemed was where they had to be, home for Christmas, whatever home meant for them, whether it was with friends, or loved ones, or working in a shelter. It was time. It was ready. The bright stars of the world were holding their breath.

Chapter Thirty-Two

On the private wing, there was bustle and fuss and soft flattering lighting and a rather bored-looking consultant still wearing his tweed jacket and clearly waiting for something to happen.

Rhonda was yelling into her phone at Reuben's siblings back in the US, while Merv was strolling up and down the corridors with his hands behind his back. Reuben was shouting about how awesome Kerensa was and how she was going to have this baby entirely naturally without any drugs, and there was some muted response from Kerensa that seemed to disagree with this theory entirely, and all in all it felt like there were a lot more people in the room than was entirely necessary, including lots of staff, and then of course Jackie burst in too, so then there were tears and hugs and Rhonda stepped back somewhat coolly, it had to be said, and Polly stood by the sidelines.

She caught Kerensa's eye, but Kerensa seemed to be

somewhere else altogether; off in another land, where pain and something very strange and new were happening, and Polly didn't think it was entirely right that they should all be there for something so very special, and certainly not her, so she squeezed Kerensa's hand, whispered, 'You'll do it, my darling,' then kissed her on her damp forehead and quietly retreated, stealing down the hospital corridors.

They were deserted, just a man in the corner cleaning with one of those big double-wheeled mops. Polly had no doubt he wanted to get home to his family for Christmas too.

She took out her phone and looked at the screen. Nothing. What was wrong with Huckle? Where was he? This was Christmas. What did it mean? Were they finished? Was it over? Surely not. She called, but there was no answer. Of course in Cornwall this didn't always mean very much. She sighed, and sent him a text.

Happy Christmas. Please can we ...

She deleted the last bit. Maybe let everything go calm for a little while. Just a while.

Then she dialled another number.

'Hello, Mum. Yes, I know it's late but the causeway's closed and ...'

They sat up with cups of tea, her mother having made it quite clear that there would never be any more booze with the two of them in the room. She'd also looked very sadly at the Range Rover and murmured that she'd always hoped Polly would have had a nice car of her own, but Polly had chosen to ignore that.

'I remember the night you were born,' Doreen said quietly, as they sat, the omnipresent television on, playing carols from Trafalgar Square. There was a small plastic tree, with fake presents underneath it, that made Polly sadder than she could bear to think. She brought in all her gifts she'd been thankfully too lazy to remove from the car, even though she knew that a Marks and Sparks dressing gown, a new scarf and a nail voucher her mother would never use were hardly the stuff dreams were made of. Likewise the basket she could see with her name on it. When she was a teenager she'd loved the Body Shop, and Doreen had helpfully never deviated from it since.

'Tell me,' said Polly, staring into the gas fire and wishing Neil was there.

'Well. Your grandad ... of course it was too much for him. I mean, they'd been very supportive and everything, even though I'd lost my job, couldn't be on the shop floor, not really, not with that bump sticking out and all the men coming in to buy hats for their wives ... It sounds a thousand years ago, but it wasn't really.'

Polly smiled.

'And your grandma, God rest her soul, I mean, she never

learned to drive. So we took a cab, an old Cortina, stank of fags. I couldn't bear the smell. When we got to the hospital, she checked me in but then left me. She had to get back, or she felt she should, or Dad needed his tea or . . . well. I don't know why. I never did really. Maybe she was worried she'd bump into one of her friends or something. They were supportive, they were, truly. We lived with them for a few years, until this house came up. And they never told me off. I mean some girls, they got thrown out. Some got sent away, you know. The Catholic girls, the things that happened to them were unbelievable. And recent, too.'

She took a long sip of her tea.

'So. Anyway. I had to . . . I had to do it all by myself. All alone. They weren't very interested, the nurses. They were too busy chatting to the nervous husbands and the doctors. They hadn't much time for a little scrubber like me. When it hurt, one of them said to me, well you should have thought about that, shouldn't you?' Her eyes filled with tears.

'I'm sorry,' said Polly.

'Not your fault,' said her mother.

'Was it awful?'

Her mother looked at her.

'Well, yes,' she said. 'Until . . . until I saw you.'

They fell silent. The swell of the carols on the television grew louder. They were singing the Coventry Carol. It was beautiful.

'I didn't even get to hold you for very long . . . they used to whisk babies off in those days. You know it was even suggested that I give you up. That was perfectly common, perfectly normal.'

'Did you consider it?' said Polly, feeling daring even for asking. Her mother frowned.

'Of course not,' she said. 'Of course not. I mean, no disrespect to women who felt they had to, none at all. But no. No, I couldn't. And I had my parents, even if they weren't ... It took my dad a little while to come round to you ...'

Polly stiffened. She had the fondest memories of her kind, reticent, pipe-smoking grandpa.

'... five whole seconds, I seem to remember.' She smiled to herself. 'You were born with that hair,' she said. 'You looked so very like your father, straight away. But I loved you ... I loved you fiercely. Everything else in my life had gone so wrong, was so awful. You ... you were so right. Maybe that's why I've fussed over you ... worried about you too much.'

'No you haven't,' said Polly uncomfortably.

Her mother shrugged.

'You were ... you are ...'

The rest of the sentence hung there in the overheated room. Now the singers were bawling out, 'Hail, thou ever blessed morn! Hail, redemption's happy dawn! Sing to all Jerusalem! Christ is born in Bethlehem,' as the clock ticked over, and it was practically down on Christmas morning.

'I'm sorry. I just always wanted you to be safe, and

happy,' said Doreen. 'By having a bit of money and a bit of freedom and some security. I mean, every parent wants that. And I never had that for you.'

Polly nodded.

'So when you dash off buying lighthouses and giving up sensible careers and demanding that I come down and appreciate the sea air and wander about in the country and things ... I do get scared. I do. I'm sorry.'

'I understand,' said Polly.

'But don't disappoint that lovely boy,' said her mum. 'Don't let me or anybody else stop you from that. Ever. I'm telling you now. Forget what happened to me. You marry him and have babies and live on fresh air if you have to. Be happy. I was never brave enough to be, never brave enough to step out there. But you could be. You can, Polly. Please, please, do it for me.'

Polly nodded, and tried not to sigh.

'Okay,' she said.

They got up to go to bed.

At the door, Doreen stopped.

'Did you see ... did you see your father in the end?' she asked.

Polly shook her head.

'No, Mum,' she said. 'You're my family.'

Doreen swallowed hard.

'I've been too proud,' she said. 'I know that. It's hard ... It's been such a long time. But if you wanted to ... well. I can't see it would make much difference now.'

Polly nodded.

'Okay,' she said. 'Thanks. And happy Christmas.'

They embraced, and Polly winced a little at how thin her mother was, and vowed that next year she would get her down to Mount Polbearne more and insist, despite her protestations, that she sit outside the bakery with a cup of tea in her hand, and no telly, and instead enjoy the sunshine and get to say hello to the passers-by, and if she didn't want to live her own life, necessarily, then she ought to share more of Polly's. And that would be her Christmas gift.

Chapter Thirty-Three

Polly slept better than she had in weeks, back in her child-hood single bed, with the posters of Leonardo DiCaprio and Kevin from the Backstreet Boys on the walls. Reuben had texted to say they were all staying at the Exeter ground. It was something about being back there, back home, and something about not having to get up and work the next day for highly demanding American guests and also something about the fact that it didn't seem to matter how late she might lie awake wondering about Huckle, it wasn't going to make a blind bit of difference, so there wasn't really any point.

Plus, she was beyond exhausted.

She woke to, amazingly, the scent of bacon and eggs frying. Was her mother actually cooking? This was unheard of. She checked her phone. Nothing except a quick text from Reuben saying that nothing much was going on, this was super boring and rubbish, please could she make some doughnuts and bring them to the hospital, and make enough for the nurses too, please, and tell Huckle to call him because he hadn't heard from him at all.

Polly was just starting to worry seriously about Huckle when he called.

'Where are you?' she said crossly, when in fact she had woken up rested, happy to be reconciled with her mum and all prepared to be sweet to him and make it up.

'Plymouth,' said Huckle.

'Plymouth? Why?'

She was suddenly filled with panic that he was waiting for a train to London to catch a flight back to the US. He couldn't be. Surely. No. No he wouldn't, would he?

'Why? Are you flying home?'

'What? What are you talking about? No!'

There was a long pause, then, 'Polly . . . Polly, I thought I had a home.'

'So did I,' said Polly miserably.

'No . . . I'm just. Polly, you understand don't you? I feel awful about all of this. Awful for Kerensa, awful for Reuben. I'm just . . . I'm just away working for a little while so I don't come and put my foot in it, or say something awful, or just get upset . . . so we don't fight. Do you understand?'

'Not really. What are you doing?'

'I told you, I'm working.'

'It's Christmas Day. How can you be working?'

'It's a city,' said Huckle. 'It's a totally normal day for loads of people here. You've been out of the loop for too long. I have a meeting with a Jewish beauty consortium.'

'Okay,' said Polly.

'Also, I thought you were working today?'

'Apparently so,' said Polly, glancing at the phone, which was lighting up with more orders and messages. 'Wish me luck with my mum's oven. I don't think it's been used since the Royal Wedding. The first one.'

'You're at your mum's?'

'Yes,' said Polly. 'The baby's coming and I don't want to risk the tides.'

'The *baby's* coming?'

'Look at your messages!'

'Yeah, well . . . But you're still working.'

'Reuben wants catering,' said Polly.

There was a pause.

'I can't get down,' said Huckle.

'Well I don't think it's imminent. I think first babies take ages.'

There was a silence.

'Okay,' said Huckle finally. 'Well, I can tell you're busy.'

Don't let me be busy, Polly tried to silently beam to him. *Come back. Whisk me out of this. Make everything lovely and fun again.*

'I guess you're busy too,' she said.

'Oh, you'd better believe it,' said Huckle.

There was another long pause.

'How's Neil?'

'Not here,' confessed Polly.

'You left him alone on Christmas Day?' said Huckle.

'I know, I know. I'll make it up to him. Can puffins eat chocolate?'

Chapter Thirty-Four

The triumphant text message had arrived before Polly had a chance to heat up the fryer for the doughnuts. She offered to take her mother, who'd declined, but nicely, and said she'd see her in a few days.

Polly walked down the hospital corridor, all nerves. The swanky private wing was, she was slightly aggrieved to note, nicer than most places she'd ever lived in. Oh well. Even so, the Christmas decorations seemed a little forced. Someone had made a gigantic star out of cardboard bed-pans. It was kind of revolting and charming at the same time. The nurses were wearing Santa hats, as were several of the patients, which looked rather sad.

She found the right room without too much trouble, partly because it was covered in hundreds of absurdly gigantic blue helium balloons, and a line of muffin baskets that stretched out the door. Americans, Polly remembered, liked to celebrate this kind of thing.

She took a deep breath, and knocked gently.

Inside, it was chaos. Kerensa was sitting up in bed looking exhausted and anxious but tender and strange all at the same time. Reuben was jabbering into his mobile by the window.

'Yeah! Yeah! He's perfect! He's awesome! Seriously, I'm telling you, you wouldn't get a better child than this. We're seriously considering getting him a special tutor, because I'm telling you now, this kid is smart. I mean, better than smart, I mean super smart . . . '

'How are you,' mouthed Polly, as she gingerly tried to embrace Kerensa without accidentally whacking the baby on the head with her handbag.

Kerensa smiled tiredly.

'Well that was interesting,' she said.

'By interesting do you mean heartily disgusting?' asked Polly.

'It's really, really disgusting,' said Kerensa. 'I don't know why anyone does it. Honestly. It's rubbish.'

Her voice went a bit wobbly and Polly thought she was about to cry, so then, of course, they both did start to cry.

Finally Polly plucked up the courage to look down.

He was just . . . he was just a baby. Dark fronds of hair on his head, eyes tightly shut, looking like an astronaut who'd just landed from another world and taken his suit off but still carried the faint aura of other-worldliness and stardust.

Polly blinked.

'He's beautiful, Kerensa.'

'I know!' said Kerensa, snuffling.

Reuben was still hollering into the phone and wasn't paying them any attention. Polly took Kerensa's hand and squeezed it very tightly. Then she offered the baby a finger, and he grabbed on to it without opening his eyes.

'That's amazing,' she said, feeling his tiny grip. His little mouth worked, looking for something.

'Oh don't be hungry,' said Kerensa. 'I tell you, breast-feeding is also disgusting. And impossible.'

'Keep at it,' said Polly.

'Oh, I will,' said Kerensa. 'He's obviously loving it. Plus Reuben says it gives you a bunch of IQ points, and we're already raising the greatest genius the world has ever known, obviously.'

Polly smiled.

'Hey, Polls!' said Reuben, finishing his call. 'Meet my awesome son, huh! Awesome son, going to take on the world, blah blah blah.'

His face went uncharacteristically soft for a moment and he lowered the phone that was usually superglued to his fingers. He moved away from the window and stared deep into the baby's face. Polly found she was holding her breath. He put his hand on the baby's head.

'Huh, dark hair,' he said. 'Normally the Finkels have, you know . . . ' He indicated his own ginger locks.

'That's just cowl hair,' said Kerensa incredibly fast. 'It'll come out. It's not his real hair.'

257

'No, no, it's cool, I like dark hair,' said Reuben, gazing at the baby. 'He's beautiful, isn't he, Polly? Don't you think he's the most beautiful baby there's ever been? And super smart. He totally aced his Apgar test. First exam he ever had, and he aced it.'

Polly blinked.

'Yes,' she said. 'What are you calling him?'

Kerensa and Reuben exchanged glances.

'Ah,' said Kerensa.

'What?' said Reuben. 'Herschel's a great family name.'

'Herschel,' said Kerensa. 'Herschel Finkel.'

'Ohh,' said Polly, putting a polite expression on her face. 'That sounds nice.'

'Hershy? Hersch? Herscho?' said Kerensa. 'What's wrong with Lowin?'

'That's lovely,' said Polly.

'Yeah, right,' said Reuben. 'Way to get him bullied at school.'

'Oh and Herschel Finkel isn't?'

'Nothing wrong with it,' said Reuben stoutly.

'We'll get round to sorting out the name,' said Kerensa.

Just then Rhonda and Merv burst into the room with huge shopping bags full of clothes and, absurdly, lots and lots of toys, which, given that the baby was at the moment not much more than a floppy fish, was a bit hard to understand.

'Here he is! The most beautiful boy in the world! Aren't you! Aren't you, my gorgeous? You're going to be a true Finkel, aren't you? You come to your bubbe!' And the new grandmother bent her teased, backcombed head and covered the tiny face in kisses, leaving bright pink lipstick traces wherever she went.

Polly noticed that Kerensa was trying hard not to cry; she was obviously exhausted, and the weariness made her lovely face droop. Rhonda looked at her.

'Are you feeling depressed?' she asked in what she obviously regarded as a low whisper and thus was only audible to the next four rooms down the corridor. 'Because you know you can watch for that.'

'I'm fine,' said Kerensa. 'Just tired.' She crossly wiped away a tear.

'There there,' said Rhonda, stroking her cheek. 'Don't you worry. Any help you need, any doctors you need, anything you need, we'll sort it for you. You're our family now. You are my daughter now too, huh? So. Anything we can do we will do for you, for you are the mother of the most beautiful Finkel man ever known.'

Kerensa couldn't speak but nodded quietly. Rhonda got up and indicated to Merv.

'Come on!' she hollered. 'Leave them alone! They clearly need a bit of peace and quiet.'

This felt a bit rich, seeing as how Merv had just been staring quietly at the baby and beaming with happiness, but he started moving towards the door anyway.

'We'll be back soon,' he said.

'We will!' said Rhonda. 'Oh, I can't bear to leave him!

My first grandchild!' She gave him one last lipstick kiss. 'That beautiful boy,' she added. 'That beautiful, beautiful boy. My grandson!'

Her mascara started to leak a little.

'I know,' she said to Kerensa, 'I know that to you this little bundle is everything. But can I say that to us too . . . to us it feels exactly the same. That we are carrying on, that our family is carrying on into the future, and it is the most wonderful feeling on earth.'

Merv passed her a large handkerchief, and she blew her nose noisily.

'So you look after yourself, huh? Because you have done a wonderful thing for us. A wonderful, wonderful thing. Now, Reuben, you show us where this restaurant is. We have to eat, yes? Everybody has to eat. We'll come back soon. Give your wife some rest and stop taking photographs. You'll damage my perfect grandson's little eyes, I'm sure it's dangerous . . . '

She kissed the baby and Kerensa once more, then, still talking, bustled her husband and son noisily out into the corridor.

The room was very quiet after they'd all left, just the gentle bleeping of a machine here or there in the distance. There were so many flowers, it looked like a greenhouse. Polly went to the window and gazed out at the garden outside.

'It's weird,' Kerensa said, her voice completely flat.

'There's all those people just walking about out there, getting on with their daily business, without the faintest idea that everything in here is just ... well, glorious and awful all at once.'

'I wonder how many people looking out of these windows feel that,' said Polly, her heart heavy. She turned round. 'Oh KEZ,' she wailed.

'Why are *you* so sad?' said Kerensa. 'You're not the one sitting here with a dark-haired baby.'

Polly burst into tears.

'What? What's this about?'

'It's Huckle,' said Polly.

'What?' said Kerensa, looking alarmed. 'Why isn't he here? What's happened to him? I thought he'd be the first to come and see Reuben's baby. I thought you wouldn't be able to keep him away.'

She stared at Polly as the truth dawned on her.

'You didn't ... '

'I had to,' said Polly. 'He knew something was up. He knew there was something I wasn't telling him. It was tearing us apart.'

Kerensa blinked.

'So now what? Where is he? Calling Reuben?'

'I don't think so,' said Polly. 'I think he's wrestling with his conscience. Also, I think he might be breaking up with me.'

'He can't be,' Kerensa said. 'He can't be. Not you two. Not Polly and Huckle. Who'd get custody of Neil?'

'Me,' said Polly quickly. 'But that's not the point.'

Kerensa shook her head.

'Oh God,' she said. 'Oh God oh God oh God. Everything ... everything so horribly, horribly ruined. Everything so messed up. Because I made one stupid mistake. One stupid, stupid thing.'

Polly blinked. 'It's always the women who pay. We always do. It's been this way for ever.'

'I'm not some Victorian parlour maid,' said Kerensa.

'You might as well be,' said Polly bitterly. 'You're a fallen woman. We're always left holding the baby. Suffering the consequences.' She thought about her mum.

Kerensa looked down at the sleeping infant.

'I love him,' she said. 'I love him so much. I can't tell you. As soon as I met him, as soon as they handed him to me I just thought, I know you. I know you. Everything about you. Everything you are. And I love it all. I think all of it is perfect, and splendid, and I always will. But I'm going to have to pay for that.'

'Not necessarily,' said Polly. 'He might not say anything.'

'But he might,' said Kerensa. 'Maybe not now. Maybe one day. In the future. When something happens. When something goes wrong.'

Polly shook her head. 'I'll beg him. I'll deny it. I'll ... I'll stand up in a court of law and swear against it.'

'It doesn't matter,' said Kerensa. 'Because already every piece of happiness I have from my boy here ... every word

Rhonda says . . . it cuts me like a knife. Stabs me through and through. And I think it always will.'

'One in ten,' said Polly. 'One in ten men are raising children that aren't theirs. That's what they say, isn't it?'

'It can't be true, though,' said Kerensa. 'It can't be. Surely. That can't be right.'

'We'll never know,' said Polly. 'Nobody will ever know. That's the point.'

She placed a hand on Kerensa's shoulder and ran a finger down the baby's cheek. His skin was so soft, so pure and new. He was perfect. None of this gigantic mess was his fault. She swore then, silently, that he would never, ever feel that it was.

She looked at Kerensa.

'I'm godmother,' she said fiercely.

Kerensa nodded. 'How are you going to reject the devil and all his works though?' she said. 'We basically *are* the devil and all his works.'

They looked at the perfect little face once more.

'You're not going to mess this up,' whispered Polly. 'Neither am I. And neither is Huckle. He'll come round. We'll sort it. We will.' She smiled. 'Friends. Not just there for the nice things in life. Although this, I will tell you, is a very, very nice thing.'

Kerensa nodded and swallowed hard.

'Yeah,' she said.

'Yeah,' said Polly.

There was nothing more to say. Polly didn't want to go, but she had to. She gave them one last hug.

'I hate leaving you alone.'

'Reuben will be back in a second,' said Kerensa. 'Don't worry, I'm sure he'll manage to keep both sides of the conversation going, as usual.'

'He's happy,' said Polly. 'Your mum has headed off to contact everyone she's ever known. Rhonda and Merv are happy. The baby is gorgeous. Everyone is happy. Our job is to keep it that way, don't you think? Who knows. Maybe then we get to be happy too.'

She thought of Huckle's haunted, handsome face. Was it possible? Could it ever be? How careless life was.

Chapter Thirty-Five

Polly left the private wing profoundly and utterly choked and yet strangely happy at the same time – meeting the new baby had brought about in her some odd deep joy she hadn't anticipated; something pure and lovely and wonderful. She'd expected to be worried when he arrived – as worried as Kerensa felt – but in fact he was so gorgeous she could feel nothing but hope. Surely everyone could love a baby enough. Even if Reuben found out? Even if the kid was taller than him and could grow more facial hair by the age of nine? He wouldn't desert his family, would he?

Except Polly herself had had a father who hadn't wanted her. Who hadn't wanted to know her. It was possible. Was it ever possible?

As she reached the main entrance, deep in thought, she nearly collided with the woman who was standing stock still in the middle of the hallway, staring at her.

'Sorry,' she mumbled, but to her surprise, the woman put up a hand to stop her.

'Polly,' she said.

Polly focused, dragged herself away from her musings, and was brought up short in shock.

'Carmel,' she said, her mouth moving but making barely any sound.

Carmel was equally startled, but her face was joyful and full of excitement.

'Polly! You came!'

There was a silence. Polly swallowed hard.

'Well ... ' she said. Carmel's expression was so radiant, Polly hated to disappoint her. But she couldn't ... she just couldn't ...

She should have realised that this might happen, but it just hadn't crossed her mind – the hospital was vast, and the private maternity wing was tucked away in a pleasant building overlooking the gardens at the back. But of course, nothing was impossible.

'No,' she said. 'I'm here seeing somebody else.'

Carmel's face fell.

'Oh,' she said. 'Oh, I'm sorry. I thought ... I thought ... '

'I never had a dad,' said Polly. 'I never had one.'

Carmel nodded. 'I realise that. Completely and utterly. I do. I was wrong to contact you and I want to apologise.'

'Thanks,' said Polly.

'I shouldn't have dropped a bomb in your life like that. It was wrong of me ... I was distraught. Everything was so awful and I was thinking of him and what he was begging me to do, and not about you.'

Polly nodded. 'I understand that,' she said. She couldn't help it, she liked Carmel.

There was a pause, and Polly moved to walk away.

'But,' said Carmel. 'Perhaps you could see it as a favour . . . a favour to a stranger. Something you might do for anyone. For a dying man. I know he's nothing to you. I think if I'd let him, you might have been a lot to him. It's me you have to forgive,' she went on. 'I had children of my own. I couldn't risk . . . couldn't risk my own family. Couldn't. I told him if he ever went near your mother, if he risked our family again for somebody else, then I couldn't be held responsible for my actions.'

She blinked.

'I hope one day you'll understand what I did. I would have fought tooth and nail for my children to have a full-time father. I'm sorry about how that's made you feel. I'm not sorry for keeping my family together.'

Her eyes flashed as she said it. And Polly thought how she didn't blame Carmel for fighting for her family. She wished her own mother had been better equipped to fight for hers. But that was what it was.

'Okay,' she said.

'Okay what?' said Carmel. 'Okay with what I did, or okay you'll come and see him?'

Polly thought for a long time. She thought of Kerensa's innocent little baby, and how he deserved access to anybody who might ever love him. She wished Huckle was here. She wished she could somehow speak to her mum about it, but she'd already asked so much.

She felt very, very lonely.

'Are . . . are any of your children there?' she asked.

Carmel shook her head.

'No,' she said. 'They're coming this afternoon.'

Polly nodded. She would go in, say hello, say goodbye and that would be it. She would have done her duty, fulfilled the last request of a dying man. It was the right thing to do. Then she would call Huckle and tell him to go and see the baby, no matter what was going on between the two of them. And then she would . . . well. She didn't know. Get back to work, she supposed.

'Yeah, all right then,' she said.

The men's oncology ward wasn't anything like as nice as the private maternity wing. It was grey, and there was a lot of coughing, and so much sadness.

The Christmas decorations looked even more miserable here than elsewhere. Men grey around the gills sat with tracheotomy holes in their throats. Bored children rolled around eating sweets and complaining. Here and there curtains were drawn around the beds, with who knew what mysterious events happening inside. There was a strong smell of Dettol and spilled tea and something else Polly didn't want to experience too intimately.

She glanced around, unwilling to let her eyes rest on any faces. Her heart was beating strongly, too strongly. She felt her hands trembling and tucked them into the pockets of her jeans.

Right at the end of the ward there was a bed underneath a window – it was the nicest, quietest spot on the six-bed ward, and instinctively Polly knew there was a reason why you got it.

The figure lying on the bed was asleep; long, very thin. Even though his hair was mostly grey, she could see quite clearly the sandy streak in it. She wished she'd taken a minute to run a comb through her own hair, although she was at least wearing make-up; if you didn't wear a full face of slap at all times, Rhonda asked you if you were sick, or had given up.

She halted, nervous and unsure. Carmel leaned over the bed.

'Tony,' she whispered. 'Tony dear.'

There was such tenderness in her voice – a lifetime's worth, Polly reflected.

The figure on the bed – you could see his hip bones through the thin sheets; it was extremely hot on the ward – stirred slightly. There was a drip above his head, presumably morphine. Polly hoped he wasn't in pain. That whatever was eating him from the inside was being tended to carefully and effectively; that he wouldn't be made to linger on in any way.

But she didn't feel anything beyond that. She didn't

feel the need to throw herself on the bed and shout 'Daddy! My daddy!' She barely knew how daddies worked. Instead she stood there, her hands plunged in her pockets, trying to compose herself; trying to make her face into the right kind of expression: concerned without being fake or weird. Her mouth twisted a little, and she bit the inside of her cheek.

'Tony,' said Carmel again, and he blinked and slowly opened his eyes.

They were the exact same shade of blue-green as Polly's own.

Polly shuffled a little closer, into his field of vision. Carmel gently picked up a pair of horn-rimmed glasses from the bedside table and fitted them round his pale, narrow head. He stared at Polly as if he were looking at a total stranger.

'Is it the nurse?'

His voice was a little quavery, but she could hear him well enough.

'No,' said Carmel, holding his hand. 'No, Tony. This is Polly.'

There was a long silence.

'Polly?' came the voice finally. It cracked a little.

'Yes,' said Carmel.

Tony drew a long breath. It took him a while; he wheezed slowly, in and out. It sounded absolutely horrible.

'Polly. Pauline?'

Polly nodded.

'Hello,' she said. She didn't know what to call him, so she didn't call him anything.

Those blue-green eyes blinked again. It was absurd. Of course, what else could a baby be made up of but the information from both its parents – a toe shape here, an eyebrow there? That was all there was. She thought once again of Kerensa's baby, then shook the image out of her mind. This wasn't the time.

'Nice to meet you,' she added, her own voice trembling.

Tony's veiny hand, with its protruding drip, waved feebly in the air in her direction. Polly, rather reluctantly, moved forward and put her own hand out. He grabbed it with slightly surprising force and she felt him squeeze. She glanced down and almost couldn't stifle her shock: the same square nails; the same very long forefinger. She had her father's hands.

'It's uncanny,' said Carmel. 'Sorry. It's why I couldn't stop staring at you. Sorry.'

Polly looked at her.

'Well,' Carmel went on. 'It's just how it is, but none of your . . . none of your siblings look quite as much like him.'

Polly couldn't do anything other than nod.

'I'm so sorry,' said Tony, his voice croaky. 'I . . . It was . . . '

'It's all right,' said Polly. 'I understand.'

And as she said it, she felt a weight fall off her; something she had barely realised had been heavy on her her entire life. As she looked at the wasted figure of the man in the bed, she realised he wasn't the perfect father figure she'd been dreaming of, that she'd wanted so very badly. Neither was he the bad bogeyman of her mother's imagination, the implacable enemy to be hated for ever. He was just a man who had made a mistake, exactly like the one Kerensa had made, more or less, and then had to live with it for the rest of his life.

It was just there, nothing you could change or prevent. Once upon a time, perhaps, it could have been made better, but not now. And that was okay. Well, it wasn't, but it had to be. Because it was all there was.

'Are you ... are you having a good life?' croaked Tony.

Polly nodded. 'Yes,' she said. She thought about Huckle and suppressed the thought that things might be unravelling at pace. 'Yes, I am having a good life. It wasn't always. Then I found out what I really wanted to do ...'

'You're the girl that makes bread, aren't you? I saw you in the paper.'

'I am the girl who makes bread,' agreed Polly.

'You should teach her to cook then, she's always been rubbish,' he said, grinning a slightly ghastly grin in Carmel's direction.

'Shut up you,' said Carmel, and Polly could see again the massive weight of affection that had obviously survived everything life could throw at it, still more or less shining brightly. Would she ever have that?

She tried to smile at him.

'Yes,' she said. 'I love what I do. It took me a while to

get there, and I'm massively overworked and exhausted all the time and I don't make any money and all that stuff, but I'm happier than I've ever been in my entire life.'

Tony nodded. 'Good,' he said. 'That's really good, isn't it, Carmel?'

Carmel smiled. 'She must have had a wonderful mother,' she said softly, and all three of them fell silent for a moment.

'Is she ... Do you want to meet the others?' said Tony hopefully, as if he knew already that he was asking too much.

'No,' said Polly. 'No. I don't think so. I have my life and they have theirs, and I wouldn't want to complicate matters. Complicate everyone's lives.'

'It was me who did that,' said Tony.

Polly took her hand back and stepped away from the bed.

'It was nice to meet you,' she said softly. 'But I'm going to go now.'

'Aye,' said Tony. 'Aye, yeah, that's all right. Of course.'

He looked at her, and his eyes were glistening with tears.

'Do you forgive me?'

Polly nodded. 'Of course,' she said.

'Thank you. Do you have little ones?'

'No.'

'Oh well. I know this will sound wrong, but ... you should, you know. It's ... Having a family ... I shouldn't be telling you this, but ... it's wonderful. It's a wonderful thing. A family of your own.'

Polly felt this was going too far.

'Goodbye,' she said.

Carmel jumped up. Her eyes were full of tears.

'Sorry about that,' she said, walking her to the ward door.

'It's all right,' said Polly stiffly. 'He was being honest. He chose you. And that's all right. He's lucky to have you.'

Carmel bit her lip.

'Thank you,' she said. 'Thank you for doing this for him. I know you didn't want to. It means ... It means so much.'

And instinctively she threw her arms around Polly, who stood, a tad reluctantly, then found herself hugging her back.

'Okay. Goodbye now,' said Polly. This would have to do. She turned.

At the end of the corridor, she heard a yell. It was Carmel, calling her name. She turned back.

'Sorry!' said Carmel. 'Sorry. Sorry to bother you, sorry to keep bothering you, I really am. But: can I ask you for one last thing? Sorry. I know it's too much. But it is Christmas ...'

Polly blinked and stood still, not saying anything.

'Could I ... could I possibly have a photograph of the two of you together?'

Polly nodded. 'Of course,' she said.

Their first ever photo. The first father-and-daughter photograph Polly had ever had.

She sat down on the bed feeling weird and awkward, with a stupid lump in her throat she couldn't dispel, and took her father's wizened hand fully in her own, grasped it, fingers interlaced, for the first and the very last time, and squeezed it, and he squeezed back as if they could connect with each other just here, just this one time, and then the photo was taken and it was time to go.

'Any time you need me,' said Carmel, 'come and find me. Here's my number. Anything. Any questions. Come and find me.'

And Polly turned and walked slowly out of the hospital, into the car park, where the first snow of the season was starting to fall; blanketing the ugly hospital buildings, covering the pain and sadness, turning the world fresh and white and new again, starting over with a clean slate.

Chapter Thirty-Six

Polly had picked up Nan the Van – which Reuben had kindly got a flunky to bring over when she'd explained she only had one mode of transport, and Nan was it. She drove slowly away from the hospital, the world changed in front of her eyes. The gently falling flakes turned into a flurry, then began to fall steadily, silently, covering the ground. The light was fading from the afternoon and Polly tried not to worry about how she would manage the causeway. She would get home somehow, back home to her puffin and her lighthouse and her oven, and she could figure everything else out later. Or maybe sooner.

Because the thing was, she guessed, you always thought you had time – time to fix the relationships that had broken down; to do all the things you thought you'd get round to; to finish everything, tie it up with a neat bow and that was it.

But life wasn't like that at all. Things festered for years.

Things that ought to be got over never were. Bitterness became a defining characteristic of people's lives. And she could see it happening. It had happened to her mother. It might happen to Kerensa and that little baby. And she understood why, at the end, her father had tried to make sure that it didn't happen to him.

She wasn't going to go through the same thing. She and Huckle had been so happy together. Could they get it back? Could they make it right?

She turned on the radio, which was playing jaunty Christmas music intercut with ominous snow warnings and suggestions that you didn't travel unless it was absolutely necessary. Polly ignored these. The A road was fine, the trails of the many cars in front of her making it easy to follow. She was not looking forward to the turn-off, though. The snow hadn't been forecast, so the gritters wouldn't have had a chance to get out. The problem was, unless she found a hotel before the turn-off – which she didn't have the money for – there was absolutely nothing between there and Mount Polbearne. If she did turn off, she was stuffed.

Her thoughts drifted to Huckle. What was he doing? What on earth was he thinking? Whatever else happened, she had to get home.

As the exit loomed, several things happened very quickly.

Lost in her thoughts, Polly had to indicate in a fluster. A huge truck behind her honked menacingly, which startled her, just as her telephone rang. As the van twisted towards the exit ramp, a tiny rabbit flashed out from the undergrowth and straight across her path; she caught a glimpse of the little pawprints in the fresh snow. Nan struggled to get purchase on the road, failed, lurched forward and headed straight down the hill towards the road at the bottom, which was thankfully empty, shooting straight across it and coming to rest, rocking menacingly, in the snowdrift that had already started to build on the opposite verge, just out of reach of the oncoming traffic.

Polly didn't realise she was screaming, nor that she had somehow in her panic pressed the answer button on her phone.

'It's all right, it's all right, it's all right!' she heard a desperate voice saying on the other end of the line. 'It's all right! It's going to be—'

'GAAAAA!'

'Polly! Polly! Are you there? What is it? What is it?'

Polly desperately tried to catch her breath, but it came in tearing sobs. The voice became more alarmed.

'Polly? Polly, what is it? What's happened?'

Finally she found the breath to speak, a great ripped-out gasp.

'Hu ... Huckle?'

'Yes. What happened? What's the matter? It wasn't because of me, was it? You haven't done anything stupid? Please tell me you're okay!'

Polly blinked and looked around. Nan the Van appeared to be slowly sinking sideways into the snowdrift.

'Nan ... the van came off the road,' she whispered. 'We're off the road. We're ... I don't know where ... '

'Oh my God,' said Huckle. 'Oh God. Are you all right? I told you to check the tyres.'

'You told me to check the tyres?!' exclaimed Polly. 'I just nearly died in a horrible accident and you're making sure that I know it was my own fault?'

'No, no. Sorry. I'm sorry. You gave me such a fright ... At first I thought you'd heard the news and were just upset about it – God knows we're all upset, so it could have been that, could have been anything ... Jesus. Are you all right?'

'I think so,' said Polly, trying to breathe out through her nose like she'd read somewhere, even though it felt weird. 'I think I might be slightly stuck.' She paused, trying to think straight. 'Where are you?'

'Didn't you get the news?'

'The news that you're back?'

'No, the news from the hospital.'

'What news? What's happening?'

'It's the baby,' said Huckle.

Polly didn't say anything.

'What?' she said finally. 'What? What's happened with the baby? You didn't ... '

'Of course not,' said Huckle crossly. 'No. No. The doctor came and looked at the baby ... I was just leaving, and calling to find out if you knew. Apparently there's something wrong with it.'

Chapter Thirty-Seven

It was as if a bell was tolling deep inside Polly's soul. Everything else fell away; all the little petty things, all the worries and concerns and jealousies and getting-bys, they all left, immediately, to be replaced by her deepest, darkest fears.

'Oh my God,' she said. 'Are you coming? It's filthy out here.'

The snow was falling more heavily than ever.

'Of course.'

'What's wrong with him?'

'I don't know. I think Kerensa was trying to get you. She sounded hysterical.'

Polly blinked. Oh God.

'Are you really stuck?' said Huckle.

'Yes,' said Polly. 'And there's nobody on the road. Nobody on the road at all.'

'Well you'll need me then, won't you? To pull you out.'

'Can the motorbike do that?' said Polly sceptically.

'EXCUSE ME,' said Huckle. 'Don't diss the bike when you're upside down in a ditch.'

Polly turned up the heating, but it didn't make a lot of difference.

'Hurry up,' she said, meaning it. 'Hurry up. I need you, Huckle.'

Over an hour later, Polly was still sitting stock still, too scared to try and get out of the van, even as she could feel the snow piling up around her; too petrified with fear. She had tried to call Kerensa but couldn't get through, and Reuben's number just went to voicemail.

But the baby had been perfect. Utterly perfect. She'd seen him; held him. Everything had been fine.

She thought again. Babies could have fits; or the doctors could have done all those tests and come back with something awful. Cystic fibrosis or spina bifida or any of those terrible, terrible things that haunted parents' worst nightmares.

She was trapped in a cycle of desperate fear, huddling deeper and deeper into her coat, wondering where on earth Huckle was – it shouldn't be taking him this long. There was only one exit to Mount Polbearne. Had he tried to get that bloody motorbike over the causeway? Had he just skidded off into the water, lost to the sea, like so many boats around the ragged Cornish coastline;

so many men beneath the waves in high winds and weather?

A fragment of an old song about a shipwreck came to her, 'And many was the fine feather beds floating on the foam/ And many was the little lords' sons who never did come home.'

Where was he? Where was *she*? The road was quiet: the occasional passing lights of a traveller trundling on through the darkening afternoon and the whirling flakes, but they didn't stop.

She huddled deeper in her seat. Perhaps everything was over now, everything was done, and there was nothing to do but stay here. Everything had gone wrong and she'd lost the only thing she'd ever wanted and . . .

TAP TAP TAP!

Polly realised she was sinking into a stupor; that she was half asleep. She didn't know where the noise was coming from.

TAP TAP TAP!

She glanced around blearily. Something or someone was tapping on the window. Was it a tree? Where was she?

She leaned over and wound down the window. There, hovering outside, beating his little wings frantically, was Neil. He *eep*ed furiously at her.

'Neil!' said Polly, feeling a stupid smile spread across her face. Why did she feel so weird?

'Polly!' came a voice, and charging up behind Neil

was a headlamp, and behind *that* was Huckle's face. Polly stared at him woozily.

'I thought you were dead,' she said, smiling at him in a funny way.

Huckle wrenched open the van door and pulled her out, shoving her unceremoniously on to the ground. The shock of the cold air felt like someone had poured a bucket of cold water over her head. She coughed and choked on the freezing snow bank.

'Oh my God!' Huckle was saying. 'The stink in there! There's some gas feeding back; you must have bumped something when you came to rest. Oh my God, Polly! You could have poisoned yourself! You can't ... I can't believe ... It's a deathtrap, that van! Everyone's been telling you that!'

Polly shook her head.

'Didn't you feel weird? Woozy?'

'Yes,' said Polly, frowning. 'It felt nice.'

'Oh God,' said Huckle, pulling her to him, then letting her go again as she suddenly had to turn away and vomit into the snow. He handed her some water.

'Jesus, Polly.' He was almost as white as she was. 'JESUS. Shit. When did everything go so wrong?'

Polly shook her head. 'I don't know,' she said tearfully. 'I don't know. I wish I did so I could go back and fix it.'

'You didn't do anything,' said Huckle, holding her. 'It's not your fault, my darling. It's not your fault. Oh my God, you're shivering.'

Huckle flagged down a car, finally, and a very kind lady called Maggie let Polly sit in it whilst he rigged up the motorbike to pull Nan the Van out of the snowdrift. He parked her up carefully by the side of the road, with all the windows open, then thanked the woman.

'Where are you going?' she asked.

'We have to get to the hospital in Plymouth,' Huckle explained.

'In that thing?' she said, indicating the motorbike. She was a teacher, of the very nicest sort, and had a way of telling you what to do without beating around the bush. 'Don't be ridiculous. Get in the car. I'll take you.'

'It's a Mini,' said Huckle. 'I'm not sure it'll do much better than—'

'Get in,' she said.

Neil flew in and sat on Polly's lap. Maggie stared at him for a bit.

'Ah,' said Huckle.

'Is he going to poo in the car?' she asked, as they took to the cleared, gritted A road.

'Can't promise he won't,' said Huckle, grinning apologetically, and luckily, it turned out that Maggie had a soft spot for smiling young men.

Chapter Thirty-Eight

Polly wanted to run straight to the private wing, but Huckle stopped and made her drink a strong coffee from the vending machine. Then he looked into her eyes.

'Are you okay?'

'Apart from the nine weird things that have happened today,' said Polly. She gave herself a quick internal check. 'I think I am,' she said. She looked up at him. 'Oh my, I must be the most bedraggled mess.'

'If you're thinking *that*, you must be on the mend,' said Huckle.

'That's obviously a yes, then,' said Polly, feeling her damp hair in dismay.

Huckle took her in his arms.

'Oh Polly Waterford,' he said. 'You are lovely to me in every way.'

'I just threw up,' said Polly.

'Yeah, okay, forget about that bit,' said Huckle.

'Because I don't think you're hearing what I'm trying to say to you.'

'That you aren't going to leave me any more because of not telling you about Kerensa?'

Huckle shook his head.

'I wasn't ever going to leave you,' he said. 'It's just ... you know. I've been cheated on in the past, and it was so hard. It hurt so much. And I thought I knew you so well, and I panicked. But you can't ... you can't ever know another person. Not through and through. People have their reasons for things. And you can choose to love them for who they are, and, well, that's the deal. That's how it is. I understand why you did what you did. I'd rather you hadn't ... No. I wish the entire thing hadn't happened.'

Polly nodded.

'But I can live with it. I can.'

She laid her head on his shoulder and let out an enormous juddering sigh.

'I love you so much,' she said.

'We're going to have to love each other,' said Huckle soberly. 'Because we have to be there for Reuben and Kerensa. When they need us. Which I think starts now.'

Holding hands, and dreading what they were about to discover, they moved towards the lift, both of them trying not to dwell on the worst. That beautiful, innocent little baby. That something could be wrong with him, that something could have happened ... it was horrifying. So unfair. So wrong, that a baby could be born to pain.

The lift took forever to arrive. Up in the private wing, the great displays of winter flowers in the corridors seemed to mock them, as did the balloons and gift baskets outside Kerensa's door.

Polly and Huckle glanced at one another, squeezed hands tightly, and knocked.

Inside the room, things were eerily quiet. In fact, given that the room contained Reuben, Kerensa, Jackie, Merv, Rhonda and a brand-new baby, things were utterly, bizarrely quiet.

'Hey,' whispered Polly. 'We came as soon as we could.'

'Any trouble getting here?' asked Merv, who was staring out at the heavy snowfall still coming down over the garden.

'Neh,' said Polly, deciding that now was not the time to explain. She turned towards the bed. The baby was lying peacefully asleep in his bassinet. Kerensa, white-faced, didn't meet her eyes.

Reuben was pacing up and down.

'Well,' he said to Polly and Huckle. 'Now you know.'

Polly went cold.

'Yup, now it's out. Now I'm going to be a laughing stock all over the world. Oh good. People laughing at

Reuben Finkel. It doesn't matter how much money I have or how well I do, I just can't get away from it, can I, Pa?'

He spat the last part bitterly.

'C'mon now, Reuben,' said Merv, but Reuben shook him off.

'It's your fault,' he said.

'It's nobody's fault,' said Merv. 'Seriously, son.'

Polly was frozen to the spot. This wasn't going to be nice.

'All I wanted was for my son to be perfect. Is that too much to ask?'

Polly stared desperately at Kerensa. This couldn't be all about Reuben, surely. He couldn't just go on and on like this. There was a baby to think of. A mother to think of.

And then Kerensa did the most surprising thing.

She winked at Polly.

At first Polly thought – she was still feeling a little bleary – that she might have imagined it. But no. It was definitely there.

And was that a little colour stealing back into Kerensa's face?

Huckle grasped the nettle.

'Reuben, what's up? What's wrong with little Herschel?'

'Um,' said Kerensa. 'Actually I think you'll find that's not his name.'

Huckle ignored her and stepped forward. 'What is it, bro?'

Reuben looked up at him.

'I can't believe it,' he said. 'Seriously, dude. I can't believe it.'

'What?'

A nurse bustled in.

'Oh look at you all,' she said. 'Listen, there's lots that can be done, okay?'

'Can you ... show them?' said Reuben.

'Reuben,' said Merv. 'Is this necessary?'

'Yeah,' said Reuben. 'Yeah, it is.'

Polly's teeth were chattering. Actually chattering out loud.

The nurse shrugged and picked up the baby like he was a little football. To Polly's eyes she handled him quite roughly, but then she herself was hardly versed in picking up brand-new infants. She'd have to assume the woman knew what she was doing.

She unwrapped his swaddling, then his fresh organic cotton babygro. The baby didn't like that at all and started bawling lustily. His hair really was very dark.

His nappy looked ridiculously large on the tiny form. Polly had never seen such a new baby naked; she hadn't realised they were like tadpoles really, all head, with kind of little flippery arms and legs.

'Okay,' said the nurse. 'Well here it is.'

Polly was gripping Huckle's hand so hard it was going white. They peered over.

Right across the baby's tiny bottom was a bright streak

of red; a huge strawberry mark that made him look as if he'd been spanked.

Polly's hand shot to her mouth, and for just a second she was unutterably terrified that she might laugh.

'A *birthmark*?' said Huckle, astonished. 'You called us out here because you're worried about a birthmark?'

'Yeah,' said Reuben. 'Not just any old birthmark, though. A huge, ass-obliterating satellite of a birthmark! Just like I had and my dad has. Thanks, Pa!'

'You should have told Kerensa!' said Merv, his hand drifting behind his back. 'I told Rhonda!'

'No, Ma found it!' said Reuben. 'They couldn't get rid of them in those days.' He turned to Kerensa, whose hand was also over her mouth. 'Aw, honey, I'm so sorry. I had mine lasered off when I got my legal emancipation. So I'm not a fricking lizard skin like Pops. You've been awesome about this,' he added tenderly.

Kerensa couldn't do anything except wave her free hand about. She was half smiling, half crying, as was Polly.

'It's nothing!' scolded the nurse. 'You have to stop getting your knickers in a twist about it. He's a lovely healthy baby.'

'Why didn't it show up on the scan?' asked Huckle, probably more crossly than he intended.

'Well it wouldn't. Plus he's a very wriggly baby,' said the nurse. 'I wonder who he gets that from.'

Reuben stopped fidgeting with his phone for long enough to look up.

'Huh?' he said. 'Yeah, whatever.'

The nurse expertly rebuttoned the baby into his babygro and swaddled him so tightly he couldn't move. Polly thought he would hate it, but in fact the little body relaxed and turned into a parcel, and the nurse handed him straight back to Kerensa, who took him cheerfully and snuggled him right up the front of her nightie, as if she was a kangaroo and he her joey.

They didn't say anything in the lift. They didn't say anything to each other in the long hallway, quiet now with as many beds as possible empty so people could be with their families for Christmas; plus it was late, after the normal visiting hours that applied to the rest of the hospital. This was just them.

They didn't say anything until they finally reached the end of the corridor and the automatic doors opened silently into the whirling wonderland beyond, the flakes illuminated by the lurid orange of the hospital's external lights but the ugly car park and the squat buildings hidden by the beautiful soft white. The trees beyond were lit dimly by the glow from the city, and had transformed into a Narnian wood, and without a word to one another they ran towards it.

Once safely inside, both of them screamed, 'YESSSS!' at the top of their lungs, then grabbed one another and whirled each other round and round in the snow until they were pink-cheeked and sparkling-eyed with delight, and bursting with happiness. Huckle crushed Polly to him and she laughed, and Neil fluttered down from a tree he'd been exploring and watched them jump up and down with joy, then joined in.

At last the cold drove them back inside, both of them beaming. They went to the lobby to call a cab.

'Where are we going?' said Polly.

'Aha!' said Huckle.

'What?'

'You'll see,' he said. 'Stay here, I'm going to make a call.'

Polly waited, her heart completely full. Oh, the mind-bending, world-crushing relief. She took out her nearly-dead phone and texted Kerensa. She didn't know what to say, so in the end she just put five hearts and loads of kisses, then some more hearts and a very small emoti-con of the closest thing she could find. That was going to have to do.

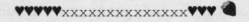

She glanced up and back into the main body of the hospital, wondering where Huckle had gone.

And that was when she saw them. A large group of people walking along the corridor, quietly, slowly. They had their arms around one another, as if they were consoling each other. One, a woman around Polly's age, was weeping, and a man was holding her close. There were a couple of children, walking solemnly, as if they knew something bad was happening but weren't quite clear as to what it was. Someone was carrying a very small child, fast asleep, nuzzled against his mother's neck.

And bringing up the rear, weeping copiously and supported by two older men – her brothers, by the look of them – was Carmel.

Polly shrank back, hidden by the vending machine, watching the sad parade of people walk past.

They looked – well, they looked normal. Nice. Mixed race, married to black and white, just a totally average, supportive, well-dressed family.

She turned away, in case Carmel saw her face, but Carmel was bowed over and blinded by tears.

Tony must have died, thought Polly. This was it. The father she had never had was no more. The kind of father he must have been, she supposed, she could see in the utterly distraught faces of the men and women passing by.

She stood stock still and watched, feeling incredibly sad and strange, as the party made its way out into the freezing night.

'Okay!' said Huckle, bouncing round the corner. 'Madam, your carriage awaits. Hey hey!'

A cab had pulled up outside.

'Where are we going?' said Polly, glancing around the car park, but the family had dispersed.

'Just get in,' said Huckle, winking at the driver. Neil followed close behind.

Polly desperately needed to talk to him about her father, but she didn't get a chance, as Huckle was bouncing up and down in his seat and talking about how amazing it was, and how great things were, and weren't they lucky, and surely Kerensa would never, ever do anything like that again, and how now they would all appreciate every moment . . .

Polly looked at him.

'Yes,' she said quietly. 'Yes. I want to appreciate every moment.'

Just at that moment the car swung off the deserted road and through the massive gates of an enormous stately home.

'Where are we?' said Polly suspiciously.

Huckle smiled.

'Ah,' he said. 'Hang it. Sometimes you have to do these things. It's too dangerous to go home. This is the nearest hotel to the hospital.'

'Yes, but it's . . .'

The gravel drive seemed a mile long. The trees were bent over with the weight of snow. A white winter moon shone through the clouds.

'It totally is.'

'We can't afford this!'

'Sssh,' said Huckle.

'And I'm wearing a pinafore!'

'Yeah, yeah, you are.'

Polly sat up in alarm. 'What's up?'

'I called them and explained the situation,' said Huckle. 'It's either this or a night sheltering in Accident and Emergency pretending we've got broken wrists.'

A liveried man rushed out to open the taxi door, and they were ushered through a grand entrance into the most ridiculous stately home. There were precious antiques and oil paintings everywhere, and the wallpaper was made out of some sort of material. It was stunning. Polly looked round and fiddled nervously with her pinafore buttons.

'Now, Mr Freeman.' The receptionist came forward smiling. 'We heard all about you being caught in the storm. We know about your clothes situation, so if you need anything, just let us know and we'll see what we can do. Also, we've taken the liberty of upgrading you to a suite.'

Polly turned on Huckle.

'What is this?'

'Nothing!' said Huckle. 'I just said we'd had some fabulous news and could they look after us.'

'Pets are welcome here aren't they?'

Neil pretended to be lifting his foot to examine his claws and not eating the tinsel. 'Um,' said the receptionist who was very nice and absolutely desperate to get home.

'Sure! Also,' she confided, 'we had a massive group coming tonight and they've all had to call off because of the weather. So you are definitely in luck. Enjoy.'

She glanced back at Huckle.

'I like your boyfriend's accent,' she said.

'So do I,' said Polly.

The room was absolutely immense, with a four-poster bed in the middle of it. Polly nearly cried with happiness when she saw it. There was an enormous claw-footed bath in the bathroom, which had a heated floor and two incredibly fluffy robes hanging up, with slippers.

'Oh my God,' said Polly. Huckle grinned. He knew how much she absolutely loved a bath, and while she turned on the taps and filled it full of foam from a selection of expensive smellies, he went and poured them both very large gin and tonics from the minibar.

As Polly wallowed blissfully in the endless superhot water, sipping her G&T, Huckle knelt down beside the bath.

'You know,' he said, 'I don't like doing it very often. But being a workaholic like you sometimes really pays dividends.'

'Your meeting went well?'

He frowned. 'Better than well. I always work better when I'm miserable. It's so weird.'

'What happened?'

'I've sold the new range to a whole chain of beauticians. Fresh honeycomb wax, all local, all organic.'

Polly looked at him in astonishment.

'Seriously?'

'Seriously. Common or garden wax is no longer good enough for the tender mimsies of the south-west.'

'So you're paying for this place with pubes?'

Huckle grinned. 'Is it worth it?'

Polly beamed. 'Oh my God, yes! You clever thing! Yes!'

'Just don't ask me to work like that every week. It's exhausting!'

After she'd soaked for long enough, but before she passed out from utter fatigue, they got into bed and ordered far too much from room service, then she told him everything that had happened with her father, and he, in his perfect, gentle Huckle way, simply listened; properly listened to everything she had to say, in the way she'd missed so very much.

When she was finished, he didn't ask how she was feeling or say anything stupid about closure. He just said, 'Oh.' And 'That sounds hard.'

And Polly nodded, and thought about the odd counter-balance of weights in the universe – how bad things could happen, and sometimes wonderful, wonderful things could happen, but you weren't always fated to be in the heart of the story; sometimes it simply wasn't about you; you didn't always get all the answers.

And some days, when you were lying in a four-poster

bed, with the person you loved more than anything else in the world asking if you would like more club sandwich, and should you curl up and watch a film together, and saying that you might have to stay tomorrow too because everything and everyone would be snowed in ...

Well. Sometimes that was all right in itself. Sometimes that was more than enough. Sometimes it was everything.

Chapter Thirty-Nine

Polly woke on Boxing Day feeling happy and sad at the same time and didn't know why, then she blinked and realised.

Outside, the beautiful grounds of the hotel were completely covered in a thick blanket of snow. Amazingly, someone had come in the night and taken away her clothes, and returned them laundered and folded up in tissue paper. This was, she thought, as nuts as all the extraordinary things that had happened over the last couple of days.

They ate a ridiculously huge breakfast, then went for a wander around the grounds, kicking up snow with their feet. Polly had spoken to Jayden, who was still trying to talk Flora round, and now she was fretting about the old ladies, who might not be able to get down the treacherous cobbled pathways to the bakery or Muriel's little supermarket. She would need to go back soon, to make deliveries to her elderly customers, who relied on her. There were always plenty of emergency supplies on Mount Polbearne, because of its often sticky winters, but it was good just to have a quick check in on everyone, make sure they were all all right.

'Hush,' said Huckle. 'It's Boxing Day. Everyone in Britain has far more in their house than they can possibly eat in a million years. Everyone will be fine for a few hours. Please. Trust me. Relax.'

So they walked in the beautiful, sunny, snowy grounds, talking of this and that: of Huckle's new business line, how he was going to have to outsource production even more, beyond Dave, his regular bee man, and how it ought to work; and of what Kerensa and Reuben would call the baby – Huckle was fairly sure Herschel would win, and Polly accused him of only liking it because it sounded like Huckle.

Then there was a pause as they walked, and Polly said, 'I am so sorry,' and Huckle said, 'Me too.'

Then Polly said, 'Will that do?' and Huckle thought, just for a brief moment, about bringing up how the hotel might be a nice place to get married one of these days, but decided they'd been through enough for now. He was so relieved that they were back, that they were Polly and Huckle again, that he was determined never to rock the boat about anything, not even when Neil had made pancake-butter footprints across the posh restaurant table and the maître d' had pulled a face that Polly had patently ignored. No. Not even then.

He tugged her braids under the big woollen hat.

'Of course.'

And they squeezed hands again, and thought they had had a very narrow escape after all.

After a while Huckle said, 'Do you think you might go to the funeral?'

Polly blinked.

'No,' she said. 'I met him. I kind of understand – I do understand. The stuff people do in their twenties ... they're not grown up really. And in the end ... Well. He learned his lesson, didn't he? He went back and raised his family and he obviously really loved them and was a wonderful father. I was his mistake, but that wasn't my fault. My mum could maybe have dealt with it slightly differently, but it was a great love affair for her, and it wasn't for him. And that's nobody's fault either; sometimes these things just don't shake down. But no,' she said. 'I don't think I need to hear lots of people stand up and say what a great guy he was, you know?'

Huckle nodded. 'Of course.'

They walked on in silence.

'What about his children?' he asked.

Polly thought back with a pang to the close-knit-looking group of smartly dressed people. How nice it must be, when things were really tough, to have people to lean on like that. She'd never known what it was like to have brothers and sisters. Huckle's brother was a bit of a rogue, but he was family. She would have liked something like that.

'Mmm,' she said. 'They all ... I'm sure they all have their own lives. I'm the last thing they need to complicate matters.'

'Yes, well, wait till they discover you make the world's most awesome bread. You'll be welcomed with open arms,' said Huckle cheerfully.

Polly shook her head. 'God, no. What if they think I'm there to cause trouble, or to get at his will?'

'Do you think there's any money?'

Polly shrugged. 'Dunno. Don't care.' She frowned. 'I wonder if my mum will keep brooding.'

'Maybe she'll have to get a job,' said Huckle.

'Huck!'

'What? There's nothing wrong with her. Do her good to get out of the house a bit.'

'She's fragile,' said Polly.

'Maybe she's like that because everyone's been tiptoeing around her for so long.'

'She looked after her own parents very well.'

'That's true,' allowed Huckle. 'She should look after other people's. For money.'

'Hmm,' said Polly.

They'd made a full circle of the grounds and were back at the grand entrance. Polly was looking longingly at the posh indoor spa arrangement.

'I'd love a swim.'

And as if by magic, a swimsuit in her size was found, and they went and swam under an indoor waterfall and bathed in clouds of puffy steam in the steam room and giggled in the jacuzzi, and despite the fact that they spent less than twelve hours at the beautiful country house hotel, it was one of the nicest holidays Polly had ever had in her life.

Chapter Forty

The snow was settling in, possibly for a long stay, but the sun was out, the roads were clear and there was hardly any traffic – people were obviously staying in, settling down for the lovely hazy days between Christmas and New Year with chocolate and liqueurs and a general sense of having nowhere to go and nothing to do except a jigsaw and some audio books.

Polly and Huckle took a cab to Nan the Van, which was still parked safely by the side of the road. When Polly turned the key in the ignition, amazingly the engine roared into life first time, and she climbed behind the wheel while Huck went to start the motorbike. Before they headed off, Polly called Kerensa, who announced cheerfully that she was coming home with Lowin, whereupon Reuben yelled, 'Herschel!' in the background and a squabble commenced, which sounded exactly like Kerensa and Reuben getting back to normal.

'Are you sure you should be coming home so soon?' said Polly.

'Oh yes,' said Kerensa, a sparkle in her voice. 'I know most people are meant to feel a bit tired and washed out after childbirth. But I feel oddly good.'

'Because my baby is awesome,' came the voice in the background. 'Totally the most awesome.'

Polly smiled down the phone.

'My godson too,' she said.

And still the snow came down.

Polly started making batches of bread every morning and delivering it to the elderly of the village, and eventually, when people kept catching her on her rounds, to just about everybody else as well. She'd given Jayden some time off – he rather looked like he needed it – and when she finished in the bakery, she headed back to the lighthouse, where they kept the stove running day and night for once, keeping the sitting room at the top of the house warm and cosy, and heating the bedroom too.

And when the day's work was done – for Huckle had a lot to do too, with the business taking off – they ate buns and crackers and cheese and drank champagne and lazed in bed, watching films and looking at the snow coming down and listening to reports recommending that people didn't travel unless it was absolutely necessary, and smugly chinked their glasses together because they didn't want to travel at all.

Reuben and Kerensa were, if the hourly photographs were anything to go by, completely immersed in a baby-moon of gigantic proportions, cuddling and cooing and sending loved-up pictures of their three hands or feet, or of them all snuggled up in a bed the size of Polly's mother's front room, beaming mightily and joyously, Reuben fully back to his bouncy King of the World persona; the baby looking more like him every day.

Kerensa looked exquisite; a large, soft, beaming earth mother, the drawn look gone from her eyes. It helped that the baby was a perfect eater and sleeper – according to his father – and that they had absolutely oodles of help around the place, but regardless, she was a changed person; back to the fun, confident, wonderful best friend Polly had always known, and she was entirely thrilled for her.

Polly phoned her mum every day – which she didn't normally do – and somehow, because they'd had to throw everything up in the air, because they'd had to talk about things that nobody had ever wanted to talk about, she finally felt she understood a huge great tranche of her life that had formerly been a mystery to her. And because she understood this, it was as if things had become lighter, easier between them; as if her mother was no longer holding up massive barriers, desperately trying to control what Polly knew and how she felt.

She thought of her dad from time to time, with a slight air of melancholy. But it was what it was. Nobody had a life untouched by sadness, not in the real world. And for now, looking at Huckle playing ping-pong football with Neil in front of the fire, his long body stretched out, his shaggy hair glinting golden in the firelight, she felt that in so many areas of her life, she was so blessed that she couldn't complain. Lots of people didn't have what she had. And she had so very much.

She knew that at some point next year they would get married, but that would be next year. She could think about the organising and the costs and everything then. It would be lovely. Fine. Small. Just what they wanted. She didn't need to get superstitious about it any more, terrified about it, or just worried in general because she'd never known how it was meant to go. It would just be her and Huckle. She wasn't desperately looking forward to it, but it would be fine. It really would. Marriage, babies; whatever came next. She was ready for it all.

She came and lay next to Huckle and helped him blow the ping-pong ball about, which drove Neil bananas. He'd *eep* and hop and get so cross they'd stop playing, whereupon he'd flutter down and push the ball straight towards them until they agreed to play with him again.

She cuddled up against Huckle's warm body on the rug, relishing the incredibly unusual feeling of having nothing – absolutely nothing, apart from the morning run – planned for the rest of the week. It was too snowy to go out; there was no need to take any exercise, or organise or arrange anything. It was just hours of clear nothingness ahead, with little more to do than make love, watch films, eat Quality Street and drink fizz. That would do.

Chapter Forty-One

Early on New Year's Eve, after Polly had done her rounds and was crawling back into bed, the phone rang deep in the bowels of the lighthouse.

'Kill them,' said Huckle. 'Whoever it is. Seriously. I'm not answering the phone.'

They let it ring out. It went on for ages and ages. Huckle groaned.

'No,' he said. 'No. Everything is exactly how I wanted it.'

Polly checked her phone, but as usual she couldn't get a signal.

'It will be a sales call,' she said. 'Don't worry. I've spoken to Mum today. Let's just ignore them and they'll go away.'

The ringing stopped as she smiled sleepily and cuddled up to Huckle even more closely. 'See,' she said.

'You have magic powers,' said Huckle, leaning in to

kiss her. The phone started again. It sounded oddly more insistent than before.

'Go away!' said Huckle.

Polly made a groaning noise. 'Oh God, I'd better answer it.'

'If it's Reuben or Kerensa, can you tell them we're out of their ridiculous lives now? Please?'

'Why am I going downstairs anyway?' said Polly, wincing as the freezing air on the stairwell hit her.

'Because you'll enjoy it so much more when you come back into the warm,' said Huckle. 'I'll build us a nest.'

Polly smiled and inched her way downstairs to pick up the heavy black Bakelite phone.

'Polly!'

'No,' said Polly.

'What do you mean, no?' said Reuben, offended.

'Whatever it is,' said Polly, 'I'm not doing it. I'm kind of on holiday, which also includes feeding everyone in town. So. No.'

'Maybe I'm not calling you to get you to do anything for me.'

'Okay, so what is it?' said Polly.

'Ah,' said Reuben.

'NO!' said Polly. 'Absolutely not. No. I'm not doing it.'

There was a pause.

'Polls . . . '

'No!'

'Because the thing is,' said Reuben, 'you know I agreed

to pay for you to cater Christmas? Well actually, technically speaking, Christmas morning and that box day thing you have after Christmas . . . '

'Christmas morning when you were at the hospital because your wife was giving birth and I was driving your mother-in-law?'

'Yeah,' said Reuben. 'You see, you weren't technically there.'

'That wasn't my fault!' said Polly. 'That was your baby decided to come early!'

'Yeah, nevertheless . . . ' said Reuben.

'NO!'

'Because, you know, that puffin sanctuary is looking mighty hard up . . . '

It was absolutely freezing downstairs in the little office. Ice patterns had formed on the windows. Huckle had cleared the path down the stone steps to the harbour every morning, but the snow was still piling up. It was unusual for quite so much to lie on the island; normally the wind and the salt in the air cleared it quickly. But this year they were totally inundated.

Polly thought with some sadness about the *Back to the Future* triple bill they'd had scheduled for that afternoon. And then she thought of all the puffins that would be absolutely decimated if left to their own devices in Cornish waters. She sighed.

'What do you need?'

'I've got all the ingredients here,' said Reuben. 'Just

come over. Say hi to everyone. Herschel is dying to see you.'

'Is that how it's going to go?' said Polly. 'You're going to use the baby to guilt me every time you want a sandwich until the end of time?'

'He is your only godson.'

Huckle crept down behind her with the duvet pulled around him.

'Work?' he said crossly.

'Bring Huckle,' said Reuben authoritatively down the phone.

'No!' said Huckle, but it was too late. Reuben had already hung up.

'Oh for heaven's sake,' said Polly. 'Seriously. I don't think being friends with those two is remotely good for us. And I don't even know if we can get there.'

Huckle glanced out of the window.

'I don't think that's going to be an issue,' he said.

A tiny dot in the sky grew larger and larger and eventually came into focus, the noise growing louder and louder.

'He sent the *helicopter*?' said Polly. 'This is utterly ridiculous. Honestly. For a few pastries!'

'The best pastries,' said Huckle, and Polly rolled her eyes.

The helicopter touched down carefully on the harbour front, which Polly was sure was entirely illegal. The snow had stopped, and it was a bright, freezing, crunchy day;

a beautiful day in fact. Which didn't change the fact that she didn't want to be out in it at all.

The pilot beckoned to them to hurry up, and Polly pulled on a coat and grabbed her bag. Neil hopped up to the helicopter to have a look at it – he obviously thought it was a really big puffin – and Polly let him come inside. Huckle looked grumpy, then followed her out of the house.

'This is annoying,' he said. 'Because obviously Reuben is being a total pain in the arse, but I've always really wanted to go in a helicopter.'

'Me too,' said Polly. They grinned at each other as the pilot gave them both a set of headphones and strapped them in, then off they went.

They held hands as the helicopter lurched sideways and they circled the lighthouse once; it was odd to see it veer away below them at an angle that felt quite close to being in the sea, which was beating up against the rocks with white-crested waves. There were very few fishing boats out today; even the men were taking a little time off to reconnect with their families at Christmas.

Mount Polbearne from above, under its mantle of snow, looked like a postcard, the little rambling cottages and streets jammed up against each other, tumbling over one another, all the way down the cobbles to the busy harbour, and Polly snapped some pictures on her phone.

She could see Muriel's shop, still resolutely open when the rest of the world was taking a break. She saw Patrick out walking one of the stray dogs he seemed to collect around him at all times – he couldn't bear to let an animal go to the pound or anywhere it might be put down, so often had the most motley collection of fleabags around his heels. She saw two of the toddlers of the town, done up like little Michelin men in their winter zip-up outfits, tumbling and playing with stones on the beach, whilst their parents clutched their arms tightly around themselves and – from the look of it – shot evil glances at the door of the Little Beach Street Bakery for being shut when they clearly needed hot chocolate now more than ever.

Then the helicopter turned and flew over the sea – Mount Polbearne was a proper island this morning, cut off completely, its own little world, and Polly felt, as she often did, a little pang for leaving it, even if it was only for the day.

'I've had worse commutes,' she told Huckle, who smiled back, enjoying the trip as much as she was.

They flew over the mainland of Cornwall, its rocky crags giving way to fertile fields, now all laid out in white stripes and white hedges; tangles of woodland as old as the legends of the land King Arthur once strode through silent under their blanket of snow; creatures deep in the undergrowth below. An owl searching for field mice glanced up at them as they passed above. The few cars on the roads looked like toys; horses turned out loose in their fields started a little at the noise of the helicopter, which made Polly feel guilty.

Away from the coastal towns, it felt like the beautiful county was spread out below for them alone; almost no people, just the soft, silent countryside they had both taken so much to their hearts, and Huckle squeezed her hand tightly, and she returned it, as the sound of a church bell reached them through the roar, and then the northern tip of the county came into view on the horizon and the helicopter turned towards the great house on the top of the cliff, Reuben's mansion, with its huge H painted on the ground. Reuben, Kerensa and the baby were out front, waving furiously.

'Okay, ready to go,' said Polly as they landed and thanked the pilot. Neil hopped around with a confused look on his face. Probably slightly noisier flying than he'd been used to.

Reuben and Kerensa looked utterly delighted; Kerensa far better than any woman who'd given birth less than a week ago had the right to. Baby Herschel-Lowin was sleeping happily in his father's arms. Rhonda and Merv also came out to greet them. This felt odd; Polly had expected to be hustled into the kitchen to start getting on with things.

'What's up?' she said.

Everyone was beaming at them in a slightly peculiar way, especially Kerensa. She and Reuben exchanged glances. Reuben's staff were also lined up out front, in a weird, presidential visit kind of a way.

'So anyway,' said Kerensa, 'I was trying to ... we were

trying to find a way to say thank you. For your support. For everything you've done for us over the years. To give you a Christmas present.'

'I should say now,' said Reuben, 'that this was mostly a way for Kerensa to keep shopping when she was all miserable about being pregnant.'

'Shut up,' said Kerensa, beaming happily at him.

'What's going on?' said Polly, feeling nervous.

Kerensa came up and took both their hands.

'Look,' she said. 'You absolutely don't have to do this if you don't want to.'

'Do what?' said Polly with suspicion. Kerensa beamed and pulled her inside.

The house had once again been totally transformed. White orchids and lilies lined the entrance hall, their heavy scent hanging amongst the smell of cranberries and oranges that had filled the house throughout the Christmas season. There were runs of flowers up and down the circular banister. And ahead were rows of white seats with bows on the back, laid out in front of the huge conservatory . . .

There was a long silence.

'Oh,' said Polly, in deep shock. It couldn't be. They couldn't possibly mean . . .

Kerensa looked at her.

'Because you see,' she said, so excited she could barely get the words out. 'Well. I wanted to thank you. For. You know. Everything. And so did lots of other people. And I know you were busy and didn't want fuss and don't like buying stuff and don't have any money ... '

'Thanks,' said Polly.

'And so I thought ... when everything was really tough ... I thought, why don't we do it for you! Then you'll be all married and you can just get on with your lives.'

'I can't get married!' said Polly. 'I need to lose half a stone and get everything arranged and grow my nails and ... ' She petered out.

'Of course you don't have to,' said Kerensa, looking slightly concerned. 'I mean, there's a few people coming, but we can just have like a New Year's party.'

'What do you mean, a few people?' said Polly, feeling panicky.

'Well. Obviously all our old crowd from school ... and your college crowd ... and your mum ... and ... Well, I wasn't sure who to ask from the village, so I just invited everyone.'

'Everyone?'

'Well, yeah.'

'You invited every single person in the entire village?'

'They won't all come,' said Kerensa uncertainly.

'They will,' said Polly. 'Oh my God. Oh. No. Kerensa ... I mean ... I mean, it's a fun idea and ... I mean, I don't know how you could possibly want to do this a week after having a baby ... '

'Because I have the most awesome wife and baby in the world,' said Reuben smugly. 'They can do anything.'

317

'Yeah, right,' said Polly. 'But this is just ... it's just ... '

Caterers arrived with a massive ice swan. They all stopped and watched it pass.

'Can't you marry Jayden and Flora instead? They're definitely up for it.'

Kerensa's face fell.

'Oh,' she said. 'I'm so sorry. I thought ... I thought it would be an amazing idea. I thought you guys would be absolutely delighted. You know, to not have to worry about the stress and the cost and everything.'

'Stop talking about how skint we are,' said Polly. 'Look, I'm sorry, Kerensa, I know you meant well, but I didn't ... I mean, we wouldn't ever want a big thing ... '

She paused.

'Are Huckle's parents here?'

Kerensa didn't say anything. Polly swore. Then she turned to look at Huckle.

'This is awkward, eh?' she whispered. 'Shall we just tell them thanks, and maybe sneak out? Or stay for a bit, possibly ... '

Huckle looked at her, straight into her eyes.

'Or,' he said quietly, 'we could just do it.'

'You knew about this?'

'No,' he said. 'But, you know. We're here now.'

'I'm wearing dungarees! And thermal pants.'

'Ah,' said Kerensa. 'I might be able to help you with that.'

'And, you know, WAXING, and my eyebrows need plucking and my hair is a mess and ...'

Huckle blinked.

'I think you look beautiful,' he said.

And suddenly, for Polly, it felt like all the anxieties, all the frustrations and worries of keeping the bakery running and the lighthouse warm and her friends happy and dealing with her own deep-buried issues ... it suddenly felt as if everything, every one of those was lifted from her shoulders, everything was taken away and the world seemed a brighter place, as the sun glinted off the snow outside and the huge fire crackled merrily in the grate, and all her fears about marriage, about that step, and what it meant, and what it had meant for her family, seemed to vanish as she looked at the handsome, open, guileless face of the man she absolutely adored ...

And everything else fell away.

'And I would like to marry you,' he said.

'Are you *sure* you weren't in on this?' said Polly suspiciously.

'I promise I wasn't.' He shook his head. 'Although my parents did mention they'd suddenly changed their plans.'

'So you had a hint?'

'Come on!' said Kerensa. 'Come with me! I have lots of stuff to show you, all of which you can fit into but I can't because my tits have exploded into milk-filled HHs and I still appear to look eight months pregnant despite the fact that the baby is officially out and not in any more.'

And she spirited Polly, whose head was in a whirl, upstairs to her room.

Chapter Forty-Two

Polly walked into the room.

'What the hell? What is this?'

Kerensa beamed with happiness.

'I know!' she said.

The dressing room annexe, normally full of Kerensa's ridiculous collection of shoes and bags that Reuben insisted on buying her, had been completely transformed into a white boudoir. And in every available space a different style of wedding dress was hanging – strapless; lacy; a ridiculous princess number over the door.

'What . . . what is this?' Polly blinked.

'Choose one.'

And there, at a little table at the side, looking slightly concerned but sipping from a flute of champagne nonetheless, was Polly's mum.

'Mum?' said Polly.

Doreen stood up and they embraced.

'You knew about this?'

Her mother, who was all done up in a fuchsia suit that had last seen use in about 1987 – and still fitted – smiled and nodded.

'You have a very good friend in Kerensa.'

'What did you . . . I mean, are we really getting married, or is it a fake one?'

'We posted the banns for you,' said Kerensa. 'They've been up in the church for six weeks.'

'Why did nobody tell us?'

'We swore everyone to secrecy and threatened them with not being invited. We knew there was absolutely no way you two heathens would be setting foot inside a church anyway. You have to go to the registrar in a couple of days, but apart from that, it's the real thing, baby.'

Polly shook her head.

'And *this* is what you were doing all that time?'

Kerensa shrugged. 'You know how miserable I was. I hated thinking about the baby; hated thinking about how I'd ruined my life. And I was worried, you know. Worried about you.'

'YOU were worried about ME?' said Polly.

'Yes! You had this fabulous guy standing right there and you were all like, oh, I'm too stressed out to get married, oh, I'm not ready, blah blah blah.'

'But he always knew I loved him,' said Polly.

'He's a bloke!' said Kerensa. 'Blokes don't know ANYTHING unless you spell it out in foot-high letters and stick it in front of their noses. All he'd have been thinking is "Polly no marry Huckle. Huckle so sad. So so sad. Huckle go marry twenty-year-old."'

'No he wasn't,' said Polly.

'"Huckle so sad and lonely!"'

'She's right, you know,' said Doreen, and it was to Polly's great credit that she didn't immediately turn around and say what on earth would you know about it?

Kerensa beamed.

'My mum's here too, saying I should have done it like this instead of dressing up like Princess Leia, and it's actually even more annoying because she has a point.'

'How did you get here, Mum?' said Polly.

'That nice young American boy sent a car for me,' said Doreen. 'He's looked after me so well! Such a lovely chap.'

'Reuben?'

'He's a darling,' said Doreen.

'He is,' said Kerensa, looking fondly at the crib in the corner where she'd laid Herschel-Lowin.

Polly looked around.

'And you promise me Huckle knew nothing about this?'

'Nope,' said Kerensa. 'Reuben thought he'd pitch a fit and insist that you needed a chance to do it your way. Whereas we've decided that it's just time for the two of you.'

'Seriously?'

'You're so busy, you'd never have got round to it.'

Kerensa knelt down.

'You're not cross, are you?'

Polly looked around again. Planning her own wedding wasn't at all the kind of thing she'd dreamed of as a child. Everything she'd dreamed of – running her own business, being independent, baking things people wanted to buy – those things she'd done. But in this big, mad, beautiful house . . .

'Who else is coming?' she asked weakly.

'Everyone,' said Kerensa, with a wicked glint in her eye, and sure enough, there were already fleets of cars crunching up the drive towards the house, and laughing, shouting people disgorging from them.

'Oh Lord,' said Polly.

There was a woman lingering by the door carrying a huge box of what was clearly make-up. Polly turned to her.

'Okay,' she said. 'Whatever it is you do – do it all. Twice. Then add some more for luck.'

Kerensa poured them all glasses of champagne.

'Don't look at me like that,' she said. 'I have a breast pump.'

'I really don't deserve this,' said Polly. 'I don't deserve any of this. Not really.'

Kerensa blinked. 'You've been the best friend in the world,' she said hoarsely. 'Anyway, choose a dress, the rest are going back. Reuben hired the entire shop. Plus you'll need an hour for Anita to paint your nails and stick extra hair in.'

'What do you mean, extra hair?'

'All the brides these days have extra hair,' said Kerensa. 'Well, they have lots extra in some places and lots less in other places. We can do that too.'

Polly thought of how often Huckle had said he liked her strawberry-blonde hair natural and curly rather than how she normally did it, ironed flat and sprayed down.

'Actually,' she said. 'I think I'll just leave it like it is.'

'But it's all curly.'

'Maybe curly is all right.'

'My God, your children are going to have, like, the world's curliest hair.'

Polly smiled to think of it.

'Well,' she said. 'Maybe I've made my peace with that.'

She started trying on the dresses, having a giggle at the really massive princess one – she couldn't help it; it looked stiff and strange and not like her at all, and was profoundly uncomfortable to wear.

'No,' she said. 'Definitely not.'

'It's okay,' said Kerensa. 'I've taken lots of nice pictures of you in it anyway, so if you want to you can substitute that frock in the wedding pictures later. Reuben can do all the computer stuff.'

'Hmm,' said Polly. And then she saw it. It was just behind the cupboard, and wasn't at all like the rest of the showy diamanté numbers. In fact it was rather plain:

a simple vintage dress with a boat-neck lace top and a deep V at the waist. If anything, it was slightly medieval. It didn't have petticoats or hoops or sparkles or ruffles or bows. Neither did it cut her off as the strapless numbers did, making her look like the top half of her was cavorting about naked. This dress was subtle, sweet, understated . . .

She slipped the cool silk underskirt over her head. It flowed down her body and fitted immediately, perfectly, as if it had been made for her. It shimmered as she moved; it wasn't too tight or too puffy; not too fussy and not too plain. The tiny glinting vintage sequins caught the light in a subtle way; the pale ivory colour set off her red hair perfectly. She looked in the mirror and barely recognised herself.

'Oh,' Doreen said quietly. 'Oh. That's exactly what I'd have chosen. For you,' she added quickly, looking up and wiping her eyes. 'I mean for you, of course. That's what I would have chosen for you.'

Polly came over and hugged her mother for a long time and they had a small cry together. Then Anita, the hair and make-up girl, unpacked her box and started work.

Polly could see more cars arriving.

'Oh my Lord,' she said. 'I'm quite nervous now.'

She turned to Kerensa. 'What music are we having?'

'Just the normal stuff,' said Kerensa quickly. 'Don't worry about it.'

Polly blinked.

'Oh my God, what about rings?'

326

'We've borrowed a couple for you,' said Kerensa. 'They have to go back and then you can choose your own.'

Polly shook her head.

'No, it's all right,' she said. 'I think we have a better idea.' And she sent a quick text to Huckle.

After half an hour of painting and polishing and primping – at one point there were three people working on her at once – Kerensa gave Polly some fresh underwear and declared her ready.

'I still think I should have had more notice and I wouldn't have eaten all that toast and leftover canapés over Christmas.'

'Shut up,' said Kerensa. 'You look beautiful.'

And she did. Exquisitely beautiful and perfect and gorgeous in the pale winter sunlight that reflected off the snow and streamed in through the huge windows overlooking the bay. Polly blinked as she watched the activity on the drive. Old Mrs Corning was being helped out of a large car by Pat the vet. Everyone was here.

'How?' she said. 'Seriously? Everyone's known about this for weeks?'

'Yup,' said Kerensa smugly.

Polly shook her head, bemused.

'This is mad.'

'I think it's the funnest thing to happen to Mount Polbearne for ages.' Kerensa peered out of the window. 'Oh wow.'

'What?' said Polly. She glanced out. It was Huckle's

mum and dad, looking cheery and bemused, and with them was Huckle's very troublesome brother DuBose.

'Whoa,' said Polly. 'You really did get everyone.'

'Just lock up the jewellery,' said Kerensa. 'Oh! I almost forgot. I have a present for you.'

'On top of what?' said Polly. 'Oh my God, Kerensa, this is totally mad already.'

'Sssh,' said Kerensa. 'Doing this has been about the only nice time I've had this year.' She looked adoringly at the baby in the cot. 'Worth it, though.'

She brought out a velvet jewellery case and handed it to Polly, who opened it. Inside was a delicate necklace on a platinum chain, with a tiny row of puffins, each with a little diamond. You couldn't even tell what they were unless you got close; otherwise it just looked like a lovely piece of filigree.

'Oh my God,' said Polly.

'Hah!' said Kerensa. 'I knew you'd like it.'

'I love it!' said Polly, her eyes filling with tears. 'Oh my God, I don't know what I did to deserve this.'

'Everything,' said Kerensa. 'Come here. I told them to use the waterproof mascara.'

The two girls held one another tightly.

'I'm going to do this,' said Polly disbelievingly. 'I'm actually going to do this.'

'Unless you reckon anyone better's going to come along,' said Kerensa, and they both burst out laughing.

Doreen stood up cautiously, still a little nervous. Polly

noticed that she had had her nails done and was even wearing a tiny bit of make-up. She had made the most massive effort. Polly blinked.

'This is . . . ' Doreen swallowed hard. 'This is all I ever wanted for you. No. I wanted whatever you wanted for you,' she said with some difficulty. 'And I should have been better at letting you see . . . letting you know that whatever you wanted was fine. And . . . I should have . . . '

'Mum,' said Polly. 'Forget about that. Forget about everything. It's fine. It's all fine. Please.'

And they embraced too, just as a very trendy photographer in cowboy boots and a bald spot came in and started taking shots of them with an unnecessarily complex-looking camera.

'Reportage,' hissed Kerensa. 'Nothing cheesy.'

'Yes, because this isn't at all cheesy,' wept Polly. The photographer ignored them completely and kept snapping away.

'Hang on,' said Polly. 'What about music? And readings? And all that stuff?'

'Well you told me all that,' said Kerensa.

'What do you mean? No I didn't. How?'

'When we were at school,' said Kerensa. 'Remember? I made plans then. We wrote it all down in an exercise book. You helped.'

Polly went white.

'You didn't . . . '

'What?' said Kerensa innocently. '"I Want It That Way"

329

is a perfectly good song to walk down the aisle to. I did actually speak to their management, so they're on their way . . . '

'YOU DIDN'T?'

Kerensa grinned. 'I didn't.'

'Oh,' said Polly, mostly relieved and a teensy-tiny bit disappointed.

'Ha! I knew it! You totally look disappointed!'

Polly shook her head.

'Trust me, I am so round the bend with shock and terror, disappointment is the furthest thing from my mind.'

'Don't worry,' said Kerensa, squeezing her hand. 'We've gone very trad.'

She glanced at her watch. It was coming up to two o'clock.

'Okay,' she said. 'You know, I think it's nearly time.'

'Oh my God,' said Polly. 'Oh my God. I'm not ready. I'm not ready. Where's Neil?'

'He's with Huckle,' said Kerensa. 'The groomsmen stick together. Don't worry. And you're never ready. Oh, and Huckle's fraternity brothers are here too. I'm amazed you didn't hear them before now. Reuben wouldn't let them stay in the house; we had to put them up in a hotel.'

'Because they're frat boys?'

'And he wanted to be one and they wouldn't let him. He says he's working on a disease to eradicate them all.'

Polly shook her head.

'This is mad.'

'I had a lot of displacement energy,' said Kerensa grimly.

Marta came in, beaming and giggling, and exclaimed at Polly's transformation. Polly hugged her too.

'Mr Finkel says it's time,' Marta said. 'He says come on, and bring the baby with you.'

Kerensa nodded. She hopped into the bathroom and shimmied into a pale silk slouchy dress that immediately eliminated all the lumps and bumps and made her look like she hadn't had a baby at all. In fact she looked stunningly lovely, all her spark, her mojo right back.

'Chief bridesmaid,' she announced.

Outside the door was a tiny gaggle of children from the village, as well as Reuben's youngest sister. They were an orgy of cream and flowers and giggles and gorgeousness, and as Polly emerged, they burst into spontaneous applause.

'Hello, you lot!' she said cheerfully. She crept forward and peered over the balcony.

Kerensa hadn't been lying. Everybody was there. Absolutely everyone. The entire gang from school, and her college friends – obviously word had got out – all done up in their wedding best. Polly hated to think what would have happened if she'd said no. The logistics of everything were mind-boggling. She glanced down the big staircase, her heart beating terribly fast.

'Are you ready?' said Kerensa.

'Yes! No! Oh my God,' said Polly. She stepped back.

'Actually,' she said. 'Mum. It is totally up to you to say no, honestly. Completely. But I was . . . '

She was so confused and emotional, she could barely get the words out.

'I just wondered if maybe . . . '

'Anything,' said Doreen.

'I thought I might . . . maybe we could call Carmel? Just . . . I mean, there's . . . I mean, I have a whole bunch of half-brothers and sisters out there who I don't know or anything, and well, I mean. If I was. If I wanted to get to know them. Maybe. One day. Well.'

'You want to invite them?'

'Maybe just Carmel,' said Polly. 'To start with. But if I was . . . if I was ever to get to know them, this might not be a bad way of beginning it.'

They looked at each other.

'On it,' said Kerensa, pulling out Polly's phone from the handbag she'd spirited it into.

'Hang on,' said Polly, raising her hand.

Doreen stared at the floor for a moment, then looked up again with something resolute about her eyes.

'Yes,' she said. 'Yes. If there is a family out there for you, Polly . . . more of a family, I mean. Yes. It's so far in the past now . . . Yes. It's fine.'

Polly nodded. 'Thanks.'

'I'm texting right now,' said Kerensa.

They hung on with bated breath. Then Kerensa looked up.

'They'll be here in time for the afternoon tea,' she said.

'No way,' said Polly.

There was a sound of scuffling and some impatient throat-clearing from behind them.

'Right,' said Kerensa.

'Right,' said Polly. And Doreen put out her arm to walk her down the aisle.

Chapter Forty-Three

Polly stood for just a second at the top of the stairs, looking dazedly at the whole of the life they had built together spread out before her. People were bunched around the staircase, smiling, beaming at her, dressed up in hats and wobbly on high heels, and oh my goodness, it was incredible to Polly that they'd all managed to keep it a secret.

And then a path was made, with a red carpet running down it, running through the throng of giggling delighted people, and she saw, just for a second, Huckle's broad back, in a black jacket. Neil was perched on his shoulder, wearing a bow tie, obviously caught up in the solemnity of the moment. Reuben, a head shorter, was standing next to him. Polly just stood for a second, a thrill going through her as suddenly, gradually, the crowd became aware of her, and Reuben glanced round and nudged Huckle, who turned too, both of them with white Cornish heather in their buttonholes, and Polly's heart leapt, and the same swing band as before – but now looking not at all so snotty – started playing a song it took Polly a moment to recognise.

Huckle spotted her, and his face lit up in a way she would never forget for as long as she lived.

And he gave her the biggest wink as she started down the stairs in the pretty low-heeled shoes she'd picked out, biting her lip, desperately hoping she wouldn't stumble, a bevy of bridesmaids around her, one throwing rose petals that were spilling out all round the long skirt of her dress and the new shoes that she hadn't had a chance to practise walking in, and it was quite useful, in fact, that she had to concentrate so hard on not falling down the stairs that she didn't really have a moment to start crying or get terribly anxious about it.

But then suddenly the fact that everyone was there, the way the entire world appeared to have known about her big day before she did; the fact that she had had absolutely no idea about what was planned or how she was going to react . . . suddenly all of that melted away. Because Huckle was holding her gaze with his strong blue eyes. And Neil was hopping on his shoulder in his bow tie, and in his claws he held two entwined rings of fresh seaweed from the low tide on the shore.

The song continued. *'It must be love! Love! Love!'*

The rest was more or less a blur, although Polly had heard lots of people say that about their wedding day. She remembered amazing food; and Mattie the vicar doing the traditional vows with a huge beaming smile; and loads and loads of champagne; and constantly being surprised by people she hadn't seen for too long, buried as she had been in work and her own problems. She remembered Reuben's speech, which had somehow turned into a massive tribute to how brilliant he was, and she remembered Huckle's because he simply stood up and said, 'This is love and I am in it' and sat down again, and she remembered his face when his mum and dad came up to embrace them; and she remembered Merv dancing with Doreen, and Jayden saying to Flora, 'We could get married like this' and her face being absolutely horrified, and Bernard throwing himself on her and thanking her for saving the sanctuary, which meant Reuben had clearly paid her invoice before she'd even sent it, and she'd made a mental note that turning the puffin café into something would have to be her summer project, but before she could start discussing it with him, Huckle had pulled her away, and Selina, looking absolutely foxy in red satin, had slipped in and grabbed Bernard's elbow.

And she remembered, later, Carmel turning up, looking very nervous – alone, but with her camera – and she'd hugged her, and Carmel had toasted her, just once, smiling a smile with heartbreak behind it, before they were both whirled into the massive hora that had started.

And then, late at night, the cars started to arrive,

including a huge limo for Polly and Huckle and Neil, and they cuddled up in the back seat, giggling occasionally, kissing often, shaking their heads at the madness and the joy of it all, and when they reached the causeway across to Mount Polbearne, the tide was out, and the way was lit, incredibly, astonishingly, all the way to the island with huge proud braziers.

God knows how Reuben had managed it, or how he'd got permission. But it looked like a magical winding path leading straight out to sea; a secret golden road, known only to them, that would close as soon as they had passed, sinking back beneath the waves.

The local cars all drove on over. But the wedding cars stopped, refusing to venture on to dangerous territory they didn't know.

So Polly and Huckle, right at the back of the convoy, had to get out of their car, the tiny waves already lapping at their toes, and Polly took off her absurdly expensive shoes and hitched up her skirts, and both of them, floating on champagne and bubbles of pure happiness, giggling their heads off, charged along the causeway as the waves closed over behind them, the flaming torches snuffed out one by one, so that from the mainland it must have looked as if Mount Polbearne was nothing but a mirage in the distance; a lost dream.

Andy was already opening the Red Lion, and the fiddles were starting up, but Huckle simply took Polly in his arms and carried her up the steps to the lighthouse.

And in that moment, as the old year paused before the new arrived, it was as if the world took a breath.

Polly didn't believe in magic, but even so, as they crossed the threshold, in a flash, in a vision, she could see it; feel it all.

Even though the lighthouse was dark and cold and empty, it was as if, suddenly, she could hear her name being called; the bath running; Neil *eep*ing, children charging up and down the stairs – and falling, from time to time – banging and making noise and charging in and out, and it sped up, it went so fast, the oven turning over, and the village children playing together, and friends arriving, and Reuben's new school . . . and it sped up again, and the lamp in the lighthouse whizzed round and round as the boats followed the tide in and out and the freezing winters turned to perfect summers and the children came and went and shouted and grew and the bread filled the air with its scent and the children ran back from school and grabbed great handfuls of banana cake and dashed out again to dabble in rock pools with Neil, tousle-haired, shrimping nets in little fingers, clamouring to be allowed in the sidecar, and Herschel-Lowin, with his bright red hair and freckles, ran round pretending to be in charge . . .

Polly blinked and shook away the vision – far too much champagne, she thought, too much excitement, and tiredness, and emotion. All of those things.

'I love you, my darling,' said Huckle. 'But I am going to have to put you down. It's your dress that's heavy.'

'I know,' she said, still half caught in the dream. 'It's definitely the dress.'

'Definitely,' said Huckle. 'Shall I go and put the electric blanket on?'

'Yes please,' said Polly.

And as he vanished upstairs, she turned, watching the lighthouse beam sweep over the harbour, the little town, out to the mainland, where the fireworks were already starting to pop, one two three, and just before she switched out the light, she went into the kitchen in her wedding dress, and she laid out the yeast and the flour and the eggs for the morning bread, and kissed Neil, already snuggled in front of the Aga, and put out the light, then ran upstairs, her skirt and a faint wake of flour trailing behind her.

AWESOME HOT CHOCOLATE

NB: Don't add TOO much cream, otherwise it will turn into pudding. But do add marshmallows, even though those two statements contradict each other. Also keep an eye on the chocolate. If it gets above a simmer when it's melting, it's all over.

One large bar of milk chocolate (the size of one they offer you in shops when you buy a newspaper. The branding is completely up to you.)
One small bar of dark chocolate (Bournville or similiar but go posh as you like. If you like, e.g., chilli flavouring (I don't judge), go for that at this point.)
Brandy or Cointreau (optional)
750ml whole milk
A dollop of single cream
Vanilla, to taste
Ginger or cinnamon, to taste
2 tsp sugar (optional)

Melt the chocolate INCREDIBLY slowly stirring over a very low heat. If you've got small people chuntering around, they may need a distraction whilst you get this together. If you don't, a small slug of brandy or Cointreau is practically *de riguer*.

When the chocolate is melted, add up to 750ml of whole milk – the precise consistency is up to you – and a dollop of single cream. It should be lovely and thick but not dessert.

A spot of vanilla; a tiny pinch of ginger or cinnamon to taste. Some people add a teaspoon or two of sugar at this point, and that is entirely to your taste. I do.

If you have a foamer, use that; otherwise carefully whisk and pour.

Small marshmallows or tiny ones are up to you. I prefer the little ones because it feels like I get more. Don't look at me like that.

Drink slowly. Possibly with this book in your hands.

KNISHES

Knishes are basically the Jewish version of a pasty. You can make your own pastry or just buy it; it should be very thin. They can be filled with meat or potatoes and onion or cream cheese. I don't like the cream cheese one so much, so here's the classic.

2kg potatoes	*For the pastry*
2 large onions	800g flour
3 tspn veg oil	2 eggs
Salt and pepper, to taste	4 tspn veg oil
Chopped parsley	Cup of warm water
	1 tspn of salt

Boil the potatoes and sauté (softly fry) the onions in the oil. Mash together with plenty of salt and pepper and parsley, and set aside to cool.

Mix the wet ingredients for the pastry, then gradually add the flour until its firm enough for kneading. Knead for a few minutes, then set aside to rest.

You want to roll the dough out as thin as possible, then put dollops of the potato mixture at intervals. Roll the whole thing up like a long sausage roll, but when you slice it up, you should be able to 'wrap up' the entire thing in pastry, because the potato mixture isn't touching – they should be round little parcels, if that makes sense.

Brush with eggwash and bake at 190°C for around 35 minutes. Perfect finger food. Dip in sour cream if so inclined.

MINCEMEAT TWISTS

I love making my own mincemeat. It feels like the start of Christmas and it will make you feel better about using puff pastry.

Mincemeat (prepare at least two weeks before)
275g currants
100g sultanas
250g raisins
3 tbspn lemon juice
Lemon zest
300g suet
300g brown sugar
100g mixed peel
Pinch of nutmeg
2 x peeled apples (firm green ones best)
QUITE a lot of brandy.

SQUISH SQUISH SQUISH.

Then leave.

After a couple of hours, fill sterilised jam jars (I run them through a dishwasher on a boil setting), make sure the air is out (put one of those little gingham flat hats on it), and lock so they're airtight otherwise will spoil. Stick in the cupboard for two weeks. If I make extra, I give it away as gifts. When we lived in France I gave it to my French friends and they all looked at me like I was a MANIAC.

I am sure the jars are still in their cupboards.

To make a twist, cut triangles out of the puff pastry. Put a spoonful of the mincemeat at the bottom and roll up. It doesn't matter if they look slightly messy, that's all part of the fun!

Brush with egg wash, sprinkle with brown sugar and bake for 30 mins at 200 degrees, or until brown.

GALETTE DES ROIS

Where we live in France, the big thing to eat at Christmas is yule log (coming next) and, after Christmas, galette des rois up to the feast of the Ephiphany, or Twelfth Night. There are little ceramic creatures, called fêves, or favours, hidden in each cake. They can be angels or religious figures, but these days you can also get Scooby Doo. Whoever finds it is crowned the Roi with the gold paper crown that traditionally goes around the outside. Then it is their turn to host the next galette des rois. We have found through trial and error it is usually prudent to push the fêve piece towards the youngest person in the room. If you can't lay your hand on some fêves, a coin wrapped in greaseproof paper should have the same cheerful effect in warding off the post-chrimbo blues.

1 roll ready-made puff pastry, unless you are a fantastic pastry nut (I worship you)	100g soft butter
	100g caster sugar
	100g ground almonds
1 egg, beaten	1 tbspn brandy
2 tbspn jam	

Preheat the oven to 190 degrees. Divide the ready-made puff pastry in half, roll out each piece into two circles. Put one of the circles on a baking sheet and spread with the jam.

Whisk the butter and sugar until fluffy. Beat in most of the egg. Stir in the almonds, brandy, and add the *fêve*.

Spread the mix on top of the jam, then cover with the second piece of pastry. Seal up with a pinch. You can decorate the top of the *galette* with a fork if you like.

Bake for 25 minutes or until crisp and golden. Serve warm or cold.

Acknowledgements

Thanks to everyone who's been so incredibly supportive of Polly, Neil and the gang over the last three years, particularly:

Maddie West, Rebecca Saunders, David Shelley, Charlie King, Manpreet Grewal, Amanda Keats, Jen and the sales team, Emma Williams, Stephanie Melrose, Jo Wickham, Kate Agar, and all at Little, Brown; Jo Unwin, Isabel Adamakoh Young, the Amble Puffin Festival, and all our many, dear rabbit friends and relations who were there so staunchly for me during an unusually tricky time. Love, and a very, very merry Christmas to you all.

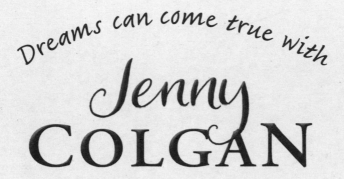

Dreams can come true with

Jenny
COLGAN

Read on for an exclusive chapter from
Jenny Colgan's next bestseller,

THE ENDLESS
BEACH

Coming early 2018

Once upon a time there was a prince who lived in a high tower made entirely of ice. But he never noticed, as he had never seen anything else, nor been anything else, and to him, being cold was simply the way of things for he had not known anything different. He was the prince of a vast wasteland; he ruled over bears and wild things and answered to nobody.

And wise advisers told him to travel; to take a bride; to learn from others. But he refused, saying, 'I am comfortable here,' and eventually the tower of ice grew thick and impossible to enter and nothing grew and it could not be climbed and dragons circled the tower and it became perilous and still the prince would not leave. And many people tried to climb the tower to rescue the prince, but none succeeded. Until one day . . .

Chapter One

Even in early spring, Mure is pretty dark.

Flora didn't care; she loved waking up in the morning, curled up close, together in the pitch black. Joel was a very light sleeper (Flora didn't know that before he had met her, he had barely slept at all) and was generally awake by the time she rubbed her eyes, his normally tense watchful face softening as he saw her, and she would smile, once again surprised and overwhelmed and scared by the depth of how she felt; how she trembled at the rhythm of his heartbeat.

She even loved the frostiest mornings, when she had to pull herself up to get everything going. It was different, when you didn't have an hour-long commute pressed up against millions of other commuters breathing germs and pushing against you and making your life more uncomfortable than it had to be.

Instead, she would rake up the damped peat in the wood-burner in the beautiful guest cottage Joel was staying in while working for Colton Rogers, the billionaire who owned half the island. She would set the flames into life – and the room became even cosier in an instant, the flickering light from the fire throwing shadows on the white-washed walls.

The one thing Joel had insisted on in the room was a highly expensive state-of-the-art coffee machine, and she would let him fiddle with that while he logged on to the day's work and made his customary remark about the many and varied failures of the island's internet reliability.

Flora would take her coffee, pull on an old jumper and wander to the window of the cottage, where she could sit on the top of the old oil-fired radiator, the type you get in schools but had now cost Colton a fortune. Here she would stare out at the dark sea; sometimes with its white tips showing if it was going to be a breezy day; sometimes astonishingly clear, in which case, even in the morning, you could raise your eyes and see the brilliant cold stars overhead. There was no light pollution on Mure. They were bigger than Flora remembered from being a child.

She wrapped her hands round her mug and smiled. The shower started up. 'Where are you off to today?' she shouted.

Joel popped his head out the door. 'Hartford for starters,' he said. 'Via Reykjavik.'

'Can I come?'

Joel gave her a look. Work wasn't funny.

'Come on. We can make out on the plane.'

'I'm not sure . . .'

Colton had a plane he used to get in and out of Mure, and Flora was absolutely incensed that it was strictly for company business and she'd never been allowed on it. A private plane! Such a thing was unimaginable, really. Joel was impossible to tease where work was involved. Actually, he was quite difficult to tease about anything. Which worried Flora sometimes.

'I bet there is absolutely nothing the stewardesses

haven't seen,' said Flora. This was undoubtedly true, but Joel was already scrolling through the *Wall Street Journal* and not really listening.

'Back two weeks Friday. Colton is consolidating literally ... well ...'

Flora wished he could talk more about his work, like he could when she was still in the law trade. It wasn't just confidentiality. Colton was dating her brother, so it wasn't even her business.

Flora pouted. 'You'll miss the Argylls.'

'The what?'

'It's a band. They tour and they're coming to the Harbour's Rest. They're really brilliant.'

Joel shrugged. 'I don't really like music.'

Flora went up to him. Music was in the lifeblood of everyone on Mure. Before the ferries and the aeroplanes came, they'd had to make their own entertainment, and everyone joined in with enthusiasm, if not always too much talent. Flora danced well and could just about play a bodhrán if there wasn't anyone better around. Her brother Innes was a better fiddler than he let on. The only one who couldn't play anything was big Hamish; their mother had just tended to give him a pair of spoons and let him get on with it.

She put her arms around him. 'How can you not like music?' she said.

Joel blinked and looked over her shoulder. It was silly, really, a small thing in the endless roundabout that had been his difficult childhood, that every new school was a new chance to get it wrong: to wear the wrong thing; to like the wrong band. The fear of doing so. His lack of ability, or so it seemed, to learn the rules. The cool bands varied so widely, it was absolutely impossible to keep track.

He had found it easier to abdicate responsibility altogether. He'd never quite made his peace with music. Never dared to find out what he liked. Never had an older sibling to point the way.

It was the same with clothes. He only wore two colours – blue and grey, impeccably sourced, from the best fabrics – not because he had taste, but because it seemed absolutely the simplest. He never had to think about it. Although he'd gone on to date enough models to learn a lot more about clothes: that was something they had been helpful for.

He glanced over at Flora. She was staring out at the sea again. Sometimes he had trouble distinguishing her from the environment of Mure. Her hair was the fronds of seaweed that lay across the pale white dunes of her shoulders; her tears the sprays of saltwater in a storm; her mouth a perfect shell. She wasn't a model – quite the opposite. She felt as grounded, as solid as the earth beneath her feet; she was an island, a village, a town, a home. He touched her gently, almost unable to believe she was his.

Flora knew this touch of his, and she could not deny it. It worried her, the way that he looked at her sometimes: as if she were something fragile, precious. She was neither of those things. She was just a normal girl, with the same worries and faults as anyone else. And eventually he was going to realise this, and she was terrified about what would happen when he realised that she wasn't a selkie; that she wasn't some magical creature who'd materialised to solve everything about his life ... She was terrified what would happen when he realised she was just a normal person who worried about her weight and liked to dress very badly on Sundays ... What would happen when they had to argue about washing-up liquid? She kissed his hand gently.

'Stop looking at me like I'm a water sprite.'

He grinned. 'Well, you are to me.'

'What time's your ...? Oh.'

She always forgot that Colton's plane left to their schedule, not an airline's.

Joel glanced at his watch. 'Now. Colton has a real bug up his ass ... I mean ... There's lots to do.'

'Don't you want breakfast?'

Joel shook his head. 'Ridiculously, they'll be serving Seaside Kitchen bread and scones on board.'

Flora smiled. '*Well*, aren't *we* fancy?' She kissed him. 'Come back soon.'

'Why, where are you going?'

'Nowhere,' said Flora, pulling him close. 'Absolutely nowhere.'

And she watched him leave without a backwards glance, and sighed.

Oddly it was only during sex that she knew, one hundred per cent, that he was there. Absolutely and completely there, with her, breath for breath, movement for movement. It was not like anything she had ever known before. She had known selfish lovers and show-off lovers, and purely incompetent lovers, their potential ruined by pornography before they were barely men.

She hadn't ever known anything like this – the intensity, almost desperation – as if he were trying to fit the whole of himself inside her skin. She felt utterly known and as if she knew him perfectly. She thought about it constantly. But he was hardly ever here. And the rest of the time she wasn't any clearer about where his head was than when they'd first met.

And now, a month later, it wasn't so dark, but Joel was still away, busy on one job after another. Flora was travelling today but nowhere quite so interesting, and alas, she was back in the farmhouse.

There was something Flora felt as an adult about being closeted in the bedroom – in the single bed she grew up in, no less, with her old highland dancing trophies, dusty and still lining the wall – that made her irritable, as well as the knowledge that however early she had to get up – and it felt very, very early – her three farmworking brothers and her father would already have been up milking for an hour.

Well, not Fintan. He was the food genius of the family and spent most of his time making cheese and butter for the Seaside Kitchen and, soon they hoped, Colton's new hotel, the Rock. But the other boys – strong, dim Hamish and Innes, her eldest brother – were out, dark or light, rain or shine, and however much she tried to get her father, Eck, to slow down, he tended to head out too. When she had worked down in London as a paralegal, they had joked that she was lazy. Now that she ran an entire café single-handedly, she'd hoped to prove them wrong, but they still saw her as a lightweight, only getting up at 5 a.m.

She should move out – there were a few cottages to rent in Mure town, but the Seaside Kitchen wasn't turning enough money for her to afford to do something as extravagant as that. She couldn't help it. They had such amazing produce here on Mure – fresh organic butter churned in their own dairies; the most astonishing cheese, made by Fintan; the best fish and shellfish from their crystal-clear waters; the rain that grew the world's sweetest grass, that fattened up the coos. But it all cost money.

She immediately worked out in her head what time it was in New York, where Joel, her boyfriend – it felt ridiculous, she realised, calling him her boyfriend – was working.

He had been her own boss, sent up with her to work on some legal business for Colton Rogers. But being her boss was only a part of it. She'd had a massive crush on him for years, since the first moment she'd set eyes on him. He, on the other hand, spent his life dating models and not noticing her. She hadn't ever thought she could get his attention. And then, finally, when they had worked together last summer, he had thawed enough to notice her: enough, in the end, to relocate his business to work with Colton on Mure.

Except of course it hadn't quite turned out like that. Colton had assigned him a guest cottage, a beautifully restored hunting lodge, while the Rock was preparing to officially open, which was taking its time. Then he'd shot off all round the world, looking after his various billionaire enterprises – which seemed to require Joel with him at all times. She'd barely seen him all winter. Right now, he was in New York. Things like setting up home – things like sitting down to have a conversation – seemed completely beyond him.

Flora had known theoretically that he was a workaholic; she'd worked for him for years. She just didn't realise what that meant when it came to their relationship. She seemed to get the leftovers. And there wasn't much. Not even a message to indicate he was aware she was going to London today, to formally sign her leaving papers.

Flora hadn't been sure if they could keep the Seaside Kitchen going over the winter, when the tourists departed and the nights drew down so low it was never light at all, not really, and the temptation was very much to stay in bed all day with the covers over her head.

But to her surprise, the Kitchen was busy every single day. Mothers with babies; old people stopping to chat to their friends over a cheese scone; the knitting group that handled spillover Fair Isle orders and normally met in each other's kitchens had decided to make the Seaside Kitchen their home, and Flora never got tired of watching the amazing speed and grace of gnarled old fingers producing the beautiful repeating patterns on every type of wool.

So much so that she'd realised: this was her job now. This was where she belonged. Her firm in London had originally given her a leave of absence to work with Colton, but that was over and she had to formally resign. Joel was too: he was working for Colton full time. Flora had been putting off going to London, hoping they'd be able to go together to sign off the paperwork, but it didn't seem to be very likely.

So she helped Isla, one of the two young girls who worked with her, open up the Seaside Kitchen for the day. They'd repainted it the same pale pink it had been until it had gone to seed and started to peel. Now it fitted in nicely with the black-and-white Harbour's Rest hotel, the pale blue of the tackle shop and the cream of many tourist shops that lined the front, selling big woollen jumpers, souvenir shells and stone carvings, tartan (of course), small models of

Highland coos, tablet and toffee. Many of them were shut for the winter.

The wind was ripping off the sea, throwing handfuls of spray and rain into her face and she grinned and ran down the hill from the farmhouse, the commute that was all she had these days. It might be freezing – although she had a huge puffed jacket on that basically insulated her from absolutely everything – but she still wouldn't swap it in a second for an overheated, overstuffed tube carriage; a great outpouring of humanity pushing up the stairs; hot, cold, hot, cold, pushing past more and more people; witnessing shouts and squabbles and cars bumping each other and horns going off and cycle couriers screaming at cabbies and tubes roaring past, free sheets being blown by the wind up and down the street with fast food wrappers and cigarette butts ... No, Flora thought, even on mornings like this. You could keep your commute. She didn't miss it.

Annie's Seaside Kitchen was lit up and golden. It was plain, with ten mismatched bric-a-brac tables scattered artfully around the large room. The counter, currently empty, would soon be filled with scones, cakes, quiche, homemade salads and soups as Iona and Isla busied themselves in the back. Mrs Laird, a local baker, dropped off two dozen loaves a day, which went fairly speedily, and the coffee machine didn't stop from dawn till dusk. Flora still couldn't quite believe it existed, and that it was down to her. Somehow, coming back to her old stamping ground and finding her late mother Annie's own recipe book – it had felt like a happy choice, not a desperate one, or a sad one.

It had felt like a great, ridiculous leap at the time. Now in retrospect it felt entirely obvious, as if it was the only thing she should have done. As if this was home, and the same people she remembered from her childhood – older now, but the faces were the same, handed down the generations – were as much a part of her world as they ever were, and the important things in her world – Joel, the Seaside Kitchen, the weather forecast, the farm, the freshness of the produce – were more important to her somehow than Brexit, than global warming, than the fate of the world. It wasn't as if she was in retreat. She was in renewal.

NEW FOR KIDS

Polly and her puffin friend Neil have wrapped presents, practised for the village nativity and written their lists for Santa. But Christmas is taking a very long time to arrive. And Polly isn't enjoying the wait.

What's worse, Neil is busy helping to keep an egg warm, so he hasn't got much time to play.

Will it EVER be Christmas? And will a tiny little puffling hatch in time for the big day?

Perfect for bedtime stories and early readers, with fun festive recipes and activities at the back!

Also available

NEW FOR YOU FROM
Jenny COLGAN

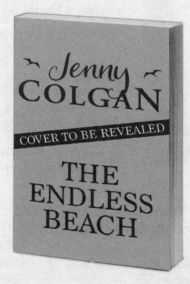

On the quayside next to the Endless Beach sits the Summer Seaside Kitchen, a haven for tourists and islanders alike. Flora, who runs the cafe, feels safe and content – unless she thinks too hard about her relationship with Joel, her gorgeous but emotionally (and physically) distant boyfriend.

While Flora is in turmoil about her relationship. her best friend Lorna is pining after the local doctor. Saif came to the island as a refugee, having lost all of his family. But he's about to get some shocking news which will change everything for him.

As cold winter nights shift to long summer days, can Flora find her happy-ever-after with Joel?

AVAILABLE TO PRE-ORDER NOW

'Gorgeous, glorious, uplifting'
MARIAN KEYES

Can baking mend a broken heart?

Polly Waterford is recovering from a toxic relationship. Unable to afford their flat, she has to move to a quiet seaside resort in Cornwall, where she lives alone. And so Polly takes out her frustrations on her favourite hobby: making bread. With nuts and seeds, olives and chorizo, and with reserves of determination Polly never knew she had, she bakes and bakes and bakes. And people start to hear about it ...

Is Polly about to lose everything she loves?

Summer has arrived in the Cornish town of Mount Polbearne and Polly Waterford couldn't be happier. Because Polly is in love. And yet there's something unsettling about the gentle summer breeze that's floating through town. Polly sifts flour, kneads dough and bakes bread, but nothing can calm the storm she knows is coming: Is Polly about to lose everything she loves?

'Sheer indulgence from start to finish'
SOPHIE KINSELLA

Meet Issy Randall, proud owner of *The Cupcake Café*

After a childhood spent in her beloved Grampa Joe's bakery, Issy Randall has undoubtedly inherited his talent so when she's made redundant from her job, Issy decides to seize the moment. Armed with recipes from Grampa, The Cupcake Café opens its doors. But Issy has absolutely no idea what she's let herself in for ...

One way or another, Issy is determined to have a merry Christmas!

Issy Randall is in love and couldn't be happier. Her new business is thriving and she is surrounded by close friends. But when her boyfriend is scouted for a possible move to New York, Issy is forced to face up to the prospect of a long-distance romance, and she must decide what she holds most dear.

'An evocative, sweet treat'
JOJO MOYES

Remember the rustle of the pink and green striped paper bag?

Rosie Hopkins thinks leaving her busy London life, and her boyfriend Gerard, to sort out her elderly Aunt Lilian's sweetshop in a small country village is going to be dull. Boy, is she wrong. Lilian Hopkins has spent her life running Lipton's sweetshop, through wartime and family feuds. As she struggles with the idea that it might finally be time to settle up, she also wrestles with the secret history hidden behind the jars of beautifully coloured sweets.

Curl up with Rosie, her friends and her family as they prepare for a very special Christmas...

Rosie is looking forward to Christmas. Her sweetshop is festooned with striped candy canes, large tempting piles of Turkish Delight, crinkling selection boxes and happy, sticky children. She's going to be spending it with her boyfriend, Stephen, and her family, flying in from Australia. She can't wait. But when a tragedy strikes at the heart of their little community, all of Rosie's plans are blown apart. Is what's best for the sweetshop also what's best for Rosie?

'A fun, warm-hearted read'
WOMAN & HOME

There's more than one surprise in store for Rosie Hopkins this Christmas...

Rosie Hopkins, newly engaged, is looking forward to an exciting year in the little sweetshop she owns and runs. But when fate strikes Rosie and her boyfriend, Stephen, a terrible blow, threatening everything they hold dear, it's going to take all their strength and the support of their families and their Lipton friends to hold them together.

After all, don't they say it takes a village to raise a child?

Meet Nina

Given a back-room computer job when the beloved Birmingham library she works in turns into a downsized retail complex, Nina misses her old role terribly – dealing with people, greeting her regulars, making sure everyone gets the right books for their needs. Then a new business nobody else wants catches her eye: owning a tiny little bookshop bus up in the Scottish highlands. Out all hours in the freezing cold; driving with a tiny stock of books ... can Nina really make it work?

LOOK OUT FOR
Jenny COLGAN

writing as Jenny T. Colgan in

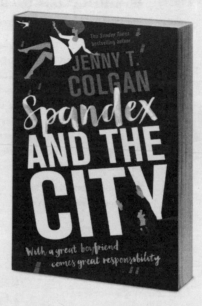

LOCAL GIRL SWEPT OFF HER FEET

Mild-mannered publicist Holly Phillips is unlucky in love. She's embarrassed beyond belief when the handsome stranger she meets in a bar turns out to be 'Ultimate Man' – a superpowered hero whose rescue attempt finds her hoisted over his shoulder and flashing her knickers in the newspaper the next day.

But when Holly's fifteen minutes of fame make her a target for something villainous, she only has one place to turn – and finds the man behind the mask holds a lot more charm than his crime-fighting alter-ego.

Can Holly find love, or is superdating just as complicated as the regular kind?

WATCH OUT FOR
Jenny COLGAN

Writing as Jane Beaton in

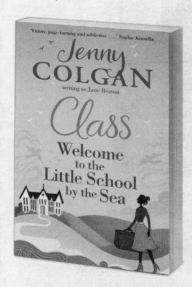

Escape to a beautiful Cornish boarding school by the sea
with the wonderfully warm and funny *Class* and *Rules*.

'Funny, page-turning and addictive ... just like
Malory Towers for grown-ups' SOPHIE KINSELLA

'A brilliant boarding school book, stuffed
full of unforgettable characters, thrilling
adventures and angst ...' LISA JEWELL

Keep in touch with
Jenny COLGAN

Chat with Jenny and meet her other readers:

 /JennyColganBooks /@jennycolgan

Check out Jenny's website and sign up
to her newsletter for all the latest book news
plus mouth-watering recipes.

www.jennycolgan.com

LOVE TO READ?

Join **The Little Book Café** for competitions,
sneak peeks and more.

 /TheLittleBookCafe

 /@littlebookcafe